Online Research Aids

Whether students want to investigate the ideas behind a thought-provoking topic or conduct in-depth research for a paper, our online research aids can help them refine their research skills, find what they need in the library or on the Web, and then use and document their sources effectively.

A Student's Online Guide to History, Eighth Edition
www.bedfordstmartins.com/benjamin

Jules R. Benjamin, *Ithaca College*

The online edition of Jules Benjamin's brief yet comprehensive introduction to the study of history contains abbreviated content from the print version and is accessible to students wherever they have a connection to the Internet.

Links Library

www.bedfordstmartins.com/historylinks

Links Library is a database of more than 350 carefully reviewed and annotated American and Western history Web links searchable by topic or by textbook chapter. Spanning history from ancient Mesopotamia to the present, the database contains diverse links to resources such as historical archaeology sites, primary documents collections, photograph and illustration galleries, map collections, secondary sources, and audio.

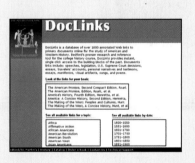

DocLinks

www.bedfordstmartins.com/doclinks

DocLinks is a database of over 1000 annotated Web links to primary documents online for the study of American and Western history. Documents in this database include speeches, legislation, U.S. Supreme Court decisions, essays, travelers' accounts, personal narratives and testimony, essays, e-books, manifestos, visual artifacts, songs, and poems. Documents are searchable by topic and date and are also indexed to the chapters of our major survey textbooks.

Research and Documentation Online

www.bedfordstmartins.com/resdoc

Diana Hacker, *Prince George's Community College*

This online version of Diana Hacker's popular booklet provides clear advice across the disciplines on how to find, evaluate, and integrate outside material into a paper, how to cite sources correctly, and how to format in MLA, APA, CBE, and *Chicago* styles.

www.bedfordstmartins.com/history

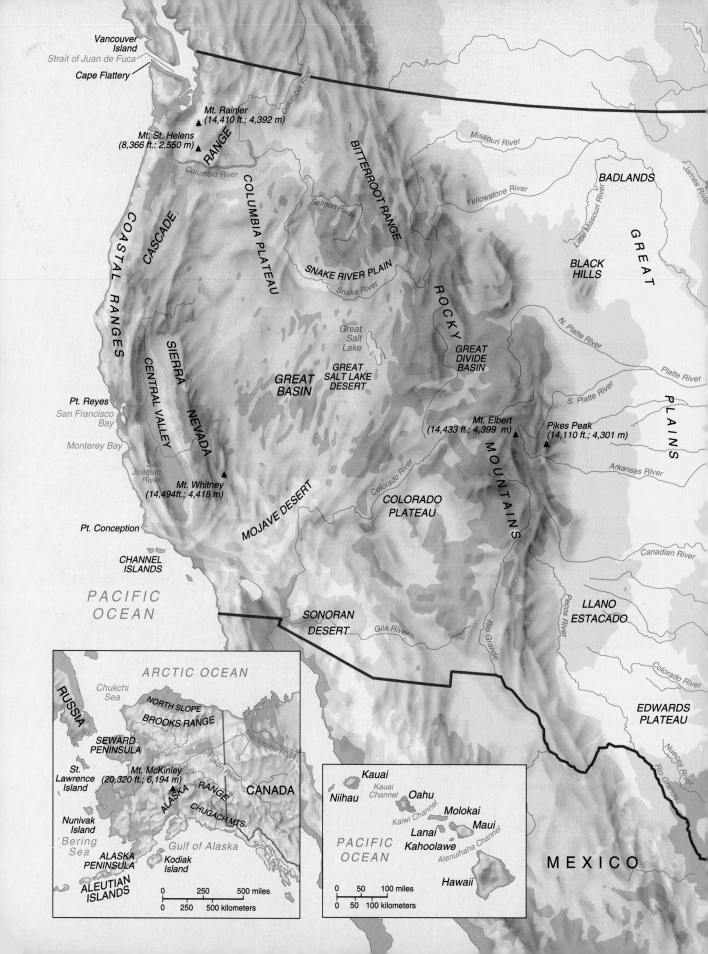

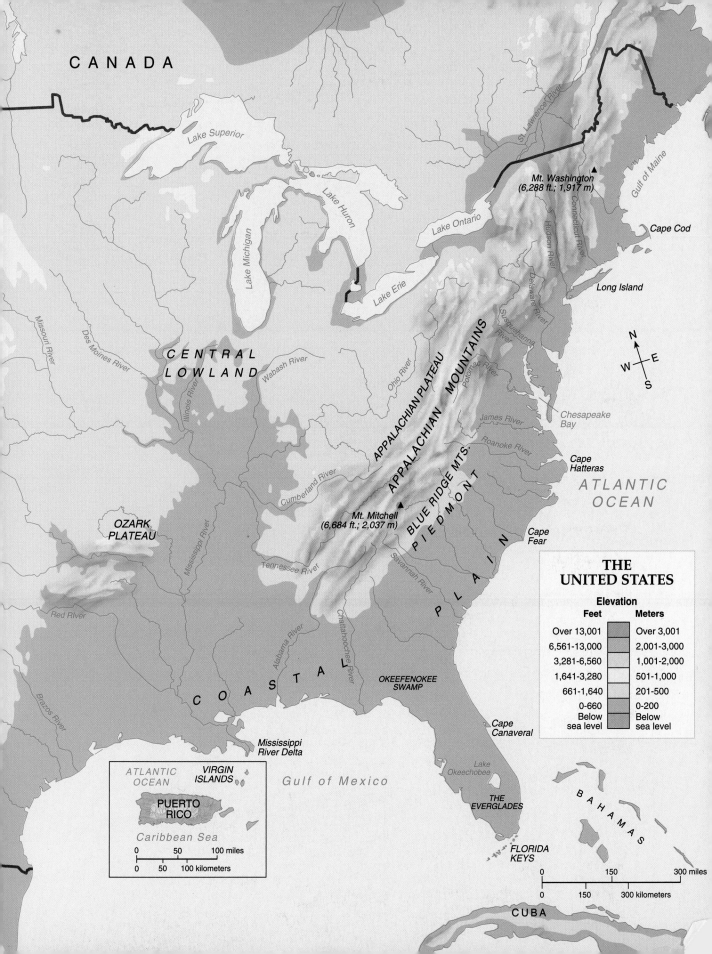

CANADA

Lake Superior

Lake Michigan

Lake Huron

Lake Ontario

Lake Erie

Mt. Washington
(6,288 ft.; 1,917 m)

St. Lawrence River

Connecticut River

Hudson River

Gulf of Maine

Cape Cod

Long Island

Delaware River

Susquehanna River

Chesapeake Bay

CENTRAL
LOWLAND

Missouri River

Des Moines River

Illinois River

Wabash River

Ohio River

APPALACHIAN PLATEAU

APPALACHIAN MOUNTAINS

Potomac River

James River

Roanoke River

Cape Hatteras

ATLANTIC
OCEAN

N
W   E
S

Cumberland River

Mt. Mitchell
(6,684 ft.; 2,037 m)

BLUE RIDGE MTS.

PIEDMONT

Cape Fear

OZARK
PLATEAU

Mississippi River

Tennessee River

Savannah River

Red River

C O A S T A L

P L A I N

**THE
UNITED STATES**

Elevation

Feet		Meters
Over 13,001		Over 3,001
6,561-13,000		2,001-3,000
3,281-6,560		1,001-2,000
1,641-3,280		501-1,000
661-1,640		201-500
0-660		0-200
Below sea level		Below sea level

Brazos River

Alabama River

Chattahoochee River

OKEEFENOKEE
SWAMP

Cape
Canaveral

Lake
Okeechobee

THE
EVERGLADES

B A H A M A S

Mississippi
River Delta

Gulf of Mexico

ATLANTIC
OCEAN

VIRGIN
ISLANDS

PUERTO
RICO

Caribbean Sea

0   50   100 miles
0   50   100 kilometers

FLORIDA
KEYS

0   150   300 miles
0   150   300 kilometers

CUBA

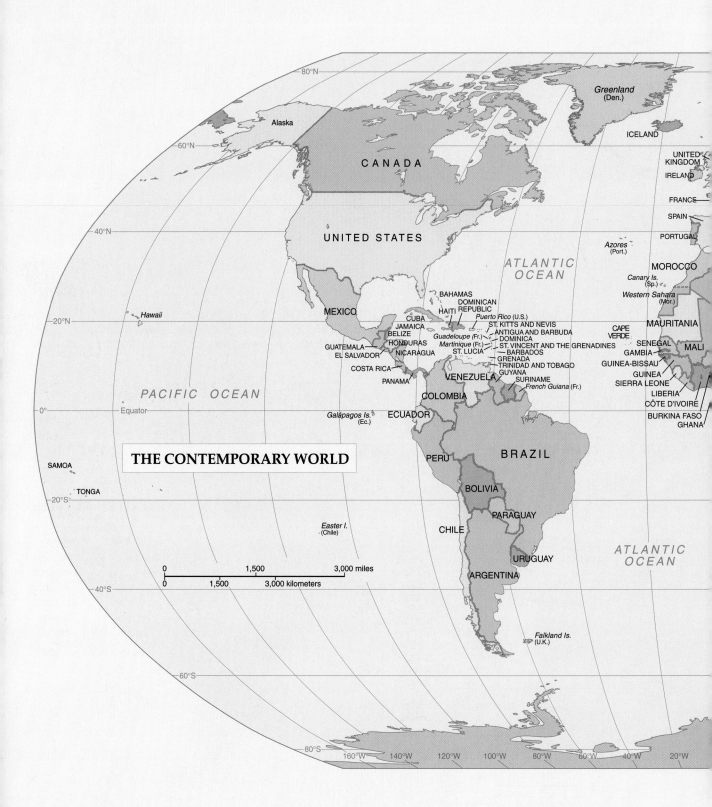

THE CONTEMPORARY WORLD

80°N

Greenland
(Den.)

ICELAND

60°N

Alaska

CANADA

UNITED
KINGDOM

IRELAND

FRANCE

SPAIN

40°N

UNITED STATES

PORTUGAL

Azores
(Port.)

ATLANTIC
OCEAN

MOROCCO

Canary Is.
(Sp.)

Western Sahara
(Mor.)

Hawaii

20°N

MEXICO

BAHAMAS
DOMINICAN
REPUBLIC

HAITI

Puerto Rico (U.S.)

ST. KITTS AND NEVIS

ANTIGUA AND BARBUDA

DOMINICA

ST. VINCENT AND THE GRENADINES

BARBADOS

GRENADA

TRINIDAD AND TOBAGO

GUYANA

SURINAME

French Guiana (Fr.)

CUBA

JAMAICA

BELIZE

HONDURAS

GUATEMALA

EL SALVADOR

NICARAGUA

COSTA RICA

PANAMA

Guadeloupe (Fr.)

Martinique (Fr.)

ST. LUCIA

MAURITANIA

CAPE
VERDE

SENEGAL

GAMBIA

GUINEA-BISSAU

GUINEA

SIERRA LEONE

LIBERIA

CÔTE D'IVOIRE

BURKINA FASO

GHANA

MALI

VENEZUELA

COLOMBIA

PACIFIC OCEAN

0° Equator

ECUADOR

Galápagos Is.
(Ec.)

SAMOA

PERU

BRAZIL

BOLIVIA

TONGA

20°S

Easter I.
(Chile)

CHILE

PARAGUAY

ATLANTIC
OCEAN

URUGUAY

ARGENTINA

40°S

0   1,500   3,000 miles
0   1,500   3,000 kilometers

Falkland Is.
(U.K.)

60°S

80°S

160°W   140°W   120°W   100°W   80°W   60°W   40°W   20°W

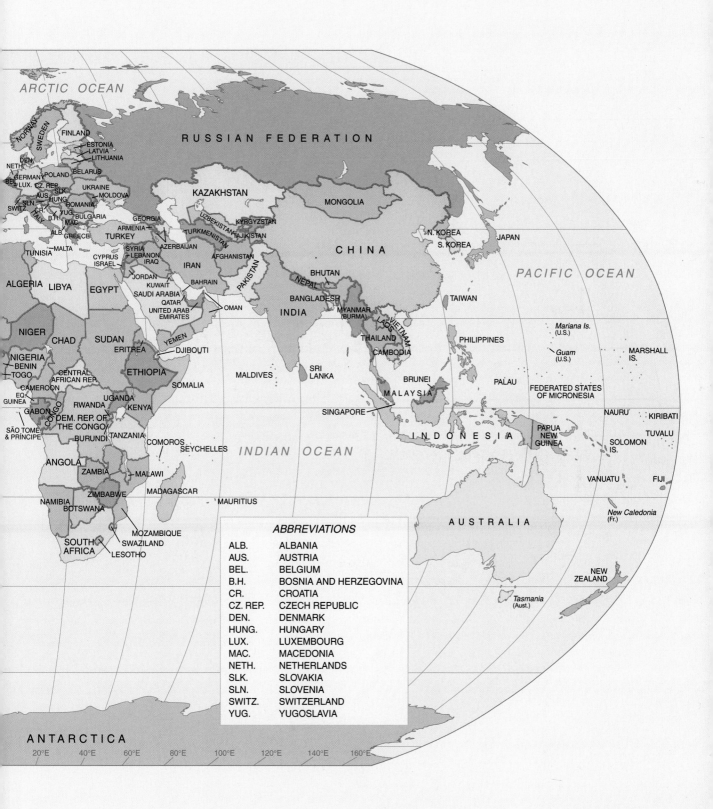

ARCTIC OCEAN

NORWAY
SWEDEN
FINLAND
ESTONIA
LATVIA
LITHUANIA
DEN.
NETH.
GERMANY
BEL.
LUX.
CZ. REP.
POLAND
BELARUS
SLK.
AUS.
HUNG.
UKRAINE
MOLDOVA
SWITZ.
SLN.
CR.
B.H.
ROMANIA
ITALY
YUG.
BULGARIA
MAC.
ALB.
GREECE
GEORGIA
ARMENIA
TURKEY
AZERBAIJAN
TUNISIA
MALTA
CYPRUS
ISRAEL
SYRIA
LEBANON
IRAQ

RUSSIAN FEDERATION

KAZAKHSTAN

MONGOLIA

UZBEKISTAN
KYRGYZSTAN
TURKMENISTAN
TAJIKISTAN
AFGHANISTAN
IRAN
PAKISTAN

CHINA

N. KOREA
S. KOREA
JAPAN

PACIFIC OCEAN

ALGERIA
LIBYA
EGYPT

JORDAN
KUWAIT
SAUDI ARABIA
QATAR
UNITED ARAB
EMIRATES
BAHRAIN
OMAN

BHUTAN
NEPAL
BANGLADESH
INDIA
MYANMAR
(BURMA)
LAOS
VIETNAM
THAILAND
CAMBODIA

TAIWAN

Mariana Is.
(U.S.)

Guam
(U.S.)

MARSHALL
IS.

NIGER
CHAD
SUDAN
ERITREA
YEMEN
DJIBOUTI

PHILIPPINES

NIGERIA
BENIN
TOGO
CENTRAL
AFRICAN REP.
ETHIOPIA
SOMALIA

MALDIVES

SRI
LANKA

BRUNEI

PALAU

FEDERATED STATES
OF MICRONESIA

CAMEROON
EQ.
GUINEA
GABON
CONGO
RWANDA
UGANDA
KENYA
MALAYSIA

NAURU
KIRIBATI

SÃO TOMÉ
& PRÍNCIPE
DEM. REP. OF
THE CONGO
BURUNDI
TANZANIA

SINGAPORE

INDONESIA

PAPUA
NEW
GUINEA

SOLOMON
IS.

TUVALU

COMOROS
SEYCHELLES

INDIAN OCEAN

ANGOLA
ZAMBIA
MALAWI

VANUATU
FIJI

NAMIBIA
BOTSWANA
ZIMBABWE
MADAGASCAR
MAURITIUS

New Caledonia
(Fr.)

AUSTRALIA

SOUTH
AFRICA
MOZAMBIQUE
SWAZILAND
LESOTHO

NEW
ZEALAND

Tasmania
(Aust.)

ANTARCTICA

20°E   40°E   60°E   80°E   100°E   120°E   140°E   160°E

ABBREVIATIONS

ALB.	ALBANIA
AUS.	AUSTRIA
BEL.	BELGIUM
B.H.	BOSNIA AND HERZEGOVINA
CR.	CROATIA
CZ. REP.	CZECH REPUBLIC
DEN.	DENMARK
HUNG.	HUNGARY
LUX.	LUXEMBOURG
MAC.	MACEDONIA
NETH.	NETHERLANDS
SLK.	SLOVAKIA
SLN.	SLOVENIA
SWITZ.	SWITZERLAND
YUG.	YUGOSLAVIA

THE
AMERICAN
PROMISE

A HISTORY OF THE UNITED STATES

Second Compact Edition

BATTLE OF BUNKER HILL, JUNE 17, 1775 by Alonzo Chappel. *Chicago Historical Society.*

THE AMERICAN PROMISE

A HISTORY OF THE UNITED STATES

Second Compact Edition

Volume I: To 1877

JAMES L. ROARK
Emory University

MICHAEL P. JOHNSON
Johns Hopkins University

PATRICIA CLINE COHEN
University of California at Santa Barbara

SARAH STAGE
Arizona State University West

ALAN LAWSON
Boston College

SUSAN M. HARTMANN
The Ohio State University

BEDFORD / ST. MARTIN'S
Boston   ◆   New York

FOR BEDFORD/ST. MARTIN'S

Publisher of History: Patricia A. Rossi
Director of Development for History: Jane Knetzger
Developmental Editors: Heidi Hood, Gretchen Boger, Louise Townsend
Project Manager: Tina Samaha
Senior Production Supervisor: Joe Ford
Marketing Manager: Jenna Bookin Barry
Associate Editor for New Media: William J. Lombardo
Editorial Assistants: Brianna R. Germain, Rachel L. Siegel, Elisabeth Stark
Production Assistant: Kerri Cardone
Copyeditor: Lisa Wehrle
Text Design: Wanda Kossak
Photo Research: Pembroke Herbert/Sandi Rygiel, Picture Research Consultants & Archives, Inc.
Cartography: Mapping Specialists Limited
Indexer: Maro Riofrancos
Cover Design: Donna Dennison
Composition: TechBooks
Printing and Binding: RR Donnelley & Sons Company

President: Joan E. Feinberg
Editorial Director: Denise B. Wydra
Director of Marketing: Karen Melton
Director of Editing, Design, and Production: Marcia Cohen
Managing Editor: Elizabeth M. Schaaf

Library of Congress Control Number: 2002108121

7   6   5   4   3
f   e   d   c

For information, write: Bedford/St. Martin's, 75 Arlington Street, Boston, MA 02116
(617-399-4000)

ISBN: 0–312–40358-5 (combined edition)
        0–312–40359-3 (Vol. I)
        0–312–40360-7 (Vol. II)

Cover Art: *American Fantasy,* a cutwork picture. Lebanon County, Pennsylvania, c. 1840–1860. Layered cut paper and applique on original vibrant blue paper background. Courtesy, David Schorsch/American Antiques, Inc.

BRIEF CONTENTS

CONTENTS

CHAPTER 16

Reconstruction, 1863–1877   387

MAPS, FIGURES, AND TABLES

SPECIAL FEATURES

PREFACE

THE COMPACT EDITION OF *The American Promise: A History of the United States* grew from the authors' desire to provide a fresh alternative for fellow instructors searching for the most teachable and readable text available: a unique midsized book that pairs all the color, pedagogy, and features of a full-length text with a briefer narrative at a lower price. The unique size of the Compact Edition allows us to meet the needs of students and instructors who want the flexibility of a briefer text without sacrificing coverage or readability. In writing the Second Compact Edition, we continued to draw from our experiences as longtime teachers of the survey course to help us identify the essentials of American history as well as the stories and voices that make this history memorable for students. Our collective experience teaching introductory American history in a wide range of institutions, from community colleges and state universities to private colleges and research institutions, taught us that the survey course is the most difficult to teach and the most difficult to take. It is this knowledge that has informed every decision we have made in creating this text.

Our teaching experience was invaluable in making the choices necessary to create the Second Compact Edition from its parent text, *The American Promise,* Second Edition. To preserve the narrative strengths of *The American Promise,* all of the authors revised their own chapters. To maintain the strong story line and balanced narrative in a midsized format, we reorganized material and combined thematically related sections throughout the text. In short, we did not create the Second Compact Edition simply by cutting; we also reimagined, reorganized, and rewrote.

Our experience as teachers also informed the framework of our text. Most survey texts emphasize either a social or political approach to history; by focusing on one, they inevitably slight the other. In our classrooms, students need **both** the structure a political narrative provides and the insights gained from examining social and cultural experiences. To write a comprehensive, balanced account of American history, we focused on the public arena—the place where politics intersects social and cultural developments—to show how Americans confronted the major issues of their day and created far-reaching historical change.

We also thought hard about the concerns most frequently voiced by instructors: that students often find history boring, unfocused, and difficult and their textbooks similarly lifeless and overwhelming. How could our text address these concerns and help introductory students understand and remember American history's main events and developments? We decided to explore fully the political, social, economic, and cultural changes that students need to understand by connecting them to individuals who experienced history as it happened. To make each chapter more memorable and to portray the diversity of the American experience, we stitched into the narrative the voices of hundreds of contemporaries—from presidents to pipefitters—whose ideas and actions shaped their times and whose efforts still affect our lives. By incorporating a rich selection of authentic American voices, we sought to create a vivid and compelling narrative that captures students' interest and sparks their historical imagination.

Our title, *The American Promise,* reflects our emphasis on the power of human agency and our conviction that American history is an unfinished story. For millions, the nation held out the promise of a better life, unfettered worship, representative government, democratic politics, and other freedoms seldom found elsewhere around the world. But none of these promises came with guarantees. And promises fulfilled for some meant promises denied to others. As we see it, much of American history is a continuing struggle over the definition and realization of the nation's promise. That hope, kept alive by countless sacrifices, has been marred by compromises, disappointments, and denials, but it lives today. Abraham Lincoln, in the midst of what he termed the "fiery trial" of the Civil War, pronounced the nation "the last best hope of

Earth." Ideally, *The American Promise,* Second Compact Edition, will help students become aware of the legacy of hope bequeathed to them by previous generations of Americans, a legacy that is theirs to preserve and to build on.

Features

Because students learn best when they find a subject engaging, we have made a special effort to incorporate features that bring American history to life and make it memorable. **Chapter-opening vignettes** invite students into the narrative with vivid accounts of individuals or groups who embody each chapter's main themes. Vignettes new to this edition include Pocahontas's "rescue" of John Smith, Nat Turner's war on slavery, and Fannie Lou Hamer's civil rights struggles. **Two-tiered running heads** on every page remind students where the sections they read fall chronologically. At the close of each chapter, strengthened **conclusions** critically reexamine central ideas and provide a bridge to the next chapter, and **annotated chronologies** review the key events and developments explored in the chapter. We have enhanced the well-received **appendices** by extending our collection of reference materials in a new **Online Appendix** that contains such important documents as the Articles of Confederation, the Seneca Falls Resolution, the Confederate Constitution, and Martin Luther King, Jr.'s "I Have a Dream" speech. **Cross-references to the new Online Study Guide** in each chapter encourage mastery of visual and text material and development of critical-thinking skills. Additional text **cross-references to Online Bibliographies,** organized by chapter and topic, provide students with detailed suggestions for additional reading and research.

For further reading about the topics in this chapter, see the Online Bibliography at
www.bedfordstmartins.com/roarkcompact.

For additional first-hand accounts of this period, see pages 181–195 in Michael Johnson, ed., *Reading the American Past,* Second Edition, Volume I.

To assess your mastery of the material in this chapter, see the Online Study Guide at
www.bedfordstmartins.com/roarkcompact.

An enriched array of special features reinforces the narrative and offers teachers more points of departure for assignments and discussion. With the addition of sixteen new boxed features, this edition provides a wider variety of choices for sparking students' interest while helping them understand that history is both a body of knowledge and an ongoing process of investigation. The all-new **Promise of Technology** features examine the ramifications—positive and negative—of technological developments in American society and culture such as the cultivation of corn, the printing press, hydraulic mining, and air conditioning. **Documenting the American Promise** features (formerly "Texts in Historical Context") combine three or four primary documents that dramatize the human dimension of major events and controversies with interpretive commentary. New topics in this edition include "King Philip Considers Christianity," "The Destruction of the Tea," "Rockefeller and His Critics," and "The Emerging Cold War." Questions for Analysis and Debate now follow the documents to help students analyze and squeeze meaning from primary sources. Illustrated **Historical Questions** pose and interpret specific questions of continuing interest so as to demonstrate the depth and variety of possible answers, thereby countering the belief of many beginning students that historians simply gather facts and string them together into a chronological narrative. New Historical Questions in this edition include "Did Terrorists Sink the *Maine*?" and "Was Prohibition a Bad Joke?"

We take great pride as well in our full-color design and rich art program. We have preserved the **award-winning design** and added many new **illustrations** to make *The American Promise* a visual feast. In all, more than 350 images, many in full color and all large enough to study in detail, reinforce and extend the narrative. An illustration accompanies each chapter-opening vignette, providing a visual supplement to the narrative portrait that opens every chapter. All pictures are contemporaneous with the period of the chapter, with **comprehensive captions** that draw students into active engagement with the images and help

TOURISM AND THE LURE OF NATIVE TRADITION
This advertisement for vacationing in the mountainous Indian country of New Mexico implies the benefits of high altitude for health. But commerce in native crafts is also an objective. Others at the time headed to New Mexico to attain quite different benefits. Attracted by anthropologists studying native culture and a coterie of painters and writers who began an artists' colony near the ancient pueblo at Taos, disillusioned strivers and other refugees from the stresses of modern life hoped to find a spiritual inner wisdom within Pueblo culture that would reconnect them with nature and the past.
Private collection.
www.bedfordstmartins.com/roarkcompact See the Online Study Guide for more help in analyzing this image.

them unpack the layers of meaning. Full-page **chapter-opening artifacts** combine with many other illustrations of artifacts to emphasize the importance of material culture in the study of the past.

Finally, we have extended and expanded our highly regarded **map program** to offer the most effective set of maps available in a survey text. Each chapter offers, on average, three **full-size maps** showing major developments in a wide range of areas, from environmental and technological issues to political, social, cultural, and diplomatic matters. New maps reflect this edition's increased attention to Native American peoples and to a sustained continental perspective. Each chapter includes as well an average of two new **"spot maps,"** small, single-concept maps embedded in pertinent passages of the narrative to increase students' grasp of crucial issues. Unique to *The American Promise,* the spot maps highlight such topics as ancient California, Pontiac's rebellion, the Haitian revolution, the Vicksburg campaign, Pullman's company town, the Dust Bowl, the creation of Israel, the breakup of Yugoslavia, and the recent conflict in Afghanistan. In addition, **critical-thinking map exercises**—one per chapter—combine for an **embedded map workbook.**

Haitian Revolution, 1790–1804

made other major revisions in organization and coverage.

To mesh better with most course calendars and to provide a more focused narrative, we reduced the number of chapters from 32 to 31. We also shortened the text by an additional 5 percent from the First Compact Edition (making it 30 percent shorter than its parent, *The American Promise,* Second Edition), in the process highlighting a stronger thematic development. Specifically, coverage of ancient America now appears in a refashioned and richly illustrated chapter on ancient America, to show students how and why the discussion of this crucial but obscured history differs from the historical narrative that follows in the remainder of the book. Discussion of antebellum society has been reorganized and revised to ensure a smooth, unified narrative. Throughout the text we have incorporated the most important recent scholarship, as reflected in chapter bibliographies on the companion Web site (**www.bedfordstmartins.com/roarkcompact**).

To provide an even more dynamic and memorable narrative while reinforcing the text's central theme, we expanded the number of historical actors whose interpretations of "the American promise"—sometimes shared, often competing—drove historical change. More succinct coverage of politics also permitted us to expand discussion of cultural and social topics such as the diversity of West Africa, the experience of Native Americans, and Western history. We have also made an effort to better place American history in a global context. Discussions of early modern Europe's westward expansion and the Haitian revolution, for example, strengthen the text's balanced, braided international coverage. Revised conclusions focus on and extend the chapter's central ideas, contributing to our effort to provide the introductory classroom the most teachable and readable text available.

Textual Changes

A new edition of a textbook is cause for celebration, for it proudly announces the successful reception of the previous edition. But as authors, we found little time for complacency, for we welcomed this opportunity to reconsider the original text, to take stock of what worked and what could be improved. In addition to the many changes already mentioned to condense the text, we

Supplements

Developed with the guidance of the author team and thoroughly revised to reflect changes in the new edition, our comprehensive collection of print and electronic resources provides a host of practical learning and teaching aids. Cross-references in the textbook to the groundbreaking Online Study Guide and the primary-source reader reflect the tight integration of core text with supplements.

For Students

Reading the American Past: Selected Historical Documents, **Second Edition.** This highly regarded primary-source collection, edited by Michael Johnson (Johns Hopkins University), one of the authors of *The American Promise*, complements the textbook by offering 4 or 5 documents for each chapter. The new edition provides a host of compelling features while retaining its low cost and brevity: a rich selection of over 125 documents (one-quarter of them new to this edition), balancing accounts by well-known figures with the voices of ordinary people; a wide array of sources that vividly illustrate the diversity of materials with which historians work; and user-friendly editorial apparatus such as chapter introductions, headnotes, questions, and an Introduction for Students on the goals and methods of source analysis.

Online Study Guide www.bedfordstmartins.com/roarkcompact. For each chapter, our free Online Study Guide offers an initial multiple-choice test that allows students to assess their comprehension of the material and a Recommended Study Plan that suggests specific exercises on the subject areas students still need to master. Two follow-up multiple-choice tests per chapter help students judge their command of the material. Additional exercises encourage students to think about chapter themes as well as help them develop skills of analysis. Password-protected reports for instructors allow them to monitor students' activity easily.

The Bedford Series in History and Culture. Over fifty American titles in this highly praised series combine first-rate scholarship, historical narrative, and important primary documents for undergraduate courses. Each book is brief, inexpensive, and focused on a specific topic or period. Package discounts are available.

Historians at Work Series. Brief enough for a single assignment yet substantive enough to provoke thoughtful discussion, each volume in this series combines the best thinking about an important historical issue with helpful learning aids. Selections by distinguished historians, each with a differing perspective, provide a unique structure within which to examine a single question. With headnotes and questions to guide their reading and the complete original footnotes, students are able to engage in discussion that captures the intellectual excitement of historical research and interpretation. Package discounts are available.

Links Library www.bedfordstmartins.com/historylinks. Links Library is a database of more than 350 carefully reviewed and annotated U.S. and Western history links searchable by historical topic and textbook chapter. Spanning history from ancient Mesopotamia to the present, the database contains diverse links to resources such as historical archaeology sites, primary documents collections, photograph and illustration galleries, map collections, secondary sources, and audio.

DocLinks www.bedfordstmartins.com/doclinks. DocLinks is a database of over 1000 annotated Web links to primary documents online for the study of U.S. and Western history. Documents in this database include speeches, legislation, U.S. Supreme Court decisions, essays, traveler's accounts, personal narratives and testimony, essays, e-books, manifestos, visual artifacts, songs, and poems. Documents are searchable by topic and date and are also indexed to the chapters of our major survey textbooks.

For Instructors

Instructor's Resource Manual. This popular manual by Sarah E. Gardner (Mercer University) offers extensive information for each chapter in the text-book: outlines of chapter themes and topics, lecture and discussion strategies, multiple-choice questions for quizzing, video and film resources, and advice on outside readings. In addition, the new edition offers suggestions on incorporating all the supplements for the Second Compact Edition of *The American Promise* into teaching plans; including Bedford series books relevant to each chapter; and assigning Using the Internet exercises that reinforce and extend the text. It also includes a wealth of practical suggestions for first-time teaching assistants, from suggestions on running discussion sections and designing assignments to advice on dealing with difficult students.

Online Instructor's Resource Manual www.bedfordstmartins.com/roarkcompact. The Online Instructor's Resource Manual combines all of the advantages of the print Instructor's Resource Manual along with links for Using the Internet exercises, annotated Web links for each chapter, PowerPoint slides for lectures, syllabus hosting, and the ability to track student work.

Videos. Available to all adopters of the text are two hours of video delivered in fifteen brief clips that allow instructors to intersperse their lectures with images and audio designed to engage students by giving voice to the history of early America. These segments are drawn from the award-winning telecourse "Shaping America," developed and distributed by the LeCroy Center for Educational Telecommunications, Dallas County Community College District. Bedford/St. Martin's is proud to announce that *The American Promise: To 1877*, Second Edition, has been selected for use in this distinguished distance learning program.

Computerized Test Bank CD-ROM for Windows or Macintosh. This thoroughly revised test bank by Valerie Hinton (Richland College) and Norman C. McLeod (Dixie State College) provides easy-to-use software to create and administer tests on paper or over a network. Instructors can generate exams and quizzes from the print test bank or write their own. A grade-management function helps keep track of student progress. It includes for each chapter in the text fifty multiple-choice questions, ten short-answer questions, four essay questions (all ranked as easy, medium, or difficult); an exercise in which students match important terms with definitions or examples; a chronology exercise; and a multipart map exercise. Also included are twenty-five black outline map quizzes. Answers for objective questions are provided.

Map Transparencies. Full-color transparencies of full-size maps from both the full and compact editions of *The American Promise* help instructors present the materials and teach students important map-reading skills.

Instructor Resources CD-ROM. This new CD-ROM offers all the maps and figures and numerous illustrations from the text in PowerPoint-ready files designed to enhance class presentations.

Using the Bedford Series in the U.S. History Survey www.bedfordstmartins.com/usingseries. This short guide by Scott Hovey (Boston University) gives practical suggestions for using more than sixty volumes from the Bedford Series in History and Culture and the Historians at Work Series with a core text in the survey classroom. The guide not only supplies links between the text and the supplements but also provides ideas for starting discussions focused on a single primary-source volume.

Map Central www.bedfordstmartins.com/mapcentral. Bedford/St. Martin's is proud to announce Map Central, a database of the more than 450 maps that appear in *The American Promise* and its other history survey texts. Designed to help instructors create more effective lecture presentations, Map Central is easily searchable by specific chapter or by keyword. Maps are in full color and downloadable for use in PowerPoint or other presentation software.

e-Content for Online Learning. e-Content for Online Learning helps instructors using *The American Promise*, Second Compact Edition, develop custom Web sites with WebCT, Blackboard, and other course-building systems.

Acknowledgments

We gratefully acknowledge all of the helpful suggestions that have come from those who have read and taught the previous editions of *The American Promise,* and we hope that our many classroom collaborators will see their influence in the Second Compact Edition. In particular, we wish to thank the talented scholars and teachers who gave generously of their time and knowledge to review this book; their critiques and suggestions have contributed greatly to the published work: Robert Allison, *Suffolk University;* Edward Baptist, *University of Miami;* Vernon Burton, *University of Illinois at Urbana-Champaign;* Manuel Callahan, *University of Texas;* Marvin Cann, *Lander University;* Robert Cormier, *Shrewsbury High School;* Dolores Davison Peterson, *Foothill College;* Alan C. Downs, *Georgia Southern University;* Frederick Fausz, *University of Missouri-St. Louis;* Richard M. Filipink, *SUNY College at Freedonia;* Randy Finley, *Georgia Perimeter College;* Ellen Fitzpatrick, *University of New Hampshire;* John M. Giggie, *University of Texas at San Antonio;* Valerie Hinton, *Richland College;* Tim Koerner, *Oakland Community College;* Jill Lepore, *Boston University;* Mike Light, *Grand Rapids Community College;* Barbara Loomis, *San Francisco State University;* Norman Love, *El Paso Community College;* Joanne Maypole, *Front Range Community College;* Tom Nierman, *University of Kansas;* Robert Olwell, *University of Texas at Austin;* Terry Perrin, *Austin Community College;* Nicolas W. Proctor, *Simpson College;* Peggy Renner, *Glendale Community College;* James Schick, *Pittsburgh State University;* Michael Searles, *Augusta State University;* Rebecca Shoemaker, *Indiana State University;* Rachel Standish, *Foothill College;* Richard M. Ugland, *The Ohio State University;* Elizabeth Van Beek, *San Jose State University;* Pamela West, *Jefferson State Community College;* Thomas Winn, *Austin Peay State University;* Molly M. Wood, *Wittenberg University;* Laura Woodward-Ney, *Idaho State University;* and William D. Young, *Maple Woods Community College.*

A project as complex as this requires the talents of many individuals. First, the authors would like to acknowledge our families for their support, forbearance, and toleration of our textbook responsibilities. Pembroke Herbert and Sandi Rygiel of Picture Research Consultants, Inc., contributed their imagination and research to make possible the extraordinary illustration program.

We would also like to thank the many people at Bedford/St. Martin's who have been crucial to this project. First we want to thank both Editor Heidi L. Hood, who coordinated the editorial process, and Editor Gretchen Boger, for their intelligence and commitment to excellence that guided every step of this revision. Thanks are also due to Editor Louise Townsend, whose accomplished editing of this and previous editions greatly improved our textbook. Special thanks also go to our friend, Executive Editor Elizabeth M. Welch, who contributed invaluably to past editions and advised on this revision. Brianna Germain, Rachel L. Siegel, and Elisabeth Stark helped with countless editorial tasks. Jane Knetzger, Director of Development for History, supported the efforts of the editorial team. We thank as well Patricia Rossi, Publisher for History and Communications, and Jenna Bookin Barry, Marketing Manager, for their tireless efforts in marketing the book. With great skill and professionalism, Project Manager Tina Samaha pulled all the pieces together with the assistance of Kerri Cardone. Managing Editor Elizabeth Schaaf, Assistant Managing Editor John Amburg, and Senior Production Supervisor Joe Ford oversaw production of the book. Our copy editor, Lisa Wehrle, improved our best efforts. Thanks also go to Associate Editor for New Media William J. Lombardo who guided the development of the companion Web site and supervised the editing of the book's supplements. New Media Production Coordinator Coleen O'Hanley helped transform the Companion Web site and other electronic supplements into reality. Director of New Media Denise Wydra provided support for these new media resources for history. Joan E. Feinberg, President, and Charles H. Christensen, former president, have taken a personal interest in *The American Promise* from the start and have guided all its editions through every stage of development.

ABOUT THE AUTHORS

James L. Roark

Born in Eunice, Louisiana, and raised in the West, James L. Roark received his B.A. from the University of California, Davis, in 1963 and his Ph.D. from Stanford University in 1973. His dissertation won the Allan Nevins Prize. He has taught at the University of Nigeria, Nsukka; the University of Nairobi, Kenya; the University of Missouri, St. Louis; and, since 1983, Emory University, where he is Samuel Candler Dobbs Professor of American History. In 1993, he received the Emory Williams Distinguished Teaching Award, and in 2001–2002 he was Pitt Professor of American Institutions at Cambridge University. He has written *Masters without Slaves: Southern Planters in the Civil War and Reconstruction* (1977). With Michael P. Johnson, he is author of *Black Masters: A Free Family of Color in the Old South* (1984) and editor of *No Chariot Let Down: Charleston's Free People of Color on the Eve of the Civil War* (1984). He has received research assistance from the American Philosophical Society, the National Endowment for the Humanities, and the Gilder Lehrman Institute of American History. Active in the Organization of American Historians and the Southern Historical Association, he is also a fellow of the Society of American Historians.

Michael P. Johnson

Born and raised in Ponca City, Oklahoma, Michael P. Johnson studied at Knox College in Galesburg, Illinois, where he received a B.A. in 1963, and at Stanford University in Palo Alto, California, earning a Ph.D. in 1973. He is currently professor of history at Johns Hopkins University in Baltimore, having previously taught at the University of California, Irvine; San Jose State University; and LeMoyne (now LeMoyne-Owen) College in Memphis. His publications include *Toward a Patriarchal Republic: The Secession of Georgia* (1977); *Black Masters: A Free Family of Color in the Old South* (1984); *No Chariot Let Down: Charleston's Free People of Color on the Eve of the Civil War* (1984); *Abraham Lincoln, Slavery, and the Civil War: Selected Speeches and Writings* (2001); and *Reading the American Past: Selected Historical Documents,* Second Edition, the documents reader for *The American Promise* (2002); and articles that have appeared in the *William and Mary Quarterly,* the *Journal of Southern History, Labor History,* the *New York Review of Books,* the *New Republic,* the *Nation,* and other journals. Johnson has been awarded research fellowships by the American Council of Learned Societies, the National Endowment for the Humanities, and the Center for Advanced Study in the Behavioral Sciences. He directed a National Endowment for the Humanities Summer Seminar for College Teachers and has been honored with the University of California, Irvine, Academic Senate Distinguished Teaching Award and the University of California, Irvine, Alumni Association Outstanding Teaching Award. He is an active member of the American Historical Association, the Organization of American Historians, and the Southern Historical Association.

Patricia Cline Cohen

Born in Ann Arbor, Michigan, and raised in Palo Alto, California, Patricia Cline Cohen earned a B.A. at the University of Chicago in 1968 and a Ph.D. at the University of California, Berkeley, in 1977. In 1976, she joined the history faculty at the University of California, Santa Barbara. Cohen has written *A Calculating People: The Spread of Numeracy in Early America* (1982; reissued 1999) and *The Murder of Helen Jewett: The Life and Death of a Prostitute in Nineteenth-Century New York* (1998). She has also published articles on quantitative literacy, mathematics education, prostitution, and murder in journals including the *Journal of Women's History, Radical History Review,* the *William and Mary Quarterly,* and the *NWSA Journal.* Her scholarly work has received support from the National Endowment for the Humanities, the National Humanities Center, the University of California President's Fellowship in the Humanities, the Mellon Foundation, the American Antiquarian Society, the Schlesinger Library, and the Newberry Library. She sits on the council for the Omohundro Institute of Early American History and Culture and on the advisory council of the Society for the History of the Early American Republic. She has served as chair of the Women's Studies Program and as acting dean of the humanities and fine arts at the

University of California, Santa Barbara. In 2001–2002 she was the Distinguished Senior Mellon Fellow at the American Antiquarian Society.

Sarah Stage

Sarah Stage was born in Davenport, Iowa, and received a B.A. from the University of Iowa in 1966 and a Ph.D. in American studies from Yale University in 1975. She has taught U.S. history for more than twenty-five years at Williams College and the University of California, Riverside. Currently she is professor of Women's Studies at Arizona State University West, in Phoenix. Her books include *Female Complaints: Lydia Pinkham and the Business of Women's Medicine* (1979) and *Rethinking Home Economics: Women and the History of a Profession* (1997), which is being translated for a Japanese edition. Among the fellowships she has received are the Rockefeller Foundation Humanities Fellowship, the American Association of University Women dissertation fellowship, a fellowship from the Charles Warren Center for the Study of History at Harvard University, and the University of California President's Fellowship in the Humanities. She is at work on a book entitled *Women and the Progressive Impulse in American Politics, 1890–1914*.

Alan Lawson

Born in Providence, Rhode Island, Alan Lawson received his B.A. from Brown University in 1955 and his M.A. from the University of Wisconsin in 1956. After Army service and experience as a high school teacher, he earned his Ph.D. from the University of Michigan in 1967. Since winning the Allan Nevins Prize for his dissertation, Lawson has served on the faculties of the University of California, Irvine; Smith College; and, currently, Boston College. He has written *The Failure of Independent Liberalism* (1971) and coedited *From Revolution to Republic* (1976). While completing the forthcoming *Ideas in Crisis: The New Deal and the Mobilization of Progressive Experience,* he has published book chapters and essays on political economy, the cultural legacy of the New Deal, multiculturalism, and the arts in public life. He has served as editor of the *Review of Education* and the *Intellectual History Newsletter* and contributed articles to those journals as well as to the *History of Education Quarterly.* He has been active in the field of American studies as director of the Boston College American Studies program and as a contributor to the *American Quarterly.* Under the auspices of the United States Information Agency, Lawson has been coordinator and lecturer for programs to instruct faculty from foreign nations in the state of American historical scholarship and teaching.

Susan M. Hartmann

Professor of history at Ohio State University, Susan M. Hartmann received her B.A. from Washington University in 1961 and her Ph.D. from the University of Missouri in 1966. After specializing in the political economy of the post–World War II period and publishing *Truman and the 80th Congress* (1971), she expanded her interests to the field of women's history, publishing many articles and three books: *The Home Front and Beyond: American Women in the 1940s* (1982); *From Margin to Mainstream: American Women and Politics since 1960* (1989); and *The Other Feminists: Activists in the Liberal Establishment* (1998). Her work has been supported by the Truman Library Institute, the Rockefeller Foundation, the National Endowment for the Humanities, and the American Council of Learned Societies. At Ohio State she has served as director of women's studies, and in 1995 she won the Exemplary Faculty Award in the College of Humanities. Hartmann has taught at the University of Missouri, St. Louis, and Boston University, and she has lectured on American history in Australia, Austria, France, Germany, Greece, Nepal, and New Zealand. She has served on award committees of the American Historical Association, the Organization of American Historians, the American Studies Association, and the National Women's Studies Association and currently is on the Board of Directors at the Truman Library Institute. Her current research is on gender and the transformation of politics since 1945.

THE
AMERICAN
PROMISE

A HISTORY OF THE UNITED STATES

Second Compact Edition

OLMEC RITUAL FIGURES

Ancient American artifacts sometimes portray human forms that probably bore a strong resemblance to the people for whom they were made. This astonishing group of Olmec men, crafted and buried between 900 and 600 B.C. in the ceremonial center at La Venta in what is now southern Mexico, is shown exactly as it was found when archaeologists excavated it in 1955. The men all exhibit cranial deformation, probably common among Olmecs of the era; it was created by wrapping tight bindings around the skulls of infants and children. These men seem to be engaged in an important ritual. The sandstone figure with his back to the upright stones, or celts, observes four men filing in front of him from his right, while eleven men of differing heights and distinctive physiognomies stand in a semicircle looking on. The significance of this ceremony is documented by its haunting artistry and careful burial, but exactly what the ceremony meant remains utterly mysterious, like so much else about ancient Americans.

Museo Nacional de Antropologia, Mexico City.

BEFORE THE WRITTEN RECORD: ANCIENT AMERICA

To 1492

I N AUGUST 1908, AFTER A VIOLENT RAINSTORM NEAR FOLSOM, NEW MEXICO, George McJunkin, the manager of the Crowfoot Ranch, rode out to mend fences and to look for missing cattle. An African American, McJunkin had been born a slave in Texas over fifty years earlier. After he became free at the end of the Civil War in 1865, McJunkin worked as a cowboy in Colorado and New Mexico, becoming the Crowfoot manager in 1891. As he surveyed the damage done by the recent storm, McJunkin noticed that the floodwater had exposed a deposit of stark white bones in the bank of a gulch called Wild Horse Arroyo. Curious, he dismounted and chipped away at the deposit until he uncovered an entire fossilized bone. Since the bone was considerably larger than the parched skeletons of range cattle and buffalo, McJunkin saved it, hoping someday to identify it.

In 1912, McJunkin met a white man named Carl Schwachheim, a blacksmith in Raton, New Mexico, who shared his curiosity about fossils, and the two men became friends. Ten years later, a few months after McJunkin's death, Schwachheim finally drove out to Wild Horse Arroyo, dug out several bones, and brought them back to Raton. But he could not identify animals that had such big bones.

In 1926, when Schwachheim delivered cattle to the stockyards in Denver, he took some of the old bones to the Denver Museum of Natural History and showed them to J. D. Figgins, a paleontologist who was an expert on fossils of ancient animals. Figgins immediately recognized the significance of the fossils and a few months later began an excavation of the Folsom site that revolutionized knowledge about the first Americans.

When Figgins began his dig at Folsom, archaeologists (individuals who study artifacts left by long-vanished peoples) believed that Native Americans had arrived relatively recently in the Western Hemisphere, probably no more than three or four thousand years earlier when, experts assumed, they had paddled small boats across the icy waters of the Bering Strait from what is now Siberia. At Folsom, Figgins learned that the bones McJunkin had first spotted belonged to twenty-three giant bison, a species known to have been extinct for at least 10,000 years. Far more startling, Figgins found nineteen flint projectile points (Folsom points, they have since been called) associated with the bones, proof that human beings had been alive at the same time as the giant bison. One flint point remained stuck between two ribs of a giant bison, just where a Stone Age hunter had plunged it more than 10,000

GEORGE MCJUNKIN
This photo shows McJunkin a few years after he discovered the Folsom site, but about fifteen years before anyone understood the significance of his find. He appears here in his work clothes on horseback, as he probably was when he made the discovery. The fossilized bones he discovered belonged to an extinct bison species that was much larger than modern bison; the horns of the ancient animal often spanned six feet, wide enough for McJunkin's horse to have stood sideways between the horns.

Eastern New Mexico University, Blackwater Draw Site, Portales, New Mexico 88130.

years earlier. No longer could anyone doubt that human beings had inhabited North America for at least ten millennia. 1920

The Folsom discovery sparked other major finds of ancient artifacts that continue to this day. Since the 1930s, archaeologists have tried to reconstruct the history of ancient Americans, making connections between the hunters who killed giant bison with flint points, their descendants who built southwestern pueblos and eastern burial mounds, and *their* descendants who encountered the Europeans who arrived with Christopher Columbus in 1492. Although the story they have assembled is incomplete and controversial, nonetheless scholars have learned enough about ancient Americans to bring into focus who they were, where they came from, and some basic features of their history in the thousands of years before that moment in 1492 when some of them stood on the beach of a small island in the Caribbean and watched Columbus and his men row ashore.

Archaeology and History

Archaeologists and historians share the desire to learn about people who lived in the past, but they usually employ different methods to obtain information. Both archaeologists and historians study artifacts as clues to the activities and ideas of the humans who created them. They concentrate, however, on different kinds of artifacts. Archaeologists tend to focus on physical objects such as bones, stones, pots, baskets, jewelry, textiles, clothing, graves, and buildings. Historians direct their attention mostly to writings, which encompass personal and private jottings such as diary entries and love letters, official and public pronouncements such as laws and speeches, as well as an enormous variety of other documents such as court records, censuses, business ledgers, newspapers, books, and pamphlets. Although historians are interested in other artifacts and archaeologists do not neglect written sources if they exist, the characteristic concentration of historians on writings and archaeologists on other physical objects denotes a rough cultural and chronological boundary between the human beings studied by the two groups of scholars, a boundary marked by the use of writing.

A system of symbols that record spoken language, writing originated among ancient peoples in China, Egypt, and Central America about 8,000 years ago, within the most recent 2 percent of the 400 millennia that modern human beings (*Homo sapiens*) have existed. Writing came into use even later in most other places in the world. The ancient Americans who inhabited North America in 1492, for example, possessed many forms of symbolic representation, but not writing.

The people who lived during the millennia before writing were biologically nearly identical to people today. After all, their DNA was the template for ours. But they differed from us in many other ways, among them in not using writing to communicate across space and time. They certainly had a history, both individually and collectively. They moved across the face of the globe; they invented hundreds of spoken languages; they learned to survive and even to thrive in almost every natural environment; they chose and honored leaders; they traded, warred, and worshiped; and, above all, they learned from and taught each other, not just old ways but, little by little, surprising new ways. Nonetheless, much of what we would like to know about their history remains unknown because it took place before written history existed. It is this lack of written records that has prompted the misleading label of *prehistory* for this era. These ancient people spoke to each other, but, without writing, time forever muffled their words and thus their history.

Archaeologists specialize in learning about people whose history was not documented in writing. They study the millions of artifacts created by these people, trying to decipher what the objects can tell us about their lives. By also scrutinizing soil, geological strata, pollen, climate, and other environmental features, they attempt to reconstruct the outlines of the history of ancient peoples. But much of their history remains unknown and unknowable. The absence of written sources means that ancient human beings remain anonymous. No documents chronicle their births and deaths, comings and goings, victories and defeats. Despite these silences, archaeologists have learned to make ancient artifacts tell a great deal about the people who made them.

This introductory chapter relies on the work of archaeologists to sketch a brief overview of ancient America. Calling the long history of ancient Americans an introduction reflects our present-mindedness, an outgrowth of our desire to understand the origins and development of our own society over the last five centuries or so. Ancient Americans surely did not consider their history an introduction to a future that included us. They resided in North America for thousands of years before Europeans arrived. They created societies and cultures of amazing diversity and complexity. But because they did not use written records, their history cannot be reconstructed with the detail and certainty made possible by written documents. Nonetheless, their remarkable longevity and creativity make it far preferable to abbreviate and oversimplify their history than to ignore it.

The First Americans

Human beings existed elsewhere in the world long before they reached the Western Hemisphere. The basic reason for the prolonged absence of humans from the Western Hemisphere is that millions of years before human beings came into existence North and South America became detached from the gigantic continent scientists now call Pangaea. Beginning about 240 million years ago, powerful forces deep within the earth slowly pushed the continents apart to approximately their present positions (see Map 1.1). This process of continental drift encircled the land of the Western Hemisphere with large oceans and isolated it from the other continents, long before early human beings (*Homo erectus*) evolved in Africa about 2 million years ago. Only within the last 400,000 years did modern humans (*Homo sapiens*) evolve and migrate out of Africa and into Europe and Asia. For roughly 97 percent of the time *Homo sapiens* have existed, no one set foot in the Western Hemisphere.

Asian Origins

Two major developments made it possible for human beings to reach the Western Hemisphere. First, humans successfully adapted to the frigid environment near the Arctic Circle. Second, changes in the earth's climate reconnected North America to Asia.

By about 25,000 years ago, people had learned to use bone needles to sew animal skins into warm clothing that permitted humans to become permanent residents of extremely cold regions like northeastern Siberia. Today, the Bering Strait, a body of water about sixty miles wide, separates easternmost Siberia from westernmost Alaska. But during the last great global cold spell—the Wisconsin glaciation, which endured from about 80,000 years ago to about 10,000 years ago—snow piled up in glaciers that did not melt, causing the sea level to drop as much as 350 feet below its current level. The seafloor that is now submerged 120 feet below the surface of the Bering Strait was then dry land, forming what is often called a "land bridge" between Asian Siberia and American Alaska. However, the exposed land was not a narrow bridge but a region about a thousand miles wide that scientists call Beringia.

Grasses and small shrubs covered Beringia and supported herds of mammoth, bison, and horses as well as numerous smaller animals. Siberian hunters presumably roamed into Beringia for thousands of years in search of game animals. Archaeologists speculate that hunters traveled in small bands of perhaps twenty-five people. How many such bands arrived in North America before water once again covered Beringia will never be known. When they arrived is hotly debated by experts. The first migrants probably arrived sometime after 15,000 years

The Bering Strait

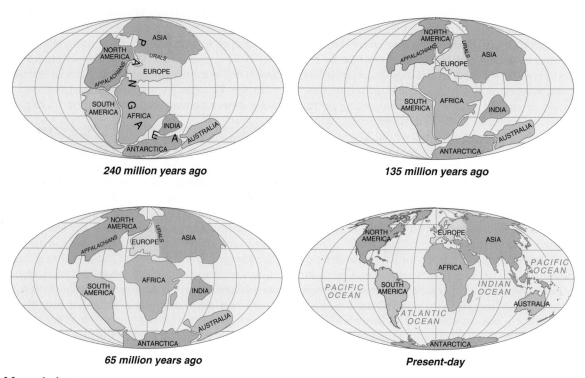

240 million years ago

135 million years ago

65 million years ago

Present-day

MAP 1.1

Continental Drift

Massive geological forces separated North and South America from other continents eons before human beings evolved in Africa in the last 1.5 million years. This continental drift explains why human life developed elsewhere on the planet for hundreds of thousands of years before the first person entered the Western Hemisphere during the last fifteen thousand years.

ago. Scattered and inconclusive evidence suggests that these first Americans may have arrived a few thousand years earlier.

Archaeologists refer to these first migrants and their descendants for the next few millennia as Paleo-Indians. Their Asian origins seem almost certain. Siberians hunted large game, and Beringia provided an attractive hunting ground that reached all the way to North America, a wide avenue to the Western Hemisphere that existed for no other humans at the time. Furthermore, Native Americans today still share certain obvious physical characteristics of Asians. Detailed analyses of Native American languages and of certain blood proteins provide additional compelling evidence of Asian origins.

Paleo-Indian Hunters

When humans first arrived in the Western Hemisphere, massive glaciers covered most of Canada. A narrow corridor not entirely obstructed by ice ran along the eastern side of the Canadian Rockies, and most archaeologists believe that Paleo-Indians migrated through it in pursuit of game. They may also have traveled along the coast in small boats, hopscotching from one desirable landing spot to another. At the southern edge of the glaciers, Paleo-Indians entered a hunters' paradise. North, Central, and South America teemed with wildlife that had never before confronted wily two-legged predators armed with razor-sharp spears. The abundance of game presumably made hunting relatively easy. Ample food permitted the Paleo-Indian population to grow. Within a thousand years or so, Paleo-Indians had reached the southern tip of South America and virtually everywhere else in the Western Hemisphere.

Paleo-Indians used a distinctively shaped spearhead known as a Clovis point, named for the place in New Mexico where it was first excavated. The discovery of Clovis points throughout North and Central America in sites dated between 11,500 and 11,000 years ago is powerful evidence that these nomadic hunters shared a common ancestry and way of life. The Paleo-Indians who used Clovis points to kill big animals probably also hunted smaller animals. But most of the artifacts that have survived from this era indicate that Paleo-Indians specialized in hunting big mammals. One mammoth kill supplied meat for weeks or, if dried, for months. The hide and bones could be used for clothing, shelter, and tools.

The Big Game extinction

About 11,000 years ago Paleo-Indians confronted a major crisis. The big-game animals they hunted became extinct. Scientists are not completely certain why the extinction occurred, although the changing environment probably contributed to it. About this time the Wisconsin glacial period came to an end, glaciers melted, and sea levels rose. Large mammals presumably had difficulty adapting to the warmer climate. Many archaeologists also believe, however, that Paleo-Indian hunters were the major cause of the New World extinctions by killing animals more rapidly than these animals could reproduce.

Paleo-Indians adapted to the big-game extinctions by making at least two important changes in their way of life. First, hunters necessarily focused their attention on smaller animals. Second, Paleo-Indians devoted more energy to foraging, that is, to collecting wild plant foods such as roots, seeds, nuts, berries, and fruits. When Paleo-Indians made these changes, the apparent uniformity of the big-game-oriented Clovis culture* was replaced by great cultural diversity. Paleo-Indians adapted to the many natural environments throughout the hemisphere, ranging from icy tundra to steamy jungles.

Post-Clovis adaptations to local environments led to the astounding variety of Native American cultures that existed when Europeans arrived in 1492. By then, more than three hundred major tribes and hundreds of lesser groups inhabited North America alone. Hundreds more lived in Central and South America. These people spoke different languages, practiced different religions, lived in different dwellings, followed different subsistence strategies, and observed different rules of kinship and inheritance. Hundreds of other ancient American cultures had disappeared or transformed themselves as their members constantly adapted to changing environmental conditions. A full account of those changes and the cultural diversity they created is beyond the scope of this textbook. But we cannot ignore the most important changes and

---

*The word *culture* is used here to connote what is commonly called "way of life." It refers not only to how a group of people supplied themselves with food and shelter but also to family relationships, social groupings, religious ideas, and other features of their way of life. For most prehistoric cultures—as for the Clovis people—more is known about food and shelter because of the artifacts that have survived. Ancient Americans' ideas, assumptions, hopes, dreams, and fantasies were undoubtedly important, but we know very little about them.

adaptations made by ancient Americans during the last eleven millennia.

Archaic Hunters and Gatherers

Archaeologists use the term *Archaic* to describe the many different hunting and gathering cultures that descended from Paleo-Indians. *Archaic* also refers to the long period of time when those cultures dominated the history of ancient America, roughly from 8000 B.C. to somewhere between 2000 and 1000 B.C. Although the cultural and the chronological boundaries of the Archaic era are not sharply defined, the term *Archaic* usefully describes the important era in the history of ancient America that followed the Paleo-Indian big-game hunters and preceded the development of agriculture. It also denotes a hunter-gatherer way of life that persisted throughout most of North America well into the era of European colonization.

Like their Paleo-Indian ancestors, Archaic Indians hunted with spears; but they also took smaller game with traps, nets, and hooks. Unlike Paleo-Indians, most Archaic peoples used a variety of stone tools to prepare food from wild plants. A characteristic Archaic artifact is a grinding stone used to pulverize seeds into edible form. Most Archaic Indians migrated from place to place to harvest plants and hunt animals. They usually did not establish permanent villages, although they often returned to the same river valley or fertile meadow from year to year to take advantage of abundant food resources. In certain regions where resources were especially rich—such as California and the Pacific Northwest—permanent settlements developed. Many Archaic groups became highly proficient basket makers in order to collect and store plant food. Above all, Archaic folk did not depend on agriculture for food. Instead, they gathered wild plants and hunted wild animals. These general traits of Archaic peoples were expressed in distinctive ways in the major environmental regions of North America (Map 1.2).

FOLSOM POINT AT WILD HORSE ARROYO
In 1927, paleontologist J. D. Figgins found this spear point (subsequently named a Folsom point) at the site discovered by George McJunkin. Embedded between the fossilized ribs of a bison that had been extinct for 10,000 years, this point proved that ancient Americans had inhabited the hemisphere at least that long. The importance of this find led one paleontologist to hold up several Folsom points and proclaim, "In my hand I hold the answer to the antiquity of man in America." Although he exaggerated (since Folsom was only part of the answer), this discovery in Wild Horse Arroyo stimulated archaeologists to rethink the history of ancient Americans and to uncover fresh evidence of their many cultures.

Great Plains Bison Hunters

After the extinction of large game such as mammoths, hunters began to concentrate on huge herds of bison that grazed the grassy, arid plains stretching for hundreds of miles east of the Rocky Mountains. For almost a thousand years after the big-game extinctions, Archaic Indians hunted bison with Folsom points like those found at the site discovered by George McJunkin.

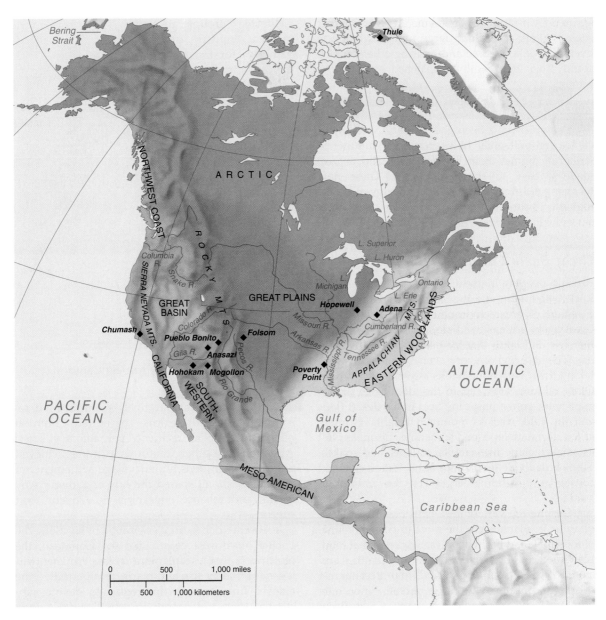

M A P   1 . 2

Native North American Cultures

Environmental conditions defined the boundaries of the broad zones of cultural similarity among ancient North Americans. Using the map, try to specify the crucial environmental features that set the boundaries of each cultural region. The topography indicated on Map 1.3, "Native North Americans about 1500," may be helpful.

Like their predecessors, Folsom hunters were nomads who moved constantly to maintain contact with their prey. Often two or three hunters from a band of several families would single out a few bison from a herd and creep up close enough to spear them. Bison hunters also developed trapping techniques that made it easier to kill large numbers of animals. At the original Folsom site, careful study of the bones McJunkin found suggests that early one winter hunters drove bison into the arroyo and speared twenty-three of them. At many other sites, hunters stampeded large numbers of bison over cliffs, killing some and injuring others, which could then be readily dispatched by waiting hunters.

Bows and arrows reached the Great Plains from the north by about A.D. 500 and largely replaced spears, which had been the hunters' weapon of choice for millennia. Bows permitted hunters to strike an animal from farther away, and arrows made it easy to shoot repeatedly. These new weapons did not otherwise alter the age-old techniques of bison hunting that had been developing since the Folsom era.

Great Basin Cultures

Archaic peoples in the Great Basin between the Rocky Mountains and the Sierra Nevada inhabited a region of great environmental diversity. Some Great Basin Indians lived along the shores of large marshes and lakes that formed during rainy periods. They ate fish of every available size and type, taking them with bone hooks as well as with nets. Other cultures survived in the foothills of mountains between the blistering heat in the desert floor and the cold, treeless mountain heights. Hunters killed deer, antelope, and sometimes bison, as well as smaller game like rabbits, rodents, and snakes. These broadly defined zones of habitation changed constantly depending largely on the amount of rainfall.

Despite the variety and occasional abundance of animals, plants were the most important source of food for Great Basin peoples. Unlike animal food, plant food could be collected in large quantities and stored in baskets for long periods to protect against shortages caused by the fickle rainfall. Piñon nuts became a dietary staple for many Great Basin peoples. By diversifying their food sources and migrating to favorable locations, Great Basin peoples adapted to environmental challenges and maintained their basic hunter-gatherer way of life until long after A.D. 1492.

Pacific Coast Cultures

The richness of the natural environment made California the most densely settled area in all of ancient North America. The abundant resources of both land and ocean offered such ample food that

California groups remained hunters and gatherers for hundreds of years after Europeans arrived in the Western Hemisphere. The diversity of California's environment encouraged corresponding diversity among native peoples. By A.D. 1492, the mosaic of settlements in California included about five hundred separate tribes speaking some ninety languages, each with local dialects. No other region of comparable size in North America exhibited such cultural variety.

The Chumash, one of the many California cultures, emerged near Santa Barbara about 5,000 years ago. Comparatively plentiful food resources—especially acorns—permitted Chumash people to establish relatively permanent villages. Although few other California cultures achieved the population density and village settlements of the Chumash, all shared the hunter-gatherer way of life and reliance on acorns as a major food source.

Another rich natural environment lay along the Pacific Northwest coast. Like the Chumash, the Northwest peoples built more or less permanent villages. Abundant fish and marine life permitted the ancient Americans in this region to devote substantial time and energy to activities other than hunting and gathering. After about 5,500 years ago, they concentrated on catching large quantities of salmon, halibut, and other fish, which they dried to last throughout the year. With time free from the demands of food gathering, Northwest peoples developed sophisticated woodworking skills. They fashioned huge canoes, some big enough to hold fifty people, which they used to fish, hunt, and conduct warfare against neighboring tribes. They also carved totem poles with images of animals, ancestors, and supernatural beings to adorn their houses.

Ancient California

OZETTE WHALE EFFIGY
This carving of a whale fin decorated with hundreds of sea otter teeth was discovered along with thousands of other artifacts of daily life at Ozette, an ancient village on the tip of the Olympic Peninsula in present-day Washington that was inundated by a catastrophic mudslide about five hundred years ago. The fin illustrates the importance of whale hunting to the residents of Ozette, who set out in canoes carrying eight men armed with harpoons to catch and kill animals weighing twenty to thirty tons.
Makah Cultural and Resource Center.

Eastern Woodland Cultures

East of the Mississippi River, Archaic peoples adapted to a forest environment that included many local variants, such as the major river valleys of the Mississippi, Ohio, Tennessee, and Cumberland; the Great Lakes region; and the Atlantic coast (see Map 1.2). Throughout these diverse locales, Archaic peoples adopted basic survival strategies.

Deer were the most important prey of nearly all Woodland hunters. In addition to food, deer supplied hides and bones that were crafted into useful items such as clothing, weapons, needles, and other tools. Like Archaic peoples elsewhere, Woodland Indians gathered edible plants, seeds, and especially nuts. Hickory nuts were the most commonly gathered plant food, but pecans, walnuts, acorns, and hazelnuts were also collected. About 4000 B.C., some Woodland groups established more or less permanent settlements of 25 to 150 people, usually near a river or lake that offered a wide variety of plant and animal resources. The existence of semipermanent settlements has permitted archaeologists to locate numerous Archaic burial sites that suggest the life expectancy at birth for these Woodland people was slightly over eighteen years.

Around 2000 B.C., the Woodland cultures incorporated two important features into their basic hunter-gatherer lifestyles: agriculture and pottery. Gourds and pumpkins that originated in Mexico spread to North America though trade and migration and began to be grown in parts of Missouri and Kentucky. After the introduction of these Mexican crops, Woodland peoples began to cultivate local species such as sunflowers. It is likely that they also grew tobacco, another import from South America, since stone pipes for smoking appeared by 1500 B.C. Corn, the most important plant food in Mexico, did not become a significant food crop until more than a thousand years later. These cultivated crops added to the quantity, variety, and predictability of Woodland food sources, but they did not fundamentally alter the hunter-gatherer way of life.

Techniques for making ceramic pots probably also originated in Mexico and may have been brought north by traders and migrants along with Mexican seeds. Pots were more durable than baskets for food preparation and storage, but they were also much heavier, probably an outgrowth of more permanent settlements. Neither pottery nor agriculture caused Woodland peoples to turn away from their basic hunter-gatherer cultures, which persisted in most areas to A.D. 1492 and beyond.

Agricultural Settlements and Chiefdoms

Among Eastern Woodland peoples and other Archaic cultures, agriculture supplemented rather than replaced hunter-gatherer subsistence strategies. Reliance on wild animals and plants required most Archaic groups to remain small and mobile. But in the centuries after 2000 B.C., distinctive southwestern cultures slowly came to rely on agriculture and to build permanent settlements. Later, around 500 B.C., Woodland peoples in the vast Mississippi valley began to construct burial mounds and other earthworks that suggest the existence of social and political hierarchies that archaeologists term chiefdoms. Although the hunter-gatherer lifestyle never entirely disappeared, the development of agricultural settlements and chiefdoms represented important innovations to the Archaic way of life.

Southwestern Cultures

Ancient Americans in Arizona, New Mexico, and southern portions of Utah and Colorado developed cultures characterized by agriculture and eventually by multiunit dwellings called pueblos. All southwestern peoples confronted the challenge of a dry climate and unpredictable fluctuations in rainfall that made the supply of wild plant food very unreliable. These ancient Americans probably adopted agriculture in response to this basic environmental condition.

Until about five thousand years ago, the population of the Southwest appears to have been extremely sparse. Sometime within a few centuries of 1500 B.C., southwestern hunters and gatherers began to cultivate their signature food crop, corn. Over the following centuries, corn became the basic cultivated food crop for Native American peoples throughout North America. The demands of corn cultivation encouraged southwestern hunter-gatherers to restrict their migratory habits in order to tend the crop. A vital consideration was access to water. Southwestern Indians became irrigation experts, conserving water from streams, springs, and rainfall and distributing it to thirsty crops.

Between about A.D. 200 and 900, small farming settlements appeared throughout southern New Mexico, marking the emergence of the Mogollon culture. Typically, a Mogollon settlement included about a dozen pit houses, made by digging out a

ANCIENT AGRICULTURE
Dropping seeds into holes punched in cleared ground by a pointed stick, this ancient American farmer sows a new crop while previously planted seeds— including the corn and beans immediately opposite him—bear fruit for harvest. Created by a sixteenth-century European artist, the drawing misrepresents who did the agricultural work in many ancient American cultures, namely women rather than men.
Art Resource, NY.

rounded pit about fifteen feet in diameter and a foot or two deep and then erecting poles to support a roof of branches or dirt. Larger villages usually had one or two bigger pit houses that may have been the predecessors of the circular kivas, the ceremonial rooms that became a characteristic of nearly all southwestern settlements. About A.D. 1000, Mogollon culture began to decline, for reasons that remain obscure.

About A.D. 500, people who appear to have emigrated from Mexico established the distinctive Hohokam culture in southern Arizona. Hohokam peoples made extensive use of irrigation to plant and harvest twice a year. Their comparatively high crop yields allowed the Hohokam population to grow and seek out more land to settle. Hohokam culture continued to be strongly influenced by Mexico. The people built sizable platform mounds and ball courts characteristic of cultures to the south. The Hohokam culture declined about A.D. 1400, for reasons that remain a mystery.

North of the Hohokam and Mogollon cultures, in a region that encompassed southern Utah and Colorado and northern Arizona and New Mexico, the Anasazi culture began to flourish during the

first century A.D. The early Anasazi built pit houses on mesa tops and used irrigation much like their neighbors to the south. Beginning around A.D. 1000 (again, it is not known why), the Anasazi began to move to large, multistory cliff dwellings whose spectacular ruins still exist at Mesa Verde, Colorado, and Canyon de Chelly, Arizona. Other Anasazi communities, like the one whose impressive ruins can be visited at Chaco Canyon, New Mexico, erected huge, stone-walled pueblos with enough rooms to house the entire population of the settlement. Pueblo Bonito at Chaco Canyon, for example, contained more than eight hundred rooms. Anasazi pueblos and cliff dwellings typically contained one or more kivas used for secret ceremonies, restricted to men, that sought to communicate with the supernatural world.

Around A.D. 1130, drought began to plague the region. The drought lasted for half a century and triggered the disappearance of Anasazi culture. By 1200, the large Anasazi pueblos had been abandoned. The prolonged drought may have intensified conflict among pueblos and rendered ineffective the agricultural methods that had been developed in earlier centuries. Some Anasazi

PUEBLO BONITO, CHACO CANYON
The ruins of Pueblo Bonito, the largest of many similar pueblos built centuries ago by the Anasazi in Chaco Canyon, New Mexico, can still be visited today. The numerous circular structures were kivas, underground ceremonial chambers that were originally covered with wooden roofs. What do the number, size, and arrangement of kivas at Pueblo Bonito suggest about the Anasazi who lived and visited there?
Richard Alexander Cooke III.

migrated toward regions with more reliable rainfall and settled in Hopi, Zuñi, and Acoma pueblos that their descendants in Arizona and New Mexico have occupied ever since.

Burial Mounds and Chiefdoms

No other ancient Americans created dwellings similar to pueblos, but around 500 B.C., Woodland cultures throughout the vast drainage of the Mississippi River began to build burial mounds. The size of the mounds, the labor and organization required to erect them, and the differences in the artifacts buried with certain individuals suggest the existence of a social and political hierarchy that archaeologists term a chiefdom.

Between about 500 and 100 B.C., Adena people built hundreds of burial mounds radiating from central Ohio (see Map 1.2). In the mounds, the Adena usually deposited a wide variety of grave goods, including spear points and stone pipes as well as decorative and ritualistic items such as thin sheets of mica (a glasslike mineral) crafted into naturalistic shapes. Once the body and grave goods were in place, dirt was piled into a mound one basketful at a time. Sometimes mounds were constructed all at once, but often they were built up over many years.

About 100 B.C., Adena culture evolved into the more elaborate Hopewell culture, which lasted about 500 years. It too was centered in Ohio but extended throughout the Ohio and Mississippi valleys. Hopewell people built larger mounds and filled them with more magnificent grave goods than had their Adena predecessors. Burial was probably reserved for the most important members of Hopewell groups. Most people were cremated.

Grave goods at Hopewell sites testify not only to the high quality of Hopewell crafts but also to the existence of a trade network ranging from Wyoming to Florida. After about A.D. 400, Hopewell culture declined, for reasons that are obscure. Some archaeologists believe that the bow and arrow and increasing reliance on agriculture may have made small settlements more self-sufficient and less dependent on the central authority of the chiefs responsible for the burial mounds.

Four hundred years later, another mound-building culture flourished. The Mississippian culture emerged in the floodplains of the major southeastern river systems about A.D. 800 and lasted until about 1500. Major Mississippian sites included huge mounds with platforms on top for ceremonies

WOODLAND EAGLE CARVING
This eagle effigy topped a post in a charnel house where Woodland Indians deposited the remains of their dead ancestors sometime between 1,500 and 1,000 years ago at a site in present-day Florida. The significance of the eagle is unknown; it may have represented the clan of the deceased in the charnel house.
Florida Museum of Natural History, photograph © 1985 The Detroit Institute of Arts.

Major Mississippian Mounds, A.D. 800–1500

and for the residences of great chiefs. The largest Mississippian site was Cahokia, just across the Mississippi River from St. Louis, Missouri.

At Cahokia, more than one hundred mounds of different sizes and shapes were grouped around large open plazas. Monk's Mound, the largest, covered sixteen acres at its base and was one hundred feet tall. Dwellings at one time covered five square miles and may have housed as many as thirty thousand inhabitants, easily qualifying Cahokia as the largest settlement in North America. At Cahokia and other Mississippian sites, people evidently worshiped a sun god; perhaps the mounds were a way to elevate elites nearer to the sun.

One Cahokia burial mound suggests the authority a great chief exercised. One man—presumably the chief—was buried with the bodies of fifty-seven people who had evidently been killed at the time of burial. Such a mass sacrifice shows the power a Cahokian chief wielded and the obedience he commanded.

Cahokia and other Mississippian sites had dwindled by A.D. 1500. By the time of European contact, most of the descendants of Mississippian cultures lived in small dispersed villages supported by agriculture, hunting, and gathering.

Native Americans in 1492

By the time Europeans arrived, North American tribes had incorporated and adapted many of the cultural achievements of their ancestors. The rigors of the continent's natural environments required that they maintain time-tested adaptations.

Eastern Woodland peoples clustered into three major groups. Algonquian tribes inhabited the Atlantic seaboard, the Great Lakes region, and much of the upper Midwest (Map 1.3). The relatively mild climate along the Atlantic permitted the coastal Algonquians to grow corn and other crops as well as to hunt and fish. Around the Great Lakes and in northern New England, however, cool summers and severe winters made agriculture impractical. Instead, the Abenaki, Penobscot, Chippewa, and other tribes hunted and fished, using canoes both for transportation and for gathering wild rice.

Inland from the Algonquians were the territories of the Iroquoian tribes, centered in Pennsylvania and upstate New York, as well as the hilly upland regions of the Carolinas and Georgia. Several features distinguished Iroquoian tribes from their neighbors. First, their success in cultivating corn and other crops allowed them to build permanent settlements, usually consisting of several bark-covered longhouses up to one hundred feet long and housing five to ten families. Second, Iroquoian societies were thoroughly matriarchal. Property of all sorts, including land, children, and inheritance, belonged to women. Women headed family clans and even selected the chiefs (normally men) who governed tribes. Third, for purposes of war and diplomacy, the Seneca, Onondaga, Mohawk, Oneida, and Cayuga tribes formed the League of Five Nations, an Iroquoian confederation that remained powerful well into the eighteenth century.

Muskogean peoples spread throughout the Southeast, south of the Ohio River and east of the Mississippi. Including Creek, Choctaw, Chickasaw, and Natchez tribes, Muskogeans inhabited a bountiful natural environment that provided abundant food from hunting, gathering, and agriculture. Remnants of the Mississippian culture existed in the religious rites common among the Muskogean. They practiced a form of sun worship, and the Natchez even built temple mounds modeled after those of their Mississippian ancestors.

West of the Mississippi River, Great Plains peoples straddled the boundary between the Eastern Woodland and the western tribes. Many of the tribes had migrated to the plains within the century or two before 1500, forced westward by Iroquoian and Algonquian tribes. They were in the process of increasing their reliance on buffalo, although some tribes—especially the Mandan and Pawnee—were successful farmers, growing both corn and sunflowers. The Teton Sioux, Blackfeet, Comanche, Cheyenne, and Crow on the northern plains and the Apache and other nomadic tribes on the southern plains depended on buffalo. Tribes in the Great Basin region, such as the Comanche and Shoshone, also continued to follow earlier subsistence practices, as did Pacific coast cultures.

In the Southwest, descendants of the Mogollon, Hohokam, and Anasazi cultures lived in settled agricultural communities, many of them pueblos. However, a large number of warlike Athapascan tribes had invaded the area within the two hundred years before 1500. The Athapascans—principally Apache and Navajo—were skillful warriors who preyed on the sedentary pueblo Indians, reaping the fruits of agriculture without the work of farming.

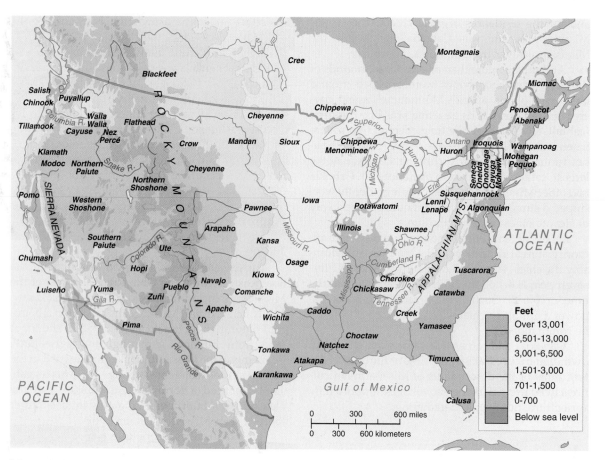

MAP 1.3

Native North Americans about 1500

Distinctive Native American peoples resided throughout the area that, centuries later, would become the United States. This map indicates the approximate location of some of the larger tribes about 1500. In the interest of legibility, many other peoples who inhabited North America at the time are omitted from the map.

By the time Columbus arrived, the comparatively small Native American settlements in North America supported a population estimated to be about four million, slightly less than the population of the British Isles at the time. All of them depended on hunting and gathering for a major portion of their food. Most of them also practiced agriculture, some far more than others. All of them used bows and arrows, as well as other weapons, for hunting and warfare. None of them employed writing, expressing themselves instead in many other ways. They made drawings on stones, wood, and animal skins; wove patterns in baskets and textiles; painted designs on pottery; and crafted beadwork, pipes, and other decorative items. They danced, sang, and

played music. They performed elaborate burial ceremonies and other religious rites.

Ancient Americans' rich and varied cultural resources did not include certain common features of life in late-fifteenth-century Europe: They did not use wheels; sailing ships were unknown; they had no large domesticated animals like horses, cows, or oxen; their use of metals was restricted to copper; and metallurgy did not exist in North America. However, the absence of these European conveniences was profoundly irrelevant to ancient North Americans. Their cultures had developed as adaptations to the natural environment local to each tribe. That great similarity underlay all the cultural diversity among native North Americans.

The Mexica:
A Meso-American Culture

By 1492, the indigenous population of the New World numbered roughly 80 million, about the same as the population of Europe. All but about 4 million of these people lived in Central and South America. Like their North American counterparts, they too lived in a natural environment of tremendous diversity. They too developed hundreds of cultures, far too numerous to catalog here. But among all the Central and South American cultures, the Mexica stood out. (Europeans often called these people Aztecs, a name the Mexica did not use.) Their empire stretched from coast to coast across central Mexico, encompassing as many as 25 million people. We know more about the fifteenth-century Mexica than about any other Native American society of the time, principally because of their written sources, massive monuments, and their Spanish conquerors' well-documented interest in subduing them. Their significance in the history of the New World after 1492 dictates a brief consideration of their culture and society.

The Mexica began their rise to prominence about A.D. 1325 when small bands settled on a marshy island in Lake Texcoco, the site of the future city of Tenochtitlán. Resourceful, courageous, and cold-blooded warriors, the Mexica often were hired as mercenaries by richer, more settled tribes. By 1430, the Mexica succeeded in asserting their dominance over their former allies and leading their own military campaigns in an ever-widening arc of empire building. Despite pockets of resistance, by 1500 the Mexica ruled an empire that covered more land than Spain and Portugal combined and contained almost three times as many people.

The empire exemplified the central values of Mexican society. The Mexica worshiped the war god Huitzilopochtli. Warriors held the most exalted positions in the Mexican social hierarchy, even above the priests who performed the sacred ceremonies that won Huitzilopochtli's favor. In the almost constant battles necessary to defend and extend the empire, young Mexican men exhibited the courage and daring that would allow them to rise in the carefully graduated ranks of warriors. The Mexica considered capturing prisoners the ultimate act of bravery. The captives usually were turned over to the priests, who sacrificed them to Huitzilopochtli by cutting out their hearts. (See "Historical Question," page 18.)

The empire contributed far more to Mexican society than victims for sacrifice. At the most basic level, the empire was a military and political system for collecting tribute from subject peoples. The Mexica forced conquered tribes to pay tribute in goods, not money. Tribute redistributed to the

HUMAN SACRIFICE
Many ancient American peoples practiced human sacrifice as a sacred rite of communion with the gods. The Inca, a powerful people whose empire stretched down the west coast of South America, required each village to send one or two especially beautiful children to the capital, where they were honored in religious ceremonies and other festivities and then given an intoxicating drink and buried in a prepared tomb, where they died. This mummy was probably a child sacrificed in such a ritual about 500 years ago. Discovered in Chile at an altitude of about 20,000 feet, where the dry, intense cold preserved the body, the mummy was accompanied by a tiny female votive figure wrapped in finely woven cloth and capped with a bright feather headdress, a llama figurine, a bag of coca leaves, and other objects.
Loren McIntyre.

Why Did the Mexica Practice Human Sacrifice?

MEXICAN CEREMONIAL SKULL
This human skull, decorated by Mexican artisans with a mosaic of turquoise, jet, and shell, represented Tezcatlipoca, the Mexican deity who governed human fate. A handsome young man was selected for the great honor of impersonating Tezcatlipoca for eighteen months. The Mexican emperor gave the impersonator riches and privileges of all sorts, and even allowed him to rule Tenochtitlán for the last five days of his life. On the last day, the impersonator climbed the steps of a temple where priests cut out his heart and decapitated him. This skull from the Tezcatlipoca ceremony presumably belonged to one of the impersonators. The skull is said to have been a gift from the emperor Montezuma to Cortés, leader of the Spanish conquest of Mexico.
Copyright © The British Museum.

THE MEXICA PRACTICED HUMAN SACRIFICE on a scale unequaled in human history. That does not mean, of course, that they intentionally killed more people than any other society. Plenty of other societies, both before and since, have systematically killed other human beings. Only a partial accounting of the years from 1930 to 1945, for example, would include millions of Jews and others murdered by the Nazis, millions of Russians killed by the Soviet leader Joseph Stalin, hundreds of thousands of Chinese slaughtered by the Japanese, and hundreds of thousands of Japanese annihilated by the atomic bombs dropped by the United States on Hiroshima and Nagasaki. Warfare of any kind involves intentional sacrifice of human life. However, the human sacrifice practiced by the Mexica was different. For them, human sacrifice was an act of worship—in fact, the ultimate act of worship.

Looking back from our vantage point five hundred years later, we may find it difficult to understand why the Mexica accepted human sacrifice as a normal and reasonable activity. Yet it is perfectly clear that they did. Although the precise number of victims is unknown, experts estimate that roughly 20,000 people were sacrificed each year throughout the Mexican empire. Celebration of an important victory or the appointment of a new emperor often involved the sacrifice of hundreds, sometimes thousands.

Most of the victims were prisoners captured in battle or rendered in tribute. Nonetheless, ordinary Mexican citizens—especially young men, women, and children—were often sacrificed in religious rituals. Every eighteen months, for example, a greatly honored young man was sacrificed to Tezcatlipoca, the god of human fate. From time to time, all Mexica practiced sacrificial bloodletting, piercing themselves with stingray spines or cactus thorns to demonstrate their religious devotion. Both as symbol and reality, human sacrifice was an integral part of daily life in Mexican communities.

Mexica employed several different techniques of sacrifice, all supervised and carried out by priests. By far the most common sacrifice was performed at an altar on the top of a temple where a priest cut out the still-beating heart of a victim and offered it to the gods. The victim's head and limbs were then severed and the torso fed to wild animals kept in cages in and near the temple. The heads were displayed on large racks at the base of the temple, while the limbs were cooked and eaten in sacred rituals. It is likely that participation in this ritualistic cannibalism was restricted to a minority of Mexica, principally warriors, priests, and wealthier merchants. However, every Mexica participated in symbolic cannibalism by eating small cakes made of flour mixed with blood and shaped into human forms.

To us, these rituals may seem ghoulish and disgusting, as they certainly did to sixteenth-century Europeans who eventually witnessed them. Yet the Mexica devoted so much time, energy, and resources to such rituals that it is impossible to doubt their importance to them. But why was human sacrifice so important?

In recent times, some scholars have argued that the Mexica practiced human sacrifice and cannibalism to remedy protein deficiencies in their diet. However, the Mexica's diet contained many sources of protein, including turkeys, chickens, fish, turtles, and eggs as well as corn and beans. For most Mexica, dietary protein was adequate or better. Protein deficiency interprets human sacrifice as a solution to a problem that, evidently, did not actually exist.

Mexican religious beliefs offer a far more persuasive explanation for human sacrifice. Scholars know a good deal about Mexican religion because, in the years immediately following European conquest, Catholic priests studied Mexican religion in order to convert the people more readily to Christianity. These sources make clear that the Mexica inhabited a world suffused with the power of supernatural beings. A special deity oversaw nearly every important activity. Mexica believed that their gods communicated with human beings through omens, signs that the gods were either happy or displeased. In turn, the people communicated their own reverence for the gods by observing appropriate rituals. Bad omens such as an unexplained fire or a lightning bolt striking a temple meant that a god was angry and needed to be appeased with the proper rituals. Since almost every occurrence could be in-terpreted as an omen that revealed the will of a god, the routine events of daily life had a profound, supernatural dimension.

The Mexica's most powerful gods were Huitzilopochtli, the war god, and Quetzalcoatl, the god who gave sustenance to human beings. Mexica believed that these two gods had created the world, the sun, the moon, the first human beings, the whole array of lesser deities, and everything else in the universe. Since the moment of creation, the earth had passed through four different epochs, which Mexica called the Four Suns, each of which had ended in catastrophe. It fell to Quetzalcoatl and other potent deities to begin the Fifth Sun by recreating human beings and all the other features of the universe. After years of work, Quetzalcoatl and the other gods had accomplished everything except the creation of the sun. Finally, two gods agreed to sacrifice themselves by jumping into a fire. Thereby they became the sun and the moon, and other gods quickly followed them into the fire to keep the sun burning. But the sacrifice of the gods was sufficient only to ignite the sun. To maintain the light of the sun and keep it moving across the sky every day required human beings to follow the example of the gods and to feed the sun with human blood. Without the sacrificial blood, the world would go dark and time would stop. Mexica considered the Fifth Sun the final stage of the universe, which would end when cataclysmic earthquakes destroyed the earth and supernatural monsters ravaged human life. By feeding the sun with human sacrifices, Mexica believed they could delay that horrible final reckoning.

For the Mexica, human sacrifice was absolutely necessary for the maintenance of life on earth. Victims of sacrifice fulfilled the most sacred of duties. Through the sacrifice of their own lives they fed the sun and permitted others to live. The living demonstrated their respect and reverence for victims of sacrifice by eating their flesh. As one sixteenth-century Catholic priest explained, "The flesh of all those who died in sacrifice was held truly to be consecrated and blessed. It was eaten with reverence, ritual, and fastidiousness—as if it were something from heaven." From the Mexica's perspective, it was not wrong to engage in human sacrifice; it was wrong not to.

Mexica as much as one-third of the goods produced by conquered tribes. It included everything from candidates for human sacrifice to basic food products like corn and beans as well as exotic luxury items like gold, turquoise, and rare bird feathers.

Tribute reflected the fundamental relations of power and wealth that pervaded the Mexican empire. The relatively small nobility of Mexican warriors, supported by a still smaller priesthood, possessed the military and religious power to command the obedience of thousands of nonnoble Mexicans and of millions of other non-Mexicans in subjugated provinces. The Mexican elite exercised their power to obtain tribute and thereby to redistribute wealth from the conquered to the conquerors, from the commoners to the nobility, from the poor to the rich. This redistribution of wealth made possible the achievements of Mexican society that eventually amazed Europeans: the fabulous temples, markets, and gardens, not to mention the storehouses stuffed with gold and other treasures.

On the whole, the Mexica did not interfere much with the internal government of conquered regions. Instead, they usually permitted the traditional ruling elite to stay in power—so long as they paid tribute. For their efforts, the conquered provinces received very little from the Mexica, except immunity from punitive raids by the dreaded Mexican warriors. Subjugated communities felt exploited by the constant payment of tribute to the Mexica. By depending on military conquest and constant collection of tribute, the Mexica failed to create among their subjects a belief that Mexican domination was, at some level, legitimate and equitable. The high level of discontent among subject peoples constituted the soft, vulnerable underbelly of the Mexican empire. Instead of making friends for the Mexica, the empire created many bitter and resentful opponents, a fact Spanish intruders eventually exploited to conquer the Mexica.

SALADO RITUAL FIGURE
About A.D. 1350—more than a century before Columbus arrived in the New World—this figure was carefully wrapped in a reed mat with other items and stored in a cave in a mountainous region of New Mexico by people of the Salado culture, descendants of the Mimbres who had flourished three centuries earlier. The face of this figure is as close to a self-portrait of ancient Americans on the eve of their encounter with Europeans as we are ever likely to have. Adorned with vivid pigments, cotton string, bright feathers, and stones, the effigy testifies to the human complexity of all ancient Americans, a complexity visible in artifacts that have survived the millennia before the arrival of Europeans.
The Art Institute of Chicago.

Conclusion: The World of Ancient Americans

Ancient Americans shaped the history of human beings in the New World for more than twelve thousand years. They established continuous human habitation in the Western Hemisphere from the time the first big-game hunters crossed Beringia until 1492 and beyond. Much of their history remains irretrievably lost because they relied on oral rather than written communication. But much can be pieced together from artifacts they left behind, like the bones discovered at Folsom by George McJunkin. Ancient Americans achieved their success through resourceful adaptation to the hemisphere's many and ever-changing natural environments. They also adapted to social and cultural changes caused by human beings—such as marriages, deaths, political struggles, and warfare—but the sparse evidence that has survived renders those adaptations almost entirely unknowable. Their creativity and artistry are unmistakably documented in the artifacts they left behind at kill sites, camps, and burial mounds. Those artifacts sketch the only likenesses of ancient Americans we will ever have—blurred, shadowy images that are indisputably human but forever silent.

In the five centuries after 1492—just 4 percent of the time human beings have inhabited the Western Hemisphere—Europeans and their descendants began to shape and eventually to dominate Ameri-

can history. Native American peoples continued to influence major developments of American history after 1492. But the new wave of strangers that at first trickled and then flooded into the New World from Europe and Africa forever transformed the peoples and places of ancient America.

FOR FURTHER READING ABOUT THE TOPICS IN THIS CHAPTER, see the Online Bibliography at www.bedfordstmartins.com/roarkcompact.

FOR ADDITIONAL FIRST-HAND ACCOUNTS OF THIS PERIOD, see pages 1–8 in Michael Johnson, ed., *Reading the American Past,* Second Edition, Volume I.

TO ASSESS YOUR MASTERY OF THE MATERIAL IN THIS CHAPTER, see the Online Study Guide at www.bedfordstmartins.com/roarkcompact.

CHRONOLOGY

c. 80,000– 10,000 B.C.	Wisconsin glaciation exposes Beringia, land bridge between Siberia and Alaska.
c. 13,000– 10,000 B.C.	First humans arrive in North America.
c. 9500– 9000 B.C.	Paleo-Indians in North and Central Americas use Clovis points to hunt big game.
c. 9000 B.C.	Mammoths and many other big-game prey of Paleo-Indians become extinct.
c. 8000– 1000 B.C.	Archaic hunter-gatherer cultures dominate ancient America.
c. 5000 B.C.	Corn cultivation begins in Central and South Americas.
c. 2000 B.C.	Some Eastern Woodland people grow gourds and pumpkins and begin making pottery.
c. 1500 B.C.	Southwestern cultures begin corn cultivation.
	Stone pipes for tobacco smoking appear in Eastern Woodland.
c. 500 B.C.	Eastern Woodland cultures start to build burial mounds.
c. 500– 100 B.C.	Adena culture develops in Ohio.
c. 300 B.C.	Some Eastern Woodland peoples begin to cultivate corn.
c. 100 B.C.– A.D. 400	Hopewell culture emerges in Ohio and Mississippi valleys.
c. A.D. 200– 900	Mogollon culture emerges in New Mexico.
c. A.D. 500	Bows and arrows appear in North America south of Arctic.
	Pacific Northwest cultures denote wealth and status with elaborate wood carvings.
c. A.D. 500– 1400	Hohokam culture develops in Arizona.
c. A.D. 800– 1500	Mississippian culture flourishes in Southeast.
c. A.D. 1000– 1150	Anasazi peoples build cliff dwellings at Mesa Verde, Colorado, and pueblos at Chaco Canyon, New Mexico.
c. A.D. 1325– 1500	Mexica conquer neighboring peoples and establish Mexican empire.
A.D. 1492	Christopher Columbus arrives, beginning European conquest of New World.

TAINO ZEMI BASKET

This basket is an example of the effigies Tainos made to represent **zemis**, *their deities. The effigy illustrates not only the artistry of the basket maker—probably a Taino woman— but also the basket maker's use of European mirrors in a sacred object. Crafted sometime between 1492 and about 1520, the effigy suggests that Tainos readily incorporated goods obtained through contacts with Europeans into their own traditional beliefs and practices.*

Archìvio Fotogràfico del Museo Preistòrico Etnografico L. Pigorini, Rome.

EUROPEANS AND THE NEW WORLD

2

1492–1600

A HALF HOUR BEFORE SUNRISE ON AUGUST 3, 1492, Christopher Columbus commanded three ships to catch the tide out of a harbor in southern Spain and sail west. Just over two months later, in the predawn moonlight of October 12, 1492, Columbus glimpsed an island on the western horizon. At last, he believed, he had found what he had been looking for—the western end of a route across the Atlantic Ocean to Japan, China, and India. At daybreak, Columbus could see people on the shore who had spotted his ships. He rowed ashore and, as the curious islanders crowded around, he claimed possession of the land for Ferdinand and Isabella, king and queen of Spain, who had sponsored his voyage.

A day or two afterward, Columbus described that first encounter with the inhabitants of San Salvador in an extensive diary he kept during his voyage. He called these people Indians, assuming that their island lay somewhere in the East Indies near Japan or China. The Indians were not dressed in the finery Columbus expected. "All of them go around as naked as their mothers bore them; and the women also," he observed. Their skin color was "neither black nor white." This first encounter led Columbus to conclude, "They should be good and intelligent servants, for I see that they say very quickly everything that is said to them; and I believe that they would become Christians very easily, for it seemed to me that they had no religion."

The people Columbus called Indians called themselves Tainos, which to them meant "good" or "noble." They inhabited most of the Caribbean islands Columbus visited on his first voyage, as had their ancestors for more than two centuries. The Tainos were an agricultural people who grew cassava, a nutritious root, as well as sweet potatoes, corn, cotton, tobacco, and other crops. To fish and to travel from island to island, they built canoes from hollowed-out logs. The Tainos worshiped gods they called *zemis*, the spirits of ancestors and of natural objects like trees and stones. They made effigies of *zemis* and performed rituals to honor them. "It seemed to me that they were a people very poor in everything," Columbus wrote. But the Tainos mined gold in small quantities, enough to catch the eye of Columbus and his men.

What the Tainos thought about Spaniards we can only surmise, since they left no written documents. At first, Columbus believed that the Tainos thought he and his men came from heaven. After six weeks of contact, Columbus concluded that in fact he did not understand Tainos. Late in November 1492, he wrote that "the people of these lands do not understand me nor do I, nor anyone else that I have with me, them. And many times I understand one thing said by these Indians . . . for another, its contrary."

The confused communication between Europeans and Tainos suggests how different, how strange, each group seemed to the other. Columbus's perceptions of

CACIQUE'S CANOE
This sixteenth-century drawing of a large canoe carrying a cacique, or chief, and powered by twenty oarsmen probably resembles the canoes used by Tainos and the other native Americans who paddled out to visit the ships of Columbus and other European explorers. The influence of such European contacts may be reflected in the flags flying from the corners of the leafy awning that enthrones the cacique.
Art Resource, NY.

Tainos were shaped by European ideas, attitudes, and expectations, just as Tainos's perceptions of Europeans must have been colored by their own culture. Yet the word that Columbus coined for the Tainos—*Indians*, a word that originated in a colossal misunderstanding—hinted at the direction of the future. To Europeans, *Indians* came to mean all native inhabitants of the New World, the name they gave to the lands in the Western Hemisphere. After 1492, the perceptions, the cultures, and even the diseases of Europeans began to exert a transforming influence on the New World and its peoples.

Long before 1492, certain Europeans restlessly expanded the limits of the world known to them. Their efforts made possible Columbus's encounter with the Tainos. In turn, Columbus's landfall in the Caribbean changed the history not only of the Tainos, but also of Europe and the rest of the world. Beginning in 1492, the promise of the New World lured more and more Europeans to venture their lives and fortunes on the western shores of the Atlantic, a promise realized largely at the expense of New World peoples like Tainos.

Europe in the Age of Exploration

Historically, the East—not the West—attracted Europeans. Wealthy Europeans developed a taste for luxury goods from Asia and Africa, and merchants competed to satisfy that taste. As Europeans traded with the East and with one another, they acquired new information about the world they inhabited. A few people—sailors, merchants, aristocrats—took the risks of exploring beyond the limits of the world known to Europeans. Those risks were genuine and could be deadly. But sometimes they paid off in new information, new opportunities, and eventually in the discovery of a world entirely new to Europeans.

Mediterranean Trade and European Expansion

From the twelfth through the fifteenth centuries, spices, silk, carpets, ivory, gold, and other exotic goods traveled overland from Persia, Asia Minor,

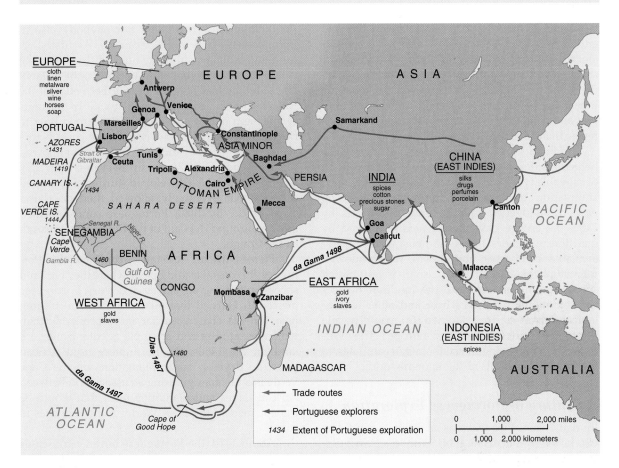

MAP 2.1

European Trade Routes and Portuguese Exploration in the Fifteenth Century

The strategic geographic position of Italian cities as a conduit for overland trade from Asia was slowly undermined during the fifteenth century by Portuguese explorers who hopscotched along the coast of Africa and eventually found a sea route that opened the rich trade of the East to Portuguese merchants.

India, and Africa and then were funneled into continental Europe through Mediterranean trade routes (Map 2.1). Dominated primarily by the Italian cities of Venice, Genoa, and Pisa, this lucrative trade enriched Italian merchants and bankers. Instead of trying to displace the Italians, merchants in other European countries chose the safer alternative of trading with them. The vitality of the Mediterranean trade offered few incentives to look for alternatives. New routes to the East and the discovery of new lands were the stuff of fantasy.

Preconditions for turning fantasy into reality developed in fifteenth-century Europe. In the mid-fourteenth century, Europeans suffered a catastrophic epidemic of bubonic plague. The Black Death, as it was called, killed about a third of the European population. Understandably, most Europeans perceived the world as a place of alarming risks where the delicate balance of health, harvests, and peace could quickly be tipped toward disaster by epidemics, famine, and violence. Curiously, the insecurity and uncertainty of fifteenth-century European life encouraged a few people to take greater chances, such as embarking on a dangerous sea voyage through uncharted waters to points unknown.

Monarchs who hoped to enlarge their realms and enrich their dynasties also had reasons to sponsor journeys of exploration. More territory meant more subjects who could pay more taxes, provide more soldiers, and participate in more commerce, magnifying monarchs' power and prestige. Explorers, both nobles and commoners like Columbus, sought to earn rewards and prestige in European society.

Scientific and technological advances also helped set the stage for exploration. The invention of movable type made printing easier and cheaper, stimulating diffusion of information, including news of discoveries, among literate Europeans. By 1400, the crucial navigational aids employed by maritime explorers like Columbus were already available: compasses; hourglasses, which allowed calculation of elapsed time, useful in estimating speed; and the astrolabe and the quadrant, devices for determining latitude. These and other technological advances were known to many people throughout fifteenth-century Europe. The Portuguese were the first to use them in a campaign to sail beyond the limits of the known world.

A Century of Portuguese Exploration

In many ways, Portugal was an unlikely candidate to take the lead in exploration. With less than 2 percent of the population of Christian Europe, the country devoted far more energy and wealth to the geographical exploration of the world between 1415 and 1460 than all the other countries of Europe combined.

Facing the Atlantic on the Iberian peninsula, the Portuguese lived on the fringes of the thriving Mediterranean trade. As a Christian kingdom, Portugal cooperated with Spain in the Reconquest, the centuries-long drive to expel Muslims from the Iberian peninsula. The religious zeal that propelled the Reconquest also justified expansion into what the Portuguese considered heathen lands.

The most influential advocate of Portuguese exploration was Prince Henry the Navigator, son of the Portuguese king. From 1415 until his death in 1460, Henry collected the latest information about sailing techniques and geography, supported new crusades against the Muslims, encouraged fresh sources of trade to fatten Portuguese pocketbooks, and pushed explorers to go farther still. African conquests also promised to wrest wheat fields from their Moroccan owners and to obtain gold, the currency of European trade.

Neither the Portuguese nor anybody else in Europe knew how big Africa was. At first, Portuguese mariners cautiously hugged the west coast of Africa, seldom venturing beyond sight of land. By 1434, they had reached the northern edge of the Sahara Desert, where strong westerly currents swept them out to sea. They soon learned how to ride those currents far away from the coast before sailing back toward land, a technique that allowed them to reach Cape Verde by 1444 (see Map 2.1). The Portuguese also developed sturdier ships called caravels that eventually allowed them to round Cape Verde. By 1480, Portuguese caravels sailed into and around the Gulf of Guinea and as far south as the Congo.

Fierce African resistance confined the Portuguese to coastal trading posts where they bartered successfully for gold, slaves, and ivory. Portuguese merchants learned that relatively peaceful trading posts on the coast were far more profitable than violent conquests and attempts at colonization inland. In the 1460s, the Portuguese used African slaves to develop sugar plantations on the Cape Verde Islands, inaugurating an association between African slaves and plantation labor that would be transplanted to the New World in the centuries to come.

About 1480, the Portuguese began a conscious search for a sea route to Asia. In 1488, Bartolomeu Dias sailed around the Cape of Good Hope at the southern tip of Africa and hurried back to Lisbon with the exciting news that it appeared to be possible to sail on to India and China. In 1498, after ten years of careful preparation, Vasco da Gama commanded the first Portuguese fleet to sail to India. Portugal quickly capitalized on the commercial potential of da Gama's new sea route. By the early sixteenth century, the Portuguese controlled a far-flung commercial empire in India, Indonesia, and China (collectively referred to as the East Indies). Their new sea route to the East eliminated overland travel and the numerous intermediate merchants and markups of the old Mediterranean trade routes controlled by the Italians.

Through its century of African explorations, Portugal broke the monopoly of the old Mediterranean trade with the East, dramatically expanded the known world, established a network of Portuguese outposts in Africa and Asia, and developed methods of sailing the high seas that Columbus employed on his revolutionary voyage west.

YORUBA QUEEN
This expressive terracotta head, discovered in Nigeria in 1957, was once part of a large sculpture of a Yoruba queen memorialized in a shrine built between 800 and 900 years ago, centuries before the arrival of Portuguese explorers.
The National Commission for Museums and Monuments & Life, Nigeria.

A Surprising New World in the Western Atlantic

In retrospect, the Portuguese seemed ideally qualified to venture across the Atlantic. They had pioneered the frontiers of seafaring, exploration, and geography for almost a century. However, the knowledge and experience gained in navigating around Africa made them cautious about the risks of trying to sail across the Atlantic. Most European experts believed it could not even be done. The European discovery of America required someone bold enough to believe that the experts were wrong and the risks were surmountable. That person was Christopher Columbus.

The Explorations of Columbus

Born in 1451 into the family of an obscure master weaver in Genoa, Italy, Columbus went to sea when he was about fourteen. By about 1476, he lived in Lisbon, venturing frequently to the Madeira Islands and at least twice sailing all the way to the coast of central Africa.

Like other educated Europeans, Columbus believed that the earth was a sphere and that theoretically it was possible to reach the East Indies by sailing west. Most Europeans believed, however, that the earth was simply too big for anyone to sail west from Europe to Asia. Sailors would die of thirst and starvation long before they reached Asia. Columbus rejected this conventional wisdom. With flawed calculations, he estimated that Asia lay about 2,500 miles from the westernmost boundary of the known world, a shorter distance than Portuguese ships routinely sailed between Lisbon and the Congo. Convinced by his erroneous calculations, Columbus became obsessed with a scheme to prove he was right.

In 1492, after years of unsuccessful lobbying for support from Portugal, England, and France, Columbus finally won financing for his journey from Spain's King Ferdinand and Queen Isabella. After barely three months of hurried preparation, Columbus and his small fleet—the *Niña* and *Pinta*, both caravels, and the *Santa María*, a larger merchant vessel—headed west. Six weeks after leaving the Canary Islands, where he stopped for supplies, Columbus landed on a tiny Caribbean island about three hundred miles north of the eastern tip of Cuba, which he named San Salvador.

Columbus and his men understood that they had made a momentous discovery. Yet they found it frustrating. Although the Tainos proved friendly, they did not have the riches Columbus expected to find in the East. For

Columbus's First Voyage to the New World, 1492–1493

three months Columbus cruised from island to is-land, looking for the king of Japan. In mid-January 1493, he started back, taking seven Tainos with him. When he reached Isabella and Ferdinand, they were overjoyed by his news. With a voyage that had lasted barely eight months, Columbus appeared to have catapulted Spain from a secondary position in the race for a sea route to Asia into that of a serious challenger to Portugal (whose explorers had not yet sailed to India or China).

To protect their claims, the Spanish monarchs negotiated the Treaty of Tordesillas with Portugal in 1494, drawing an imaginary line eleven hundred miles west of the Canary Islands (Map 2.2). Land discovered west of the line belonged to Spain, while Portugal claimed land to the east.

Before Columbus died in 1506, he returned to the New World two more times without relinquishing his belief that the East Indies were there, someplace. Explorers continued to search for a passage to the East or some other source of profit. Before long, prospects of beating the Portuguese to Asia began to dim along with the hope of finding vast hoards of gold. Nonetheless, Columbus's discoveries forced sixteenth-century Europeans to think about the world in new ways. He proved that it was possible to sail from Europe to the western rim of the Atlantic and return to Europe. Most important, Columbus made clear that beyond the western shores of the Atlantic lay lands entirely unknown to Europeans.

The Geographic Revolution and the Columbian Exchange

Within thirty years of Columbus's initial discovery, Europeans' understanding of world geography underwent a revolution. But it took a generation of additional exploration before they could comprehend the general contours of what Columbus had found.

In 1497, King Henry VII of England sent another Genoese sailor, John Cabot, to look for a passage to the Indies across the North Atlantic, referred to as a "Northwest Passage" (see Map 2.2). Cabot managed to reach the tip of Newfoundland, which he believed was part of Asia. He hurried back to England, assembled a small fleet to follow up his discovery, and returned in 1498. But he was never heard from again. In 1499, a Spanish expedition landed on the northern coast of South America, accompanied by Amerigo Vespucci, an Italian businessman whose avocation was geography. In 1500,

Pedro Álvars Cabral commanded a Portuguese fleet bound for the Indian Ocean that accidentally made landfall on the coast of Brazil as it looped westward into the Atlantic.

By 1500, it was clear that several large chunks of land cluttered the western Atlantic. A few cartographers speculated that these chunks were connected to one another in a landmass that was not Asia. In 1507, Martin Waldseemüller, a German cartographer, published the first map that showed the New World separate from Asia; he named the land America, in honor of Amerigo Vespucci.

Two additional discoveries confirmed Waldseemüller's speculation. In 1513, Vasco Núñez de Balboa crossed the isthmus of Panama and reached the Pacific Ocean. Clearly, more water lay between the New World and Asia. How much water Ferdinand Magellan discovered when he led an expedition to circumnavigate the globe in 1519. Sponsored by King Charles I of Spain, Magellan's voyage took him first to the New World, around the southern tip of South America, and into the Pacific late in November 1520. Crossing the Pacific took almost four months. When he reached the Philippines, his crew had been decimated by extreme hunger and thirst. Magellan himself was killed by Philippine tribesmen. A remnant of his expedition continued into the Indian Ocean and managed to transport a cargo of spices back to Spain in 1522.

In most ways Magellan's voyage was a disaster. One ship and 18 men crawled back from an expedition that had begun with five ships and more than 250 men. But the geographic information it provided left no doubt that America was a continent separated from Asia by the enormous Pacific Ocean. The voyage made clear that Columbus was dead wrong about the identity of what he had discovered. It was possible to sail west to reach the East Indies, but that was a terrible way to go. After Magellan, most Europeans who sailed west had their sights set on the New World, not on Asia.

Columbus's arrival in the Caribbean anchored the western end of what might be imagined as a sea bridge spanning the Atlantic and connecting the New World to Europe. That sea bridge ended the age-old separation of the hemispheres and initiated the Columbian exchange, a transatlantic exchange of goods, people, and ideas that has continued ever since. Spaniards brought things that were novelties in the New World but commonplace in Europe, including Christianity, iron technology, sailing ships, firearms, wheeled vehicles, and horses and other

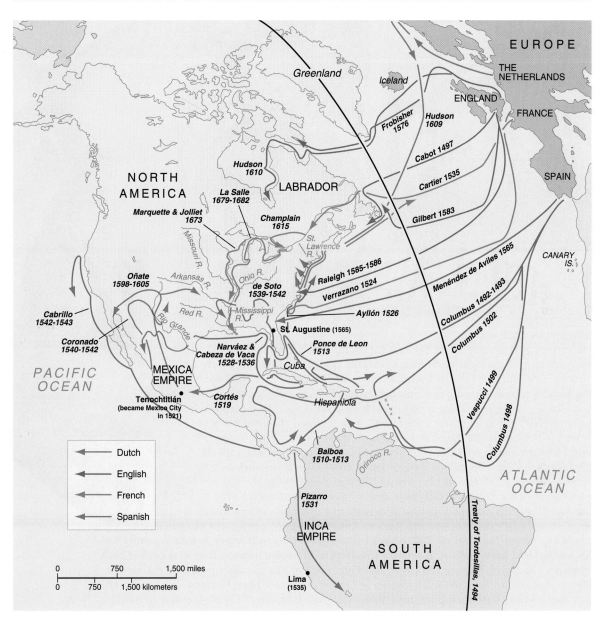

MAP 2.2

European Explorations in Sixteenth-Century America

This map illustrates the approximate routes of early European explorations of the New World.

READING THE MAP: Which countries were most actively exploring the New World? Which countries were exploring later than others?

CONNECTIONS: What were the motivations behind the explorations? What were the motivations for colonization?

www.bedfordstmartins.com/roarkcompact SEE THE ONLINE STUDY GUIDE for more help in analyzing this map.

COLUMBIAN EXCHANGE

The arrival of Columbus in the New World initiated an unending transatlantic exchange of goods, people, and ideas. Spaniards brought domesticated animals from the Old World, including horses, cattle, goats, chickens, cats, and sheep (left). The novelty of such animals is demonstrated by the Nahua words the Mexican people initially used to refer to these strange new beasts: for horses, they used the Nahua word for deer; a cow was "one with horns"; a goat was a "bearded one with horns"; a chicken was a "Spanish turkey hen"; a cat was a "little cougar"; a sheep was referred to with the word for cotton, linking the animal with its fibrous woolen coat. Spaniards brought many other alien items such as cannon, which the Mexica at first termed "fat fire trumpets," and guitars, which the Mexica called "rope drums." Spaniards also carried Old World microorganisms that caused devastating epidemics of smallpox, measles, and other diseases (center). Ancient American people, goods, and ideas made the return trip across the Atlantic. Columbus's sailors quickly learned to use Indian hammocks and became infected with syphilis in sexual encounters with Indian women; then they carried both hammocks and syphilis back to Europe. Smoking tobacco, like the cigar puffed by the ancient Mayan lord (right), became such a fashion in Europe that some came to believe, as a print of two men relaxing with their pipes was captioned, "Life Is Smoke." The strangeness of New World peoples and cultures also reinforced Europeans' notions of their own superiority. Although the Columbian exchange went in both directions, it was not a relationship of equality. Europeans seized and retained the upper hand.

The Bancroft Library; Arxiv Mas; Collection of Dr. Robicsek.

domesticated animals. Smuggled along unknowingly were also Old World microorganisms that caused epidemics of smallpox, measles, and other diseases that killed the vast majority of Indian peoples during the sixteenth century and continued to decimate survivors in later centuries. The catastrophic effects of European diseases made the Columbian exchange far from equal.

Ancient American goods, people, and ideas made the return trip across the Atlantic. Europeans were introduced to such vital New World crops as corn and potatoes as well as exotic items like pineapples, named for their resemblance to pinecones. Columbus's sailors became infected with syphilis in sexual encounters with New World women and then unwittingly carried the deadly parasite back to Europe. New World tobacco created a European rage for smoking that has yet to abate. But for almost a generation after 1492, this Columbian exchange did not reward Spaniards with the riches they longed to find.

Spanish Exploration and Conquest

During the sixteenth century, the New World helped Spain become the most powerful country in both Europe and the Americas. Initially, Spanish expeditions reconnoitered the Caribbean, scouted stretches of the Atlantic coast, and established settlements on the large islands of Hispaniola, Puerto Rico, Jamaica, and Cuba. Spaniards enslaved Caribbean tribes and put them to work growing crops and mining gold. But the profits from these early ventures barely covered the costs of maintaining the settlers. After almost thirty years of exploration, the promise of Columbus's discovery seemed illusory.

Soon after 1519, however, that promise was fulfilled, spectacularly. The mainland phase of exploration began in 1519 with Hernán Cortés's march into Mexico; by about 1545, Spanish conquests extended from northern Mexico to southern Chile, and New World riches filled Spanish treasure chests. Cortés's expedition served as the model for those to follow.

The Conquest of Mexico

Hernán Cortés, who would become the richest and most famous *conquistador* (conqueror), arrived in the New World in 1504, an obscure nineteen-year-old Spaniard seeking adventure and the chance to make a name for himself. He fought in the conquest of Cuba and elsewhere in the Caribbean. In 1519, the governor of Cuba authorized Cortés to organize an expedition to investigate rumors of a fabulously wealthy kingdom somewhere in the interior of the mainland. A charming, charismatic leader, Cortés quickly assembled a force of about six hundred men, loaded his ragtag army aboard eleven ships, and set out.

Cortés's confidence that he could talk his way out of most situations and fight his way out of the rest fortified the small band of Spaniards. Landing first on the Yucatán peninsula, Cortés had the good

fortune to receive a gift from a Mayan chief: a young woman named Malinali who spoke both Mayan and Nahuatl, the language of most people in Mexico and Central America. Malinali, whom the Spaniards called Marina, soon learned Spanish and became Cortés's interpreter. Marina served as the essential conduit of communication between the Spaniards and the Indians. With her help, Cortés talked and fought with Indians along the Gulf coast of Mexico, trying to discover the location of the fabled kingdom.

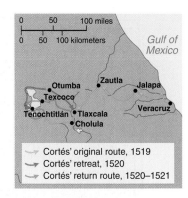

Cortés's Invasion of Tenochtitlán, 1519–1521

Leading about 350 men armed with swords, lances, and muskets, Cortés had to live off the land, making friends with the indigenous tribes when he could and killing them when he thought necessary. Montezuma, the Mexican emperor, received news of the intruders and sent scouts to try to obtain information about who they were and what they wanted. On November 8, 1519, when Cortés reached Tenochtitlán, the Mexican capital, Montezuma came out to meet him. After presenting Cortés with gifts, Montezuma welcomed the Spaniards to the royal palace and showered them with lavish hospitality. Quickly, Cortés took Montezuma hostage and held him under house arrest, hoping to make him a puppet through which the Spaniards could rule the Mexican empire. This uneasy peace existed for several months until, after a brutal massacre of many Mexican nobles by one of Cortés's subordinates, the population of Tenochtitlán revolted, murdered Montezuma, and mounted a ferocious assault on the Spaniards. On June 30, 1520, Cortés and about a hundred other Spaniards fought their way out of Tenochtitlán and retreated toward the coast about one hundred miles to Tlaxcala, a stronghold of bitter enemies of the Mexicans. The friendly Tlaxcalans—who had long resented the Mexicans' power—allowed Cortés to regroup, obtain reinforcements, and plan a strategy to conquer Tenochtitlán.

In the spring of 1521, Cortés mounted a complex campaign against the Mexican capital. The Spaniards and tens of thousands of Indian allies laid siege to the city. With a relentless, scorched-earth

MEXICAN COUNTERATTACK
This postconquest painting by a sixteenth-century Mexican artist is one of a series depicting crucial battles in the Spaniards' ultimate defeat of the Mexica. Here Mexican warriors attack the conquistadors, forcing the Spaniards to retreat from Tenochtitlán and regroup for the final siege. The distinctive shields and costumes of the Mexicans signified their military status, which was based on their battlefield prowess. The Spaniards wear uniform battle armor. The painting contrasts the colorful individuality of the Mexican warriors with the massed, anonymous Spaniards who level crossbows and firearms against the Mexicans' wooden spears. The painting does not show one of the Spaniards' deadliest weapons: steel swords.
Oronoz.

strategy, Cortés finally defeated the last Mexican defenders on August 13, 1521. The great capital of the Mexican empire "looked as if it had been ploughed up," one of Cortés's soldiers remembered. A few years later, one of the Mexica described the utter despair of the defeated:

> Broken spears lie in the roads;
> we have torn our hair in grief.
> The houses are roofless now, and their walls
> are red with blood. . . .
> We have pounded our hands in despair
> against the adobe walls,
> for our inheritance, our city, is lost and dead.

The Search for Other Mexicos

Lured by their insatiable appetite for gold, conquistadors quickly fanned out from Tenochtitlán in search of other Mexicos. The most spectacular prize fell to Francisco Pizarro, who conquered the Incan empire in Peru. The Incas controlled a vast, complex region that contained more than nine million people and stretched along the western coast of South America for more than two thousand miles. In 1532, Pizarro and his army of fewer than two hundred men captured the Incan emperor Atahualpa and held him hostage. As ransom, the Incas gave Pizarro the largest treasure yet produced by the conquests: gold and silver equivalent to half a century's worth of precious-metal production in Europe. With the ransom safely in their hands, the Spaniards executed Atahualpa.

In 1539, Hernando de Soto, a seasoned conquistador who had taken part in the conquest of Peru, set out to find another Peru in North America. Landing in Florida, de Soto literally slashed his way through much of southeastern North America for three years, searching for the rich, majestic civilizations he thought were there. After many brutal battles and much hardship, de Soto became sick and died in 1542, and his men turned back to Mexico, disappointed.

Tales of the fabulous wealth of the mythical Seven Cities of Cíbola also lured Francisco Vásquez de Coronado to search the Southwest and Great

Plains of North America. In 1540, Coronado left northern Mexico with a large expedition including a priest who claimed to know the way to what he called "the greatest and best of the discoveries." Cíbola turned out to be a small Zuñi pueblo of about a hundred families. When the Zuñi shot arrows at the Spaniards, Coronado attacked the pueblo and routed the defenders after a hard battle. Convinced that the rich cities must lie somewhere over the horizon, Coronado kept moving all the way to central Kansas before deciding in 1542 that the rumors he had pursued were just that, nothing more.

Juan Rodríguez Cabrillo led an expedition in 1542 that sailed along the coast of California. Cabrillo died on Santa Catalina Island, offshore from present-day Los Angeles, but his men sailed on to the border of Oregon, where a ferocious storm forced them to turn back toward Mexico.

These probes into North America by de Soto, Coronado, and Cabrillo persuaded Spaniards that enormous territories stretched northward, yet their inhabitants had little to loot or exploit. After a generation of vigorous exploration, Spaniards concluded that there was only one Mexico and one Peru.

New Spain in the Sixteenth Century

For all practical purposes, Spain dominated the New World in the sixteenth century (Map 2.3). Portugal claimed the giant territory of Brazil under the Tordesillas treaty but was far more concerned with exploiting its hard-won trade with the East Indies than in colonizing the New World. England and France were absorbed in the affairs of Europe and largely lost interest in America until late in the century. In the decades after 1519, Spaniards created the distinctive colonial society of New Spain that gave other Europeans a striking illustration of how the New World could be made to serve the purposes of the Old.

The Spanish monarchy claimed ownership of most of the land in the Western Hemisphere and gave the conquistadors permission to explore and plunder. (See "Documenting the American Promise," page 36.) The crown took one-fifth, called the "royal fifth," of any loot confiscated by the conquerors and allowed the conquerors to divide the rest. In the end, most conquistadors received very little after the plunder was divided among Cortés and his favorite officers. After the conquest of Tenochtitlán, Cortés decided to compensate his disappointed,

battle-hardened men by giving them the towns the Spaniards had subdued.

The distribution of conquered towns institutionalized the system of *encomienda*, which empowered conquistadors to rule the Indians and the lands in and around their towns. The concept of encomienda was familiar to the Spaniards, who had used it to govern regions recaptured from the Muslims during the Reconquest. In New Spain, encomienda transferred to the Spanish *encomendero* (the man who "owned" the town) the tribute that the town had previously paid to the Mexican empire.

In theory, encomienda involved a reciprocal relationship between the encomendero and "his" Indians. In return for the tribute and labor of the Indians, the encomendero was supposed to encourage the Indians to convert to Christianity, to be responsible for their material well-being, and to guarantee order and justice in the town. Catholic missionaries labored earnestly to convert the Indians to Christianity. After baptizing tens of thousands of Indians, the missionaries discovered that the Indians continued to worship their own gods along with the Christian God. Most friars came to believe that the Indians were lesser beings inherently incapable of fully understanding the Christian faith.

In practice, encomenderos were far more interested in what the Indians could do for them than in what they or missionaries could do for the Indians. Encomenderos subjected Indians to chronic overwork, mistreatment, and abuse. Economically, however, encomienda recognized a fundamental reality of New Spain: The most important treasure the Spaniards could plunder from the New World was not gold, but uncompensated Indian labor. To exploit that labor, the hemisphere's richest natural resource, encomienda gave encomenderos the right to force Indians to work when, where, and how the Spaniards pleased.

Encomienda engendered two groups of influential critics. A few of the missionaries were horrified at the brutal mistreatment of the Indians. The cruelty of the encomenderos made it difficult for priests to persuade Indians of the tender mercies of the Spaniards' God. "What will [the Indians] think about the God of the Christians," Fray Bartolomé de Las Casas asked, when they see their friends "with their heads split, their hands amputated, their intestines torn open? . . . Would they want to come to Christ's sheepfold after their homes had been destroyed, their children imprisoned, their wives raped, their cities devastated, their maidens

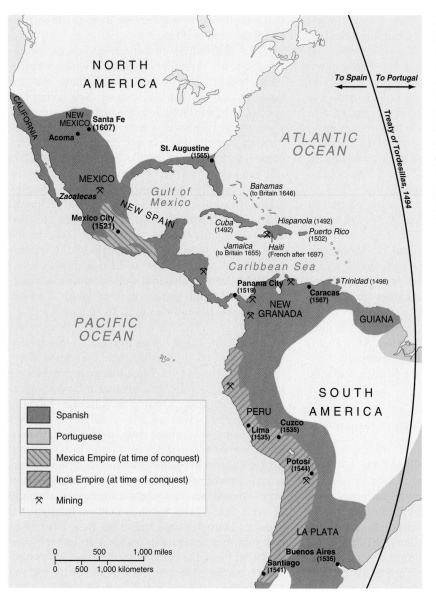

MAP 2.3
New Spain in the Sixteenth Century
Spanish control spread throughout Central and South America during the sixteenth century, with the important exception of Portuguese Brazil. North America, although claimed by Spain under the Treaty of Tordesillas, remained peripheral to Spain's New World empire.

deflowered, and their provinces laid waste?" Las Casas and other outspoken missionaries softened few hearts among the encomenderos, but they did win some sympathy for the Indians from the Spanish monarchy and royal bureaucracy.

One of the most important blows to encomienda was the imposition in 1549 of a reform called the *repartimiento*, which limited the labor an encomendero could command from his Indians to forty-five days per year from each adult male. The repartimiento, however, did not challenge the principle of forced labor, nor did it prevent encomenderos

from continuing to cheat, mistreat, and overwork their Indians. Slowly, as the old encomenderos died, repartimiento replaced encomienda as the basic system of exploiting Indian labor.

The practice of coerced labor in New Spain grew directly out of the Spaniards' assumption that they were superior to the Indians. As one missionary put it, the Indians "are incapable of learning. . . . The Indians are more stupid than asses and refuse to improve in anything." Therefore, most Spaniards assumed, Indians' labor should be organized by and for their conquerors.

Doctrina Christiana.

MISSION SCHOOL
This early-seventeenth-century woodcut depicts a mission school in New Spain. A monk instructs Indian children in Christian doctrine by leading them word by word through a printed book. The obedient students follow the monk's directions by pointing to the right passage in the book. A disobedient student is punished with a whipping administered by a fellow student at the monk's command. According to this woodcut, what lessons did mission school students learn in addition to Christian doctrine?
© Collection of the New-York Historical Society.

From the viewpoint of Spain, the single most important economic activity in New Spain after 1540 was silver mining. Spain imported more New World gold than silver in the early decades of the century, but that changed with the discovery of major silver deposits at Potosí, Bolivia, in 1545 and Zacatecas, Mexico, in 1546. As the mines swung into large-scale production during the 1540s, an ever-growing stream of silver flowed from New Spain to Spain (Figure 2.1). Overall, exports of precious metals from New Spain during the sixteenth century were worth about twenty-five times more than hides, the next most important export. The mines and their products were valuable principally for their contribution to the wealth of Spain, not to that of the colony.

During the century after 1492, about 225,000 Spaniards settled in the colonies. Virtually all of them were poor young men of common (nonnoble) lineage who came directly from Spain. Laborers and artisans made up the largest proportion, but sol-diers and sailors were also numerous. Throughout the sixteenth century, men vastly outnumbered women, although the proportion of women grew from about one in twenty before 1519 to nearly one in three by the 1580s. The gender and number of Spanish settlers shaped two fundamental features of the society of New Spain. First, despite the thousands of immigrants, Europeans never made up more than 1 or 2 percent of the total population. Although Spaniards ruled New Spain, the population was almost wholly Indian. Second, the shortage of Spanish women meant that a great deal of concubinage and intermarriage took place between Spanish men and Indian women.

The highest social status in New Spain was reserved for natives of Spain, *peninsulares* (people born on the Iberian peninsula). Below them but still within the elite were *creoles*, the children born in the New World to Spanish men and women. Below them on the social pyramid was a larger group of *mestizos*, the offspring of Spanish men and Indian

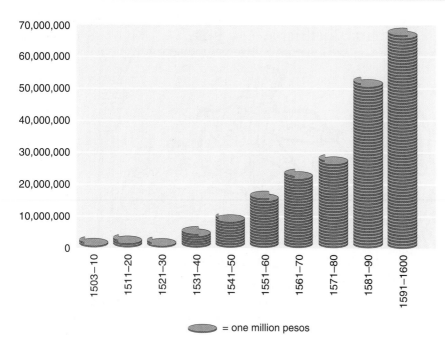

FIGURE 2.1

New World Gold and Silver Imported into Spain during the Sixteenth Century, in Pesos
Spain imported more gold than silver during the first three decades of the sixteenth century, but the total value of this treasure was quickly eclipsed during the 1530s and 1540s when rich silver mines were developed. Silver accounted for most of the enormous growth in Spain's precious-metal imports from the New World.

= one million pesos

women, who made up 4 or 5 percent of the population. So many of the mestizos were illegitimate that the term *mestizo* (from the Spanish word for "mixed") was almost synonymous with *bastard* in the sixteenth century. Some mestizos worked as artisans and labor overseers and lived well, and a few rose into the ranks of the elite, especially if their Indian ancestry was not obvious from their skin color. Most mestizos, however, were lumped with the Indians, the enormous bottom mass of the population.

The society of New Spain established the precedent for what would become a pronounced pattern in the European colonies of the New World: a society stratified sharply by social origin and race. All Europeans of whatever social origin considered themselves superior to the native Americans; in New Spain, they were a dominant minority in both power and status.

The Toll of Spanish Conquest and Colonization

By 1560, the major centers of Indian civilization had been conquered, their leaders overthrown, their religion held in contempt, and their people forced to work for the Spaniards. Profound demoralization pervaded Indian society. As a Mexican poet wrote:

Nothing but flowers and songs of sorrow
are left in Mexico . . .
where once we saw warriors and wise men. . . .
We are crushed to the ground;
we lie in ruins.
There is nothing but grief and suffering
in Mexico.

Adding to the culture shock of conquest and colonization was the deadly toll of European diseases. As conquest spread, Indians were struck by virulent epidemics of measles, smallpox, and respiratory illnesses, diseases unknown to them before the arrival of the Europeans. By 1570, only a half century after Cortés entered Tenochtitlán, the Indian population of New Spain had fallen to about 10 percent of what it had been when Columbus arrived. In little more than fifty years, nine out of ten Indians had succumbed to the severity of colonial policies and even more deadly European diseases. The destruction of the Indian population was a catastrophe unequaled in human history. A Mayan Indian recalled that when sickness struck his village, "Great was the stench of the dead. . . . The dogs and vultures devoured the bodies. The mortality was terrible. . . . So it was that we became orphans. . . . We were born to die!" For most Indians, New Spain was a graveyard.

For the Spaniards, Indian deaths meant that the most valuable resource of New Spain—Indian labor—dwindled rapidly. By the last quarter of the sixteenth century, Spanish colonists felt the pinch of a labor shortage. To help redress the need for laborers, the colonists began to import African slaves. In the years before 1550, only 15,000 slaves were imported from Africa. Even after Indian labor began to decline, the relatively high cost of African slaves kept imports low, approximately 36,000 from 1550 to the end of the century. During the sixteenth century, New Spain continued to rely primarily on a diminishing number of Indians.

Northern Outposts in Florida and New Mexico

After the explorations of de Soto, Coronado, and Cabrillo, officials in New Spain lost interest in North America. The monarchy claimed that Spain owned North America and insisted that a few North American settlements be established to give some tangible reality to its claims. Settlements in Florida would have the additional benefit of protecting Spanish ships from pirates and privateers who lurked along the southeastern coast, waiting for the Spanish treasure fleet sailing toward Spain.

In 1565, the Spanish king sent Pedro Menéndez de Avilés to create settlements along the Atlantic coast of North America. In early September, Menéndez founded St. Augustine in Florida, the first permanent European settlement within what became

Español con India, Mestizo.

Mestizo con Españolo Castizo.

Castizo con Española Español.

Español con Mora Mulato.

5

6

Mulato con Española Morisco.

Morisco con Española Chino.

7

Chino con India Salta atras.

Salta atras con Mulata Lobo.

MIXED RACES
Residents of New Spain maintained a lively interest in each person's racial lineage. These eighteenth-century paintings illustrate forms of racial mixture common in the sixteenth century. In the first painting, a Spanish man and an Indian woman have a mestizo son; in the fourth, a Spanish man and a woman of African descent have a mulatto son; in the fifth, a Spanish woman and a mulatto man have a morisco daughter. The many racial permutations of parents led residents of New Spain to develop an elaborate vocabulary of ancestry. The child of a morisco and a Spaniard was a chino; the child of a chino and an Indian was a salta abas; the child of a salta abas and a mulatto was a lobo; and so on. Can you detect hints of some of the meanings of racial categories in the clothing depicted in these paintings?
Bob Schalkwijk/INAH.

Justifying Conquest

The immense riches Spain reaped from its New World empire came largely at the expense of Indians. A few individual Spaniards raised their voices against the brutal exploitation of Indians. Their criticisms prompted the Spanish monarchy to formulate an official justification of conquest that, in effect, blamed Indians for resisting Spanish dominion.

DOCUMENT 1. Montecino's 1511 Sermon

In 1511, a Dominican friar named Antón Montecino delivered a blistering sermon that astonished the Spaniards gathered in the church in Santo Domingo, headquarters of the Spanish Caribbean.

Your greed for gold is blind. Your pride, your lust, your anger, your envy, your sloth, all blind. . . . You are in mortal sin. And you are heading for damnation. . . . For you are destroying an innocent people. For they are God's people, these innocents, whom you destroyed. By what right do you make them die? Mining gold for you in your mines or working for you in your fields, by what right do you unleash enslaving wars upon them? They have lived in peace in this land before you came, in peace in their own homes. They did nothing to harm you to cause you to slaughter them wholesale. . . . Are you not under God's command to love them as you love yourselves? Are you out of your souls, out of your minds? Yes. And that will bring you to damnation.

SOURCE: Zvi Dor-Ner, *Columbus and the Age of Discovery* (New York: William Morrow, 1991), 220–21.

DOCUMENT 2. The *Requerimiento*

Montecino returned to Spain to bring the Indians' plight to the king's attention. In 1512 and 1513, King Ferdinand met with philosophers, theologians, and other advisers and concluded that the holy duty to spread the Christian faith justified conquest. To buttress this claim, the king had his advisers prepare the Requerimiento. According to the Requerimiento, Indians who failed to welcome Spanish conquest and all its blessings deserved to die. Conquistadors were commanded to read the Requerimiento to Indians before any act of conquest. Beginning in 1514, they routinely did so, speaking in Spanish while other Spaniards brandishing unsheathed swords stood nearby.

On the part of the King . . . [and] queen of [Spain], subduers of the barbarous nations, we their servants notify and make known to you, as best we can, that the Lord our God, living and eternal, created the heaven and the earth, and one man and one woman, of whom you and we, and all the men of the world, were and are descendants. . . .

God our lord gave charge to one man called St. Peter, that he should be lord and superior to all the men in the world, that all should obey him, and that he should be the head of the whole human race, wherever men should live . . . and he gave him the world for his kingdom and jurisdiction.

And he commanded him to place his seat in Rome, as the spot most fitting to rule the world from. . . . This man was called Pope, as if to say, Admirable Great Father and Governor of men. The men who lived in that time obeyed that St. Peter and took him for lord, king, and superior of the universe. So also they have regarded the others who after him have been elected to the pontificate, and so has it been continued even till now, and will continue till the end of the world.

One of these pontiffs, who succeeded that St. Peter as lord of the world . . . made donation of these islands and mainland to the aforesaid king and queen [of Spain] and to their successors. . . .

So their highnesses are kings and lords of these islands and mainland by virtue of this donation; and . . . almost all those to whom this has been notified, have received and served their highnesses, as lords and kings, in the way that subjects ought to do, with good will, without any resistance, immediately, without delay, when they were informed of the aforesaid facts. And also they received and obeyed the priests whom their highnesses sent to preach to them and to teach them our holy faith; and all these, of their own free will, without any reward or condition have become Christians, and are so, and the highnesses have joyfully and graciously received them, and they have also commanded them to be treated as their subjects and vassals; and you too are held and obliged to do the same. Wherefore, as best we can, we ask and require that you consider what we have said to you, and that you take the time that shall be necessary to understand and deliberate upon it, and that you acknowledge the Church as the ruler and superior of the whole world, and the high priest called Pope, and in his name the king and queen [of Spain] our lords, in his place, as superiors and lords and kings of these islands and this mainland by virtue of the said donation, and that you consent and permit that these religious fathers declare and preach to you. . . .

If you do so . . . we . . . shall receive you in all love and charity, and shall leave you your wives and your children and your lands free without servitude, that you may do with them and with yourselves freely what you like and think best, and they shall not compel you to turn to Christians unless you yourselves, when informed of the truth, should wish to be converted to our holy Catholic faith. . . . And besides this, their highnesses award you many privileges and exemptions and will grant you many benefits.

But if you do not do this or if you maliciously delay in doing it, I certify to you that with the help of God we shall forcefully enter into your country and shall make war against you in all ways and manners that we can, and shall subject you to the yoke and obedience of the Church and of their highnesses; we shall take you and your wives and your children and shall make slaves of them, and as such shall sell and dispose of them as their highnesses may command; and we shall take away your goods and shall do to you all the harm and damage that we can, as to vassals who do not obey and refuse to receive their lord and resist and contradict him; and we protest that the deaths and losses which shall accrue from this are your fault, and not that of their highnesses, or ours, or of these soldiers who come with us.

Indians who heard the Requerimiento *could not understand Spanish, of course. No native documents survive to record the Indians' thoughts upon hearing the Spaniards' official justification for conquest, even when it was translated in a language they recognized. But one conquistador reported that when the* Requerimiento *was translated for two chiefs in Colombia, they responded that if the pope gave the king so much territory that belonged to other people, "the Pope must have been drunk."*

SOURCE: Adapted from A. Helps and M. Oppenheim, eds., *The Spanish Conquest in America and Its Relation to the History of Slavery and to the Government of the Colonies,* 4 vols. (London and New York, 1900–1904), 1:264–67.

QUESTIONS FOR ANALYSIS AND DEBATE

1. How did the *Requerimiento* answer the criticisms of Montecino? According to the *Requerimiento*, why was conquest justified? What was the source of Indians' resistance to conquest?

2. What arguments might a critic like Montecino have used to respond to the *Requerimiento*'s justification of conquest? What arguments might the Mexican leader Montezuma have made against those of the *Requerimiento*?

3. Was the *Requerimiento* a faithful expression or a cynical violation of Spaniards' Christian faith?

the United States. By 1600, St. Augustine had a population of about five hundred, a token Spanish presence on the vast Atlantic shoreline of North America (see Map 2.3).

More than sixteen hundred miles west of St. Augustine, the Spaniards founded another outpost in 1598. Juan de Oñate led an expedition of about five hundred people to settle northern Mexico, now called New Mexico, and claim the booty rumored to exist there. Oñate and his companions reached pueblos near present-day Albuquerque and Santa Fe, where he solemnly convened the pueblos' leaders and received their oath of loyalty to the Spanish king and to the Christian God. But when the Acoma pueblo revolted against the Spaniards, Oñate ruthlessly suppressed the uprising, killing some hundreds of men, women, and children. Although Oñate reconfirmed the Spaniards' military superiority, he did not bring peace or stability to the region. Many of Oñate's settlers returned to Mexico, disillusioned. New Mexico lingered as a small, dusty token of Spanish claims to the North American Southwest.

The New World and Europe

The riches of New Spain helped make the sixteenth century the Golden Age of Spain. After the deaths of Queen Isabella and King Ferdinand, their sixteen-year-old grandson became King Charles I of Spain in 1516. Charles used the wealth of New Spain to pursue his vast ambitions in the fierce dynastic and religious battles of sixteenth-century Europe. Spain's power spread the impact of the New World throughout Europe.

In 1519, Charles I used judicious bribes to secure his selection as Holy Roman Emperor Charles V. His empire encompassed more than that of any other European monarch. With ambitions that matched his sprawling territories, Charles V confronted an unexpected challenge from Martin Luther, an obscure Catholic priest in central Germany.

The Protestant Reformation and the European Order

In 1517, Martin Luther initiated the Protestant Reformation by publicizing his criticisms of the Catholic Church. Luther's ideas, while shared by many other Catholics, were considered extremely

dangerous by church officials and by many monarchs like Charles V, who believed firmly that, just as the church spoke for God, they ruled for God.

Luther preached a doctrine known as justification by faith: Individual Christians could obtain salvation and life everlasting only by faith that God would save them. Giving offerings to the church, following the orders of the priest, or participating in church rituals did not put believers one step closer to heaven. The only true source of information about God's will was the Bible, not the church. By reading the Bible, any Christian could learn as much about God's commandments as any priest. Indeed, Luther called for a "priesthood of all believers." In effect, Luther charged that the Catholic Church was in many respects fraudulent. Although Luther hoped his ideas would reform the Catholic Church, instead they ruptured forever the unity of Christianity in western Europe.

Charles V pledged to exterminate the Protestant heresies. The wealth pouring into Spain from the New World fueled his efforts to defend the Catholic faith against Protestants, Muslims in eastern Europe, and any nation bold or foolhardy enough to contest Spain's supremacy. As the wealthiest and most powerful monarch in Europe, Charles V, followed by his son and successor Philip II, assumed responsibility for upholding the existing order of sixteenth-century Europe.

Europe and the Spanish Example

Both Charles V and Philip II fought wars throughout the world during the sixteenth century. Mexican silver funneled through the royal treasury into the hands of military suppliers, soldiers, and sailors wherever in the world Spain's forces fought. New World treasure was dissipated in military adventures that served the goals of the monarchy but did little to benefit most Spaniards.

But sixteenth-century Spaniards did not see it that way. As they looked at their accomplishments in the New World, they saw unmistakable signs of progress. They had added enormously to their knowledge and wealth. They had built mines, cities, churches, and even universities on the other side of the Atlantic. Their military, religious, and economic achievements gave them great pride and confidence.

The lessons of sixteenth-century Spain were not lost on Spain's European rivals. Spain had shown that the distant lands of the New World could serve the interests of Europeans. The German artist Albrecht Dürer expressed amazement at "the things which were brought to the King [of Spain] from the New Golden Land: a sun entirely of gold, a whole fathom [six feet] broad; likewise a moon, entirely of silver, just as big." But even more exciting for most Europeans was that the New World seemed to be a place for the expansion of European influence, a place where, as one Spaniard wrote, Europeans could "give to those strange lands the form of our own." France and England tried to follow Spain's lead. Both nations warred with Spain in Europe, preyed on Spanish treasure fleets, and ventured to the New World, where they too hoped to find an undiscovered passageway to the East Indies or another Mexico or Peru.

In 1524, France sent Giovanni da Verrazano to scout the Atlantic coast of North America from North Carolina to Canada, looking for a Northwest Passage (see Map 2.2). Eleven years later, France probed farther north with Jacques Cartier's voyage up the St. Lawrence River. Encouraged, Cartier returned to the region with a group of settlers in 1541,

ALGONQUIAN CEREMONIAL DANCE
When the English artist John White visited the coast of present-day North Carolina in 1585 as part of Raleigh's Roanoke expedition, he painted this watercolor portrait of an Algonquian ceremonial dance. This and White's other portraits are the only surviving likenesses of sixteenth-century North American Indians that were drawn from direct observation in the New World. White's portrait captures the individuality of these Indians' appearances and gestures while depicting a ceremony that must have appeared bizarre and alien to a sixteenth-century Englishman. The significance of this ceremonial dance is still a mystery, although the portrait's obvious signs of order, organization, and collective understanding show that the dancing Indians knew what it meant.
Copyright © The British Museum.

but the colony they established—like the search for a Northwest Passage—came to nothing.

English attempts to follow Spain's lead were slower but equally ill fated. Not until 1576, almost eighty years after John Cabot's voyages, did the English try again to find a Northwest Passage. This time Martin Frobisher sailed into the frigid waters of northern Canada; his sponsor was the Cathay Company, which hoped to open trade with China (see Map 2.2). Like many other explorers who preceded and followed him, Frobisher was mesmerized by the Spanish example and was sure he had found gold. But the tons of "ore" he hauled back to England proved worthless, the Cathay Company collapsed, and English interests shifted southward.

English attempts to establish North American settlements were no more fruitful than their search for a northern route to China. Sir Humphrey Gilbert led expeditions in 1578 and 1583 that made feeble efforts to found colonies in New-foundland until Gilbert vanished at sea in 1583. Sir Walter Raleigh organized an expedition in 1585 to settle Roanoke Island off the coast of present-day North Carolina. The first group of explorers left no colonists on the island, but two years later Raleigh sent a contingent of more than one hundred settlers to Roanoke under John White's leadership. White returned to England for supplies and when he went back in 1590, the Roanoke colonists had disappeared, leaving only the word *Croatoan* (whose meaning is unknown) carved on a tree. The Roanoke colonists most likely died from a combination of natural causes and unfriendly Indians. By the end of the century, England had failed to secure a New World beachhead.

Roanoke Settlement, 1585–1590

Conclusion: The Promise of the New World for Europeans

The sixteenth century in the New World belonged to the Spaniards, who employed Columbus, and the Indians, who greeted him as he stepped ashore. Spaniards initiated the Columbian exchange between the New World and the Old that continues to this day. The exchange subjected native Americans to the ravages of European diseases and Spanish conquest. Spanish explorers, conquistadors, and colonists forced Indians to serve the interests of Spanish settlers and the Spanish monarchy. The exchange illustrated one of the most important lessons of the sixteenth century: After millions of years, the Atlantic no longer was an impermeable barrier separating the Eastern and Western Hemispheres. After the voyages of Columbus, European sailing ships regularly bridged the Atlantic and carried people, products, diseases, and ideas from one shore to the other.

No European monarch could forget the seductive lesson taught by Spain's example: The New World could vastly enrich the Old. Spain remained a New World power for almost four centuries, and its language, culture, and institutions left a permanent imprint. By the end of the sixteenth century, however, other European monarchies began to contest Spain's dominion in Europe and to make forays into the northern fringes of Spain's New World preserve. To reap some of the benefits the Spaniards enjoyed from their New World domain, the others had to learn a difficult lesson: how to deviate from Spain's example. That discovery lay ahead.

FOR FURTHER READING ABOUT THE TOPICS IN THIS CHAPTER, see the Online Bibliography at www.bedfordstmartins.com/roarkcompact.

FOR ADDITIONAL FIRST-HAND ACCOUNTS OF THIS PERIOD, see pages 9–26 in Michael Johnson, ed., *Reading the American Past,* Second Edition, Volume I.

TO ASSESS YOUR MASTERY OF THE MATERIAL IN THIS CHAPTER, see the Online Study Guide at www.bedfordstmartins.com/roarkcompact.

CHRONOLOGY

1415 Portuguese explorers begin forays along African coast.

1444 Portuguese explorers reach Cape Verde.

1451 Christopher Columbus born in Genoa, Italy.

1480 Portuguese ships reach Congo.

1488 Bartolomeu Dias rounds Cape of Good Hope.

1492 Columbus lands on Caribbean island that he names San Salvador.

1493 Columbus makes second voyage to the New World.

1494 Portugal and Spain negotiate the Treaty of Tordesillas to divide New World between them.

1497 John Cabot searches for Northwest Passage.

1498 Columbus makes third voyage to the New World and lands in Venezuela.

Vasco da Gama sails to India.

1500 Pedro Álvars Cabral makes landfall in Brazil.

1507 German mapmaker Martin Waldseemüller names New World *America*.

1513 Vasco Núñez de Balboa crosses isthmus of Panama.

1517 Protestant Reformation begins in Europe.

1519 Hernán Cortés leads expedition to find and conquer Mexico.

Ferdinand Magellan sets out to sail around the world.

Charles I of Spain becomes Holy Roman Emperor Charles V.

1521 Cortés conquers the Mexica at Tenochtitlán.

1532 Francisco Pizarro begins conquest of Peru.

1539 Hernando de Soto launches exploration of southeastern North America.

1540 Francisco Vásquez de Coronado starts to explore the Southwest and Great Plains of North America.

1542 Juan Rodríguez Cabrillo explores California coast.

1549 *Repartimiento* reforms begin to replace *encomienda*.

1565 Pedro Menéndez de Avilés establishes St. Augustine, Florida.

1576 Martin Frobisher sails into northern Canadian waters.

1578 Sir Humphrey Gilbert attempts to found colonies in Newfoundland.

1587 English colonists under Sir Walter Raleigh settle Roanoke Island.

1598 Juan de Oñate leads expedition into New Mexico.

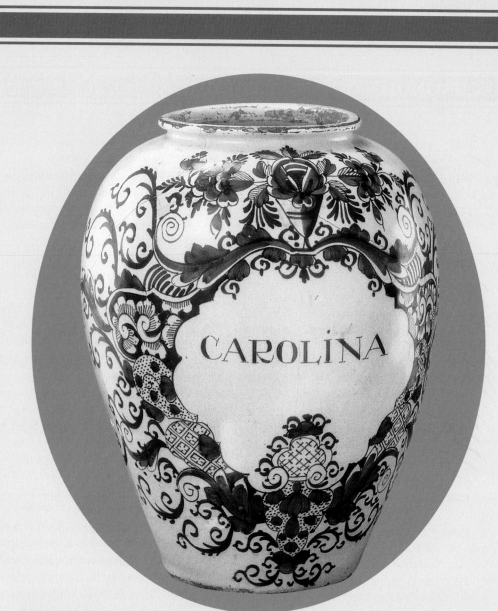

TOBACCO JAR

This tobacco storage jar combines a product and place name from the southern colonies in North America with the fine craft of decorative ceramics designed for Europeans to use in their everyday lives. The jar illustrates the many ways tobacco grown in the New World influenced life beyond tobacco fields. Grown principally by servants and slaves, the tobacco stored in this jar would have been transported to port in barrels made by coopers, ferried across the Atlantic in ships—made by shipbuilders and equipped with sails, ropes, and specialized fittings made by skilled workingmen—and insured by financiers and insurance companies. Upon arrival on the eastern shores of the Atlantic, the tobacco barrels would have been off-loaded and opened, the tobacco chopped, ground, and flavored by tobacconists, who sold it in shops along with jars like the one pictured here to consumers avid for tobacco to smoke, sniff, or chew and for an attractive repository both to store their stimulant and to display their sophisticated taste. Most tobacco came from the Chesapeake region; the label "Carolina" was a brand name rather than an accurate indication of the origin of the tobacco.

Colonial Williamsburg Foundation.

THE SOUTHERN COLONIES IN THE SEVENTEENTH CENTURY

3

1601–1700

IN DECEMBER 1607, BARELY SIX MONTHS AFTER ARRIVING AT JAMESTOWN with the first English colonists, Captain John Smith was captured by warriors of Powhatan, the supreme chief of about fourteen thousand Algonquian people who inhabited the coastal plain of present-day Virginia, near the Chesapeake Bay. According to Smith, Powhatan "feasted him after their best barbarous manner." Then, after the chief consulted with his men, "two great stones were brought before Powhatan: then as many [Indians] as could layd hands on [Smith], dragged him to [the stones], and thereon laid his head, and being ready with their clubs, to beate out his braines." At that moment, Pocahontas, Powhatan's eleven-year-old daughter, rushed forward and "got [Smith's] head in her armes, and laid her owne upon his to save him from death." Pocahontas, Smith wrote, "hazarded the beating out of her owne braines to save mine, and . . . so prevailed with her father, that I was safely conducted [back] to James towne."

This romantic story of an Indian maiden rescuing a white soldier and saving not only his life but also Jamestown and ultimately English colonization of North America has been enshrined in the writing of American history since 1624 when Smith published his *Generall Historie of Virginia* and has even been dramatized in a recent Disney movie. Historians believe that this episode actually happened more or less as Smith described it. But Smith did not understand why Pocahontas acted as she did. Many commentators have claimed that her love for Smith caused her to rebel against her father's authority.

On the contrary, when Pocahontas intervened to save Smith, she almost certainly was participating in an Algonquian ceremony that expressed Powhatan's supremacy and his ritualistic adoption of a subordinate chief, or *werowance*. Most likely, what Smith interpreted as Pocahontas's saving him from certain death was a ceremonial enactment of Powhatan's willingness to incorporate Smith and the white strangers at Jamestown into Powhatan's empire. The ceremony displayed Powhatan's power of life or death over a subordinate chief—Smith—and Powhatan's willingness to give protection to those who acknowledged his supremacy—in this case, the interlopers at Jamestown. By appearing to save Smith, Pocahontas was probably acting out Smith's new status as an adopted member of Powhatan's extended family. Rather than a rebellious, love-struck girl, Pocahontas was almost certainly a dutiful daughter playing the part prescribed for her by her father and her culture. It appears that Powhatan attempted to treat the tribe of white strangers at Jamestown as he did other tribes in his empire, an attempt that failed.

In 1613, after relations between Powhatan and the English colonists had deteriorated into bloody raids by both parties, Pocahontas was captured and held hostage at Jamestown. Within a year she converted to Christianity and married one of the colonists, a widower named John Rolfe. After giving birth to a son, Thomas, Pocahontas, her husband, and the new baby sailed for England in the spring of 1616. There, promoters of the Virginia colony dressed her as a proper Englishwoman and arranged for her to meet dignitaries.

Hearing that Pocahontas was in London, John Smith went to see her. According to Smith, Pocahontas said, "You did promise Powhatan what was yours should bee his, and he the like to you; you called him father, being in his land a stranger, and by the same reason so must I doe you." It seems likely, in other words, that Pocahontas understood what was happening to her in England as a counterpart to the ritual John Smith had experienced in Virginia back in 1607.

Pocahontas died in England in 1617. Her son, Thomas, ultimately returned to Virginia and by the time of the American Revolution his descendants numbered in the hundreds. But the world Thomas Rolfe and his descendants inhabited was shaped by a reversal of the power ritualized when his mother "saved" John Smith. By the end of the seventeenth century, native Americans were far from vanquished, but—unlike Powhatan—they no longer dominated the newcomers who had arrived in the Chesapeake with John Smith.

During the seventeenth century, the English colonists learned how to make a living growing tobacco, a crop native Americans had cultivated in small quantities for centuries. The new settlers, however, grew enormous crops of tobacco, far more than they could smoke, chew, or sniff themselves, and they exported most of it to England. Rather than incorporating Powhatan's people into their new society, the settlers appropriated lands surrounding the Chesapeake Bay that had supported ancient Americans for millennia and built new societies on the foundation of tobacco agriculture and transatlantic trade.

To produce large crop surpluses for export required hard labor and people who were willing—or could be forced—to do it. For the most part, native Americans refused to be conscripted into the colonists' fields. Instead, the settlers depended on the labor of family members, indentured servants, and, by the last third of the seventeenth century, African slaves. By the end of the century, the southern colonies had become sharply different both from the world dominated by Powhatan when the Jamestown settlers first arrived and from contemporary English society. In ways unimaginable to Powhatan, Pocahontas, or John Smith, the colonists paid homage to the international market and the English monarch by working mightily to make a good living growing crops for sale to the Old World.

POCAHONTAS IN ENGLAND

Shortly after Pocahontas and her husband John Rolfe arrived in England in 1616, an engraver made this portrait of her dressed in English clothing suitable for a princess. The portrait captures the dual novelty of England for Pocahontas and of Pocahontas for the English. Ornate, courtly clothing probably signified to English observers that Pocahontas was royalty and to Pocahontas that the English were accepting her as befitted the "Emperour" Powhatan's daughter. The mutability of Pocahontas's identity is displayed in the engraving's identification of her as "Matoaka alias Rebecca."

Library of Congress.

SECOTAN VILLAGE
This engraving, published in 1612, was copied from an original drawing John White made in 1585 when he visited the village of Secotan on the coast of North Carolina. The drawing provides a schematic view of daily life in the village, which may have resembled one of Powhatan's settlements. White noted on the original that the fire burning behind the line of crouching men was "the place of solemne prayer." The large building in the lower left was a tomb where the bodies of important leaders were kept. Dwellings lined a central space, where men and women ate. Corn is growing in the fields along the right side of the village. The engraver has included hunters shooting deer at the upper left; hunting was probably never so convenient—no such hunters or deer appear in White's original drawing. This portrait conveys the message that Secotan was orderly, settled, religious, harmonious, and peaceful (note the absence of fortifications), and very different from English villages.
Princeton University Libraries.

www.bedfordstmartins.com/roarkcompact
SEE THE ONLINE STUDY GUIDE for more help in analyzing this image.

An English Colony on the Chesapeake

By 1600, King James I eyed North America as a possible location for English colonies. In 1606, a number of "knightes, gentlemen, merchauntes, and other adventurers of our cittie of London" organized a joint stock company, the Virginia Company of London, and petitioned King James to grant them permission to establish a colony in North America. The king boldly granted the Virginia Company over six million acres and everything they might contain, in large measure because they were not his to grant. In effect, the charter was a royal license to poach on Spanish claims to the region and on Powhatan's chiefdom.

The adventurers in the Virginia Company hoped to found an empire that would strengthen England not only overseas but also at home. Jobless Englishmen would be put to work in the colony, producing goods that England currently had to import from other nations. They would also provide a ready market in the colony for English woolens.

But the main reason the Virginia Company was willing to risk its capital in Virginia was the fervent hope for quick profits. One way or another, Virginia promised to reward the adventurers. Or so they thought.

The Fragile Jamestown Settlement

In December 1606, the *Susan Constant*, *Discovery*, and *Godspeed* carried 144 Englishmen toward Virginia. They arrived at the mouth of the Chesapeake Bay on April 26, 1607. That night while the colonists rested onshore, one of them later recalled, a band of Indians "creeping upon all foure, from the Hills like Beares, with their Bowes in their mouthes," attacked and dangerously wounded two men. The attack gave the colonists an early warning that the North American wilderness was not quite the paradise described by the Virginia Company's publications in England. On May 14, they put ashore on a small peninsula in the midst of Powhatan's chiefdom. With the memory of their first night in America fresh in their minds, they quickly built a fort, the first building in the settlement they named Jamestown.

The Jamestown fort showed the colonists' awareness that native peoples were prepared to defend Virginia as their own. During May and June 1607, the settlers and Powhatan's warriors skirmished repeatedly. English muskets and cannon repelled Indian attacks on Jamestown, but the Indians' superior numbers and knowledge of the Virginia wilderness made it risky for the settlers to venture far beyond the peninsula. Late in June, Powhatan sensed a stalemate and made peace overtures.

The settlers soon confronted far more dangerous, invisible threats: disease and starvation. By September, fifty of the colonists had died. Powhatan's people came to the rescue of the weakened and distracted colonists. Early in September 1607, they began to bring corn to the colony for barter. When that was insufficient to keep the colonists fed, the settlers sent Captain John Smith to trade (and plunder) for corn with tribes upriver from Jamestown. His efforts managed to keep 38 of the original settlers alive until a fresh supply of food and 120 more colonists arrived from England in January 1608.

It is difficult to exaggerate the precarious state of the early Jamestown settlement. Although the Virginia Company sent hundreds of new settlers to Jamestown each year, few survived. During the "starving time" winter of 1609–1610, food was so short that one or two famished settlers resorted to eating their recently deceased neighbors.

Cooperation and Conflict between Natives and Newcomers

Native Americans stayed in contact with the English settlers, but maintained a cautious distance. The Virginia Company boasted that the settlers bought from the Indians "the pearles of earth [corn] and [sold] to them the pearles of heaven [Christianity]." In fact, few Indians converted to Christianity, and the English devoted scant effort to proselytizing. Marriage between Indian women and English men was also rare, despite the acute shortage of English women in Virginia in the early years. One of the few settlers who troubled to learn the Indians' language was John Smith. Powhatan's people regarded the English with suspicion, and for good reason. While the settlers often exhibited friendship toward the Indians, they did not hesitate to use their superior weapons to enforce English notions of proper Indian behavior.

The Indians retaliated against English violence, but for fifteen years they did not organize an all-out assault on the European intruders, probably for several reasons. Although the Indians felt no attraction to Christianity, they were impressed by the power of the settlers' God. One chief told John Smith that "he did believe that our God as much exceeded theirs as our guns did their bows and arrows." Powhatan probably concluded that these powerful strangers would make better allies than enemies. As allies, the English not only strengthened Powhatan's dominance over the tribes in the region; they also traded with his people, usually exchanging European goods for corn. Native Virginians had an insatiable desire for the settlers' iron and steel weapons and tools.

The trade that supplied Indians with European conveniences provided the English settlers with a prime necessity: food. But why did the settlers prove unable to feed themselves for more than a decade? First, as the staggering death rate suggests, many settlers were too sick to be productive members of the colony. Second, very few farmers came to Virginia in the early years. Instead, most of the newcomers were gentlemen and their servants, men who, in John Smith's words, "never did know what a day's work was." In the meantime, the colonists depended on the Indians' corn for food. (See "The Promise of Technology," page 50.)

Becaufe many doe defire to know the manner

of their Language, I haue inferted thefe few words.

KA katorawincs yowo. What call you this.
Nemarough, a man.
Crenepo, a woman.
Marowancheffo, a boy.
Yehawkans, Houfes.
Matchcores, Skins, or garments.
Mockafins, Shooes.
Tuffan, Beds. *Pokatawer,* Fire.
Attawp, A bow. *Attonce,* Arrowes.
Monacookes, Swords.
Aumoohhowgh, A Target.
Pawcuffacks, Gunnes.
Tomahacks, Axes.
Tockahacks, Pickaxes.
Pamefacks, Kniues.
Accowprets, Sheares.
Pawpecones, Pipes. *Mattaffin,* Copper
Vffawaffin, Iron, Braffe, Silver, or any white mettall. *Muffes,* Woods.
Attaffkuff, Leaues, weeds, or graffe.
Chepfin, Land. *Shacquohocan.* A ftone.
Wepenter, A cookold.
Suckahanna, Water. *Noughmaff,* Fifh.
Copotone, Sturgeon.
Weghfhaughes, Flefh.
Sawwehone, Bloud.
Netoppew, Friends.
Marrapough, Enemies.
Maskapow, the worft of the enemies.
Mawchick chammay, The beft of friends
Cafacunnakack, peya quagh acquintan vttafantafough, In how many daies will there come hither any more Englifh Ships.

Their Numbers.

Necut, 1. *Ningh,* 2. *Nuff,* 3. *Yowgh,* 4.
Paranske, 5. *Comotinch,* 6. *Toppawoff,* 7
Nuffwafh, 8. *Kekatawgh,* 9. *Kaskeke* 10
They count no more but by tennes as followeth.
Cafe, how many.
Ninghfapooeksku, 20.
Nuffapooeksku, 30.

Yowghapooeksku, 40.
Parankeftaffapoockfku, 50.
Comatinchtaffapoockfku, 60.
Nuffwafhtaffapoockfku, 70.
Kekataughtaffapoockfku, 90.
Necuttoughtyfimough, 100.
Necuttwevnquaaough, 1000.
Rawcofowghs, Dayes.
Kefkowghes, Sunnes:
Toppquough. Nights.
Nepawwefhowghs, Moones.
Pawpaxfoughes, Yeares.
Pummahumps, Starres.
Ofies, Heavens.
Okees, Gods.
Quiyoughcofoughs, Pettie Gods, and their affinities.
Righcomoughes, Deaths.
Kekughes, Liues.
Mowchick woyawgh tawgh noeragh kaquere mecher, I am very hungry? what fhall I eate?
Tawnor nehiegh Powhatan, Where dwels Powhatan.
Mache, nehiegh yourowgh, Orapaks. Now he dwelsa great way hence at Orapaks.
Vittapitchewayne anpechitchs nehawper Werowacomoco, You lie, he ftaid ever at Werowacomoco.
Kator nehiegh mattagh neer vttapitchewayne, Truely he is there I doe not lie.
Spaughtynere keragh werowance mawmarinough kekatë wawgh peyaquaugh. Run you then to the King Mawmarynough and bid him come hither.
Vtteke, e peya weyack wighwhip, Get you gone, & come againe quickly.
Kekaten Pokahontas patiaquagh niugh tanks manotyens neer mowchick rawrenock audowgh, Bid Pokahontas bring hither two little Baskets, and I will giue her white Beads to make her a Chaine.   *FINIS.*

The persistence of the Virginia colony, precarious as it was, created difficulties for Powhatan's chiefdom. The steady contact between natives and newcomers spread European viruses among the Indians, who suffered deadly epidemics in 1608 and between 1617 and 1619. But from the Indians' viewpoint, the most important fact about the Virginia colony was that it was proving to be a permanent settlement.

Powhatan died in 1618, and his brother Opechancanough replaced him as supreme chief. In 1622, Opechancanough organized an all-out assault

Corn, the "Life-Giver"

EUROPEANS FIRST LEARNED ABOUT CORN from Columbus. As soon as he returned to Spain in 1493, he told the royal court about amazing things he had seen on his voyage to the other side of the Atlantic, including a plant he called *maize*, his version of *mahiz*, the Taino word for corn, which meant "life-giver." Ancient Americans had been growing corn for about seven thousand years. From its origin in central Mexico, corn had spread throughout the Western Hemisphere by the time Columbus arrived. Although the rest of the world had never seen or heard of corn, within a generation after 1493 travelers carried seeds throughout the Old World. By the early sixteenth century, corn seeds sprouted in Europe, the Middle East, Africa, India, and China.

Accustomed to growing wheat and eating foods derived from it, Europeans at first did not like corn. A few years before the settlers arrived in Jamestown, an English botanist expressed the common European view that "the barbarous Indians which know no better, are constrained to make a vertue of necessitie, and think [corn is] a good food; whereas we may easily judge that it nourisheth but little, and is of hard and evill digestion, a more convenient foode for swine than for man."

Early in the seventeenth century, English settlers in North America discovered that hunger quickly made a virtue of necessity. John Smith wrote that during the spring of 1609 Jamestown residents became so hungry that "they would have sould their soules" for a half-basket of Powhatan's corn. Before settlers could reliably subsist in the Chesapeake region, they had to learn the technology of corn.

From the perspective of the twenty-first century, it may seem odd to speak of the technology of corn. Today, we tend to think that technology refers only to machinery such as engines, computer chips, or airplanes. But technology also refers to a much broader range of human experience. *Webster's* defines technology as "the science of the application of knowledge to practical purposes." Nowadays, technological knowledge has found countless practical uses for corn as food, sweetener, and oil, as well as in such products as medicines, tires, batteries, and lipstick. The roots of these modern-day uses of corn stretch back to ancient Americans who first developed the technology of growing, processing, and consuming corn, a technology English settlers of North America sought to learn for the practical purpose of eating.

Corn needs help to grow. Bury an ear of corn in the soil and the seeds that sprout strangle each other in an overcrowded quest for light. But strip the husk from a ripe ear of corn, rub the seeds out of the cob, plant the separated seeds on a spring day in a spot with sufficient heat, light, and water, and during the summer each seed is capable of producting a stalk with two or more ears, each bearing hundreds of edible corn seeds. An awestruck English visitor described corn's "marveillous great increase; of a thousand, fifteene hundred and some two thousand fold."

To obtain this impressive yield, early-seventeenth-century European settlers throughout North America watched native Americans cultivate corn. "In place of ploughs" commonly used in England, one observer reported, "they use an instrument of hard wood, shaped like a spade" to break up the soil and prepare it for planting, work usually done by men. Then women used a stick to "make a hole [in the soil] wherein they put out four grains . . . and cover them." Another colonist acknowledged that native Americans were "our first instructors for the planting of their Indian Corne, by teaching us to cull out the finest seede, to observe the fittest season, to keepe distance for holes, and fit measure for hills, to worme it, and weede it; to prune it, and dresse it as occasion shall require." Jamestown's early settlers did not depend on chance observations of this planting technology. John Smith boasted that two hostages the colonists captured from Powhatan "taught us how to order and plant our fields" while they were held as "fettered prisoners."

Along with corn, Indians usually planted beans. "When they [beans] grow up they interlace with the corn . . . and they keep the ground very free from weeds," one newcomer noticed. Ancient Americans' association of beans with corn had a sound biochemical basis. Beans fixed nitrogen in the soil, a function corn roots cannot perform. Corn plants then absorbed the nitrogen to produce higher yields. Beans also made corn more nutritious. Beans contain niacin, an essential nutrient lacking in corn. Together, corn and beans provided the basic ingredients for a healthy diet.

As every popcorn eater knows, corn kernels are hard enough to crack a tooth. European settlers had no difficulty eating green or sweet corn, the immature form of ripening corn commonly consumed today as corn on the cob. But to obtain the nutritious interior of mature corn kernels without cracking their teeth they had to learn ancient American technology. For millennia native Americans had soaked or boiled corn kernels with wood ash or other alkaline material. The alkali softened and loosened the tough hull protecting the corn's nutrients. Treated in this way, corn kernels that otherwise were rock-hard could be separated from their hulls and readily mashed into dough for tortillas or mixed with beans or other foods in tasty stews. Early colonists copied this process to make softened corn foods they called samp, or hominy, or grits.

Since settlers were accustomed to wheat ground into a fine flour, they preferred cornmeal obtained by the much more laborious process of pulverizing corn kernels with a mortar and pestle or grinding them between stones, both processes familiar to native Americans. From cornmeal dough cooked on an iron griddle or baked in the coals of a cookfire, Europeans made corn bread, corn pone, hoecake, and johnnycake—English names for ancient American food.

Unlike wheat, many varieties of corn pop open when heated, an astonishing trait Columbus duly reported to his Spanish sponsors. Archaeologists speculate that ancient Americans first thought to cultivate corn when a few grains accidentally landed in a campfire and out popped a morsel of readily edible food. For millennia ancient Americans enjoyed popcorn, not least because it so easily avoided the need to soak, boil, or grind hard corn kernels. They also ground popped corn into a nu-

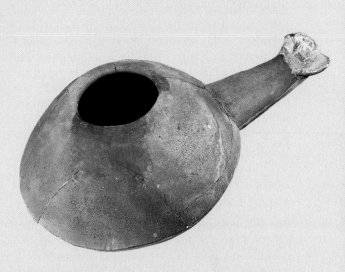

ANCIENT CORN POPPER
Long before movies and microwaves, ancient Americans munched popcorn. This corn popper comes from the Mochica culture, which thrived on the northern coast of Peru for about six hundred years after the birth of Christ. The Mochica presumably nestled the popper on a bed of coals with the opening facing up, placed corn inside, and covered the opening with a lid (not shown) while the kernels popped. The Mochica and other ancient Americans did not pop most of the corn they grew. Instead they ground it into corn meal which they incorporated in a wide variety of dishes, probably including ancient counterparts of modern tortillas.
The Field Museum #A112961c, Chicago. Photographer: Diane Alexander White.

tritious and portable powder that could be mixed with water and other foods for a satisfying meal. The New England minister Roger Williams wrote that he "made a good dinner and supper" with "a *spoonfull* of this *meale* and a *spoonfull* of water from the *Brooke*." Other colonists, too, learned the ancient technology of popcorn. Today, at the cineplex and on the couch, every American consumes about fifty quarts of popped corn each year, participating— usually unwittingly—in a technology that reaches back in unbroken continuity to a campfire in central Mexico about seven thousand years ago.

on the English settlers. Striking on March 22, the Indians killed 347 settlers, nearly a third of the English population. But the attack failed to dislodge the colonists. In the aftermath, the settlers unleashed a murderous campaign of Indian extermination that in a few years pushed Indians beyond the small circumference of white settlement. Before 1622, the settlers knew that the Indians, though dangerous, were necessary to keep the colony alive. After 1622, most colonists considered Indians their perpetual enemies.

From Private Company to Royal Government

The 1622 uprising came close to achieving Opechancanough's goal of pushing the colonists back into the Atlantic—so close that it prompted a royal investigation of affairs in Virginia. The investigators discovered that the appalling mortality among the colonists was caused by disease and mismanagement more than by Indian raids. In 1624, King James revoked the charter of the Virginia Company and made Virginia a royal colony, subject to the direction of the royal government rather than to the company's private investors, an arrangement that lasted until 1776.

The king now appointed the governor of Virginia and his council, but most other features of local government established under the Virginia Company remained intact. In 1619, for example, the company had inaugurated the House of Burgesses, an assembly of representatives (called burgesses) elected by the colony's inhabitants. (Historians do not know exactly which settlers were considered inhabitants and were thus qualified to vote.) Under the new royal government, laws passed by the burgesses had to be approved by the king's bureaucrats in England rather than by the company. Otherwise, the House of Burgesses continued as before, acquiring distinction as the oldest representative legislative assembly in the British colonies. Under the new royal government, all free adult men in Virginia could vote for the House of Burgesses, giving it a far broader and more representative constituency than the English House of Commons.

The demise of the Virginia Company marked the end of the first phase of colonization of the Chesapeake. From the first 105 adventurers in 1607, the population had grown to about 1,200 by 1624. Despite high mortality rates, new settlers still came. Their arrival and King James's willingness to take

over the struggling colony reflected a fundamental change in Virginia. After years of fruitless experimentation, it was becoming clear that English settlers could make a fortune in Virginia by growing tobacco.

A Tobacco Society

Tobacco never featured in the initial plans of the Virginia Company, but beginning in 1612, John Rolfe showed that it could be grown successfully in the

TOBACCO WRAPPER
This wrapper labeled a container of "Virginia Planters Best Tobacco." It shows a colonial planter supervising slaves who hold hoes used to chop weeds that robbed the leafy tobacco plants of nutrients and moisture. The planter enjoys a pipe in the shade of an umbrella held by a slave. Once the tobacco was harvested and dried, it was pressed tightly into barrels like those shown here for shipment overseas. How does the ad indicate the differences between the planter and the slaves?
Colonial Williamsburg Foundation.

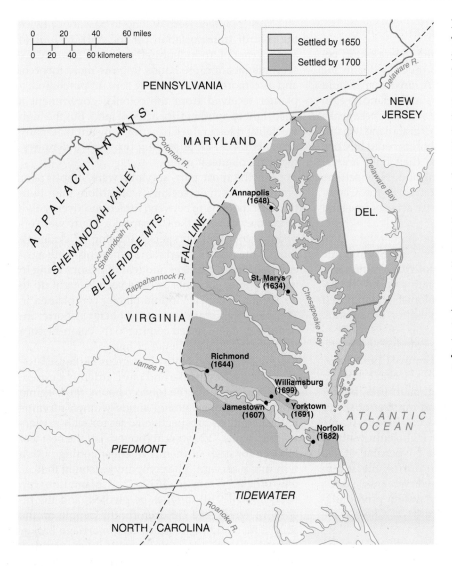

MAP 3.1

The Chesapeake Colonies in the Seventeenth Century
The intimate association of land and water in the settlement of the Chesapeake in the seventeenth century is illustrated by this map. The fall line indicates the limit of navigable water, where rapids and falls prevented further upstream travel. Why was access to navigable water so important? Although Delaware had excellent access to navigable water, it was claimed and defended by the Dutch colony at New Amsterdam (discussed in chapter 4) rather than the English settlements in Virginia and Maryland shown on this map.

new colony. In 1617, when the first commercial shipment of tobacco to England sold for a high price, the same Virginia colonists who had difficulty growing enough corn to feed themselves quickly tried to learn how to grow as much tobacco as possible. In a sense, that first commercial cargo was a pivot on which Virginia turned from a colony of rather aimless adventurers into a society of dedicated planters.

Dedicated they were. In 1620, with fewer than a thousand colonists, Virginia shipped 60,000 pounds of tobacco to England. By 1700, tobacco exports from the Chesapeake region (encompassing Virginia and Maryland) topped 35 million pounds, and more than 98,000 colonists lived in the region. Tobacco planters' endless need for labor attracted droves of indentured servants from England to work in tobacco fields and settle the Chesapeake (Map 3.1).

The requirements of tobacco agriculture shaped patterns of settlement, making the landscape of the English colonies in the Chesapeake quite different from that of rural England. English colonists professed the Protestant and Catholic faiths, but they governed their daily lives less by the dictates of religious doctrine than by the demands of tobacco cultivation.

A Servant Labor System

English settlers now were willing to work hard because they could expect to do much better in the Chesapeake than in England. A hired man would have to work two or three years in England to earn as much as he could in just one year in Chesapeake tobacco fields. Better still, in Virginia land was so abundant that even common laborers could buy one hundred acres of land for less than their annual wages—an impossibility in England. New settlers who paid their own transportation to the Chesapeake also received a grant of fifty acres of free land (a headright).

Headrights, cheap land, and high wages gave poor English folk powerful incentives to immigrate to the New World. Yet many potential immigrants could not scrape together the fare to cross the Atlantic. Their poverty and the colonists' crying need for labor formed the basic context for the creation of a servant labor system.

Today, people think of the colonial South as a slave society. The seventeenth-century Chesapeake, however, was fundamentally a servant society. Twenty Africans arrived in Virginia in 1619, but for the next fifty years, only a small number of slaves labored in Chesapeake tobacco fields. (Large numbers of slaves came in the eighteenth century, as chapter 5 explains.) About 80 percent of the immigrants to the Chesapeake during the seventeenth century were indentured servants. Along with tobacco, the servant labor system profoundly influenced nearly every feature of Chesapeake society.

To buy passage aboard a ship bound for the Chesapeake, an English immigrant had to come up with about £5, roughly a year's wages for an English servant or laborer. Lacking that much money, poor immigrants signed a contract called an indenture specifying that the holder of the indenture would pay for the immigrant's transportation to the Chesapeake. In return, the immigrant agreed to work for a period—usually four to seven years—without pay. During this period of indentured servitude, the immigrant received food and shelter from an employer in the colonies. When the indenture expired, the employer was required to give the former servant "freedom dues," usually three barrels of corn and a suit of clothes. In effect, indentures allowed poor immigrants to trade their most valuable asset—their ability to work—for a trip to the New World.

Most planters were willing to pay about twice the cost of transportation for the right to four to seven years of an indentured servant's labor. More servants meant more hands to grow more tobacco, and also more land. For every servant purchased, a planter received from the colonial government a headright of another fifty acres of land. But the high mortality rates in the Chesapeake meant that many servants died before serving out their indentures, reducing planters' gains.

For the most part, servants were simply poor young Englishmen seeking work. More than two-thirds of them were between fifteen and twenty-five when they came to the Chesapeake. Many were orphans. Most had no special training or skills, although the majority had some experience with agricultural work. "Hunger and fear of prisons bring to us onely such servants as have been brought up to no Art or Trade," a Virginia planter complained in 1662. A skilled craftsman could obtain a shorter indenture, but few risked coming to the colonies since their prospects were better at home.

Women were almost as rare as skilled craftsmen in the Chesapeake and more ardently desired. In the early days of the tobacco boom, the Virginia Company shipped young single women servants to the colony as prospective wives for male settlers willing to pay "120 weight [pounds] of the best leaf tobacco for each of them," in effect getting both a wife and a servant. The company reasoned that, as one official wrote in 1622, "the plantation can never flourish till families be planted, and the respect of wives and children fix the people on the soil." The company's efforts as a marriage broker proved no more successful than its other ventures. Men continued to outnumber women by a wide margin until late in the seventeenth century, since only one in four indentured servants was a woman.

Servant life was harsh by the standards of seventeenth-century England and even by the frontier standards of the Chesapeake. Severe laws were designed to keep servants in their place. Punishments for petty crimes like running away or stealing a pig stretched servitude far beyond the original terms of indenture. Just after midcentury, the Virginia legislature added at least three years to the servitude of most servants by requiring them to serve until they were twenty-four years old.

Women servants were subject to special restrictions and risks. They were prohibited from marrying until their servitude had expired. A servant

INDENTURE CONTRACT
Indenture contracts were so common that forms were printed, leaving blank spaces for the details. Here, in mid-November 1698, fifteen-year-old Mathew Evans, a friendless boy from Harfordshire, agreed to serve mariner Thomas Graves, or anybody to whom Graves sold his rights, for four years in Virginia. The contract specified that Graves would carry Evans to Virginia and provide during the term of the indenture, "all necessary Cloathes, Meat, Drink, Washing, Lodging and other necessaryes, fit and convenient for him according to the Custom of the said Plantation, as other Servants in such Cases are usually Provided for. . . ."
The Library of Virginia.

woman, the law assumed, could not serve two masters at the same time: one who owned her indentured labor and another who was her husband. However, the overwhelming predominance of men in the Chesapeake population inevitably pressured women to engage in sexual relations. As a rule, if a woman servant gave birth to a child, she had to serve two extra years and pay a fine.

Masters could not easily hire free men and women because land was so readily available that those who were free preferred to work for themselves on their own land. Furthermore, most masters could not depend on much labor from family members. The preponderance of men meant that families were few, were started late, and thus had few children. And, until the 1680s and 1690s, slaves were expensive and hard to come by. Before then, masters who wanted to expand their labor force and grow more tobacco had few alternatives to buying indentured servants.

Cultivating Land and Faith

Villages and small towns dotted the rural landscape of seventeenth-century England, but in the Chesa-peake acres of wilderness were interrupted here and there by tobacco farms. Tobacco was such a labor-intensive crop that one field worker could tend only about two acres of the plants in a year (an acre is slightly smaller than a football field), plus a few more acres for food crops. A successful farmer needed a great deal more land, however, because tobacco quickly exhausted the fertility of the soil. Since each farmer cultivated only 5 or 10 percent of his land at any one time, a "settled" area comprised swatches of cultivated land surrounded by virgin forest. Arrangements for marketing tobacco also contributed to the dispersion of settlements.

TOBACCO PLANTATION

This print illustrates the tobacco harvest on a seventeenth-century plantation. Workers cut the mature plants and put the leaves in piles to wilt (left foreground and center background). After the leaves had dried somewhat, they were suspended from poles in a drying barn (right foreground), where they were seasoned before being packed in casks for shipping. Sometimes they were also dried in the fields (center background). The print suggests the labor demands of tobacco by showing twenty-two individuals, all but two of them actively at work with the crop. The one woman depicted (hand in hand with a man in the left foreground) may be on her way to work in the harvest, but it appears more likely that she and the man are overseeing the labor of their servants or employees.

From "About Tobacco," Lehman Brothers.

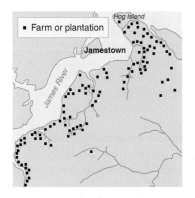

Settlement Patterns along the James River

Tobacco planters sought land that fronted a navigable river in order to minimize the work of transporting the heavy hogsheads of tobacco onto ships. A settled region thus resembled a lacework of farms stitched around waterways.

Most Chesapeake colonists were nominally Protestants. Attendance at Sunday services and conformity to the doctrines of the Church of England were required of all Englishmen and women. Certainly some colonists took their religion seriously. But on the whole, religion did not awaken the zeal of Chesapeake settlers, certainly not as it did the New England settlers in these same years (see chapter 4). Although the religion of the Chesapeake colonists was Anglican, their faith lay in the turbulent, competitive, high-stakes gamble of survival as tobacco planters.

The situation was similar in the Catholic colony of Maryland. In 1632, King Charles I granted his Catholic friend Lord Baltimore about six and a half million acres in the northern Chesapeake region. Lord Baltimore intended to create a refuge for Catholics, who suffered severe discrimination in England. He fitted out two ships, the *Ark* and the *Dove*, gathered about 150 settlers, and sent them to the new colony, where they arrived on March 25, 1634. However, the population of Maryland grew very slowly for the next twenty years, and most settlers were Protestants rather than Catholics. The religious turmoil of the Puritan Revolution in England (discussed in chapter 5) spilled across the Atlantic, creating conflict between Maryland's few Catholics—most of them wealthy and prominent—and the Protestant majority, most of them neither wealthy nor prominent. During the 1660s, Maryland began to attract settlers as readily as Virginia, mostly Protestants. Although Catholics and the Catholic faith continued to exert influence in Maryland, the colony's society, economy, politics, and culture became virtually indistinguishable from Virginia's. Both colonies shared a devotion to tobacco, the true faith of the Chesapeake.

The Evolution of Chesapeake Society

The system of indentured servitude sharpened inequality in Chesapeake society by the mid-seventeenth century, propelling social and political polarization that culminated in 1676 with Bacon's Rebellion. The rebellion ultimately prompted reforms that stabilized relations between elite planters and their lesser neighbors and paved the way for a social hierarchy based less overtly on land and wealth than on race. Amidst this social and political evolution, one thing did not change: the dedication of Chesapeake colonists to growing tobacco.

Social and Economic Polarization

The first half of the seventeenth century in the Chesapeake was the era of the yeoman planter—that is, a farmer who owned a small plot of land sufficient to support a family and tilled largely by family members and perhaps a few servants. A few elite planters had larger estates and commanded ten or more servants. But for the first several decades, few men lived long enough to accumulate a fortune sufficient to set them much apart from their neighbors. Until midcentury, the principal division in Chesapeake society was less between rich and poor planters than between free farmers and unfree servants. While these two groups contrasted sharply in their legal and economic status, their daily lives had many similarities. Servants looked forward to the time when their indentures would expire and they would become free and eventually own land. On the whole, a rough, frontier equality characterized free families in the Chesapeake until about 1650.

Three major developments splintered that equality during the third quarter of the century. First, as tobacco production increased, prices declined. Cheap tobacco reduced planters' profits and made it more difficult for freed servants to save enough to become landowners. Second, because the mortality rate dropped, more and more servants survived their indentures. As landless freemen became more numerous, they grew more discontent. Third, declining mortality also encouraged the formation of a planter elite. By living longer, the most successful planters compounded their success. The wealthiest planters also began to serve as merchants, marketing crops for their less successful neighbors, importing English goods for sale, and giving credit to hard-pressed customers.

By the 1670s, the social structure of the Chesapeake had become polarized. Landowners—the planter elite and the more numerous yeoman planters—clustered around one pole. Landless colonists, mainly freed servants, gathered at the other. Each group eyed the other with suspicion and mistrust. For the most part, planters saw landless freemen as a dangerous rabble rather than as fellow colonists with legitimate grievances.

Government Policies and Political Conflict

In general, government and politics amplified the distinctions in Chesapeake society. The most vital distinction separated servants and masters, and the colonial government enforced it with an iron fist. Poor men like William Tyler complained that "nether the Governor nor Counsell could or would doe any poore men right, but that they would shew favor to great men and wronge the poore." The poor had plenty of ammunition for such views. After 1640, no former servant ever served in either the governor's council or the House of Burgesses. Until 1670, all freemen could vote, and they routinely elected prosperous planters to the legislature. Most Chesapeake colonists, like most Europeans, assumed that the responsibilities of government were best borne by men of wealth and status.

In the 1660s and 1670s, colonial officials began to seek additional security as discontent mounted among the poor. Beginning in 1661, for example, Governor Berkeley did not call an election for the House of Burgesses for fifteen years. In 1670, the House of Burgesses limited voting rights to landowners and householders.

In 1660, the king himself began to tighten the royal government's control of trade and to collect substantial revenue from the Chesapeake. The Navigation Act passed that year required all tobacco and other colonial products to be sent only to English ports. The act supplemented laws of 1650 and 1651 that specified that colonial goods had to be transported in English ships with predominantly English crews. A 1663 law stipulated that all goods sent to the colonies must pass through En-

glish ports and be carried in English ships by English sailors. Together, these navigation acts were designed to funnel the colonial import trade exclusively into the hands of English merchants and shippers and reflected the English government's mercantilist assumptions about the colonies: What was good for England should determine colonial policy.

These mercantilist assumptions underlay the import duty on tobacco inaugurated by the 1660 Navigation Act. The law assessed an import duty of two pence on every pound of colonial tobacco brought into England, about the price a Chesapeake tobacco farmer received. The duty gave the king a major financial interest in the size of the tobacco crop.

Bacon's Rebellion

Colonists, like residents of European monarchies, accepted social hierarchy and inequality as long as they believed government officials ruled for the general good. When rulers violated that precept, ordinary people felt justified in rebelling. In 1676, Bacon's Rebellion erupted as a dispute over Indian policy. Before it was over, the rebellion convulsed Chesapeake politics and society, leaving in its wake death, destruction, and a legacy of hostility between the great planters and their poorer neighbors.

Opechancanough, the old chief who had led the Indian uprising of 1622 in Virginia, mounted another surprise attack in 1644 and killed about five hundred colonists in two days. During the next two years of bitter fighting, the colonists eventually gained the upper hand, capturing and murdering Opechancanough. The treaty that concluded the war established policies toward the Indians that the government tried to maintain for the next thirty years. The Indians relinquished all claims to land already settled by the English. Wilderness land beyond the fringe of English settlement was supposed to be reserved exclusively for Indian use. The government hoped to minimize contact between settlers and Indians and thereby maintain the peace.

Had the Chesapeake population remained constant, the policy might have worked. But the number of land-hungry colonists, especially poor, recently freed servants, continued to multiply. In their quest for land, they pushed beyond the treaty limits of English settlement and encroached steadily on Indian land. During the 1660s and 1670s, violence between colonists and Indians repeatedly flared along the advancing frontier. The government, headquartered in the tidewater region near the coast, far from the danger of Indian raids, took steps to calm the disputes and reestablish the peace. Frontier settlers thirsted for revenge against what their leader, Nathaniel Bacon, termed "the protected and Darling Indians." Bacon minced no words about his intention: "Our Design [is] not only to ruine and extirpate all Indians in Generall but all Manner of Trade and Commerce with them." Indians were not the only enemies Bacon and his men singled out. Bacon also urged colonists to "see what spounges have suckt up the Publique Treasure." He charged that "Grandees," or elite planters, operated the government for their private gain, a charge that made sense to many colonists. Bacon crystallized the grievances of the small planters and poor farmers against both the Indians and the colonial rulers in Jamestown.

Hoping to maintain the fragile peace on the frontier in 1676, Governor Berkeley pronounced Bacon a rebel, threatened to punish him for treason, and called for new elections of burgesses who, Berkeley believed, would endorse his get-tough policy. To Berkeley's surprise, the elections backfired. Almost all the old burgesses were voted out of office, their places taken by local leaders, including Bacon. The legislature was now in the hands of minor grandees who, like Bacon, chafed at the rule of the elite planters.

In June 1676, the new legislature passed a series of reform measures known as Bacon's Laws. Among other changes, the laws gave local settlers a voice in setting tax levies, forbade officeholders from demanding bribes or other extra fees for carrying out their duties, placed limits on holding multiple offices, and restored the vote to all freemen. Under pressure, Berkeley pardoned Bacon and authorized his campaign of Indian warfare. But elite planters soon convinced Berkeley that Bacon and his men were a greater threat than Indians.

When Bacon learned that Berkeley had once again branded him a traitor, he declared war against Berkeley and the other grandees. For three months, Bacon's forces fought the Indians and sacked the grandees' plantations. Berkeley's loyalists retaliated by plundering the homes of Bacon's supporters. The fighting continued until late October, when Bacon unexpectedly died, most likely from dysentery, and

several English ships arrived to bolster Berkeley's strength. With the rebellion crushed, Berkeley hanged several of Bacon's allies and destroyed farms that belonged to Bacon's supporters.

The rebellion did not dislodge the grandees from their positions of power. If anything, it strengthened their position. When the king learned of the turmoil in the Chesapeake and its devastating effect on tobacco exports and customs duties, he ordered an investigation. The royal officials replaced Berkeley with a governor more attentive to the king's interests, nullified Bacon's Laws, and instituted an export tax on every hogshead of tobacco as a way of paying the expenses of government without having to obtain the consent of the tight-fisted House of Burgesses. In a sense, the grandees of the Chesapeake were put in their place by still grander royal officials.

In the aftermath of Bacon's Rebellion, tensions between great planters and small farmers gradually lessened. By 1700, the new export duty on tobacco allowed the government to cut other taxes to just one-fourth what they had been in 1660, a move welcomed by all freemen. In the long run, however, the most important contribution to political stability was the declining importance of the servant labor system. During the 1680s and 1690s, fewer servants arrived in the Chesapeake, partly because of improving economic conditions in England. Accordingly, the number of poor, newly freed servants also declined, reducing the size of the lowest stratum of free society. In 1700, as many as one-third of the free colonists still worked as tenants on land owned by others, but the social and political distance between them and the great planters, enormous as it was, did not seem as profound as it had been in 1660. The main reason was that by 1700 the Chesapeake was in the midst of transition to a slave labor system that minimized the differences between poor farmers and rich planters and magnified the differences between whites and blacks.

Toward a Slave Labor System

Spaniards and Portuguese engaged in an extensive African slave trade in the sixteenth century, and they established slavery as a major form of coerced labor in the New World. In the seventeenth century,

British colonies in the West Indies followed the Spanish and Portuguese examples and developed sugar plantations with slave labor. In the British North American colonies, however, a slave labor system did not emerge until the last quarter of the seventeenth century. During the 1670s, settlers from Barbados brought slavery to the new English mainland colony of Carolina, where the imprint of the West Indies remained strong for decades. In Chesapeake tobacco fields at about the same time, slave labor began to replace servant labor, marking the transition toward a society of freedom for whites and slavery for Africans.

The West Indies: Sugar and Slavery

The most profitable part of the British New World empire in the seventeenth century lay in the Caribbean (Map 3.2). The tiny island of Barbados, colonized in the 1630s, was the jewel of the British West Indies. During the 1640s, Barbadian planters began to grow sugarcane, with such success that a colonial official proclaimed Barbados "the most flourishing Island in all those American parts, and I verily beleive in all the world for the production of sugar." Sugar commanded high prices in England, and planters rushed to grow as much as they could. By midcentury, annual sugar exports from the British Caribbean totaled about 150,000 pounds; by 1700, exports reached nearly 50 million pounds.

Sugar transformed Barbados and other West Indian islands. Poor farmers could not afford the expensive machinery that extracted and refined the sugarcane juice. Planters who had the necessary capital to grow sugar got rich. By 1680, the wealthiest Barbadian sugar planters were, on average, four times richer than tobacco grandees in the

SUGAR MILL
This seventeenth-century drawing of a Brazilian sugar mill highlights the heavy equipment needed to extract the juice from sugarcane. A vertical waterwheel turns a large horizontal gear that exerts force on the jaws of a press, which squeezes the cane. Workers constantly remove crushed cane from the press and replenish it with freshly harvested cane as it is unloaded from an oxcart. Note that except for the overseer (just to the right of the waterwheel), all of the workers are black, presumably slaves from Africa, as suggested by their clothing. All of the mill workers appear to be men, a hint of the predominance of men among newly imported African slaves.
Musées Royaux des Beaux-Arts de Belgique.

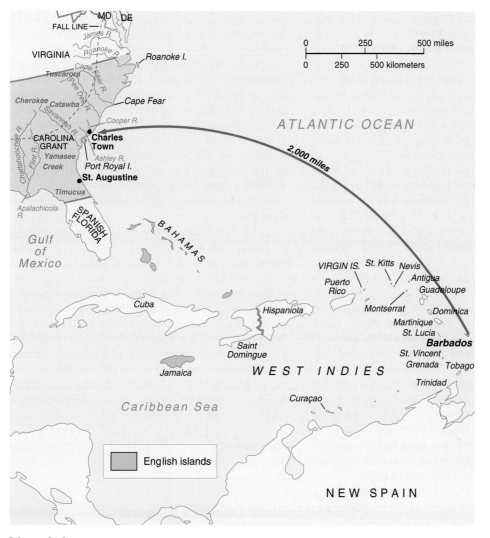

MAP 3.2

The West Indies and Carolina in the Seventeenth Century

Although Carolina was geographically closer to the Chesapeake colonies, it was cultur-ally closer to the West Indies in the seventeenth century since its early settlers—both blacks and whites—came from Barbados. South Carolina retained close ties to the West Indies for more than a century, long after many of its subsequent settlers came from England, Ireland, France, and elsewhere.

READING THE MAP: Locate English colonies in America and English holdings in the Caribbean. Which European country controlled most of the mainland bordering the Caribbean? Where was the closest mainland English territory?

CONNECTIONS: Why were colonists in Carolina so interested in Barbados? What goods did they export? Describe the relationship between Carolina and Barbados in 1700.

www.bedfordstmartins.com/roarkcompact SEE THE ONLINE STUDY GUIDE for more help in analyzing this map.

Chesapeake. The sugar grandees differed from their Chesapeake counterparts in another crucial way: The average sugar baron in Barbados in 1680 owned 115 slaves.

African slaves planted, cultivated, and harvested the sugarcane that made West Indian planters wealthy. Whites commonly assumed that people of African descent were degraded and inferior, and hence deserved bondage. Beginning in the 1640s, Barbadian planters purchased thousands of slaves to work their plantations, and the African population on the island mushroomed. During the 1650s, when blacks made up only 3 percent of the Chesapeake population, they had already become the majority on Barbados. By 1700, slaves constituted more than three-fourths of the island's population.

For slaves, work on a sugar plantation was a life sentence to brutal, unremitting labor. Slaves' life expectancy was short and their death rate high. Furthermore, since slave men outnumbered slave women two to one, the vast majority of slaves could not form a family and have children. These grim realities meant that in Barbados and elsewhere in the West Indies, the slave population did not grow by natural reproduction. Instead, planters continually purchased slaves from Africa. Although sugar plantations did not gain a foothold in North America in the seventeenth century, the West Indies nonetheless exerted a powerful influence on the development of slavery in the mainland colonies.

Carolina: A West Indian Frontier

The early settlers of what became South Carolina were immigrants from Barbados. In 1663, a Barbadian planter named John Colleton and a group of seven other men obtained a charter from King Charles II to establish a colony south of the Chesapeake and north of the Spanish territories in Florida. Colleton and his colleagues, known as the "proprietors," hoped to siphon settlers from Barbados and other colonies and encourage them to develop a profitable export crop comparable to West Indian sugar and Chesapeake tobacco. Following the Chesapeake example, the proprietors offered headrights of up to 150 acres of land for each settler. In 1670, they established the first permanent English beachhead in the colony, on the west bank of the Ashley River just across from the penin-

sula where the king's namesake city, Charles Towne (later spelled Charleston), was founded (see Map 3.2).

As the proprietors had planned, most of the settlers were from Barbados. In fact, Carolina was the only seventeenth-century English colony to be settled principally by colonists from other colonies rather than from England. The Barbadian immigrants brought their slaves with them. More than a fourth of the early settlers were black, and as the colony continued to attract settlers from Barbados, the black population multiplied. By 1700, blacks made up about half the population of Carolina.

The Carolinians experimented unsuccessfully to match their semitropical climate with profitable export crops of tobacco, cotton, indigo, and olives. In the mid-1690s, colonists identified a hardy strain of rice and took advantage of the knowledge of rice cultivation among their many African slaves, inaugurating a flourishing industry. During the first generation of settlement, however, Carolina remained an economic colony of Barbados. Settlers sold livestock and timber to the West Indies. They also exploited another "natural resource": They captured and enslaved several thousand local Indians and sold them to Caribbean planters. Both economically and socially, seventeenth-century Carolina was a frontier outpost of the West Indian sugar economy.

Slave Labor Emerges in the Chesapeake

By 1700, more than eight out of ten people in the southern colonies of British North America lived in the Chesapeake. Until the 1670s, almost all Chesapeake colonists were white people from England. In 1700, however, one out of eight people in the region was a black person from Africa. Although a few blacks had lived in the Chesapeake since the 1620s, the black population increased fivefold between 1670 and 1700 as hundreds of tobacco planters made the transition from servant to slave labor, purchasing slaves rather than servants to work in their tobacco fields. For planters, slaves had several obvious advantages over servants. Although slaves cost three to five times more than servants, slaves never became free. Since the mortality rate had declined by the 1680s, planters could reasonably expect slaves to live longer than a servant's period of indenture. Slaves also promised to be a perpetual labor force, since children of slave mothers inherited the status of slavery.

For planters, slaves had another important advantage over servants: They could be controlled politically. Bacon's Rebellion had demonstrated how disruptive former servants could be when their expectations were not met. A slave labor system promised to avoid the political problems caused by the servant labor system. Slavery kept discontented laborers in permanent servitude, and their color was a badge of their bondage.

The slave labor system polarized Chesapeake society along lines of race and status: All slaves were black and nearly all blacks were slaves; almost all free people were white and all whites were free or only temporarily bound in indentured servitude. Unlike Barbados, however, the Chesapeake retained a vast white majority. Among whites, huge differences of wealth and status still existed. In fact, the emerging slave labor system sharpened the economic differences among whites because only prosperous planters could afford to buy slaves. By 1700, more than three-quarters of white families had neither servants nor slaves. Nonetheless, poorer white farmers enjoyed the privileges of free status. Distinctions between slaves and free people made lesser white folk feel they had a genuine stake in the existence of slavery, even if they did not own a single slave. By emphasizing the privileges of freedom shared by all white people, the slave labor system reduced the tensions between poor folk and grandees that had plagued the Chesapeake region in the 1670s.

In contrast to Barbados, most slaves in the seventeenth-century Chesapeake colonies had frequent and close contact with white people. Slaves and white servants performed the same tasks on tobacco plantations, often working side by side in the fields. For slaves, work on a tobacco plantation was less onerous than on a sugar plantation. But slaves' constant exposure to white surveillance made Chesapeake slavery especially confining. Slaves took advantage of every opportunity to slip away from white supervision and seek out the company of other slaves, "going abroad" to visit slaves on neighboring plantations. More than once, slaves turned such seemingly innocent social pleasures to political ends, either to run away or to conspire to strike against their masters.

While slavery resolved the political unrest caused by the servant labor system, it created new political problems. By 1700, the bedrock political issue in the Chesapeake was keeping slaves in their place, at the business end of a hoe in a tobacco field. The Chesapeake was developing a slave labor system that stood midway, both geographically and socially, between the sugar plantations and black majority of Barbados to the south and the small farms and homogeneous villages that developed in seventeenth-century New England to the north.

Conclusion: The Growth of English Colonies Based on Export Crops and Slave Labor

By 1700, the colonies of Virginia, Maryland, and Carolina were firmly established. The staple crops they grew for export provided a livelihood for many, a fortune for a few, and valuable revenues for shippers, merchants, and the English monarchy. Their societies differed markedly from English society in most respects, yet the colonists considered themselves English people who happened to live in North America. They claimed the same rights and privileges as English men and women while they denied those rights and privileges to native Americans and African slaves.

The English colonies also differed from the sixteenth-century example of New Spain. Large quantities of gold and silver never materialized in the Chesapeake. The system of encomienda (see chapter 2) was never adopted because Indians were too few and too hostile and their communities too small and decentralized compared with those of the Mexica. Yet forms of coerced labor and racial distinction that developed in New Spain had North American counterparts, as English colonists employed servants and slaves and defined themselves as superior to Indians and Africans.

By 1700, the remnants of Powhatan's people still survived. As English settlement pushed north, west, and south of the Chesapeake Bay, the various Indian peoples were faced with the new colonial world that Powhatan and Pocahontas had encountered when John Smith and the first settlers arrived at Jamestown. By 1700, the many descendants of

Pocahontas's son, Thomas, as well as other colonists and native Americans, understood that the English had come to stay.

For further reading about the topics in this chapter, see the Online Bibliography at www.bedfordstmartins.com/roarkcompact.

For additional first-hand accounts of this period, see pages 27–42 in Michael Johnson, ed., *Reading the American Past,* Second Edition, Volume I.

To assess your mastery of the material in this chapter, see the Online Study Guide at www.bedfordstmartins.com/roarkcompact.

CHRONOLOGY

1606 Virginia Company of London receives royal charter to establish colony in North America.

1607 English colonists found Jamestown settlement; Pocahontas "rescues" John Smith.

1609 Starvation plagues Jamestown.

1612 John Rolfe begins to plant tobacco in Virginia.

1617 First commercial tobacco shipment leaves Virginia for England. Pocahontas dies in England.

1618 Powhatan dies and Opechancanough becomes supreme chief.

1619 First Africans arrive in Virginia. House of Burgesses begins to meet in Virginia.

1622 Opechancanough leads Indian uprising against Virginia colonists.

1624 Virginia becomes royal colony.

1632 King Charles I grants Lord Baltimore land for colony of Maryland.

1634 Colonists begin to arrive in Maryland.

1640s Barbados colonists begin to grow sugarcane with labor of African slaves.

1644 Opechancanough leads Indian uprising against Virginia colonists.

1660 Navigation Act requires colonial tobacco to be shipped to English ports and to be assessed customs tax.

1663 Carolina proprietors receive charter from King Charles II for Carolina colony.

1670 Charles Towne, South Carolina, founded.

1670–1700 Slave labor system emerges first in Carolina and more gradually in Chesapeake colonies.

1676 Bacon's Rebellion convulses Virginia.

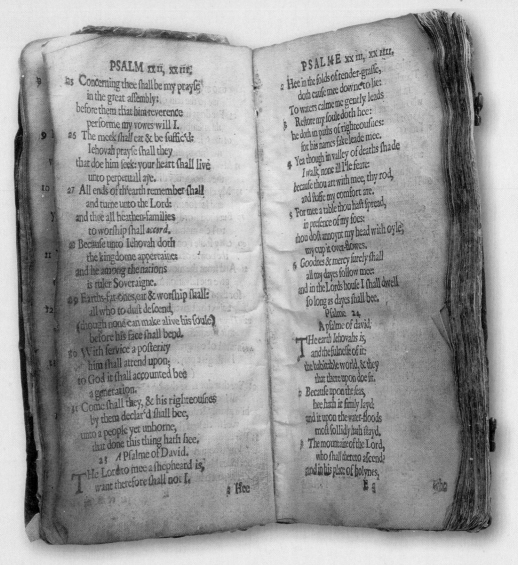

AMERICA'S FIRST BOOK

The first book printed in what is now the United States, this well-thumbed copy of **The Whole Booke of Psalmes Faithfully Translated into English Metre** *was published in Cambridge, Massachusetts, in 1640. Puritan services banned musical instruments and other diversions from God's holy word. Worshippers used this book and others to sing psalms, celebrating with a chorus of voices the wonders of God's Truth. The famous Twenty-third Psalm begins near the bottom of the left-hand page and concludes on the facing page. Read the psalm aloud to re-create the experience of seventeenth-century New England Puritan congregations.*

Library of Congress.

THE NORTHERN COLONIES IN THE SEVENTEENTH CENTURY

4

1601–1700

ANNE HUTCHINSON ARRIVED IN THE MASSACHUSETTS BAY COLONY in 1634 with her husband and family. She was a devout Puritan, steeped in Scripture and absorbed by sermons. A brilliant woman, Hutchinson had received an excellent education from her father in England. The mother of fourteen children, she served her neighbors as a skilled midwife. After she settled into her new home in Boston, women gathered there to hear her Thursday lectures on recent sermons, a proper female activity since, according to one minister, it "water[ed] the seeds *publikely* sowen." But as the months passed, the meetings increased to twice a week and the crowds grew to sixty or more women and men. One of those who attended praised Hutchinson as a "Woman that Preaches better Gospell then any of your black-coates that have been at the Ninneversity."

Hutchinson expounded on the sermons of John Cotton, her favorite minister. Cotton emphasized that individuals could be saved only by God's grace in choosing them to be members of the elect, a doctrine Cotton termed the "covenant of grace." Cotton contrasted this familiar Puritan tenet with the "covenant of works," the belief that one's behavior—one's works—could win God's favor and, ultimately, salvation. Cotton's sermons strongly hinted that many Puritans, even ministers, leaned toward this heretical covenant of works. Anne Hutchinson agreed. In her lectures to the groups assembled at her home, she amplified Cotton's somewhat muted message that the leaders of Massachusetts were repudiating the covenant of grace, the true basis of Puritan faith.

The meetings at Hutchinson's house alarmed her nearest neighbor, former governor John Winthrop, who believed that she was subverting the good order of the colony. In 1637, Winthrop had formal charges brought against Hutchinson and confronted her in court as her chief accuser. "You have stept out of your place," he said, "*you have rather bine a Husband than a Wife and a preacher than a Hearer; and a Magistrate than a Subject.*"

Winthrop and other Puritan elders referred to Hutchinson and her followers as "Antinomians," that is, people who opposed the law. Hutchinson's opponents charged that she believed that Christians could be saved by faith alone and that they therefore did not need to act according to God's law as set forth in the Bible and as interpreted by the colony's leaders. Hutchinson nimbly defended herself against this accusation. Yes, she believed that men and women were saved by faith alone; but no, she did not deny the need to obey God's law. "The Lord hath let me see which was the clear ministry and which the wrong," she said. Finally, her interrogators cornered her. How could she tell which was which? "By an immediate revelation," she replied, "by the voice of [God's] own spirit to my soul." Here was the crime Winthrop had been searching for, the erroneous view that God revealed his will directly to a believer instead of exclusively through the Bible, as every good Puritan knew.

In 1638, the Boston church formally excommunicated Hutchinson. The minister decreed, "I doe cast you out and . . . deliver you up to Satan that you may learne no more to blaspheme to seduce and to lye. . . . I command you . . . as a Leper to withdraw your selfe out of the Congregation." Banished, Hutchinson and her family moved first to Rhode Island and then to Long Island, where all but her ten-year-old daughter were killed by Indians.

Hutchinson's admission of divine revelation was a departure from standard Puritan belief. Yet by urging believers to search for evidence of God's grace, Puritanism encouraged the faithful to listen for a whisper from God. Puritanism combined rigid insistence on conformity to God's law and aching uncertainty about how to identify and act upon it. Despite the best efforts of Winthrop and other New England leaders to render God's instructions in no uncertain terms, Puritanism inspired believers like Anne Hutchinson to draw their own conclusions and stick to them.

During the seventeenth century, New England's Puritan zeal—exemplified by both Anne Hutchinson and her persecutors—cooled, and the goal of founding a holy New England faded. Late in the century, new "middle" colonies—New York, New Jersey, and Pennsylvania—were founded that featured greater religious and ethnic diversity than New England. Religion remained important throughout all the colonies, but it competed with a growing faith that the promise of a better life required less of the Puritans' intense focus on salvation and more attention to the mundane affairs of family, work, and trade.

By 1700, all the North American colonies had become more integrated into the English empire. Although located an ocean away from England, the colonists shipped North American wares east and off-loaded Old World goods on western shores. The continual exchange of products, people, and ideas was the lifeblood of empire that pulsed between England and the colonies, energizing both.

Puritan Origins: The English Reformation

The religious roots of the Puritans who founded New England reached back to the Protestant Reformation, which arose in Germany in 1517 (see chapter 2). The Reformation spread quickly to other countries, but the English church initially remained within the Catholic fold. King Henry VIII, who reigned from 1509 to 1547, understood that the Reformation offered him an opportunity to break with Rome and take control of the church in England. In 1534, Henry formally initiated the English Reformation. At his insistence, Parliament passed the Act of Supremacy, which outlawed the Catholic Church and proclaimed the king "the only supreme head on earth of the Church of England." The vast properties of the Catholic Church in England were now the king's, as was the privilege of appointing bishops and other members of the church hierarchy.

In the short run, the English Reformation allowed Henry VIII to achieve his political goal of controlling the church. In the long run, however, the English Reformation brought to England the political and religious turmoil that Henry had hoped to avoid. Henry himself sought no more than a halfway Reformation. Many English Catholics wanted no Reformation at all; they hoped to return the Church of England to the pope and to maintain Catholic doctrines and ceremonies. But many other English people insisted on a genuine, thoroughgoing Reformation; these people came to be called Puritans.

During the sixteenth century, Puritanism was less an organized movement than a set of ideas and religious principles that appealed strongly to many dissenting members of the Church of England. They sought to purify the Church of England by eliminating what they considered the offensive features of Catholicism. For example, they demanded that the church hierarchy be abolished and that ordinary Christians be given greater control over religious life. They wanted to do away with the rituals of Catholic worship and instead emphasize an individual's relationship with God developed through Bible study, prayer, and introspection. Although there were many varieties and degrees of Puritanism, all Puritans shared a desire to make the English church thoroughly Protestant.

You shall be led before Princes and rulers for my names sake. *Math*, 10.

PERSECUTION OF ENGLISH PROTESTANTS
This sixteenth-century drawing shows the persecution of Protestants during the reign of Queen Mary, a staunch Catholic. Here Protestant prisoners are being marched to London to be tried for heresy. This pro-Protestant drawing emphasizes the severity of royal tyranny by depicting four well-armed guards, two of them mounted, escorting some fifteen prisoners, including at least five women. The women are roped together, but not because they appear to be menacing or likely to run away. The guards seem to be necessary less to maintain order among the prisoners than to prevent sympathetic citizens from rushing toward the marchers and freeing the prisoners. The drawing assumes that most citizens opposed the queen's persecution of Protestants. The Bible verse from the Book of Matthew underscored Protestants' fealty to Christ rather than to mere "Princes and rulers" like Queen Mary.
Folger Shakespeare Library.

The fate of Protestantism waxed and waned under the monarchs who succeeded Henry VIII, until the reign of his daughter, Elizabeth I (1558–1603). She reaffirmed the English Reformation and tried to position the English church between the extremes of Catholicism and Puritanism. By the time she died, many people in England looked on Protestantism as a defining feature of national identity. When her successor, James I, came to the throne, English Puritans petitioned for further reform of the Church of England. However, neither James I nor his son Charles I, who became king in 1625, was receptive to the ideas of Puritan reformers. James and Charles moved the Church of England away from Puritanism rather than toward it. They enforced conformity to the Church of England and punished dissenters, both ordinary Christians and ministers. In 1629, Charles I dissolved Parliament—where Puritans were well represented—and initiated aggressive anti-Puritan policies. Many Puritans despaired about continuing to defend their faith in England and began to make plans to emigrate. The largest number set out for America.

Puritans and the Settlement of New England

Puritans who emigrated aspired to escape the turmoil and persecution of England and to build a new, orderly society that resembled a Puritan version of England. Their faith shaped the colonies they established in virtually every way. Although many New England colonists were not Puritans, Puritanism remained a paramount influence in New England's religion, politics, and community life during the seventeenth century.

The Pilgrims and Plymouth Colony

One of the earliest groups to emigrate, known subsequently as Pilgrims, espoused a heresy known as separatism: They sought to withdraw and separate from the Church of England, actions that would be punished severely in England. Hoping that they might preserve their community in America, the Pilgrims obtained permission to settle in the extensive lands granted to the Virginia Company. To finance their journey, they formed a joint stock company with London investors. In August 1620, 102 settlers, mostly families, finally boarded the *Mayflower*. After eleven weeks at sea, all but one of them arrived at the outermost tip of Cape Cod, in present-day Massachusetts.

The Pilgrims realized immediately that they had landed far north of the Virginia grant and had no legal authority from the king to settle in the area. To provide order and security as well as a claim to legitimacy, they drew up the Mayflower Compact on the day they arrived. In signing the document, they agreed to "covenant and combine ourselves together into a civil Body Politick, for our better Ordering and Preservation"; the signers (all men) agreed to enact and obey necessary and just laws.

The Pilgrims soon settled at Plymouth and elected William Bradford their governor. That first winter "was most sad and lamentable," Bradford wrote later. "In two or three months' time half of [our] company died." In the spring, Indians rescued the floundering Plymouth settlement. First Samoset, then Squanto—both of whom understood English—befriended the settlers. Samoset arranged for the Pilgrims to meet and establish good relations

with Massasoit, the chief of the Wampanoags, whose territory included Plymouth. Squanto, Bradford recalled, "was a special instrument sent of God for their [the Pilgrims'] good. . . . He directed them how to set their corn, where to take fish, and to procure other commodities, and was also their pilot to bring them to unknown places." With Squanto's help and their own hard labor, the Pilgrims managed to store enough food to guarantee their survival through the coming winter, an occasion they celebrated in the fall of 1621 with a feast of thanksgiving attended by Massasoit and many of his warriors.

The colony's status remained precarious. But the Pilgrims lived quietly and simply, coexisting in relative peace with the Indians, paying Massasoit when settlers gradually encroached on Wampanoag territory. By 1630, Plymouth had become a permanent settlement, although it failed to attract many other English Puritans.

The Founding of Massachusetts Bay Colony

In 1629, shortly before Charles I dissolved Parliament, a group of Puritan merchants and country gentlemen obtained a royal charter for the Massachusetts Bay Company that provided the usual privileges granted to joint stock companies. It granted land for colonization that spanned the present-day states of Massachusetts, New Hampshire, Vermont, Maine, and upstate New York. In addition, the charter contained a unique provision that allowed the government of the company to be located in the colony rather than in England. With this royal permission, Puritans could exchange their position as a harassed minority in England for self-government in Massachusetts.

To lead the emigrants, the stockholders of the Massachusetts Bay Company elected John Winthrop, a prosperous lawyer and landowner, to serve as governor. In March 1630, eleven ships crammed with seven hundred passengers sailed for Massachusetts. Winthrop's fleet arrived in Massachusetts Bay in early June. Unlike the Pilgrims, Winthrop's Puritans aspired to reform the corrupt Church of England (rather than separate from it) by setting an example of godliness in the New World. Winthrop and a small group chose to settle on the peninsula that became Boston,

SEAL OF MASSACHUSETTS BAY COLONY
In 1629 the Massachusetts Bay Company designed this seal depicting an Indian man inviting English settlers to "Come Over And Help Us." Of course, such an invitation was never issued. Instead, the seal was an attempt to lend an aura of altruism to the Massachusetts Bay Company's colonization efforts. In English eyes, the Indian man obviously needed help. The only signs that he was more civilized than the pine trees flanking him were his girdle of leaves, his bow and arrow, and his miraculous use of English. In reality, colonists in Massachusetts and elsewhere were far less interested in helping Indians than in helping themselves. For the most part that suited Indians, since they did not want the colonists' "help."
Courtesy of Massachusetts Archives.

www.bedfordstmartins.com/roarkcompact SEE THE ONLINE STUDY GUIDE for more help in analyzing this image.

and other settlers clustered at promising locations nearby (Map 4.1).

In a sermon to his companions aboard the *Arbella* while they were still at sea—probably the most famous sermon in American history—Winthrop explained the cosmic significance of their journey. The

Puritans had "entered into a covenant" with God to "work out our salvation under the power and purity of his holy ordinances," Winthrop proclaimed. The Puritans had to subordinate their individual interests to the common good. "We must be knit together in this work as one man," Winthrop declared. "We must delight in each other, make others' conditions our own, rejoice together, mourn together, labor and suffer together, always having before our eyes . . . our community as members of the same body." The stakes could not be higher, Winthrop told his listeners. "We must consider that we shall be as a city upon a hill. The eyes of all people are upon us."

That belief shaped seventeenth-century New England as profoundly as tobacco shaped the Chesapeake. The vision of a city on a hill announced the Puritans' fierce determination to keep their covenant and live according to God's laws, unlike the backsliders and compromisers who accommodated to the Church of England. Their determination to adhere strictly to God's plan charged nearly every feature of life in seventeenth-century New England with a distinctive, high-voltage piety.

The new colonists, as Winthrop's son John wrote later, had "all things to do, as in the beginning of the world." Unlike the early Chesapeake settlers, the first Massachusetts Bay colonists encountered few Indians because the local population had been almost entirely exterminated by an epidemic more than a decade earlier. Still, as in the Chesapeake, the colonists fell victim to deadly ailments. But each year from 1630 to 1640, ship after ship followed Winthrop's fleet. In all, more than twenty thousand new settlers came, their eyes fixed on the Puritans' city on a hill.

Often, when the Church of England cracked down on a Puritan minister in England, he and many of his followers uprooted and moved together to New England. By 1640, New England had one of the highest ratios of preachers to population in all of Christendom. A few ministers sought to carry the message of Christianity to Indians, accompanied by instructions about proper civilized (that is, English) behavior to replace what missionary John Eliot termed Indians' "unfixed, confused, and ungoverned . . . life, uncivilized and unsubdued to labor and order." (See "Documenting the American Promise," page 74.)

The occupations of the New England immigrants reflected the social origins of English Puritans. On the whole, the immigrants came from the middle ranks of English society. The vast majority

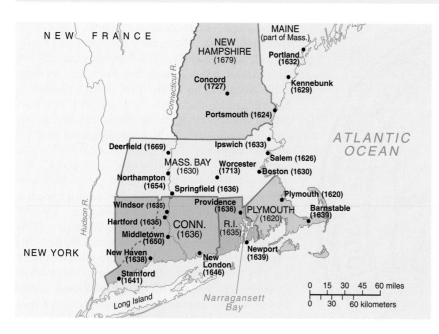

MAP 4.1

New England Colonies in the Seventeenth Century
New Englanders spread across the landscape town by town during the seventeenth century. (For the sake of legibility, only a few of the more important towns are shown on the map.) Why were towns so much more a feature of seventeenth-century New England than of the Chesapeake?

of immigrants were either farmers or tradesmen, including carpenters, tailors, and textile workers. Servants, whose numbers dominated the Chesapeake settlers, accounted for only about a fifth of those headed for New England.

In contrast to the Chesapeake, New England immigrants usually arrived as families. In fact, more Puritans came with family members than did any other group of immigrants in all of American history. These families were not democracies, of course. As Winthrop reminded the first settlers in his *Arbella* sermon, each family was a "little commonwealth" that mirrored the hierarchy among all God's creatures. Just as humankind was subordinate to God, so young people were subordinate to their elders, children to their parents, and wives to their husbands. The immigrants' family ties reinforced their religious beliefs with a form of government defined by the interlocking institutions of family, church, and community.

The Evolution of New England Society

The New England colonists, unlike their counterparts in the Chesapeake, settled in small towns, usually located on the coast or a river (see Map 4.1).

Church members' fervent piety, buttressed by the institutions of local government, enforced remarkable religious and social conformity in the small New England settlements. During the century, tensions within the Puritan faith and changes in New England communities splintered religious orthodoxy and weakened Puritan zeal. By 1700, however, Puritanism still maintained a distinctive influence in New England.

Church, Covenant, and Conformity

To Puritans, the church was composed of men and women who had entered a solemn covenant with one another and with God. Winthrop and three other men signed the original covenant of the first Boston church in 1630, agreeing to "Promisse, and bind our selves, to walke in all our wayes according to the Rule of the Gospell, and in all sincere Conformity to His holy Ordinaunces." A new member of the covenant also had to persuade existing members that she or he had fully experienced conversion. The fervent Puritans among the early colonists had little difficulty meeting the test of covenant membership. By 1635, the Boston church had added more than 250 names to the 4 original subscribers to the covenant.

Puritan views on church membership derived from John Calvin, a sixteenth-century Swiss Protes-

THE

World turn'd upfide down:

OR,

A briefe defcription of the ridiculous Fafhions
of thefe diftracted Times.

By T. J. a well-willer to King, Parliament and Kingdom.

London : Printed for John Smith. 1647.

THE PURITAN CHALLENGE TO THE STATUS QUO
*This title page of "The World Turn'd Upside Down,"
satirizes the Puritan notion that the contemporary
world was deeply flawed. Printed in London in
1647, the pamphlet refers to the "distracted Times"
of the Puritan Revolution in England. The drawing
ridicules criticisms of English society that were also
common among New England Puritans. The drawing
shows at least a dozen examples of the conventional
world of seventeenth-century England turned upside
down. Can you identify them? Puritans, of course,
would claim that the drawing had it wrong—that
instead the conventional world turned God's order
upside down. How might the drawing have been
different if a devout Puritan had drawn it?*
By permission of The British Library.

tant theologian. Calvin stressed the doctrine of pre-
destination, which held that before the creation of
the world, God exercised his divine grace and chose
a few human beings to receive eternal life. Only God
knew who these fortunate individuals—the "elect"
or "visible saints"—were. Nothing a person did
could change God's inscrutable choice.

Puritans, however, believed that if one were
among the elect, then one would surely act like it.
To a certain extent, one's sainthood would become
visible in one's behavior, especially if one were privileged to know God's Word as revealed in the Bible.
However, the connection between sainthood and
saintly behavior was far from firm. But the Puritans
thought that passing the demanding test of membership in one of their churches was a promising
clue that one was in fact among God's elect.

Members of Puritan churches ardently hoped
that they were visible saints and tried to act that
way. Their covenant bound them to help each other
attain this lofty goal and to discipline the entire
community by saintly standards. Church members
kept an eye on the behavior of everybody in town.
Infractions of morality, order, or propriety were reported to the elders, who summoned the wayward
to a church inquiry. Church members enforced a remarkable degree of righteous conformity in Puritan
communities.

Despite the central importance of religion,
churches had no direct role in the civil government
of New England communities. Puritans did not
want to emulate the Church of England, which they
considered a puppet of the king rather than an independent body that served the Lord. They were
determined to insulate New England churches from
the contaminating influence of the civil state and its
merely human laws. Although ministers were the
most highly respected figures in New England
towns, they were prohibited from holding government office.

Puritans had no qualms, however, about their
own beliefs influencing New England governments.
As much as possible, the Puritans tried to bring
public life into conformity with their view of God's
law. On the Sabbath, townsfolk could not work,
play, or travel. Fines were issued for Sabbath-
breaking activities such as playing a flute, smoking
a pipe, and visiting neighbors. Puritans mandated
other purifications of what they considered corrupt
English practices. They refused to celebrate either
Christmas or Easter, since the Bible did not mention
such rituals. They outlawed religious wedding ceremonies. They prohibited elaborate, colorful clothing and banned cards, dice, shuffleboard, and other
games of chance, as well as music and dancing. On
special occasions, Puritans proclaimed days of
fasting and humiliation, which, as one preacher
boasted, amounted to "so many Sabbaths more."

King Philip Considers Christianity

Beginning in 1646, Puritan minister John Eliot served as a missionary to New England's Indians, trying to teach both the doctrines of Christianity and the orthodoxies of proper English behavior. During his half-century tenure as the leader of the Puritan congregation in Roxbury, Massachusetts, Eliot studied the languages, customs, and beliefs of native Americans, hoping to help them along the path to Christian piety and to strengthen them against colonists' unscrupulous encroachment on Indian lands. The efforts of Eliot and other missionaries convinced some Indians to leave their own communities and settle in "praying towns" populated by native Americans who had agreed to live in conformity with English ways. Most Indians, however, did not move into praying towns or adopt the faith or manners of the colonists.

In Indian Dialogues, *a book published in 1671, Eliot illustrated the challenge he and other missionaries confronted as they tried to convince native Americans of the errors of their ways. Based upon his decades of missionary experience, Eliot created imaginary conversations between converted Indians and those who resisted Christianity. Eliot's invented conversations echoed arguments he and other missionaries had encountered repeatedly. The following selection from an imaginary dialogue between two praying Indians, Anthony and William, and King Philip (or Metacomet), the chief (or sachem) of the powerful Wampanoags, documents Eliot's perception of the attractions of Christianity and one Indian leader's doubts about it. These doubts ultimately prevailed when King Philip led the Wampanoags in an all-out attack against the settlers in 1675.*

Anthony. Sachem, we salute you in the Lord, and we declare unto you, that we are sent by the church, in the name of our Lord Jesus Christ, to call you, and beseech you to turn from your vain conversation unto God, to pray unto God, and to believe in Jesus Christ for the pardon of your sins, and for the salvation of your soul. . . . So we are come this day unto you, in the name of Jesus Christ, to call you to come unto the Lord, and serve him. [W]e hear that many of your people do desire to pray to God, only they depend on you. We pray you to consider that your love to your people should oblige you to do them all the good you can. . . . You will not only yourself turn from sin unto God . . . , but all your people will turn to God with you, so that you may say unto the Lord, oh Lord Jesus, behold here am I, and all the people which thou hast given me. We all come unto thy service, and promise to pray unto God so long as we live. . . . Oh how happy will all your people be. . . . It will be a joy to all the English magistrates, and ministers, and churches, and good people of the land, to hear that Philip and all his people are turned to God, and become praying Indians. . . .

Philip. Often have I heard of this great matter of praying unto God, and hitherto I have refused. . . . Mr. Eliot himself did come unto me. He was in this town, and did persuade me. But we were then in our sports, wherein I have much delighted, and in that temptation, I confess, I did neglect and despise the offer, and lost that opportunity. Since that time God hath afflicted and chastised me, and my heart doth begin to break. And I have some serious thoughts of accepting the offer, and turning to God, to become a praying Indian, I myself and all my people. But I have some great objections, which I cannot tell how to get over, which are still like great rocks in my way, over which I cannot climb. And if I should, I fear I shall fall down the precipice on the further side, and be spoiled and undone. By venturing to climb, I shall catch a deadly fall to me and my posterity.

The first objection that I have is this, because you praying Indians do reject your sachems, and refuse to pay them tribute, in so much that if any of my people turn to pray unto God, I do reckon that I have lost him. He will no longer own me for his sachem, nor pay me any tribute. And hence it will come to pass, that if I should pray to God, and all my people with me, I must become as a common man among them, and so lose all my power and authority over them. This is such a temptation as . . . I, nor any of the other great sachems, can tell how to get over. Were this temptation removed, the way would be more easy and open for me to turn praying Indian. I begin to have some good likance of the way, but I am loth to buy it at so dear a rate.

William. . . . I say, if any of the praying Indians should be disobedient (in lawful things) and refuse to pay tribute unto their sachems, it is not their religion and praying to God that teaches them so to do, but their corruptions. . . . I am sure the word of God commandeth all to be subject to the higher powers, and pay them tribute. . . . And therefore, beloved sachem, let not your heart fear that praying to God will alienate your people from you . . . for the more beneficent you are unto them, the more obligation you lay upon them. And what greater beneficence can you do unto them than to further them in religion, whereby they may be converted, pardoned, sanctified, and saved? . . .

Philip. I have another objection stronger than this, and that is, if I pray to God, then all my men that are willing to pray to God will (as you say) stick to me, and be true to me. But all such as love not and care not to pray to God, especially such as hate praying to God, all these will forsake me, yea will go and adjoin themselves unto other sachems that pray not to God. And so it will come to pass, that if I be a praying sachem, I shall be a poor and weak one, and easily trod upon by others, who are like to be more potent and numerous. And by this means my tribute will be small, and my people few, and I shall be a great loser by praying to God. In the way I am now, I am full and potent, but if I change my way and pray to God, I shall be empty and weak. . . .

William. . . . Suppose all your subjects that hate praying to God should leave you. What shall you lose by it? You are rid of such as by their sins vitiate others, and multiply transgression, and provoke the wrath of God against you and yours. But consider what you shall gain by praying to God . . . all the praying Indians will rejoice at it, and be your friends, and they are not a few. [And] you shall gain a more intimate love of the Governor, and Magistrates. . . . They will more honor, respect, and love you, than ever they did. [T]he Governor and Magistrates of the Massachusetts will own

you, and be fatherly and friendly to you. . . . Yea more, the King of England, and the great peers who . . . yearly send over means to encourage and promote our praying to God, they will take notice of you.

Philip. I perceive that in your praying to God, and in your churches, all are brought to an equality. Sachems and people they are all fellow brethren in your churches. Poor and rich are equally privileged. The vote of the lowest of the people hath as much weight as the vote of the sachem. Now I doubt [i.e., worry] that this way will lift up the heart of the poor to too much boldness, and debase the rulers to[o] low. This bringing all to an equality will bring all to a confusion. [T]here is yet another thing that I am much afraid of, and that is your church admonitions and excommunications. I hear that your sachems are under that yoke. I am a sinful man as well as others, but if I must be admonished by the church, who are my subjects, I know not how I shall like that. I doubt [i.e., worry] it will be a bitter pill, too hard for me to get down and swallow. . . . I feel your words sink into my heart and stick there. You speak arrows. . . . I desire to ponder and consider of these things. . . . I am willing they should still lie soaking in my heart and mind.

SOURCE: John Eliot, *Indian Dialogues* (Cambridge, 1671), in Henry W. Bowden and James P. Ronda, eds., *John Eliot's Indian Dialogues: A Study in Cultural Interaction* (Westport, Conn., 1980), 120–31.

QUESTIONS FOR ANALYSIS AND DEBATE

1. To what degree is Eliot's dialogue a reliable guide to Philip's doubts about the wisdom of becoming a praying Indian?

2. According to Eliot, was Philip's religion a stumbling block to his acceptance of Christianity? What made Philip fear that he would "fall down the precipice"?

3. If Philip had written a dialogue proposing that Eliot convert to the Wampanoag way of life, what arguments might it have made?

NEW ENGLAND GREAT CHAIR

This throne-like chair belonged to Michael Metcalf, a teacher in seventeenth-century Dedham, Massachusetts. The oldest known piece of New England furniture inscribed with a date, 1652, the chair was made in Dedham specifically for Metcalf (note the initials flanking the date), who turned sixty-six in that year. Metcalf stored books, presumably including a Bible, in the enclosed compartment under the seat. No overstuffed recliner, the chair is suited less for a relaxing snooze than for alert concentration. The panels under the arms served to block chilly drafts. Otherwise, the chair shows few concessions to comfort or ease. The carved chair back—rigidly upright—displays motifs often found on Puritan tombstones. The grand austerity of the chair hints at the importance of serious Bible study and unflinching introspection in Puritan New England.

Dedham Historical Society/photo by Forrest Frazier.

Government by Puritans for Puritanism

It is only a slight exaggeration to say that seventeenth-century New England was governed by Puritans for Puritanism. The charter of the Massachusetts Bay Company empowered the company's stockholders, or freemen, to meet as a body known as the General Court and make the laws to govern the company's affairs. The colonists transformed this arrangement for running a joint stock company into a structure for governing the colony. In 1631, the General Court ruled that freemen must be male church members, hoping to ensure that godly men would decide government policies. When new settlers continued to be admitted as freemen, the number became too large for the group to meet conveniently. In 1634, the freemen in each town agreed to send two deputies to the General Court to act as the colony's legislative assembly.

All other men were classified as "inhabitants," and they had the right to vote, hold office, and participate fully in town government. A "town meeting," composed of all the town's inhabitants and freemen, chose the selectmen and other officials who administered local affairs. New England town meetings routinely practiced a level of popular participation in political life that was unprecedented elsewhere during the seventeenth century. Almost every adult man could speak out in town meetings and fortify his voice with a vote. However, all women—even church members—were prohibited from voting, and towns did not permit "contrary-minded" men to become or remain inhabitants. Although town meeting participants wrangled from time to time, widespread political participation tended to reinforce conformity to Puritan ideals.

One of the most important functions of New England government was land distribution. Settlers who desired to establish a new town entered a covenant and petitioned the General Court for a grant of land. The court granted town sites to suitably pious petitioners but did not allow settlement until the Indians who inhabited a grant agreed to relinquish their claim to the land, usually in exchange for manufactured goods. Having obtained their grant, town founders apportioned land among themselves and any newcomers they permitted to join them. Although there was a considerable difference between the largest and smallest family plots, most clustered in the middle range—roughly fifty to one hundred acres—giving New England a more equal distribution of land than the Chesapeake. Towns reserved some common land, which all inhabitants could use for grazing livestock and cutting wood, and saved the rest for new settlers and the descendants of the founders. The physical layout of the towns encouraged settlers to look inward toward their neighbors, multiplying the opportunities for godly vigilance.

The Splintering of Puritanism

Almost from the beginning, John Winthrop and other leaders had difficulty enforcing their views of Puritan orthodoxy. In England, persecution as a dissenting minority unified Puritan voices in opposition to the Church of England. But in New England, the promise of a godly society and the Puritans' emphasis on individual Bible study led New Englanders toward different visions of godliness. Puritan leaders, however, interpreted dissent as an error caused either by a misguided believer or by the malevolent power of Satan. Whatever the cause, errors could not be tolerated. As one Puritan minister proclaimed, "The Scripture saith . . . there is no Truth but one."

Among the immigrants who arrived in Massachusetts in 1630 was Roger Williams, a lively young minister who counted Winthrop and other Puritan elders among his friends. From the start, Williams needled the colony's leadership with his outspoken views that their church was fatally impure. Williams declared that the government of Massachusetts contaminated the purity of the church, which had to be kept absolutely separate from civil influence. For these opinions and others, Massachusetts banished Williams in 1635. He helped found the colony of Rhode Island, which became a refuge for dissenters from Puritan orthodoxies.

Strains within Puritanism exemplified by Williams and Anne Hutchinson caused it to splinter repeatedly during the seventeenth century. The prominent minister Thomas Hooker, for example, clashed with Winthrop and other leaders over the composition of the church. Hooker argued that men and women who lived godly lives should be admitted to church membership, even if they had not experienced conversion. This question, like most others in New England, had both religious and political dimensions, since only church members

could vote in Massachusetts. In 1636, Hooker led an exodus of more than eight hundred colonists from Massachusetts to the Connecticut River valley, where they founded Hartford and neighboring towns. In 1639, the towns adopted the Fundamental Orders of Connecticut, a quasi-constitution that could be altered by vote of the freemen, who did not have to be church members, though nearly all of them were. Other Puritan churches divided and subdivided throughout the seventeenth century as acrimony developed over doctrine and church government. These schisms arose from the ambiguities and tensions within Puritan belief. As the colonies matured, other tensions developed as well.

Religious Controversies and Economic Changes

A revolutionary transformation in the fortunes of Puritans in England had profound consequences in New England. Disputes between King Charles I and Parliament escalated in 1642 to civil war in England, known as the Puritan Revolution. The parliamentary forces led by the staunch Puritan Oliver Cromwell were victorious, executing Charles I in 1649 and proclaiming a Puritan Republic. From 1649 to 1660, England's rulers were not monarchs who suppressed Puritanism but believers who championed it. In a half century, English Puritans rose from a harassed group of religious dissenters to a dominant power in English government.

When the Puritan Revolution began, the stream of immigrants to New England dwindled to a trickle, creating hard times for the colonists. They could no longer consider themselves a city on a hill setting a godly example for humankind. English society was being reformed by Puritans in England, not New England. Furthermore, when immigrant ships became rare, the colonists faced sky-high prices for scarce English goods and few customers for their own colonial products. As they searched to find new products and markets, they established the enduring patterns of New England's economy.

New England's rocky soil and short growing season ruled out cultivating the southern colonies' crops of tobacco and rice that found a ready market in Atlantic ports. Exports that New Englanders could not get from the soil they took instead from the forest and the sea. During the first decade of settlement, colonists traded with Indians for animal pelts, which were in demand in Europe. By the

1640s, fur-bearing animals were scarce unless traders ventured far beyond the frontiers of English settlement. Trees from the seemingly limitless forests of New England proved a longer-lasting resource. Masts for ships and staves for barrels of Spanish wine and West Indian sugar were crafted from New England timber.

But the most important New England export was fish. During the religious and political turmoil of the 1640s, English ships withdrew from the rich North Atlantic fishing grounds and New England fishermen quickly took their place. Dried, salted codfish found markets in southern Europe and the West Indies. The fish trade also stimulated colonial shipbuilding and trained generations of fishermen, sailors, and merchants, creating a commercial network that endured for more than a century.

Although immigration came to a standstill in the 1640s, the population continued to boom, doubling every twenty years. In New England, almost everyone married and women often had eight or nine children. Long, cold winters prevented the warm-weather ailments of the southern colonies and reduced New England mortality. The descendants of the immigrants of the 1630s multiplied and remultiplied, boosting the New England population to roughly equal that of the southern colonies (Figure 4.1).

Under the pressures of steady population growth and integration into the Atlantic economy, the white-hot piety of the founders cooled during the last half of the seventeenth century. By the 1680s, women were the majority of full church members throughout New England. In some towns, only 15 percent of the adult men were members. Most alarming to Puritan leaders, the children of visible saints often failed to experience conversion and attain full church membership. The problem became urgent during the 1650s when the children of saints —people who had grown to adulthood in New England but who had not experienced conversion— began to have children themselves. These babies, the grandchildren of visible saints, could not receive the protection baptism afforded against the terrors of death because their parents were not converted.

Puritan churches debated what to do. In 1662, a synod of Massachusetts ministers reached a compromise known as the Halfway Covenant. The unconverted children of saints were permitted to become "halfway" church members. Like regular church members, they could baptize their infants. But unlike full church members, they could not par-

ticipate in communion or have the voting privileges of church membership. The Halfway Covenant generated a controversy that sputtered through Puritan churches for the remainder of the century. With the Halfway Covenant, Puritan churches came to terms with replacing the founders' burning zeal with what one called "luke-warm Indifferency."

Nonetheless, during the last half of the seventeenth century, New England communities continued to enforce piety with holy rigor. Beginning in 1656, small bands of Quakers began to arrive in Massachusetts. Quakers—or members of the Society of Friends, as they called themselves—believed that God spoke directly to each individual through an "inner light." Neither a preacher nor the Bible was necessary to discover God's Word. Furthermore, since all human beings were equal in God's eyes, Quakers refused to conform to mere temporal

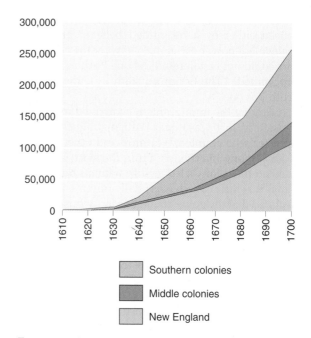

Figure 4.1

Population of British North American Colonies in the Seventeenth Century

The colonial population grew at a steadily accelerating rate during the seventeenth century. On the whole, New England and the southern colonies each comprised about half the total colonial population until after 1680, when the growth in Pennsylvania and New York contributed to a surge in the population of the middle colonies.

A NEW ENGLAND CHILD
This 1668 painting of young Alice Mason illustrates the drift away from the intense piety and plain dress of New England's founding generation. The elaborately decorated dress, especially the slashed sleeves, reflects the prosperity that some New Englanders had achieved by the 1660s, prosperity they displayed in their clothing and homes in ways the founders would have deemed profane.
Adams National Historic Site.

New Englanders' partial success in realizing the promise of a godly society ultimately undermined the intense appeal of Puritanism. In the pious communities of New England, leaders tried to eliminate sin. In the process, they diminished the sense of utter human depravity that was the wellspring of Puritanism. By 1700, New Englanders did not doubt that human beings sinned, but they were more concerned with the sins of others than with their own, as the Salem witch trials demonstrated. In 1692, more than one hundred individuals were accused of witchcraft, a capital crime, in the frenzied Salem proceedings. Most of the accused witches were middle-aged women who, their accusers charged, were in thrall to Satan who had caused misfortune to befall the accusers. Accusing vulnerable older women of witchcraft made it somewhat easier for their accusers to consider themselves saints who were victimized by evil witches, rather than sinners who were largely responsible for their own deviations from piety. The Salem court executed nineteen accused witches, signalling enduring belief in the supernatural origins of evil and gnawing doubt about the strength of New Englanders' faith.

The Founding of the Middle Colonies

The English colonies of New York, New Jersey, and Pennsylvania originated as proprietary colonies—that is, colonies granted by the crown to one or more proprietors, who then possessed both the land and extensive, almost monarchical, powers of government (see Map 4.2). Before the 1670s, few Europeans settled in any of these middle colonies. For the first two-thirds of the seventeenth century, the most important European outpost in the region north of the Chesapeake and south of New England was the relatively small Dutch colony of New Netherland. By 1700, however, the English monarchy had seized New Netherland, renamed it New York, and encouraged the creation of a Quaker colony led by William Penn.

From New Netherland to New York

In 1609, the Dutch East India Company dispatched Henry Hudson to search for a Northwest Passage to the Orient. Hudson sailed along the Atlantic coast and ventured up the large river that now bears his

powers such as laws and governments, unless God requested otherwise. Quakers affronted Puritan doctrines of faith and social order. They refused to observe the Sabbath, for example, because they insisted that God did not set aside any special day for worship but instead expected the faithful to worship every day.

New England communities treated Quakers with ruthless severity. Some Quakers were branded on the face "with a red-hot iron with [an] H. for heresie." Several Quaker women were stripped to the waist, tied to the back of a cart, and whipped as they were paraded through towns. When Quakers refused to leave Massachusetts, the Boston magistrates sentenced two men and a woman to be hanged in 1659.

MAP 4.2

Middle Colonies in the Seventeenth Century
For the most part, the middle colonies in the seven-
teenth century were inhabited by settlers who clus-
tered along the Hudson or Delaware River. The vast
geographic extent of the colonies shown in this map
represented land grants authorized in England but
still inhabited by native Americans rather than
settled by colonists.

name until it dwindled to a stream that obviously did not lead to China. A decade later, the Dutch government granted the West India Company—a group of Dutch merchants and shippers—exclusive rights to trade with the Western Hemisphere. In 1626, Peter Minuit, the resident director of the company, purchased Manhattan Island from the Manhate Indians for trade goods worth the equivalent of a dozen beaver pelts. New Amsterdam, the small settlement established at the southern tip of Manhattan Island, became the principal trading center in New Netherland and the colony's headquarters. Unlike the English colonies, New Netherland did not attract many European immigrants. Like New England and the Chesapeake colonies, New Netherland never realized the profits of its sponsors' dreams.

Although few in number, the New Netherlanders were remarkably diverse, especially compared with the homogeneous English settlers to the north and south. Religious dissenters and immigrants from Holland, Sweden, France, Germany, and else-

where made their way to the colony. A minister of the Dutch Reformed Church complained to his superiors in Holland that several groups of Jews had recently arrived, adding to the religious mixture of "Papists, Mennonites and Lutherans among the Dutch [and] many Puritans . . . and many other atheists . . . who conceal themselves under the name of Christians."

The West India Company struggled to govern the motley colonists. Peter Stuyvesant, governor from 1647 to 1664, tried to enforce conformity to the Dutch Reformed Church, but the company declared that "the consciences of men should be free and unshackled," making a virtue of New Netherland necessity. The company never permitted the colony's settlers to form a representative government. Instead, the company appointed government officials who set policies, including taxes, which many colonists deeply resented.

In 1664, New Netherland became New York. Charles II, who became king of England in 1660, gave his brother James, the Duke of York, an enormous grant of land that included New Netherland. Of course, the Dutch colony did not belong to the king of England. But that legal technicality did not impede the king or his brother. The duke quickly organized a small fleet of warships, which appeared off Manhattan Island in late summer 1664, and demanded that Stuyvesant surrender. With little choice, he did.

As the new proprietor of the colony, the Duke of York exercised almost the same unlimited authority over the colony as had the West India Company. The duke never set foot in New York, but his governors struggled to impose order on the unruly colonists. Like the Dutch, the duke permitted "all persons of what Religion soever, quietly to inhabit . . . provided they give no disturbance to the publique peace, nor doe molest or disquiet others in the free exercise of their religion." This policy of religious toleration was less an affirmation of liberty of conscience and more a recognition of the reality of the most heterogeneous colony in seventeenth-century North America.

New Jersey and Pennsylvania

The creation of New York led indirectly to the founding of two other middle colonies, New Jersey and Pennsylvania (Map 4.2). In 1664, the Duke of York subdivided his grant and gave the portion between the Hudson and Delaware Rivers to two of his friends. The proprietors of this new colony, New Jersey, soon discovered that Puritan and Dutch settlers already in the region stubbornly resisted the new government. The continuing strife persuaded one of the proprietors to sell his share to two Quakers. When the Quaker proprietors began to quarrel, they called in a prominent English Quaker, William Penn, to arbitrate their dispute. Penn eventually worked out a settlement that continued New Jersey's proprietary government but did little to end the conflict with the settlers. In the process, Penn became intensely interested in what he termed a "holy experiment" of establishing a genuinely Quaker colony in America.

The Quakers' concept of an open, generous God who made his love equally available to all people manifested itself in unusually egalitarian worship services and in social behavior that continually brought Quakers into conflict with the English government. Quaker leaders were ordinary men and women, not specially trained preachers. More than any other seventeenth-century sect, Quakers allowed women to assume positions of religious leadership. "In souls there is no sex," they said. Since all people were equal in the spiritual realm, Quakers considered social hierarchy false and evil. They called everyone "friend" and shook hands instead of curtsying or removing their hats—even when meeting the king. These customs enraged many non-Quakers and provoked innumerable beatings and worse. Penn was jailed four times for such offenses, once for nine months.

Despite his many run-ins with the government, Penn remained on good terms with Charles II, who granted him land to found a Quaker colony in America. Partly to rid England of the troublesome Quakers, in 1681 Charles made Penn the proprietor of 45,000 square miles for his new colony, called Pennsylvania.

Toleration and Diversity in Pennsylvania

When Penn announced the creation of his colony, Quakers flocked to English ports in numbers exceeded only by the great Puritan migration to New England fifty years earlier. Between 1682 and 1685, nearly eight thousand immigrants arrived in Pennsylvania, most of them Quakers from England, Ireland, and Wales. They represented a cross section of the artisans, farmers, and laborers who predominated among English Quakers. Quaker missionaries also encouraged immigrants from the European continent, and many came, giving Pennsylvania greater ethnic diversity than any other English colony except New York. Pennsylvania prospered, and the capital city, Philadelphia, soon rivaled New York—though not yet Boston—as a center of commerce. By 1700, the city's five thousand inhabitants participated in a thriving trade exporting flour and other food products to the West Indies and importing textiles and manufactured goods.

WILLIAM PENN
This portrait of William Penn was drawn about a decade after the founding of Pennsylvania. At a time when extravagant clothing and fancy wigs proclaimed that their wearer was an important person, Penn is portrayed informally, lacking even a coat, his natural hair neat but undressed—all a reflection of his Quaker faith. Penn's full face and double chin show that his faith did not make him a stranger to the pleasures of the table. No hollow-cheeked ascetic or wild-eyed enthusiast, Penn appears sober and observant, as if sizing up the viewer and reserving judgment. The portrait captures the calm determination—anchored in his faith—that inspired Penn's hopes for his new colony.
Historical Society of Pennsylvania.

Penn was determined to live in peace with the Indians who inhabited the region. His Indian policy expressed his Quaker ideals and contrasted sharply with the hostile policies of the other English colonies. Penn instructed his agents to obtain the Indians' consent by purchasing their land, respecting their claims, and dealing with them fairly.

Penn declared that the first principle of government was that every settler would "enjoy the free possession of his or her faith and exercise of worship towards God." Accordingly, Pennsylvania tolerated Protestant sects of all kinds as well as Roman Catholics. All voters and officeholders had to be Christians, but the government did not compel settlers to attend religious services, as in Massachusetts, or to pay taxes to maintain a state-supported church, as in Virginia.

Despite its toleration and diversity, Pennsylvania was as much a Quaker colony as New England was a stronghold of Puritanism. Penn had no hesitation about using civil government to enforce religious morality. The ethnic and religious diversity of Pennsylvania prevented strict enforcement of pious behavior, but Quaker expectations of godly order and sobriety set the tone of Pennsylvania society.

As proprietor, Penn had extensive powers, subject only to review by the king. He appointed a governor who maintained the proprietor's power to veto any laws passed by the colonial council, which was elected by property owners who possessed at least one hundred acres of land or who paid taxes. The council had the power to originate laws and administer all the affairs of government. A popularly elected assembly served as a check on the council; its members had the authority to reject or approve laws framed by the council.

Penn stressed that the exact form of government mattered less than the men who served in it. In Penn's eyes, "good men" staffed Pennsylvania's government because Quakers dominated elective and appointive offices. Quakers, of course, differed among themselves. Members of the assembly struggled to win the right to debate and amend laws, especially tax laws. They finally won the battle in 1701 when a new Charter of Privileges gave the proprietor the power to appoint the council and in turn stripped the council of all its former powers and gave them to the assembly, which became the only unicameral legislature in all the British colonies.

The Colonies and the British Empire

From the king's point of view, proprietary grants of faraway lands to which he had tenuous claims were a cheap way to reward friends. As the colonies grew, however, the grants became more valuable. After 1660, the king took initiatives to channel colonial trade through English hands and to consolidate royal authority over colonial governments. These initiatives defined the basic relationship between the colonies and England that endured until the American Revolution (Map 4.3).

Royal Regulation of Colonial Trade

English economic policies toward the colonies were designed to yield customs revenues for the monarchy and profitable business for English merchants and shippers. In addition, the policies were intended to divert the colonies' trade from England's enemies, the Dutch and the French.

The Navigation Acts of 1650, 1651, and 1660 set forth two fundamental regulations governing colonial trade. First, all colonial goods imported into England had to be transported in English ships using primarily English crews. Second, the Navigation Acts listed specific colonial products that could be shipped only to England or to other English colonies. The Staple Act of 1663 imposed a third regulation on colonial trade. It required all goods imported into the colonies to pass through England (see chapter 3).

By the end of the seventeenth century, colonial commerce was defined by regulations that subjected merchants and shippers to royal supervision and gave them access to markets throughout the British Empire. In addition, colonial commerce received protection from the British navy. By 1700, colonial goods (including those from the West Indies) accounted for one-fifth of all British imports and for two-thirds of all goods reexported from England to the continent. In turn, the colonies absorbed more than one-tenth of British exports. The commercial regulations gave economic value to England's proprietorship of American colonies.

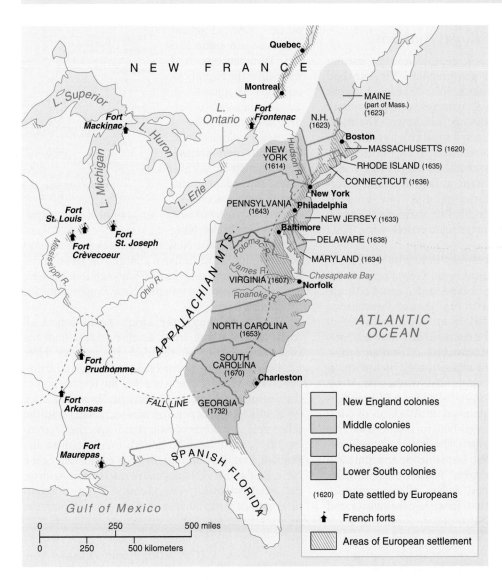

MAP 4.3
American Colonies at the End of the Seventeenth Century
By the end of the seventeenth century, settlers inhabited a narrow band of land that stretched more or less continuously from Boston to Norfolk, with pockets of settlement farther south. The colonies' claims to enormous tracts of land to the west were contested by native Americans as well as the ambitions of France and Spain.

READING THE MAP: What geographic feature acted as the boundary for colonial territorial claims? Which colonies were the most settled and which the least?

CONNECTIONS: The map divides the colonies into four regions; can you think of alternative organizations? On what criteria would they be based?

www.bedfordstmartins.com/roarkcompact SEE THE ONLINE STUDY GUIDE for more help in analyzing this map.

Consolidation of Royal Authority

The monarchy also took steps to exercise greater control over colonial governments. Virginia had been a royal colony since 1624; Maryland, South Carolina, and the middle colonies were proprietary colonies with close ties to the crown. The New England colonies possessed royal charters, but they had developed their own distinctively Puritan governments. Charles II, whose father, Charles I, had been executed by Puritans in England, took a particular interest in harnessing the New England colonies more firmly to the British Empire. The occasion was a royal investigation following King Philip's War.

In 1675, warfare between Indians and colonists erupted in the Chesapeake and New England. Although Massachusetts settlers had massacred hundreds of Pequot Indians in 1637, they had established relatively peaceful relations with the more potent Wampanoags. But in the decades that followed, New Englanders steadily encroached on Indian lands, and, in 1675, the Wampanoags struck back with attacks on settlements in western Massachusetts. Metacomet—whom the colonists called King Philip—was the chief of the Wampanoags and the son of Massasoit, who had befriended William Bradford and his original band of Pilgrims. The Indians utterly destroyed thirteen English settlements and partially burned another half dozen. By the spring of 1676, Indian warriors ranged freely within seventeen miles of Boston. Militias from Massachusetts and

other New England colonies counterattacked the Wampanoags and their allies the Nipmucks and the Narragansetts in a deadly sequence of battles that killed over a thousand colonists and thousands more Indians. The colonists finally defeated the Indians, principally with a scorched-earth policy of burning their food supplies. King Philip's War left the New England colonists with an enduring hatred of Indians, a large war debt, and a devastated frontier. And in 1676, an agent of the king arrived to investigate whether New England abided by English laws.

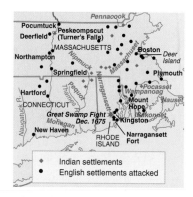

King Philip's War, 1675

Not surprisingly, the king's agent found all sorts of deviations from English rules, and the English government decided to govern New England more directly. In 1684, an English court revoked the Massachusetts charter, the foundation of the distinctive Puritan government. Two years later, royal officials incorporated Massachusetts and the other colonies north of Maryland into the Dominion of New England. To govern the dominion, the English sent Sir Edmund Andros to Boston. Some New England merchants cooperated with Andros, but most colonists were offended by his flagrant disregard of such Puritan traditions as keeping the

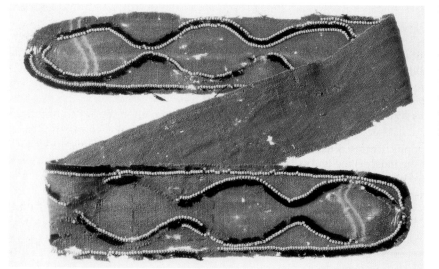

KING PHILIP'S SASH
This woolen sash belonged to Metacomet, or King Philip. Small white glass beads, obtained through trade with Europeans, embroider the sash in the shape of a serpent.
Peabody Museum, Harvard University.

Sabbath. Worst of all, the Dominion of New England invalidated all land titles, confronting every landowner in New England with the horrifying prospect of losing his or her land.

Events in England, however, permitted Massachusetts colonists to overthrow Andros and retain title to their property. When Charles II died in 1685, he was succeeded by his brother James II, a zealous Catholic. James's aggressive campaign to appoint Catholics to government posts engendered such unrest that in 1688 a group of Protestant noblemen invited the Dutch ruler William of Orange to claim the English throne. When William landed in England at the head of a large army, James fled to France and William became king in the bloodless Glorious Revolution, which reasserted Protestant influence in England and its empire. Rumors of the revolution raced across the Atlantic and emboldened colonial uprisings against royal authority in Massachusetts, New York, and Maryland.

In Boston, rebels reestablished the former charter government, destroying the Dominion of New England. New Yorkers under the leadership of Jacob Leisler followed the Massachusetts example. But when King William's governor of New York arrived in 1691, he executed Leisler for treason. In Maryland, the Protestant Association, led by John Coode, overthrew the colony's pro-Catholic government in 1689, fearing it would not recognize the new Protestant king. Coode's men ruled until the new royal governor arrived in 1692 and ended both Coode's rebellion and Lord Baltimore's proprietary government.

Much as they chafed under increasing royal control, the colonists still valued English protection from hostile neighbors. While the northern colonies were distracted by the Glorious Revolution, French forces from the fur trading regions along the Great Lakes and in Canada attacked villages in New England and New York. Known as King William's War, the conflict with the French was a colonial outgrowth of William's war against France in Europe. The war dragged on until 1697 and ended inconclusively in both Europe and the colonies. But it made clear to many colonists that along with English royal government came a welcome measure of military security.

In Massachusetts, John Winthrop's city on a hill became another royal colony in 1691, when a new charter was issued. Under the charter, the governor was appointed by the king rather than elected by the colonists' representatives. But perhaps the most unsettling change was the new qualification for voting. Possession of property replaced church membership as a prerequisite for voting in colony-wide elections. Wealth replaced God's grace as the defining characteristic of Massachusetts citizenship.

Conclusion: An English Model of Colonization in North America

By 1700, the diverse English colonies in North America had developed along lines quite different from the example New Spain had set in 1600. In the North American colonies, English immigrants and their descendants created societies of settlers, unlike the largely Indian societies in New Spain ruled by a tiny group of Spaniards. Although many settlers came to North America from other parts of Europe and a growing number of Africans arrived in bondage, English laws, habits, ideas, and language dominated all the colonies.

Economically, the English colonies thrived on agriculture and trade instead of mining silver and exploiting Indian labor as in New Spain. Southern colonies grew huge crops of tobacco and rice with the labor of indentured servants and slaves, while farmers in the middle colonies planted wheat and New England fishermen harvested the sea. Although servants and slaves could be found throughout the North American colonies, many settlers depended principally on the labor of family members. Relations between settlers and native Americans often exploded in bloody warfare, but Indians seldom served as an important source of labor for settlers, as they did in New Spain.

Protestantism prevailed in the North American settlements, relaxed in some colonies and straitlaced in others. The convictions of Puritanism that motivated John Winthrop and others to build a new England in the colonies became muted as the New England colonies matured and dissenters like Anne Hutchinson multiplied. Catholics, Quakers, Anglicans, Jews, and others settled in the middle and southern colonies, creating considerable religious toleration, especially in Pennsylvania and New York.

Politics and government differed from colony to colony, although the imprint of English institutions and practices existed everywhere. And everywhere, local settlers who were free adult white men had an extraordinary degree of political influence, far beyond that of colonists in New Spain or ordinary citizens in England. A new world of settlers that Columbus could not have imagined, that Powhatan only glimpsed, had been firmly established in English North America by 1700. During the next half century, that English colonial world would undergo surprising new developments built upon the achievements of the seventeenth century.

FOR FURTHER READING ABOUT THE TOPICS IN THIS CHAPTER, see the Online Bibliography at www.bedfordstmartins.com/roarkcompact.

FOR ADDITIONAL FIRST-HAND ACCOUNTS OF THIS PERIOD, see pages 43–59 in Michael Johnson, ed., *Reading the American Past,* Second Edition, Volume I.

TO ASSESS YOUR MASTERY OF THE MATERIAL IN THIS CHAPTER, see the Online Study Guide at www.bedfordstmartins.com/roarkcompact.

CHRONOLOGY

1534 Henry VIII breaks with Roman Catholic Church and initiates English Reformation.

1609 Henry Hudson searches for Northwest Passage for Dutch East India Company.

1620 English Puritans found Plymouth colony and elect William Bradford governor.

1626 Peter Minuit purchases Manhattan Island for Dutch West India Company and founds New Amsterdam.

1629 Massachusetts Bay Company receives royal charter for colony.

1630 John Winthrop leads Puritan settlers to Massachusetts Bay.

1635 Roger Williams, banished from Massachusetts, establishes Rhode Island colony.

1636 Thomas Hooker leaves Massachusetts and helps found Connecticut colony.

1637 Anne Hutchinson accused of Antinomianism; excommunicated from Boston church in 1638.

1642 Civil war inflames England, pitting Puritans against royalists.

1649 English Puritans win civil war and execute King Charles I.

1656 Quakers arrive in Massachusetts and are persecuted there.

1660 Monarchy restored in England; Charles II becomes king.

Navigation Act requires colonial goods to be shipped in English vessels through English ports.

1662 Many Puritan congregations adopt Halfway Covenant.

1663 Staple Act requires all colonial imports to come from England.

1664 English seize New Netherland colony from Dutch and rename it New York.

Duke of York subdivides his colony, creating new colony of New Jersey.

1675 Indians and colonists clash in King Philip's War.

1681 King Charles II grants William Penn charter for colony of Pennsylvania.

1686 Royal officials create Dominion of New England.

1688 James II overthrown by Glorious Revolution; William of Orange becomes king.

1691 Massachusetts becomes royal colony.

1692 Witch trials flourish at Salem, Massachusetts.

**"DUMMY BOARD" OF PHYLLIS,
A NEW ENGLAND SLAVE**

*This life-size portrait of a slave
woman named Phyllis, a mulatto who
worked as a domestic servant for her
owner, Elizabeth Hunt Wendell, was
painted sometime before 1753. Known
as a "dummy board," it was evidently
propped against a wall or placed in a
doorway or window to suggest that
the residence was occupied and to discourage thieves. Phyllis is portrayed as a demure,
well-groomed woman whose dress and demeanor suggest that she was capable, orderly,
and efficient. Although tens of thousands of slaves were brought from Africa to the British
North American colonies during the eighteenth century, it does not appear that Phyllis was
one of them. Instead, she was probably born in the colonies of mixed black and white
parentage. Like thousands of other slave women who labored in the homes of prosperous
white families, Phyllis illustrates the integration of the mundane tasks of housekeeping
with the shifting currents of transatlantic commerce.*

Courtesy of the Society for the Preservation of New England Antiquities/photo by David Bohl.

COLONIAL AMERICA IN THE EIGHTEENTH CENTURY

5

1701–1770

ARLY ON A SUNDAY MORNING IN OCTOBER 1723, young Benjamin Franklin stepped from a wharf along the Delaware River onto the streets of Philadelphia. As he wrote later in his autobiography, "I was dirty from my Journey; my Pockets were stuff'd out with Shirts and Stockings; I knew no Soul, nor where to look for Lodging. I was fatigu'd with Travelling, Rowing and Want of Rest. I was very hungry."

Born in 1706, Benjamin Franklin grew up in Boston, where his father, Josiah, worked making soap and candles. The father of seventeen children, Josiah apprenticed each of his sons to learn a trade. At the age of twelve, Benjamin signed an indenture to serve for nine years as an apprentice to his brother James, a printer. In James's shop, Benjamin learned the printer's trade and had access to the latest books and pamphlets, which he read avidly. In 1721, James inaugurated the *New England Courant*, avowing to "expose the Vice and Follies of Persons of all Ranks and Degrees" with articles written "so that the meanest ploughman . . . may understand them."

Benjamin's responsibilities in the print shop grew quickly, but he chafed under his brother's supervision. "My Brother was passionate and had often beaten me," he remembered. Benjamin resolved "to assert my Freedom" and run away to New York, nearly three hundred miles from anyone he knew. When he could not find work, he wandered to the Delaware River and then talked his way aboard a small boat heading toward Philadelphia. After rowing half the night, Franklin arrived in the city and went straight to a bakery where he purchased "three great Puffy Rolls." Then he set off for the wharf, "with a Roll under each Arm," to wash down the bread with "a Draught of the River Water." After quenching his thirst, Franklin followed "many clean dress'd People . . . to the great Meeting House of the Quakers. . . . I sat down among them, and . . . I fell fast asleep, and continu'd so till the Meeting broke up."

Franklin's account of his life in Boston and his arrival in Philadelphia is probably the most well-known portrait of life in eighteenth-century America. It illustrates everyday experiences that Franklin shared with many other colonists: a large family; long hours of labor subject to the authority of a parent, relative, or employer; and a restless quest for escape from the ties that bound, for freedom. Franklin's account hints at other, less tangible trends: an ambition to make something of oneself in this world rather than worry too much about the hereafter; an eagerness to

PHILADELPHIA WHARF
This early-nineteenth-century drawing of the Arch Street wharf in Philadelphia approximates the world Benjamin Franklin entered when he stepped ashore in 1723. The wharf was a center of industrious activity; almost everyone depicted appears to be working. The pulse of Atlantic commerce propels casks of products from the deck of the small local sailboat (right) toward the hold of large oceangoing ships (center) bound for England and Europe. The small rowboat carrying four people (just to the right of the large ships) is probably similar to the boat Franklin rowed to the city. Coordinating the complicated comings and goings of people and goods that moved through the wharf required individuals who combined intelligence, energy, and discipline with efficiency, reliability, and trustworthiness—traits Franklin and other eighteenth-century colonists sought to cultivate.
Rare Book Department, The Free Library of Philadelphia.

subvert orthodox opinion by publishing dissenting views expressed in simple, clear language understandable by "the meanest ploughman"; a confidence that, with a valued skill and a few coins, a young man could make his way in the world, a confidence few young women could dare assert; and a slackening of religious fervor displayed, for example, in Franklin's quiet snooze—rather than rapt attention—during the Quaker meeting he wandered into on his first day in Philadelphia.

Franklin's story introduces some of the major changes that affected all the colonies in eighteenth-century British North America. Social and economic changes tended to reinforce the differences among New England, the middle colonies, and the southern colonies, while important cultural and political developments tugged in the opposite direction, creating common experiences, aspirations, and identities. In 1776, when *E Pluribus Unum* (Latin meaning "From Many, One") was adopted as the motto for the Great Seal of the United States, the changes in eighteenth-century America that strengthened *Pluribus* also planted the seeds of *Unum*.

A Growing Population and Expanding Economy

The most important fact about eighteenth-century colonial America was its phenomenal population growth. In 1700, colonists numbered about 250,000; by 1770, they tallied well over 2 million. An index of the emerging significance of colonial America is that in 1700 there were 19 people in England for every American colonist, whereas by 1770 there were only 3. The eightfold growth of the colonial population signaled the maturation of a distinctive colonial society. That society was by no means homogeneous. Colonists of different ethnic groups, races, and religions lived in varied environments under thirteen different colonial governments, all of them part of the British Empire.

In general, the growth and diversity of the eighteenth-century colonial population derived from two sources: immigration and natural increase (that is, growth through reproduction). Natural increase contributed about three-fourths of the population growth, immigration about one-fourth. Immigration shifted the ethnic and racial balance among the colonists, making them by 1770 less English and less white than ever before. Fewer than 10 percent of eighteenth-century immigrants came from England; about 36 percent were Scots-Irish, mostly from northern Ireland; 33 percent arrived from Africa, almost all of them slaves; nearly 15 percent had left the many German-language principalities (the nation of Germany did not exist until 1871); and almost 10 percent came from Scotland. In 1670, more than 9 out of 10 colonists were of English ancestry, and only 1 out of 25 was of African ancestry. By 1770, only about half the colonists were of English descent, while more than 20 percent descended from Africans. By 1770, the people of the colonies had a distinctive colonial—rather than English—profile (Map 5.1).

The booming population of the colonies hints at a second major feature of eighteenth-century colonial society: an expanding economy. Today, societies with rapidly growing populations often have more people than they can adequately feed; or, put another way, they have a high ratio of people to land. In the eighteenth-century colonies, very different conditions prevailed.

In 1700, after almost a century of settlement, nearly all the colonists lived within fifty miles of

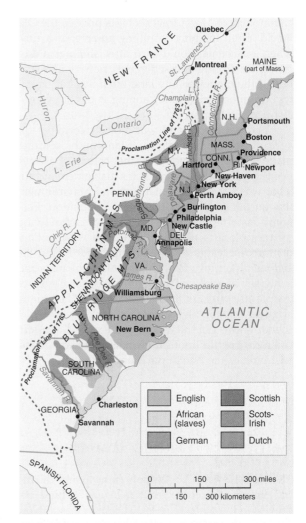

MAP 5.1

Europeans and Africans in the Eighteenth Century
This map illustrates regions where Africans and certain immigrant groups clustered. It is important to avoid misreading the map. Predominantly European regions, for example, also contained colonists from other places. Likewise, regions where African slaves resided in large numbers also included many whites, their masters among them. The map suggests the polyglot diversity of eighteenth-century colonial society.

the Atlantic coast, on the edge of a vast wilderness peopled by native Indians and a few trappers and traders. The almost limitless wilderness gave the colonies an extremely low ratio of people to land. Consequently, land was cheap. Land in the colonies commonly sold for a fraction of its price in the Old World, often for only a shilling an acre, at a time when a carpenter could earn three shillings a day. Along the frontiers of settlement, newcomers who lacked the money to buy land often lived as squatters on unoccupied land, hoping it might eventually become theirs.

Without labor, land was almost worthless for agriculture. The abundance of land in the colonies made labor precious, and the colonists always needed more. The colonists' insatiable demand for labor was the fundamental economic environment that sustained the mushrooming population. Economic historians estimate that the standard of living of free colonists (that is, those who were not indentured servants or slaves) improved during the eighteenth century: By 1770, most free colonists had a higher standard of living than the majority of people elsewhere in the Atlantic world. The unique achievement of the eighteenth-century colonial economy was not the wealth of the most successful colonists but the modest economic welfare of the vast bulk of the free population.

New England: From Puritan Settlers to Yankee Traders

The New England population grew sixfold during the eighteenth century, but it lagged behind the growth in the other colonies. The main reason New England failed to keep pace was that most immigrants chose other destinations because of New England's relatively densely settled land and because Puritan orthodoxy made these colonies comparatively inhospitable. As the population grew, many settlers in search of farmland dispersed from towns, and Puritan communities lost much of their cohesion. Nonetheless, networks of economic exchange laced New Englanders to Atlantic commerce. In many ways, trade became a faith that competed strongly with the traditions of Puritanism.

Natural Increase and Land Distribution

The New England population grew mostly by natural increase, much as it had during the seventeenth century. Nearly every adult woman married. Most married women had children and, thanks to the rel-

atively low mortality rate in New England, often many children. The burgeoning New England population pressed against a limited amount of land. The interior of New England was smaller than that of colonies farther south (see Map 5.1). Moreover, as the northernmost group of colonies, New England had a contested northern and western frontier. Powerful Indian tribes, especially the Iroquois and Mahicans, jealously guarded their territories.

In the seventeenth century, New Englanders practiced partible inheritance (that is, they subdivided land more or less equally among sons). By the eighteenth century, the original land allotments had to be further subdivided to accommodate grandsons and great-grandsons, causing many plots of land to become too small for subsistence. Sons who could not hope to inherit sufficient land to farm had to move away from the town where they were born.

During the eighteenth century, colonial governments in New England abandoned the seventeenth-century policy of granting land to towns. Needing revenue, the governments of both Connecticut and Massachusetts sold land directly to individuals, including speculators. Now money, rather than membership in a community bound by a church covenant, determined whether a person could obtain land. The new land policy eroded the seventeenth-century pattern of settlement. As colonists moved into western Massachusetts and Connecticut and north into present-day New Hampshire and Maine, they tended to settle on individual farms rather than in the towns and villages that characterized the seventeenth century. New Englanders still depended on their relatives and neighbors, but far more than in the seventeenth century, they regulated their behavior in newly settled areas by their own individual dictates.

Farms, Fish, and Trade

A New England farm was a place to get by, not to get rich. New England farmers grew food for their families, but their fields did not produce a huge marketable surplus. Instead of one big crop, farmers grew many small ones. If they had extra, they sold to or traded with neighbors. By 1770, New Englanders had only one-fourth as much wealth as free colonists in the southern colonies.

As consumers, New England farmers made up the foundation of a diversified commercial economy that linked remote farms to markets through-

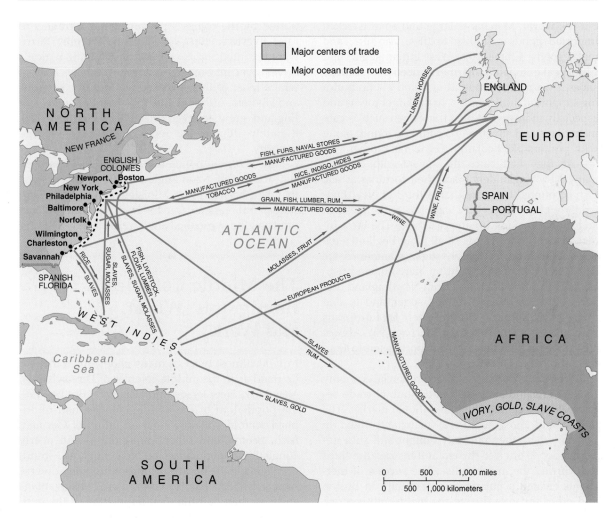

MAP 5.2

Atlantic Trade in the Eighteenth Century

This map illustrates the economic outlook of the colonies in the eighteenth century: that is, east toward the Atlantic world rather than west toward the interior of North America. The long distances involved in the Atlantic trade and the uncertainties of seaborne travel suggest the difficulties Britain experienced governing the colonies and regulating colonial commerce.

READING THE MAP: What were the major markets for trade coming out of Europe? What goods did the English colonies import and export?

CONNECTIONS: In what ways did the flow of raw materials from the colonies affect English industry? How did English colonial trade policies influence the Atlantic trade?

www.bedfordstmartins.com/roarkcompact SEE THE ONLINE STUDY GUIDE for more help in analyzing this map.

out the world. Merchants large and small stocked imported goods—English textiles, ceramics, and metal goods; Chinese tea; West Indian sugar; and Chesapeake tobacco. Farmers' needs for sturdy shoes, a warm coat, a sound cart, and a solid building supported local artisans. In the larger towns and especially in Boston, skilled tradesmen such as cabinetmakers and silversmiths could be found, along with printers like Benjamin Franklin's brother.

As they had since the seventeenth century, many New Englanders made their fortunes at sea. Fish accounted for more than a third of New England's eighteenth-century exports, with livestock and timber making up another third. The West Indies absorbed two-thirds of all New England's exports. Slaves on Caribbean sugar plantations ate dried, salted codfish caught by New England fishermen, filled barrels crafted from New England timber with molasses and refined sugar, and loaded them aboard ships bound ultimately for Europeans with a sweet tooth (see Map 5.2, page 93). Almost all the rest of New England's exports went to England and continental Europe.

Merchants dominated the commercial economy of New England and stood at the hub of trade between local folk and the international market. The largest and most successful merchants lived in Boston, where they not only bought and sold imported goods but also owned and insured the ships that carried the merchandise. The success of merchants created a polarization of wealth in Boston and other seaports during the eighteenth century. By 1770, the richest 5 percent of Bostonians owned about half the city's wealth; the poorest two-thirds of the population owned less than one-tenth.

Although the rich got richer, and everybody else had a smaller share of the total wealth, the incidence of genuine poverty did not change much. A Connecticut traveler wrote from England in 1764, "We in New England know nothing of poverty and want, we have no idea of the thing, how much better do our poor people live than 7/8 of the people on this much famed island."

The contrast with English poverty had meaning, since the overwhelming majority of New Englanders traced their ancestry to England, making the region more homogeneous than any other. The population of African ancestry (almost all slaves) in the region remained small. New Englanders had no hesitation about acquiring slaves, and many Puritan ministers owned one or two. In the Narragansett region of Rhode Island, numerous slaves were im-

ported by the colony's prominent slave traders to raise livestock. But New England's family farms were unsuited for slave labor. Instead, the region's slaves concentrated in towns, especially Boston, where most of them worked as domestic servants and laborers. Although the black population of New England grew to over fifteen thousand by 1770, it barely diluted the region's 97 percent white majority.

By 1770, the population, wealth, and commercial activity of New England differed from what they had been in 1700. Ministers still enjoyed high status, but Yankee traders had replaced Puritan saints as the symbolic New Englanders.

The Middle Colonies: Immigrants, Wheat, and Work

In 1700, almost twice as many people lived in New England as in the middle colonies of Pennsylvania, New York, New Jersey, and Delaware. But by 1770, the population of the middle colonies had multiplied tenfold—mainly from an influx of German, Irish, Scotch, and other immigrants—and nearly equaled the population of New England. Immigrants made the middle colonies a uniquely diverse society. By 1800, barely one-third of Pennsylvanians and less than half the total population of the middle colonies traced their ancestry to England.

German and Scots-Irish Immigrants

Germans made up the largest contingent of migrants from the European continent to the middle colonies. By 1770, about 85,000 Germans had arrived in the colonies. Their fellow colonists often referred to them as "Pennsylvania Dutch," an English corruption of *Deutsch*, the word the immigrants used to describe themselves.

Most German immigrants came from what is now southwestern Germany, although some hailed from German-speaking parts of Switzerland, Austria, and the Netherlands. Throughout Europe, peasants suffered from exploitation by landowners and governments, and they had few opportunities to improve their lives. Many German peasants, one observer noted, were "not as well off as cattle elsewhere." German immigrants included numerous artisans and a few merchants, but the great majority were farmers and laborers. Economically, they represented "middling" folk, neither the poorest (who could not afford the trip) nor the better off (who did not want to leave).

By the 1720s, Germans who had established themselves in the colonies wrote back to their friends and relatives, as one reported, "of the civil and religious liberties [and] privileges, and of all the goodness I have heard and seen." Such letters prompted still more Germans to pull up stakes and embark for America, to exchange the miserable certainties of their lives in Germany for the uncertain attractions of life in the colonies.

Similar motives propelled the Scots-Irish, who considerably outnumbered German immigrants. The term *Scots-Irish* was another misleading label coined in the colonies. Immigrants labeled Scots-Irish actually hailed from the north of Ireland, Scotland, and northern England. Some of the Scots-Irish were Irish natives who had no personal or ancestral connection whatever with Scotland.

Like the Germans, the Scots-Irish were Protestants, but with a difference. Most German immigrants worshiped in Lutheran or German Reformed churches; many others belonged to dissenting sects like the Mennonites, Moravians, and Amish, whose adherents sought relief from persecution they had suffered in Europe for their refusal to bear arms and to swear oaths, practices they shared with Quakers. In contrast, the Scots-Irish tended to be militant Presbyterians who seldom hesitated to bear arms or swear oaths. Like German settlers, however, Scots-Irish immigrants were clannish, residing when they could among relatives or neighbors from the old country.

In the eighteenth century, wave after wave of Scots-Irish immigrants arrived, beginning in 1717, cresting every twelve or fifteen years thereafter and culminating in a flood of immigration in the years just before the American Revolution. Deteriorating economic conditions in northern Ireland, Scotland, and England pushed many toward America. Most of the immigrants were farm laborers or tenant farmers fleeing droughts, crop failures, high food prices, or rising rents.

Both Scots-Irish and Germans probably heard the common saying that "Pennsylvania is heaven for farmers [and] paradise for artisans," but they almost certainly did not fully understand the risks of their decision to leave their native lands. Gottfried Mittelberger, a musician who traveled from Germany to Philadelphia in 1750, described the grueling passage to America commonly experienced by eighteenth-century emigrants. Mittelberger's trip from his home village in the interior to the port of Rotterdam took seven weeks and cost four times more than the trip from Rotterdam to Philadelphia. Nearly two-thirds of all German emigrants arrived at their port of departure with no money to stock up on extra provisions for the trip or even to buy a ticket. Likewise, they could not afford to go back home. Ship captains, aware of the hunger for labor in the colonies, eagerly signed up the penniless emigrants as "redemptioners," a variant of indentured servants. A captain would agree to provide transportation to Philadelphia, where redemptioners would obtain the money to pay for their passage from a friend or relative who was already in the colonies or, as most did, by selling themselves as servants. Impoverished Scots-Irish emigrants, especially the majority who traveled alone rather than with families, typically paid for their passage by contracting to become indentured servants before they sailed.

Unlike indentured servants, redemptioners negotiated independently with their purchasers about their period of servitude. Typically, a healthy adult redemptioner agreed to four years of labor. Indentured servants commonly served five, six, or seven years, as did weaker, younger, and less skilled redemptioners. Children ten years old or younger usually had to become indentured servants until they were twenty-one.

Pennsylvania: "The Best Poor [White] Man's Country"

New settlers, whether free or in servitude, poured into the middle colonies because they perceived unparalleled opportunities, particularly in Pennsylvania, "the best poor Man's Country in the World," as indentured servant William Moraley wrote in 1743. Although Moraley reported that "the Condition of bought Servants is very hard" and masters often failed to live up to their promise to provide decent food and clothing, opportunity abounded because there was more work to be done than workers to do it.

Most servants toiled in Philadelphia, New York City, or one of the smaller towns or villages. From the masters' viewpoint, servants were a bargain. A master could purchase five or six years of a servant's labor for approximately the wages a common laborer would earn in four months. Wage workers could walk away from their jobs when they pleased, and they did so often enough to be troublesome to employers. Servants, however, were legally bound to work for their masters until their terms expired.

A few black slaves worked in shops and homes in Philadelphia and New York City. After Benjamin Franklin became prosperous, he purchased five slaves. Since a slave cost at least three times as much as a servant, only affluent colonists could afford the long-term investment in slave labor. While the population of African ancestry (almost all slaves) in the middle colonies grew to over thirty thousand in 1770, it represented only about 7 percent of the total population, and in most of the region much less. The reason more slaves were not brought to the middle colonies was that farmers, the vast majority of the population, had little use for them. Most farms operated with family labor.

During the eighteenth century, most slaves came to the middle colonies and New England from the West Indies. Enough arrived to prompt colonial assemblies to pass slave codes that punished slaves much more severely than servants for the same transgressions. "For the least trespass," servant Moraley reported, slaves "undergo the severest Punishment." Even the few free African Americans did not escape whites' firm convictions about black inferiority and white supremacy. Whites' racism and blacks' lowly social status made African Americans scapegoats for European Americans' suspicions and anxieties. In 1741, when arson and several unexplained thefts plagued New York City, officials suspected a murderous slave conspiracy. On the basis of little more than evidence of slaves' "insolence" (that is, refusal to conform fully to whites' expectations of servile behavior), city authorities had thirteen slaves burned at the stake and eighteen others hanged.

Immigrants swarmed to the middle colonies because of the availability of land. The Penn family encouraged immigration to bring in potential buyers for their enormous tracts of land in Pennsylvania. From the beginning, Pennsylvania followed a policy of negotiating with Indian tribes to purchase additional land. This policy greatly reduced the violent frontier clashes evident elsewhere in the colonies. Few colonists drifted beyond the northern boundaries of Pennsylvania. The Iroquois dominated the lucrative fur trade of the St. Lawrence valley and eastern Great Lakes, and they had the po-

litical and military strength to defend their territory from colonial encroachment.

Since the cheapest land always lay at the margin of settlement, would-be farmers tended to migrate to promising areas just beyond already improved farms. From Philadelphia, settlers moved north along the Delaware River and west along the Schuylkill and Susquehanna Rivers. By midcentury, settlement had reached the eastern slopes of the Appalachian Mountains, and newcomers spilled down the fertile valley of the Shenandoah River into western Virginia and the Carolinas. Thousands of settlers migrated from the middle colonies through this back door to the South.

Patterns of Settlement, 1700–1770

Farmers made the middle colonies the breadbasket of North America. They planted a wide variety of crops to feed their families, but they grew wheat in abundance. Flour milling was the number one industry and flour the number one export, constituting nearly three-fourths of all exports from the middle colonies. Pennsylvania flour fed residents in other colonies, in southern Europe, and, above all, in the West Indies.

The standard of living in rural Pennsylvania was probably higher than in any other agricultural region of the eighteenth-century world. The comparatively widespread prosperity of all the middle colonies permitted residents to indulge in a half-century shopping spree for English imports. The middle colonies' per capita consumption of imported goods from England more than doubled between 1720 and 1770, far outstripping the per capita consumption of English goods in New England and the southern colonies.

At the crossroads of trade in wheat exports and English imports stood Philadelphia. By 1776, Philadelphia had a larger population than any other city in the entire British Empire except London.

BETHLEHEM, PENNSYLVANIA

This view of the small community of Bethlehem, Pennsylvania, in 1757 dramatizes the profound transformation of the natural landscape in the eighteenth century by highly motivated human labor. Founded by Moravian immigrants in 1740, Bethlehem must have appeared at first like the dense woods on the upper left horizon. In fewer than twenty years, precisely laid-out orchards and fields had replaced forests and glades. Carefully penned livestock (lower center right) and fenced fields (lower left) kept the handiwork of farmers separate from the risks and disorders of untamed nature. Not only individual farmsteads (lower center) but impressive multistory brick town buildings (upper center) combined the bounty of the land with the delights of community life. Few eighteenth-century communities were as orderly as Bethlehem, but many effected a comparable transformation of the environment.

Miriam and Ira D. Walsh Division of Art, Prints, and Photographs, The New York Public Library. Astor, Lenox, and Tilden Foundations.

www.bedfordstmartins.com/roarkcompact SEE THE ONLINE STUDY GUIDE for more help in analyzing this image.

Merchants occupied the top stratum of Philadelphia society. In a city where only 2 percent of the residents owned enough property to qualify to vote, merchants built grand homes and dominated local government. Many of Philadelphia's wealthiest merchants were Quakers. Quaker traits of industry, thrift, honesty, and sobriety encouraged the accumulation of wealth.

The ranks of merchants reached downward to aspiring tradesmen like Benjamin Franklin. After he started to publish the *Pennsylvania Gazette* in 1728, Franklin opened a shop, run mostly by his wife, Deborah, that sold a little bit of everything: cheese, codfish, coffee, goose feathers, sealing wax, soap, and now and then a slave. In 1733, Franklin began to publish *Poor Richard's Almanack*, a calendar of weather predictions, astrological alignments, and pithy epigrams. Poor Richard preached the likelihood of long-term rewards for tireless labor. The *Almanack* sold thousands of copies, quickly becoming Franklin's most profitable product.

William Penn's Quaker utopia became a center of worldly affluence whose most famous citizen, Franklin, was neither a Quaker nor a utopian. Quakers remained influential, but Franklin spoke for most colonists with his aphorisms of work, discipline, and thrift that echoed Quaker rules for outward behavior. Franklin's maxims did not look to the Quakers' divine inner light for guidance. They depended instead on the spark of ambition and the glow of gain.

The Southern Colonies: Land of Slavery

Between 1700 and 1770, the population of the southern colonies of Virginia, Maryland, North Carolina, South Carolina, and Georgia grew almost ninefold. By 1770, about twice as many people lived in the South as in either the middle colonies or New England. As elsewhere, natural increase and immigration accounted for this rapid population growth. Many Scots-Irish and German immigrants funneled from the middle colonies into the southern backcountry. Other immigrants were indentured servants (mostly English and Scots-Irish) who followed their seventeenth-century predecessors. But slaves made the most striking contribution to the booming southern colonies, transforming the racial composition of the population and shaping the region's economy, society, and politics.

The Atlantic Slave Trade and the Growth of Slavery

The number of southerners of African ancestry (nearly all of them slaves) rocketed from just over 20,000 in 1700 to well over 400,000 in 1770. The black population increased nearly three times faster than the South's briskly growing white population. Consequently, the proportion of southerners who were black grew from 20 percent in 1700 to 40 percent in 1770. Slavery became the defining characteristic of the southern colonies during the eighteenth century.

Southern colonists clustered into two distinct geographic and agricultural zones. The colonies in the upper South, surrounding the Chesapeake Bay, specialized in growing tobacco, as they had since the early seventeenth century. Throughout the eighteenth century, nine out of ten southern whites and eight out of ten southern blacks lived in the Chesapeake region. The upper South retained a white majority during the eighteenth century.

In the lower South, a much smaller cluster of colonists inhabited the coastal region and specialized in the production of rice and indigo (a plant used to make blue dye). Lower South colonists made up only 5 percent of the total population of the southern colonies in 1700 but inched upward to 15 percent by 1770. South Carolina was the sole British colony along the South Atlantic coast until 1732, when Georgia was founded. (North Carolina, founded in 1711, was largely an extension of the Chesapeake region.) In contrast to every other British mainland colony, blacks in South Carolina outnumbered whites almost two to one; in some low country districts, the ratio of blacks to whites exceeded ten to one.

The enormous growth in the South's slave population occurred through natural increase and the flourishing Atlantic slave trade (see Map 5.3 and Table 5.1). Slave ships brought almost 300,000 Africans to British North America between 1619 and 1780. Of those Africans, 95 percent arrived in the South and 96 percent arrived during the eighteenth century. Unlike indentured servants or redemptioners, the Africans did not choose to come to the colonies. Most of them had been born into free families in villages located within a few hundred miles of the West African coast. Although they shared African origins, they came from many different African cultures, including Akan, Angolan, Asante, Bambara, Gambian, Igbo, Mandinga, and others. They spoke different languages, worshiped different deities, followed different rules of kinship, grew different crops, and recognized different rulers. The most important experience they had in common was enslavement. Captured in war, kidnapped, or sold into slavery by other Africans, they were brought to the coast, sold to African traders who assembled slaves for sale, and sold again to European or colonial slave traders or ship captains who bought them for shipment to the New World. Packed aboard a slave ship with two to three hundred or more other slaves, they were subjected to the infamous Middle Passage—the crossing of the Atlantic in the hold of a slave ship—and then sold yet again by the ship captain to a colonial slave merchant or to a southern planter.

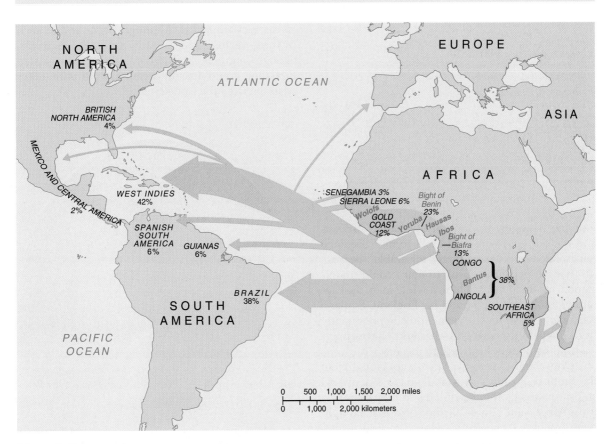

MAP 5.3

The Atlantic Slave Trade

Although the Atlantic slave trade endured from about 1450 to 1870, its heyday occurred during the eighteenth century, when more than six million African slaves were imported to the New World. Only a small fraction of the African slaves imported to the Western Hemisphere were taken to British North America; most went to sugar plantations in Brazil and the Caribbean. Why were so many more African slaves sent to the West Indies and Brazil than to British North America?

The voices of Africans who were swept up in the slave trade have been enveloped by a deafening historical silence, with one major exception. In 1789, Olaudah Equiano published *The Interesting Narrative*, an account of his own enslavement that hints at the stories that might have been told by the thousands of silenced Africans. Equiano was born in 1745 in the interior of what is now Nigeria. "I had never heard of white men or Europeans, nor of the sea," he recalled. One day when Equiano was eleven years old, two men and a woman, all Africans, broke into his home, seized him and his sister, and carried them off. The kidnappers soon separated Equiano from his sister, leaving him "in a state of distraction not to be described."

During the next six or seven months, Equiano was sold to several different African masters, each of whom moved him closer to the coast. When he arrived at the coast, a slave ship waited offshore. Equiano feared that he had "gotten into a world of bad spirits," that he was going to be killed and "eaten by those white men with horrible looks, red faces, and loose hair." Once the ship set sail, many slaves died from sickness, crowded together in suffocating heat fouled by filth of all descriptions. "The shrieks of the women and the groans of the dying rendered the whole a scene of horror almost inconceivable," Equiano recalled. Most of the slaves on the ship were sold in Barbados, but Equiano and other leftovers were shipped off to Virginia, where

TABLE 5.1
SLAVE IMPORTS, 1451–1870

Estimated Slave Imports to the
Western Hemisphere

1451–1600	275,000
1601–1700	1,341,000
1701–1810	6,100,000
1811–1870	1,900,000

slaves they imported. Although slaves within each of these regions spoke many different languages, enough linguistic and cultural similarities existed that they could usually communicate with other Africans from the same region.

Equiano "saw few or none of our native Africans and not one soul who could talk to me." Equiano felt isolated and "exceedingly miserable" because he "had no person to speak to that I could understand." He finally was sold to a white man, the captain of a tobacco ship bound for England. Equiano remained a slave for ten years, traveling frequently from England to the West Indies and North America until he bought his freedom in 1766.

Only about 15 percent of the slaves brought into the southern colonies came as Equiano did, aboard ships from the West Indies. All the rest came directly from Africa, and almost all the ships that brought them (roughly 90 percent) belonged to British merchants. Most slaves on board were young adults, men usually outnumbering women two to one. Children under the age of fourteen, like Equiano, were typically no more than 10 or 15 percent of a cargo. Mortality during the Middle Passage varied considerably from ship to ship. On average, about 15 percent of the slaves died, but sometimes half or more perished. The average mortality among the white crew of slave ships was often nearly as bad. In general, the longer the voyage, the larger the number of deaths.

Normally an individual planter purchased at any one time a relatively small number of newly arrived Africans, or "new Negroes," as they were called. Planters preferred to purchase small groups of slaves to permit the newcomers to be trained by the planters' other slaves. Planters' preferences for slaves from specific regions of Africa aided slaves' acculturation (or "seasoning," as it was called) to the routines of bondage in the southern colonies. Chesapeake planters preferred slaves from Senegambia, the Gold Coast, or—like Equiano—the Bight of Biafra, the origin of 40 percent of all Africans imported to the Chesapeake. South Carolina planters favored slaves from the central African Congo and Angola regions, the origin of about 40 percent of the African

OLAUDAH EQUIANO
This portrait of Olaudah Equiano was painted by an unknown English artist about 1780, when Equiano was in his mid-thirties, more than a decade after he had bought his freedom. The portrait evokes Equiano's successful acculturation to the customs of eighteenth-century England. His clothing and hairstyle reflect the fashions of respectable young Englishmen. In **The Interesting Narrative,** *Equiano explained that he had learned to speak and understand English while he was a slave. He wrote that he "looked upon [the English] . . . as men superior to us [Africans], and therefore I had the stronger desire to resemble them, to imbibe their spirit and imitate their manners; I therefore embraced every occasion of improvement, and every new thing that I observed I treasured up in my memory." Equiano's embrace of English culture did not cause him to forsake his African roots. He honored his dual identity by campaigning against slavery. His* **Narrative** *was one of the most important and powerful antislavery documents of the time.*
Olaudah Equiano: Royal Albert Memorial Museum, Exeter, Devon, UK/Bridgeman Art Library.

Negro's houses

a fire

Boys plaving under that Rooff

a Woman with her Child on her back

ỹ door

THE AFRICAN SLAVE TRADE

The African slave trade supplied the New World's demand for labor and Europe's voracious appetite for such New World products as sugar, tobacco, and rice with millions of enslaved Africans to work for their New World purchasers. African men, women, and children, like those pictured in this early-eighteenth-century engraving of a family residence in Sierra Leone, were kidnapped or captured in wars—typically by other Africans—and enslaved. Uprooted from their homes and kin, they were usually taken to coastal enclaves where African traders and European ship captains negotiated prices, made deals, and often branded the newly enslaved people. The significance of this diabolical collaboration between Europeans and their African trading partners is illustrated by the seventeenth-century Benin bronze box, which depicts a royal palace in Nigeria, whose slave trading and other activities are guarded by massive birds and two Portuguese soldiers. Jammed into the holds of slave ships, enslaved Africans made the dreaded Middle Passage to the New World. The model of a slave ship shown here was used in parliamentary debates by antislavery leaders in Britain to demonstrate the inhumanity of shipping people as if they were just so much tightly packed cargo. The model does not show another typical feature of slave ships: weapons. Slaves vastly outnumbered the crews aboard the ships, and crew members justifiably feared slave uprisings.

Museum für Volkerkunde, Berlin/Courtesy, Earl Gregg Swen Library, College of William and Mary, Williamsburg, Virginia/ Wilberforce House Museum, Hull City Museum, Art Gallery, and Archives, UK/Bridgeman Art Library.

Seasoning acclimated new Africans to the physical as well as the cultural environment of the southern colonies. Slaves who had just endured the Middle Passage were poorly nourished, weak, and sick. In this vulnerable state they encountered the alien diseases of North America without having developed a biological arsenal of acquired immunities. As many as 10 or 15 percent of newly arrived Africans, sometimes more, died during their first year in the southern colonies.

While newly enslaved Africans poured into the southern colonies, slave women made an even greater contribution to the growth of the black population by giving birth to slave babies, which caused the slave population to mushroom. Slave owners encouraged these births. Thomas Jefferson explained, "I consider the labor of a breeding [slave] woman as no object, that a [slave] child raised every 2 years is of more profit than the crop of the best laboring [slave] man." The high rate of natural increase in the southern colonies meant that by the 1740s the majority of southern slaves were native-born.

Slave Labor and African American Culture

Southern planters expected slaves to work from sunup to sundown and beyond. The conflict between the masters' desire for maximum labor and the slaves' reluctance to do more than necessary made the threat of physical punishment a constant for eighteenth-century slaves. Masters preferred black slaves over white indentured servants not just because slaves served for life, but also because colonial laws did not limit the force masters could use against slaves. As a traveler observed in 1740, "A new negro . . . will require more discipline than a young spaniel. . . . let a hundred men show him how to hoe, or drive a wheelbarrow; he'll still take the one by the bottom and the other by the wheel and . . . often die before [he] can be conquered." Slaves, the traveler noted, were not stupid or simply obstinate; despite the inevitable punishment, they resisted their masters' demands because of their "greatness of soul," their stubborn unwillingness to conform to their masters' definition of them as merely slaves.

Some slaves escalated their acts of resistance to direct physical confrontation with the master, mistress, or an overseer. But a hoe raised in anger, a punch in the face, or a desperate swipe with a knife led to swift and predictable retaliation by whites. Throughout the southern colonies, the balance of physical power rested securely in the hands of whites.

Rebellion occurred, however, at Stono, South Carolina, in 1739. Before dawn on a September Sunday, a group of about twenty slaves attacked a country store, killed the two storekeepers, confiscated the store's guns, ammunition, and powder, and set out toward Spanish Florida. Enticing other rebel slaves to join the march south, the group plundered and burned more than a half dozen plantations and killed more than twenty white men, women, and children. A mounted force of whites suppressed the rebellion. The Stono rebellion illustrated that eighteenth-century slaves had no chance of overturning slavery and very little chance of defending themselves in any bold strike for freedom. No other similar uprising occurred during the colonial period.

Slaves maneuvered constantly to protect themselves and to gain a measure of autonomy within the boundaries of slavery. In Chesapeake tobacco fields, most slaves were subject to close supervision by whites. In the lower South, the task system gave slaves some control over the pace of their work and some discretion in the use of the rest of their time. A task was typically defined as a certain area of ground to be planted, cultivated, and harvested or a specific job to be completed. A slave who completed the assigned task could use the remainder of the day to work in a garden, fish, hunt, spin, weave, sew, or cook.

Eighteenth-century slaves also planted the roots of African American lineages that branch out to the present. Historians are only beginning to explore the kin networks slaves built; much remains unknown. But it is clear that slaves valued family ties and that, as in West African societies, kinship structured slaves' relations with one another. Slave parents often gave a child the name of a grandparent, aunt, or uncle. In West Africa, kinship not only identified a person's place among living relatives; it also linked the person to ancestors among the dead and to descendants in the future. Newly imported African slaves usually arrived alone, like Equiano, without kin. Often slaves who had traversed the Middle Passage on the same ship adopted one another as "brothers" and "sisters." Likewise, as new Negroes were seasoned and incorporated into existing slave communities, established families often adopted them as "fictive" kin.

When possible, slaves expressed many other features of their West African origins in their lives on New World plantations. They gave their children African names such as Cudjo or Quash, Minda or Fuladi. They grew food crops familiar to them in Africa such as yams and okra. They constructed huts with mud walls and thatched roofs similar to African residences. They fashioned banjos, drums, and other musical instruments, held dances, and observed funeral rites that echoed African practices. In these and many other ways, slaves drew upon their African heritages to endow their personal lives with relationships and meanings that they controlled, as much as the oppressive circumstances of slavery permitted.

Tobacco, Rice, and Prosperity

Slaves' labor bestowed prosperity on their masters, British merchants, and the monarchy. The southern colonies supplied 90 percent of all North American exports to England. Rice exports from the lower South exploded from less than half a million pounds in 1700 to eighty million pounds in 1770, virtually all of it grown by slaves. Exports of indigo also boomed. Together, rice and indigo made up three-fourths of lower South exports, nearly two-thirds of them going to England and most of the rest to the West Indies, where sugar-growing slaves ate slave-grown rice. Tobacco was by far the most important export from British North America; by 1770, it represented almost one-third of all colonial exports and three-fourths of all Chesapeake exports. And under the provisions of the Navigation Acts (see chapter 4), nearly all of it went to England, where the monarchy collected a lucrative tax on each pound. British merchants then reexported more than 80 percent of the tobacco to the European continent, pocketing a nice markup for their troubles.

These products of slave labor made the southern colonies by far the richest in North America. The per capita wealth of free whites in the South was four times greater than that in New England and three times that in the middle colonies. At the top of the wealth pyramid stood the rice grandees of the lower South and the tobacco gentry of the Chesapeake. These elite families commonly resided on large estates adorned by handsome mansions and luxurious gardens, maintained and supported by slaves.

The vast differences in wealth among white southerners engendered envy and occasional ten-

PLANTATION MISTRESS
Enslaved Africans made possible the opulence of Mrs. Barnard Elliott, the wife of a wealthy South Carolina rice planter. Mrs. Elliott appears to be a discriminating consumer. Although she probably made most of her purchases in the best Charleston shops, her custom-made fashions would not have been out of place in the drawing rooms of the English gentry. Sensuous textiles, billowing lace-encrusted sleeves, a daring neckline, and dazzling jewels demonstrate Mrs. Elliott's cosmopolitan tastes despite her colonial residence. Her formal, almost regal pose evokes the enormous distance between the luxurious refinements of elite planters and workaday plantation realities. Contrast the appearance of Mrs. Elliott with that of her approximate contemporary, the New England household slave Phyllis (page 88).
The Gibbes Museum of Art, Carolina Art Association.

sion between rich and poor, but remarkably little open hostility. In private, the planter elite spoke disparagingly of humble whites, but in public they acknowledged their lesser neighbors as equals, at least in belonging to the superior—in their minds—white race. Looking upward, white yeomen and tenants (who owned neither land nor slaves) sensed the gentry's condescension and veiled contempt.

But they also appreciated the gentry for granting favors, upholding white supremacy, and keeping slaves in their place. While racial slavery made a few whites much richer than others, it also gave those who did not get rich a powerful reason to feel similar (in race) to those who were so different (in wealth).

The slaveholding gentry dominated the politics and economy of the southern colonies. In Virginia, only adult white men who owned at least one hundred acres of unimproved land or twenty-five acres of land with a house could vote. This property-holding requirement prevented about 40 percent of white men in Virginia from voting for representatives to the House of Burgesses. In South Carolina, only fifty acres of land were required to vote, and most adult white men qualified. But in both colonies, voters elected members of the gentry to serve in the colonial legislature. The gentry passed elected political offices from generation to generation, almost as if they were hereditary. Politically, the gentry built a self-perpetuating oligarchy—rule by the elite few—with the votes of their many humble neighbors.

The gentry also set the cultural standard in the southern colonies. They entertained lavishly, gambled regularly, and attended Anglican church services more for social than religious reasons. Above all they cultivated a life of leisurely pursuit of happiness. They did not condone idleness, however. Their many pleasures and responsibilities as plantation owners kept them busy. Thomas Jefferson, a phenomenally productive member of the gentry, recalled that his earliest childhood memory was of being carried on a pillow by a family slave—a powerful image of the slave hands beneath the gentry's leisure and achievement.

Unifying Experiences

While the societies of New England, the middle colonies, and the southern colonies became more sharply differentiated during the eighteenth century, colonists throughout British North America shared certain unifying experiences. The first was economic: The economies of all three regions had their roots in agriculture. But the tempo of commerce quickened during the eighteenth century. Colonists sold their distinctive products in markets that, in turn, offered to consumers throughout the

colonies a more or less uniform array of goods. A second unifying experience was a decline in the importance of religion. Although some settlers called for a revival of religious intensity, for most people throughout the colonies religion mattered less, the affairs of the world more, than they did in the seventeenth century. Third, white inhabitants throughout North America became aware that they shared a distinctive identity as British colonists. Thirteen different governments presided over the North American colonies, but all of them answered to the British monarchy. Royal officials who expected loyalty from the colonists often had difficulty obtaining obedience. The North American colonists asserted their prerogatives as British subjects to defend their special colonial interests.

Commerce and Consumption

Eighteenth-century commerce whetted the appetite to consume. Colonial products spurred the development of mass markets throughout the Atlantic world (Figure 5.1). Huge increases in the supply of colonial tobacco and sugar brought the price of these small luxuries within reach of most free whites. Colonial goods brought into focus an important lesson of eighteenth-century commerce. Ordinary people, not just the wealthy elite, would buy the things that they desired in addition to what they absolutely needed. Even news, formerly restricted mostly to a few people through face-to-face conversations or private letters, became an object of public consumption through the innovation of newspapers. (See "The Promise of Technology," page 106.) With the appropriate stimulus, market demand seemed unlimited.

The Atlantic commerce that took colonial goods to markets in England brought objects of consumer desire back to the colonies. English merchants and manufacturers recognized that colonists made excellent customers, and the Navigation Acts gave English exporters privileged access to the colonial market. English exports to North America multiplied eightfold between 1700 and 1770, outpacing the rate of population growth after midcentury. When the colonists' eagerness to consume exceeded their ability to pay, English exporters willingly extended credit, and colonial debts soared.

Imported mirrors, silver plate, spices, bed and table linens, clocks, tea services, wigs, books, and more infiltrated parlors, kitchens, and bedrooms throughout the colonies. Despite the many

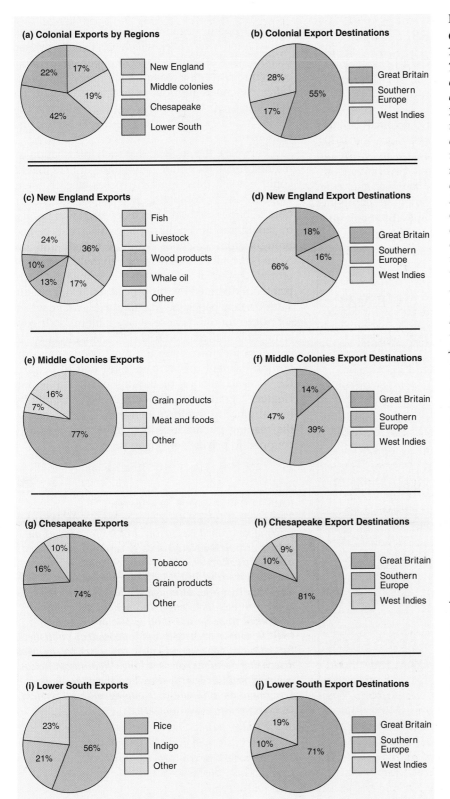

(a) Colonial Exports by Regions

- 17% New England
- 19% Middle colonies
- 42% Chesapeake
- 22% Lower South

(b) Colonial Export Destinations

- 55% Great Britain
- 17% Southern Europe
- 28% West Indies

(c) New England Exports

- 36% Fish
- 17% Livestock
- 13% Wood products
- 10% Whale oil
- 24% Other

(d) New England Export Destinations

- 18% Great Britain
- 16% Southern Europe
- 66% West Indies

(e) Middle Colonies Exports

- 77% Grain products
- 7% Meat and foods
- 16% Other

(f) Middle Colonies Export Destinations

- 14% Great Britain
- 39% Southern Europe
- 47% West Indies

(g) Chesapeake Exports

- 74% Tobacco
- 16% Grain products
- 10% Other

(h) Chesapeake Export Destinations

- 81% Great Britain
- 10% Southern Europe
- 9% West Indies

(i) Lower South Exports

- 56% Rice
- 21% Indigo
- 23% Other

(j) Lower South Export Destinations

- 71% Great Britain
- 10% Southern Europe
- 19% West Indies

FIGURE 5.1

Colonial Exports, 1768–1772

These pie charts provide an overview of the colonial export economy in the 1760s. The first two show that almost two-thirds of colonial exports came from the South and that the majority of the colonies' exports went to Great Britain. The remaining charts illustrate the distinctive patterns of exports in each colonial region. Fish, livestock, and wood products were New England's most important exports; they were sent primarily to the West Indies, only a small fraction going to Great Britain. From the colonial breadbasket in the middle colonies, grain products made up three-fourths of all exports, most of which went to the West Indies or to southern Europe. The Chesapeake also exported some grain, but tobacco accounted for three-fourths of the region's export trade, nearly all of it bound for Great Britain as mandated by the Navigation Acts. Rice and indigo comprised three-fourths of the exports from the lower South, the bulk of which was sent to Great Britain. Taken together, these charts reveal Britain's economic interest in the exports of the North American colonies.

The Printing Press: "The Spring of Knowledge"

I N THE EIGHTEENTH CENTURY, colonial printers began to publish newspapers. Since the 1630s, colonial printers had used presses to churn out books, pamphlets, broadsides, government announcements, legal forms, invitations, and even promissory notes. The innovation of compiling newsworthy information and publishing it on a regular schedule began in 1704 with the appearance of the *Boston News-Letter*, which was usually printed on both sides of a single sheet of paper smaller than conventional typing paper. Each week the *News-Letter* contained reprints of articles that had appeared in English newspapers, along with a few tidbits of local news such as deaths, fires, storms, and ship arrivals.

For years, the audience for such information remained small; the editor complained in 1719 that he could not sell three hundred copies of each issue. Nonetheless, a competing newspaper, the *Boston Gazette*, began publication in that year. It was printed by James Franklin on his press (right), which he had brought from England. Both the *Gazette* and the *News-Letter* submitted their copy to the governor for official approval before the newspapers were printed. Frustrated by this official scrutiny, Franklin started a new paper, the *New England Courant*, which set out to thumb its nose at officialdom, both governmental and religious. The *Courant* pledged "to entertain the Town with the most comical and diverting Incidents of Humane Life" and to "expose the Vice and Follies of Persons of all Ranks and Degrees." Franklin's press—operated faithfully by his apprentice brother, Benjamin—broadcast to the reading public dissenting opinions previously confined to private conversations.

JOHN PETER ZENGER'S NEWSPAPER
This issue of John Peter Zenger's **New-York Weekly Journal** *contained on the third of its four pages an article criticizing New York's governor. For this and other critical articles, the governor had Zenger tried for seditious libel in 1735. The jury sided with Zenger and acquitted him, although the law favored the governor. Printers like Zenger throughout the colonies continued to be harassed by public officials who tried to censor irreverent and independent publishers. But colonial governments were too weak to suppress dissenting opinions for very long. Vigorous political commentary like that featured on the page shown here found an avid audience among colonial readers.*
Courtesy, American Antiquarian Society.

By 1740, more than a dozen newspapers were published in the colonies and their numbers continued to increase. The relatively high rates of literacy gave them a large reading audience. In the northern colonies, readers included well over half of adult men and nearly half of adult women. In the southern colonies, literacy rates among whites were slightly lower, but still considerably above those in Europe. Since whites tried to prevent slaves from learning to read, literacy rates remained low among southern blacks.

But the information printed by newspapers spread far beyond readers. Newspapers were often read aloud not just at home but in workshops, taverns, and courthouses. In these public places, people who could not read listened to the controversial ideas, partisan accusations, and salacious rumors that printers relished. An eighteenth-century poem illustrates the many connections between news and audiences cultivated by colonial newspapers:

JAMES FRANKLIN'S PRINTING PRESS
Newport Historical Society.

News'papers are the spring of knowledge,
The gen'ral source throughout the nation.
Of ev'ry modern conversation.
What would this mighty people do,
If there, alas! were nothing new?

A New-paper is like a feast,
Some dish there is for ev'ry guest;
Some large, some small, some strong, some tender,
For ev'ry stomach, stout or slender;
Those who roast beef and ale delight in,
Are pleas'd with trumpets, drums, and fighting;
For those who are more puny made,
Are arts and sciences, and trade;
For fanciful and am'rous blood,
We have a soft poetic food;
For witty and satyric folks,
High-season'd, acid, BITTER JOKES;
And when we strive to please the mob,
A jest, a quarrel, or a job.

If any gentleman wants a wife,
(A partner, as 'tis termed, for life)
An advertisement does the thing,
And quickly brings the pretty thing.

If you want health, consult our pages,
You shall be well, and live for ages. . . .

Our services you can't express,
The good we do you hardly guess;
There's not a want of human kind,
But we a remedy can find.

When newspapers employed the technology of printing to publish everything from political news to advertisements for a spouse, all kinds of information and ideas began to diffuse more readily beyond official channels and to help form public opinion. Eighteenth-century newspapers combined the old technology of printing with the new currents of commerce, dissent, and enlightenment, creating a novel awareness of the problems and possibilities of public life.

differences among the colonists, the consumption of English exports built a certain material uniformity across region, religion, class, and status, and even made the colonists look and feel more British. The rising tide of colonial consumption had other less visible but no less important consequences. Consumption presented women and men with a novel array of choices. In many respects the choices might appear trivial: whether to buy knives and forks, teacups, or a clock. But such small choices confronted eighteenth-century consumers with a big question: "What do you want?" As colonial consumers defined and expressed their desires with greater frequency during the eighteenth century, they became accustomed to thinking of themselves as individuals who had the power to make decisions that influenced the quality of their lives—attitudes of significance in the hierarchical world of eighteenth-century British North America.

Religion, Enlightenment, and Revival

Eighteenth-century colonists could choose from almost as many religions as consumer goods. Virtually all of the bewildering variety of religious denominations represented some form of Christianity, almost all of them Protestant. Slaves made up the largest group of non-Christians. A few slaves converted to Christianity in Africa or after they arrived in North America, but most continued to embrace elements of indigenous African religions. Roman Catholics concentrated in Maryland as they had since the seventeenth century, but even there they were outnumbered by Protestants.

The varieties of Protestant faith and practice ranged across an extremely broad spectrum. The thousands of immigrants in the middle colonies and the southern backcountry included militant Baptists and Presbyterians. Huguenots who had fled persecution in Catholic France peopled congregations in several cities. In New England, old-style Puritanism splintered into strands of Congregationalism that differed over fine points of theological doctrine. The Congregational Church was the official established church in New England, and all residents paid taxes for its support. Throughout the plantation South, and in urban centers like Charleston, New York, and Philadelphia, prominent colonists belonged to the Anglican Church. The Anglican Church in the South, like the Congregational Church in New

England, received support in the form of tax monies. But in both regions, dissenting faiths grew, and in most colonies adherents of other faiths won the right to worship publicly, although the established churches retained official sanction.

Many educated colonists became deists, looking for God's plan in nature more than in the Bible. Deists shared the ideas of eighteenth-century European Enlightenment thinkers. Representing a multifaceted intellectual movement that challenged many conventional ideas, Enlightenment thinkers tended to agree that science and reason could disclose God's laws in the natural order. In the colonies as well as in Europe, Enlightenment ideas encouraged people to study the world around them, to think for themselves, and to ask whether the disorderly appearance of things masked the principles of a deeper, more profound natural order. From New England towns to southern drawing rooms, individuals met to discuss such matters. Among the purposes of these discussions was to find ways to improve society. Franklin's interest in electricity, stoves, and eyeglasses exemplified the shift of focus among many eighteenth-century colonists from heaven to the here and now.

Most eighteenth-century colonists went to church seldom or not at all, although they probably considered themselves Christians. A minister in Charleston observed that on the Sabbath "the Taverns have more Visitants than the Churches." In the leading colonial cities, church members were a small minority of eligible adults, no more than 10 to 15 percent. Anglican parishes in the South rarely claimed more than one-fifth of eligible adults as members. In some regions of rural New England and the middle colonies, church membership embraced two-thirds of eligible adults, while in other areas only one-quarter of the residents belonged to a church. The dominant faith overall was religious indifference.

The spread of religious indifference, of deism, of denominational rivalry, and of comfortable backsliding profoundly concerned many Christians. To combat what one preacher called the "dead formality" of church services, some ministers set out to convert nonbelievers and to revive the piety of the faithful with a new style of preaching that appealed more to the heart than to the head. Historians have termed this wave of revivals the "Great Awakening." In Massachusetts during the mid-1730s, the fiery Puritan minister Jonathan Edwards

GEORGE WHITEFIELD
An anonymous artist portrayed George Whitefield preaching, emphasizing the power of his sermons to transport his audience to a revived awareness of divine spirituality. Light from above gleams off Whitefield's forehead. His crossed eyes and faraway gaze suggest that he spoke in a semihypnotic trance. Note the absence of a Bible at the pulpit. Rather than elaborating on God's word as revealed in Scripture, Whitefield speaks from his own inner awareness. The young woman bathed in light below his hands appears transfixed, her focus not on Whitefield but on some inner realm illuminated by his words. Her eyes and Whitefield's do not meet, yet the artist's use of light suggests that she and Whitefield see the same core of holy Truth. The other people in Whitefield's audience appear not to have achieved this state. They remain intent on Whitefield's words, failing so far to be ignited by the divine spark.
National Portrait Gallery, London.

reaped a harvest of souls by reemphasizing traditional Puritan doctrines of humanity's utter depravity and God's vengeful omnipotence.

The most famous revivalist in the eighteenth-century Atlantic world was George Whitefield. An Anglican, Whitefield preached well-worn messages of sin and salvation to large audiences in England using his spellbinding, unforgettable voice. Whitefield visited the North American colonies seven times, staying for more than three years during the mid-1740s and attracting tens of thousands, including Benjamin Franklin, to his sermons. His preach-

ing transported many in his audience to emotion-choked states of religious ecstasy. About one revival, he wrote, "Some of the people were as pale as death; others were wringing their hands; others lying on the ground; others sinking into the arms of their friends; and most lifting their eyes to heaven, and crying to God for mercy."

Whitefield's successful revivals spawned many lesser imitations. Itinerant preachers, many of them poorly educated, toured the colonial backcountry after midcentury, echoing Whitefield's medium and message as best they could. Educated and established ministers often regarded them with disgust. Bathsheba Kingsley, a member of Jonathan Edwards's flock, preached the revival message informally—as did an unprecedented number of other awakened women throughout the colonies—causing her congregation to brand her a "brawling woman" who had "gone quite *out* of her place." But the revivals nonetheless awakened and refreshed the spiritual energies of thousands of colonists struggling with the uncertainties and anxieties of eighteenth-century America. The conversions at revivals did not substantially boost the total number of church members, however. After the revivalists moved on, the routines and pressures of everyday existence reasserted their primacy in the lives of many converts. But revivals imparted an important message to colonists, both converted and unconverted. They communicated that every soul mattered, that men and women could choose to be saved, that individuals had the power to make a decision for everlasting life or death. Colonial revivals expressed in religious terms many of the same democratic and egalitarian values expressed in economic terms by colonists' patterns of consumption. One colonist noted the analogy by referring to itinerant revivalists as "Pedlars in divinity." Like consumption, revivals contributed to a set of common experiences that bridged colonial divides of faith, region, class, and status.

Bonds of Empire

The plurality of peoples, faiths, and communities that characterized the North American colonies arose from the somewhat haphazard policies of the eighteenth-century British Empire. Since the Puritan Revolution of the mid-seventeenth century, British monarchs had valued the colonies' contributions to trade and encouraged their growth and development. Unlike France—whose policy of excluding Protestants and foreigners kept the population of its territory tiny—Britain kept the door to its colonies open to anyone, and tens of thousands of non-British immigrants settled in the North American colonies and raised families. The open door did not extend to trade, however, as the seventeenth-century Navigation Acts restricted colonial trade to British ships and traders. These policies evolved because they served the interests of the monarchy and of influential groups in England and the colonies, but they gave the colonists a common framework of political expectations and experiences.

At a minimum, British power defended the colonists from foreign enemies. Each colony organized a militia, and privateers sailed from every port to prey on foreign ships. But the British navy and army bore responsibility for colonial defense. Royal officials warily eyed the settlements of New France and New Spain for signs of threats to the colonies. Alone, neither New France nor Spanish Florida jeopardized British North America, but with Indian allies they became a potent force that kept colonists on their guard.

All along the ragged edge of settlement, colonists encountered Indians. Indians' impulse to defend their territory from colonial incursions warred with their desire for trade, which tugged them toward the settlers. The fur trade was the principal medium of exchange between the two groups.

HURON BONNET
This dazzling bonnet illustrates the trade between Native Americans and colonists. Beads of Venetian glass were one of the many items colonists imported from Europe to exchange for animal skins offered by Indian hunters and trappers. Native American women in turn incorporated these European beads into designs they had previously wrought with porcupine quills, shells, and bones. European needle and thread were also used to craft this bonnet. Native American artistry transformed these simple trade goods into a beautiful bonnet useful and valuable among the Huron, who lived near the Great Lakes.
Musée de l'Homme.

To trade for goods manufactured largely by the British, Indians trapped animals throughout the interior, and colonial traders competed for the furs. British officials monitored the trade to prevent French, Spanish, and Dutch competitors from deflecting the flow of hides toward their own markets. Indians took advantage of this competition to improve their own prospects, playing one trader off against another. And Indian tribes and confederacies competed for favored trading rights with one colony or another, a competition colonists encouraged.

The shifting alliances and complex dynamics of the fur trade struck a fragile balance along the frontier. The threat of violence from all sides was ever present, and the threat became reality often enough for all parties to be prepared for the worst. In the Yamasee War of 1715, Yamasee and Creek Indians—with French encouragement—mounted a coordinated attack against colonial settlements in South Carolina and inflicted heavy casualties. The Cherokees, traditional enemies of the Creeks, refused to join the attack. Instead, they protected their access to British trade goods by allying with the colonists and turning the tide of battle, thus triggering a murderous rampage of revenge by the colonists against the Creeks and Yamasees.

Relations between Indians and the colonists differed from colony to colony and from year to year. But the colonists' nagging perceptions of menace on the frontier kept them continually hoping for help from the British in keeping the Indians at bay and in maintaining the essential flow of trade. In 1754, the colonists' endemic competition with the French flared into the French and Indian War, which would inflame the frontier for years (see chapter 6). Before the 1760s, neither the colonists nor the British developed a coherent policy toward Indians. But both agreed that Indians made profitable trading partners, powerful allies, and deadly enemies.

British attempts to exercise political power in colonial governments met with success so long as British officials were on or very near the sea. Colonists acknowledged—although they did not always readily comply with—British authority to collect customs duties, inspect cargoes, and enforce trade regulations. But when royal officials tried to wield their authority on land, in the internal affairs of colonies, they invariably encountered colonial resistance. A governor appointed by the king in each of the nine royal colonies (Rhode Island and Connecticut selected their own governors) or by the proprietors in Maryland and Pennsylvania headed the government of each colony. The British envisioned colonial governors as mini-monarchs able to exert influence in the colonies much as the king did in England. But colonial governors were not kings, and the colonies were not England.

Eighty percent of colonial governors had been born in England, not in the colonies. Some governors stayed in England, close to the source of royal patronage, and delegated the grubby details of colonial affairs to subordinates. Even the best-intentioned colonial governors had difficulty developing relations of trust and respect with influential colonists because their terms of office averaged just five years and could be terminated at any time. In obedience to England, colonial governors fought incessantly with the colonial assemblies. They battled over governors' vetoes of colonial legislation, removal of colonial judges, creation of new courts, dismissal of the representative assemblies, and other local issues. Some governors developed a working relationship with the assemblies. But during the eighteenth century, the assemblies gained the upper hand.

British policies did not clearly define the powers and responsibilities of colonial assemblies. In effect, the assemblies made many of their own rules and established a strong tradition of representative government analogous, in their eyes, to the English Parliament. Voters often returned the same representatives to the assemblies year after year, building continuity in power and leadership that far exceeded that of the governor. By 1720, colonial assemblies had won the power to initiate legislation, including tax laws and authorizations to spend public funds. Although all laws passed by the assemblies (except in Maryland, Rhode Island, and Connecticut) had to be approved by the governor and then by the Board of Trade in England, the difficulties in communication about complex subjects over long distances effectively ratified the assemblies' decisions.

The heated political struggles between royal governors and colonial assemblies that occurred throughout the eighteenth century taught colonists a common set of political lessons. They learned to employ traditionally British ideas of representative government to defend their own interests. They learned that power in the British colonies rarely belonged to the British government.

Conclusion: The Dual Identity of British North American Colonists

During the eighteenth century, a distinctive society emerged in British North America, a society that was both distinctively colonial and distinctively British. Tens of thousands of immigrants and slaves gave the colonies an unmistakably colonial complexion. People of different ethnicities and faiths sought their fortunes in the colonies, where land was cheap, labor was dear, and—as Benjamin Franklin preached—work promised to be rewarding. Indentured servants and redemptioners risked a temporary period of bondage for the potential reward of better opportunities than on the Atlantic's eastern shore. Slaves endured lifetime servitude that they neither chose nor desired but from which their masters greatly benefited.

Identifiably colonial products from New England, the middle colonies, and the southern colonies flowed across the Atlantic. Back came unquestionably British consumer goods along with fashions in ideas, faith, and politics. The bonds of the British Empire required colonists to think of themselves as British subjects and, at the same time, encouraged them to consider their status as colonists.

At midcentury, colonists could not imagine that their distinctively dual identity—as British and as colonists—would soon become a source of intense conflict. But by 1776, colonists in British North America had to choose whether they were British or American.

FOR FURTHER READING ABOUT THE TOPICS IN THIS CHAPTER, see the Online Bibliography at www.bedfordstmartins.com/roarkcompact.

FOR ADDITIONAL FIRST-HAND ACCOUNTS OF THIS PERIOD, see pages 60–77 in Michael Johnson, ed., *Reading the American Past*, Second Edition, Volume I.

TO ASSESS YOUR MASTERY OF THE MATERIAL IN THIS CHAPTER, see the Online Study Guide at www.bedfordstmartins.com/roarkcompact.

CHRONOLOGY

1711 North Carolina founded.

1715 Yamasee War pits South Carolina colonists against Yamasee and Creek Indians.

1717 Scots-Irish immigration to American colonies begins to increase.

1721 *New England Courant* begins publication.

1723 Benjamin Franklin arrives in Philadelphia.

1730s Jonathan Edwards leads New England religious awakening.

1732 Georgia founded.

1733 Benjamin Franklin begins to publish *Poor Richard's Almanack.*

1739 Slave insurrection occurs at Stono, South Carolina.

1740s George Whitefield preaches revival of religion throughout England and British North America.

Majority of southern slaves are born in colonies rather than in Africa.

1741 New York City officials suspect slave conspiracy and execute thirty-one slaves.

1745 Olaudah Equiano born in present-day Nigeria.

1750s Colonists begin to move down Shenandoah Valley from Pennsylvania into southern backcountry.

Colonists increasingly become indebted to English merchants.

1754 French and Indian War begins.

PATRICK HENRY'S MAP DESK

Patrick Henry's father, John Henry of Virginia, was both a county judge and a surveyor, and his son absorbed well the importance of both professions. Patrick studied law, and in 1763, he stunned a courtroom crowd by exclaiming that the king was a tyrant, for voiding an act of the Virginia House of Burgesses relating to ministers' salaries. Shocked onlookers muttered "treason," but the judge in the case—none other than John Henry—allowed his son's incendiary remark to stand. Two years later, Patrick's reputation for brilliant, unrestrained oratory was well established, and his county elected him to the House of Burgesses where he immediately created another sensation, skillfully maneuvering the burgesses into a startling repudiation of British power known as the Virginia Resolves. But Patrick Henry was not a reckless firebrand full-time. His father's surveying and mapmaking skills inclined him to attend to frontier real estate, the sure way to wealth in eighteenth-century Virginia. This map desk sat in Henry's law office. Its fold-out extensions provided support for the large maps required to represent Virginia's vast western land claims. Its light weight allowed Henry to move it near the window with the best light, depending on the time of day and year. Patrick Henry ultimately had seventeen children, fourteen of whom survived to adulthood. Through astute land purchases, he managed to establish each with a landed estate.

Courtesy of Scotchtown, photo by Katherine Wetzel.

THE BRITISH EMPIRE AND THE COLONIAL CRISIS

1754–1775

6

THOMAS HUTCHINSON WAS A FIFTH-GENERATION DESCENDANT of Anne Hutchinson, the woman of conscience who so rattled the Puritan town of Boston in the 1630s. Thomas Hutchinson likewise was a man of conscience, but there the resemblance to his famous ancestor ended. A Harvard-educated member of the Massachusetts elite, from a family of successful merchants, Hutchinson was also a measured and cautious man. "My temper does not incline to enthusiasm," he once wrote.

After serving two decades in the Massachusetts general assembly, Hutchinson was appointed lieutenant governor in 1758, as well as chief justice of the highest court in 1760. In 1771, with Boston politics a powder keg, he agreed to become the royal governor, knowing full well the risks. Despite his family's deep roots in American soil, Hutchinson remained steadfastly loyal to England. His love of order and tradition inclined him to unconditional support of the British Empire, but loyalty was a dangerous choice in Boston after 1765. Hutchinson faced agitated crowds during demonstrations over the Stamp Act, the Townshend duties, the Boston Massacre, and the Boston Tea Party, all landmark events on the road to the American Revolution. Privately, he lamented the stupidity of the British acts that provoked trouble, but his sense of duty required him to defend the king's policies, however misguided. Quickly, he became an inspiring villain to the emerging revolutionary movement. The man not inclined to enthusiasm unleashed popular enthusiasm all around him. He never appreciated that irony.

As early as anyone, Thomas Hutchinson recognized the difficulties of maintaining full rights and privileges for Americans so far from their supreme government, the king and Parliament in England. In 1769, soon after British troops had come to occupy Boston, he wrote privately to a friend in England, "There must be an abridgment of what are called English liberties. . . . I doubt whether it is possible to project a system of government in which a colony three thousand miles distant from the parent state shall enjoy all the liberty of the parent state." What he could not imagine was the possibility of giving up the parent state altogether and creating an independent government closer to home.

Thomas Hutchinson was a loyalist; in the 1750s, most English-speaking colonists were affectionately loyal to England. But the French and Indian War, which England and its colonies fought together as allies, shook that affection, and imperial policies in the decade following the war (1763–1773) shattered it completely. Over the course of that decade, serious questions about American liberties and rights were raised insistently and repeatedly, especially over the issues of taxation and representation. Many on the American side came to believe what

THOMAS HUTCHINSON
The only formal portrait of Thomas Hutchinson still in existence shows an assured young man in ruffles and hair ribbons. Decades of turmoil in Boston failed to puncture his self-confidence. Doubtless he sat for other portraits, as did all the Boston leaders in the 1760s to 1780s, but no other likeness has survived. Hutchinson was hated; any portrait that fell into his enemies' hands would probably have been mutilated.
Courtesy of the Massachusetts Historical Society ©.

Thomas Hutchinson could never credit, that a tyrannical Britain had embarked on a course to enslave the colonists by depriving them of their traditional English liberty. The opposite of liberty was slavery, a condition of unfreedom and of coercion. Political rhetoric about liberty, tyranny, and slavery heated up emotions during the many crises of the 1760s and 1770s. But this rhetoric turned out to be a two-edged sword. The call for an end to tyrannical slavery meant one thing when sounded by Boston merchants whose commercial shipping rights had been revoked; the same call meant something quite different when sounded by black Americans in 1775, locked in the bondage of perpetual slavery.

The French and Indian War, 1754–1763

For nearly half of the first fifty years of the eighteenth century, England was at war intermittently, with either France or Spain. Often the colonists in America experienced reverberations from these conflicts, most acutely along the French frontier in northern New England. In the 1750s, tensions mounted again, but this time over events originating in America. The conflict involved contested land in the Ohio valley, variously claimed by Virginians, by Pennsylvanians, by the French in Canada—and of course by the Indians living on that land. The result was the costly French and Indian War, which first brought the British and Americans together as allies but then began to split them over questions of war-related expenses.

French-English Rivalry in the Ohio Valley

In 1753, French soldiers advanced from Canada south into Indian territory in the Ohio valley, a region encompassing present-day western Pennsylvania and eastern Ohio. For more than a decade, the French had cultivated alliances with the Indian tribes there, cementing their relationship with trade and gifts. But in the late 1740s, aggressive Pennsylvania traders pushed into the Ohio valley and began to poach on their business, underselling French goods and threatening to reorient Indian loyalties. In response, the French began building a series of forts, hoping to create a western barrier to British-American expansion.

Ohio River Valley, 1753

The same region was also claimed by Virginia, and in 1747, a group of wealthy Virginians, including the brothers Lawrence and Augustine Washington, formed the Ohio Company and obtained a large land grant from the English king. The Virginians were interested in profits from the even-

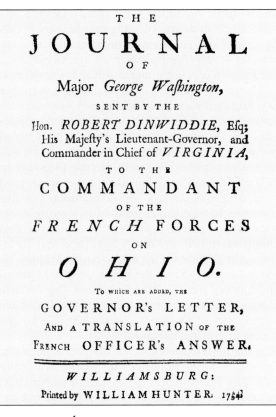

THE

JOURNAL

OF

Major *George Wafhington,*

SENT BY THE

Hon. *ROBERT DINWIDDIE,* Efq;
His Majefty's Lieutenant-Governor, and
Commander in Chief of *VIRGINIA,*

TO THE

COMMANDANT

OF THE

FRENCH FORCES

ON

O H I O.

To WHICH ARE ADDED, THE

GOVERNOR's LETTER,

AND A TRANSLATION OF THE

FRENCH OFFICER's ANSWER,

WILLIAMSBURG:

Printed by WILLIAM HUNTER. 1754.

WASHINGTON'S JOURNAL, 1754
*When George Washington returned from his first
mission to the French, Governor Dinwiddie asked
him to write a full report of what he had seen of the
countryside, of the Indians, and of French troop
strength. Washington obliged, writing about 7,000
words in less than two days (about equivalent to a
25-page double-spaced typescript paper of today). He
coolly narrated scenes of personal danger: of traveling in deep snow and freezing temperatures, of
falling off a raft into an icy river, of being shot at by
a lone Indian. Dinwiddie printed Washington's report, along with his own letter and the French commander's defiant answer, in a 32-page pamphlet;
shortly thereafter it was reprinted in London. The
governor's aim was to inform Virginians and British
leaders about the French threat in the west. But the
pamphlet suited Washington's aims as well: at age
22, he was now known on both sides of the Atlantic
for resolute and rugged courage.*
Huntington Library.

tual resale of the land; the British government was
more interested in blocking the French. By 1753, the
enterprising Virginians had built a trading post near

present-day Pittsburgh. The royal governor of
Virginia, Robert Dinwiddie, himself a shareholder
in the Ohio Company, sent a messenger to warn the
French that they were trespassing on Virginia land.

The messenger on this dangerous mission was
George Washington, younger half-brother of the
Ohio Company leaders. Although he was only
twenty-one, Washington was an ambitious youth
whose imposing height (six feet two) and air of silent
competence convinced the governor he could do the
job. The middle child in a family of eight, Washington did not stand to inherit great wealth, so he
sought to gain public reputation and impress the
Virginia elite by volunteering for this perilous duty.

Washington returned from his mission with
crucial intelligence about French military plans. Impressed, Dinwiddie appointed the youth to lead a
small military force to chase off the adversaries.
Washington went west with several hundred soldiers and met bitter defeat by French troops. Thus
began the French and Indian War, as well as young
Washington's military career. By 1756, the war had
escalated to include a half dozen countries. In
Europe, it would be known as the Seven Years' War,
after it concluded in 1763. But for Americans, with
their two-year head start, it actually lasted nine
years.

The Albany Congress and Intercolonial Defense

To succeed in even a limited war, the British needed
help from the colonists as well as support, or at least
neutrality, from the Indians. Colonies from Virginia
northward were instructed to send delegates to a
meeting in Albany, New York. One goal of the
Albany Congress was to form an intercolonial
agency to coordinate the mutual defense of the
colonies. A second and perhaps more crucial goal
was to woo with gifts and promises selected tribes
of the powerful Iroquois Nation of western New
York.

In June 1754, twenty-four delegates from seven
colonies met in Albany, among them Benjamin
Franklin of Pennsylvania and Thomas Hutchinson
of Massachusetts. These two men, both rising political stars in their home colonies, coauthored a
document, the Albany Plan of Union, which proposed a unified but limited administration over all
the colonies. A president general, appointed by the
crown, together with a grand council, would have
powers only over defense and Indian affairs. The

Albany Plan humbly reaffirmed Parliament's authority; this was no bid for enlarged autonomy of the colonies.

To Franklin's surprise, not a single colony approved the Albany Plan. The Massachusetts assembly feared it was "a Design of gaining power over the Colonies," especially the power of taxation. Others objected that it would be impossible to agree on unified policies toward hundreds of quite different Indian tribes. Oddly enough, the British government never backed the Albany Plan either, which perplexed both Franklin and Hutchinson, who were earnestly trying to solidify British authority. Many years later, after the Revolution, Franklin wistfully reflected that if the Albany Plan "had been adopted and carried into Execution, the subsequent Separation of the Colonies from the Mother Country might not so soon have happened."

Representatives of the Iroquois League, embracing the Seneca, Mohawk, Onondaga, Cayuga, Oneida, and Tuscarora tribes, also attended the Albany Congress. They collected thirty wagon loads of gifts and made ambiguous promises to the colonists, but left without pledging to fight the French. The Iroquois preferred to stall and play off the English against the French, for their interests were best served by being on the winning side, which in 1754 looked to be the French.

The War and Its Consequences

By 1755, Washington's frontier skirmish had turned into a major mobilization of British and American troops against the French. At first, the British hoped for quick victory by throwing armies at the French in three strategic places. General Edward Braddock from England was to attack the French at Fort Duquesne in western Pennsylvania, accompanied by George Washington's Virginia militia. In Massachusetts, Governor William Shirley aimed his soldiers at Fort Niagara, critically located between Lakes Erie and Ontario. And finally, forces under William Johnson of New York moved north toward Lake Champlain to push the French back to Canada (Map 6.1).

Unfortunately for the British, the French were prepared to fight. In July 1755, General Braddock's army of 2,000 British and Virginian troops was ambushed by a combined French and Indian force a day short of their march to Fort Duquesne, leaving 976 killed or wounded. Washington was unhurt, though two horses in succession were shot from under him; Braddock was killed. Despite the humiliation of defeat, Washington's bravery in battle caused the governor to promote him to commander of the Virginia army. At age twenty-two, Washington was beginning to realize his ambitions.

News of Braddock's defeat alarmed the other two British armies, then hacking their way through dense New York forests, and they retreated from action. For the next two years, the British stumbled badly on the American front, with inadequate soldiers and supplies. But with the rise to power in 1757 of William Pitt in England, the war was turned around. Pitt's strategy of committing massive resources to all-out war resulted in a string of resounding successes, including the capture of Fort Duquesne in 1758 and Fort Niagara and Fort Ticonderoga in 1759. When the British navy advanced up the St. Lawrence River, the French cities of Montreal and Quebec were isolated from help. The decisive victory was the capture of the seemingly invincible fortress city of Quebec in September 1759 by the young British general James Wolfe.

The fall of Quebec broke the backbone of the French in North America. The victory was completed by the surrender of the French at Montreal in late 1760. American colonists rejoiced, but the war was not officially over yet. Battles continued in the Caribbean, where the French sugar islands Martinique and Guadeloupe fell to the English. After further fighting in Europe and India, France and Spain capitulated, and the Treaty of Paris was signed in 1763.

The triumph of victory was sweet but short-lived. The complex peace negotiations reorganized the map of North America but stopped short of providing the full spoils of victory to England. Canada was transferred to England, which eliminated the French threat from the north and west. But all French territory west of the Mississippi River,

---

MAP 6.1

European Areas of Influence and the French and Indian War, 1754–1763
In the mid-eighteenth century, France, England, and Spain claimed vast areas of North America, many of them already inhabited by various Indian peoples. The early flash points of the French and Indian War occurred in regions of disputed claims where the French had allied with powerful native groups—the Iroquois and the Algonquin—to put pressure on the westward-moving English.

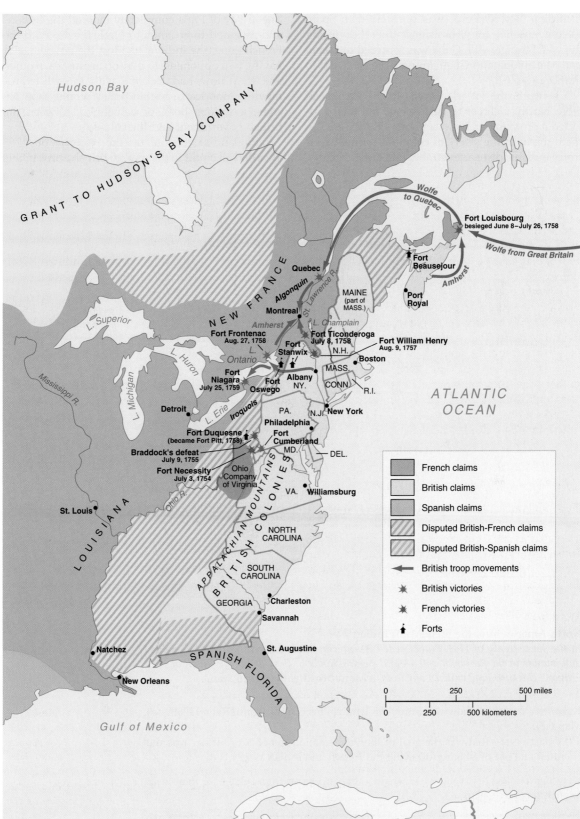

Hudson Bay

GRANT TO HUDSON'S BAY COMPANY

Wolfe
to Quebec

Fort Louisbourg
besieged June 8–July 26, 1758

Wolfe from Great Britain

NEW FRANCE

Quebec

Algonquin

St. Lawrence R.

MAINE
(part of
MASS.)

**Fort
Beausejour**

Amherst

Montreal

L. Superior

Amherst

L. Champlain

**Port
Royal**

Fort Frontenac
Aug. 27, 1758

Fort Ticonderoga
July 8, 1758

Fort William Henry
Aug. 9, 1757

L. Huron

*L.
Ontario*

**Fort
Stanwix**

N.H.

Mississippi R.

L. Michigan

**Fort
Niagara**
July 25, 1759

**Fort
Oswego**

Albany
NY.

Boston

MASS.

CONN.

L. Erie

Iroquois

R.I.

Detroit

ATLANTIC
OCEAN

PA.

N.J.

New York

Fort Duquesne
(became Fort Pitt, 1758)

Philadelphia

**Fort
Cumberland**

Braddock's defeat
July 9, 1755

MD.

DEL.

Fort Necessity
July 3, 1754

Ohio
Company
of Virginia

Ohio R.

VA.

Williamsburg

St. Louis

LOUISIANA

APPALACHIAN MOUNTAINS

BRITISH COLONIES

NORTH
CAROLINA

SOUTH
CAROLINA

	French claims
	British claims
	Spanish claims
	Disputed British-French claims
	Disputed British-Spanish claims
←	British troop movements
✳	British victories
✳	French victories
⚑	Forts

GEORGIA

Charleston

Savannah

Natchez

SPANISH FLORIDA

St. Augustine

New Orleans

0		250		500 miles
0	250	500 kilometers		

Gulf of Mexico

including New Orleans, was transferred to Spain as compensation for its assistance to France during the war. Stranger still, Cuba was returned to Spain, and Martinique and Guadeloupe were returned to France (Map 6.2).

In truth, the French islands in the Caribbean were hardly a threat to Americans, for they provided a profitable trade in smuggled molasses. The main threat to the safety of colonists came instead from Indians disheartened by England's victory.

The Treaty of Paris completely ignored the Indians and assigned their lands to English rule. With the French gone, the Indians had lost the advantage of having two opponents to play off against each other, and they now had to cope with the westward-moving Americans. Indian policy would soon become a serious bone of contention between the British government and the colonists.

England's version of the victory of 1763 awarded all credit to the mighty British army. In this

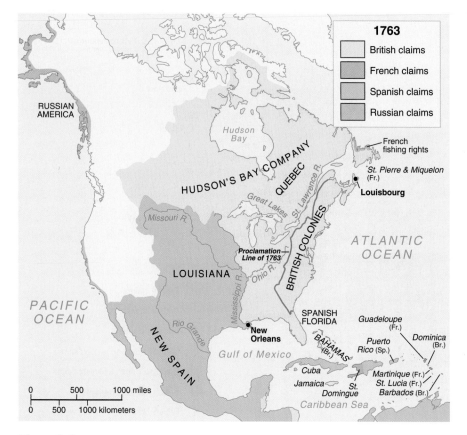

MAP 6.2

North America after the French and Indian War

In the peace treaty of 1763, France ceded its interior lands but retained fishing rights and islands in the far north and several sugar islands in the Caribbean. Much of France's claim to land called Louisiana went not to England but to Spain.

READING THE MAP: How did European land claims change from 1750 to 1763 (see Map 6.1)?

CONNECTIONS: What was the goal of the Proclamation Act of 1763? What was the eventual fate of Louisbourg following the French and Indian War?

www.bedfordstmartins.com/roarkcompact   SEE THE ONLINE STUDY GUIDE for more help in analyzing these maps.

version, ungrateful colonists had provided inadequate support for a war fought to save them from the French. In defiance of British law, colonists had engaged in smuggling, notably a lively trade in beaver pelts with French fur traders and an illegal molasses trade in the Caribbean. American traders, grumbled the British leaders, were really traitors. William Pitt was convinced that the illegal trade "principally, if not alone, enabled France to sustain and protract this long and expensive war."

Colonists read the lessons of the war differently. American provincial soldiers had turned out in force, they claimed, but the troops had been relegated to grunt work by arrogant British military leaders. General Braddock had foolishly bragged to Benjamin Franklin that "these savages may, indeed, be a formidable enemy to your raw American militia, but upon the king's regular and disciplined troops, sir, it is impossible they should make any impression." Braddock's defeat "gave us Americans," Franklin wrote, "the first suspicion that our exalted ideas of the prowess of British regulars had not been well founded."

The human costs of the war were also etched sharply in the minds of New England colonists, who had contributed most of the colonial troops. About one-third of all Massachusetts men between age fifteen and thirty had seen service. Many families lost loved ones, and this cost would not soon be forgotten. The enormous expense of the war caused by Pitt's no-holds-barred military strategy cast another huge shadow over the victory. By 1763, England's national debt, double what it had been when Pitt took office, posed a formidable challenge to the next decade of leadership in England. At the heart of the matter was disagreement about the relative responsibility the colonists should bear in helping to pay off that debt.

Tightening the Bonds of Empire

Throughout the 1760s, inconsistent leadership in England pursued a hodgepodge of policies toward the colonies. A new and inexperienced king gained the throne in 1760, and he spent the next ten years searching for a prime minister he could trust. Nearly half a dozen ministers in succession took their turns formulating policies designed to address one basic, underlying British reality: A huge war

debt needed to be serviced, and the colonists, as British subjects, should expect to pay. From the American side, however, these policies deeply violated what colonists perceived to be their rights and liberties as British subjects.

British Leadership and the Indian Question

In 1760, in the middle of the French and Indian War, George III, age twenty-two, came to the British throne, underprepared for his monarchical duties. The previous king, George II, was his grandfather;

MOHAWK WARRIOR
This rear view of a Mohawk warrior highlights clothes and body decoration: arm and ankle bracelets, earrings, a hair ornament, and body paint. The English watercolor artist includes an important element of frontal display—the warrior's tomahawk.
Musée du Nouveau Monde, Hotel Fleuriau, La Rochelle.

his father's death, when young George was thirteen, thrust the boy suddenly into the role of heir apparent. Timid and insecure, the new King George trusted only his tutor, the earl of Bute, a Scotsman who was an outsider to power circles in London. George III immediately installed Bute as head of his cabinet of ministers. Bute made blunders and did not last long, but in his short time in office he made one very significant decision—to keep a standing army in the colonies. In terms of money and political tension, this was a costly move.

The ostensible reason for keeping ten thousand British troops in America was to maintain the peace between the colonists and the Indians. This was not a misplaced concern. The defeat and withdrawal of the French from North America had left their Indian allies—who did not accept defeat—in suspension. Just three months after the Treaty of Paris was signed, Pontiac, chief of the Ottawa tribe in the northern Ohio region, attacked the British garrison near Detroit in late April 1763. Quickly, six more attacks on forts occurred; American settlements were also hit. Joining the Ottawa were tribes from western New York, the Ohio valley, and the Great Lakes region: the Chippewa, Huron, Potawatomi, Miami, Kickapoo, Mascouten, Wea, Shawnee, Mingo, Delaware, and Seneca tribes. By fall, these dozen tribes had captured every fort west of Detroit; more than four hundred British soldiers were dead, and another two thousand colonists had been killed or taken captive. Pontiac's uprising was quelled finally in December 1763 by the combined efforts of British and colonial soldiers, plus the realization that French aid to the Indians would not materialize. Pontiac later said to the British, "All my young men have buried their hatchets."

The potential for continued and costly wars with the Indians, so well illustrated by Pontiac's uprising, caused the British government to issue an order called the Proclamation Act of 1763, which forbade colonists to settle west of a line drawn from Canada to Georgia along the crest of the Appalachian Mountains. The line promised to protect

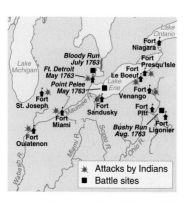

Pontiac's Rebellion, 1763

not only the Indians but also the lucrative fur trade, now in British rather than French hands. But the pressure of population growth meant that the proclamation line would be very difficult to enforce. Settlers had already moved west of the line, as had land speculators, such as those of Virginia's Ohio Company, who stood to lose opportunities for profitable resale of their claims. Bute's decision to leave a standing army in the colonies was thus a cause for concern for western settlers and eastern speculators alike.

Growing Resentment of British Authority

The mission of George Grenville, the king's next chief minister, was to tackle the problem of the war debt, which in 1763 amounted to £123 million, a shockingly high figure. To find increased revenue, Grenville first scrutinized the customs service, a division of the government responsible for monitoring the flow of ships and collecting duties on specified trade items in both England and America. Grenville found that customs officers' salaries cost the government four times what was collected in revenue. The shortfall was due in part to bribery and smuggling, and so Grenville began to insist on rigorous attention to paperwork and a strict accounting of collected duties.

The hardest duty for Grenville to enforce was the one imposed by the Molasses Act of 1733—a stiff tax of six pence per gallon on any molasses purchased from non-British sources. The purpose of the tax was to discourage trade with French Caribbean islands and redirect the molasses trade to British sugar islands. But it did not work: French molasses remained cheap and abundant because French planters on Martinique and Guadeloupe had no use for it. A by-product of sugar production, molasses was a key ingredient in making rum, a drink the French scorned. Rum-loving Americans were eager to buy French molasses, and they ignored the tax law for decades.

Grenville's ingenious solution to this problem was the Revenue Act of 1764, popularly dubbed the Sugar Act. It lowered the duty on French molasses to three pence, making it more attractive for shippers to obey the law, and at the same time raised penalties for smuggling. The act appeared to be in the tradition of navigation acts, meant to regulate trade, but Grenville's actual intent was to raise revenue. He was using an established form of law for new ends, and he was doing it by the novel means of lowering a duty.

The Sugar Act set out tougher enforcement policies. From now on, all British naval crews could act as impromptu customs officers, boarding suspicious ships and seizing cargoes found to be in violation. Smugglers caught without proper paperwork would be prosecuted, not in a friendly civil court with a local jury, but in a vice-admiralty court located in Halifax, Nova Scotia, where a single judge presided without a jury. The implication was that justice would be more sure and severe.

Grenville hoped that his tightening of the customs service and the lowered duties of the Sugar Act would reform American smugglers into law-abiding shippers and in turn generate income for the empire. Unfortunately, the decrease in duty was not sufficient to offset the attractions of smuggling. The vigilant customs officers made bribery harder to accomplish, and several ugly confrontations occurred in port cities. Reaction to the Sugar Act foreshadowed questions about England's right to tax Americans, but in 1764 objections to the act came principally from Americans in the shipping trades inconvenienced by the law.

From the British point of view, the 1763 Proclamation Act and the Sugar Act seemed to be reasonable efforts to administer the colonies. To the Americans, however, the British supervision appeared to be a disturbing intrusion into colonial practices.

The Stamp Act Crisis, 1765

By his second year in office, Grenville had made almost no dent in the national debt. Continued evasion prevented the Sugar Act from becoming the moneymaker he had hoped it would be. So in February 1765, he escalated his revenue program with the Stamp Act, which precipitated the first major conflict between England and the colonies over Parliament's right to tax.

Taxation and Consent

The Stamp Act imposed a tax on paper used for various colonial documents—newspapers, pamphlets, court documents, licenses, wills, ships' bills of lading—and required that a special stamp be affixed

TAX ASSESSMENT BOOK *American colonists routinely paid property taxes to local authorities. This 1772 tax book from Rowley, Massachusetts, records amounts due in pounds, shillings, and pence. The several entries for each name indicate assessments on real estate, personal property, and a poll (per head) tax. Notice that two women identified as Mrs. owe taxes. Since married women by law owned no property, we can conclude that these were widows. What do you think the seven large X marks meant? Why might "Capt Samuel Pike" lack one?* Chicago Historical Society.

to the paper proving that the tax had been paid. While the Sugar Act regulated trade, the Stamp Act was designed plainly and simply to raise money. It affected nearly everyone who used any official paper, but it fell heaviest on the business and legal communities, whose repeated use of documents would now tax them the most.

Grenville was no fool; anticipating that the stamp tax would be unpopular—Thomas Hutchinson had forewarned him—he delegated the administration of the act to Americans, to avoid the problem of hostility to British enforcers. In each colony, local stamp distributors would be hired at a handsome salary of 8 percent of the revenue collected.

The colonists already paid taxes to support their local governments, but the taxing bodies were always the colonial assemblies, composed of elected representatives. English tradition held that taxation was a gift of the people to the king offered by the people's representatives. This view of taxes, as a freely given gift, preserved an essential concept of English political theory, the idea that citizens have the liberty to enjoy and use their property without fear of confiscation. The king could not simply demand money; only the House of Commons could grant it. Grenville quite agreed with the notion of taxation by consent, but he argued that the colonists were already "virtually" represented in Parliament; the House of Commons represented all British subjects, wherever they were. Colonial leaders emphatically rejected this British view, arguing that virtual representation could not withstand the stretch across the Atlantic. The stamp tax itself illustrated the problem, levied by a distant Parliament on unwilling colonies. "The MINISTER'S *virtual representation* in Support of the TAX on us is fantastical and frivolous," Maryland inhabitants complained.

Resistance Strategies and Crowd Politics

The Stamp Act was to take effect on November 1, 1765. News of its passage arrived in the colonies in April 1765, leaving colonial leaders seven months to contemplate a response. Colonial governors were unlikely to challenge the law, since most of them owed their office to the king. Instead, the colonial assemblies took the lead; eight of them held discussions on objections to the Stamp Act.

Virginia's assembly was the first to object to the Stamp Act. At the very end of the May 1765 session,

when two-thirds of the members had already gone home, a twenty-nine-year-old lawyer and political newcomer named Patrick Henry presented a series of resolutions on the Stamp Act that were debated and passed, one by one. They came to be called the Virginia Resolves.

Henry's successive resolutions inched the assembly toward radical opposition to the Stamp Act. The first three resolutions stated the obvious: that Virginians were British citizens, that they enjoyed the same rights and privileges as Britons, and that self-taxation was one of those rights. The fourth resolution noted that Virginians had always taxed themselves, via their representatives in the House of Burgesses. The fifth took the radical leap, by pushing the other four unexceptional statements to one logical conclusion—that the Virginia assembly alone had the sole right to tax Virginians.

Two more fiery resolutions were debated, but majority support eroded as Henry pressed the logic of his case to the extreme. The sixth resolution denied legitimacy to any tax law originating outside Virginia, and a seventh boldly called anyone who disagreed with these propositions an enemy of Virginia. This was too much for the burgesses. They backed away from resolutions six and seven and later rescinded their vote on number five as well.

Their caution hardly mattered, however, because newspapers in other colonies printed all seven Virginia Resolves, creating the impression that a daring first challenge to the Stamp Act had taken place in Virginia. This made it easier for other assemblies to consider more radical questions, such as: By what authority could Parliament legislate for the colonies without also taxing them? No one disagreed, in 1765, that Parliament had legislative power over the colonists, who were, after all, British subjects. Several assemblies advanced the argument that there was a distinction between *external* taxes, imposed to regulate trade, and *internal* taxes, such as a stamp tax or a property tax, which could only be self-imposed.

Reaction to the Stamp Act ran far deeper than the politicians in assemblies. Every person whose livelihood required the use of official paper had to decide whether to comply with the act. Hence, local communities strategized their responses. Should they boycott all paper use? While this kept noncompliance within the law, it also was very inconvenient; if enough people ceased using stamped paper, the information network of newspapers, the legal system, and the world of trade might grind to a halt. Should they defy the law and conduct business as usual on unstamped paper, running the risk of fines or jail? A third strategy promised the surest success: to destroy the stamped paper or prevent its distribution at the source, before the law took effect, thus ensuring universal noncompliance.

The first organized resistance to the Stamp Act began in Boston, under the leadership of Samuel Adams, at forty-three a town politician with a history of opposition to then Lieutenant Governor Thomas Hutchinson. Unlike Hutchinson, Adams cared nothing for status, high office, or fine material goods. He was the Harvard-educated son of a Boston brewer, a man with shrewd political instincts and gift for organizing. He mobilized numbers of shopkeepers, master craftsmen, dockworkers, and laborers into a group of protestors who called themselves—and anyone who joined them—the Sons of Liberty.

The plan hatched by Samuel Adams and others called for a large street demonstration highlighting a ritualized mock execution, designed to convince Andrew Oliver, the stamp distributor, that his personal safety would best be served by resigning. With no stamp distributor, no stamps could be sold. On the morning of August 14, 1765, an effigy (stuffed dummy) of Oliver was found hanging from a tree. The royal governor of Massachusetts, Francis Bernard, took no action, in an effort to keep tensions under control. By evening, a large crowd of two to three thousand people paraded the effigy around town, using it as a prop in short plays demonstrating the dangers of selling stamps before beheading and burning it. The crowd also pulled down a small building on Oliver's dock, reported to be the future stamp office. The flesh-and-blood Oliver stayed in hiding; the next day he resigned his office in a well-publicized announcement.

There were lessons from the August 14 demonstration for everyone. Oliver learned that stamp distributors would be very unpopular people. Bernard and Hutchinson learned the limitations of their own powers to govern, with no police to call on. The demonstration's leaders learned that street action was very effective. And hundreds of laborers, sailors, and apprentices not only learned what the Stamp Act was all about but also gained pride in their ability to have a decisive impact on politics.

Twelve days later, a second crowd action, more properly termed a riot, showed just how well some of these lessons had been learned. On August 26, a crowd visited the houses of four detested officials.

SAMUEL ADAMS BY JOHN COPLEY
Samuel Adams consented to pose for Boston artist John Singleton Copley in 1770. The portrait highlights Adams's face, which projects a dramatic intensity and dominates the bulky body, subdued by dark clothes. Adams stares thoughtfully and silently at the viewer and points to important legal documents before him, including the Massachusetts charter of 1689. Wealthy merchant John Hancock commissioned the portrait, which hung in his house. Copley painted scores of Boston's leaders in the 1760s, both loyalists and patriots. He maintained neutrality until 1773, when his father-in-law became an official East India tea distributor. Copley's home was threatened by a crowd, and he left for England in 1774.
Deposited by the City of Boston, Museum of Fine Arts, Boston.

One was a customs officer and two others were officers of the admiralty courts, where smugglers were tried; the crowd broke windows and raided wine cellars. The fourth house was the finest dwelling in Massachusetts, owned by the stiff-necked Thomas Hutchinson. Rumors abounded that Hutchinson had urged Grenville to adopt the Stamp Act. In fact, he had done the opposite, but he refused to set the record straight, saying curtly, "I am not obliged to give an answer to all the questions that may be put me by every lawless person." The crowd attacked his house, and by daybreak only the exterior walls were standing.

The destruction of Hutchinson's house brought a temporary halt to crowd activities in Boston. The Boston town meeting issued a statement of sympathy; but a reward of £300 for the arrest and conviction of riot organizers failed to produce a single lead. The Sons of Liberty denied planning the event.

Essentially, the opponents of the Stamp Act in Boston had won the day; no one volunteered to replace Oliver as distributor. When November 1 arrived, the day the Stamp Act took effect, customs officers were unable to prevent ships from passing through the harbor without properly stamped clearance papers.

Liberty and Property

Boston's crowd actions of August sparked similar eruptions by groups calling themselves Sons of Liberty in virtually every colony, and stamp distributors everywhere hastened to resign. One Connecticut distributor was forced by a crowd to throw his hat and powdered wig in the air while shouting a cheer for "Liberty and property!" This man fared better than the stamp agent who was nearly buried alive by Sons of Liberty. Only when the thuds of dirt sounded on the coffin did he have a sudden change of heart, shouting out his resignation to the crowd above. In Charleston, South Carolina, the stamp distributor resigned after crowds burned effigies and chanted "Liberty! Liberty!"

Some colonial leaders, disturbed about the riots, hastened to mount a more moderate challenge to Parliamentary authority. Twenty-seven delegates representing nine colonial assemblies met in New York City in October 1765 as the Stamp Act Congress. For two weeks the men hammered out a petition about taxation addressed to the king and Parliament. Their statement closely resembled the first five Virginia Resolves, claiming taxes were "free gifts of the people" that only the people's representatives could give. They dismissed virtual representation: "The people of these colonies are not, and from their local circumstances, cannot be represented in the House of Commons." But the delegates also took great care to affirm their subordination to Parliament and monarch in deferential language. Nevertheless, the Stamp Act Congress, by the mere fact of its meeting, advanced a radi-

cal potential, the notion of intercolonial political action.

The rallying cry "Liberty and property" made perfect sense to many white Americans of all social ranks, who feared that the Stamp Act threatened their traditional right to liberty as British subjects. The opposite of liberty was slavery, the condition of being under the control of someone else. Civil society required some interference in perfect freedom in the form of laws, but Englishmen preserved liberty by making sure that only representative governments passed the laws. Up to 1765, Americans consented to accept Parliament as a body that in some way represented them, at least for purposes of legislation. But the right to own property was a special kind of liberty, requiring even stricter safeguards. This was why the tradition arose that only a representative body could tax British subjects.

To Americans, the Stamp Act violated this principle of liberty and property, and some Americans began to speak and write about a plot by British leaders to enslave them. A Maryland writer warned that if the colonies lost "the right of exemption from all taxes without their consent," that loss would "deprive them of every privilege distinguishing freemen from slaves." The opposite meanings of liberty and slavery were utterly clear to white Americans, but they stopped short of applying similar logic to the one million black Americans they held in bondage. Many blacks, however, could see the contradiction. When a crowd of Charleston blacks paraded with shouts of "Liberty!" just a few months after white Sons of Liberty had done the same, the town militia turned out to break up the demonstration.

Politicians and merchants in England reacted with alarm to the American demonstrations and petitions. Merchants particularly feared trade disruptions and pressured Parliament to repeal the Stamp Act. By late 1765, yet another new minister, the marquess of Rockingham, headed the king's cabinet. His dilemma was to find a dignified way to repeal the act that did not yield to the Americans' claim that Parliament could not tax them. The solution came in March 1766: The Stamp Act was repealed, but with it came the Declaratory Act, which asserted Parliament's right to legislate for the colonies "in all cases whatsoever." Perhaps the stamp tax had been inexpedient, but the power to tax—one prime case of a legislative power—was stoutly upheld.

The Townshend Acts and Economic Retaliation, 1767–1770

Rockingham did not last long as prime minister. By the summer of 1766, George III had persuaded William Pitt to resume that role. Pitt then appointed Charles Townshend to be chancellor of the exchequer, the chief financial minister. Townshend faced both the old war debt problem and the continuing cost of stationing the British army in America, and he turned again to taxation. But Townshend's knowledge of the developing political climate in the colonies was unfortunately limited; his simple idea to raise revenue turned into a major mistake.

The Townshend Duties

Townshend proposed new taxes in the old form of a navigation act. Officially called the Revenue Act of 1767, it established new duties on tea, glass, lead, paper, and painters' colors imported into the colonies, to be paid by the importer but passed on to consumers in the retail price. A year before, the duty on French molasses had been reduced from three pence down to one pence per gallon, and finally the Sugar Act was pulling in a tidy revenue of about £45,000 annually. So it was not unreasonable to suppose that duties on additional trade goods might also improve the cash flow. Townshend assumed that external taxes—that is, duties levied on the transatlantic trade—would be more acceptable to Americans than internal taxes, such as the stamp tax.

The Townshend duties were not especially burdensome, but the principle they embodied— taxation extracted through trade duties—looked different to the colonists now, in the wake of the Stamp Act crisis. If Americans once distinguished between external and internal taxes, that distinction was wiped out by an external tax meant only to raise money. John Dickinson, a Philadelphia lawyer, articulated this view in a series of articles titled *Letters from a Farmer in Pennsylvania*, widely reprinted in the winter of 1767–68. "We are taxed without our consent. . . . We are therefore—SLAVES," Dickinson wrote, calling for "a total denial of the power of Parliament to lay upon these colonies any 'tax' whatever."

A controversial provision of the Townshend duties directed that some of the revenue generated would be used to pay the salaries of royal governors. Before 1767, local assemblies set the salaries of their own officials, giving them significant influence over crown-appointed officeholders. Townshend wanted to strengthen the governors' position, as well as to curb the growing independence of the assemblies.

In New York, for example, the assembly had refused to enforce a British rule of 1765 called the Quartering Act, which directed the colonies to furnish shelter and provisions for the British army. The assembly argued that the Quartering Act was really a tax measure because it required New Yorkers to pay money by order of Parliament. Townshend came down hard on the New York assembly: He orchestrated a parliamentary order, the New York Suspending Act, which declared all the assembly's acts null and void until it met its obligations to the army. Both these measures—the new way to pay royal governors' salaries and the suspension of the governance functions of the New York assembly— struck a chill throughout the colonies. Many wondered if legislative government was at all secure.

The Massachusetts assembly took the lead in protesting the Townshend duties. Samuel Adams, now a member from Boston, argued that any form of parliamentary taxation was unjust because Americans were not represented in Parliament. The assembly circulated a letter with Adams's arguments to other colonial assemblies and urged their endorsement. As with the Stamp Act Congress of 1765, colonial assemblies were starting to coordinate their protests.

In response to Adams's letter, the new man in charge of colonial affairs in Britain, Lord Hillsborough, instructed the Massachusetts governor, Francis Bernard, to dissolve the assembly if it refused to rescind its statement. The assembly refused, by a vote of 92 to 17, and Governor Bernard carried out his instruction. In the summer of 1768, Boston was in an uproar.

Nonconsumption and the Daughters of Liberty

The Boston town meeting had already passed resolutions, termed "nonconsumption agreements," calling for a boycott of British-made goods. Dozens of other towns passed similar resolutions in 1767 and 1768. For example, prohibited purchases in the town of New Haven, Connecticut, included carriages, furniture, hats, clothing, shoes, lace, iron plate, clocks, jewelry, toys, textiles, malt liquors, and cheese. The idea was to encourage home manufacture of such items and to hurt trade with Britain, causing London merchants to pressure Parliament for repeal of the duties.

But nonconsumption agreements were very hard to enforce. With the Stamp Act, there was one hated item, a stamp, and a limited number of official distributors. In contrast, an agreement to boycott all British goods required serious personal sacrifice. Some merchants were wary of nonconsumption because it hurt their pocketbooks, and a few con-

EDENTON TEA LADIES
American women in many communities renounced British apparel and tea during the early 1770s. Women in Edenton, North Carolina, publicized their pledge and drew hostile fire in the form of a British cartoon. The cartoon's message is that brazen women who meddle in politics will undermine their femininity. Neglected babies, urinating dogs, wanton sexuality, and mean-looking women are some of the dire consequences, according to the artist. The cartoon works as humor for the British because of the gender inversions it predicts and because of the insult it poses to American men.
Library of Congress.

tinued to import in readiness for the end of nonconsumption (or to sell on the side to people choosing to ignore nonconsumption). In Boston, such merchants found themselves blacklisted in newspapers and broadsides.

A more direct blow to trade came from nonimportation agreements, but it proved even more difficult to get merchants to agree to these. There was always the risk that merchants in other colonies might continue to trade and thus receive handsome profits if neighboring colonies prohibited trade. Not until late 1768 could Boston merchants agree to suspend trade through a nonimportation agreement lasting from January 1, 1769, to January 1, 1770. Sixty signed the agreement. New York merchants soon followed suit, as did Philadelphia and Charleston merchants in 1769.

Doing without British products, either luxury goods or basics such as tea or textiles, no doubt was a hardship. But it also presented an opportunity, for many of the British products specified in nonconsumption agreements were household goods traditionally under the control of women. By 1769, male leaders in the patriot cause clearly understood that women's cooperation in nonconsumption and home manufacture was essential. The Townshend duties thus provided an unparalleled opportunity for developing and showcasing female patriotism. During the Stamp Act crisis, Sons of Liberty took to the streets in protest. During the difficulties of 1768–1769, the Daughters of Liberty emerged to give shape to a new idea—that women could play a role in public affairs.

Any woman could express affiliation with the colonial protest by boycotting goods and taking up home manufacture of items previously imported from England. Women in at least three towns met together to sign their own nonconsumption agreements. In Boston, over three hundred women signed a petition to abstain from tea, "sickness excepted." A nine-year-old girl visiting the royal governor's house in New Jersey took the tea she was offered, curtsied, and tossed the beverage out a nearby window. Homespun cloth also became a prominent symbol of patriotism, with dozens of towns organizing public "frolics" or bees where women competed in spinning and weaving. Cloth making was no longer simply a family chore but a task invested with political content. A Connecticut girl who spun ten knots of wool in one day proclaimed in her journal that her work made her feel "Nationly." On the whole, the year of boycotts was a success. British imports fell by more than 40 percent, and British merchants felt the pinch.

Military Occupation and "Massacre" in Boston

By summer 1768, Boston's royal officials felt alarm. On August 15, a rollicking anniversary celebration of the Stamp Act demonstration of 1765 put crowds in the street and apprehension in the hearts of Governor Bernard and Lieutenant Governor Hutchinson. With no police force and no reasonable hope of controlling the town militia, Bernard concluded that he needed British soldiers to keep the peace.

In the fall, three thousand uniformed troops arrived to occupy Boston. The soldiers drilled conspicuously on the Common, played loud music on the Sabbath, and in general grated on the nerves of Bostonians. Although the situation was frequently tense, no major troubles occurred during that winter and through most of 1769. But as January 1 approached, marking the end of the nonimportation agreement, it was clear that some

merchants could no longer be kept in line. Thomas Hutchinson's two sons, for example, were both importers hostile to the boycott, and they had already ordered new goods from England. The early months of 1770 were thus bound to be a conflict-ridden period in Boston.

Serious troubles began in January. The Hutchinson sons' shop was visited by a crowd that smeared "Hillsborough paint," a potent mixture of human excrement and urine, on the door. In mid-February, a crowd surrounded the house of Ebenezer Richardson, a cranky, low-level customs official. When Richardson panicked and fired his musket to scare off the crowd, he accidentally killed a boy. The Sons of Liberty mounted a massive funeral procession to mark this first instance of violent death in the struggle with England.

For the next week, heightened tensions gripped Boston, and frequent brawls occurred. The climax came on Monday evening, March 5, 1770, when a small crowd taunted a soldier guarding the customs house. British Captain Thomas Preston sent a seven-man guard to join the lone sentry. Meanwhile, the hostile crowd grew, and the soldiers raised their

THE BLOODY MASSACRE PERPETRATED IN KING STREET, BOSTON, ON MARCH 5, 1770
This mass-produced engraving by Paul Revere sold for six pence per copy. In this patriot version, the soldiers fire on an unarmed crowd under orders of their captain. The tranquil dog is an artistic device to signal the crowd's peaceful intent; not even a deaf dog could actually hold that pose during the melee. Among the five killed was Crispus Attucks, a black sailor, but Revere shows only whites among the casualties.
Anne S. K. Brown Military Collection, Providence, R.I.

www.bedfordstmartins.com/ roarkcompact See the Online Study Guide for more help in analyzing this image.

loaded muskets in defense. Onlookers threw snowballs and sticks, daring the soldiers to fire. Finally one of the soldiers, hit by some object, pulled his trigger. After a short pause, during which time someone yelled "Fire!" the other soldiers fired as well. Eleven men in the crowd were hit, five of them fatally.

The Boston Massacre, as it quickly became called, was over in minutes. In the immediate aftermath, Hutchinson (now acting governor after Bernard's recall to England) showed courage in confronting the crowd personally, from the balcony of the customs house. By daybreak of March 6, he ordered the removal of the regiments to an island in the harbor to prevent further bloodshed. Hutchinson also jailed Preston and the eight soldiers, as much for their own protection as to appease the townspeople, and promised they would be held for trial.

That trial came in the fall of 1770. The soldiers were defended by two young Boston attorneys, Samuel Adams's cousin John Adams and Josiah Quincy. Because Adams and Quincy had direct ties to the leadership of the Sons of Liberty, their decision to defend the British soldiers at first seems odd. But John Adams was deeply committed to the idea that even unpopular defendants deserve a fair trial. Samuel Adams respected his cousin's decision to take the case, for there was a tactical benefit as well. It showed that the Boston leadership was not lawless but could be seen as defenders of British liberty and law.

The five-day trial, with dozens of witnesses, resulted in acquittal for Preston and for all but two of the soldiers, who were convicted of manslaughter, branded on the thumbs and released. Nothing materialized in the trial to indicate a conspiracy or concerted plan, either by the British or by the leaders of the Sons of Liberty, to provoke trouble. To this day, the question of who was responsible for the Boston Massacre remains obscure.

The Tea Party and the Coercive Acts, 1770–1774

In the same week as the Boston Massacre, yet another new British prime minister, Frederick North, contemplated the decrease in trade caused by the Townshend duties and recommended repeal. A skillful politician, Lord North took office in 1770 and kept it for twelve years; at last King George had stability at the helm. North sought peace with the colonies and prosperity for British merchants, so all the Townshend duties were removed, except the tax on tea, a pointed reminder of Parliament's ultimate power. North hoped to cool tensions without sacrificing principles.

Those few Americans who could not abide the symbolism of the tea tax turned to smuggled Dutch tea. The renewal of trade and the return of cooperation between England and the colonies gave men like Thomas Hutchinson hope that the worst of the crisis was behind them. For nearly two years, peace seemed possible.

The Calm before the Storm

Repeal of the Townshend duties brought an end to nonimportation, despite the tax on tea. Trade boomed in 1770 and 1771. Moreover, the leaders of the popular movement seemed to be losing their power. Samuel Adams, for example, ran for a minor local office in Boston and lost to a conservative merchant.

In 1772, however, several incidents brought the conflict with England into focus again. One was the burning of the *Gaspée*, a Royal Navy ship chasing down suspected smugglers off the coast of Rhode Island. Although a royal investigating commission failed to arrest anyone, it announced that it would send suspects, if it found any, to England for trial on charges of high treason.

This decision seemed to fly in the face of the traditional English right to a trial by a jury of one's peers. When the news of the *Gaspée* investigation spread, it was greeted with disbelief in other colonies. Patrick Henry, Thomas Jefferson, and Richard Henry Lee from the Virginia House of Burgesses proposed that a network of standing committees be established to link the colonies and pass along alarming news. By mid-1773, every colonial assembly except Pennsylvania had a "committee of correspondence."

Another British action in 1772 further spread the communications network. Lord North proposed to pay the salaries of superior court justices out of the tea revenue, in a move parallel to Townshend's plan for royal governors. The Boston town meeting, alarmed that judges would now be in the pockets of their new paymasters, established a committee of correspondence and urged other towns to do likewise. The first vital message, circulated in

December 1772, attacked the judges' salary policy as the latest proof of a British plot to undermine traditional "liberties": unjust taxation, military occupation, massacre, now capped by the subversion of justice. By spring 1773, half the towns in Massachusetts had set up their own committees of correspondence, providing local forums for debate. These committees politicized ordinary townspeople and bypassed the official flow of power and information through the colony's royal government.

The third and final incident that irrevocably shattered the relative calm of the early 1770s was the Tea Act of 1773. Americans had been drinking moderate amounts of English tea and paying the tea duty without objection, but they were also smuggling large quantities of Dutch tea, cutting into the British East India Company's sales. So Lord North proposed special legislation giving favored status to the East India Company, allowing it to sell its tea through special government agents rather than through public auction to independent merchants. The hope was that the price of the East India tea, even with the duty, would then fall below that of the smuggled Dutch tea, motivating Americans to obey the law as well as boosting sales for the East India Company.

Tea in Boston Harbor

In the fall of 1773, news of the Tea Act reached the colonies. Parliamentary legislation to make tea inexpensive struck many colonists as an insidious plot to trick Americans into buying large quantities of the duffied tea. The real goal, some argued, was the increased revenue, which would then be used to pay the royal governors and judges. The Tea Act

TOSSING THE TEA
This colored engraving appeared in an English book published in 1789, recounting the history of North America from its earliest settlement to "becoming united, free, and independent states." Men on the ship break into the chests and dump the contents; a few are depicted in Indian disguise, with feathers on their heads or topknots of hair. A large crowd on the shore looks on. The red rowboat is clearly stacked with tea chests, suggesting that some of the raiders were stealing rather than destroying the tea. However, the artist, perhaps careless, shows the rowboat heading toward the ship instead of away. This event was not dubbed the "Tea Party" until the 1830s when a later generation celebrated the illegal destruction of the tea and made heroes out of the few surviving participants, by then men in their eighties and nineties.
Library of Congress.

was thus a sudden and painful reminder of Parliament's claim to the power to tax and legislate for the colonies.

As with the Stamp Act and the Townshend duties, the colonists' strategy was crucial. Nonimportation was not a viable option, because the trade was too lucrative to expect colonial merchants to give it up willingly. Consumer boycotts of tea had proved ineffective since 1770, chiefly because it was impossible to distinguish between duties tea (the object of the boycott) and smuggled tea (illegal but politically clean) once it was in the teapot. Like the Stamp Act, the Tea Act mandated special agents to handle the tea sales, and that requirement pointed to the solution for anti-tea activists. In every port city, revived Sons of Liberty pressured tea agents to resign.

The Boston Sons of Liberty were slower to act at first, but their action—more direct and illegal than anywhere else—ultimately provoked the most alarmed and alarming reprisals from England. Three ships bearing tea arrived in Boston in late November 1773. They cleared customs and unloaded their other cargoes, but not the tea. Sensing the extreme tension, the captains wished to return to England, but because the ships had already entered the harbor, they could not get clearance to leave without first paying the tea duty. On top of that, there was a twenty-day limit on the stay allowed in the harbor, by which time either the duty had to be paid or the tea would be confiscated and sold by the authorities. Governor Hutchinson refused to bend any rules.

For the full twenty days, pressure built in Boston. Daily mass meetings energized the citizenry not only from Boston but from surrounding towns, alerted by the committees of correspondence. On the final day, December 16, a large crowd gathered at Old South Church to hear Samuel Adams declare, "This meeting can do nothing more to save the country." This was a signal to adjourn to the harbor, where between 100 and 150 men, many dressed as Indians, dumped ninety thousand pounds of tea into the water while a crowd of two thousand watched. (See "Documenting the American Promise," page 134.)

The Coercive Acts

Lord North's response was swift and stern. Within three months he persuaded Parliament to issue the first of the Coercive Acts, a series of four laws meant to punish Massachusetts for the destruction of the tea. The laws were soon known as the Intolerable

Acts in America, along with a fifth one not aimed at Massachusetts alone, the Quebec Act.

The first, the Boston Port Act, closed Boston harbor to all shipping traffic as of June 1, 1774, for as long as the destroyed tea was not paid for. In effect, England was obliterating the commercial life of the city.

The second act, called the Massachusetts Government Act, altered the colony's charter (in itself an unprecedented step, underscoring Parliament's claim to supremacy over Massachusetts). The royal governor's powers were greatly augmented; the council became an appointive, not elective, body; and no town meeting beyond the annual spring election of town selectmen could be held unless the governor expressly permitted it. Not only Boston but every Massachusetts town felt the punitive sting.

The third of the Coercive Acts, the Impartial Administration of Justice Act, stipulated that any royal official accused of a capital crime—for example, Captain Preston and his soldiers at the Boston Massacre—would now be tried in a court in England. It did not matter that Preston in fact got a fair trial in Boston. What this act ominously suggested was that down the road, there might be more Captain Prestons and soldiers firing into crowds.

The fourth of the Coercive Acts was a new amendment to the 1765 Quartering Act, permitting military commanders to lodge soldiers wherever necessary, even in private households. For Boston this was no idle gesture, for in a related move Lord North appointed General Thomas Gage, commander of the Royal Army in New York, to be the new governor of Massachusetts. Thomas Hutchinson was out, relieved at long last of his duties, and military rule, including soldiers, returned once more to Boston.

The fifth Intolerable Act, the Quebec Act, had little to do with the first four but, ill-timed, it greatly fed the fear of Americans. It confirmed the continuation of French civil law, government form, and Catholicism for Quebec, all an affront to Protestant New Englanders denied their own representative government. The act also gave Quebec control of disputed lands (and hence control of the lucrative fur trade) throughout the Ohio valley, lands claimed variously by Virginia, Pennsylvania, and Connecticut.

The Coercive Acts spread alarm to all the colonies. If England could step on Massachusetts and change its charter, suspend government, inaugurate military rule, and on top of that give Ohio to Catholic Quebec, then what liberties were secure? Fearful royal governors in a half dozen colonies suspended sitting assemblies, adding to the sense of urgency; some suspended assemblies defiantly continued to meet in new locations. Via the committees of correspondence, the colonial leaders agreed to meet in Philadelphia in the fall of 1774 to respond to the crisis.

The First Continental Congress

Every colony except Georgia sent delegates to Philadelphia for the meeting of the First Continental Congress in September 1774. The gathering included the leading patriots, such as Samuel and John Adams from Massachusetts and George Washington and Patrick Henry from Virginia. A few colonies purposely sent men who were cool to provoking a crisis with England, like Pennsylvania's Joseph Galloway. Whatever their views, most of the delegates were the leading statesmen of their localities.

Two difficult tasks confronted the congress: The delegates wanted to agree on exactly what liberties they claimed as English subjects and what powers Parliament held over them, and they needed to make a unified response to the Coercive Acts. Some delegates wanted a total ban on trade with England, to force a repeal of the Coercive Acts, but others—especially those from southern colonies heavily dependent on the export of tobacco and rice—opposed halting trade. Samuel Adams and Patrick Henry were eager for a ringing denunciation of all parliamentary control, whereas the conservative Joseph Galloway proposed a plan (quickly defeated) to create a miniparliament in America to assist the British Parliament in ruling the colonies.

The congress met for seven weeks in Carpenter's Hall, Philadelphia, and produced a declaration of rights, couched in traditional language: "We ask only for peace, liberty and security. We wish no diminution of royal prerogatives, we demand no new rights." Yet the rights assumed already to exist were in fact radical, from England's point of view. Chief among them was the claim that Americans were not represented in Parliament and so each colonial government had the sole right to legislate for and tax its own people. The one slight concession to England was a carefully worded agreement that the colonists would "cheerfully consent" to trade regulations for the larger good of the empire—so long as trade regulation was not a covert means of raising revenue.

To put pressure on England, the delegates agreed to a staggered and limited boycott of trade—imports prohibited this year, exports the following, and rice totally exempted, to keep South Carolinians happy. To enforce the boycott, they created the Continental Association, with chapters in each town, variously called committees of public safety or of inspection, to monitor all commerce and punish suspected violators of the boycott (sometimes with a bucket of tar and a bag of feathers). Its work done, the congress disbanded in October 1774, with agreement to reconvene the following May.

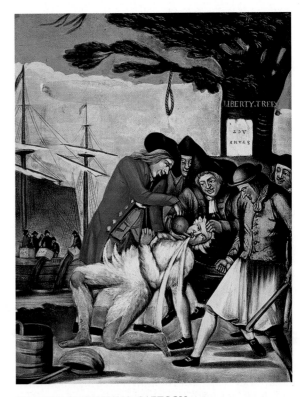

TAR AND FEATHERING CARTOON
In 1774, a Boston customs collector named John Malcolm felt the sting of pain at the hands of a Boston crowd which tarred and feathered him as punishment for extorting extra money from shippers. This ritualized humiliation involved stripping a man, painting him with tar, and dipping him in chicken feathers. Local committees of public safety often used threats of this treatment as a weapon to enforce boycotts; it happened far less often in actuality. This cartoon, of English origin, is hostile to Americans, who are shown with cruelly gleeful faces, forcing tea down Malcolm's throat. The Liberty Tree has become a gallows; posted to it is the Stamp Act, upside down, and the dumping of tea in the harbor is shown in the background.
Library of Congress.

The Destruction of the Tea

*O*n the night of December 16, 1773, over a hundred men disguised as Indians threw 342 chests of tea into Boston harbor. Here are three accounts by participants close to the action.

DOCUMENT 1. Governor Hutchinson's Account, Published in 1828

In exile in England, Thomas Hutchinson wrote a long history of Massachusetts, which was first published in 1828, decades after his death. In narrating Boston events of the 1760s and 1770s, Hutchinson referred to himself in the third person, but his point of view was definitely weighted toward self-vindication. Here he describes the consequences of his final rejection of a demand by the town meeting that he permit the vessels to leave port without paying the tea tax.

It was not expected the governor would comply with the demand; and, before it was possible for the owner of the ship to return . . . with an answer, about fifty men had prepared themselves, and passed by the house where the people were assembled, to the wharf where the vessels lay, being covered with blankets, and making the appearance of Indians. The body of the people remained until they had received the governor's answer; and then, after it had been observed to them, that, every thing else in their power having been done, it now remained to proceed in the only way left . . . the meeting was declared to be dissolved, and the body of the people repaired to the wharf, and surrounded the immediate actors, as a guard and security, until they finished their work. In two or three hours, they hoisted out of the holds of the ships, three hundred and forty-two chests of tea, and emptied them into the sea. The governor was unjustly censured by many people in the province, and much abused by the pamphlet and newspaper writers in England, for refusing his pass, which, it was said, would have saved the property thus destroyed; but he would have been justly censured, if he had granted it. He was bound, as all the king's governors were, by oath, faithfully to observe the acts of trade. . . . His granting a pass to a vessel which had not cleared at the custom-house, would have been a direct violation of his oath, by making himself an accessory in the breach of those laws which he had sworn to observe. It was out of his power to have prevented this mischief, without the most imminent hazard of much greater mischief. The tea could have been secured in the town in no other way than by landing marines from the men of war, or bringing to town the regiment which was at the castle, to remove the guards from the ships, and to take their places. This would have brought on a greater convulsion than there was any danger of in 1770, and it would not have been possible . . . for so small a body of troops to have kept possession of the town. Such a measure the governor had no reason to suppose would have been approved of in England. He was not sure of support from any one person in authority. The house of representatives openly avowed principles which implied complete independency. The council, appointed by charter to be assisting to him, declared against any advice from which might be inferred an acknowledgment of the authority of parliament in imposing taxes. . . . There was not a justice of peace, sheriff, constable, or peace officer in the province, who would venture to take cognizance of any breach of law, against the general bent of the people.

SOURCE: Excerpt from "Governor Hutchinson's Account, 1828." In *The History of the Colony and Province of Massachusetts-Bay:* Volume II by Thomas Hutchinson, edited by Lawrence Shaw Mayo. Copyright © 1936 by the President and Fellows of Harvard College. Reprinted by permission of the publisher, Harvard University Press.

DOCUMENT 2. George Robert Twelves Hewes's Recollection, Transcribed in 1834

George Robert Twelves Hewes, a thirty-one-year-old Boston shoemaker, was first stirred to political action by witnessing the Boston Massacre. During the struggle over tea, he joined the "Indian" boarding party and found himself thrust into a leadership role, a singular moment of glory that he proudly recounted when he was in his nineties. As one of the last surviving participants of that famous event, he enjoyed enormous celebrity in the 1830s. His life came to symbolize the Revolution's power to lift up the common man and endow him with a sense of political significance.

The commander of the division to which I belonged, as soon as we were on board the ship, appointed me boatswain, and ordered me to go to the captain and demand of him the keys to the hatches and a dozen candles. I made the demand accordingly, and the captain promptly replied, and delivered the articles; but requested me at the same time to do no damage to the ship or rigging. We then were ordered by our commander to open the hatches, and take out all the chests of tea and throw them overboard, and we immediately proceeded to execute his orders; first cutting and splitting the chests with our tomahawks, so as thoroughly to expose them to the effects of the water. In about three hours from the time we went on board, we had thus broken and thrown overboard every tea chest to be found in the ship; while those in the other ships were disposing of the tea in the same way, at the same time. We were surrounded by British armed ships, but no attempt was made to resist us. We then quietly retired to our several places of residence, without having any conversation with each other, or taking any measures to discover who were our associates.

SOURCE: [James Hawkes], *A Retrospect of the Boston Tea-Party, with a Memoir of George R. T. Hewes, a Survivor of the Little Band of Patriots Who Drowned the Tea in Boston Harbour in 1773* (New York, 1834), reprinted in Alfred F. Young, *The Shoemaker and the Tea Party: Memory and the American Revolution* (Boston: Beacon Press, 1999), 44.

DOCUMENT 3: John Adams's Diary Entry of December 17, 1773

John Adams reveled in the bold destruction of the tea in his diary the day after the event. He also gave thought to the legal consequences that might follow, rehearsing the justifications that motivated "the People."

Last Night 3 Cargoes of Bohea Tea were emptied into the Sea. This Morning a Man of War sails.

This is the most magnificent Movement of all. There is a Dignity, a Majesty, a Sublimity, in this last Effort of the Patriots, that I greatly admire. . . . This Destruction of the Tea is so bold, so daring, so firm, intrepid and inflexible, and it must have so important Consequences, and so lasting, that I cant but consider it as an Epocha in History.

This however is but an Attack upon Property. Another similar Exertion of popular Power, may produce the destruction of Lives. Many Persons wish, that as many dead Carcasses were floating in the Harbour, as there are Chests of Tea:—a much less Number of Lives however would remove the Causes of all our Calamities.

The malicious Pleasure with which Hutchinson the Governor, the Consignees of the Tea, and the officers of the Customs, have stood and looked upon the distresses of the People, and their Struggles to get the Tea back to London, and at last the destruction of it, is amazing. Tis hard to believe Persons so hardened and abandoned.

What Measures will the Ministry take, in Consequence of this?—Will they resent it? will they dare to resent it? will they punish Us? How? By quartering Troops upon Us?—by annulling our Charter?—by laying on more duties? By restraining our Trade? By Sacrifice of Individuals, or how.

The Question is whether the Destruction of this Tea was necessary? I apprehend it was absolutely and indispensably so.—They could not send it back, the Governor, Admiral, and Collector and Comptroller would not suffer it. It was in their Power to have saved it—but in no other. It could not get by the Castle, the Men of War &c. Then there was no other Alternative but to destroy it or let it be landed. To let it be landed, would be giving up the Principle of Taxation by Parliamentary Authority, against which the Continent have struggled for 10 years, it was loosing all our labour for 10 years and subjecting ourselves and our Posterity forever to Egyptian Taskmasters—to Burthens, Indignities, to Ignominy, Reproach and Contempt, to Desolation and Oppression, to Poverty and Servitude.

SOURCE: Excerpt from "John Adams' Diary Entry of December 17, 1773." In *The Adams Papers: Diary and Autobiography of John Adams*, Volume II 1771–1781, edited by L. H. Butterfield. Copyright © 1961 by the Massachusetts Historical Society. Reprinted by permission of the publisher, The Belknap Press of Harvard University Press.

QUESTIONS FOR ANALYSIS AND DEBATE

1. Does Thomas Hutchinson persuade you that he had no other option than to refuse to let the ship either leave or land? Why did he reject the use of troops to guard the tea?

2. How might men like Hewes be politicized by hacking open chests of tea?

3. John Adams says that Hutchinson took a malicious pleasure in forcing the tea crisis to its conclusion. Was he right or wrong in your judgment? Why?

4. What is at stake, for John Adams, in the showdown over tea, when he speaks of ten years of struggle by "the Continent" and of poverty and servitude to "Egyptian Taskmasters"? How does he feel about the possibility of deaths in the building struggle?

The committees of public safety, the committees of correspondence, the regrouped colonial assemblies, and the Continental Congresses were all functioning political bodies without any formal constitutional authority. British officials did not recognize them as legitimate, but many Americans who supported the patriot cause instantly accepted them. A key reason for the stability of such unauthorized bodies throughout the Revolutionary period was that they were composed of the same men, by and large, who had composed the official bodies now disbanded.

England's severe reaction to Boston's destruction of the tea finally succeeded in making many colonists from New Hampshire to Georgia realize that the problems of British rule went far beyond questions of taxation. The Coercive Acts infringed on liberty and denied self-government; they could not be ignored. With one colony subordinated to military rule now, and a British army at the ready in Boston, the threat of a general war was at the doorstep.

Domestic Insurrections, 1774–1775

Before the Second Continental Congress could meet, war broke out in Massachusetts. General Thomas Gage, military commander and new governor, at first thought he faced a domestic insurrection that needed only a show of force to quiet it. The rebels saw things differently: They were defending their homes and liberties against an intrusive power bent on enslaving them. To the south, a different and inverted version of the same story began to unfold, as thousands of enslaved black men and women seized an unprecedented opportunity to mount a different kind of insurrection, against planter-patriots who looked over their shoulders uneasily whenever they called out for liberty from the British.

Lexington and Concord

Over the winter of 1774–75 Americans pressed on with boycotts. Some hoped for the repeal of the Coercive Acts, while pessimists started accumulating arms and ammunition. In Massachusetts, gunpowder and shot were secretly stored, and militia units called minutemen prepared to respond on a

minute's notice to any threat from the British in Boston.

Thomas Gage soon realized how desperate the British position was. The people, Gage wrote Lord North, were "numerous, worked up to a fury, and not a Boston rabble but the freeholders and farmers of the country." Gage requested twenty thousand reinforcements. He also strongly advised repeal of the Coercive Acts, but leaders in England could not admit failure. Instead, Gage was ordered in mid-April 1775 to arrest the troublemakers immediately, before the Americans got better organized.

Gage quickly planned a surprise attack on a suspected ammunition storage site at Concord, a village about eighteen miles west of Boston (Map 6.3). Near midnight on April 18, 1775, British soldiers moved west across the Charles River. Boston silversmith Paul Revere raced ahead to alert the minutemen. When the British soldiers got to Lexington, a village five miles east of Concord, they met with some seventy armed American men assembled on the village green. The British commander barked out, "Lay down your arms, you damned rebels and disperse." The militiamen hesitated and began to comply, turning to leave the green, but then someone—unknown—fired. In the next two minutes, more firing left eight Americans dead and ten wounded.

The British units then marched to Concord, any pretense of surprise gone. Three companies of minutemen nervously occupied the center of Concord but offered no challenge to the British troops as they searched in vain for the ammunition storage. Finally, at the Old North Bridge in Concord, shots were exchanged, killing two Americans and three British soldiers.

By now both sides were very apprehensive. The British had failed to find the expected arms storage, and the Americans had failed to stop their raid. As the British returned to Boston along a narrow road, militia units attacked from the sides in the bloodiest fighting of the day. In the end, 273 British soldiers were wounded or dead; the toll for the Americans stood at about 95. It was April 19, 1775, and the war had begun.

Another Rebellion against Slavery

News of the battles of Lexington and Concord spread rapidly. Within eight days, Virginians had heard of the fighting, and, as Thomas Jefferson reflected, "A phrenzy of revenge seems to have seized all ranks of people." The royal governor of Virginia,

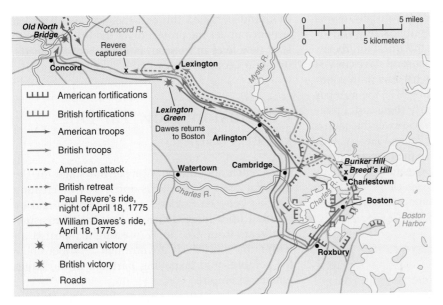

MAP 6.3

Lexington and Concord, April 1775

Under pressure from England, British forces at Boston staged a raid on a suspected rebel arms supply in Concord, Massachusetts, starting the first battle of the Revolutionary War.

Lord Dunmore, removed a large quantity of gunpowder from the Williamsburg powder house and put it on a ship in the dead of night, out of reach of any frenzied Virginians. Next, Dunmore threatened to arm the slaves, if necessary, to ward off attacks by colonists.

This was an effective threat; Dunmore understood full well how to produce panic among the planters. He did not act on it until November 1775, when he issued an official proclamation promising freedom to defecting, able-bodied slaves who would fight for the British. Dunmore's dilemma was that while he wanted to scare the planters, he had no intention of liberating all slaves or of starting a real slave rebellion. So his offer was limited to able-bodied men. Female, young, and elderly slaves were not welcome behind British lines, and many were sent back to face irate masters. Astute blacks noticed that Dunmore neglected to free his own slaves. A Virginia barber named Caesar declared that "he did not know any one foolish enough to believe him [Dunmore], for if he intended to do so, he ought first to set his own free."

In the northern colonies as well, slaves clearly recognized the evolving political struggle with England as an ideal moment to bid for freedom. A twenty-one-year-old Boston domestic slave employed biting sarcasm in a 1774 newspaper essay to call attention to the hypocrisy of local slave owners: "How well the Cry for Liberty, and the reverse Disposition for exercise of oppressive Power over others agree,—I humbly think it does not require the

Penetration of a Philosopher to Determine." This extraordinary young woman, Phillis Wheatley, had already gained international recognition through a book of poems, endorsed by Governor Thomas Hutchinson and Boston merchant John Hancock and published in London in 1773. Possibly neither man fully appreciated the irony of his endorsement, however, for Wheatley's poems spoke of "Fair Freedom" as the "Goddess long desir'd" by Africans enslaved in America. At the urging of his wife, Wheatley's master freed the young poet in 1775.

Wheatley's poetic ideas about freedom found concrete expression among other discontented groups. Some slaves in Boston petitioned Thomas Gage, promising to fight for the British if he would liberate them. Gage turned them down. In Ulster County, New York, along the Hudson River, two blacks were overheard discussing gunpowder, and thus a plot unraveled that involved at least twenty slaves in four villages discovered to have ammunition stashed away.

The numerical preponderance of black slaves in the southern colonies deepened white fears of rebellion. In Maryland, soon after the news of the Lexington battle arrived, slaves exhibited impatience with their status, in light of the revolutionary movement unfolding around them. One Maryland planter reported that "the insolence of the Negroes in this county is come to such a height, that we are under a necessity of disarming them. . . . We took about eighty guns, some bayonets, swords, etc." In North Carolina, a planned uprising was uncovered and scores of slaves were arrested; ironically, it was the revolutionary committee of public safety that ordered the whippings to punish this quest for liberty.

In 1775, probably several thousand slaves in Virginia took Lord Dunmore up on his offer of freedom for joining the British side, and by 1778 the number had escalated to as many as thirty thousand. Possibly eighty thousand southern blacks over the course of the Revolutionary War voted against slavery with their feet. Some failed to achieve the liberation they were seeking. The British army generally used them for menial labor; and disease, especially smallpox, devastated encampments of runaways. But several

thousand persisted through the war and later left America under the protection of the British army to start new lives in freedom in Nova Scotia, Canada, or Sierra Leone in Africa.

Conclusion: How Far Does Liberty Go?

The French and Indian War set the stage for the imperial crisis of the 1760s and 1770s by creating distrust between England and its colonies and by running up a huge deficit in the British treasury. The years from 1763 to 1775 brought repeated attempts by the British government to subordinate the colonies into taxpaying partners in the larger scheme of empire.

American resistance grew slowly but steadily over those years. In 1765, Thomas Hutchinson shared with Samuel Adams the belief that it was exceedingly unwise for England to assert a right to taxation, because Parliament did not adequately represent Americans. But by temperament and office, Hutchinson had to uphold British policy; Adams, in contrast, protested the policy and made political activists out of thousands in the process.

By 1775, events propelled many Americans to the conclusion that a concerted effort was afoot to deprive them of all their liberties, the most important of which were the right to self-taxation, the right to live free of an occupying army, and finally their right to self-rule. Hundreds of minutemen converged on Concord, prepared to die for these American liberties. April 19 marked the start of their rebellion.

Another rebellion under way in 1775 was doomed to be short-circuited. Black Americans who had experienced actual slavery now listened to shouts of "Liberty!" from white crowds and appropriated the language of revolution swirling around them that spoke to their deepest needs and hopes. Defiance of authority was indeed contagious.

The emerging leaders of the patriot cause were mindful of a delicate balance they felt they had to strike. To energize the American public about the crisis with England, they had to politicize masses of men—and eventually women too—and infuse them with a keen sense of their rights and liberties. But in so doing, they became fearful of the unintended consequences of teaching a vocabulary of rights and liberties. They worried that the rhetoric of enslavement might go too far.

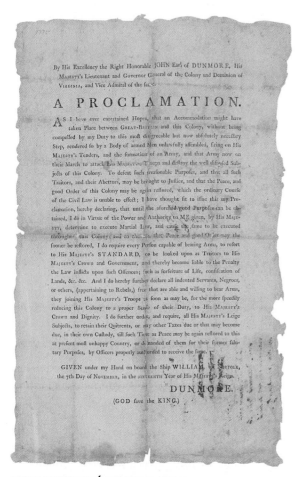

LORD DUNMORE'S PROCLAMATION
In November 1775, Lord Dunmore of Virginia offered freedom to "all indented Servants, Negroes, or others (appertaining to Rebels)" who would help put down the rebellion. Dunmore issued multiple printed copies in broadside form from the safety of a ship anchored at Norfolk, Virginia.
Special Collections, University of Virginia, Alderman Library.

The question of how far the crisis could be stretched before something snapped was largely unexamined in 1765. Patriot leaders in that year wanted a correction, a restoration of an ancient liberty of self-taxation that Parliament seemed to be ignoring. But events from 1765 to 1775 convinced many that no return to the old ways was possible. A challenge to Parliament's right to tax had led, step by step, to a challenge to Parliament's right to legislate over the colonies in any matter. If Parliament's sovereignty was set aside, then who actually had authority over the American colonies? By 1775, with the outbreak of fighting and the specter of slave rebellions, American leaders turned to the king for the answer to that question.

FOR FURTHER READING ABOUT THE TOPICS IN THIS CHAPTER, see the Online Bibliography at www.bedfordstmartins.com/roarkcompact.

FOR ADDITIONAL FIRST-HAND ACCOUNTS OF THIS PERIOD, see pages 78–92 in Michael Johnson, ed., *Reading the American Past,* Second Edition, Volume I.

TO ASSESS YOUR MASTERY OF THE MATERIAL IN THIS CHAPTER, see the Online Study Guide at www.bedfordstmartins.com/roarkcompact.

CHRONOLOGY

1747 Ohio Company of Virginia formed.

1754 French and Indian War begins in America.

Albany Congress proposes Plan of Union and courts Iroquois support.

1755 General Edward Braddock defeated by French and Indians in Pennsylvania.

1757 William Pitt, prime minister in Britain, fully commits to war effort.

1759 Quebec falls to British.

1760 George III becomes British king.

1763 Treaty of Paris ends French and Indian War.

Pontiac's uprising provokes fear and destruction in western frontier settlements.

Proclamation Act of 1763 prohibits settlement west of Appalachians.

1764 The Revenue (Sugar) Act lowers tax on foreign molasses to promote compliance with trade duty.

1765 Stamp Act imposes tax on documents.

May. Patrick Henry sponsors Virginia Resolves.

August. Crowd actions in Boston inaugurate Sons of Liberty.

October. Stamp Act Congress meets in New York City.

1766 Stamp Act repealed; Declaratory Act asserts Parliament's control over colonies.

1767 Townshend duties reinstate revenue-raising taxes.

1768 **Fall.** British troops stationed in Boston.

1769 Year of nonimportation agreements; Daughters of Liberty appear.

1770 **March 5.** Boston Massacre.

Townshend duties repealed; Lord North comes to power.

1772 **June.** *Gaspée* attacked off Rhode Island.

Committees of correspondence formed.

1773 Tea Act lowers price of tea to encourage Americans to purchase legal rather than smuggled tea.

December 16. Destruction of tea in Boston harbor.

1774 Parliament passes Coercive Acts (Intolerable Acts): Boston Port Act, Massachusetts Government Act, Impartial Administration of Justice Act, a new amendment to the 1765 Quartering Act, and the Quebec Act.

September. First Continental Congress meets. Continental Association formed.

1775 **April 19.** Battles of Lexington and Concord.

Virginia's Lord Dunmore promises freedom to defecting slaves.

PAINTED DRUM

Drums were essential military equipment in eighteenth-century wars. Small to carry but loud in use, they provided a percussive beat that penetrated the din of the battlefield to signal troop advances, retreats, or other field movements. Drummers often stood right behind soldiers in firing formation, regulating the timing of each volley of shots. The eagle painted on this Revolutionary-era drum from Fort Ticonderoga in New York holds a banner inscribed "Sons of Liberty," a name adopted in 1765 to distinguish protesters of British policies toward the colonies.

Fort Ticonderoga Museum.

THE WAR FOR AMERICA

1775–1783

ABIGAIL ADAMS WAS IMPATIENT for American independence. While her husband, John, was away in Philadelphia as a member of the Second Continental Congress, Abigail tended house and farm in Braintree, Massachusetts, just south of British-occupied Boston. She had four young children to look after, and in addition to her female duties, such as cooking, sewing, and making soap, she also had to shoulder male duties in her husband's absence—hiring farm help, managing rental property, selling the crop. John wrote to her often, approving of the fine "Farmeress" who was conducting his business so well. She replied, conveying news of the family along with shrewd commentary on revolutionary politics. In December 1775, she chastised the congress for being too timid and urged that independence be declared. A few months later, she astutely observed to John that southern slave owners might shrink from a war in the name of liberty: "I have sometimes been ready to think that the passion for Liberty cannot be Equally strong in the Breasts of those who have been accustomed to deprive their fellow Creatures of theirs."

"I long to hear that you have declared an independency," she wrote in March 1776. "And by the way in the new Code of Laws which I suppose it will be necessary for you to make I desire you would Remember the Ladies, and be more generous and favourable to them than your ancestors." If Abigail was politically precocious in favoring independence and questioning slave owners' devotion to liberty, she was positively visionary in this extraordinary plea to her husband to "Remember the Ladies." "Do not put such unlimited power into the hands of the Husbands," she advised. "Remember all Men would be tyrants if they could." Abigail had put her finger on another form of tyranny that was rarely remarked on in her society: that of men over women. "If particular care and attention is not paid to the Ladies," she jokingly threatened, "we are determined to foment a Rebellion, and will not hold ourselves bound by any Laws in which we have no voice, or Representation."

John Adams dismissed his wife's provocative idea as a "saucy" suggestion: "As to your extraordinary Code of Laws, I cannot but Laugh." The Revolution had perhaps unleashed discontent among other dependent groups, he allowed; children, apprentices, students, Indians, and blacks had grown "disobedient" and "insolent." "But your Letter was the first Intimation that another Tribe more numerous and powerful than all the rest were grown discontented." Men were too smart to repeal their "Masculine Systems," John assured her, for otherwise they would find themselves living under a "despotism of the petticoat."

This clever exchange between husband and wife in 1776 says much about the cautious, limited radicalism of the American Revolution. Both John and Abigail Adams understood (Abigail probably far more than John) that ungluing the hierarchical bond between the king and his subjects potentially unglued other kinds of

ABIGAIL ADAMS
Abigail Smith Adams was twenty-two when she sat for this pastel portrait in 1766. A wife for two years and a mother for one, Adams exhibits a steady, intelligent gaze. Pearls and a lace collar anchor her femininity, while her facial expression projects a confidence and maturity not often credited to young women of the 1760s.
Courtesy of the Massachusetts Historical Society ©.

social inequalities. John was surely joking in listing the groups made unruly in the spirit of a challenge to authority, for children, apprentices, and students were hardly rebellious in the 1770s. But it would soon prove to be an uncomfortable joke, because Indians and blacks did take up the cause of their own liberty during the Revolution, and the great majority of them saw their liberty best served by joining the British side in the war.

Though Abigail Adams was impatient for independence, many other Americans feared separation from Britain. What kind of civilized country had no king? Who, if not Britain, would protect Americans from the French and Spanish? How could the colonies possibly win a war against the most powerful military machine on the globe? Rec-

onciliation, not independence, was favored by many.

Members of the Continental Congress, whether they were pro-independence like John Adams or more cautiously hoping for reconciliation, had their hands full in 1775 and 1776. The war had already begun, and it fell to the congress to raise an army, finance it, and explore diplomatic alliances with foreign countries. In part a classic war with professional armies and textbook battles, the Revolutionary War was also a civil war in America, at times even a brutal guerrilla war, of committed rebels versus loyalists.

In one glorious moment, the congress issued a ringing statement about how social hierarchy would be rearranged in America after submission to the king was undone. That was on July 4, 1776, when the Declaration of Independence asserted that "all men are created equal." But this striking phrase went completely unremarked in the two days of congressional debate spent tinkering with the language of the Declaration. The solvent to dissolve social inequalities in America was created at that moment, but none of the men at the congress, or even Abigail Adams up in Braintree, fully realized it at the time.

The Second Continental Congress

On May 10, 1775, nearly one month after the fighting at Lexington and Concord, the Second Continental Congress assembled in Philadelphia. The congress immediately set to work on two crucial and seemingly contradictory tasks: to raise and supply an army and to negotiate a reconciliation with England. But as the war progressed and hopes of reconciliation faded, delegates at the congress began to ponder the treasonous act of declaring independence.

Assuming Political and Military Authority

As with the First Continental Congress, the delegates to the second were well-established figures in their home colonies, but they still had to learn to know and trust each other; they did not always agree. The Adams cousins John and Samuel defined the radical end of the spectrum, favoring indepen-dence. John Dickinson of Pennsylvania, no longer the eager revolutionary who had dashed off *Letters from a Farmer* back in 1767, was now a moderate, seeking reconciliation with England. Benjamin Franklin, fresh off a ship from an eleven-year resi-dence in England, was feared by some to be a British spy. Mutual suspicions flourished easily when the undertaking was so dangerous, opinions were so varied, and a misstep could spell disaster.

Most of the delegates were not yet prepared to break with England. Several legislatures instructed their delegates to oppose independence. Some felt that government without a monarchical element was unworkable, while others feared it might be suicidal to lose England's protection against the tra-ditional enemies, France and Spain. Colonies that traded actively with England feared undermining their economies. Nor were the vast majority of or-dinary Americans able to envision independence from the British monarchy. From the Stamp Act of 1765 to the Coercive Acts of 1774, the constitutional struggle with England had turned on the issue of parliamentary power. During that decade, almost no one had questioned the legitimacy of the monarchy.

The few men at the Continental Congress who did think that independence was desirable were, not surprisingly, from Massachusetts. Their colony had been stripped of civil government under the Coercive Acts and their capital was occupied by the British army. Even so, those men knew that it was premature to push for a break with England. John Adams wrote to Abigail in June 1775: "America is a great, unwieldy body. Its progress must be slow. It is like a large fleet sailing under convoy. The fleetest sailors must wait for the dullest and slowest."

As slow as the American colonies were in sail-ing toward political independence, they needed to take swift action to coordinate a military defense, for the Massachusetts countryside was under threat of further attack. Even the hesitant moderates in the congress agreed that a military buildup was neces-sary. Around the country, militia units from New York to Georgia collected arms and drilled on vil-lage greens in anticipation. On June 14, the congress voted to create the Continental army. Choosing the commander in chief offered an opportunity to demonstrate that this was no local war of a single rebellious colony. Congress bypassed Artemas Ward from Massachusetts, then already command-

ing the soldiers massed around Boston, and instead chose a southerner, George Washington. Washing-ton's appointment sent the message to England that there was widespread commitment to war beyond New England.

Next the congress drew up a document titled "A Declaration of the Causes and Necessity of Tak-ing Up Arms," which rehearsed familiar arguments about the tyranny of Parliament and the need to de-fend traditional English liberties. This declaration was first drafted by a young Virginia planter, Thomas Jefferson, a newcomer to the congress and a radical on the question of independence. The moderate John Dickinson, fearing that the declara-tion would offend England and rule out reconcilia-tion, was allowed to rewrite it; however, he still left much of Jefferson's highly charged language about choosing "to die freemen rather than to live slaves." Even a man as reluctant for independence as Dick-inson acknowledged the necessity of military de-fense against an invading army.

To pay for the military buildup, the congress authorized a currency issue of two million dollars. The Continental dollars were merely paper; they did not represent gold or silver, for the congress owned no precious metals. The delegates somewhat naively expected that the currency would be ac-cepted as valuable on trust as it spread in the pop-ulation through the hands of soldiers, farmers, munitions suppliers, and beyond.

In just two months, the Second Continental Congress had created an army, declared war, and issued its own currency. It had taken on the major functions of a legitimate government, both military and financial, without any legal basis for its auth-ority, for it had not—and would not for a full year—declare independence from the authority of the king.

Pursuing Both War and Peace

Three days after the congress voted to raise the Con-tinental army, one of the bloodiest battles of the Rev-olution occurred. The British commander in Boston, Thomas Gage, had recently received troop rein-forcements, three talented generals (William Howe, John Burgoyne, and Henry Clinton), and new in-structions to root out the rebels around Boston. But before Gage could take the offensive, the Americans fortified the hilly terrain of Charlestown, a penin-sula just north of Boston, on the night of June 16, 1775.

The British generals could have nipped off the peninsula where it met the mainland, to box in the Americans. But General Howe insisted on a bold frontal assault, sending his 2,500 soldiers across the water and up the hill, in an intimidating but potentially costly attack. The American troops, 1,400 strong, held their fire until the British were about twenty yards away. At that distance, the musket volley was sure and deadly, and the British turned back. Twice more General Howe sent his men up the hill to receive the same blast of firepower; each time they had to step around the bodies felled in the previous attempts.

On the third assault, the British took the hill, mainly because the American ammunition supply gave out, and the defenders quickly retreated. The Battle of Bunker Hill was thus a British victory, but an expensive one. The dead numbered 226 on the British side, with more than 800 wounded; the Americans suffered 140 dead, 271 wounded, and 30 captured. As General Clinton later remarked, "It was a dear bought victory; another such would have ruined us."

Instead of pursuing the fleeing Americans, Howe pulled his army back to Boston, unwilling to risk more raids into the countryside. If the British had had any grasp of the basic instability of the American units gathered around Boston, they might have pushed westward and perhaps decisively defeated the core of the Continental army in its infancy. Instead they lingered in Boston, abandoning it without a fight nine months later. Howe used the time in Boston to inoculate his army against smallpox, because a new epidemic of the deadly disease was growing in port cities along the Atlantic. Inoculation worked by producing a light but real (and therefore risky) case of smallpox, followed by lifelong immunity. Howe's instinct here was right: from 1775 to 1782, the years coinciding with the American Revolution, some 130,000 people on the

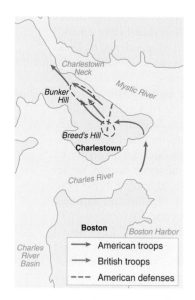

The Battle of Bunker Hill, 1775

American continent, most of them Indians, died of smallpox.

A week after Bunker Hill, when General Washington arrived to take charge of the new Continental army, he found enthusiastic but undisciplined troops. Sanitation was an unknown concept, drunkenness on duty was common, and soldiers came and went at will. The amazed general attributed the disarray to the New England custom of letting militia units elect their own officers, a custom he felt undermined deference. Washington quickly imposed more hierarchy and authority.

While military plans moved forward, the Second Continental Congress pursued its second, contradictory objective, reconciliation with England. Delegates from the middle colonies (Pennsylvania, Delaware, and New York) whose merchants depended on trade with England urged that channels for negotiation remain open. Congressional moderates led by John Dickinson engineered an appeal to the king, called the Olive Branch Petition, in July 1775. The petition affirmed loyalty to the monarchy and blamed all the troubles on the king's ministers and on Parliament. It proposed that the American colonial assemblies be recognized as individual parliaments, under the umbrella of the monarchy. By late fall 1775, however, reconciliation was out of the question. King George rejected the Olive Branch Petition and heatedly condemned the Americans, calling them rebels and traitors. It was thereafter hard to maintain the illusion that ministers and not the king himself were to blame for the conflict.

Thomas Paine and the Case for Independence

Pressure for independence mounted starting in January 1776, when a pamphlet titled *Common Sense* appeared in Philadelphia. Thomas Paine, its author, was an English artisan and coffeehouse intellectual who had come to America in the fall of 1774. He landed a job with the *Pennsylvania Magazine* and soon met delegates from the Second Continental Congress. With their encouragement, he wrote *Common Sense* to lay out a lively and compelling case for complete independence.

In simple yet forceful language, Paine elaborated on the absurdities of the British monarchy. Why should one man, by accident of birth, claim extensive power over others? he asked. A king might be foolish or wicked. "One of the strongest

RHODE ISLAND REGIMENT FLAG
In the absence of an official American flag, regiments often commissioned their own symbolic banners. Almost certainly the elaborate stitchery and even the design work of this Rhode Island artillery company flag came from female hands wielding needle and thread. There were thus dozens, not just one, "Betsy Ross," the legendary Philadelphia woman credited with designing the prototype of the stars and stripes. A popular 1770s flag-theme portrayed a coiled rattlesnake paired with the slogan "Don't Tread on Me." Such a flag conveyed a dire warning and a clear point of view about who had started the war in America: the rattler, uniquely American, was deadly only when aroused or provoked. This 1775 flag offers an unusual variant, using the more formal "do not" instead of "don't." The slogan endures today, showing up on state license plates and as lyrics in popular songs. Note as well another nearly familiar motto: "In God We Hope." It precedes by almost a century the Civil War–era origins of the modern-day motto on U.S. coinage, "In God We Trust."
Collection of Mr. and Mrs. Boleslaw Mastai.

natural proofs of the folly of hereditary right in kings," Paine wrote, "is that nature disapproves it; otherwise she would not so frequently turn it into ridicule by giving mankind an *ass for a lion*." Calling the king of England an ass broke through the automatic deference most Americans still had for the monarchy. To replace monarchy, he advocated republican government, based on the consent of the people. Rulers, according to Paine, were only representatives of the people, and the best form of government relied on frequent elections to achieve the most direct democracy possible.

Paine's pamphlet sold more than 150,000 copies in a matter of weeks. Newspapers reprinted it; men read it aloud in taverns and coffeehouses; John Adams sent a copy to Abigail Adams, who passed it around to neighbors. Another of John Adams's correspondents wrote him in late February that many New Englanders desired an official declaration of independence. Middle and southern colonies, under no immediate threat of violence, remained cautious. But by May, all but four colonies were in favor of independence. Two of the holdouts were New York and South Carolina, both with large loyalist populations.

In early June, the Virginia delegation introduced a resolution calling for independence. The moderates still commanded enough support to postpone a vote on the measure until July, so they could go home and consult about this extreme step. In the meantime, the congress appointed a committee, with Thomas Jefferson and others, to draft a longer document setting out the case for independence.

On July 2, after intense politicking, all but one state voted for independence; New York abstained. The congress then turned to the document drafted by Thomas Jefferson and his committee. Jefferson began with a preamble that articulated philosophical principles about natural rights, equality, the right of revolution, and the consent of the governed as the only true basis for government. He then listed more than two dozen grievances against King George. The congress merely glanced at the political philosophy, finding nothing exceptional in it; the ideas about natural rights and the consent of the governed were seen as "self-evident truths," just as the document claimed. In itself, this absence of comment showed a remarkable transformation in political thinking since the end of the French and Indian War. The single phrase declaring the natural equality of "all men" was also passed over without comment; no one elaborated on its radical implications.

For two days, the congress wrangled over the list of grievances, especially the issue of slavery. Jefferson had included an impassioned statement blaming the king for slavery, which delegates from Georgia and South Carolina struck out. They had no intention of denouncing their labor system as an evil practice. But the congress let stand another of Jefferson's fervent grievances, blaming the king for mobilizing "the merciless Indian Savages" into bloody frontier warfare.

On July 4, the amendments to Jefferson's text were complete and the document was formally adopted. (See appendix, pages A-1–A-3.) Nearly a month later, on August 2, the delegates gathered to

DECLARATION OF INDEPENDENCE READ TO A CROWD *Printed copies of the Declaration of Independence (see appendix, pages A-1–A-3) were read aloud in public places throughout America in the week after July 4, 1776, often accompanied by carefully orchestrated celebrations.* Library of Congress.

www.bedfordstmartins.com/roarkcompact SEE THE ONLINE STUDY GUIDE for more help in analyzing this image.

sign the official parchment copy, handwritten by an exacting scribe. Four men, including John Dickinson, declined to sign; several others "signed with regret . . . and with many doubts," according to John Adams. The document was then printed, widely distributed, and read aloud in celebrations everywhere. A crowd in New York listened to a public reading of it and then toppled a lead statue of George III on horseback to melt it down for bullets. On July 15, the New York delegation switched from abstention to endorsement, making the vote on independence truly unanimous.

The First Year of War, 1775–1776

Both sides had cause to approach the war for America with uneasiness. The Americans, with only inexperienced and undertrained militias, opposed the mightiest military power in the world, and many thought it was foolhardy to expect victory. Further, pockets of loyalism remained strong; the country was not united. But the British faced serious obstacles as well. Their utter disdain for the fighting abilities of the Americans had to be reevaluated in light of their costly Bunker Hill victory. The logistics of supplying an army with food across three thousand miles of water were daunting. And since the British goal was to regain allegiance, not to destroy and conquer, the army was often constrained in its actions.

The American Military Forces

Americans claimed that the initial months of war were purely defensive, triggered by the British army's invasion. But quickly the war also became a rebellion, an overthrowing of long-established authority. As both defenders and rebels, Americans were generally highly motivated to fight, and the potential manpower that could be mobilized was in theory very great.

From the earliest decades of settlement, local defense in the colonies rested with a militia requiring participation from nearly every able-bodied man over age sixteen. When the main threat to public safety was the occasional Indian attack, the local militia made sense. But such attacks were now mostly limited to the frontier. Southern militias trained with potential slave rebellions in mind, but these too were rare. The annual muster day in most communities had evolved into a holiday of drinking, marching, and perhaps shooting practice with small fowling guns or muskets. (See "The Promise of Technology," page 148.)

Militias were best suited to limited engagements, when a local community was under immediate attack. But they were not appropriate for extended wars requiring military campaigns far from home. In forming the Continental army, the congress set enlistment at one year, but army leaders soon learned that that was not enough time to train soldiers and carry out campaigns. A three-year enlistment earned a new soldier a twenty-dollar bonus, while men who committed for the duration

of the war were promised a postwar land grant of one hundred acres. To make this inducement effective, of course, recruits had to believe that the Americans would win. By early 1777, the army was the largest it would ever be.

Women also served in the Continental army. They were needed to do the daily cooking and washing, and after battle they nursed the wounded. The British army established a ratio of one woman to every ten men; in the Continental army, the ratio was set at one woman to fifteen men. Close to twenty thousand women served during the war, probably most of them wives of men in service. Children tagged along as well, and babies were born in the camps and on the road.

Black Americans were at first excluded from the Continental army, a rule that slave owner George

BLACK REVOLUTIONARY WAR SAILOR
Thousands of black men served on the patriot side as soldiers and sailors, usually at the rank of private or ordinary seaman. Their names are preserved in regiment records and crew lists; rarely, however, were their faces preserved. This 1780 portrait by an unknown artist shows an unnamed man, sword and scabbard at hand, dressed in military finery with a ship in view to establish his naval connection.
Collection of A. A. McBurney.

Arming the Soldiers: Muskets and Rifles

How combat-ready was the American side of the Revolutionary War? Were there adequate numbers of firearms along with men trained in their use? These are lively and important questions that have generated sharp debate among twenty-first-century historians and that speak to the question of the centrality and significance of guns in the founding days of the United States.

In theory, all towns in the colonies were expected to maintain a local militia, at the ready to protect their own communities. All able-bodied adult men were supposed to participate in annual training days, bringing their own guns, but in many communities, such "muster" or "train-band" days had been gradually transformed into festive town holidays. Male camaraderie as expressed in displays of parading and shooting competitions often took precedence over military drill and serious musket practice, an altogether understandable relaxation in coastal or northern towns not feeling any imminent threat of Indian attack or slave rebellion.

Guns were not the weapon of choice for procuring everyday food; table meat came mainly from domesticated animals slaughtered with large knives. But they were useful for the small-game hunting of ducks and wild turkeys, or raccoons and squirrels killed as farm pests. Americans used guns known as fowling pieces that fired shot (small pellets) to kill such game at close range. Households on the frontier would need larger guns for shooting deer, bears, or wolves; but residents of Lexington and Concord, not to mention Boston, rarely encountered bears.

Muskets firing one-ounce lead balls were the preferred weapon of eighteenth-century warfare. Muskets were a sixteenth-century invention, featuring by the mid-eighteenth century an improved flintlock ignition system in which the trigger released a spring-held cock that caused a hammer to strike a flint, a special rock that sparks easily. The sparks set off a small charge in a priming pan leading directly to a larger explosion in the barrel. To load the gun, a soldier first put the it on half-cock, to prevent an accidental firing. He next put a small quantity of powder (carried in a powder horn) in the priming pan and closed it, poured more powder down the smooth gun barrel, dropped in the lead projectile, and then wadded paper down the barrel with a ramrod to hold the loose ball in place. He would then raise the gun to firing position, put it on full cock, and fire. The whole procedure took highly experienced shooters from 45 to 90 seconds.

The range of muskets extended only about 50 to 100 yards. They were notoriously inaccurate, owing to the poor fit between ball and barrel and

POWDER HORN

James Pike, a twenty-three-year-old New England militiaman, made and then personalized this powder horn, a hollow cow's horn capped on both ends with leather. The stopper was designed to be pulled off by the teeth, leaving the hands to hold the musket barrel and pour the powder. Pike's carvings suggest his motivation for fighting. Above his name he depicts a scene dated April 19, 1775, in which British soldiers, labeled "the Aggressors," fire through the Liberty Tree at "Provincials, Defending." Pike was not at Lexington or Concord; his first combat experience came two months later at the Battle of Bunker Hill, where he saw his brother killed and was himself wounded in the shoulder.

Chicago Historical Society.

to the considerable kick produced by firing, which interfered with aiming. Far more accurate were longer-barreled rifles, used in frontier regions where big-game hunting was more common. The interior of a rifle barrel carried spiral grooves that imparted spin to the ball as it traversed the barrel, stabilizing and lengthening its flight, and enabling expert marksmen to hit small targets at 150 or 200 yards. Yet military commanders much preferred muskets to rifles. Rifles took twice as long to load and fire, and their longer barrels made them unwieldy for soldiers on the march. Inaccurate muskets were quite deadly enough when fired in unison at 50 yards.

How many American men actually owned fowling pieces, muskets, or rifles? Evidence on this point is complicated and controversial. Probate inventories, many thousands of which exist in county courthouses, offer a partial answer. An inventory, taken soon after the owner's death, listed the contents of an estate in order to establish its value, both for inheritance purposes and for paying off the deceased person's creditors. Yet these sources are fraught with thorny problems that make them something less than an accurate indicator of possessions. For one thing, they are often not complete: If few inventories itemize clothing, can we conclude the decedents went nude? Clearly not. Further, they list possessions of a recently deceased person who owned property of interest to creditors and heirs, so they are biased by age (older), sex (male), and wealth (more). No doubt many men and women died without having their property inventoried at all.

Despite these and other complexities, scholars have worked with probate inventories as the best available source of information. Current careful studies based on this source yield estimates for the 1770s on overall gun ownership (including guns of all kinds) that range from 40 to 50 percent of all probated estates, with significant regional variations.

A second way to assess gun ownership is to look at the arms procurement experiences of state legislatures and the Continental Congress as they geared up for war. Soldiers were requested to report for duty with muskets, gunpowder, and cartridges; when they were underarmed, their officers let superiors know. A New Hampshire captain complained of his unit's plight in June 1775: "We are in want of both arms and ammunition. There is but very little, or none worth mentioning—perhaps one pound of powder to twenty men, and not one-half our men have arms." A militia officer in Pennsylvania noted that men who owned high-quality muskets and rifles were often reluctant to report for duty with them unless assured they would be reimbursed in the event of loss of the valuable possession. A Prussian general, who volunteered his expertise to the Continental army, arrived at Valley Forge in 1778 and was shocked to find "muskets, carbines, fowling pieces, and rifles" all in the same company of troops. While this evidence points to an underarmed soldiery, the opposite evidence—militia captains who failed to register complaints—did not leave a paper trail for historians.

Certainly the Continental Congress understood that obtaining more muskets was essential to the war effort. Before 1774, American ironworks artisans imported British-made gunlocks, the central firing mechanism, and added the wooden stock and iron barrel to produce muskets. But the British Parliament, anticipating trouble, prohibited all gunlock and firearm exports to the colonies in October 1774. Congress turned to French and Dutch suppliers to purchase gunlocks, gunpowder, and finished muskets.

Muskets and even fowling pieces worked well enough for the Revolutionary War, where combatants on both sides were similarly armed and engaged in choreographed and synchronized firing at close range. Not until the fourth and fifth decades of the nineteenth century would the United States begin to manufacture firearms whose components were machine-tooled rather than handcrafted, leading to a faster and cheaper manufacturing process and more accurate and deadly weapons. With handguns like the Colt revolver and rifles like the Remington, both with repeat-fire capability, America entered an entirely new stage in gun history.

Washington made as commander in chief. But as manpower needs increased, the northern states began to welcome free blacks into service; even slaves could serve in some states, with their masters' permission. About five thousand black men served in the Revolutionary War on the rebel side, mostly from the northern states. Black Continental soldiers sometimes were segregated into separate units; two battalions from Rhode Island were entirely black. Just under three hundred blacks joined regiments from Connecticut. While some of these were draftees, others were clearly inspired by the ideals of freedom being voiced in a war against tyranny. For example, twenty-three blacks gave "Liberty," "Freedom," or "Freeman" as their surname at the time of enlistment.

Military service helped to politicize Americans during the early stages of the war. In early 1776, independence was a risky idea, potentially treasonous. But as the war heated up and recruiters demanded commitment, some Americans discovered that apathy had its dangers as well. Anyone who refused to serve ran the risk of being called a traitor to the cause. Military service established one's credentials as a patriot; it became a prime way of defining and demonstrating political allegiance.

The American army was at times raw and inexperienced and much of the time woefully undermanned. It never had the precision and discipline of European professional armies. But it was never as bad as the British continually assumed. The British were to learn that it was a serious mistake to underrate the enemy.

The British Strategy

The American strategy was relatively straightforward—to repulse and defeat an invading army. The British strategy was not nearly so clear. England wanted to put down a rebellion and restore monarchical power in the colonies, but the question was how to accomplish this. A decisive defeat of the Continental army was essential but not sufficient to end the rebellion, for the British would still have to contend with an armed and highly motivated insurgent population.

Furthermore, there was no single political nerve center whose capture would spell certain victory. The Continental Congress floated from place to place, staying just out of reach of the British. During the course of the war, the British captured and

for a time occupied every major port city—Boston, New York, Newport, Philadelphia, and Charleston—essential for receiving their constant caravan of supply ships. But capturing them brought no serious loss to the Americans, 95 percent of whom lived in the countryside.

England's delicate task was to restore the old governments, not to destroy an enemy country. Hence, the British generals were usually reluctant to ravage the countryside, confiscate food, or burn villages and towns. There were thirteen distinct political entities to capture, pacify, and then restore to the crown, and they were spread out in a long line from New Hampshire to Georgia. Clearly a large land army was required for the job. Without the willingness to seize food from the locals, such an army needed hundreds of supply ships that could keep several months' worth of food in storage. Another ingredient of the British strategy was the untested assumption that many Americans remained loyal to the king and would come to their aid. Without substantial numbers of loyal subjects, the plan to restore old royal governments made no sense.

The overall British plan was a divide-and-conquer approach, focusing first on New York, the state judged to harbor the greatest number of loyal subjects. New York offered a geographic advantage as well: Control of the Hudson River would allow the British to isolate those troublesome New Englanders. Armies could descend from Canada and move up from New York City along the Hudson River into western Massachusetts. Between a naval blockade on the eastern coast and army raids in the west, Massachusetts could be driven to surrender. New Jersey and Pennsylvania would fall in line, the British thought, due to loyalist strength. Virginia was a problem, like Massachusetts, but the British were confident that the Carolinas would help them isolate and subdue Virginia. Or so the British hoped.

Quebec, New York, and New Jersey

In late 1775, an American expedition was swiftly launched to capture the British cities Montreal and Quebec before British reinforcements could arrive. This offensive was a clear sign that the war was not purely a reaction to the invasion of Massachusetts. A force of New York Continentals commanded by General Richard Montgomery took Montreal easily in September 1775 and then advanced on Quebec.

Meanwhile, a second contingent of Continentals led by Colonel Benedict Arnold moved through Maine to Quebec, a punishing trek through freezing rain with woefully inadequate supplies; many men died. Arnold's determination to get to Quebec was heroic, but in human costs the campaign was a tragedy. Arnold and Montgomery jointly attacked Quebec in December but failed to take the city (Map 7.1). Worse yet, they encountered smallpox, which killed more men than had been felled by the British.

The main action of the first year of war came not in Canada, however, but in New York, so crucial to England. In August 1776, some 45,000 British troops (including 8,000 German mercenaries, called Hessians) landed south of New York City, under the command of General Howe. General Washington had anticipated that New York would be Howe's target and had moved his army, numbering about 20,000, south from Massachusetts. The Battle of Long Island, in late August 1776, pitted the well-trained British redcoats against a very green Continental army. Howe attacked, inflicting many casualties (1,500 dead and wounded) and spreading panic among the American soldiers, who fled under fire to the eastern edge of Long Island. Howe failed to press forward, however, perhaps remembering the costly victory of Bunker Hill, and in the meantime Washington evacuated his troops to Manhattan Island in the dead of a foggy night.

Washington knew it would be hard to hold Manhattan, so he further withdrew north to two critical forts on either side of the Hudson River. For two months, the armies engaged in limited skirmishing, but in November, Howe finally captured Fort Washington and Fort Lee, taking thousands of prisoners. Washington retreated quickly across New Jersey into Pennsylvania. Yet again, Howe unaccountably failed to press his advantage. Had he attacked Washington's army at Philadelphia, he probably would have taken the city. Instead he parked his German troops in winter quarters along the Delaware River. Perhaps he knew that many of the Continental soldiers' enlistment periods ended on December 31, so he felt confident that the Americans would not attack him. But he was wrong. On Christmas—a holiday Germans celebrated with much more spirit (and spirits) than did Americans—Washington recrossed the Delaware River at night with 2,400 men and made a quick capture of the unsuspecting German soldiers at Trenton. This impressive victory did much to restore the sagging morale of the patriot side. For the next two weeks, Washington remained on the offensive, capturing supplies in a clever attack on British units at Princeton on January 3. Soon he was safe in Morristown, in northern New Jersey, settled in for the winter, finally with time enough to administer mass smallpox inoculations and see the men through the abbreviated course of the disease. Future recruits would also face inoculation.

All in all, in the first year of declared war, the rebellious Americans had a few isolated moments to feel proud of but also much to worry about. The very inexperienced Continental army had barely hung on in the New York campaign. Washington had shown exceptional daring as well as admirable restraint, but what really saved the Americans may have been the repeated reluctance of the British to follow through militarily when they had the advantage.

The Home Front

Battlefields alone did not determine the outcome of the war. Struggles on the home front were equally important. In 1776, each community contained small numbers of highly committed people on both sides and far larger numbers who were uncertain about whether independence was worth a war. The contest for the allegiance of the many neutrals thus was a major factor, and both persuasion and force were used. Revolutionaries who took control of local government often used it to punish loyalists and intimidate neutrals. On their side, loyalists worked to reestablish British authority. The struggle to secure political allegiance was complicated greatly by the wartime instability of the economy. The creative financing of the fledgling government brought hardships as well as opportunities, forcing Americans to confront new manifestations of virtue and corruption.

Patriotism at the Local Level

Committees of correspondence, of public safety, and of inspection dominated the political landscape in patriot communities. These committees took on more than customary local governance; they enforced boycotts, picked army draftees, and policed suspected traitors. They sometimes invaded homes to search for contraband goods.

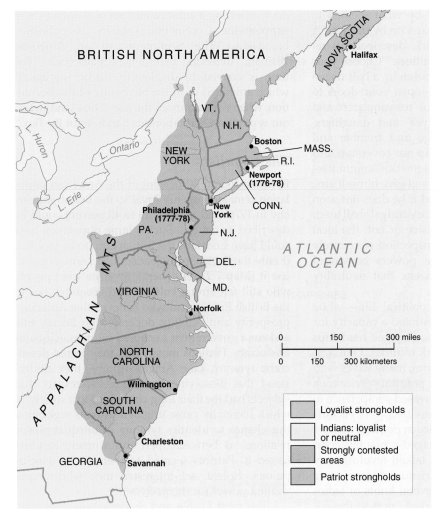

MAP 7.2
Loyalist Strength and Rebel Support
The exact number of loyalists can never be known. No one could have made an accurate count at the time; in addition, political allegiance often shifted with the winds. This map shows the pockets of loyalist strength on which the British relied— the lower Hudson valley and the Carolina Piedmont.

READING THE MAP: Which forces were stronger, those loyal to Britain or those rebelling? What areas were contested? If the contested areas ultimately sided with the British, how would the balance of power change?
CONNECTIONS: Who was more likely to be a loyalist, and why? How many loyalists left the United States, and where did they go?

www.bedfordstmartins.com/ roarkcompact SEE THE ON-LINE STUDY GUIDE for more help in analyzing this map.

eventually most were drawn in, many taking the British side. The powerful Iroquois confederacy divided, with Mohawks, Cayugas, Senecas, and Onondagas lining up with the British, while the Oneidas and Tuscaroras aided the Americans. One young Mohawk leader, Thayendanegea (known to Americans as Joseph Brant), traveled to England in 1775 to complain to King George about how the colonists repeatedly deceived the Mohawks. "It is very hard when we have let the King's subjects have so much of our lands for so little value," he wrote, "they should want to cheat us in this manner of the small spots we have left for our women and children to live on. We are tired out in making complaints & getting no redress." Thayenda-

negea negotiated Indian support for the king in exchange for protection from encroaching settlers, under a revived implementation of the Proclamation Act of 1763.

Pockets of loyalism thus existed everywhere, in the middle colonies, in the backcountry of the southern colonies, and out beyond the Appalachian Mountains in Indian country. Even New England towns at the heart of turmoil, like Concord, Massachusetts, had a small and increasingly silenced core of loyalists who refused to countenance armed revolution.

The loyalists were most vocal between 1774 and 1776, when the possibility of a full-scale rebellion against England was still uncertain. Loyalists chal-

JOSEPH BRANT
The Mohawk leader Thayendanegea, called Joseph Brant by Americans, had been educated in English ways at Eleazar Wheelock's New England school (which became Dartmouth College in 1769). In 1775, the thirty-four-year-old Brant traveled to England with another warrior to negotiate Mohawk support for the British. While there, he had his portrait painted by English artist George Romney. Notice that Brant wears a metal gorget around his neck over his English shirt, along with Indian armbands, sash, and headdress. A gorget was a symbolic piece of armor, a shrunken version of a throatpiece from the feudal days of metal-clad knights. Many military men, both white and Indian, wore gorgets when they dressed formally for portraits — or for war.
National Gallery of Canada, Ottawa.

lenged the emerging patriot side using pamphlets, broadsides, and newspapers. In New York City in 1776, some loyalists even circulated a broadside titled "A Declaration of Dependence," in rebuttal to the congress's July 4 manifesto, denouncing this "most unnatural, unprovoked Rebellion that ever disgraced the annals of Time."

Who Is a Traitor?

In June 1775, the First Continental Congress passed a resolution declaring loyalists to be traitors. Over the next year, state laws defined as treason acts such as joining or provisioning the British army, saying or printing anything that undermined patriot morale, or discouraging men from enlisting in the Continental army. Punishments ranged from house arrest and suspension of voting privileges to confiscation of property and deportation. And sometimes self-appointed committees of Tory hunters bypassed the judicial niceties and terrorized loyalists, raiding their houses or tarring and feathering them.

A question rarely asked in the heat of the revolutionary moment was whether the wives of loyalists were traitors as well. When loyalist families fled the country, property held in the name of the family patriarch was then confiscated. But what if the wife stayed? One Connecticut woman brought witnesses to testify that she was "a steady and true and faithful friend to the American states in opposition to her husband, who has been of quite a different character." In such cases, the court typically allowed the woman to keep one-third of the property, the amount she was due if widowed, and confiscated the rest. But even when the wife fled with her husband, was she necessarily a traitor? If he insisted, was she not obligated to go? Such questions came up in several lawsuits after the Revolution, where descendants of refugee loyalists sued to regain property that had entered the family through the mother's inheritance. In one well-publicized Massachusetts case in 1805, the outcome confirmed the traditional view of women as political blank slates; the American son of loyalist refugee Anna Martin recovered her property on the grounds that she had no independent will to be a loyalist.

Tarring and feathering, property confiscation, deportation, terrorism—to the loyalists, such denials of liberty of conscience and of freedom to own private property proved that democratic tyranny was more to be feared than the monarchical variety. A Boston loyalist, Mather Byles, aptly expressed this point: "They call me a brainless Tory, but tell me . . . which is better—to be ruled by one tyrant three thousand miles away, or by three thousand tyrants not a mile away?" Byles was soon sentenced to deportation.

Throughout the war, probably 7,000 to 8,000 loyalists fled to England, while 28,000 found closer haven in Canada. But many chose to remain in the new United States and tried to swing with the changing political fortunes. In some instances, that proved difficult. In New Jersey, for example, 3,000 Jerseyites felt protected (or scared) enough by the occupying British army in 1776 to swear an oath of allegiance to the king. But then General Howe drew back to New York City, leaving them to the mercy of local patriot committees. British strategy depended on using loyalists to hold occupied territory, but the New Jersey experience showed just how poorly that strategy was carried out.

Financial Instability and Corruption

Wars cost money—for arms and ammunition, for food and uniforms, for soldiers' pay. The Continental Congress printed money, but within a few short years its value had deteriorated since the congress held no reserves of gold or silver to back the currency. In practice, the currency was worth only what a buyer and seller agreed it was worth. The dollar eventually bottomed out at one-fortieth of its face value; a loaf of bread that once sold for two and a half cents now sold for a dollar. States too were printing their own paper money to pay for wartime expenses, further complicating the economy.

Soon the congress had to resort to other means to procure supplies and labor. One method was to borrow hard money (coins, not paper) from wealthy men, who would get certificates of debt (also called public securities) promising repayment with interest. In effect, the wealthy men had bought government bonds. To pay soldiers, the congress offered land bounties, which amounted to a promise of a tangible form of wealth. Public securities and land bounties quickly became a form of negotiable currency. For example, a soldier with no cash might sell his land bounty certificate to get food for his family. These certificates also fluctuated in value, mainly depreciating.

Depreciating currency inevitably led to rising prices, as sellers compensated for the falling value of the money. The wartime economy of the late 1770s, with its unreliable currency and price inflation, was extremely demoralizing to Americans everywhere. So local committees of public safety in 1778 began to fix prices on goods such as flour, bread, and other essentials for short periods in an effort to impose some stability.

Inevitably, some Americans turned this unstable situation to their advantage. Money that fell fast in value needed to be spent quickly; being in debt was suddenly advantageous because the debt could be repaid weeks later in devalued currency. A brisk black market sprang up in prohibited luxury imports, such as tea, sugar, textiles, and wines. No matter that these items came from Britain. A New Hampshire delegate to the congress denounced the extravagance that flew in the face of the virtuous homespun association agreements of just a few years before: "We are a crooked and perverse generation, longing for the fineries and follies of those Egyptian task masters from whom we have so lately freed ourselves."

The Campaigns of 1777–1779: Highs and Lows

In early 1777, the Continental army had a bleak road ahead. Washington had shown considerable skill in avoiding outright defeat, but the minor victories in New Jersey lent only faint optimism to the American side. The British moved large numbers of soldiers into Quebec, readying their plan to isolate New England by controlling the Hudson River.

Burgoyne's Army and the Battle of Saratoga

In 1777, British General John Burgoyne assumed command of an army of 7,800 soldiers in Canada and began the northern squeeze on the Hudson River valley. His goal was to capture Albany, a town 150 miles north of New York City near the intersection of the Hudson and Mohawk Rivers (see Map 7.1). In addition to his soldiers, Burgoyne traveled with another 1,000 assorted "camp followers" (cooks, laundresses, musicians) and some 400 Indian warriors and scouts. This very large army did not travel light, requiring food supplies not only for 9,200 people but also for the more than 400 horses needed to haul heavy artillery. Burgoyne, who was nicknamed "Gentleman Johnny," also carted thirty trunks of personal belongings, including fine wines and elegant clothing.

Burgoyne first captured Fort Ticonderoga with ease. Some 3,000 American troops stationed there

spotted the approaching British and, low on food and supplies, abandoned the fort without a fight. The British continued to move south, but the large army moved slowly on primitive roads through heavily forested land.

The logical second step in isolating New England should have been to advance troops up the Hudson from New York City to meet Burgoyne. American surveillance indicated that General Howe in Manhattan was readying his men for a major move in August 1777. George Washington, watching from New Jersey, was astonished to see Howe's men sail south; Howe had decided to try to capture Philadelphia.

The third prong of British strategy involved troops moving east from the Great Lakes down the Mohawk River, aided by Mohawks and Senecas of Joseph Brant's Iroquois League. The British believed that the Palatine Germans living in the Mohawk valley were heavily loyalist, so they expected little trouble getting to Albany. But a hundred miles west of their goal they encountered American soldiers at Fort Stanwix, reinforced by Palatine Germans and Oneida Indians. The Seneca ambushed the Germans and their onetime allies the Oneida in a narrow ravine called Oriskany and inflicted heavy losses. But Fort Stanwix held back the British and Seneca and eventually sent them into retreat (see Map 7.1).

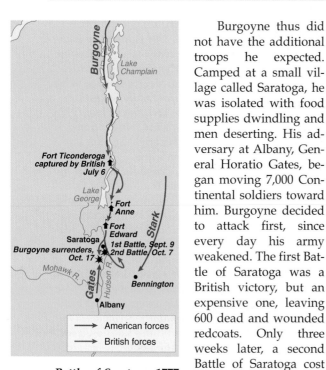

Battle of Saratoga, 1777

Burgoyne thus did not have the additional troops he expected. Camped at a small village called Saratoga, he was isolated with food supplies dwindling and men deserting. His adversary at Albany, General Horatio Gates, began moving 7,000 Continental soldiers toward him. Burgoyne decided to attack first, since every day his army weakened. The first Battle of Saratoga was a British victory, but an expensive one, leaving 600 dead and wounded redcoats. Only three weeks later, a second Battle of Saratoga cost the British another 600 men and most of their cannons. Burgoyne finally surrendered to the American forces on October 17, 1777.

General Howe, meanwhile, had succeeded in occupying Philadelphia in September 1777. Figuring that the Saratoga loss was balanced by the capture of Philadelphia, the British government proposed a negotiated settlement—not including independence—to end the war. But the American side refused.

Their optimism was not well founded, however, in the winter of 1777–78. Spirits ran high, but arms and food supplies ran precariously low. Washington moved his troops into winter quarters at Valley Forge, a day's march west of occupied Philadelphia. Quartered in drafty sheds, the men lacked blankets, boots, and stockings. Washington complained to the congress that nearly 3,000 of his men were "unfit for duty because they are bare foot and otherwise naked"; without blankets, large numbers were forced to "set up all Night by fires, instead of taking comfortable rest in a natural way." Food was also scarce. Local farms had produced adequate grain that year, but Washington was sure that the farmers were selling it to the British, who could pay with the king's silver.

The evidence of corruption indeed appeared abundant. Army suppliers too often provided defective food, clothing, and gunpowder. Washington's men unfolded a shipment of blankets only to discover that they were a quarter of their customary size. Teamsters who hauled barrels of preserved salted meat might drain out the brine to lighten their load and then refill the barrels later, allowing the meat to rot in transit. Selfishness and greed seemed to infect the American side. As one Continental officer said, "The people at home are destroying the Army by their conduct much faster than Howe and all his army can possibly do by fighting us."

The War in Indian Country

By 1779, it was clear that neutrality was not a viable option for the approximately 150,000 Indians living just west of the Appalachian Mountains. Despite the 1763 Proclamation Act, by 1778 something like 50,000 American settlers, many of them recent Scots-Irish immigrants to the colonies, had penetrated Indian country. The British maintained military outposts at Niagara and Detroit, but Fort Pitt was now an American garrison.

Even though the 1776 Declaration of Independence blamed the British for inciting "Savages," a significant group of Delaware and Shawnee Indians sought peace with the Americans—until 1778, when a series of murderous actions by frontier soldiers converted them to enemies. A Delaware leader named White Eyes negotiated a treaty with the Americans at Fort Pitt in mid-1778, pledging Indian support in the war in exchange for supplies and trade goods. But supplies and goods were not forthcoming, and escalating violence undermined the agreement. In one incident, American soldiers captured and killed friendly Shawnee chiefs Cornstalk and Red Hawk. A short time later, White Eyes himself was murdered by militiamen. Despite Indian professions of support, American military leaders repeatedly had trouble honoring distinctions between allied and enemy Indians.

Soon, isolated instances of violence escalated into anti-Indian campaigns. In North Carolina, militias attacked Cherokee settlements, destroying thirty-six villages and burning fields and livestock. To the north, Continental army troops carried out a planned campaign of terror and destruction against the Iroquois in western New York in late summer of 1779. Forty Indian towns met with total destruction; the soldiers looted and torched the dwellings, then burned cornfields and fruit orchards. Smallpox soon followed. The Delaware and Shawnee town of Coshocton, west of Fort Pitt, consisting of some two thousand inhabitants and still, amazingly, pro-American, was attacked and burned to the ground by militiamen in 1781. In these and other violent raids, Indians were driven into the hills, into starvation, and into the arms of the British at Detroit and Niagara, or into the arms of the Spanish west of the Mississippi River.

The French Alliance

On their own, the Americans could not have defeated England, and the western pressure from hostile Indians magnified their task. But essential help arrived as a result of the victory at Saratoga, which convinced the French to enter the war; a formal alliance was signed in February 1778. France recognized the United States as an independent nation and promised full military and commercial support throughout the war. The most crucial support was the French navy, which now could challenge England's transatlantic pipeline of supplies and troops.

Although France had been waiting for a promising American victory to justify a formal declaration of war, since 1776 the French had provided aid to the Americans in the form of cannons, muskets, gunpowder, and highly trained military advisors. Still, monarchical France was understandably cautious about endorsing a democratic revolution that attacked the principles of kingship. The main attraction of an alliance for France was simply the opportunity to defeat England, its archrival. A victory would also open pathways to trade and perhaps result in France acquiring the coveted British West Indies. Even American defeat was not a full disaster for France, if the war took many years and drained England of men and money.

The French support materialized slowly. The navy arrived off the coast of Virginia in July 1778 but then went south to the West Indies to defend the sugar islands. By 1781, the French proved indispensable to the American victory, but the first months of the alliance brought no dramatic victories, leading some Americans to grumble that the partnership would prove worthless.

The Southern Strategy and the End of the War

When France joined the war, some British officials wondered whether the fight was worth continuing. A troop commander, arguing for an immediate negotiated settlement, shrewdly observed that "we are far from an anticipated peace, because the bitterness of the rebels is too widespread, and in regions where we are masters the rebellious spirit is still in them. The land is too large, and there are too many people. The more land we win, the weaker our army gets in the field." The commander of the British navy argued for abandoning the war, and even Lord North, the prime minister, agreed. But the king was determined to crush the rebellion, and he encouraged a new strategy for victory. It was a brilliant but desperate plan.

Georgia and South Carolina

The new strategy abandoned New England and instead focused on the South, perhaps easier to recapture for the crown. The southern region had valuable crops—tobacco, rice, and indigo—worth keeping under the British flag. Further, the large slave population was a powerful destabilizing factor from which the British hoped to benefit. White southerners feared the instability of all-out war, which might unleash violence from slaves seizing the moment to claim freedom. Georgia and the Carolinas also looked promising for victory because of the large pockets of loyalists presumed to be militant. The British hoped to recapture the southern colonies one by one, restore the loyalists to power, and then move north to the more problematic middle colonies, saving prickly New England for last.

Georgia, the first target, fell at the end of December 1778 (Map 7.3). A small army of British soldiers occupied Savannah and Augusta, and a new royal governor and loyalist assembly were quickly installed. Taking Georgia was easy because the bulk of the Continental army was in New York and New Jersey, keeping an eye on General Henry Clinton, Howe's replacement as commander in chief, and the French were in the West Indies. The British in Georgia quickly organized twenty loyal militia units, and 1,400 Georgians swore an oath of allegiance to the king. So far, the plan looked as if it might work.

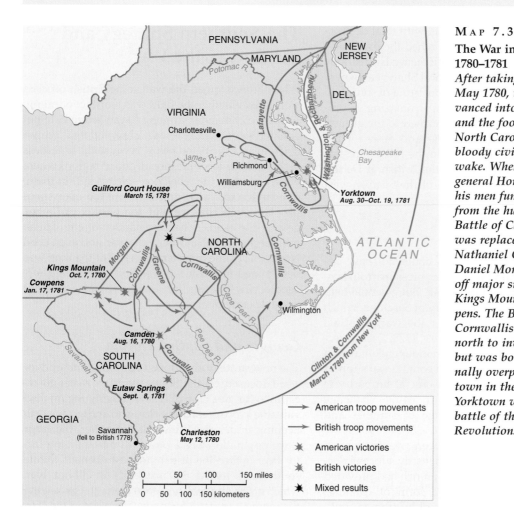

MAP 7.3

The War in the South, 1780–1781

After taking Charleston in May 1780, the British advanced into South Carolina and the foothill region of North Carolina, leaving a bloody civil war in their wake. When the American general Horatio Gates and his men fumbled and fled from the humiliating Battle of Camden, Gates was replaced by Generals Nathaniel Greene and Daniel Morgan, who pulled off major successes at Kings Mountain and Cowpens. The British general Cornwallis then moved north to invade Virginia, but was bottled up and finally overpowered at Yorktown in the fall of 1781. Yorktown was the last battle of the American Revolution.

The next target was South Carolina. General Clinton moved British troops south from New York, while the Continental army put ten regiments into Charleston to defend it. For five weeks in early 1780, the British laid siege to the city, which finally surrendered in mid-May 1780, sending 3,300 soldiers, a tremendous loss, into British captivity. Again, the king's new strategy seemed to be on target.

Clinton returned to New York, leaving the task of pacifying South Carolina to General Charles Cornwallis and 4,000 troops. The boldest of all the British generals in the war for America, Lord Cornwallis quickly moved into action. He chased out the remaining Continental army units and established military control of the province by midsummer 1780. He purged rebels from government office and disarmed potential rebel militias. The export of

South Carolina's main crop, rice, resumed, and, as in Georgia, pardons were offered to Carolinians who swore loyalty oaths to the crown and then proved their loyalty by taking up arms for the British.

In August 1780, the Continental army was ready to strike back at Cornwallis. General Gates, the hero of the Battle of Saratoga, arrived in South Carolina with more than 3,000 troops, some of them experienced army units and others green militiamen. They met Cornwallis's army at Camden, South Carolina, on August 16 (Map 7.3). Gates put the militiamen into the center of the battle, where a contagious panic gripped them at the sight of the approaching enemy cavalry. Men threw down unfired muskets and ran from the field of battle. When regiment leaders tried to regroup the next day, only

BENEDICT ARNOLD
This portrait shows Benedict Arnold in 1776, when he was the hero of the Quebec campaign. Probably the final straw for Arnold came when he failed to earn promotion, while men he considered inferior were elevated to higher rank.
Anne S. K. Brown Military Collection, Providence, R.I.

700 showed up, the rest dead, captured, or still in flight. Camden was a devastating defeat; prospects now seemed very grim for the Americans.

The new British strategy succeeded in 1780 partly because of improved information about American troop movements that was secretly furnished to the British by Benedict Arnold, the one-time American hero of several key battles. Arnold was a brilliant military talent but also a deeply insecure man who never felt he got his due, in either honor or financial reward. Sometime in 1779, he opened secret negotiations with General Clinton in New York, trading information for money and hinting he could deliver far more of value. When he was assigned the command of West Point, a new fort sixty miles north of New York City on the Hudson River, his plan crystallized. West Point controlled the Hudson; its easy capture by the British might well have meant instant victory in the war.

Arnold's treasonous plot to sell a West Point victory to the British was foiled by the capture of the messenger between Arnold and Clinton. News of the Arnold treason created shock waves. Arnold represented all of the patriots' worst fears: greedy self-interest like that of the war profiteers, unprincipled abandonment of war aims like that of the turncoat Tories of the South, panic like that of the terrified soldiers with Gates at Camden. But instead of symbolizing all that was troubling about the American side of the war, the treachery of Arnold became celebrated in a kind of displacement of the anxieties of the moment. Vilifying Arnold allowed Americans to stake out a wide distance between themselves and dastardly conduct. It inspired a renewal of patriotism at a particularly low moment.

The Other Southern War: Guerrillas

Shock over Gates's defeat at Camden and Arnold's treason revitalized rebel support in western South Carolina, an area that Cornwallis had believed to be pacified and loyal. The backcountry of the South soon became the site of a guerrilla war. In hit-and-run attacks, both sides burned and ravaged not only opponents' property but the property of anyone claiming to be neutral. The loyalist militia units organized by the British were met by fierce rebel militia units who now figured they had little to lose. Guerrilla warfare soon spread to Georgia and North Carolina. In South Carolina, some six thousand men became active partisan fighters, and they entered into at least twenty-six engagements with loyalist units. Some of these were classic battles; but on other occasions the fighters were more like bandits than soldiers. Both sides committed murders and atrocities and plundered property, clear deviations from standard military practice.

The British southern strategy counted on sufficient loyalist strength to hold reconquered territory as the army moved north. The backcountry civil war proved this assumption false. The Americans won few major battles in the South, but they ultimately succeeded by harassing the British forces and thus preventing them from foraging for food. Cornwallis boldly moved the war into North Carolina in late 1780, not because he thought South Carolina was secure—it was not—but because the North Carolinians were supplying the South Carolina rebels with arms and men (see Map 7.3). But news of a brutal massacre of loyalist units in western South Carolina at Kings Mountain, at the hands of 1,400 frontier riflemen, sent him hurrying back. The British were stretched too thin to hold even two of their onetime colonies.

Surrender at Yorktown

In the early months of 1781, Cornwallis set out to try his North Carolina plan again; if successful, it would isolate South Carolina and Georgia. For months, he moved his army around the province, taking land but not holding it. So Cornwallis decided to push the war farther north, into Virginia. He captured Williamsburg, which had been the colony's old seat of royal government. He raided Charlottesville, where Virginia's revolutionary government was meeting, and seized members of the assembly. As late as the start of September, Cornwallis was not wrong to think he had the upper hand in Virginia.

What changed the picture dramatically was an infusion of French military support. A large French army under the command of the comte de Rochambeau had joined Washington in Rhode Island in mid-1780. News that a large fleet had sailed from France in the spring of 1781 set in motion Washington's plan to defeat the British. The fleet, commanded by the comte de Grasse, was bound for the Chesapeake Bay, so Washington and Rochambeau fixed their attention on Virginia. Bypassing New York (where Clinton had been expecting an attack), thousands of American and French soldiers headed south in August 1781.

By the time British ships arrived to defend the Chesapeake, the French had already taken control of it. A five-day naval battle in early September sent the British ships limping away and left the French in clear command of the Virginia and North Carolina coasts. This proved to be the decisive factor in ending the war, because it eliminated a water escape route for Cornwallis's land army, encamped at Yorktown, Virginia.

General Cornwallis and his 7,500 troops now faced a combined French and American army numbering over 16,000. For twelve days, the Americans and French bombarded the British fortifications at Yorktown; Cornwallis ran low on food and ammunition. An American observer keeping a diary noted that "the enemy, from want of forage, are killing off their horses in great numbers. Six or seven hundred of these valuable animals have been killed, and their carcasses are almost continually floating down the river." Realizing escape was impossible, Cornwallis signaled his intention to surrender. On October 19, 1781, he formally capitulated.

What had begun as a promising southern strategy by the British in 1778 had turned into a discouraging defeat by 1781. British attacks in the South energized American resistance, as did the timely exposure of Benedict Arnold's treason. The arrival of the French fleet sealed the fate of Cornwallis at

Siege of Yorktown, 1781

Yorktown, and the military war quickly came to a halt.

The Losers and the Winners

The surrender at Yorktown proved to be the end of the war, but it took some time for the principals to realize that. The peace treaty was nearly two years in the making, with both the American and the British armies still in the field, in case the treaty fell through. King George tenaciously clung to the idea of pursuing the war, but the sentiment for a formal peace was growing in Parliament. The war had become unpopular among the British citizenry in general, and support for it dwindled until finally the king had to realize it was over.

It took six months for the three American commissioners, Benjamin Franklin, John Adams, and John Jay of New York, to negotiate the three-way settlement in Paris, but at last, in November 1782, eighty-two articles of peace were agreed to. The first article went to the heart of the matter: "His Britannic Majesty acknowledges the said United States to be free Sovereign and independent States." Other articles described the boundaries of the new country and guaranteed that creditors on both sides could collect debts owed them in sterling money, a provision especially important to British merchants. England agreed to withdraw its troops quickly; more than a decade later, this promise would still not be fully kept. The final, official peace treaty—

the Treaty of Paris—was signed nearly a year later, on September 2, 1783.

As at the end of the French and Indian War, no article in this treaty recognized the Indians as players in the war. Indian lands were assigned to the victors as though they were uninhabited. Many Indian refugees had fled, some west into Missouri and Arkansas, others into Canada, and yet others into Spanish Florida. Their movements helped spread the deadly smallpox epidemic to the far ends of the continent. But significant numbers remained within the new United States, displaced from their ancestral homelands. For them, the peace of 1783 was only a temporary lull in a much longer war that would extend at least until 1795. As one delegation of Indians reported to the Spanish governor at St. Louis in 1784, the Revolutionary War was "the greatest blow that could have been dealt us, unless it had been our total destruction."

With the treaty finally signed, the British began their evacuation of New York, Charleston, and Savannah, a process complicated by the sheer numbers involved—soldiers, fearful loyalists, and runaway slaves by the thousands. In New York City, more than 27,000 soldiers and 30,000 loyalists sailed on hundreds of ships for England in late fall 1783. In a final act of mischief, on the November day when the last ships left, the losing side raised the British flag at the southern tip of Manhattan, cut away the ropes used to hoist it, and greased the flagpole.

Conclusion: Why the British Lost

The British began the war for America convinced that they could not lose. They had the strongest and best-trained army and navy in the world; they were familiar with the American landscape from the French and Indian War; they outnumbered their opponents in uniform; and they easily captured every port city of consequence in America. Probably one-fifth of the population was loyalist, and another two-fifths were undecided. Why, then, did they lose?

One continuing problem the British faced was the uncertainty of supplies. Unwilling to ravage the countryside, the army depended on a steady stream of supply ships from home. Insecurity about food helps explain the repeated reluctance of Howe and

Clinton to pursue the Continental army aggressively.

A second obstacle to British success was their continual misuse of loyalist energies. Any plan to repacify the colonies required the cooperation of the loyalists as well as new support from the many neutrals. But again and again, the British failed to back the loyalists, leaving them to the mercy of vengeful rebels. In the South, they allowed loyalist militias to engage in vicious guerrilla warfare that drove away potential converts among the rest of the population.

The French alliance looms large in any explanation of the British defeat. The artillery and ammunition the French supplied even before 1778 were critical necessities for the Continental army. In 1780, the French army brought a fresh infusion of troops to a war-weary America, and the French navy made the Yorktown victory possible. The major naval defeat in the Chesapeake, just before the Yorktown siege, dissolved the pro-war spirit in England and forced the king to admit it was over.

Finally, the British abdicated civil power in the colonies in 1775 and 1776, when royal officials were forced to flee to safety, and they never really regained it. For nearly seven years, of necessity the Americans created their own government structures, from the Continental Congress to local committees and militias. Staffed by many who before 1775 had been the political elites, these new government agencies had remarkably little trouble establishing their authority to rule. The basic British goal—to turn back the clock to imperial rule—receded into impossibility as the war dragged on.

The war for America had taken five and a half years to fight, from Lexington to Yorktown; negotiations and the evacuation took two more. It profoundly disrupted the lives of Americans everywhere. It was a war for independence from England, but it was more. It was a war that required men and women to think about politics and the legitimacy of authority. The precise disagreement with England about representation and political participation had profound implications for the kinds of governance the Americans would adopt, both in the moment of emergency, and in the longer run of the late 1770s and early 1780s when states began to write their constitutions. The rhetoric employed to justify the revolution against England put words like *liberty, tyranny, slavery, independence,* and *equality* into common usage. These words carried far deeper meanings than a mere complaint over taxation without representation. As Abigail Adams and others saw, the Revolution unleashed a dynamic of equality and liberty. That it was largely unintended and unwanted by the revolutionary leaders of 1776 made it all the more potent a force in American life in the decades to come.

FOR FURTHER READING ABOUT THE TOPICS IN THIS CHAPTER, see the Online Bibliography at www.bedfordstmartins.com/roarkcompact.

FOR ADDITIONAL FIRST-HAND ACCOUNTS OF THIS PERIOD, see pages 93–112 in Michael Johnson, ed., *Reading the American Past,* Second Edition, Volume I.

TO ASSESS YOUR MASTERY OF THE MATERIAL IN THIS CHAPTER, see the Online Study Guide at www.bedfordstmartins.com/roarkcompact.

CHRONOLOGY

1775   **May 10.** Second Continental Congress convenes in Philadelphia.

June 14. Continental Congress creates Continental army.

June 17. Battle of Bunker Hill won by the British, though at a great cost.

July. Congress offers Olive Branch Petition in attempt at reconciliation with king.

September. American army marches on Montreal and Quebec.

1776   **January.** Americans lose assault on Quebec.

Thomas Paine's *Common Sense* published.

March. British evacuate Boston.

July 4. Declaration of Independence adopted.

August 27. Battle of Long Island results in heavy American casualties.

September. British take Manhattan when American army retreats to Fort Washington and Fort Lee.

November. Americans retreat to Philadelphia.

Howe's troops capture Fort Washington and Fort Lee.

December 26. Washington surprises British and Hessians at Trenton.

1777   **January.** American army winters at Morristown, New Jersey.

July. Burgoyne takes Fort Ticonderoga for British.

August. Seneca ambush at Oriskany, but Americans hold Fort Stanwix against British attack.

September. Howe and the British occupy Philadelphia.

October 17. Burgoyne surrenders at Saratoga.

December. Washington leads army into winter quarters at Valley Forge, Pennsylvania.

1778   **February.** France enters war on American side.

July–August. French fleet threatens British occupation of New York and Newport, Rhode Island.

December. Savannah, Georgia, falls to British.

1779   **January–June.** Skirmishes in South Carolina and Georgia.

October. British evacuate Newport.

1780   Philadelphia Ladies Association raises money for soldiers.

March–May. British lay siege to Charleston, South Carolina.

July. Comte de Rochambeau and French army arrive at Newport.

August 16. Battle of Camden, South Carolina, dims hopes for Americans.

September–October. Benedict Arnold's treason exposed.

September–December. Guerrilla warfare starts in South Carolina and spreads to Georgia and North Carolina.

October 7. Battle of Kings Mountain, South Carolina, results in heavy loyalist casualties.

1781   **January 17.** Battle of Cowpens, South Carolina.

May–August. Cornwallis pushes army into Virginia, capturing Williamsburg.

August. Cornwallis occupies Yorktown, Virginia.

September 5. French fleet takes Chesapeake Bay.

September 28–October 19. Siege of Yorktown.

October 19. Cornwallis surrenders.

1783   Treaty of Paris ends war.

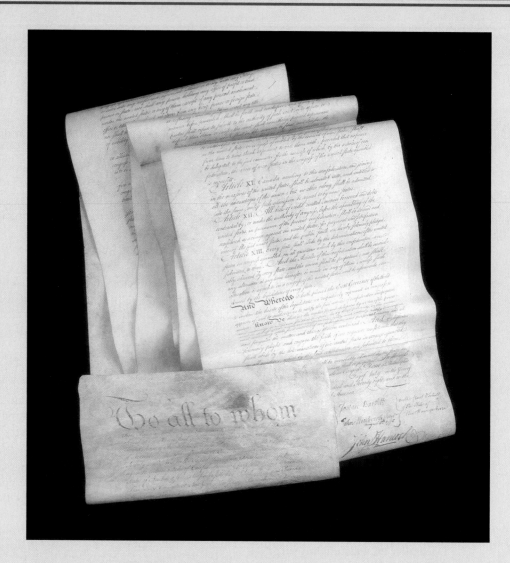

ARTICLES OF CONFEDERATION

The first written frame of government that bound together the thirteen rebelling provinces was called the Articles of Confederation. Delegates to the Second Continental Congress hammered out the plan over many months in 1776 and 1777, working on it when there was time free from the more pressing problems of pursuing the war. Once Congress agreed on it, the plan was printed and distributed to state legislatures for ratification, a process that took nearly five years because it required the assent of all thirteen. After ratification, in February 1781, this parchment copy became the official original version. As was often done with significant manuscript documents, the professional scribe wrote the opening words of the Articles in very large print, to proclaim the news. How does TO ALL TO WHOM *compare with such famous opening words as* IN CONGRESS, JULY 4, 1776—*the start of the Declaration of Independence—and later,* WE THE PEOPLE *for the U.S. Constitution, which replaced the Articles in 1788? Do you think* TO ALL TO WHOM *would have become a slogan or catchword had the Articles persisted as the country's sacred text? Why or why not?*

National Archives.

BUILDING A REPUBLIC

1775–1789

8

J AMES MADISON GRADUATED FROM PRINCETON COLLEGE in New Jersey in 1771, not knowing what to do next with his life. Certainly the twenty-year-old had an easy fallback position. As the firstborn son of a wealthy plantation master, he could return home to the foothills of Virginia and wait to inherit substantial land and a large force of slaves. But James was an intensely studious young man, uninterested in farming, and reluctant to leave the collegiate environment. Five years at boarding school had given him fluency in Greek, Latin, French, and mathematics, and three years at Princeton acquainted him with the great thinkers, both ancient and modern. Driven by a thirst for learning, young Madison slept only five hours a night, perhaps undermining his health. Protesting he was too ill to travel, he hung around Princeton six months after graduation.

In 1772, he returned home, still adrift. He swapped reading lists and ideas about political theory by letter with a Princeton classmate, prolonging his student life. While Madison struggled for direction, the powerful winds before the storm of the American Revolution swirled through the colonies; the youth's drifting would abruptly end. In May 1774, Madison traveled north to deliver his brother to boarding school and was in Philadelphia when the startling news broke that Britain had closed the port of Boston in retaliation for the destruction of the tea. Turbulent protests over the Coercive Acts turned him into a committed revolutionary.

Back in Virginia, Madison joined his father on the newly formed Committee of Public Safety. For a few days in early 1775, the twenty-four-year-old took up musket practice, but his continued poor health ruled out the soldier's life, and he quickly gave it up. His special contribution to the revolution lay along a different path. In spring 1776, Madison was elected to the Virginia Convention, an extralegal assembly replacing the defunct royal government. The convention's main task was to hammer out a state constitution featuring revolutionary goals such as frequent elections and a limited executive power. Madison, shy, self-effacing, and still learning the ropes, mostly stayed on the sidelines. Still, Virginia's elder statesmen noted the young man's logical, thoughtful contributions. When his county failed to return him to the assembly in the next election, he was appointed to the governor's council, where he spent two years gaining experience helping to manage a wartime government.

In early 1780, Madison represented Virginia in the Continental Congress. Not quite twenty-nine, unmarried, and supported by his father's money, Madison was free of the burdens that made distant political service difficult for so many others. Madison stayed in the North for three years, working with men like Alexander Hamilton of New York and Robert Morris of Pennsylvania as the congress wrestled with the chaotic economy and the ever-precarious war effort. In one crisis Madison's negotiating skills proved crucial: He broke the deadlock over the ratification of the Articles of Confederation by arranging for the cession of Virginia's western lands. More often, service in the congress proved frustrating to Madison because the confederation government seemed to lack essential powers.

Madison resumed a seat in the Virginia state assembly in 1784. But he did not retreat to a local point of view. He worked hard to bring about an all-state

JAMES MADISON BY CHARLES WILLSON PEALE
James Madison, a short and slight man, was often mistaken for being younger than he was. With natural hair (no wig) and smooth face, as shown here, he could pass for a youth of 20. This miniature portrait was made in 1783 when Madison was 32. That year he experienced his first serious romance, with a young woman who was just 16. She lived in his boarding house in Philadelphia, along with her father, a congressional delegate from New York. But the girl dropped him for another suitor. Madison waited eleven years to try romance again. New York congressman Aaron Burr introduced him to a Quaker widow named Dolley Payne Todd, who came from Virginia but lived in Philadelphia. Madison was 43 and Dolley was 26; they married four months after meeting.
Library of Congress.

convention in Philadelphia in the late spring of 1787, where he took the lead in steering the delegates to a complete rewrite of the structure of the national government, investing it with considerably greater powers. True to form, Madison spent the months before the convention in feverish study of the great thinkers he had read in college, searching out the best way to constitute a government on republican principles. His lifelong passion for scholarly study, seasoned by a dozen years of energetic political experience, paid off handsomely. The U.S. Constitution was the result.

By the end of the 1780s, James Madison had had his finger in every kind of political pie, on the local, state, confederation, and finally national level. He had transformed himself from a directionless and solitary youth into one of the leading political thinkers of the Revolutionary period. His personal history over the 1780s mirrored the path of the emerging United States.

The Articles of Confederation

For five years, from independence in 1776 until 1781, the Second Continental Congress continued to meet in Philadelphia and other cities. It existed without any formal constitutional basis, while its members groped to establish a government that embodied Revolutionary principles. With monarchy gone, where did sovereignty lie? What was the nature of representation? Who held the power of taxation? Who should vote; who should rule?

The initial answers to these questions took the form of a plan called the Articles of Confederation. The plan, however, proved to be surprisingly difficult to implement.

Congress, Confederation, and the Problem of Western Lands

Only after declaring independence did the Continental Congress turn its attention to the need for a written document that would specify what powers the congress had and by what authority it existed. There was widespread agreement on key government powers: pursuing war and peace, conducting foreign relations, regulating trade, and running a postal service. But there was serious disagreement about the powers of congress over the western boundaries of the states. Virginia and Connecticut, for example, had old colonial charters that located their boundaries along the Mississippi River. States without extensive land grants could not abide such grandiose claims.

For over a year, the congress tinkered with drafts of the Articles of Confederation, reaching agreement only in November 1777. The Articles defined the union as a loose confederation of states, characterized as "a firm league of friendship" existing mainly to foster a common defense. The structure of the government paralleled that of the existing Continental Congress. There was no national executive (that is, no president) and no national judiciary. The congress was composed of two to seven delegates from each state, selected annually by the state legislatures and prohibited from serving more than three years out of any six. The actual number of delegates was not critical, since each state delegation cast a single vote.

Routine decisions in the congress required a simple majority of seven states; for momentous powers, such as declaring war, nine states needed to agree. But to approve or amend the Articles required the unanimous consent both of the thirteen state delegations and of the thirteen state legislatures. The congressional delegates undoubtedly thought they were guaranteeing that no individual state could be railroaded by the other twelve in fundamental constitutional matters. But what this requirement really did was to hamstring the government. One state could—and did—hold the rest of the country hostage to its demands.

On the delicate question of deriving revenue to run the government, specifically to finance the war, the Articles provided an ingenious but ultimately troublesome solution. Each state was to contribute in proportion to the property value of the state's land. Large and populous states would give more than small or sparsely populated states. The actual taxes would be levied by the state legislatures, not by the congress, to preserve the Revolution's principle of taxation only by direct representation. However, no mechanism was created to compel states to contribute their fair share.

The lack of centralized authority in the confederation government was exactly what many state leaders wanted in the late 1770s. A league of states with rotating personnel, no executive branch, no power of taxation, and a requirement of unanimity for any major change seemed to be a good way to avoid the potential tyranny of government. But right away, the inherent weaknesses of these features became apparent.

The requirement for unanimous approval, for example, stalled the acceptance of the Articles for five years. The key dispute involved the problem of lands west of the existing states and east of the Mississippi River. Five states, all lacking land claims, insisted that the congress control those lands as a national domain that would eventually constitute new states. The other eight states refused to yield their colonial-era claims and opposed giving congress power to alter boundaries (Map 8.1). In all the heated debate, few seemed to remember that those same western lands were inhabited by many thousands of Indians not party to the disputes.

The eight land-claiming states were ready to sign the Articles of Confederation in 1777. Rhode Island, Pennsylvania, and New Jersey eventually capitulated and signed, "not from a Conviction of the Equality and Justness of it," said a New Jersey delegate, "but merely from an absolute Necessity there was of complying to save the Continent." But Delaware and Maryland continued to hold out, insisting on a national domain policy. In 1779, the disputants finally compromised: Any land a state volunteered to relinquish would become the national domain. When congressmen James Madison and Thomas Jefferson ceded Virginia's huge land claim in 1781, the Articles were at last accepted by all states.

The western lands issue demonstrated that powerful interests divided the thirteen new states; the apparent unity of purpose inspired by fighting the war against England papered over sizable cracks in the new confederation.

Running the New Government

No fanfare greeted the long-awaited inauguration of the new government. The congress continued to sputter along, its problems far from solved by the signing of the Articles. Day-to-day activities were often hampered by the lack of a quorum. The Articles required representation from seven states to conduct business, with a minimum of two men from each state's delegation. But some days fewer than fourteen men in total showed up.

State legislatures were slow to select delegates; those appointed were often reluctant to attend, especially if they had wives and children at home,

MAP 8.1

Cession of Western Lands, 1782–1802

The thirteen new states found it hard to ratify the Articles of Confederation without settling their conflicting land claims in the west, an area larger than the original states and occupied by Indian tribes. The five states objecting to the Articles' silence over western lands policy were Maryland, Delaware, New Jersey, Rhode Island, and Pennsylvania.

READING THE MAP: Which states had the largest claims on western territory? What disputed territory became the fourteenth state?

CONNECTIONS: In what context did the first dispute regarding western lands arise? How was it resolved? Does the map suggest a reason why Pennsylvania, a large state, joined the four much smaller states on this issue?

www.bedfordstmartins.com/roarkcompact SEE THE ONLINE STUDY GUIDE for more help in analyzing these maps.

and absenteeism was a constant problem. Consequently, some of the most effective and committed delegates were young bachelors like James Madison and men in their fifties and sixties whose families were grown, like Samuel Adams. Many active politicians preferred to devote their energies to their state governments, especially when the congress seemed deadlocked or, worse, irrelevant. Often, more exciting political work was going on at the state level, especially during the creative burst of state constitution writing in the late 1770s.

It also did not help that the congress had no permanent home. During the war, when the British army threatened Philadelphia, the congress relocated to small Pennsylvania towns like Lancaster and York and then to Baltimore. After hostilities ceased, the congress moved from Trenton to Princeton to Annapolis to New York City.

To address the difficulties of an inefficient congress, executive departments of war, finance, and foreign affairs were created to handle purely administrative functions. When the department heads were ambitious—as was Robert Morris, a wealthy Philadelphia merchant who served as superintendent of finance—they could exercise considerable executive power. The Articles of Confederation had deliberately refrained from setting up an executive branch, but a modest one was being invented by necessity.

The Sovereign States

In the first decade of independence, the states were sovereign and all-powerful. Relatively few functions, like that of declaring war and peace, had been transferred to the confederation government. Familiar and close to home, state governments claimed the allegiance of their citizens. As Americans discarded their English identity, they thought of themselves instead as Virginians or New Yorkers or Rhode Islanders. State government was thus the arena in which the Revolution's innovations would first be tried.

The State Constitutions

In May 1776, the congress in Philadelphia recommended that all the states draw up constitutions based on "the authority of the people." By 1778, ten

had done so, and two more (Connecticut and Rhode Island) adopted and updated their original colonial charters. Having been denied unwritten British liberties, Americans wanted written contracts that guaranteed basic principles.

A shared feature of all the state constitutions was the conviction that government ultimately rests on the consent of the governed. Political writers in the late 1770s embraced the concept of republicanism as the underpinning of the new governments. Republicanism meant more than just popular elections and representative institutions. For some, republicanism invoked a way of thinking about who leaders should be—ideally autonomous, virtuous citizens who placed civic values above private interests. For others, it suggested direct democracy, with nothing standing in the way of the will of the people. For all, it meant government that promoted the people's welfare.

Widespread agreement about the virtues of republicanism went hand in hand with the idea that republics could succeed only in relatively small units, so the people could make sure their interests were being served. Nearly every state continued the colonial practice of a two-chamber assembly but greatly augmented the powers of the lower house. Two states, Pennsylvania and Georgia, did away with the upper house altogether. Most states made their lower houses very responsive to popular majorities, with annual elections and guaranteed rotation in office. If a representative displeased his constituents, he could be out of office in a matter of months. Virtually all of the state constitutions severely limited the powers of the governor, and some restricted the governor's term to one year. Pennsylvania and Georgia abolished the office of governor altogether.

Six of the state constitutions included bills of rights, lists of basic individual liberties that governments could not abridge. Virginia debated and passed the first bill of rights in June 1776, and many of the other states borrowed from it. Its language bears a close resemblance to the wording of the Declaration of Independence, which Thomas Jefferson was composing that same June in Philadelphia: "That all men are by nature equally free and independent, and have certain inherent rights, of which, when they enter into a state of society, they cannot by any compact deprive or divest their posterity; namely, the enjoyment of life and liberty, with the means of acquiring and possessing property, and pursuing and obtaining happiness and safety." Along with these inherent rights went more specific rights to freedom of speech, freedom of the press, and trial by jury.

Who Are "the People"?

When the Continental Congress called for state constitutions based on "the authority of the people," and when the Virginia bill of rights granted "all men" certain rights, who was meant by "the people"? Who exactly were the citizens of this new country, and how far did the principle of democratic government extend? Different people answered these questions differently, but in the 1770s certain limits to full political participation by all Americans were widely agreed upon.

One limit was defined by property. In nearly every state, candidates for the highest offices—the governorship and membership in the upper house—needed to meet substantial property qualifications. In Maryland, for example, a candidate for governor had to be worth £5,000, quite a large sum of money. Voters in Maryland had to own fifty acres of land or £30. Only property owners were presumed to possess the necessary independence of mind and sense of community to make wise political choices. Are not propertyless men, asked John Adams, "too little acquainted with public affairs to form a right judgment, and too dependent upon other men to have a will of their own?"

Probably one-quarter to one-half of adult white males in all the states were disfranchised by property qualifications. Not all of them took their non-voter status quietly. One Maryland man wondered what was so special about being worth £30: "Every poor man has a life, a personal liberty, and a right to his earnings; and is in danger of being injured by government in a variety of ways." Why then restrict such a man from voting for his representatives? Others pointed out that propertyless men were fighting and dying in the Revolutionary War; surely they were expressing an active concern about politics. Finally, a very few radical voices challenged the notion that owning property transformed men into good citizens. Perhaps it did the opposite: The richest men might well be greedy and selfish and therefore bad citizens.

But ideas like this were clearly outside the mainstream. The writers of the new constitutions, themselves men of property, viewed the Revolution as an effort to guarantee people the right to own property and to prevent unjust governments from appropriating it through taxation. John Adams urged the framers of the Massachusetts constitution not even to discuss the scope of suffrage but simply to adopt the traditional colonial property qualifications. If suffrage is brought up for debate, he warned, "there will be no end of it. New claims will arise; women will demand a vote; lads from twelve to twenty-one will think their rights not enough attended to; and every man who has not a farthing, will demand an equal voice with any other." Adams was astute enough to anticipate complaints about excluding women, youth, and poor men from political life, but it did not even occur to him to worry about another group: slaves.

Equality and Slavery

Restrictions on political participation did not mean that propertyless people enjoyed no civil rights and liberties. The various state bills of rights applied to all individuals who had, as the Virginia bill so carefully phrased it, "enter[ed] into a state of society." No matter how poor, a free person was entitled to life, liberty, property, and freedom of conscience. Unfree people, however, were another matter.

The author of the Virginia bill of rights was George Mason, a plantation owner with 118 slaves. When he penned the sentence "all men are by nature equally free and independent," he did not have his slaves in mind; he meant that Americans were the equals of the British and could not be denied the liberties of British citizens. Other Virginia legislators, however, worried about misinterpretations, added the phrase specifying that rights belonged only to people who had entered civil society. As one wrote, with relief, "Slaves, not being constituent members of our so-

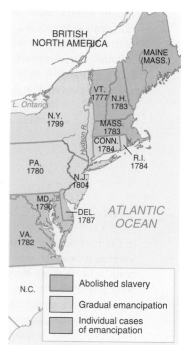

Legal Changes to Slavery, 1777–1804

ciety, could never pretend to any benefit from such a maxim."

One month later, the Declaration of Independence used essentially the same phrase about equality, this time without the modifying clause about entering society. Two state constitutions, for Pennsylvania and Massachusetts, also picked it up. In Massachusetts, one town suggested that the sentence on equality be reworded to read "All men, whites and blacks, are born free and equal." But the suggestion fell on deaf ears.

Nevertheless, after 1776, the ideals of the Revolution about natural equality and liberty began to erode the institution of slavery. Sometimes enslaved blacks led the challenge. In 1777, several Massachusetts slaves petitioned the state legislature, claiming a "natural & unalienable right to that freedom which the great Parent of the Universe hath bestowed equally on all mankind." They modestly asked for freedom for their children at age twenty-one and were turned down. In 1779, similar petitions in Connecticut and New Hampshire met with no success. Seven Massachusetts freemen, including the mariner brothers Paul and John Cuffe, refused to pay taxes for three years on the grounds that they could not vote and so were not represented. The Cuffe brothers landed in jail in 1780 for tax evasion, but their petition to the state legislature spurred the extension of suffrage to taxpaying free blacks in that state.

Another way to bring the issue before lawmakers was to sue in court. In 1781, a Massachusetts slave named Quok Walker charged his master with assault and battery, arguing he was a free man, under the state constitution's promise that "all men are born free and equal." Walker won and was set free; several similar cases followed, and by 1789 slavery had been effectively abolished by judicial decision in Massachusetts.

In other northern states, untold numbers of blacks simply ran away from owners and claimed their freedom, sometimes with the help of sympathetic whites. One estimate holds that more than half of young slave men in Philadelphia took flight in the 1780s. By 1790, free blacks outnumbered slaves in Pennsylvania by nearly a factor of two.

Pennsylvania was the first state to legislate an end to slavery by statute, in 1780. Yet the law provided for a very gradual emancipation: Only infants born to a slave mother on or after March 1, 1780, would be freed, and then not until age twenty-eight.

That meant that no current slave in Pennsylvania would gain freedom until 1808, and well into the nineteenth century some blacks would still be slaves. Rhode Island and Connecticut adopted gradual emancipation laws in 1784. In 1785, New York expanded the terms under which individual owners could free slaves, but only in 1799 did the state adopt a gradual emancipation law; New Jersey followed suit in 1804. These were the two northern states with the largest number of slaves: New York in 1800 with 20,000, and New Jersey, more than 12,000. In contrast, Pennsylvania had just 1,700. Gradual emancipation illustrates the tension between radical and conservative implications of republican ideology. Republican government protected people's liberties and property; yet slaves were both people and property. Gradual emancipation balanced the civil rights of blacks and the property rights of their owners by delaying the promise of freedom.

South of Pennsylvania, in Delaware, Maryland, and Virginia, where slavery was so important to the economy, general emancipation bills were rejected. All three states, however, eased legal restrictions and allowed individual acts of emancipation for adult slaves below the age of forty-five, under new manumission laws passed in the 1780s and 1790s. By 1790, close to 10,000 freed Virginia slaves had formed local free black communities complete with schools and churches.

In the deep South—the Carolinas and Georgia—freedom for slaves was unthinkable for whites. Yet more than 10,000 slaves from South Carolina achieved freedom in 1783 by leaving with the British army from Charleston, and another 6,000 set sail under the British flag from Savannah, Georgia. This was by far the largest emancipation of blacks in the entire country. Some went to Canada, some to England, and a small number to Sierra Leone, on the west coast of Africa. Additionally, many hundreds of ex-slaves took refuge with Seminole and Creek Indians, becoming permanent members of their communities in Spanish Florida and western Georgia.

Although emancipation affected fewer blacks in the North, simply because there were many fewer of them to begin with, its symbolic importance was enormous. Every state from Pennsylvania northward acknowledged that slavery was fundamentally inconsistent with revolutionary ideology; "all men are created equal" was beginning to acquire real force as a basic principle.

The Critical Period

From 1781 to 1786, a sense of crisis gripped some of the revolutionary leaders who feared the Articles of Confederation were too weak. But others defended the Articles as the best guarantee of individual liberty, because real governance occurred at the state level, closer to the people. Political theorizing about the proper relation among citizen, state, and confederation remained active and controversial throughout the decade as Americans confronted questions of finance, territorial expansion, and civil disorder.

Financial Chaos and Paper Money

Seven years of war produced a booming but chaotic economy in the 1780s. The confederation and the individual states had run up huge war debts, financed by printing paper money and borrowing from private sources. Some $400 to $500 million in paper currency had been injected into the economy, and prices and wages fluctuated wildly. Private debt and rapid expenditure flourished, and debtors' prisons became crowded. A serious postwar depression settled in by the mid-1780s and did not lift until the 1790s.

The confederation government was itself in a terrible financial fix. Continental dollars had lost almost all value: It took 146 of them to buy what a dollar had bought in 1775. Desperate times required desperate measures. The congress turned to Robert Morris, a merchant and newly reelected delegate from Pennsylvania, appointing him superintendent of finance. Six years earlier, the wealthy Morris had procured from Europe much-needed muskets for the army but had resigned from the congress in 1778 under suspicion that he had unfairly profited from his public service efforts; indeed, he had left public life many thousands of dollars richer than he had entered it. Nevertheless, the congress called on him from 1781 to 1784 to apply his considerable talent to the confederation's economic problems.

To augment the government's revenue, Morris first proposed a 5 percent import tax (called an *impost*). Since there was no authority in the Articles of Confederation for such a tax, Morris's plan required an amendment to the Articles approved unanimously by the thirteen states. But unanimous agreement was impossible. Rhode Island and New York, whose bustling ports provided ample state revenue, preferred to keep their money and simply refused to agree to the national impost.

SCALE OF DEPRECIATION
This chart shows the monthly value of U.S. Continental dollars from January 1777 to February 1781, as stipulated by the government of Massachusetts. For example, in March 1780, it took 3,736 Continental dollars to equal the buying power of $100 in gold or silver based on values of the dollar in January 1777. By April 1780, the same value of hard money required $4,000 Continentals. Such a chart was needed when debtors and creditors settled accounts contracted at one time and paid off later in greatly depreciated dollars. How easy would you find it to keep your head above water in an economy with such fast currency depreciation? What level of arithmetic skills were required? chart-reading skills? Notice the hand-written figuring at the bottom of the chart. Do these arithmetic operations look familiar to you?
Courtesy, American Antiquarian Society.

Morris's next idea was the creation of the Bank of North America. This private bank would enjoy a special relationship with the confederation, holding the government's hard money as well as private deposits, and providing it with short-term loans. The bank's contribution to economic stability came in the form of banknotes, pieces of paper inscribed with a dollar value. Unlike paper money, banknotes were backed by hard money in the bank's vaults and thus would not depreciate. Morris hoped that the new banknotes would function like paper money without its drawbacks. Congress agreed and voted to approve the bank in 1781.

The Bank of North America, located in Philadelphia, had limited success curing the confederation's economic woes. In the short run, the bank supplied the government with a currency that held its value, but it issued so little that the impact was very small. When its charter expired in 1786, the Pennsylvania legislature refused to renew it.

If Morris could not resuscitate the economy in the 1780s, probably no one could have done it. Because the Articles of Confederation reserved most economic functions to the states, congress was helpless to tax trade, control inflation, or pay the mounting public debt. But the confederation had acquired one source of potential enormous wealth: the huge territory ceded by Virginia, which in 1784 became the national domain.

Land Ordinances and the Northwest Territory

The Continental Congress appointed Thomas Jefferson to draft a national domain policy. Jefferson proposed dividing the territory north of the Ohio River and east of the Mississippi—called the Northwest Territory—into ten new states, each divided into townships ten miles square. He advocated giving the land to settlers, rather than selling it, on the grounds that the improved lands would so enrich the country through future property taxes that there was no need to make the settlers pay twice. Jefferson's aim was to encourage rapid and democratic settlement of the land, to build a nation of freeholders (as opposed to renters), and to avoid speculative frenzy.

Jefferson also insisted that the new states have representative governments equal in status to those of the original states once they reached a certain population. This ensured that the new United States, so recently released from colonial dependency, would

THOMAS JEFFERSON BY JOHN TRUMBULL
This miniature shows Thomas Jefferson at age forty-five, during his years as a diplomat in Paris. The American artist John Trumbull visited France in 1788 and painted Jefferson's likeness in this five-by-four-inch format so he could later copy it into his planned large canvas depicting the signing of the Declaration of Independence. Jefferson requested three replicas of the miniature to bestow as gifts. One went to his daughter Martha, another to an American woman in London, and the third to Maria Cosway, a British artist with whom the widower Jefferson shared an intense infatuation during his stay in France. Jefferson never remarried, but a scandal over his private life erupted in 1802, when a journalist charged that he had fathered several children by his slave Sally Hemings. In 1998, a careful DNA study concluded that uniquely marked Jefferson Y-chromosomes were common to both Hemings's and Jefferson's descendants. The DNA evidence, when combined with historical evidence about Jefferson's whereabouts at the start of each of Hemings's six pregnancies, makes it extremely likely that Jefferson fathered some or perhaps all of her children. What cannot be known is the nature of the relationship between the two. Was it coerced or voluntary, or somewhere in between? In all his voluminous writings, Jefferson left no comment about Sally Hemings, and the record on her side is entirely mute.
Monticello.

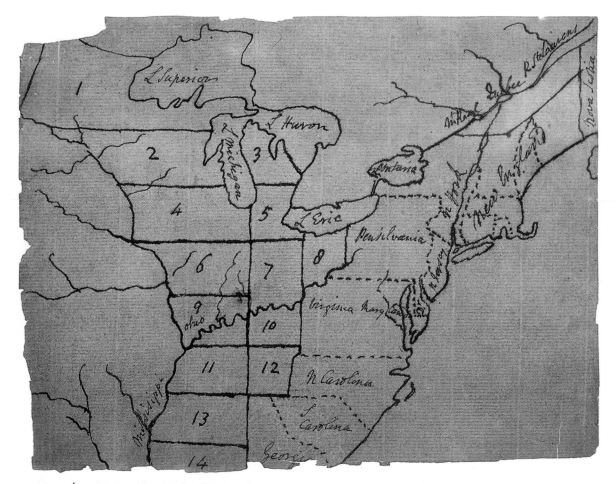

JEFFERSON'S MAP OF THE NORTHWEST TERRITORY
Thomas Jefferson sketched out borders for ten new states in his initial plan for the Northwest Territory in 1784. Straight lines and right angles held a strong appeal for him. But such regularity ignored inconvenient geographic features like rivers and even more inconvenient political features like Indian territorial claims, most unlikely to be ceded by treaty in orderly blocks. Jefferson also submitted ten distinctive names for the states. Number 9, for example, was Polypotamia, or "land of many rivers" in Greek.
William L. Clements Library.

www.bedfordstmartins.com/roarkcompact SEE THE ONLINE STUDY GUIDE for more help in analyzing this image.

not itself become a colonial power. Finally, Jefferson's draft prohibited slavery in the ten new states.

The congress adopted parts of Jefferson's plan in the Ordinance of 1784: the rectangular grid, the ten states, and the guarantee of self-government and eventual statehood. What the congress found too radical was the proposal to give away the land; the national domain was the confederation's only source of independent wealth. And the slavery prohibition failed by only one state's vote.

A year later, the congress reconsidered the land act and passed a new version, the Ordinance of 1785. The new plan called for walkable townships six miles square, each containing thirty-six sections; each section contained 640 acres, enough for four family farms. The 1785 ordinance reduced Jefferson's plan for ten rectangular states down to three to five states, with boundaries conforming to natural geographic features like the Great Lakes and major rivers instead of abstractly drawn survey lines. Land sales would occur by public auction, with minimum price one dollar an acre, but market forces could drive up the prices of the most desirable land. Two further restrictions applied: Land was sold in minimum parcels of 640 acres each, and payment had to be in hard money or in certificates of debt from Revolutionary days. This effectively meant that the land's first owners would be prosperous speculators.

Speculators usually held the land for resale rather than settling on it. Thus they avoided direct contact with the most serious obstacle to settlement: the dozens of Indian tribes that claimed the land as their own. Treaties signed at Fort Stanwix in 1784 and Fort McIntosh in 1785 coerced partial cessions of land from Iroquois, Delaware, Huron, and Miami tribes, but a united Indian meeting near Detroit in 1786 issued an ultimatum: No cession would be valid without unanimous consent. The Indians advised the United States to "prevent your surveyors and other people from coming upon our side of the Ohio river." For two more decades, violent Indian wars in Ohio and Indiana would continue to impede white settlement.

In 1787, a third land act, called the Northwest Ordinance, promised eventual self-government for a territory when the white male population reached five thousand, but it devised an interim plan for sparsely settled territories with a congressionally appointed governor. The other landmark feature of the 1787 act was a prohibition on slavery in the entire region, which this time passed without debate. A North-South sectionalism, based on slavery, was slowly taking shape.

Shays's Rebellion, 1786–1787

Without an impost amendment, the confederation turned to the states to contribute revenue voluntarily. Struggling with their own war debts, most state legislatures were reluctant to tax their constituents too heavily. Massachusetts, however, had a tough-minded, fiscally conservative legislature, dominated by the coastal commercial centers, which wanted to retire the state debt by raising taxes. Worse yet, it insisted that taxes be paid in hard money, not cheap paper. Farmers in the western half of the state found it difficult to comply, and by 1786 sheriffs frequently confiscated property and jailed tax delinquents.

However, the western farmers had learned from the American Revolution how to respond to

SILVER BOWL FOR ANTI-SHAYS GENERAL
The militia of Springfield in western Massachusetts presented its leader, General William Shepard, with this silver bowl to honor his victory over the insurgents in Shays's Rebellion. Presentational silver conveyed a double message. It announced gratitude and praise in engraved words, and it transmitted considerable monetary value in the silver itself. General Shepard could display his trophy on a shelf, use it as a punch bowl, will it to descendants to keep his famous moment alive in memory, or melt it down in hard times. Not only is Shepard's name commemorated on the silver; SHAYS *too appears in the last line, there for the ages to remember.*
Yale University Art Gallery, Mabel Brady Garvan Collection.

oppressive taxation. They called conventions to discuss their grievances and circulated petitions demanding tax reductions, paper money, and debt relief legislation. In the fall of 1786, about 2,500 armed men marched on the courthouses in three western Massachusetts counties. The leader of this tax revolt was a farmer and onetime captain in the Continental army, Daniel Shays.

The governor of Massachusetts, James Bowdoin, who had once organized protests against British taxes, now characterized the Shaysites as illegal rebels. Another former rebel, Samuel Adams, took the extreme position that "the man who dares rebel against the laws of a republic ought to suffer death." These aging revolutionaries had given little thought to the possibility that popular majorities, embodied in a state legislature, could seem to be oppressive, just as monarchs could. The Shaysites challenged the idea that popularly elected governments would always be fair and just.

In January 1787, Governor Bowdoin sent a volunteer army to quell the rebellion. When Shaysites numbering about 1,500 attacked a federal armory in Springfield, they were met with gunfire; 4 rebels were killed and another 20 wounded. The final and bloodless encounter came at Petersham, where the army surprised the rebels on a freezing morning and took 150 prisoners; the others fled into the woods. Shays took off for Canada and other leaders left the state, but more than 1,000 dissidents were rounded up and jailed. No one was executed for rebellion, but the rebels were prohibited from ever again voting, holding public office, working as schoolmasters, or operating taverns. The first two prohibitions denied the men a political voice, and the second two denied them occupations in which they could instruct or influence others.

Shays's Rebellion, 1786–1787

Shays's Rebellion caused leaders throughout the country to worry whether the confederation could handle problems of civil disorder. Perhaps there were similar "combustibles" in other states, awaiting the spark that would set off a dreadful political conflagration. New York lawyer and diplomat John Jay wrote to George Washington, "Our affairs seem to lead to some crisis, some revolution—something I cannot foresee or conjecture. I am uneasy and apprehensive; more so than during the war." Benjamin Franklin, in his eighties, shrewdly observed that in 1776 Americans had feared "an excess of power in the rulers," whereas now the problem was "a defect of obedience" in the subjects. To some, the sense of crisis in the confederation had greatly deepened.

The United States Constitution

Events in the fall of 1786 provoked an odd mixture of fear and hope that the government under the Articles of Confederation was losing its grip on power. A small circle of Virginians decided to try one last time to augment the powers granted to the government by the Articles. Their call for a meeting to discuss trade regulation led, more quickly than they could have imagined in 1786, to a total reworking of the national government.

From Annapolis to Philadelphia

The Virginians, led by James Madison, convinced the congress of the confederation government to allow a meeting of delegates at Annapolis, Maryland, in September 1786, to try again to revise the trade regulation powers of the Articles. But only five states participated. Like Madison, the dozen men who attended sensed an impending crisis, and they rescheduled the meeting for Philadelphia in May 1787. Congress reluctantly endorsed the Philadelphia meeting and tried to limit its scope to "the sole and express purpose of revising the Articles of Confederation." But at least one representative at the Annapolis meeting had far more ambitious plans. Alexander Hamilton of New York hoped the Philadelphia meeting would do whatever was necessary to strengthen the federal government.

Alexander Hamilton by character was suited for such bold steps. The illegitimate son of a poor mother in the West Indies, at age sixteen the bright lad greatly impressed an American trader, who sent him to New York City for a college education. Hamilton soon got swept up in the military enthusiasm of 1776 and by 1777 had joined George Washington's staff, serving at the general's side through much of the Revolution. After the war, he studied law, married into a New York mercantile family, and sat in the Continental Congress for two years. Despite his stigmatized and impoverished childhood, the aspiring Hamilton identified with the elite classes and their fear of democratic disorder.

The fifty-five men who assembled at Philadelphia in May 1787 to consider the shortcomings of the Articles of Confederation were generally those most concerned about weaknesses in the present government. Few attended who were opposed to revising the Articles. Patrick Henry, author of the Virginia Resolves in 1765 and more recently state governor, refused to go, saying he "smelled a rat." Two New York representatives left in dismay in the middle of the convention, leaving Hamilton as the sole New York delegate.

This gathering of white men included no artisans or day laborers or even farmers of middling wealth. Two-thirds of the delegates were lawyers. The majority had served in the confederation congress and knew its strengths and weaknesses; fully half had been officers in the Continental army. Seven men had been governors of their states and knew firsthand the frustrations of thwarted executive power. A few elder statesmen attended, such as

Benjamin Franklin and George Washington, but on the whole, the delegates were young, like Madison and Hamilton.

The Virginia and New Jersey Plans

The convention worked in secrecy, so the men could freely explore alternatives without fear that their honest opinions would come back to haunt them. The Virginia delegation first laid out a fifteen-point plan for a complete restructuring of the government. This Virginia Plan was a total repudiation of the principle of a confederation of states. Largely the work of Madison, the plan set out a three-branch government composed of a two-chamber legislature, a powerful executive, and a judiciary. It virtually eliminated the voices of the smaller states by pegging representation in both houses of the congress to population. The theory was that government operated directly on people, not on states. Among the breathtaking powers assigned to the congress were the rights to veto state legislation and to coerce states militarily to obey national laws. To prevent the congress from having absolute power, the executive and judiciary could jointly veto the actions of the congress.

In mid-June, delegates from New Jersey, Connecticut, Delaware, and New Hampshire, all small states, unveiled an alternative proposal. The New Jersey Plan, as it was called, resembled the existing Articles of Confederation in that it set out a single-house congress in which each state had one vote. Acknowledging the need for an executive, it created a plural presidency to be shared by three men elected by the congress from among its membership. Where it sharply departed from the existing government was in the sweeping powers it gave to the congress: the right to tax, to regulate trade, and to use force on unruly state governments. In favoring national power over states' rights, it aligned itself with the Virginia Plan. But the New Jersey Plan retained the confederation principle that the national government was to be an assembly of states, not of people.

For two weeks, delegates debated the two plans, focusing on the key issue of representation. The small-state delegates conceded that one house in a two-house legislature could be apportioned by population, but they would never agree that both houses could be. Madison was equally vehement about bypassing representation by state, which he viewed as the fundamental flaw in the Articles.

THE PENNSYLVANIA STATEHOUSE
The constitutional convention assembled at the Pennsylvania statehouse to sweat out the summer of 1787. Despite the heat, the delegates nailed the windows shut to eliminate the chance of being heard by eavesdroppers, so intent were they on secrecy. The statehouse, built in the 1740s to house the colony's assembly, accommodated the Continental Congress at various times in the 1770s and 1780s. The building is now called Independence Hall, in honor of the signing of the Declaration of Independence within its walls in 1776.
Historical Society of Pennsylvania.

The debate seemed deadlocked, and for a while the convention was "on the verge of dissolution, scarce held together by the strength of a hair," according to one delegate. Only in mid-July did the so-called Great Compromise break the logjam and produce the basic structural features of the emerging United States Constitution. Proponents of the competing plans agreed on a bicameral legislature; representation in the lower house, the House of Representatives, would be apportioned by population, and representation in the upper house, the Senate, would come from all the states equally. But instead of one vote per state in the upper house, as in the New Jersey Plan, the compromise provided two senators who voted independently. Plenty of fine-tuning followed, but the most difficult problem, representation, was solved.

Representation by population turned out to be an ambiguous concept once it was subjected to rigorous discussion. Who counted? Were slaves, for example, people or property? As people, they added weight to the southern delegations in the House of Representatives, but as property they added to the tax burdens of those states. What emerged was the compromise known as the three-fifths clause: All free persons plus "three-fifths of all other Persons" constituted the numerical base for the apportionment of representatives. Using "all other Persons" as a substitute for "slaves" indicates the discomfort delegates felt in acknowledging the existence of slavery in a republican document. But though slavery was nowhere named, nonetheless it was recognized, guaranteed, and thereby perpetuated by the U.S. Constitution.

Democracy versus Republicanism

The delegates in Philadelphia made a distinction between democracy and republicanism new to American political vocabulary. Pure democracy was now taken to be a dangerous thing. As a Massachusetts delegate put it, "the evils we experience flow from the excess of democracy." The delegates still favored republican institutions, but they created a government that gave direct voice to the people only in the House and that granted a check on that voice to the Senate, a body of men elected not by direct popular vote but by the state legislatures. Senators served for six years, with no limit on reelection; they were protected from the whims of democratic majorities, and their long terms fostered experience and maturity in office.

Similarly, the presidency evolved into a powerful office out of the reach of direct democracy. The delegates devised an electoral college whose only function was to elect the president and vice president. Each state's legislature would choose the electors, whose number was the sum of representatives and senators for the state, an interesting melding of the two principles of representation. The president thus would owe his office not to the Congress, the states, or the people, but to a temporary assemblage of distinguished citizens who could vote their own judgment on the candidates.

The framers had developed a far more complex form of federal government than that provided by the Articles of Confederation. To curb the excesses of democracy, they devised a government with limits and checks on all branches. They set forth a powerful president who could veto Congress but then gave Congress power to override presidential vetoes. They set up a national judiciary to settle disputes between states and citizens of different states.

They made each branch of government as independent from the other branches as they could, by basing election on different universes of voters—voting citizens, state legislators, the electoral college.

The convention carefully listed the powers of Congress and of the president. The president could initiate policy, propose legislation, and veto acts of Congress; he could command the military and direct foreign policy; and he could appoint the entire judiciary, subject to Senate approval. Congress held the purse strings: the power to levy taxes, to regulate trade, and to coin money and control the currency. States were expressly forbidden to issue paper money. Two further powers of Congress—to "provide for the common defence and general Welfare" of the country and "to make all laws which shall be necessary and proper" for carrying out its powers—provided elastic language that came closest to Madison's wish to grant sweeping powers to the new government.

The Constitution specified a mechanism for ratification that avoided the dilemma faced earlier by the confederation government: Nine states, not all thirteen, had to ratify it, and special ratifying conventions elected only for that purpose, not state legislatures, would make the crucial decision.

Ratification of the Constitution

Had a popular vote been taken on the Constitution in the fall of 1787, it would probably have been rejected. In the three most populous states—Virginia, Massachusetts, and New York—substantial majorities opposed a powerful new national government. North Carolina and Rhode Island refused to call ratifying conventions. Seven of the eight remaining states were easy victories for the Constitution, but securing the approval of the ninth proved difficult.

The Federalists

The proponents of the Constitution moved into action swiftly. To silence the criticism that they had gone beyond their charge (which indeed they had), they sent the document to the congress. Congress withheld explicit approval but resolved to send the Constitution to the states for their consideration. The pro-Constitution forces shrewdly secured an-

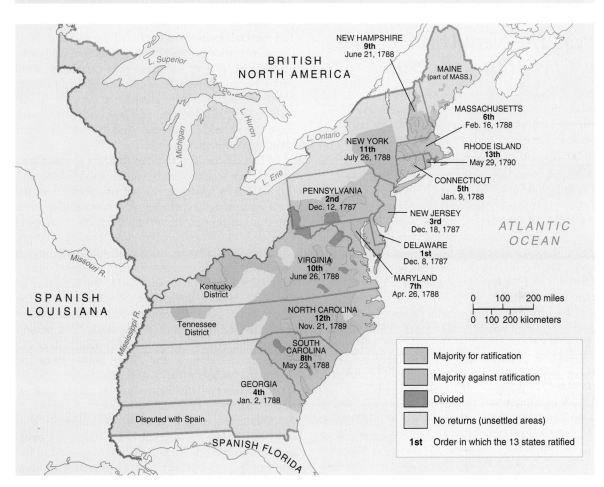

MAP 8.2
Ratification of the Constitution, 1788–1790
Populated areas cast votes for delegates to state ratification conventions. This map
shows Antifederalist strength generally concentrated in backcountry, noncoastal, and
nonurban areas, but with significant exceptions (for example, Rhode Island).

other advantage by calling themselves Federalists. By all logic, this label was more suitable for the backers of the confederation concept, since the Latin root of the word federal means "league." Their opponents became known as Antifederalists, a label that made them sound defensive and negative, lacking a program of their own.

The Federalists targeted the states most likely to ratify quickly, to gain momentum. Delaware provided a unanimous ratification by early December, before the Antifederalists had even begun to campaign. Pennsylvania, New Jersey, and Georgia followed within a month (Map 8.2). Delaware and New Jersey were small states surrounded by more

powerful neighbors; a government that would regulate trade and set taxes according to population was an attractive proposition. Georgia sought the protection a stronger national government would afford against hostile Indians and Spanish Florida to the south.

Another three easy victories came in Connecticut, Maryland, and South Carolina. As in Pennsylvania, merchants, lawyers, and urban artisans in general favored the new Constitution, as did large landowners and slaveholders. This tendency for the established political elite to be Federalist enhanced the prospects of victory, for Federalists already had power disproportionate to their numbers.

Was the New United States a Christian Country?

REBECCA SAMUEL, a Jewish resident of Virginia, conveyed her excitement about the new U.S. Constitution when she wrote her German parents in 1791 that finally "Jew and Gentile are as one" in the realm of politics and citizenship. Other voices were distinctly less approving. An Antifederalist pamphlet warned that the pope could become president; another feared that "a Turk, a Jew, a Roman Catholic, and what is worse than all, a Universalist, may be President."

The document that produced such wildly different readings was indeed remarkable in its handling of religion. The Constitution did not invoke Christianity as a state religion. It made no reference to an almighty being, and it specifically promised, in Article 6, section 3, that "no religious test shall ever be required as a qualification to any office or public trust under the United States." (See appendix, page A-8.) The six largest congregations of Jews—numbering about two thousand and located in Newport, New York, Philadelphia, Baltimore, Charleston, and Savannah—were delighted with this nearly unprecedented statement of political equality and wrote George Washington to express their hearty thanks.

But more than a few Christian leaders were stunned at the Constitution's near silence on religion. It seemed to represent a complete turnabout from the state constitutions of the 1770s and 1780s. A New Yorker warned that, "should the Citizens of America be as irreligious as her Constitution, we will have reason to tremble, lest the Governor of the universe . . . crush us to atoms." A delegate to North Carolina's ratifying convention played on anti-immigrant fears by predicting that the Constitution was "an invitation for Jews and pagans of every kind to come among us." A concerned Presbyterian minister asked Alexander Hamilton why religion was not in the Constitution, and Hamilton reportedly quipped, "Indeed, Doctor, we forgot it."

Measured against the practices of state governments, Hamilton's observation is hardly credible.

The men who wrote and debated the state and federal constitutions from 1775 to 1787 actively thought about principles of inclusion and exclusion when they defined citizenship, voting rights, and officeholding. They carefully considered property ownership, race, gender, and age in formulating rules about who could participate. And they also thought about religious qualifications.

Most leaders of the 1780s took for granted that Christianity was the one true faith and the essential foundation of morality. All but two state constitutions assumed the primacy of Protestantism, and one-third of them collected public taxes to support Christian churches. Every state but New York required a Christian oath as a condition for officeholding. Every member of Pennsylvania's legislature swore to "acknowledge the Scripture of the Old and New Testament to be given by divine inspiration." North Carolina's rule was even more restrictive, since it omitted Catholics: "No person who shall deny the being of God or the truth of the Protestant religion, or the divine authority of the Old or New Testaments" could hold office. South Carolina went much further and required that all voters had to be Protestants.

Other common political practices affirmed that the United States was a Christian country. Governors proclaimed days of public thanksgiving in the name of the Holy Trinity. Chaplains led legislatures in Christian prayer. Jurors and witnesses in court swore Christian oaths. New England states passed Sabbath laws prohibiting all work or travel on Sunday. Blasphemy laws punished people who cursed the Christian God or Jesus.

Close to half the state constitutions included the right to freedom of religion as an explicit guarantee. But freedom of religion meant only that difference would be tolerated; it did not guarantee political equality. How then did the U.S. Constitution come to be such a break from the immediate past? Had the framers really just forgotten about religion?

Not James Madison of Virginia. Madison arrived at the 1787 convention fresh from a hard-won victory in Virginia to establish religious liberty. At the end of 1786, he had finally secured passage of a bill written by Thomas Jefferson seven years earlier called the Virginia Statute of Religious Freedom. "All men shall be free to profess, and by argument to maintain, their opinions in matters of religion, and that the same shall in no wise diminish, enlarge,

TOURO SYNAGOGUE
A Jewish community inhabited the coastal shipping city of Newport, Rhode Island, as early as the 1650s. In 1759, the thriving group built a synagogue, the oldest Jewish house of worship still standing in the United States. The building blends a Georgian brick exterior with elements of Sephardic Jewish origin and is sited diagonally on its property so that worshipers face east, the direction of Jerusalem. President Washington visited Newport in 1790 and wrote to "the Hebrew Congregation" a few days later: "It is now no more that toleration is spoken of, as if it was by the indulgence of one class of people, that another enjoyed the exercise of their inherent natural rights."
Touro Synagogue/photo
John T. Hopf.

or affect their civil capacities," the bill read. Madison had convinced both the Episcopalians and the Baptist dissenters, at war with each other over state support, that to grant either or both churches tax money would be to concede to the state the authority to endorse one religion—and by implication to crush another. The statute separated church from state to protect religion. Further, it went beyond mere toleration to guarantee that religious choice was independent of civil rights.

In Madison's judgment, it was best for the U.S. Constitution to say as little as possible about religion, especially since state laws reflected a variety of positions. When Antifederalists demanded a bill of rights, Madison drew up a list for the first Congress to consider. Two items dealt with religion, but only one was approved. One became part of the First Amendment: "Congress shall make no law respecting an establishment of religion, or prohibiting the free exercise thereof." In a stroke, Madison set religious worship and the privileging of any one church beyond Congress's power. Significantly, his second proposal failed to pass: "No State shall violate the equal rights of conscience." Evidently, the states wanted to be able to keep their Christian-only rules without federal interference. Different faiths would be tolerated—but not guaranteed equal standing. And the very same session of Congress proceeded to hire Christian chaplains and proclaim days of thanksgiving.

Gradually, states deleted restrictive laws, but as late as 1840 Jews still could not hold public office in four states. Into the twentieth century, some states maintained Sunday laws that forced business closings on the Christian Sabbath, working enormous hardship on those whose religion required Saturday closings. The guarantee of freedom of religion was embedded in state and federal founding documents in the 1770s and 1780s, but it has taken many years to fulfill Jefferson's vision of what true religious liberty means: the freedom for religious belief to be independent of civil status.

Antifederalists in these states tended to be rural, western, and noncommercial, men whose access to news was limited and whose participation in state government was tenuous.

Massachusetts was the only early state that gave the Federalists difficulty. The vote to select the ratification delegates was decidedly Antifederalist; Shays's Rebellion was of recent memory there. One rural delegate from Worcester County voiced widely shared suspicions: "These lawyers and men of learning and money men that talk so finely, and gloss over matters so smoothly, to make us poor illiterate people swallow down the pill, expect to get into Congress themselves; they expect to be the managers of the Constitution and get all the power and all the money into their own hands, and then they will swallow up all us little folks." Nevertheless, the Antifederalist lead was slowly eroded by a vigorous newspaper campaign. In the end, the Federalists won by a very slim margin and only with promises that amendments to the Constitution would be taken up in the first Congress.

By May 1788, eight states had ratified; only one more was needed. North Carolina and Rhode Island were hopeless for the Federalist cause, and New Hampshire seemed nearly as bleak. More worrisome was the failure to win over the largest and most important states, Virginia and New York.

The Antifederalists

Antifederalists were a composite group, united mainly in their desire to block the Constitution. Although much Antifederalist strength came from backcountry areas long suspicious of eastern elites, many Antifederalist leaders came from the same social background as Federalist leaders; economic class alone did not differentiate them. Antifederalism also drew strength in states already on sure economic footing, like New York, that could afford to remain independent. Probably the biggest appeal of antifederalism lay in the long-nurtured fear that distant power might infringe on people's liberties. The language of the earlier revolutionary movement was not easily forgotten.

For example, in the proposed House of Representatives, the only directly democratic element of the Constitution, one member represented some thirty thousand people. How could that member really know or communicate with his whole constituency, the Antifederalists wondered. In contrast,

one wrote, "The members of our state legislatures are annually elected—they are subject to instructions—they are chosen within small circles—they are sent but a small distance from their respective homes. Their conduct is constantly known to their constituents. They frequently see, and are seen, by the men whose servants they are."

The Antifederalists also worried that elected representatives would always be members of the elite. Such men "will be ignorant of the sentiments of the middling and much more of the lower class of citizens, strangers to their ability, unacquainted with their wants, difficulties, and distress," worried a Maryland man. None of this would be a problem under a confederation system, according to the Antifederalists, because real power would continue to reside in the state governments.

The Federalists generally agreed that the elite would be favored for election to the House of Representatives, not to mention the Senate and the presidency. That was precisely what they hoped. The Federalists wanted power to flow to intelligent, virtuous, public-spirited leaders like themselves. They did not envision a government constituted of every class of people. "Fools and knaves have voice enough in government already," argued a New York Federalist, without being guaranteed representation in proportion to the total population of fools. Alexander Hamilton claimed that mechanics and laborers preferred to have their social betters represent them. The Antifederalists challenged the notion that any class could be sufficiently selfless to rule disinterestedly for others. They feared that the Federalists were resurrecting rule by aristocracy.

Antifederalists fretted over many specific features of the Constitution. It prohibited state-issued paper money. It regulated the time and place of congressional elections, leading to fears that only one inconvenient polling place might be authorized, to disfranchise rural voters. The most widespread objection to the Constitution was its lack of any guarantees of individual liberties in a bill of rights, like those contained in many state constitutions.

Despite the Federalists' campaigns in the large states, it was a small state—New Hampshire—that provided the decisive ninth vote for ratification, on June 21, 1788. Federalists there succeeded in getting the convention postponed from February to June and in the interim conducted an intense and successful lobbying effort on specific delegates.

The Big Holdouts:
Virginia and New York

Four states still remained outside the new union, and a glance at a map demonstrated the necessity of pressing the Federalist case in the two largest, Virginia and New York (see Map 8.2). Though Virginia was home to Madison and Washington, an influential Antifederalist group led by Patrick Henry and George Mason made the outcome uncertain. The Federalists finally but barely won ratification by proposing twenty specific amendments that the new government would promise to consider.

New York voters tended to Antifederalism out of a sense that a state so large and powerful need not relinquish so much authority to the new federal government. But New York was also home to some of the most persuasive Federalists. Starting in October 1787, Alexander Hamilton collaborated with James Madison and New York lawyer John Jay on a series of eighty-five essays on the political philosophy of the new Constitution, published in New York newspapers and later republished as *The Federalist*. The essays brilliantly set out the failures of the Articles of Confederation and offered an analysis of the complex nature of federalism. In one of the most compelling essays, number 10, Madison challenged the Antifederalists' heartfelt conviction that republican government had to be small scale. Madison argued that a large and diverse population was itself a guarantee of liberty. In a national government, no single faction could ever be large enough to subvert the freedom of other groups. "Extend the sphere, and you take in a greater variety of parties and interests; you make it less probable that a majority of the whole will have a common motive to invade the rights of other citizens," Madison asserted. He called it "a republican remedy for the diseases most incident to republican government."

At New York's ratifying convention, Antifederalists predominated, but impassioned debate and lobbying—plus the dramatic news of Virginia's ratification—finally tipped the balance to the Federalists. New York's ratification assured the solidity and legitimacy of the new government. It took another year and a half for the Antifederalists in North Carolina to come around. Fiercely independent Rhode Island held out until May 1790, and even then it ratified by only a two-vote margin.

In less than twelve months, the U.S. Constitution was both written and ratified. (See appendix, pages A-3–A-8.) An amazingly short time by twentieth-century standards, it is even more remarkable for the late eighteenth century, with its horse-powered transportation and hand-printed communications. The Federalists had faced a formidable task, but by building momentum and assuring a bill of rights, they did indeed carry the day.

Conclusion:
The "Republican Remedy"

Thus ended one of the most intellectually tumultuous and creative decades in American history. Americans leaders experimented with ideas and drew up plans to embody their evolving and conflicting notions of how a society and a government ought to be formulated. While there was widespread agreement that government should derive its power and authority from the people, there was fierce disagreement over the degree of democracy—the amount of direct control of government by the people—that was truly workable in American society.

The decade began in 1776 with a confederation government that could barely be ratified because of its requirement of unanimity, but there was no reaching unanimity on the western lands, on the impost amendment, or on the proper way to respond to unfair taxation in a republican state. The new Constitution offered a different approach to these problems, by loosening the grip of impossible unanimity and by embracing the ideas of a heterogeneous public life and a carefully balanced government that together would prevent any one part of the public from tyrannizing another. The genius of James Madison was to anticipate that diversity of opinion was not only an unavoidable reality but a hidden strength of the new society beginning to take shape. This is what he meant in his tenth Federalist essay when he spoke of the "republican remedy" for the troubles most likely to befall a government where the people are the source of authority.

Despite Madison's optimism, political differences remained keen and worrisome to many. The Federalists still hoped for a society in which leaders of exceptional wisdom would discern the best path for public policy. They looked backward to a society of hierarchy, rank, and benevolent rule by an aristocracy of talent, but they created a government with forward-looking checks and balances as a guard against corruption, which they figured would most likely emanate from the people. The Antifederalists also looked backward, but to an old order of small-scale direct democracy and local control, where virtuous people kept a close eye on potentially corruptible rulers. Antifederalists feared a national government led by distant, self-interested leaders who needed to be held in check. In the 1790s, these two conceptions of republicanism and of leadership would be tested in real life.

FOR FURTHER READING ABOUT THE TOPICS IN THIS CHAPTER, see the Online Bibliography at

www.bedfordstmartins.com/roarkcompact.

FOR ADDITIONAL FIRST-HAND ACCOUNTS OF THIS PERIOD, see pages 113–131 in Michael Johnson, ed., *Reading the American Past,* Second Edition, Volume I.

TO ASSESS YOUR MASTERY OF THE MATERIAL IN THIS CHAPTER, see the Online Study Guide at

www.bedfordstmartins.com/roarkcompact.

CHRONOLOGY

1775 **May.** Second Continental Congress begins.

1776 Virginia adopts state bill of rights.

1777 **November.** Final draft of Articles of Confederation approved by congress and sent to states.

1778 State constitutions completed.

1780 Pennsylvania institutes gradual emancipation.

Cuffe brothers petition Massachusetts state legislature for extension of suffrage to tax-paying free blacks.

1781 Articles of Confederation ratified.

Creation of executive departments; Robert Morris appointed superintendent of finance.

Bank of North America formed.

Slave Quok Walker sues for freedom in Massachusetts.

1782 Virginia relaxes state manumission law.

1783 Treaty of Paris signed.

1784 Gradual emancipation laws passed in Rhode Island and Connecticut.

Treaty of Fort Stanwix cedes Iroquois land to confederation government.

1786 Bank of North America charter expires, not renewed.

Virginia adopts Statute of Religious Freedom.

Farmer Shays leads rebellion in western Massachusetts.

Annapolis meeting proposes convention to revise Articles of Confederation.

1787 Northwest Ordinance allows self-government and prohibits slavery in Northwest Territory.

Delaware provides manumission law.

May–September. Constitutional convention meets in Philadelphia.

1788 U.S. Constitution ratified.

1790 Maryland provides manumission law.

1799 Gradual emancipation in New York.

1804 Gradual emancipation in New Jersey.

WASHINGTON STANDS OUTSIDE OF TIME

A French clockmaker and artist produced this piece
of Washington memorabilia after the death of the president. Washington's trim
figure, rendered in gilt bronze, sports a spiffy uniform complete with epaulets
on the shoulders. One gloved hand rests on a sword while the other holds a
rolled parchment, offered up in front of an eagle, the symbol of America's
strength. Below the eagle a familiar motto is inscribed: "E Pluribus Unum,"
or, "out of many, one," a reference to the political unity of the sovereign
states. Below the clock is another motto that quickly became a commonplace
one about Washington: "First in War, First in Peace, and First in the Hearts of
his Countrymen." In his lifetime and for years after, Washington attained
celebrity status, and Americans immortalized him in many souvenirs.

The Warner Collection of Gulf States Paper Corporation.

THE NEW NATION TAKES FORM

9

1789–1800

THE ELECTION OF GEORGE WASHINGTON in February 1789 was quick work. Seven months earlier, right after Virginia and New Hampshire ratified the Constitution, many July 4 orators and newspaper editors considered the Virginia planter as good as president, and the tallying of the unanimous votes by the electoral college became a mere formality. Washington was everyone's first choice. He perfectly embodied the republican ideal of disinterested, public-spirited leadership; indeed, he cultivated that image. At the end of the war, he had dramatically surrendered his sword to the Continental Congress, symbolizing the subservience of military power to the law.

Although somewhat reluctant, Washington ultimately accepted the presidency. He journeyed from Virginia to the capital, New York City, in six days, encountering cheering crowds, large triumphal arches, and military parades at many villages en route. In New York City, he rode a white horse down Broadway while a crowd of thirty thousand cheered. He took the oath of office at the newly built Federal Hall at Broad and Wall Streets; a cannon salute in the harbor signaled his inauguration.

The pageantry was a kind of hero worship for Washington as an individual. But the question, as yet unresolved, was whether the office of the presidency itself would be grandly heroic. The arches, the grand entry on a white horse, the gun salute—all were uneasy reminders of the trappings of monarchy. In its first month, Congress debated the proper form of address for the president, raising explicitly the issue of how kingly this new presidency was to be. Titles such as "His Highness, the President of the United States of America and Protector of Their Liberties" and "His Majesty, the President" were floated as possibilities, while Washington himself favored "His High Mightiness." Several former Antifederalists sitting in Congress held out for a less exalted title. The final version was simply "President of the United States of America," and the established form of address became "Mr. President," a subdued yet dignified title in a society where only property-owning adult white males could presume to be called "Mister."

Washington's genius in establishing the presidency lay in his capacity for implanting his own reputation for integrity into the office itself. He was not a particularly brilliant thinker, nor was he a shrewd political strategist. He was not even a very congenial man. In the political language of the day, he was virtuous. Washington was studiously aloof, resolute, and dignified, to the point of appearing wooden at times. He encouraged pomp and ceremony to create respect for the presidency, traveling with no fewer than six horses drawing his coach, hosting formal balls, and surrounding himself with servants in livery. He even held weekly levees, as European monarchs did, hour-long audiences granted to distinguished

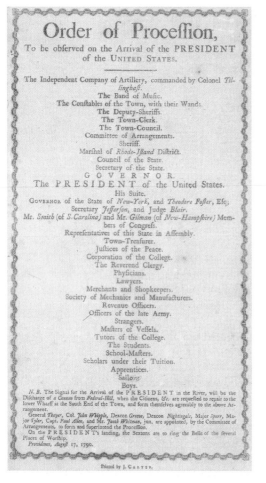

Order of Procession,
To be observed on the Arrival of the PRESIDENT
of the UNITED STATES.

The Independent Company of Artillery, commanded by Colonel Til-
lingbaſt.
The Band of Muſic.
The Conſtables of the Town, with their Wands.
The Deputy-Sheriffs.
The Town-Clerk.
The Town-Council.
Committee of Arrangements.
Sheriff.
Marſhal of Rhode-Iſland Diſtrict.
Council of the State.
Secretary of the State.
GOVERNOR.
The PRESIDENT of the United States.
His Suite.
GOVERNOR of the State of New-York, and Theodore Foſter, Eſq;
Secretary Jefferſon, and Judge Blair.
Mr. Smith (of S. Carolina) and Mr. Gilman (of New-Hampſhire) Mem-
bers of Congreſs.
Repreſentatives of this State in Aſſembly.
Town-Treaſurer.
Juſtices of the Peace.
Corporation of the College.
The Reverend Clergy.
Phyſicians.
Lawyers.
Merchants and Shopkeepers.
Society of Mechanics and Manufacturers.
Revenue Officers.
Officers of the late Army.
Strangers.
Maſters of Veſſels.
Tutors of the College.
The Students.
School-Maſters.
Scholars under their Tuition.
Apprentices.
Sailors.
Boys.
N. B. The Signal for the Arrival of the PRESIDENT in the River, will be the
Diſcharge of a Cannon from Federal-Hill, when the Citizens, &c. are requeſted to repair to the
lower Wharf at the South End of the Town, and form themſelves agreeably to the above Ar-
rangement.
General Thayer, Col. John Whipple, Deacon Greene, Deacon Nightingale, Major Spurr, Ma-
jor Tyler, Capt. Paul Allen, and Mr. Jacob Whitman, jun. are appointed, by the Committee of
Arrangements, to form and ſuperintend the Proceſſion.
On the PRESIDENT's landing, the Sextons are to ring the Bells of the ſeveral
Places of Worſhip.
Providence, Auguſt 17, 1790.

Printed by J. CARTER.

ORDER OF PROCESSION
*When President Washington visited Providence,
Rhode Island, the town government prepared an
"Order of Procession" to inform citizens of their
exact place in the welcoming parade. Soldiers, a
band, and town officers preceded the honored guest,
whose immediate entourage included two governors, a cabinet member, a judge, and two members
of Congress. Next came town politicians, professors
in the local college (Brown), clergy, doctors,
lawyers, and merchants. Further along came masters of ships, tutors at Brown, college students,
and, bringing up the rear, apprentices, sailors, and
boys. Who was excluded from the procession? How
might merchants or sailors feel about their place in
line? Several such "orders of procession" exist for
other towns; were such elaborate rituals consistent
with a non-monarchical political system? In what
other ways might President Washington have
entered a town?*
The Huntington Library and Art Collections, San Marino, California.

visitors, at which Washington appeared attired in
black velvet, a feathered hat, and a polished sword.
The president and his guests bowed, avoiding the
egalitarian familiarity of handshakes. But he always
managed, perhaps just barely, to avoid the extreme
of royal splendor.

The thirteen American states had just come
through a difficult decade, swinging between a distrust of executive power on the one hand and a fear
of turbulent factional politics on the other. Washington's reputation for integrity boosted confidence
that executive power could be compatible with the
public good. And his strong pronouncements about
the evils of divisive factions raised hopes that at last
America was on a steady course.

National harmony proved elusive, however.
Political divisions emerged in the 1790s, despite the
best intentions. Even men who had worked together to ratify the Constitution found that the
process of implementing it exposed serious disagreement. Economic policy and foreign affairs
proved to be the two most significant fissures in
the political leadership of the 1790s. The disagreements were articulated around particular events
and policies, but at heart they arose out of opposing ideological stances about the nature of democracy and of leadership, and the limits of federal
power. By 1800, these divisions had begun to crystallize into political parties, the Federalists and the
Republicans.

The Search for Stability

Conventional wisdom today praises the development of a party system: Parties organize conflict, legitimize disagreement, and mediate among competing political strategies. Yet they were entirely
unanticipated by the writers of the Constitution. Instead, leaders in the early 1790s sought stability to
heal divisions of the 1780s. Veneration for President
Washington provided one powerful source of unity.
People trusted him to initiate the untested and perhaps elastic powers of the presidency. Congress
quickly agreed on passage of the Bill of Rights in
1791, which satisfied many Antifederalist critics.
And the private virtue of women was mobilized to
bolster the public virtue of male citizens; republicanism was forcing a rethinking of women's relation to the state.

Washington's Cabinet

Congress immediately set up departments of war, treasury, and state, leaving to Washington the selection of secretaries over each. The president picked talented and experienced individuals for each post, regardless of their deep philosophical differences. For the Department of War, he chose General Henry Knox, one-time secretary of war in the confederation government. For the Treasury—an especially tough job, in view of revenue conflicts during the confederation—Washington picked Alexander Hamilton of New York, known for his general brilliance and financial astuteness. To lead the Department of State, the foreign policy arm of the executive branch, Washington chose Thomas Jefferson, a master of the intricacy of diplomatic relations, who was then serving as minister to France.

In addition, for attorney general Washington picked Edmund Randolph, a Virginian who had attended the Constitutional Convention but had turned Antifederalist during ratification. For chief justice of the Supreme Court, Washington designated John Jay, the New York lawyer who vigorously defended the Constitution along with Madison and Hamilton in *The Federalist*.

Washington liked and trusted all these men, and by 1793, in his second term, he was meeting regularly with them, thereby establishing the precedent of a presidential cabinet. (Vice President John Adams did not join these meetings; his only official duty was to preside over the Senate, a job he found "a punishment" because he could not actually participate in legislative debates. He complained to his wife, Abigail, "My country has in its wisdom contrived for me the most insignificant office.") No one anticipated that two decades of party turbulence would emerge from the brilliant but explosive mix of Washington's first cabinet.

The Bill of Rights

Many Antifederalists had complained about the absence of guarantees of individual liberties and limitations to federal power in the Constitution, and seven states had ratified on the condition that a bill of rights be swiftly incorporated. Many state constitutions already protected freedom of speech, press, peaceable assembly, and the rights to petition and to have jury trials. In the final days of the 1787 Philadelphia convention, the delegates had decided an enumeration of

rights was unnecessary. But the complaint surfaced continually in the ratification process, and so in 1789, in response to Antifederalist criticisms, James Madison drew up a set of amendments.

Final agreement from both House and Senate on the first ten amendments to the Constitution, collectively known as the Bill of Rights, came in September 1789. Amendments 1–8 dealt with individual liberties, and 9 and 10 concerned the boundary between federal and state authority. (See the U.S. Constitution in the appendix, pages A-9–A-12.) The amendments had the immediate effect of cementing a sense of national unity. The process of state ratification took another two years, but there was no serious doubt about the outcome.

Still, not everyone was entirely satisfied. Some eighty proposed amendments had been submitted by state ratifying conventions. Proposals to change the structural details of the new government were never considered by Congress; Madison had no intention of reopening debates about the length of term for the president or the power to levy excise taxes.

Significantly, no one complained about one striking omission in the Bill of Rights: the right to vote. Only much later was voting seen as a fundamental liberty requiring protection by constitutional amendment—indeed, by four amendments. The 1788 Constitution deliberately left definition of voters to the states, which set differing property qualifications. Any uniform federal voting law would run the double risk of excluding some who could already vote in state elections or including too many new voters deemed undesirable in the more restrictive states.

Unlike most states, which routinely restricted voting to free, white males, New Jersey in 1776 enfranchised all free inhabitants worth over £50, thereby including free blacks as well as unmarried women who met the property requirement. (Married women owned no property, for by law their husbands held title to everything.) Little fanfare accompanied this radical shift, and some historians have inferred that the inclusion of blacks and unmarried women was accidental, the result of an unstated assumption that voters would be white and male. Yet other parts of the suffrage clause pertaining to residency and property were extensively debated when it was put in the state constitution, and no objections were raised at that time to its gender- and race-free language. Thus other historians have concluded that the law was intentionally inclusive. By 1790, a revised election law used the words *he* or *she* in reference to voters, thus making woman suffrage explicit. As one New Jersey legislator boasted, "Our Constitution gives this right to maids or widows black or white."

In 1790, only about 1,000 free black adults of both sexes lived in New Jersey, a state with a population of 184,000. The number of unmarried adult white women was probably also small and predominantly widows. Considering the property requirement, the voter bloc enfranchised under this law could not have been decisive in elections. Still, this highly unusual state of affairs lasted until 1807, when a new state law specifically disfranchised both blacks and women. Henceforth, independence of mind, that essential precondition of voting, was redefined to be sex- and race-specific.

The Republican Wife and Mother

The general exclusion of women from political activity did not mean they had no civic role or responsibility. A flood of periodical articles of the 1790s by both male and female writers reevaluated courtship, marriage, and motherhood in light of republican ideals. Tyrannical power in the ruler, whether king or husband, was now declared a thing of the past. Affection, not duty, bound wives to their husbands and citizens to their government. In republican marriages, the writers claimed, women had the capacity to reform the morals and manners of men. One male author promised women that "the solidity and stability of the liberties of your country rest with you; since Liberty is never sure, 'till Virtue reigns triumphant." By upholding public virtue, women bolstered political liberty.

Until the 1790s, public virtue was strictly a masculine quality. But another sort of virtue loomed in importance: sexual chastity, a private asset prized as a feminine quality. Essayists of the 1790s explicitly advised young women to use sexual virtue to produce more public virtue in men. "Love and courtship . . . invest a lady with more authority than in any other situation that falls to the lot of human beings," one male essayist proclaimed. If women spurned selfish suitors, they could promote good morals more than any social institution could, essayists promised.

Republican ideals also cast motherhood in a new light. Throughout the 1790s, advocates legitimized female education, still a controversial propo-

REPUBLICAN WOMANHOOD:
JUDITH SARGENT MURRAY
The twenty-one-year-old in this portrait would become known eighteen years later as America's foremost public spokeswoman for the idea of woman's equality to man. Judith Sargent Murray wrote frequent essays for the **Massachusetts Magazine** *under the penname "Constantia." In one essay published in 1790, "On the Equality of the Sexes," she confidently asserted that women had "natural powers" of mind fully the equal of men's. Murray, the wife of a Universalist minister, wrote plays that were performed on the Boston stage, and in 1798 she published her collected "Constantia" essays in a book titled* **The Gleaner;** *George Washington and John Adams each bought a copy. Murray is the only woman of her era to keep an indexed letter book, containing copies of nearly two thousand of her own letters written over her lifetime.*

John Singleton Copley, Portrait of Mrs. John Stevens (Judith Sargent, later Mrs. John Murray), 1770–1772, oil on canvas, 50 x 40 inches, Terra Foundation for the Arts, Daniel J. Terra Art Acquisition Endowment Fund, 2000.6; Photograph courtesy of Terra Foundation for the Arts, Chicago.

sition, through the claim of significant maternal influence on the future male citizenry. Benjamin Rush, a Pennsylvania physician and educator, called for female education because "our ladies should be qualified . . . in instructing their sons in the principles of liberty and government." A series of essays by Judith Sargent Murray of Massachusetts favored education that would remake women into self-confident, competent, rational beings, poised to become the equals of men. But even Murray had to dress her advanced ideas in the cloak of republican motherhood, justifying female education in the context of family duty.

Although women's domestic obligations as wives and mothers were now infused with political meaning, traditional gender relations remained unaltered. The analogy between marriage and civil society worked precisely because of the self-subordination inherent in the term *virtue*. Men should put the public good first, before selfish desires, just as women must put their husbands and families first, before themselves. Women might gain literacy and knowledge, but only in the service of improved domestic duty.

Hamilton's Economic Policies

Compared to the severe economic instability of the 1780s, the 1790s seemed flush with opportunity and prosperity, as seen in increased agricultural trade, transportation, and banking improvements. The federal government moved from New York City to Philadelphia, a more central location. Alexander Hamilton, the secretary of the Treasury, proposed several pioneering yet controversial economic programs.

Agriculture, Transportation, and Banking

Dramatic increases in the international price of grain in the 1790s motivated American farmers to boost agricultural production and trade. Europe's rising population needed grain, and the Napoleonic Wars after 1793 compromised production there. From the Connecticut River valley to the Chesapeake, farmers responded by planting more wheat. The increase in overseas grain trade generated a host of new jobs in related areas as the number of millers, coopers, and ship and wagon builders expanded.

Cotton production also underwent a boom, spurred by market growth and a mechanical invention. Limited amounts of smooth-seed cotton had long been grown in the low-lying coastal areas

of the South; but this variety of cotton did not prosper in the drier, inland regions. Green-seed cotton grew well inland, but it contained many rough seeds that adhered tenaciously to the cotton fibers, making it very labor-intensive to clean. In 1793, a Yale graduate named Eli Whitney, visiting a Georgia plantation, invented the cotton gin, a device to separate out the seeds. Use of the gin spurred cotton production, from 138,000 pounds in 1792 to 35 million in 1800. Most of it was shipped to English factories to be made into textiles.

A surge of road building helped propel the prosperous economy. Only one continuous and improved road existed before 1790, the Post Road running for sixteen hundred miles from Maine to Georgia near the coast. This was joined, in the 1790s, by the Lancaster Turnpike, the first private toll road in the nation, connecting Philadelphia with Lancaster. Soon another turnpike connected Boston with Albany and continued west. Private companies chartered by state governments financed and built these turnpikes, and collected fees from all vehicles. Further inland, a major road extended south-

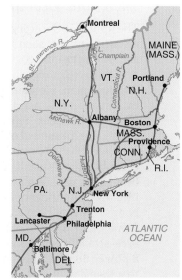

Major Roads in the 1790s

west down the Shenandoah Valley, while another road linked Richmond, Virginia, with the Tennessee towns of Knoxville and Nashville.

By 1800, a dense network of dirt, gravel, or plank roadways connected cities and towns in southern New England and the Middle Atlantic states, while isolated roadways and old Indian trails fanned out to the west. Commercial stage lines connected major eastern cities, offering four-day travel time between New York and Boston and an exhausting but speedy one-and-one-half-day trip between New York and Philadelphia. In 1790, only three stagecoach companies operated out of Boston, but by 1800 there were twenty-four. Transport of goods by roads was still expensive per mile, compared to water transport on navigable rivers or along the coast, but at least it was possible now.

A third development signalling economic resurgence was the growth of commercial banking. During the 1790s, the number of banks nationwide multiplied tenfold, from three to twenty-nine in 1800. Banks drew in money chiefly through the sale of stock. They then made loans in the form of banknotes, paper currency backed by the gold and silver paid in by stockholders. Because they issued two or three times as much money in banknotes as they held in hard money, banks were really creating new money for the economy.

The Public Debt and Taxes

The upturn in the economy suggested that the government might soon repay its wartime debts, amounting to some $52 million owed to foreign and domestic creditors. But Hamilton had a slightly different plan. He issued a *Report on Public Credit* in January 1790, recommending that the debt be funded—but not repaid immediately—at full value. This meant that old certificates of debt would be rolled over into new bonds, which earned interest until retired several years later. There would still be a public debt, but it would be secure, supported by citizens' confidence in the new government. The bonds would circulate, injecting new valuable money into the economy. "A national debt if not excessive will be to us a national blessing; it will be a powerfull cement of our union," Hamilton wrote to a financier.

A large part of the old debt had been bought up cheaply by speculators in the 1780s; these men would now have a direct financial stake in the new government, support that Hamilton regarded as essential to the country's stability. He was also providing those same men with more than $40 million released for new investment, a distinct improvement over the old depreciated bonds, which had circulated in daily transactions at a fraction of their face value.

If the *Report on Public Credit* had gone only this far, it would have been somewhat controversial. But Hamilton took a much bolder step by augmenting the debt with another $25 million still owed by state governments to individuals. All the states had obtained supplies during the war by issuing IOUs to farmers, merchants, and moneylenders. Some states, such as Virginia and New York, had paid off these debts entirely, while others, like Massachusetts, had partially paid them through

ALEXANDER HAMILTON BY JOHN TRUMBULL
Alexander Hamilton posed for this portrait in 1792, at age thirty-seven and at his height of power. Ever a prodigy, Hamilton at age nineteen became an indispensable wartime aide to George Washington. In his mid-twenties he gained admission to the bar after only three months of study. In 1789, he became Washington's youngest cabinet member.
Yale University Art Gallery.

heavy taxation of the inhabitants; about half the states had made little headway. Hamilton called for the federal government to assume these state debts and add them to the federal debt, in effect consolidating federal power over the states.

A national debt swollen to some $77 million required extra taxation to meet the interest payments. Hamilton did not propose raising import duties, in deference to the merchant class whose support he was seeking. Instead, he convinced Congress in 1791 to pass a 25 percent excise tax on whiskey, to be paid by the farmer when he brought his grain to the distillery. Members of Congress favored the tax, especially those from New England where the favorite drink was rum, an imported beverage already taxed under the import laws. A New Hampshire representative pointed out that the country would be "drinking down the national debt," an idea he evidently found acceptable.

Congressman James Madison objected to Hamilton's funding plan, fearing that windfall profits would go mainly to speculators who had bought the original IOUs at bargain prices. He also strenuously objected to assumption of all the states' debts. A large debt was dangerous, Madison warned, especially because it would lead to high taxation. But he lost the vote in Congress. Madison and Hamilton, so recently allies in writing *The Federalist,* were becoming opponents. Secretary of State Jefferson also was fearful of Hamilton's proposals. "No man is more ardently intent to see the public debt soon and sacredly paid off than I am. This exactly marks the difference between Colonel Hamilton's views and mine, that I would wish the debt paid tomorrow; he wishes it never to be paid, but always to be a thing where with to corrupt and manage the legislature."

The First Bank of the United States and the Report on Manufactures

The second and third major elements of Hamilton's economic plan were his proposal for a national Bank of the United States and his program to encourage domestic manufacturing. Believing that banks were the "nurseries of national wealth," Hamilton modeled his plan on the Bank of England, a private corporation that worked primarily for the public good. In Hamilton's plan, 20 percent of the bank's stock would be bought by the federal government. In effect, the bank would become the fiscal agent of the new government, holding and handling its revenues derived from import duties, land sales, and the whiskey excise tax. The other 80 percent of the bank's capital would come from private investors, who could buy stock in the bank with either hard money (silver or gold) or federal securities. By its size and the privilege of being the only national bank, the bank would help stabilize the economy by exerting prudent control over credit, interest rates, and the value of the currency.

Madison, concerned that the bank gave a handful of rich men undue influence over the economy, tried but failed to stop the plan in Congress. Jefferson advised Washington that the Constitution did not permit Congress to charter banks. Hamilton, however, argued that the Constitution listed certain powers to regulate commerce ending with a broad grant of the right "to make all laws which shall be necessary and proper for carrying into execution the foregoing powers." Washington agreed with Hamilton and signed the Bank of the United States into law in February 1791, providing it with a charter to operate for twenty years. When the bank's privately held stock went on sale in New York City in July, it sold out in a few hours, touching off an immediate mania of speculation in resale. A discouraged Madison reported that "the Coffee House is an eternal buzz with the gamblers," some of them self-interested congressmen intent on "public plunder."

The third component of Hamilton's plan was issued in December 1791 in the *Report on Manufactures,* a proposal to encourage the production of American-made goods. Manufacturing was in its infancy in 1790, the result of years of dependence on British imports. Hamilton recognized that a balanced and self-reliant economy required the United States to produce its own cloth and iron products. His plan mobilized the new powers of the federal government to impose tariffs and grant subsidies to encourage the growth of local manufacturing. Hamilton had to be careful not to undercut his important merchant allies who traded with England and generated over half the government's income. A high tariff would either seriously dampen that trade or force merchants into smuggling. So Hamilton favored a moderate tariff, with extra bounties paid to American manufacturers to encourage production. The *Report on Manufactures* was the one Hamiltonian plan that was not approved by Congress.

The Whiskey Rebellion

Hamilton's excise tax on whiskey proved very unpopular with cash-short grain farmers and whiskey drinkers. In 1791, farmers in the western parts of Pennsylvania, Virginia, Maryland, and the Carolinas and throughout Kentucky conveyed to Congress their resentment of Hamilton's tax. Congress responded with modest modifications in the tax in 1792; but even so, discontent was rampant.

Simple evasion of the law was the most common response; the tax proved hard to collect. Crowds threatened to tar and feather federal tax collectors, while some distilleries underreported their production. With embarrassment, Hamilton admitted to Congress that the revenue was far less than anticipated. But rather than abandon the law, he tightened up the prosecution of tax evaders.

WHISKEY REBELLION "FIRE COPPER"
*This forty-gallon "fire copper" produced Monongahela rye whiskey in the 1790s in
western Pennsylvania. Mashed rye grain was mixed and heated with mash from a previously distilled brew. The distiller next added yeast and water and let the mixture ferment for several days. The mixture was then heated to 175 degrees, the boiling point of
alcohol, in this three-foot copper vessel (called a "still"). Alcohol-laden vapor from the
boiling brew cooled and condensed in a spiral copper tubing that dripped whiskey into
a jug. High-proof, expensive whiskey required a second processing in the still to concentrate the vapors. The owner of this fire copper was James Miller, whose nephew Oliver
Miller Jr. was one of the few fatalities in the Whiskey Rebellion.*
Photo by Andrew Wagner. Courtesy of *American History* magazine.

In western Pennsylvania, Hamilton had one
ally, a stubborn tax collector named John Neville
who had refused to quit even after a group of spir-
ited farmers had burned him in effigy. In May 1794,
Neville filed charges against seventy-five farmers
and distillers for tax evasion. In July, he and a federal marshal were ambushed in Allegheny County
by a group of forty men, and then Neville's house
was burned to the ground by a crowd estimated at
five hundred. Seven thousand farmers staged a
march on Pittsburgh to protest the hated tax.

In response, Washington nationalized the Pennsylvania militia, donned his old military garb, and
set out, with Hamilton at his side urging him on, at
the head of fifteen thousand soldiers. By the time
the army arrived, in late September, the demon-
strators had all gone home. No battles were fought,
and no fire was exchanged. Twenty men were
rounded up as rebels and charged with high trea-

son, but only two were convicted, and both were
soon pardoned by Washington.

Had the government overreacted? Or was
Hamilton right to think that the whiskey rioters
posed a serious threat to the stability of the federal
government? The long colonial tradition of crowd
action to protest unfair practices had worked well
when colonists had limited formal access to power.
But in a republic, laws were passed by the supposed
representatives of the people, not by tyrannical
kings or distant parliaments. Burning effigies of
stamp tax collectors in 1765 made sense as an
effective contribution to the political process. Burning effigies of whiskey tax collectors in 1792 appeared to many to be an unlawful rejection of the
will of the people as expressed through Congress.

The whiskey rebels, however, recognized oppressive taxes for what they were and felt entitled
to resort to protest and demonstration. Representa-

tive government had not worked to their benefit. The Whiskey Rebellion was an early example of what would prove to be a long-term conflict: the tension between minority rights and majority rule.

Conflicts West, East, and South

Washington's second term began in 1793, with his unanimous reelection. But as the Whiskey Rebellion demonstrated, the widespread admiration for the individual man did not translate to complete domestic tranquility. While the whiskey rebels challenged federal leadership from within the country, disorder threatened the United States from external sources as well. To the west, a powerful confederation of Indian tribes in the Ohio country resisted white encroachment, resulting in a brutal war. At the same time, conflicts between the major European powers forced Americans to take sides and nearly thrust the country into another war, this time across the Atlantic. And to the south, a Caribbean slave rebellion raised fears of racial war imported to the United States.

To the West: The Indians

By the Treaty of Paris of 1783, England had given up all land east of the Mississippi River to the United States—but without consulting their one-time allies, the Indian tribes who inhabited 25,000 square miles of that territory. When they learned of the treaty terms, the Indians expressed astonishment. "They told me they never could believe that our king could pretend to cede to America what was not his own to give," the British commander at Fort Niagara wrote of the Iroquois. In southern Ohio, British Indian agents assured the Shawnees and Delawares that England had relinquished only political control to the United States but that Indians still had the right to occupy the land over the claims of American settlers. Such confusion and misrepresentation aggravated an already volatile situation.

A doubled American population, from two million in 1770 to nearly four million in 1790, created an insistent pressure for western land. Several thousand settlers a year moved down the Ohio River in the mid-1780s, some bound for Kentucky but many others eyeing the fresh forests and fields north of the Ohio River. By the late 1780s, government land sales in eastern Ohio commenced (Map 9.1).

Even western Ohio was not safe from American incursions. Downriver, at the site of present-day Cincinnati, an outpost named Fort Washington was constructed in 1789 and put under the command of General Arthur St. Clair, who was also governor of the entire Northwest Territory. St. Clair's mission was to displace the Indians and clear the way for permanent American settlement in Ohio. He first tried peaceful tactics and got an assortment of Indians to sign a treaty yielding land near the Muskingum River in eastern Ohio. But these Indians were not chiefs authorized to undertake negotiations, so the dubious treaty did nothing to improve the chances for peace.

Bloody frontier raids and skirmishes between settlers and Indians led the United States to expand its military force. Finally, St. Clair took direct action. In the fall of 1791, more than two thousand men (and two hundred women camp followers) marched north from Fort Washington to engage in battle with Miami and Shawnee Indians. The Indians attacked first, at daybreak on November 4, at the headwaters of the Wabash River in western Ohio. The ferocious battle was a disaster for the Americans, 55 percent of whom were dead or wounded before noon; only three of the women escaped alive. It was the worst American defeat in the entire history of the U.S.-Indian wars. The Indians captured valuable weaponry, scalped and dismembered the dying, and pursued fleeing survivors for miles. The grisly tales of St. Clair's defeat became instantly infamous, increasing, if this were possible, the level of sheer terror that Americans brought to their confrontations with the Indians.

President Washington doubled the American military presence in Ohio and appointed a new commander, General Anthony Wayne of Pennsylvania, nicknamed "Mad Anthony" for his headstrong style of leadership. About the Ohio natives he wrote, "I have always been of the opinion that we never should have a permanent peace with those Indians until they were made to experience our superiority." With some 3,500 men, Wayne established two new military camps, Fort Greenville and Fort Recovery, deep in Indian territory in western Ohio.

Throughout 1794 Wayne's army engaged in skirmishes with the Shawnees and Delawares. The decisive action came in August 1794 at the Battle of Fallen Timbers, near the Maumee River where a recent severe rainstorm had felled many trees. The con-

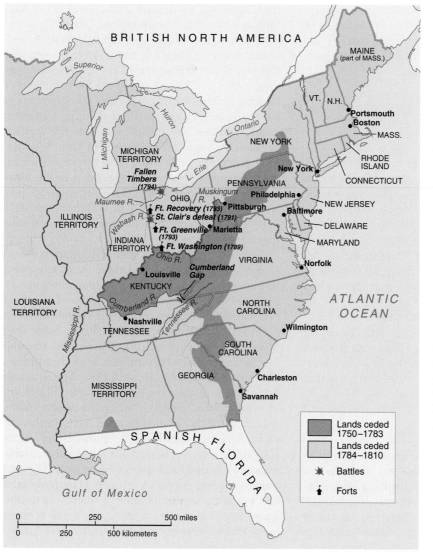

MAP 9.1

Western Expansion and Indian Land Cessions to 1810
By the first decade of the nineteenth century, the period of intense Indian wars had resulted in significant cessions of land to the U.S. government by treaty.

READING THE MAP: Locate the Appalachians. What line of 1763 ran along the mountains? What was that line's purpose, and how well was that purpose met?

CONNECTIONS: How much did the population of the United States grow between 1750 and 1790? How did this growth affect western settlement?

www.bedfordstmartins.com/roarkcompact SEE THE ONLINE STUDY GUIDE for more help in analyzing this map.

---

federated Indians—mainly Ottawas, Potawatomis, and Delawares, numbering around 800—first ambushed the Americans, but they were underarmed, many having only tomahawks. Wayne's well-disciplined troops made effective use of their guns and bayonets, and in just over an hour the Indians had retreated and scattered.

Fallen Timbers was a major defeat for the Indians. The Americans had destroyed cornfields and villages on the march north, and, with winter approaching, the Indians' confidence was sapped. They reentered negotiations in a much less powerful bargaining position. In 1795, about a thousand Indians representing nearly a dozen tribes met with

Wayne and other American emissaries to work out the Treaty of Greenville. The Americans offered $25,000 worth of treaty goods (calico shirts, axes, knives, blankets, kettles, mirrors, ribbons, thimbles, and abundant wine and liquor casks) and promised additional shipments every year. The government's idea was to create a dependency on American goods to keep the Indians friendly. In exchange, the Indians ceded most of Ohio to the Americans; only the northwest region of the territory was reserved solely for the Indians.

The treaty brought peace to the region, but it did not bring back a peaceful life to the Indians. The annual allowance from the United States too often

TREATY OF GREENVILLE, 1795
General Anthony Wayne meets with Chief Little Turtle of the Miamis and Chief Tarhe
the Crane of the Wyandots to sign the Treaty of Greenville in Ohio in 1795.
Chicago Historical Society.

came in the form of liquor. "More of us have died since the Treaty of Greenville than we lost by the years of war before, and it is all owing to the introduction of liquor among us," said Little Turtle, chief of the Miami people, in 1800. "This liquor that they introduce into our country is more to be feared than the gun and tomahawk."

Across the Atlantic: France and England

Since 1789, a violent revolution had been raging in France. At first, the general American reaction was positive, for it was flattering to think that the American Revolution had inspired imitation in France. Monarchy and privilege were overthrown in the name of republicanism; towns throughout America celebrated the victory of the French people with civic feasts and public festivities.

But news of the beheading of King Louis XVI quickly dampened the uncritical enthusiasm for everything French. Those who fondly remembered the excitement and risk of the American Revolution were still apt to regard France with optimism. However, the reluctant revolutionaries of the 1770s and 1780s, who had worried about excessive democracy and social upheaval in America, deplored the far greater violence occurring in the name of republicanism as France moved into the Reign of Terror.

Support for the French Revolution could remain a matter of personal conviction until 1793, when England and France went to war and French versus British loyalty became a critical foreign policy question. France had helped America substantially during the American Revolution, and the confederated government had signed an alliance in 1778 promising aid if France were ever under attack. Americans still optimistic about the eventual outcome of the French Revolution wanted to deliver on that promise now. But others, including those shaken by the guillotining of thousands of French people as well as those with strong commercial ties to England, sought ways to stay neutral.

In May 1793, President Washington issued a Neutrality Proclamation, with friendly assurances to both sides. But tensions at home flared in response to official neutrality. "The cause of France is the cause of man, and neutrality is desertion," wrote H. H. Brackenridge, a western Pennsylvanian, voicing the sentiments of thousands. Dozens of pro-French political clubs sprang up around the country, called Democratic or Republican Societies. The societies mobilized farmers and mechanics, issued circular letters, injected pro-French and anti-British feelings into local elections, and in general heightened popular participation and public interest in foreign policy. The activities of these societies disturbed Washington and Hamilton intensely, for they vented opposition to the policies of the president.

The Neutrality Proclamation was in theory a fine idea, in view of Washington's goal of staying out of European wars. Yet American ships continued to trade between the French West Indies and France, and in late 1793 and early 1794, the English expressed their displeasure by capturing more than three hundred of these vessels near the West Indies. At such a moment, even pro-British politicians like Hamilton agreed that it was necessary to deal firmly with England.

President Washington sent John Jay, the chief justice of the Supreme Court and a man of strong pro-British sentiments, to England to negotiate commercial relations and to secure compensation for the seizure of American ships. In addition, Jay was supposed to resolve several long-standing problems dating from the end of the Revolution. Southern planters wanted reimbursement for the slaves lured away by the British army during the war, and western settlers wanted England to vacate the western forts still occupied—twelve years after the end of the Revolution—for their strategic proximity to the Indian fur trade.

Jay returned from his diplomatic mission with a treaty that almost no one liked. First, the treaty made no direct provision for the captured ships or the lost property in slaves. Second, it granted the British eighteen more months to withdraw from the western forts while guaranteeing them continued rights in the fur trade. Finally, the Jay Treaty called for repayment with interest of the debts some American planters still owed to British firms dating from the Revolutionary War. In exchange for such generous terms, Jay secured some favorable commercial agreements for the United States, but even there the results were mixed. The treaty was widely regarded as exchanging the country's strong moral

bargaining power (the outrage over the seized ships) for an improved trading status beneficial to only a handful of merchants.

When newspapers published the terms of the treaty, powerful opposition emerged from Maine to Georgia. Nevertheless, the Jay Treaty passed the Senate in 1795 by a vote of twenty to ten. Some representatives in the House, led by Madison, tried to undermine the Senate's approval by insisting on a separate vote on the funding provisions of the treaty, on the grounds that the House controlled all money bills. Finally, in 1796, the House approved funds to implement the various commissions mandated by the treaty, but by only a three-vote margin. The cleavage of votes in both houses of Congress divided along the same lines as the Hamilton-Jefferson split on economic policy.

To the South: The Haitian Revolution

In addition to the Indian wars in Ohio and the European wars across the Atlantic, a third bloody conflict to the south polarized and even terrorized many Americans in the 1790s. The western third of the large Caribbean island of Hispaniola, just to the east of Cuba, became engulfed in revolution starting in 1791. The eastern portion of the island was a Spanish colony called Santo Domingo; the western part, in bloody conflagration, was the French

Haitian Revolution, 1790–1804

Saint Domingue. War raged there for over a decade, resulting in the birth of the Haitian Republic in 1804, distinguished as the first and only independent black state to arise out of a successful slave revolution.

The Haitian Revolution was a complex event involving many participants, including the diverse local population and, eventually, three European countries. Some 30,000 whites ruled the island in 1790, running sugar and coffee plantations with close to half a million slaves, two-thirds of them of African birth. The white French colonists were not the only plantation owners, however. About 28,000 free coloreds (*gens de couleur*) of mixed race also lived in Saint Domingue; they owned one-third of the island's plantations and nearly a quarter of the slave labor force. Despite their economic status, the free coloreds were barred from political power; but they aspired to it.

The French Revolution of 1789 was the immediate catalyst for rebellion in this already tense society. First, white colonists challenged the white royalist government in an effort to link Saint Domingue with the new revolutionary government in France. Next the free coloreds rebelled in 1791, demanding equal civil rights with the whites. No sooner was this revolt viciously suppressed than another part of the island exploded, this time involving thousands of slaves armed with machetes and torches who wreaked devastation and slaughter. In 1793, the civil war escalated to include French, Spanish, and British troops fighting the inhabitants and also each other. The slaves, led by Toussaint L'Ouverture in alliance with Spain, destroyed the northern regions of the island, leaving a thousand plantations in ruins and tens of thousands of people dead. Thousands of whites and free coloreds, along with some of their slaves, fled to Spanish Louisiana and southern cities of the United States.

White Americans followed the revolution in fascinated horror through newspapers and refugees' accounts. A few sympathized with the impulse for liberty, but many more shuddered at the violent atrocities. Many black American slaves also followed the revolution, for the amazing news of the success of a first-ever, massive revolution by slaves traveled quickly in this oral culture. Whites complained of behaviors that might prefigure plots and conspiracies, such as increased insolence and higher runaway rates among slaves.

The Haitian Revolution provoked naked fear in white Americans. Jefferson, agonizing over the contagion of liberty in 1797, wrote another Virginia slaveholder that "if something is not done, and soon done, we shall be the murderers of our own children . . . ; the revolutionary storm, now sweeping the globe, will be upon us, and happy if we make timely provision to give it an easy passage over our land. From the present state of things in Europe and America, the day which brings our combustion must be near at hand; and only a single spark is wanting to make that day to-morrow."

Federalists and Republicans

Political statesmen of the early 1790s had always believed that a division into political factions was a sign of failure, but this assumption was soon put to a severe test. In Washington's second term, consistent voting blocs first appeared in Congress on economic issues. By the time of the Jay Treaty, distinctive labels—Federalist and Republican—had come into use for rival politicians and rival newspapers. These words summarized conflicting ideologies and principles; they did not yet describe organized political parties. Washington's decision not to seek a third term opened the floodgates to serious partisan electioneering.

The Election of 1796

Washington struggled to appear to be above party politics, and in his farewell address of September 1796 he stressed the need to maintain a "unity of government" reflecting a unified body politic. He also urged the country to "steer clear of permanent alliances with any portion of the foreign world." The leading contenders for his position, John Adams of Massachusetts and Thomas Jefferson of Virginia, in theory agreed with him, but around them raged a party contest split along pro-English versus pro-French lines.

Adams and Jefferson were not adept politicians in the modern sense, skilled in the arts of persuasion and intrigue. Bruised by his conflicts with Hamilton, Jefferson had resigned as secretary of state in 1793 and retreated to Monticello, his home in Virginia. Adams's job as vice president kept him closer to the political action, but his personality often put people off. He was temperamental, thin-skinned, and quick to take offense.

The leading Federalists and Republicans informally caucused to choose candidates. The Federalists picked Thomas Pinckney of South Carolina to run with Adams; the Republicans settled on Aaron Burr of New York to pair with Jefferson. The Constitution did not anticipate parties and tickets. Instead, each electoral college voter could cast two votes for any two candidates, but on only one ballot; the top vote-getter became president and the next highest assumed the vice presidency. (This procedural flaw was corrected by the Twelfth Amendment, adopted in 1804.) With only one ballot, careful maneuvering was required to make sure the chief rivals for the presidency did not land in the top two spots.

Into that maneuverable moment stepped Alexander Hamilton. No longer in the cabinet, Hamilton had returned to his law practice in 1795, but he kept a firm hand on political developments. Hamilton did not trust Adams; he preferred Pinckney, and he tried to influence electors to throw their support to the South Carolinian. But his plan backfired: Adams was elected president with seventy-one electoral votes, and Jefferson came in second with sixty-eight and thus became vice president. Pinckney got fifty-nine votes, while Burr trailed with thirty.

Adams's inaugural speech pledged neutrality in foreign affairs and respect for the French people, which made Republicans hopeful. To please Feder-

JOHN ADAMS BY JOHN TRUMBULL
In 1793, a year after the youthful Secretary of the Treasury Alexander Hamilton posed for him (see page 194), John Trumbull painted Vice President John Adams, then age fifty-eight. A friend once listed Adams's shortcomings as a politician: "He can't dance, drink, game, flatter, promise, dress, swear with gentlemen, and small talk and flirt with the ladies."
National Portrait Gallery, Smithsonian Institution/Art Resources, N.Y.

alists, Adams retained three cabinet members from Washington's administration, the secretaries of state, treasury, and war. But the three were Hamilton loyalists, passing on Hamilton's judgments as their own to the unwitting Adams. Vice President Jefferson expected to work closely with his old friend Adams, but the Hamiltonian cabinet ruined the honeymoon. Jefferson's advice was spurned, and he withdrew from active counsel of the president.

The XYZ Affair

From the start, Adams's presidency was in crisis. France retaliated for the Jay Treaty by abandoning its 1778 alliance with the United States. French privateers—armed private vessels—started detaining American ships carrying British goods; by March 1797, more than three hundred American vessels had been seized. To avenge these insults, Federalists started murmuring openly about war with France. Adams preferred negotiations and dispatched a three-man commission to France in the fall of 1797. When the three arrived in Paris, French officials would not receive them. Finally the French minister of foreign affairs, Talleyrand, sent three French agents, unnamed and later known to the American public as X, Y, and Z, to the American commissioners with the recommendation that $250,000 might grease the wheels of diplomacy and that a $12 million loan to the French government would be the price of a peace treaty.

Americans reacted to the XYZ affair with shock and anger. Even staunch pro-French Republicans began to reevaluate their allegiance. The Federalist-dominated Congress appropriated money for an army of ten thousand soldiers. It repealed all prior treaties with France, and in 1798 twenty naval warships launched the United States into its first undeclared war, called the Quasi War by historians to underscore its uncertain legal status. The main scene of action was the Caribbean, where more than one hundred French privateers were captured.

But there was no homefront unification in this time of undeclared war; antagonism only intensified between Federalists and Republicans. Republican newspapers heaped abuse on Adams; Federalist newspapers celebrated over bonfires of rival papers, and one Federalist editor ominously declared that "he who is not for us is against us." Pro-French mobs roamed the capital city, and Adams, fearing for his personal safety, stocked weapons in his presidential quarters.

The Alien and Sedition Acts

If the United States had actually declared war on France, the pro-French Republicans could have been subject to laws of treason. But without a declared war, Federalists had to create another law to muffle opposition. In mid-1798, Congress hammered out a Sedition Act that mandated a heavy fine or a jail sentence for anyone engaged in conspiracies or revolts or convicted of speaking or writing anything that defamed the government. Criticisms of government leaders were now criminal utterances. In all, twenty-five men, almost all newspaper editors, were charged with sedition; twelve were convicted. (See "Documenting the American Promise," page 204.)

Congress also passed two Alien Acts. The first extended the waiting period for an alien to achieve citizenship from five to fourteen years and required all aliens to register with the federal government. The second empowered the president in time of war to deport or imprison without trial any foreigner

CARTOON OF MATTHEW LYON FIGHT IN CONGRESS
The political tensions of 1798 were not merely intellectual. A February session in Congress degenerated from name-calling to a brawl. Roger Griswold, a Connecticut Federalist, called Matthew Lyon, a Vermont Republican, a coward. Lyon responded with some well-aimed spit, the first departure from the gentleman's code of honor. Griswold responded by raising his cane to Lyon, whereupon Lyon grabbed nearby fire tongs to beat back his assailant. Madison wrote to Jefferson that the two should have dueled: "No man ought to reproach another with cowardice, who is not ready to give proof of his own courage" by negotiating a duel, the honorable way to avenge insults. What is the picture on the wall of the House chambers?
Library of Congress.

www.bedfordstmartins.com/roarkcompact SEE THE ONLINE STUDY GUIDE for more help in analyzing this image.

The Crisis of 1798: Sedition

*A*s President John Adams inched toward an undeclared war on France, criticism of his foreign policy reached an all-time high. Newspaper editors and politicians favorable to France blasted him with such intemperate language that his supporters feared the country could be pushed to the brink of civil war. Federalists in Congress tried to muffle the opposition by criminalizing seditious words, believing it the only path to preserve the country. Republicans just redoubled their opposition.

DOCUMENT 1. Abigail Adams Complains of Sedition, 1798

Throughout the spring of 1798, a beleaguered Abigail Adams complained repeatedly in confidential letters to her sister Mary Cranch about the need for a sedition law to put a stop to the political criticisms of her husband, the president, by Benjamin Bache, pro-French editor of the Philadelphia Aurora.

(April 26): . . . Yet dairingly do the vile incendaries keep up in Baches paper the most wicked and base, voilent & caluminiating abuse—It was formerly considerd as leveld against the Government, but now it . . . insults the Majesty of the Sovereign People. But nothing will have an Effect untill congress pass a Sedition Bill. . . . (April 28): . . . we are now wonderfully popular except with Bache & Co who in his paper calls the President old, querilous, Bald, blind, cripled, Toothless Adams. (May 10): . . . This Bache is cursing & abusing daily. If that fellow . . . is not surpressd, we shall come to a civil war. (May 26): . . . I wish the Laws of our Country were competant to punish the stirer up of sedition, the writer and Printer of base and unfounded calumny. This would contribute as much to the Peace and harmony of our Country as any measure. . . . (June 19): . . . in any other Country Bache & all his papers would have been seazd and ought to be here, but congress are dilly dallying about passing a Bill enabling the President to seize suspisious persons, and their papers. (June 23): . . . I wish our Legislature would set the example & make a sedition act, to hold in order the base Newspaper calumniators. In this State, you could not get a verdict, if a prosecution was to be commenced.

SOURCE: Stewart Mitchell, ed., *New Letters of Abigail Adams, 1788–1801* (Boston: Houghton Mifflin, 1947), 165, 167, 172, 179, 193, 196.

DOCUMENT 2. The Sedition Act of 1798

On July 14, 1798, the Congress approved a bill making sedition with malicious intent a crime.

SECTION 1. . . . if any persons shall unlawfully combine or conspire together, with intent to oppose any measure or measures of the government of the United States . . . , or to impede the operation of any law of the United States, or to intimidate or prevent any person holding . . . office in or under the government of the United States, from undertaking, performing or executing his trust or duty, and if any person or persons, with intent as aforesaid, shall counsel, advise or attempt to procure any insurrection, riot, unlawful assembly, or combination . . . , he or they shall be deemed guilty of a high misdemeanor, and on conviction . . . shall be punished by a fine not exceeding five thousand dollars, and by imprisonment during a term not less than six months nor exceeding five years. . . .

SEC. 2. . . . if any person shall write, print, utter or publish, or shall cause or procure to be written, printed, uttered or published . . . , any false, scandalous and malicious writing or writings against the government of the United States, or either house of the Congress of the United States, or the President of the United States, with intent to defame the said government . . . or to bring them . . . into contempt or disrepute; or to excite against them . . . the hatred of the good people of the United States . . . , or to aid, encourage or abet any hostile designs of any foreign nation against the United States . . . , then such person, being thereof convicted thereof . . . shall be punished by a fine not exceeding two thousand dollars, and by imprisonment not exceeding two years.

SOURCE: United States Statutes at Large; Containing the Laws and Concurrent Resolutions . . . and Proclamations, Treaties, International Agreements Other Than Treaties and Reorganized Plans (Washington: U.S. Government Printing Office, 1789–1845). Avalon Project, Yale Law School, 1996, **<www.yale.edu/lawweb/avalon/statutes/sedact.htm>**.

DOCUMENT 3. Matthew Lyon Criticizes John Adams, 1798

Matthew Lyon, a member of Congress from Vermont, published this criticism of President Adams in a letter to the editor of Spooner's Vermont Journal *(July 31, 1798). It became the first of three counts against him in a sedition trial. Lyon drew a four-month sentence and a fine of $1,000. From jail he ran for reelection to Congress—and won.*

As to the Executive, when I shall see the efforts of that power bent on the promotion of the comfort, the happiness, and the accommodation of the people, that Executive shall have my zealous and uniform support. But when I see every consideration of the public welfare swallowed up in a continual grasp for power, in an unbounded thirst for ridiculous pomp, foolish adulation, or selfish avarice; when I shall behold men of real merit daily turned out of office for no other cause but independence of sentiment; when I shall see men of firmness, merit, years, abilities, and experience, discarded on their application for office, for fear they possess that independence; and men of meanness preferred for the ease with which they take up and advocate opinions, the consequence of which they know but little of; when I shall see the sacred name of religion employed as a State engine to make mankind hate and persecute one another, I shall not be their humble advocate.

SOURCE: Matthew Lyon, Letter in *Spooner's Vermont Journal,* July 31, 1798. Quoted in Aleine Austin, *Matthew Lyon: New Man of the Democratic Revolution, 1749–1822* (Pennsylvania State University Press, 1981), 108–109.

DOCUMENT 4. James Bayard Defends the Law, 1799

James Bayard, a Federalist representative from Delaware, led the charge in the House to expel Matthew Lyon from his seat in Congress. Bayard argued that Lyon was guilty of subverting the government.

This Government . . . depends for its existence upon the good will of the people. That good will is maintained by their good opinion. But, how is that good opinion to be preserved, if wicked and unprincipled men, men of inordinate and desperate ambition, are allowed to state facts to the people which are not true, which they know at the time to be false, and which are stated with the criminal intention of bringing the Government into disrepute among the people? This was falsely and deceitfully stealing public opinion; it was a felony of the worst and most dangerous nature.

SOURCE: Annals of Congress (1799). Quoted in Richard Buel, *Securing the Revolution: Ideology in American Politics* (Ithaca, N.Y.: Cornell University Press, 1972), 256.

DOCUMENT 5. The Virginia Resolution, December 24, 1798

James Madison drafted the Virginia Resolution and had a trusted ally present it to the Virginia legislature, which was dominated by Republicans. (Jefferson did the same for Kentucky.) The Virginia document denounces the Alien and Sedition Acts and declares that states have the right to "interpose" to stop unconstitutional actions by the federal government.

RESOLVED . . . That this assembly most solemnly declares a warm attachment to the Union of the States, to maintain which it pledges all its powers; and that for this end, it is their duty to watch over and oppose every infraction of those principles which constitute the only basis of that Union, because a faithful observance of them, can alone secure its existence and the public happiness.

That this Assembly doth explicitly and peremptorily declare, that it views the powers of the federal government, as resulting from the compact, to which the states are parties; as limited by the plain sense and intention of the instrument constituting the compact; as no further valid that they are authorized by the grants enumerated in that compact; and that in case of a deliberate, palpable, and dangerous exercise of other powers, not granted by the said compact, the states who are parties thereto, have the right, and are in duty bound, to interpose for arresting the progress of the evil, and for maintaining within their respective limits, the authorities, rights and liberties appertaining to them. . . .

That the General Assembly doth particularly protest against the palpable and alarming infractions of the Constitution, in the two late cases of th["Alien and Sedition Acts" . . . ; the first of exercises a power no where delegated to the federal government . . . ; and the other of which acts, exercises in like manner, a power not delegated by the constitution, but on the contrary, expressly and positively forbidden by one of the amendments thereto; a power, which more than any other, ought to produce universal alarm, because it is levelled against that right of freely examining public characters and measures, and of free communication among the people thereon, which has ever been justly deemed, the only effectual guardian of every other right.

SOURCE: Avalon Project, Yale Law School, 1996, <www.yale.edu/lawweb/avalon/virres.htm>.

QUESTIONS FOR ANALYSIS AND DEBATE

1. Why did Federalists believe a Sedition Act was necessary? What exactly was the threat, according to Abigail Adams? James Bayard? What is the threat implied by the wording of the act?

2. Does Matthew Lyon's criticism of President Adams rise to the level of threat that Federalists feared? How do you explain his guilty verdict? His reelection to Congress?

3. What might Madison have meant by "interpose" as the desired action by states? What could states actually do?

4. How would Adams and Bayard square the Sedition Act with the First Amendment's protection of free speech? Did critics of the law invoke freedom of speech and press?

5. Which side had the stronger argument in 1798–1799? Do you think there should be limits on what can be said publicly about high government officials?

suspected of being a danger to the United States. The clear intent of the alien laws was to harass French immigrants in the United States and discourage others from coming.

Republicans strongly opposed the Alien and Sedition Acts on the grounds that they were in conflict with the Bill of Rights, but they did not have the votes to revoke the acts in Congress, nor could the federal judiciary, dominated by Federalist judges, be counted on to challenge them. Jefferson and Madison turned to the state legislatures, the only other competing political arena, to press their opposition. Each man drafted a set of resolutions condemning the acts and had the legislatures of Virginia and Kentucky present them to the federal government in late fall 1798. The Virginia and Kentucky Resolutions tested the novel argument that state legislatures have the right to judge the constitutionality of federal laws and to nullify laws that infringe on the liberties of the people as defined in the Bill of Rights. The resolutions made little dent in the Alien and Sedition Acts, but the idea of a state's right to nullify federal law did not disappear. It surfaced several times in decades to come, most notably in a major tariff dispute in 1832 and in the sectional arguments that led to the Civil War.

Amidst all the war hysteria and sedition fears in 1798, President Adams regained his balance. He was uncharacteristically restrained in pursuing opponents under the Sedition Act, and he finally refused to declare war on France, as extreme Federalists wished. No doubt he was beginning to realize how much he had been the dupe of Hamilton. He also shrewdly realized that France was not in fact eager for war and that a peaceful settlement might be close at hand. In January 1799, a peace initiative from France arrived, in the form of a letter assuring Adams that diplomatic channels were open again and that new commissioners would be welcomed in France. Adams accepted this overture and appointed a new negotiator; by late 1799, the Quasi War with France had subsided. But in responding to the French initiative, Adams lost the support of a significant part of his own party and sealed his fate as the first one-term president of the United States.

The election of 1800 was openly organized along party lines, with the self-designated national leaders of each group meeting to handpick their candidates for president and vice president. Adams's chief opponent was Thomas Jefferson. When the election was finally over, President Jefferson mounted the inaugural platform to announce, "We are all republicans, we are all federalists," an appealing rhetoric of harmony appropriate to an inaugural address. But his formulation perpetuated a denial of the validity of party politics, a denial that ran deep in the founding generation of political leaders.

Conclusion:
Parties Nonetheless

The Federalists had dominated Congress and the presidency throughout the 1790s and persisted in thinking of themselves as the legitimate, disinterested rulers who could give the country enlightened leadership. President Washington sought unity for the new Union and deplored party strife, which in his view resulted from a misguided but vocal minority. Yet under Federalist presidencies, the issues that divided the country—Hamilton's economic program, the whiskey tax, the Jay Treaty, the Quasi War, and the Alien and Sedition Acts—engendered serious opposition.

The emerging Republicans were not a small minority. Many were onetime Federalists in Congress, like Madison, now in strenuous disagreement with Federalist policies. Others were 1780s Antifederalists, still suspicious of a powerful federal government; the Sedition Act seemed an especially clear example of what the Republicans feared. The Federalists were pro-British, pro-commerce, and ever alarmed about the potential excesses of democracy, while the Republicans celebrated, up to a point, the radical republicanism of France.

When Jefferson offered his conciliatory assurance that Americans were at the same time "all republicans" and "all federalists," he was possibly thinking of widely shared ideas that undergirded the country's political institutions. Certainly his listeners favored republican government, where power derived from the people, and likewise they favored the unique federal system of shared governance structured by the Constitution. But by 1800, these same two words, adapted to be the proper names of parties, had come to signify competing philosophies of government. Federalists and Republicans had strong disagreements that had developed over a decade of decision making and would continue to grow in the coming years. Jefferson's speech was spoken aloud; his listeners could not hear the presence or absence of capital letters. For at least some of his listeners, Jefferson's assertion of harmony across party lines could only have seemed bizarre.

FOR FURTHER READING ABOUT THE TOPICS IN THIS CHAPTER, see the Online Bibliography at

www.bedfordstmartins.com/roarkcompact.

FOR ADDITIONAL FIRST-HAND ACCOUNTS OF THIS PERIOD, see pages 132–147 in Michael Johnson, ed., *Reading the American Past*, Second Edition, Volume I.

TO ASSESS YOUR MASTERY OF THE MATERIAL IN THIS CHAPTER, see the Online Study Guide at

www.bedfordstmartins.com/roarkcompact.

CHRONOLOGY

1789 George Washington inaugurated first president.

French Revolution begins.

First Congress meets in New York City.

1790 Alexander Hamilton's plans for funding the government—debts and assuming states' debts—approved.

Government moves from New York City to Philadelphia.

1791 Bill of Rights ratified by states.

Bank of the United States chartered by Congress.

General Arthur St. Clair's forces thoroughly defeated by Miami and Shawnee Indians in western Ohio.

Congress passes whiskey tax.

Haitian Revolution begins.

1793 Washington's second term begins.

Napoleonic Wars break out between France and England.

Washington issues Neutrality Proclamation over war between France and England.

Eli Whitney invents cotton gin.

1794 Farmers stage Whiskey Rebellion in western Pennsylvania.

Lancaster Turnpike, first private toll road, constructed.

General Anthony Wayne's forces defeat Shawnee and Delaware Indians at Battle of Fallen Timbers in western Ohio.

1795 Treaty of Greenville cedes most Indian land in Ohio to United States.

Senate approves Jay Treaty with England.

1796 John Adams elected president, Thomas Jefferson vice president.

1797 XYZ affair with France.

1798 Quasi War with France.

Alien and Sedition Acts passed by Congress.

Virginia and Kentucky Resolutions drafted by Jefferson and Madison.

1800 Jefferson elected president.

A JEFFERSON FAN

Ladies' fans became increasingly popular fashion accessories in the late eighteenth and early nineteenth centuries. This folding fan of vellum and carved ivory, made in the early 1800s, features a medallion portrait of President Thomas Jefferson. Carried by the ribbon on a woman's wrist, the fan could be flicked open to announce a partisan political statement. Fans and other handheld articles such as parasols and handkerchiefs expanded the repertoire of nonverbal expression for women, who by the custom and training of the time were expected to be less assertive than men in mixed-sex conversation. Many emotions and messages—from modesty, coyness, and flirtatiousness to anger, irritability, and boredom— could be communicated by the expert deployment of this delicate emblem of femininity.

Collection of David J. and Janice L. Frent.

REPUBLICAN ASCENDANCY 10

1800–1824

T HE NAME *TECUMSEH* translates to "the Shooting Star," a fitting name for the Shawnee chief who reached meteoric heights of fame among Indians during Thomas Jefferson's presidency. From Canada to Georgia and west to the Mississippi, Tecumseh was accounted a charismatic leader. White Americans, too, praised (and feared) him as a would-be Moses of the Indians. Graceful, eloquent, magnetic, astute: Tecumseh was all these things and more, a gifted natural leader, equal parts politician and warrior.

The Ohio country, where Tecumseh was born in 1768, had become home to some dozen Indian tribes, including the Shawnee, recently displaced from the South. Soon Ohio was ground zero in the struggle with the Big Knives, as the Shawnees called the Americans, producing perpetual conflict from the Revolution to the 1790s Indian wars. Tecumseh's childhood was marked by repeated violence and the loss of his father and two brothers in battle.

Tecumseh honed his warrior skills by ambushing pioneers flatboating down the Ohio. He fought at the Battle of Fallen Timbers, a major Indian defeat, but avoided the 1795 negotiations of the Treaty of Greenville, in which a half dozen dispirited tribes ceded much of Ohio to the Big Knives. With frustration he watched as seven further treaties between 1802 and 1805 whittled away more Indian land.

Some Indians, resigned and tired, looked for ways to accommodate to new realities, taking up farming, trade, and even intermarriage with the Big Knives. Others spent their treaty payments on deadly alcohol. Tecumseh's younger brother Tenskwatawa led an embittered life of idleness and drink. But Tecumseh rejected assimilation and inebriation, and embarked on a campaign to return his people to their ancient ways. Donning traditional animal-skin garb, he traveled around the Great Lakes area, persuading tribes to join his pan-Indian confederacy. The American territorial governor of Indiana, William Henry Harrison, reported, "For four years he has been in constant motion. You see him today on the Wabash, and in a short time hear of him on the shores of Lake Erie or Michigan, or on the banks of the Mississippi, and wherever he goes he makes an impression favorable to his purpose." In 1811, he toured the South, visiting tribes from Mississippi to Georgia.

Even his once-dissolute brother was born anew. After a near-death experience in 1805, Tenskwatawa miraculously revived and recounted a startling vision, a meeting with the Master of Life. Renaming himself the Prophet, Tenskwatawa urged Indians everywhere to return to tradition. He preached that the white Americans were children of the Evil Spirit, destined to be destroyed. Headquartered at a new village called Prophetstown, located in present-day Indiana along Tippecanoe Creek, Tecumseh and his brother pledged a potent blend of spiritual regeneration and political unity that attracted thousands of followers. Governor Harrison

France. Insults over shipping rights, the capture of vessels, and impressment of sailors escalated tensions. Jefferson tried to avoid war through trade embargoes against both countries, but this policy greatly alienated Federalist New England, whose economy depended on overseas trade. While New Englanders hoped to avoid a war, some western politicians in areas like Kentucky were actually eager for armed conflict with Britain, hoping it would provide an opportunity to seize extensive land not only from Indians confederated under Tecumseh but also from Canadians.

James Madison, Jefferson's successor, was not able to contain the opposing forces and deepening party strife. As had happened in the late 1790s, the country approached a crisis as it struggled to identify the real enemy, England or France. Congress finally declared war on England in 1812.

As expected, Tecumseh allied his confederacy with the British and delivered eight hundred warriors to augment British strength. Unfortunately for the Indians, the British concentrated on protecting Canada, not the Indians' country. Tecumseh died on Canadian soil at the Battle of the Thames in the fall of 1813, defending Canada against an army led by General William Henry Harrison. In the end, the War of 1812 settled little between the Americans and the British, but it was tragically conclusive for the Indians. No Tecumseh would emerge again east of the Mississippi.

TECUMSEH

Several portraits of Tecumseh exist, but they all present a different visage, and none of them enjoys a verified authenticity. This one perhaps comes closest: it is an engraving adapted from an earlier drawing that no longer exists, sketched by a French artist named Pierre Le Dru in a live sitting with the Indian leader. The engraver has given Tecumseh a British army officer's uniform, showing that Tecumseh fought on the British side in the War of 1812. Note the head covering and the medallion around the neck, marking Tecumseh's Indian identity.

Library of Congress.

admired and feared Tecumseh, calling him "one of those uncommon geniuses which spring up occasionally to produce revolutions." President Jefferson had great reason to worry about an organized Indian opposition, and more, its potential for a renewed alliance with the British in Canada.

Jefferson's first term in office was marked by notable successes, like the Louisiana Purchase and the Lewis and Clark expedition, but his second term was consumed by the threat of war with Britain and

Jefferson's Presidency

Thomas Jefferson called his election the "revolution of 1800." Certainly the turmoil in John Adams's last years in office suggested revolutionary potential, and the election itself, the first one decided in the House of Representatives, was highly suspenseful. Quite a different "revolution of 1800" nearly materialized, when a Virginia slave named Gabriel plotted rebellion, figuring it might succeed when white men were so badly divided. Gabriel was wrong, but his plot added greatly to the turbulence of the times.

Jefferson also radically transformed the presidency, away from the Federalists' vision of a powerful, even regal, executive branch to republican simplicity and limited government. Yet he found that circumstances sometimes required him to draw on the expansive powers of the presidency.

The Election of 1800

John Adams headed the Federalist ticket for reelection in 1800, even though he had angered many Federalists by his diplomatic overtures with France. New England Federalists supported him, but others from the middle and southern states hoped to ease him out in favor of his running mate, Charles Cotesworth Pinckney of South Carolina, through a careful manipulation of the electoral college votes. Alexander Hamilton went public with a contemptuous and abusive condemnation of Adams, so the surprise in the election tally was not that Adams lost but that the two Republican candidates tied each other, an outcome possible because of the single balloting to choose both president and vice president. Thomas Jefferson and his running mate, Senator Aaron Burr of New York, both got seventy-three votes. Burr, driven by ambition and vanity, declined to concede the presidency to Jefferson. So the election moved to the Federalist-dominated House of Representatives for decision.

In February 1801, the House met to choose. Each state delegation commanded one vote, and the winner needed nine votes. Some Federalists preferred Burr, believing his character flaws made him more susceptible to Federalist pressure. "His very selfishness prevents his entertaining any mischievous predilections for foreign nations," wrote one senator privately. But Hamilton, although no friend to Jefferson, recognized that the high-strung and arrogant Burr would be more dangerous in the presidency than Jefferson, with his hated but steady habits of republicanism. Jefferson was a fanatic and a "contemptible hypocrite" to Hamilton, but at least he was not corrupt. Jefferson had the votes of eight states on the first ballot; it took thirty-six more ballots and six days to get a ninth vote (and also a tenth) in his column. In the end, anti-Burr Federalist representatives in three states abstained from voting to allow Jefferson the victory without actually having to cast a ballot for him.

The election of 1800 demonstrated a remarkable feature of the new constitutional government. No matter how hard-fought the campaign, this election showed that leadership of the nation could shift from one group to a distinctly different one, in a peaceful transfer of power effected by ballots, not bullets.

Gabriel's Rebellion

As the country struggled over its white leadership, a twenty-four-year-old blacksmith named Gabriel plotted his own revolution of 1800 in Virginia. Gabriel, the slave of Thomas Prosser, recruited hundreds of co-conspirators from five counties. Inspired by the Haitian revolution, Gabriel and his followers planned to march on the state capitol at Richmond, set fires, capture an arsenal, and take the governor, James Monroe, hostage. Gabriel would spare Methodists and Quakers, known to hold antislavery views, and he also expected Indians and "the poor white people" of Richmond to join him. Taking seriously Federalist rhetoric about Republican Francophiles, Gabriel assumed that a pro-French (and thus liberty-loving) Republican Governor Monroe might prove sympathetic to their cause.

Gabriel's revolt never materialized. A massive thunderstorm scuttled it on the appointed day in August, and a few nervous slaves spilled the secret. Within days, scores of implicated conspirators were jailed and brought to trial. One jailed rebel compared himself to the most venerated icon of the early Republic: "I have nothing more to offer than what General Washington would have had to offer, had he been taken by the British and put to trial by them."

Such talk invoking the specter of a black George Washington worried James Monroe and Thomas Jefferson. Over September and October, twenty-seven black men were hanged for contemplating rebellion. Finally, Jefferson advised Monroe that the hangings had gone far enough and that deportation was a better alternative. "The world at large will forever condemn us if we indulge a principle of revenge," Jefferson wrote Monroe.

Gabriel's near-rebellion failed, but it scared Virginia politicians into a serious—but secret—effort to identify a site to which future troublesome slaves could be deported. In 1801, the Virginia legislature pressed the federal government for help, since deportation required cooperation with a foreign power. Jefferson was sympathetic to this effort, but he let the idea drop. Deporting insubordinate slaves to Sierra Leone in Africa or to some Spanish colony west of the Mississippi would perhaps reduce tensions in Virginia, but it might also encourage defiance because the eventual payoff was freedom.

The Jefferson Vision of Republican Simplicity

Jefferson sidestepped the problem of slavery and turned his attention to establishing a mode of governing that was a clear contrast to that of the Federalists. On inauguration day, held for the first time in the village of Washington, D.C., he dressed in everyday wear, to strike the tone of republican simplicity, and walked to the Senate chamber in the Capitol for the modest swearing-in ceremony. Once in office, he continued to emphasize unfussy frugality. He scaled back on Federalist building plans for Washington and cut the government budget. He wore plain clothes, appearing "neglected but not slovenly," according to one onlooker. He cultivated a casual style, wearing slippers to greet important guests, avoiding the formality of state dinner parties and liveried servants. Jefferson's studied carelessness was very deliberate.

Jefferson was no Antifederalist. He had supported the Constitution in 1788, although he had qualms about the unrestricted reelection allowed to the president. But events of the 1790s caused him to worry about the stretching of powers in the executive branch. Jefferson had watched with distrust as Hamilton led the Federalists to fund the public debt, establish a national bank, and secure commercial ties with England. The Hamiltonian program seemed to Jefferson to be promoting the interests of money-hungry speculators at the expense of the rest of the country. Jefferson was not at all anticommerce. But financial schemes that seemed merely to allow rich men to become richer, without enhancing the vast and natural productivity of America, were corrupt and worthless, he believed, and their promotion had no authority under the Constitution. In Jefferson's vision, the source of true liberty in America was the independent farmer, someone who owned and worked his land both for himself and for the market.

Jefferson set out to dismantle Federalist innovations. He reduced the size of the army by a third, leaving only three thousand soldiers, and cut back the navy from twenty-five to seven ships. Peacetime defense, he felt, should rest with "a well-disciplined militia," not a standing army. With the consent of Congress, he abolished all federal internal taxes

JEFFERSON'S RED WAISTCOAT
During his presidency, Jefferson often wore this red silk waistcoat as informal daywear. The garment had a velvet collar, woolen sleeves, and a thick lining made from recycled cotton and wool stockings. The thrifty Jefferson preferred to conserve firewood by wearing layers of warm clothes. A senator visiting in 1802 reported in dismay that the president was "dressed, or rather undressed, with an old brown coat, red waistcoat, old corduroy small clothes, much soiled, woolen hose, and slippers without heels." Another guest in 1804 found him in the red waistcoat, green velveteen breeches with pearl buttons, and "slippers down at the heels" which made him look like an ordinary farmer. Such colorful clothing in silk and velveteen carries dressy or feminine connotations in the twenty-first century, but not in 1800. Jefferson did dress up in silk stockings and clean linen for fancy dinner parties; and when he lived in Paris in the 1780s, he wore an elaborately embroidered silk waistcoat under a greatcoat trimmed with gold lace. But in the 1800s, he used his simple, colorful clothes to make a point about republican manners.
Courtesy Monticello, photo by Colonial Williamsburg.

based on population or on whiskey. (Just once, in 1798, the federal government had exacted a direct tax based on population, in a task as burdensome as taking a census.) Government revenue would now derive solely from customs duties and from the sale of western lands. This maneuver was of particular benefit to the South, where the three-fifths clause of the Constitution counted slaves for both representation and taxation. Now the South enjoyed its extra weight in the House of Representatives without the threat of extra taxes. By the end of his first term, Jefferson had deeply reduced Hamilton's cherished national debt.

A properly limited federal government, according to Jefferson, was responsible merely for running a postal system, maintaining the federal courts, staffing lighthouses, collecting customs duties, and conducting a census once every ten years. Government jobs were kept to a minimum. The president had just one private secretary, a young man named Meriwether Lewis, to help with his correspondence, and Jefferson paid him out of his own pocket. The Department of State employed only 8 people: Secretary James Madison, 6 clerks, and a messenger. The Treasury Department was by far the largest unit, with 73 revenue commissioners, auditors, and clerks and 2 watchmen. The entire payroll of the executive branch amounted to a mere 130 people in 1801.

The Judiciary and the Midnight Judges

There was one set of government workers not under Jefferson's control to appoint. His predecessor, John Adams, seized the short time between his election defeat and Jefferson's inauguration to appoint 217 Federalist men to various judicial, diplomatic, and military posts.

Most of this windfall of appointments came to Adams as a result of the Judiciary Act of 1801, passed in the final month of his presidency. The new law revised the original Judiciary Act of 1789, which had established a six-man Supreme Court and six circuit courts, each presided over by a Supreme Court justice. The new act authorized sixteen circuit courts, each headed by a new judge. A fast-acting Adams could appoint sixteen judges with lifetime tenure, plus dozens more state attorneys, marshals, and clerks for each court. The 1801 act also reduced the Supreme Court from six to five justices. Adams had recently appointed solidly Federalist Virginian

John Marshall to a vacant sixth seat, but once the Judiciary Act became law, a future president would not be able to fill the next empty seat.

Adams and Marshall worked feverishly in the last weeks of February to secure agreements from the new appointees. In view of the slowness of mail, achieving 217 acceptances was astonishing. The two men were still at work until 9 P.M. on the last night Adams was president, signing and delivering commissions to the new officeholders.

The appointment of "midnight judges" infuriated the Republicans. Jefferson, upon taking office, immediately canceled the appointments of the nontenured men. A few commissions had not yet been delivered and Jefferson refused to send them out. One of them was addressed to William Marbury, who soon decided to sue the new secretary of state, James Madison, for failure to make good on the appointment. This action gave rise to a landmark Supreme Court case, *Marbury v. Madison* decided in 1803. The Court, presided over by John Marshall, ruled that although Marbury's commission was valid and the new president should have delivered it, the Court could not compel him to do so. What made the case significant was little noted at the time: The Court found that the grounds of Marbury's suit, resting in the Judiciary Act of 1789, were in conflict with the Constitution. For the first time, the Court acted to disallow a law (part of the 1789 act) on the grounds that it was unconstitutional. John Marshall quietly established the concept of judicial review; the Supreme Court in effect assumed the legal authority to nullify acts judged in conflict with the Constitution.

The Promise of the West: The Louisiana Purchase and the Lewis and Clark Expedition

The reach of the *Marbury* decision went largely unnoticed in 1803 because the president and Congress were preoccupied with other major issues, among them the acquisition of the Louisiana Territory. Until the French and Indian War, France had claimed and partly settled this land west of the Mississippi River, only to lose it to Spain in the 1763 Treaty of Paris. Spain never sent adequate forces to control or settle the land, however; Spanish power remained precarious everywhere outside New Orleans. Meanwhile, American farming families were settling Kentucky and Tennessee, along rivers

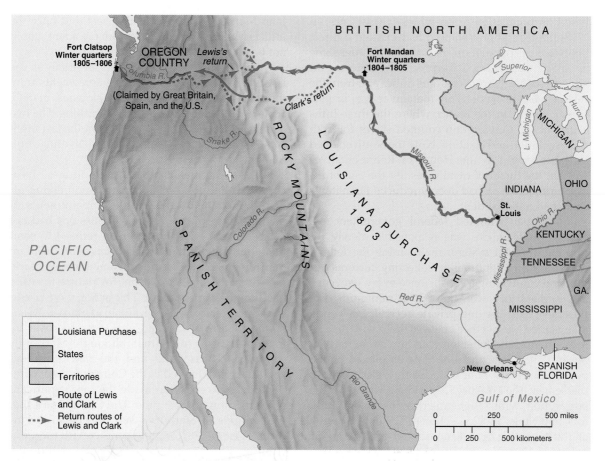

MAP 10.1

The Louisiana Purchase and the Lewis and Clark Expedition

Robert Livingston's bargain buy of 1803 far exceeded his initial assignment, to acquire just the city of New Orleans. Federalists of New England, worried that their own geographically based power in the federal government would someday be eclipsed by the West, voted against the purchase. The Indians who inhabited the vast region, unaware that their land had been sold, got their first look at Anglo-American and African American men when the Lewis and Clark expedition came exploring in 1804–1806.

emptying into the upper Mississippi, and for a time the Spanish allowed them to ship their agricultural produce downriver and even encouraged American settlements across the river, in an effort to augment the population. By 1801, Americans made up a sizable minority of the population around the lower Mississippi.

In 1802, rumors reached Jefferson that Spain had struck a secret bargain with France to hand over a large part of Spain's trans-Mississippi territory to Napoleon in exchange for a duchy in Italy. Spain had proved a weak western neighbor, but France was another story. Jefferson was sufficiently

alarmed that he instructed Robert R. Livingston, America's minister in France, to try to buy New Orleans. At first the French denied they owned the city, but when Livingston hinted that the United States might simply seize it if buying was not an option, the French negotiator suddenly asked him to name his price for the entire Louisiana Territory, from the Gulf of Mexico north to Canada. Livingston stalled, and the Frenchman made suggestions: $125 million? $60 million? Livingston shrewdly stalled some more, and within days the French sold the entire territory for the bargain price of $15 million (Map 10.1).

Jefferson and most of Congress were delighted with the outcome of the diplomatic mission. Still, Jefferson had some qualms about the Louisiana Purchase. The price was right, and the enormous territory fulfilled Jefferson's dream of abundant farmland for future generations. But by what authority in the Constitution could he justify the purchase? His frequent criticism of the Hamiltonian stretching of the Constitution came back to haunt him. His legal reasoning told him he needed a constitutional amendment to authorize the addition of territory; more expedient minds told him the treaty-making powers of the president were sufficient. Expediency won out. In late 1803, the American army took formal control of the Louisiana Territory, and the United States was now 828,000 square miles larger.

Even before the Louisiana Purchase, Jefferson had eyed the trans-Mississippi west with intense curiosity. In early 1803, he had arranged congressional funding for a secret scientific and military mission into Spanish and Indian territory. Jefferson appointed twenty-eight-year-old Meriwether Lewis, his personal secretary, to head the expedition, instructing him to investigate Indian cultures, to collect plant and animal specimens, and to chart the geography of the West. Congress had more traditional goals in mind: The expedition was to scout locations for military posts, open commercial agreements for the fur trade, and locate any possible waterway between the East and West Coasts.

For his co-leader, Lewis chose Kentuckian William Clark, a fellow veteran of the 1790s Indian wars. Together they handpicked a crew of forty-five, including expert rivermen, gunsmiths, hunters, interpreters, a cook, and a slave named York who belonged to Clark. The explorers left St. Louis in the spring of 1804, working their way northwest up the Missouri River. They camped for the winter at a Mandan village in what is now central North Dakota.

The following spring, the explorers headed west, aided by a French trapper accompanied by his wife, a sixteen-year-old Indian woman named Sacajawea, and their baby. Sacajawea's presence was to prove unexpectedly helpful. Indian tribes encountered en route withdrew their suspicion that the Americans were hostile because, as Lewis wrote in his journal, "no woman ever accompanies a war party of Indians in this quarter."

The Lewis and Clark expedition reached the Pacific Ocean at the mouth of the Columbia River in November 1805. When they returned home the following year, they were greeted as national heroes.

SACAJAWEA

Sacajawea is pictured here with her baby, as imagined by mid-nineteenth-century artist Edgar S. Paxson, who produced a series of paintings of grand moments on the Lewis and Clark expedition. The young Shoshone mother was also called Janey by the two explorers, who admired her courage and fortitude. Her baby, Jean Baptiste Charbonneau, was nicknamed Pompey. William Clark brought the boy to St. Louis when he was six years old to educate him. In the 1820s, the youth was taken to Germany by the prince of Württemberg; he returned six years later, fluent in German, French, Spanish, and English. Half Shoshone and half French, Charbonneau became a guide and interpreter for numerous trading expeditions throughout the West until his death in the 1860s.

Sacajawea oil painting by Edgar S. Paxson. The University of Montana Museum of Fine Arts Collection.

They had established favorable relations with dozens of Indian tribes; they had collected invaluable information on the peoples, soils, plants, animals, and geography of the West; and they had inspired a nation of restless explorers and solitary imitators.

Republicans in a Dangerous World

Foreign policy during Jefferson's two presidential terms was not as untroubled as his low-budget approach to the military would imply. From 1801 to 1805, the United States was drawn into belligerent exchanges off the north coast of Africa that featured hijacked ships and captured crews. His second term was dominated by the ongoing war between France and England, which continually threatened to involve the United States. As peaceful alternatives to war with a European superpower, the president experimented with economic sanctions and trade embargoes. Jefferson and his successors faced war threats not only across the Atlantic but also in the new northwest states, where Tecumseh's powerful Indian confederacy challenged the westward press of American settlement.

The Barbary Wars

For well over a century, four Arabic settlements on the Barbary coast—Morocco, Algiers, Tunis, and Tripoli—controlled shipping traffic through the Mediterranean by means of privateering. Swift vessels called *corsairs* overtook merchant ships, plundered the cargo, and captured the crew for ransom. Most European states spared their ships by paying tribute—an annual sum of money—to secure safe passage. When American ships flew under the British flag, up to 1776, they were protected. But once independent, the United States also began to pay tribute, by the mid-1790s, on the order of $50,000 to the leader of each state.

In 1801, the *pasha* (military head) of Tripoli demanded a large increase in his tribute. Jefferson had long thought such payments were extortion, and his response was to send four warships to Tripoli. A rallying slogan backed Jefferson: "Millions for defense, not one cent for tribute." Quickly, the pasha declared war on the United States.

From 1801 to 1803, American ships blockaded Tripoli and Tunis with only partial success and of-

fered escort protection to passing American merchant ships. Only a few skirmishes ensued. Then, in late 1803, the first major action by the United States floundered: the *USS Philadelphia*, a large frigate, ran aground near the Tripoli harbor. Its 300-man crew was captured, along with the ship, which greatly augmented Tripoli's naval strength.

Several months later, the Americans retaliated. Seventy men, led by twenty-five-year-old Lt. Stephen Decatur, sailed into the harbor after dark on a captured corsair with an Arabic-speaking pilot to fool harbor sentries. The corsair drew up to the *Philadelphia*, boarded it, set it on fire, and escaped. Decatur was an instant hero in America.

In summer of 1804, the U.S. forces attacked Tripoli, destroying enemy vessels, firing on the city, and also offering ransom for the captured *Philadelphia* sailors. The pasha resisted, holding out for more money, until he learned that fresh U.S. forces, aided by Egyptian and Turkish mercenaries, were headed toward Tripoli. The pasha then entered treaty negotiations, accepting $60,000 for the prisoners and agreeing to forgo tribute. One significant clause of the treaty stipulated that "no pretext arising from Religious Opinions" should interrupt good relations since the United States has "no character of enmity against the Laws, Religion or Tranquility of Musselmen" (that is, Muslims).

Although the tribute system with other Barbary states would not end until 1812, when frigates returned to the Mediterranean for further skirmishes, none of this affected the election of 1804, which proved an easy triumph for Jefferson. The Federalist candidate, Charles Cotesworth Pinckney of South Carolina, secured only 14 votes in the electoral college, in contrast to 162 for the president. Just months before the election, the Federalists had lost their shrewdest statesman: Alexander Hamilton, called by some "the brains of the Federalist Party," was tragically killed in a duel with Aaron Burr. (See "Historical Question," page 220.) Republicans would hold the presidency for another twenty years.

More Maritime Troubles: Impressment and Embargoes

When France and England resumed war in 1803, they each warned America not to aid the other. Britain acted on these threats in 1806, stopping American ships, inspecting cargoes for military aid to France, and seizing suspected deserters from the British navy, along with not a few Americans. Ultimately, 2,500 sailors were swept up—impressed—by the British. Jefferson and the American public were outraged.

One incident made the usually cautious Jefferson nearly belligerent. In June 1807, an American ship, the *Chesapeake*, harboring some British deserters, was ordered to stop by a British frigate, the *Leopard*. The *Chesapeake* refused, and the *Leopard* opened fire, killing three Americans—right at the mouth of Chesapeake Bay, well within U.S. territory. Before this incident, Jefferson had convinced Congress to pass non-importation laws banning a select list of British-made goods. But now Congress passed a total trade embargo, in December 1807. Although surely a drastic measure, the embargo was meant to forestall war. The goal was to make England suffer; and all foreign ports were banned, to discourage illegal trading through secondary ports. Jefferson was convinced that England needed America's agricultural products far more than America needed British goods.

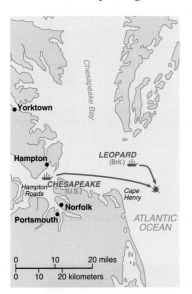

The *Chesapeake* Incident, June 22, 1807

The Embargo Act of 1807 was a total disaster. From 1790 to 1807, U.S. exports had increased fivefold; now commerce was at a standstill. In New England, the heart of the shipping industry, unemployment rose. Grain plummeted in value, river traffic halted, tobacco rotted in the South, and cotton went unpicked. Protest petitions flooded Washington. The federal government suffered too, for import duties were a significant source of revenue. Jefferson paid political costs as well. The Federalist Party, in danger of fading away after its weak showing in 1804, began to revive. Worse yet, England acquired grain from South America and seemed not to suffer particularly from American defiance.

In mid-1808, Jefferson indicated that he would not run for a third term. James Madison, Jefferson's

secretary of state, was the clear heir apparent. Disgruntled Republicans from hurting tobacco regions preferred James Monroe, a Virginia planter with experience as a diplomat to England, but Madison was the favorite among Republican caucuses. At this point, party politics, still held to be a bad thing, operated through informal caucuses that orchestrated state and local elections. The Federalist caucuses chose Charles Cotesworth Pinckney again to run against Madison. Pinckney did much better than in 1804; he received forty-seven electoral votes, nearly half Madison's total. Support for the Federalists remained centered in the New England states, but Republicans still held the balance of power nationwide.

The attacks on American ships continued, by the British and now the French. In 1809, Congress had softened the embargo by passing the Non-Intercourse Act, which prohibited trade only with England and France, opening up other trade routes to diminish the anguish of shippers, farmers, and planters. In 1810, the Non-Intercourse Act expired, and Congress replaced it with a law that permitted direct trade with either France or England, whichever first promised to stop harassing American ships. Napoleon seized the initiative and declared that France would comply. Madison too hastily accepted this offer, reopened trade with France, and notified England that he intended to reinstate the embargo in the spring of 1811 unless England rescinded its search-and-seizure policy.

Unfortunately for Madison, the duplicitous French leaders continued to seize American ships. Furthermore, the British made no move to stop impressments or to repeal trade restrictions, and Madison was forced to reactivate the embargo, much to the great displeasure of the New England shipping industry. In 1811, the country was seriously divided and in a deep quandary. To some, the United States was on the verge of war; but with France or England? To others, any war meant disaster for commerce.

A new Congress, elected in the fall of 1810, arrived in Washington in March 1811 as Madison's embargo took effect. Some of the new and much younger members were eager to avenge the insults from abroad. In particular, Henry Clay, thirty-four, from Kentucky, and John C. Calhoun, twenty-nine, from South Carolina, became the center of a group informally known as the War Hawks. Though called Republicans, these younger men had much more

How Could a Vice President Get Away with Murder?

O N JULY 11, 1804, the vice president of the United States, Aaron Burr, shot Alexander Hamilton, the architect of the Federalist Party, in a duel on a narrow ledge below the cliffs of Wee-hawken, New Jersey, across the Hudson River from New York City. The pistol blast tore through a rib, demolished Hamilton's liver, and splintered his spine. The forty-seven-year-old Hamilton died the next day, in agonizing pain.

How could it happen that a sitting vice president and a prominent political leader could put themselves at such risk? Why did men who made their living by the legal system go outside the law and turn to the centuries-old ritual of the duel? Here were two eminent attorneys, skilled in the legalistic negotiations meant to substitute for violent resolution of disputes, firing .54-caliber hair-trigger weapons at ten paces. Did anyone try to stop them? How did the public react? Was Hamilton's death a criminal act? How could Burr continue to fulfill his federal office, presiding over the U.S. Senate?

Burr challenged Hamilton in late June after learning about a newspaper report that Hamilton "looked upon Mr. Burr to be a dangerous man, and one who ought not be trusted with the reins of government." Burr knew that Hamilton had long held a very low opinion of him and had never hesitated to say so in private, but now his private disparagement had made its way into print. Compounding the insult were political consequences: Burr was sure that Hamilton's remark cost him election to the governorship of New York.

Quite possibly he was right. Knowing that Jefferson planned to dump him from the federal ticket in the 1804 election, Burr had chosen to run for New York's highest office. His opponent was an obscure Republican judge; Burr's success depended on the support of the old Federalist leadership in the state. Up to the eve of the election, he appeared to have it—until Hamilton's remark was circulated.

So on June 18, Burr challenged Hamilton to a duel if he did not disavow his comment. Over the next three weeks, the men exchanged several letters clarifying the nature of the insult that aggrieved Burr. Hamilton the lawyer evasively quibbled over words, causing Burr finally to rail against his focus on syntax and grammar. At heart, Hamilton could not deny the insult, nor could he spurn the challenge without injury to his reputation for integrity and bravery. Both Burr and Hamilton were locked in a highly ritualized procedure meant to uphold a gentleman's code of honor.

Each man had a trusted "second," in accord with the code of dueling, who helped frame and deliver the letters and finally assisted at the duel site. Only a handful of close friends knew of the challenge, and no one tried to stop it. Hamilton did not tell his wife. He wrote her a tender farewell letter the night before, to be opened in the event of his death. He knew full well the pain dueling brought to loved ones, for his nineteen-year-old son Philip had been killed in a duel three years earlier, at the same ledge at Weehawken, as a result of hotheaded words exchanged at a New York theater. Even when Hamilton's wife was called to her husband's deathbed, she was first told he had terrible spasms from an illness. Women were completely shut out of the masculine world of dueling.

AARON BURR BY JOHN VANDERLYN
Aaron Burr was fifty-three years old at the time of this portrait, painted in 1809 by the New York artist John Vanderlyn.
Collection of The New-York Historical Society.

News of Hamilton's death spread quickly in New York and then throughout the nation. On the day of the funeral, church bells tolled continuously and New York merchants shut down all business. Thousands joined the procession, and the city council declared a six-week mourning period. Burr fled to Philadelphia, fearing retribution by the crowd.

Northern newspapers expressed indignation over the illegal duel and the tragic death of so prominent a man. (Response in the South was more subdued. Dueling was fully accepted there as an extralegal remedy for insult, and Burr's grievance fit perfectly the sense of violated honor that legitimated duels. In addition, southerners had never been particularly fond of the Federalist Hamilton.) Many northern states had criminalized dueling recently, treating a challenge as a misdemeanor and a dueling death as a homicide. Even after death, the loser of an illegal duel could endure one final penalty—being buried without a coffin, having a stake driven through the body, being strung up in public until the body rotted, or, more horrible still for the time, being donated to medical students for dissection. Such prescribed mutilation of the dead showed that northern lawmakers themselves participated in the code of honor by using threats of postmortem humiliation to discourage dueling. Hamilton's body was spared such a fate. But two ministers in succession refused to administer Holy Communion to him in his dying hours because he was a duelist; finally, one relented.

The public demanded to know the reasons for the duel, so the seconds prepared the correspondence between the principals for publication. A coroner's jury in New York soon indicted Burr on misdemeanor charges for issuing a challenge; a grand jury in New Jersey indicted him for murder. By that time, Burr was a fugitive from justice hiding out with sympathetic friends in South Carolina.

But not for long. Amazingly, he returned to Washington, D.C., in November 1804 to resume presiding over sessions of the Senate, a role he continued to assume until his term ended in March 1805. Federalists snubbed him, but eleven Republican senators petitioned New Jersey to drop its indictment on the grounds that "civilized nations" do not treat dueling deaths as "common murders." New Jersey did not pursue the murder charge. Burr freely visited New Jersey and New York for three more decades, paying no penalty for killing Hamilton.

Few would doubt that Burr was a scoundrel, albeit a brilliant one. A few years later, he was in-

PISTOLS FROM THE BURR–HAMILTON DUEL
Alexander Hamilton's brother-in-law John B. Church purchased this pair of dueling pistols in London in 1797. Church used them once in a duel with Aaron Burr, occasioned by Church's calling Burr a scoundrel in public; neither man was hurt. Hamilton's son Philip had borrowed them for his own fatal duel, three years before. When Burr challenged Hamilton, the latter also turned to John Church for the weapons. The guns stayed in the Church family until 1930, when they were given to the Chase Manhattan Bank in New York City, chartered in 1799 as the Manhattan Company. (Burr, Church, and Hamilton all served on the bank's board of directors.) When the pistols were cleaned in 1874, a hidden hair trigger came to light. It could be cocked by moving the trigger forward one-eighth inch. It then required only a half-pound pull, instead of ten pounds, to fire the gun. Hamilton gained no advantage from the hair trigger, if he knew of it.
Courtesy of Chase Manhattan Archives.

dicted for treason against the U.S. government in a presumed plot to break off part of the United States and start his own country in the Southwest. (He dodged that bullet too, in a spectacular trial presided over by John Marshall, chief justice of the Supreme Court.) Hamilton certainly thought Burr a scoundrel, and when that opinion reached print, Burr had cause to defend his honor under the etiquette of dueling. The accuracy of Hamilton's charge was of absolutely no account. Dueling redressed questions of honor, not questions of fact.

Dueling continued to be a feature of southern society for many more decades, but in the North the custom became extremely rare by the 1820s, helped along by the disrepute of Hamilton's death and by the rise of a legalistic society that now preferred evidence, interrogation, and monetary judgments to avenge injury.

expansive ideas of the way the United States should meet the challenge of enemies abroad.

Indian Troubles in the West

In the atmosphere of indecision about European war, tensions mounted over difficulties with Indians. Northern tribes were already renewing ties with supportive British agents and fur traders in Canada, a potential source of food and weapons. If the United States embarked on war with England, there would be serious repercussions on the frontier.

Shifting demographics raised the stakes for both sides. The 1810 census counted some 230,000 Americans living in Ohio, only seven years after statehood. Another 40,000 Americans inhabited the territories of Indiana, Illinois, and Michigan. The Indian population of the entire region was much smaller, probably about 70,000, a number unknown (because uncounted) to the Americans but gauged by Tecumseh, based on his extensive travels.

Up to 1805, Indiana's territorial governor, William Henry Harrison, had negotiated a series of treaties in a divide-and-conquer strategy extracting Indian lands for paltry payments. But with the rise to power of Tecumseh and his brother Tenskwatawa, the Prophet, Harrison's strategy faltered. A fundamental part of Tecumseh's message was the assertion that all Indian lands were held in common by all the tribes: "No tribe has the right to sell, even to each other, much less to strangers. . . . Sell a country! Why not sell the air, the great sea, as well as the earth? Didn't the Great Spirit make them all for the use of his children?" Taking advantage of Tecumseh's absence on a recruiting trip, Harrison assembled leaders of the Potawatomi, Miami, and Delaware tribes to negotiate the Treaty of Fort Wayne in 1809. After promising (falsely) that this was the last cession of land the United States would seek, Harrison secured three million acres of land, at about two cents per acre.

When he returned, Tecumseh was furious with both Harrison and the tribal leaders. Leaving his brother in charge at Prophetstown on Tippecanoe Creek, the Shawnee chief left on a trip to seek alliances in the South. Harrison then decided to attack Prophetstown with one thousand men. The two-hour battle resulted in the deaths of sixty-two Americans and forty Indians before the Prophet's forces fled the town, which Harrison's men set on fire. The November 1811 Battle of Tippecanoe was heralded as a glorious victory for the Americans. But Tecumseh was now more ready than ever to make war on the Americans.

TENSKWATAWA

Tenskwatawa, the Shawnee Prophet, and his brother Tecumseh led the spiritual and political efforts of a number of Indian tribes to resist land-hungry Americans moving west in the decade before the War of 1812. The Prophet is shown in a portrait by George Catlin with beaded necklaces, metal arm- and wristbands, and earrings. Compare the metal gorget here with the one worn by Joseph Brant (page 155).

National Museum of American Art, Washington, D.C./Art Resource, New York.

Battle of Tippecanoe, 1811

The War of 1812

The Indian conflicts in the Northwest Territory in 1811 soon merged into the wider conflict with England known as the War of 1812. The defeat at Tippecanoe propelled Tecumseh into an alliance with British military commanders stationed at outposts in lower Canada. If there had been doubt before about who would be the enemy, France or England, it was now abundantly clear, especially to westerners living near the frontier, that England should get the honor.

The War Begins

The several dozen young War Hawks new to Congress saluted Harrison's Tippecanoe victory and urged the country to war. Mostly lawyers by profession, they came from the West and South, and they welcomed a war with England both to legitimize attacks on the Indians and to bring an end to impressment. Many were also expansionists, looking to occupy Florida and threaten Canada. And they captured prominent posts in Congress from which to wield influence. Henry Clay was elected Speaker of the House, an extraordinary honor for a young newcomer. John C. Calhoun won a seat on the Foreign Relations Committee. The War Hawks approved major defense expenditures; the army, for example, quadrupled in size.

In June 1812, Congress declared war on Great Britain in a vote that divided on sectional lines: New England and some Middle Atlantic states opposed the war, while the South and West were strongly for it. Ironically, Great Britain had just announced it would stop the search and seizure of American ships. But the war momentum would not be slowed. The Foreign Relations Committee issued an elaborate justification titled *Report on the Causes and Reasons for War*, written mainly by Calhoun and containing extravagant language about Britain's "lust for power," "unbounded tyranny," and "mad ambition." These were fighting words, in a war that was in large measure about insult and honor.

The War Hawks proposed an invasion of Canada, confidently predicting victory in four weeks. Instead, the war lasted two and a half years, and Canada never fell. The northern invasion turned out to be a series of strategic blunders that revealed the grave unpreparedness of the United States for war. The combined British and Indian forces were unexpectedly powerful, and the United States made no attempt at the outset to create a naval presence on the Great Lakes. Detroit quickly fell, as did Fort Dearborn (site of the future Chicago). By the fall of 1812, the outlook was grim.

Worse, the New England states dragged their feet in raising troops, while New England merchants carried on illegal trade with Great Britain. Britain encouraged friendly overtures with New England, hoping to create dissention among the Americans. New Englanders drank India tea in Liverpool cups, while President Madison fumed in Washington about Federalist disloyalty.

The presidential election in 1812 solidified Federalist discontent with the war. Madison was opposed by DeWitt Clinton of New York, nominally Republican but able to attract the Federalist vote. He picked up all of New England's electoral votes, with the exception of Vermont's, and also took New York, New Jersey, and part of Maryland. Madison won in the electoral college, 128 to 89, but his margin of victory was considerably smaller than in 1808.

In late 1812 and early 1813, the tide began to turn in the Americans' favor. First came some reassuring victories at sea. Then Americans attacked York (now Toronto), the capital of Upper Canada, and burned it in April 1813. A few months later, Commodore Oliver Hazard Perry defeated the British fleet at the western end of Lake Erie. Emboldened, General Harrison drove an army into Canada from Detroit and in October 1813 defeated the British and Indians at the Battle of the Thames, where Tecumseh met his death.

Indians also met defeat in the South, where a general named Andrew Jackson led 2,500 Tennessee militiamen in an attack on Creek Indians, who were fighting in solidarity with Tecumseh's confederacy. At the Battle of Horseshoe Bend in March 1814, Jackson's militia killed more than 550 Indians, including women and children.

The British Offensives of 1814

In August 1814, British ships sailed into Chesapeake Bay throwing the capital into a panic. Families evacuated, banks hid their money, and government clerks carted away boxes of important papers. One State Department worker removed the Declaration of Independence to safety. Five thousand British troops entered the city and burned the president's house, the Capitol, a newspaper office, some dockyards, and a well-stocked arsenal. August 24 was a low moment for the American side.

A BOXING MATCH, or Another Bloody Nose for JOHN BULL.

WAR OF 1812: BOXING MATCH
A battle between the American ship Enterprise *and the British ship* Boxer *off the Maine coast sparked this wishful-thinking cartoon. A bare-knuckled James Madison has just punched King George III, blackened his eye, and made his nose bleed. The king begs "Mercy, mercy on me," and acknowledges "your [Madison's] superior skill." Madison asserts "we are an Enterpriseing Nation" capable of "equal force any day." This Madison clearly does not anticipate the humiliating burning of Washington in 1814.*
Courtesy, American Antiquarian Society.

Instead of trying to hold the city, the British headed north for Baltimore and attacked it on September 11, 1814. Here a fierce defense by the Maryland militia and a steady barrage of gunfire from Fort McHenry in the harbor kept them at bay. The firing continued until midnight, motivating Francis Scott Key to compose a poem he called "The Star-Spangled Banner" the next day. The British pulled back, unwilling to try to take the city.

September 1814 brought another powerful British offensive. Marching from Canada into New York State, the British seemed to have every advantage—trained soldiers, superior artillery, cavalry. But a series of mistakes cost them a naval skirmish at Plattsburgh on Lake Champlain. It also cost them their nerve and they retreated to Canada. This nonbattle was in fact a decisive military event, for British leaders in England, hearing of the retreat, concluded that incursions by land into the United States would be costly and difficult.

This point was confirmed when a large British army landed in lower Louisiana and encountered General Andrew Jackson and his militia just outside New Orleans, in early January 1815. Jackson's forces dramatically carried the day. The British suffered between two and three thousand casualties, the Americans less than eighty. Jackson became an instant hero, and the Battle of New Orleans was the most

glorious and decisive victory the Americans had experienced. Ironically, negotiators in Europe had already signed a peace agreement two weeks earlier.

The War Ends

The Treaty of Ghent, signed in December 1814, settled few of the surface issues that had led to war. Neither country could claim victory, and no land traded hands. Instead, the treaty reflected a mutual agreement to give up certain goals. The Americans yielded on impressment and gave up any claim to Canada; and the British agreed to evacuate western forts and abandoned aid to Indians. Nothing was said about shipping rights. The most concrete result was a plan for a commission to determine the exact boundary between the United States and Canada.

Antiwar New England Federalists did not feel triumph over the war's ambiguous conclusion. Instead they felt disgrace because of a meeting convened in Hartford, Connecticut, in December 1814. Politicians at the Hartford Convention discussed possible secession from the Union. They proposed amending the Constitution, to abolish the three-fifths clause as a basis of representation; to specify that congressional powers to pass embargoes, admit states, or declare war should require a two-thirds vote instead of a simple majority; and to limit the president to one term and prohibit successive presidents from the same state. The cumulative effect of these proposals would be to reduce the South's political power and break the lock of the Virginia dynasty on national office. New England wanted to assure that no one sectional party could again lead the country into war against the clear interests of another. Coming just as peace was achieved, however, the Hartford Convention suddenly looked very unpatriotic. The Federalist Party never recovered its grip, and within a few years its hold even in New England was reduced to a shadow.

No one really won the War of 1812. Americans celebrated as though they had, however, with parades and fireworks. The war gave rise to a new spirit of nationalism. The paranoia over British tyranny evident in the 1812 declaration of war was laid to rest, replaced by pride in a more equal relationship with the old mother country.

Perhaps the biggest winners in the War of 1812 were the young men, once called War Hawks, who took up the banner of the Republican Party and carried it in new, expansive directions. These younger politicians favored trade, western expansion, internal improvements, and the energetic development of new economic markets. The biggest losers of the war were the Indians. Tecumseh was dead, the Prophet discredited, the prospects of an Indian confederacy dashed, and the British protectors vanished.

Women's Status in the Early Republic

Unlike the American Revolution, the War of 1812 had little impact on the status of women. Developments in women's status in the early Republic came not as a result of wartime emergency but instead in incremental steps. As state legislatures and the courts grappled with the legal dependency of married white women in a country whose defining characteristic was independence, religious organizations struggled to redefine the role of women in church governance.

Women and the Law

The Anglo-American view of women, implanted in British common law, was that wives had no independent legal or political personhood. The legal doctrine of *feme covert* held that a wife's civic life was completely subsumed by her husband's: A wife was obligated to obey her husband; her property was his; her domestic and sexual services were his; and even their children were legally his. Women had no right to keep their wages, to make contracts, or to sue or be sued.

State legislatures generally passed up the opportunity to rewrite the laws of domestic relations, even though they redrafted other British laws in light of republican principles. Lawyers never paused to defend, much less to challenge, the assumption that unequal power relations lay at the heart of marriage. The early Republic's conception of the "republican wife and mother" in no way altered the basic legal framework inherited from British law.

The one aspect of family law that changed in the early Republic was divorce. Before the Revolution, only New England jurisdictions had recognized a right to divorce, but by 1820, every state except South Carolina did so. Divorce was uncommon and difficult, however, and in many states could be obtained only by petition to the state's legislature, a daunting obstacle for many ordinary people. A mutual wish to terminate a marriage was never sufficient grounds for divorce. A New York judge affirmed that "it would be aiming a deadly blow at public morals to decree a dissolution of the marriage contract merely because the parties requested it. Divorces should never be allowed, except for the protection of the innocent party, and for the punishment of the guilty." States upheld the institution of marriage both to protect persons they thought of as naturally dependent (women and children) and to regulate the use and inheritance of property. Legal enforcement of marriage as an unequal relationship played a major role in maintaining gender inequality in the nineteenth century.

Single adult women could own and convey property, make contracts, initiate suits, and pay taxes. They could not vote (except in New Jersey until 1807), serve on juries, or practice law, so their civil status was limited. Single women's economic status was often limited as well, by custom as much as by law. Unless they had inherited adequate property or could live with married siblings, single adult women in the early Republic were very often poor.

None of the legal institutions that structured white gender relations applied to black slaves. As property themselves, slaves could not freely consent to any contractual obligations, including marriage. The protective features of state-sponsored unions were thus denied to black men and women in slavery, who were controlled by a more powerful authority, the slave owner. But this also meant that slave unions did not establish unequal power relations between partners, backed by the force of law, as did marriages among the free.

Women and Church Governance

In most Protestant denominations around 1800, white women made up the majority of congregants, as they had for some time. Yet the church hierarchy—ordained ministers and elders—was exclusively male, and the governance of most denominations rested in men's hands.

There were some exceptions, however. In Baptist congregations in New England, women served with men on church governance committees, where they decided admission of new members, voted on the hiring of ministers, and even debated doctrinal points. Quakers, too, had a history of recognizing women's spiritual talents. Quaker women who felt a special call were accorded the status of minister, which meant they were capable of leading and speaking in Quaker meetings.

Between 1790 and 1820, a small and highly unusual set of women emerged who actively engaged in open preaching. Most were from the Freewill Baptist groups centered in New England and upstate New York. Others were from small Methodist sects, and yet others rejected any formal religious affiliation. Probably fewer than a hundred such women existed, but several dozen traveled beyond their local communities, creating converts and controversy. They spoke from the heart, without prepared speeches, often exhibiting trances and claiming to exhort (counsel or warn) rather than to preach. But none of these women were ordained ministers, with official credentials to preach or perform baptisms.

Perhaps the most well-known exhorting woman was Jemima Wilkinson, who called herself the "Publick Universal Friend." After a near-death experience from high fever in 1776, Wilkinson proclaimed her body no longer female *or* male, but the incarnation of the "Spirit of Light." She dressed in men's clothes, wore her hair in a masculine style, shunned gender-specific pronouns, and preached openly in Rhode Island and Philadelphia. In the early nineteenth century, Wilkinson withdrew to a settlement called New Jerusalem in western New York with more than 250 followers.

WOMEN AND THE CHURCH: JEMIMA WILKINSON *Jemima Wilkinson, the "Publick Universal Friend," in an early woodcut, wears a clerical collar and body-obscuring robe, in keeping with the claim that the former Jemima was now a person without sex or gender. Her hair is pulled back tight on her head and curled at the neck in a masculine style of the 1790s.* Rhode Island Historical Society.

The decades from 1790 to the 1820s marked a period of unusual confusion, ferment, and creativity in American religion. New denominations blossomed, new styles of religiosity gripped adherents, and an extensive periodical press devoted to religion popularized all manner of theological and institutional innovations. In such a climate, the age-old tradition of gender subordination came into question here and there among the most radically democratic of the churches. But the presumption of male authority over women was deeply entrenched in American culture. Even denominations that had allowed women to participate in church governance began to pull back, and most churches reinstated patterns of hierarchy along gender lines.

Madison's Successors

With the elections of 1816 and 1820, Virginians continued their long hold on the presidency. In 1816, James Monroe beat Federalist Rufus King of New York by an electoral vote of 183 to 34. When Monroe was reelected in 1820 with all but one electoral vote, the national presence of the Federalists was fully eclipsed. The unanimity of the 1820 election did not reflect voter satisfaction with the status quo, however, for barely one-quarter of eligible voters bothered to vote.

Monroe's two terms were dubbed the "Era of Good Feelings" by a contemporary newspaper. Yet during Monroe's presidency, a major constitutional

A VIEW OF ST. LOUIS FROM AN ILLINOIS TOWN, 1835
Just fifteen years after the Missouri Compromise, St. Louis was already a booming city, having gotten its start in the eighteenth century as a French fur trading village. It was incorporated as a town in 1809 and chartered as a city in 1822. In this 1835 view, commercial buildings and steamships line the riverfront; a ferry on the Illinois shore prepares to transport travelers across the Mississippi River. Black laborers (in the foreground) handle loading tasks. The Illinois side is a free state; Missouri, where their ferry lands, is a slave state.
A View of St. Louis from an Illinois Town, 1835: Private collection.

www.bedfordstmartins.com/roarkcompact SEE THE ONLINE STUDY GUIDE for more help in analyzing this image.

crisis emerged over the admission of Missouri to the Union. Foreign policy questions animated sharp disagreements as well. The election of 1824 brought forth an abundance of candidates, all claiming to be Republicans. A one-party political system was put to the test of practical circumstances; it failed and then fractured.

The Missouri Compromise

In February 1819, Missouri applied for statehood. Since 1815, four other states had joined the Union (Indiana, Mississippi, Illinois, and Alabama). But Missouri posed a problem. Much of its area jutted up into the North, while its territorial population was already one-sixth slave. Missouri's unusual combination of geography and demography led a New York representative in Congress, James Tallmadge Jr., to propose two amendments to the statehood bill. The first stipulated that slaves born in Missouri after statehood would be free at age twenty-five, and the second declared that no new slaves could be imported into the state. Southerners in Congress loudly protested the amendments. Although gradual emancipation protected slave owners from immediate financial loss, in the long run it made Missouri a free state, tipping the national balance of power between free and slave states. Just as southern economic power rested on slave labor, southern political power drew extra strength from slaves, counted at three-fifths for purposes of representation. In 1820, the South had seventeen extra seats in the House of Representatives based on slave population.

Both of Tallmadge's amendments passed in the House, but with a close and sharply sectional vote of North against South (with a few northern Republicans taking the side of the South). The debate was ferocious, leading a Georgia representative to observe that the question had started "a fire which all the waters of the ocean could not extinguish. It can be extinguished only in blood." The Senate, with an even number of slave and free states, voted down the amendments, with some border states joining the proslavery line. Missouri statehood was postponed for the next congressional term.

In 1820, a compromise emerged in the Senate. Maine, once a part of Massachusetts, applied for statehood, which balanced Missouri as a slave state. To quiet northern fears about slavery reaching so far into the North, the Senate agreed that the southern boundary of Missouri, latitude 36° 30′, extended west would become the permanent line dividing slave from free (Map 10.2). The House also approved the compromise, thanks to expert deal brokering by Kentucky's Henry Clay, who earned the nickname the "Great Pacificator" for his superb negotiating skills.

President Monroe and Thomas Jefferson at first worried that the Missouri crisis would reinvigorate the Federalist Party as the party of the North. But even ex-Federalists agreed that the division of free versus slave states was too dangerous a fault line to let shape national politics. When new parties did develop in the 1830s, they took pains to bridge geography, each party developing a presence in both North and South. Monroe and Jefferson also worried about the future of slavery. Each understood slavery to be deeply problematic, but, as Jefferson said, "We have the wolf by the ears, and we can neither hold him, nor safely let him go. Justice is in one scale, and self-preservation in the other."

The Monroe Doctrine

New foreign policy challenges arose even as Congress struggled with the slavery issue. In 1816, American troops led by General Andrew Jackson invaded Spanish Florida in search of Seminole Indians harboring escaped slaves. Once there, Jackson declared himself the commander of northern Florida, demonstrating his power in 1818 by executing two British men who he claimed were dangerous enemies. In asserting rule over the territory, and surely in executing the two British subjects on Spanish land, Jackson had gone too far. Privately, President Monroe was distressed and pondered court-martialing Jackson, prevented only by Jackson's immense popularity as a war hero. Instead, John Quincy Adams, the secretary of state, negotiated with Spain the Adams-Onís Treaty, which delivered Florida to the United States in 1819. In exchange, the Americans agreed to abandon any claim to Texas or Cuba.

Spain at that moment was preoccupied with its colonies in South America. One after another— Chile, Colombia, Peru, and finally Mexico— declared itself independent in the early 1820s. To discourage Spain from reconquering its colonies, Monroe formulated a declaration of principles on South America, incorporated into his annual mes-

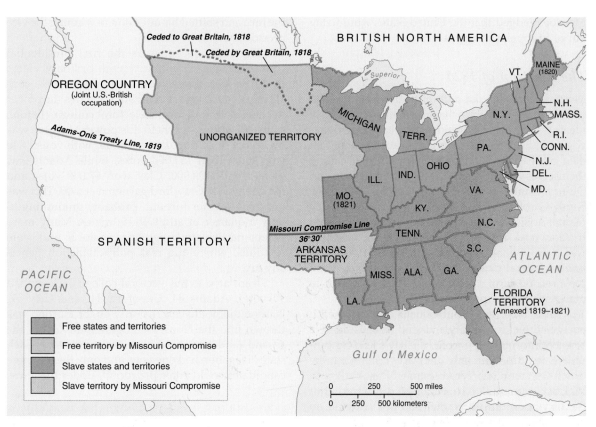

MAP 10.2

The Missouri Compromise, 1820

After a difficult battle in Congress, Missouri entered the Union in 1821 as part of a package of compromises. Maine was admitted as a free state to balance slavery in Missouri; and a line drawn at latitude 36° 30' put most of the rest of the Louisiana Territory off limits to slavery in the future.

READING THE MAP: How many free and how many slave states were there prior to the Missouri Compromise? What did the admission of Missouri as a slave state threaten to do?

CONNECTIONS: Who precipitated the crisis over Missouri, what did he propose, and where did the idea come from? Who proposed the Missouri Compromise, and who benefited from it?

www.bedfordstmartins.com/roarkcompact SEE THE ONLINE STUDY GUIDE for more help in analyzing this map.

sage to Congress in December 1823, known in later years as the Monroe Doctrine. He warned that "the American Continents, by the free and independent condition which they have assumed and maintain, are henceforth not to be considered as subjects for future colonization by any European power." Any attempt to interfere in the Western Hemisphere would be regarded as "the manifestation of an unfriendly disposition towards the United States." In exchange for noninterference by Europeans,

Monroe pledged that the United States would stay out of European struggles.

The Election of 1824

Monroe's nonpartisan administration was the last of its kind, a fitting throwback to eighteenth-century ideals, led by the last president to wear a powdered wig and knee breeches. Monroe's cabinet contained men of sharply different philosophies, all calling themselves Republicans. Secretary of State John Quincy Adams represented the urban Northeast, South Carolinian John C. Calhoun spoke for the planter aristocracy as secretary of war, and William H. Crawford of Georgia, secretary of the treasury, was a proponent of Jeffersonian states' rights and limited federal power. Well before the end of Monroe's second term, these men and others began to maneuver for the presidency.

Since 1800, the congressional caucus of each party had met to identify and lend its considerable but still informal support to its party's leading candidate. In 1824, with only one party remaining, the caucus system splintered. Some New York and Virginia representatives endorsed Crawford, but the fifty-one-year-old planter had just suffered an incapacitating stroke.

Adams felt he had a claim on the office; since 1800, every president had once been secretary of state. Henry Clay, Speaker of the House, also was a declared candidate. A man of vast congressional experience, he had engaged in high-level diplomacy, having accompanied Adams to Ghent to negotiate the 1814 peace treaty with Britain. The Kentuckian put forth a set of policies he called the American System, a package of protective tariffs to promote manufacturing and federal expenditures for extensive internal improvements, many of them roads and canals in the western states. Calhoun, a lawyer as well as planter, was another serious contender, having served in Congress and in several cabinets. Like Clay, he favored internal improvements and protective tariffs, which he figured would gain him support in northern states.

The final candidate was an outsider: General Andrew Jackson of Tennessee. Jackson had much less national political experience than the others, having served one year in the House and two in the Senate. His fame rested mainly on his reputation as a military leader, but that was sufficient to gain him a huge following, much to the surprise of the experienced politicians. Calhoun soon dropped out of

the race and shifted his attention to winning the vice presidency.

The 1824 election was the first presidential contest in which popularity with ordinary voters could be measured. Recent changes in state constitutions gave voters in all but six states the power to choose electors for the electoral college. (Before, state legislatures had held this power.) Jackson was by far the most popular candidate with voters. He won more than 153,000 votes, while Adams was second with 109,000; Clay won 47,000 votes and the debilitated Crawford garnered 46,600. This was not a large voter turnout, probably amounting to only a quarter of adult white males. Many more voters participated regularly in local and state elections, where the real political action generally lay.

Translated to the electoral college, Jackson had 99 votes, Adams 84, Crawford 41, and Clay 37. Jackson did not have a majority, so the election was thrown into the House of Representatives, for the second (and last) time in American history. Each state delegation had one vote, and only the top three candidates could enter the runoff, under the terms

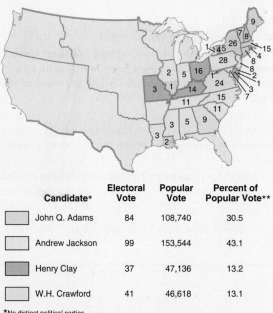

Candidate*	Electoral Vote	Popular Vote	Percent of Popular Vote**
John Q. Adams	84	108,740	30.5
Andrew Jackson	99	153,544	43.1
Henry Clay	37	47,136	13.2
W.H. Crawford	41	46,618	13.1

*No distinct political parties
**Approximate

Note: Because no candidate garnered a majority in the electoral college, the election was decided in the House of Representatives. Although Clay was eliminated from the running, as Speaker of the House he influenced the final decision in favor of Adams.

MAP 10.3
The Election of 1824

of the Twelfth Amendment to the Constitution, passed in 1804. Thus Henry Clay was out of the race and in a position now to throw his support to another candidate.

The election of 1824 came to be characterized as the "corrupt bargain" in the eyes of Jackson's supporters. Clay backed Adams, and Adams won by one vote in the House (Map 10.3). Clay's support made sense on several levels. Despite mutual dislike, he and Adams agreed on issues such as internal improvements, and Clay was uneasy with Jackson's volatile temperament and unstated political views and with Crawford's diminished capacity.

What made Clay's decision look unseemly was that immediately after the election, Adams offered to appoint Clay secretary of state—and Clay accepted. In the weeks before the vote in the House, rumors of such a deal were denied by Adams and Clay supporters, confident that two such archenemies could never cooperate. There probably was no actual bargain; Adams's subsequent cabinet appointments demonstrated his lack of political astuteness. But Andrew Jackson felt that the election had been stolen from him and wrote bitterly that "the Judas of the West has closed the contract and will receive the thirty pieces of silver."

The Adams Administration

John Quincy Adams, like his father, was a one-term president. His career had been built on diplomacy, not electoral politics, and his political horse sense was not well developed. His cabinet choices welcomed his opposition into his inner circle. He asked Crawford to stay on in the Treasury, and he retained an openly pro-Jackson postmaster general, even though that position controlled thousands of nationwide patronage appointments. Most amazingly, he asked Jackson to become secretary of war. With Calhoun as vice president (elected without opposition by the electoral college) and Clay at State, the whole argumentative crew would be thrust into the executive branch. Crawford and Jackson had the good sense to decline appointments.

Adams had lofty ideas for federal action during his presidency, and the plan he put before Congress was so sweeping that it took Henry Clay aback. Adams called for federally built roads, canals, and harbors. He proposed a national university in Washington as well as government-sponsored scientific research. He wanted to build observatories to advance astronomical knowledge

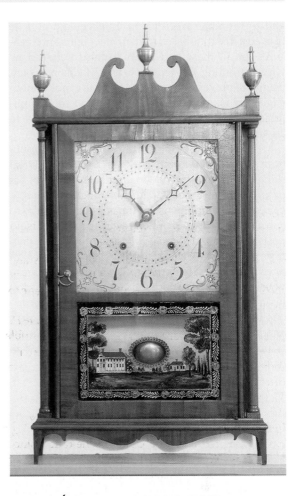

ELI TERRY'S PILLAR AND SCROLL CLOCK
Before the 1790s, sundials and church bells answered most timekeeping needs; clocks were objects of art, not utility. Connecticut clockmaker Eli Terry realized that affordable clocks might change all that. First he switched from brass to wood for the clock's internal movement, and then he designed machinery to mass-produce the parts, achieving the first successful system of "interchangeable parts" and turning out thousands of clocks a year. In 1814, Terry developed this inexpensive compact clock and sold tens of thousands over the next dozen years. Affordable clocks revolutionized timekeeping, enabling workers to arrive before the factory bell and travelers to make stagecoach and canal boat departure times. Employers could demand punctuality, a moral virtue made possible by the pervasiveness of clocks. For good or ill, clocks did not merely measure time; they helped speed up the pace of life.
American Clock & Watch Museum.

and to promote precision in timekeeping, and he backed a decimal-based system of weights and measures. In all these endeavors, Adams believed he was continuing the Jefferson and Madison legacy, using the powers of government to advance knowledge. But his opponents feared he was too Hamiltonian, using federal power inappropriately to advance commercial interests.

Whether he was more truly Federalist or Republican was a moot point, however. Lacking political skills, Adams was unable to implement much of his program. He scorned the idea of courting voters to gain support and the use of the patronage system to enhance his power. He often made appointments (to posts like customs house collectors) to placate enemies rather than reward friends. A story of a toast offered to the president may well have been mythical, but as humorous folklore it made the rounds during his term and came to summarize Adams's precarious hold on leadership. A dignitary raised a glass and pledged, "May he strike confusion to his foes . . .," to which another voice scornfully chimed in, "as he has already done to his friends."

Conclusion: Republican Simplicity Becomes Complex

The nineteenth century opened with the Jeffersonian Republicans in power, trying to undo much of what Federalists created in the 1790s. But the Republican promise of a more simple government, limited in size, scope, and power, quickly gave way to the lure of the West. The sudden acquisition of the Louisiana Purchase promised land and opportunity to settlers but also complicated the country's political future with the issues central to the Missouri Compromise. Republican simplicity also gave way in the face of increasing antagonism both from foreign nations and from Indian nations, which Jefferson and his successor Madison met with a combination of embargoes, treaties, and military action. Battles with Indians blended into the major engagement with England, the War of 1812, a war mo-

tivated less by concrete economic or political issues than by questions of honor. Its conclusion at the Battle of New Orleans allowed Americans the illusion they had fought a second war of independence.

If the War of 1812 seemed a second war of independence for the whites, how much more so it was for the Indians, who lost both times. Tecumseh's vision of an unprecedentedly large confederacy of Indian tribes that would halt western expansion by white Americans was cut short by the war and by his death. Without British support, the Indians probably could not have successfully challenged for long the westward dynamic of American settlement. But British support came at a time when Canada was under attack, and the British put their own defense higher than their promises to help the Indians.

The war elevated to national prominence General Andrew Jackson, whose sudden popularity with voters in the 1824 election surprised traditional politicians and threw the one-party rule of Republicans into a tailspin. John Quincy Adams barely occupied his office in 1825 before the election campaign of 1828 was off and running. Appeals to the people—the mass of white male voters—would be the hallmark of all elections after 1824. It was a game Adams could not easily play.

The War of 1812 started another chain of events that would prove momentous in later decades. Jefferson's long embargo and Madison's wartime trade stoppages gave strong encouragement to American manufacturing, momentarily protected from competition with English factories. When peace resumed in 1815, the years of independent development burst forth into a period of sustained economic growth that continued nearly unabated into the mid-nineteenth century.

FOR FURTHER READING ABOUT THE TOPICS IN THIS CHAPTER, see the Online Bibliography at
www.bedfordstmartins.com/roarkcompact.

FOR ADDITIONAL FIRST-HAND ACCOUNTS OF THIS PERIOD, see pages 148–163 in Michael Johnson, ed., *Reading the American Past*, Second Edition, Volume I.

TO ASSESS YOUR MASTERY OF THE MATERIAL IN THIS CHAPTER, see the Online Study Guide at
www.bedfordstmartins.com/roarkcompact.

CHRONOLOGY

1789	Judiciary Act establishes six Supreme Court justices, who preside over six circuit courts.
1800	Thomas Jefferson and Aaron Burr tie in electoral college.
	Gabriel's slave rebellion fails in Virginia.
1801	Judiciary Act reduces Supreme Court justices to five and allows for sixteen circuit courts and circuit court judges.
	Jefferson elected president by House of Representatives.
1803	*Marbury v. Madison* declares part of Judiciary Act of 1789 unconstitutional.
	Embargoes on American shipping by England and France.
	Louisiana Territory purchased from France for $15 million.
1804	Jefferson reelected president.
	Burr-Hamilton duel ends in Hamilton's death.
1804–1806	Lewis and Clark expedition.
1807	**June.** *Chesapeake* attacked and searched by British in Chesapeake Bay.
	December. Embargo Act forbids any American ship from engaging in trade with any foreign port.
1808	James Madison elected president.
1809	Treaty of Fort Wayne with Indians in Indiana Territory.

	Non-Intercourse Act forbids American trade with England, France, and their colonies.
1811	Battle of Tippecanoe won by William Henry Harrison's troops.
1812	**June.** War declared on Great Britain.
	Madison reelected president.
1813	Death of Tecumseh at the Battle of the Thames.
1814	British attack Washington, D.C., burning several buildings.
	Treaty of Ghent ends War of 1812.
	Hartford Convention proposes constitutional amendments.
1815	Battle of New Orleans won by Andrew Jackson's forces.
1816	James Monroe elected president.
1819	Spain cedes Florida to United States in the Adams-Onis Treaty.
1820	Missouri Compromise admits Missouri as slave state and Maine as free state.
	Monroe reelected president.
1823	Monroe Doctrine asserts independence of Western Hemisphere from European intervention.
1824	"Corrupt bargain" election of John Quincy Adams.

SHIP'S FIGUREHEAD OF ANDREW JACKSON
*Carved in 1834 and affixed to the bow of the
revered navy frigate* Constitution, *this figurehead of Andrew Jackson symbolized national
pride by putting "the image of the most popular man of the West upon the favorite ship
of the East," according to the commodore
who commissioned it. But when Jackson
introduced a new, strict banking policy,
his popularity in the urban East quickly
plummeted. In Boston, where the* Constitution *was docked, protesters complained that
the figurehead of a tyrant corrupted their ship.
On the night of July 3, 1834, the eve of the national
holiday, a twenty-seven-year-old mariner and ardent
Whig stole on board and decapitated the figurehead,
sawing it through just below the ears. Jackson
deflected the insult with humor, declaring "I never did like that image!
Give the man a postmaster's job." The commodore, himself alert to symbolic actions,
wrapped the headless statue in a flag and sent it to New York City where woodworkers fashioned a new head in 1835. It was reattached to the ship in another port: Jackson's banking
policies still rankled in urban financial centers, and naval authorities did not want to risk a
second mutilation of the president's image. In 1990, the original head was recovered from a
private collector in France and restored to view in the museum that now owns the figurehead.*
Museum of the City of New York.

THE EXPANDING REPUBLIC

11

1815–1840

PRESIDENT ANDREW JACKSON WAS THE DOMINANT FIGURE of his age, yet his precarious childhood little foretold the fame, fortune, and influence he would enjoy in the years after 1815. Jackson was born in the Carolina backcountry in 1767. His Scots-Irish father had recently died, leaving a poor, struggling mother to support three small boys. During the Revolution, Andrew followed his brothers into the militia, where both died of disease, as did his mother. Orphaned at fourteen, Jackson drifted around, drinking, gambling, and brawling.

But at seventeen, his prospects improved. He studied under a lawyer for three years and then moved to Nashville, a frontier community full of opportunities for a young man of legal training and aggressive temperament. He became a public prosecutor, married into a leading family, and acquired land and slaves. When Tennessee became a state in 1796, Jackson, then twenty-nine, was elected to Congress for a single term.

Jackson captured national attention in 1815 by leading the victory at the Battle of New Orleans. Songs, broadsides, and an admiring biography set him up as the original self-made man, the parentless child magically responsible for his own destiny. Jackson seemed to have created himself, a gritty, forceful personality extracting opportunities from the dynamic, turbulent frontier.

Jackson was more than a man of action, however. He was also strong-willed, reckless, and quick to anger, impulsively challenging men to duels, sometimes on slight pretexts. In one legendary fight in 1806, Jackson deliberately let his opponent, an expert marksman, shoot first. The bullet hit him in a rib, but Jackson masked all sign of injury under a loose cloak and immobile face. He then took careful aim at the astonished man and killed him. Such steely courage chilled his political opponents.

Jackson's image as a tough frontier hero set him apart from the learned and privileged gentlemen from Virginia and Massachusetts who had monopolized the presidency up to 1828. When he lost the 1824 election to John Quincy Adams, an infuriated Jackson vowed to fight a rematch. He won in 1828 and again in 1832, capturing large majorities. His appeal stretched across the urban working classes of the East, frontier voters of the West, and slaveholders in the South, who all saw something of themselves in Jackson.

The confidence and even recklessness of Jackson's personality mirrored the new confidence of American society in the years after 1815. An entrepreneurial spirit gripped the country, producing a market revolution of unprecedented scale. Old social hierarchies eroded; ordinary men dreamed of moving high on the wheel of fortune, just as Jackson had done. Stunning advances in transportation and economic productivity fueled such dreams and propelled thousands to move west or to cities. Urban growth and technological change fostered the diffusion of a distinctive and vibrant public culture, spread through newspapers and the spoken word. The development of rapid print allowed popular opinions to coalesce and intensify; Jackson's sudden nationwide celebrity was a case in point.

Expanded communication transformed politics dramatically. Sharp disagreements over the best way to promote individual liberty, economic opportunity, and national prosperity in the new market economy defined key differences between Jackson and Adams and the parties they gave rise to in the 1830s. The process of party formation brought new habits of political participation and party loyalty to many thousands more adult white males. Religion became democratized as well: A nationwide evangelical revival brought its adherents the confidence that salvation and perfection were now available to all.

As president from 1828 to 1836, Jackson presided over all these changes, fighting some and supporting others in his vigorous and volatile way. As with his own stubborn personality, there was a dark underside to the confidence and expansiveness of American society. Steamboats blew up, banks and businesses periodically collapsed, alcoholism rates soared, Indians were killed or relocated farther west, and slavery continued to expand. The brash confidence that turned some people into rugged, self-promoting, Jackson-like individuals inspired others to think about the human costs of rapid economic expansion and thus about reforming society in dramatic ways. The common denominator was a faith that people and societies can shape their own destinies.

The Market Revolution

The return of peace in 1815 unleashed powerful forces that revolutionized the organization of the economy. Spectacular changes in transportation facilitated the movement of commodities, information, and people, while textile mills and other factories created many new jobs, especially for young unmarried women. Innovations in banking, legal practices, and tariff policies promoted swift economic growth.

This was not yet an industrial revolution, but a market revolution, fueled by traditional sources—

water, wood, beasts of burden, and human muscle. What was new was the accelerated pace of economic activity and the scale of distribution of goods. Men and women were drawn out of old patterns of rural self-sufficiency into the wider realm of national market relations. At the same time, the nation's money supply enlarged considerably, leading to speculative investments in commerce, manufacturing, transportation, and land. The new nature and scale of production and consumption changed Americans' behavior, attitudes, and expectations.

Improvements in Transportation

Before 1815, transportation in the United States was slow and expensive; it cost as much to ship freight over thirty miles of domestic roads as it did to send the same cargo across the Atlantic Ocean. The fastest stagecoach trip from Boston to New York took an uncomfortable four days. But between 1815 and 1840, networks of roads, canals, steamboats, and finally railroads dramatically raised the speed and lowered the cost of travel (Map 11.1). Andrew Jackson spent weeks walking and riding west to Nashville in the 1790s along old Indian trails, but when he returned east in 1829, the new president traveled by steamboat and turnpike to Washington, D.C., in a matter of days.

Improved transportation moved goods and products into much wider markets. It moved people too, broadening the horizons of passengers on business and pleasure trips and providing means for youth to take up new employment in cities or factory towns. Transportation also facilitated the flow of political (and other) information, through a heavy traffic in newspapers, periodicals, and books.

Enhanced public transport was expensive and produced uneven economic benefits, so administrations from Jefferson to Monroe were reluctant to fund it with federal dollars. President John Quincy Adams adopted the pro-development view of Henry Clay's American System, pledging federal support for roads and canals, but Congress would not go along. Instead, private investors pooled resources and chartered stagecoach, canal, steamboat, and railroad companies, with significant aid from state governments in the form of subsidies and guarantees of monopoly rights. Turnpike and roadway mileage dramatically increased after 1815, reducing the cost of land shipment of goods. Stagecoach lines proliferated in an extensive network of passenger corridors dense in the populated East

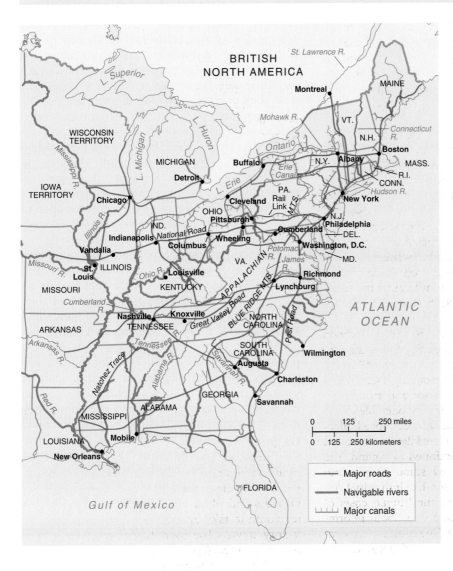

MAP 11.1
Routes of Transportation in 1840
The National Road, connecting Baltimore with the interior of Ohio, was the only federally sponsored roadway. Approved during Jefferson's presidency, it reached Ohio only in the 1830s. Its funding came from the sale of public lands in Ohio, the area that stood to benefit. Other roads and canals were the work of private companies operating under government charters. By 1840, transportation advances had cut travel times significantly. Goods and people could move from New York City to Buffalo, New York, in four days via the Erie Canal, a trip that took two weeks by road in 1800. A trip from New York to New Orleans that took four weeks in 1800 could now be accomplished in less than half that time on steamboats on the western rivers.

and fanning out to the Mississippi River. Travel time on main routes was cut in half; Boston to New York now took two days.

Water travel was similarly transformed. In 1807, Robert Fulton's steam-propelled boat, the *Clermont*, churned up the Hudson River from New York City to Albany, touching off a steamboat craze. In 1820, a dozen boats left New York City daily, and scores more operated on midwestern rivers and the Great Lakes. A voyager on one of the first steamboats to go down the Mississippi reported that the Chickasaw Indians called the vessel a "fire canoe" and considered it "an omen of evil." By the early 1830s, more than seven hundred steamboats were in operation on the Ohio and Mississippi Rivers. A journey upriver from New Orleans to Louisville, Kentucky, took only one week. Such speed came with costs, however, of boiler explosions and terrible fatalities. (See "The Promise of Technology," page 238.)

Canals were another major innovation of the transportation revolution. These shallow highways of water provided passage for barges and boats, pulled by horses or mules along a towpath beside the canal. Travel speed was slow, under five miles per hour, but the economy came from increased loads: The low-friction water allowed one horse to pull a fifty-ton barge.

Pennsylvania in 1815 and New York in 1817 commenced major state-sponsored canal enterprises.

Early Steamboats

STEAMBOATS REVOLUTIONIZED TRAVEL in the early nineteenth century. The basic technology consisted of an engine, powered by the steam from a boiler heated by a wood-burning furnace. The steam first collected in a cylinder and then cooled and condensed to create a vacuum that drove a piston, which in turn propelled a paddlewheel mounted at the side or in the stern of the boat. From the 1780s to 1807, several inventors sought the ideal combination of engine size, boat size, and paddlewheel type. Robert Fulton's *Clermont* of 1807 was not the first American steamboat, but it was the first long-distance, commercially successful endeavor.

Two advantages marked Fulton's effort: He imported a superior British-made engine, a low-pressure model built with many precision parts, and he formed a partnership with New York businessman Robert R. Livingston. Livingston had acquired from the New York state legislature in 1798 the right to a twenty-year monopoly on all steam transportation on the Hudson River, on the condition that he produce a boat capable of traveling four miles per hour upriver. The *Clermont* met that test.

In 1811, Fulton and Livingston launched the first steamboat on the Mississippi River. Their low-pressure engine, operating at about two pounds per square inch of pressure in the cylinder, failed to maneuver against the river's shifting currents and many obstructions. A high-pressure steam engine developed by Delaware entrepreneur Oliver Evans proved far more suitable. Generating pressures from eighty to one hundred pounds per square inch, it required 30 percent more fuel, but wood was plentiful along western waterways. By the 1830s, there were many hundreds of boats on the Mississippi, the Ohio, and the lower Missouri Rivers, run by companies all competing to reduce travel time. An upriver trip from New Orleans to Louisville that took nearly a month in the 1810s took less than a week in the 1830s. The American traveling public fell in love with steamboats for their speed and power.

Steamboats offered luxury as well as speed. Boats often were floating palaces, providing swank accommodations to ladies and gentlemen paying first-class fares. A few boats had private cabins, but most often there were two large rooms, one for each sex, filled with chairs that converted to beds. (The separation of sexes answered an important need in addition to bodily modesty: Women travelers often expressed their disgust over the spit-drenched carpets in the men's cabin.) Dining rooms with elegant appointments served elaborate meals. Many steamboats had gambling rooms as well. Low-fare passengers, typically men, occupied the lower decks of the boats, taking sleeping space out in the open or in crowded berths in public rooms. The largest boats could accommodate four hundred passengers.

The fire and smoke of a steamboat proved awesome and even terrifying to many. An older gent making his first trip in 1836 wrote that "I went on board, and passing the fireroom, where they were just firing up, I stopped, with unfeigned horror, and asked myself if, indeed, I was prepared to die!" But many others were enthralled by the unprecedented power represented by the belching smoke. Impromptu boat racing became a popular sport. A German traveler identified a competitive streak in American passengers: "When two steamboats happen to get alongside each other, the passengers will encourage the captains to run a race. . . . The boilers intended for a pressure of only 100 pounds per square inch, are by the accelerated generation of steam, exposed to a pressure of 150, and even 200 pounds, and this goes sometimes so far, that the trials end with an explosion."

Steamboats in fact were far from safe. Between 1811 and 1851, accidents destroyed nearly a thousand boats, a third of all steam vessels built in that period. More than half the sinkings resulted from underwater debris which penetrated hulls. Fires, too, were fearsome hazards in wooden boats that commonly carried highly combustible cargoes, such as raw cotton in burlap bags. The development of sheet metal, which strengthened hulls and protected wooden surfaces near the smokestacks from sparks, was a major safety advance.

Boiler explosions were the most horrifying cause of accidents. By far the greatest loss of life came from scalding steam, flying wreckage, and the fire that would engulf a boat in a matter of minutes. In the 1830s alone, eighty-nine boiler explosions caused 861 deaths and many more injuries. The cause of explosion was often mysterious: Was it

THE *LEXINGTON* EXPLODES IN FLAMES ON LONG ISLAND SOUND, 1840
*The **Lexington** was six years old in 1840 and equipped with many extra safety features, such as a fire engine and pump. Three lifeboats contained enough room for only half the passengers; they were quickly swamped in the emergency and rendered useless. Only four people survived; many froze to death in the cold waters. Consider this lithograph as an object made for sale: Who would buy this kind of artistic production?*
Library of Congress.

excessive steam pressure or weak metal? Exactly how much pressure could plate iron fastened with rivets really withstand? Did a dangerous or explosive gas develop in the boiler when the water level fell too low? Or was it principally human error—reckless or drunk pilots (none of them licensed) or captains bent on breaking speed records?

And who was responsible for public safety? When the three-week-old *Moselle* blew up near Cincinnati in 1838, with the loss of 150 lives, a citizen's committee fixed blame on the twenty-eight-year-old captain, who had ordered the fires stoked with pitch and the safety valves shut to build up a bigger head of steam. "Such disasters have their foundation in the present mammoth evil of our country, an inordinate love of gain," said the committee. "We are not satisfied with getting rich, but we must get rich in a day. We are not satisfied with

traveling at a speed of ten miles an hour, but we must fly. Such is the effect of competition that everything must be done cheap; boiler iron must be cheap, traveling must be done cheap, freight must be cheap, yet everything must be speedy. A steamboat must establish a reputation of a few minutes 'swifter' in a hundred miles than others, before she can make fortunes fast enough to satisfy the owners."

In 1830, the federal government awarded a grant to the Franklin Institute of Philadelphia to study the causes of boiler explosions, but it was not until 1852 that public safety became a federal responsibility with passage of regulations by the U.S. Congress mandating steamboat inspections. After the Civil War, affordable sheet steel and the development of new welding techniques produced boilers that were much stronger and safer.

Pennsylvania's Schuylkill Canal stretched 108 miles west into the state when it was completed in 1826. It was overshadowed by the impressive Erie Canal in New York, finished in 1825, stretching 350 miles between Albany on the Hudson River and Buffalo on Lake Erie. The canal was a waterbridge linking the port of New York City with the entire Northwest Territory. Wheat and flour moved east, textiles and other goods moved west, and passengers went in both directions. By the 1830s, the cost of shipping by canal fell to less than a tenth of the cost of overland transport, and New York City quickly blossomed into the premier commercial city in the United States.

In the 1830s, private railroad companies began to give canals stiff competition, and by the mid-1840s the canal-building era was over. (However, use of the canals for freight continued well into the twentieth century.) The nation's first railroad, the Baltimore and Ohio, laid thirteen miles of track in 1829. During the 1830s, three thousand more miles of track materialized nationwide, the result of a speculative fever in railroad construction masterminded by bankers, locomotive manufacturers, and state legislators, who provided subsidies, charters, and land rights-of-way. Rail lines in the 1830s were generally short, on the order of twenty to one hundred miles; they were not yet an efficient distribution system for goods. But passengers flocked to experience the marvelous travel speeds of fifteen to twenty miles per hour, enduring the frightful noise and cascades of cinders that rained on them.

Factories, Workingwomen, and Wage Labor

Transportation advances promoted a rapid expansion of manufacturing after 1815. Teamsters and bargemen hauled consumer products like shoes, textiles, clocks, and books into nationwide distribution. Some of the gain in manufacturing, especially in the textile industry, came from the development of water-driven machinery, built near fast-coursing rivers. (The steam power harnessed for steamboats and railroads had limited application in industry until the 1840s.) But much of the new manufacturing involved only a reorganization of production, still using the power and skill of human hands. Both mechanized and manual manufacturing pulled young women into the labor market for the first time.

The earliest factory, built by British immigrant Samuel Slater in Pawtucket, Rhode Island, in the 1790s, featured a mechanical spinning machine that produced thread and yarn. By 1815, nearly 170 spinning mills dotted lower New England. Unlike English manufacturing cities, where entire families worked in low-wage, health-threatening factories, American factories targeted young women as employees, cheap to hire because of their limited employment options. Mill girls would retire to marriage, replaced by fresh recruits earning a beginner's wage.

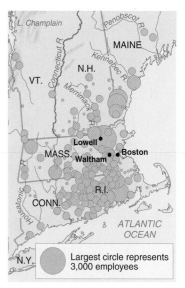

Cotton Textile Industry, 1839

In the 1820s, a group of Boston entrepreneurs founded the town of Lowell, on the Merrimack River, where all aspects of cloth production—carding, fulling, spinning, weaving, and dyeing—were centralized. By 1830, the eight mills in Lowell employed more than six thousand young women. A key innovation was the close moral supervision of the female workers, who lived in company-owned boardinghouses with housemothers, with four to six girls per bedroom. Typical mill workers were age sixteen to twenty-three; their pay averaged two to three dollars for a seventy-hour workweek, more than what a seamstress or domestic servant could earn but less than a young man's wages. The job consisted of tending noisy power looms in large rooms kept hot and humid, ideal for thread, but not for people.

Despite the discomforts, young women flocked to textile jobs. Animated by the same energy that moved Andrew Jackson westward—the faith that people can shape their own destinies—the mill workers left rural farms for factory towns in the hope of gaining more autonomy. They welcomed the unprecedented if still limited personal freedom of living in an all-female social space, away from parents and domestic tasks, and with pay in their pockets. In Lowell, the women could engage in evening self-improvement activities, like attending

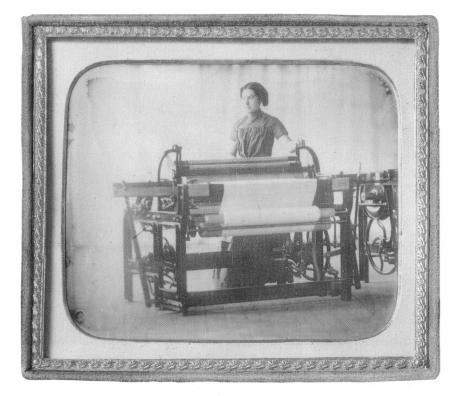

MILL WORKER TENDING A POWER LOOM, 1850
This daguerreotype—the earliest form of photograph (see page 325)—shows a young woman weaver tending a power loom in a textile mill. Her main task was to replace the shuttle bobbin, a wooden cradle that held spooled yarn, when it was empty. She also had to be constantly alert for sudden breaks in the warp yarn, which then required a quick repair. In the 1830s, women weavers generally tended two machines at a time; in the 1840s, some companies increased the workload to four.
American Textile History Museum.

lectures, or writing for the company's newspaper, *The Lowell Offering*.

In the mid-1830s, worldwide changes in the cotton market impelled mill owners to speed up work and lower wages. The workers protested, emboldened by their communal living arrangements and by their relative independence from the job as temporary employees. In 1834 and again in 1836, hundreds of women at Lowell went out on strike. All over New England, female millworkers led strikes and formed unions. Women at a mill in Dover, New Hampshire, in 1834 denounced their owners for trying to turn them into "slaves": "However freely the epithet of 'factory slaves' may be bestowed upon us, we will never deserve it by a base and cringing submission to proud wealth or haughty insolence." Their assertiveness surprised many; but ultimately their easy replaceability undermined their bargaining power, and owners in the 1840s began to shift to immigrant families as their labor source.

Other manufacturing enterprises of the 1820s and 1830s, such as shoemaking, employed women in ever larger numbers. New modes of organizing the work allowed the manufacturers to step up production, control wastage and quality, and lower wages by subdividing the tasks and by hiring women, including wives. Male workers cut leather and made soles, while the stitching of the upper part of the shoe, called shoebinding, became women's work, performed at home so that it could mesh with domestic chores. Shoebinder wives could now contribute to family income, although their wages were much smaller than men's.

In the economically turbulent 1830s, the new shoe entrepreneurs cut shoebinder wages. Unlike the mill workers, women shoebinders worked in isolation, a serious hindrance to organized protest. In Lynn, Massachusetts, a major shoemaking center, women turned to other female networks, mainly churches, as sites for meetings and to religious newspapers as forums for communication. The Lynn shoebinders who demanded higher wages in 1834 built on a collective sense of themselves as women even though they did not share daily work lives. "Equal rights should be extended to all—to the weaker sex as well as the stronger," they wrote in a document forming the Female Society of Lynn. In the end, the Lynn shoebinders' protests failed to achieve wage increases. Isolated workers all over New England continued to accept low wages, and even in Lynn, many women shied away from organized protest, preferring to situate their work in the context of family duty (helping their menfolk to finish shoes) instead of market relations.

Bankers and Lawyers

Entrepreneurs like the Lowell factory owners relied on innovations in the banking system to finance their ventures. The number of state-chartered banks in the country more than doubled in the boom years 1814–1816, from fewer than 90 to 208; by 1830, there were 330, and hundreds more by 1840. Banks stimulated the economy both by making loans to merchants and manufacturers and by enlarging the money supply. Borrowers were issued loans in the form of banknotes, certificates unique to each bank. The borrowers then used the notes exactly like money, for all transactions. Neither federal nor state governments issued paper money, so banknotes became the currency of the country.

In theory, a note could always be traded in at the bank for its equivalent in gold or silver (in a transaction known as "specie payment"). A note from a solid local bank might be worth exactly what it was written for, but if the note came from a distant or questionable bank, its value would be discounted by a fraction. The money market of Jacksonian America definitely required knowledge and caution. Not surprisingly, counterfeiting flourished under these conditions.

Bankers exercised great power over the economy in deciding who would get loans and what the discount rates would be. The most powerful bankers sat on the board of directors for the second Bank of the United States, headquartered in Philadelphia. (The first Bank of the United States, chartered in 1791, had lapsed in 1811.) The second bank opened for business in 1816 under a twenty-year charter with eighteen branches throughout the country. The rechartering of this second bank would prove to be a major issue in Andrew Jackson's reelection campaign in 1832.

Accompanying the market revolution was a revolution in commercial law. In the decades after 1815, lawyers fashioned a legal system that advanced the interests of commercial activity and enhanced the prospects of private investment. Of particular significance was the changing practice of legal incorporation, the chartering of businesses by states. Earlier, charters were generally limited to businesses formed to serve the public good,

OFFICE SAFE
Financial records, ledgers, banknotes, and stock certificates required safekeeping in the stepped-up commercial world of the 1830s. This small office safe opened by key.
Eric Long/Smithsonian Institution.

such as to build a bridge. Under new state laws from 1811 on, corporations could be formed for any reasonable purpose; a key value of incorporation was legal protection for individual investors. In 1800, there were perhaps twenty corporations in the United States; by 1817, there were eighteen hundred.

Rising numbers of young men obtained legal training in the years after the War of 1812. By 1820, most representatives in the U.S. Congress were lawyers, and a similar wave of legal professionals moved into state politics. They rewrote commercial laws to promote the entreprenuerial marketplace, for example by defining employee strikes as illegal conspiracies. They wrote the laws of eminent domain, empowering states to buy land for roads and canals, even from unwilling sellers. They drafted legislation on contributory negligence, relieving employers from responsibility for workplace injuries. In such ways, entrepreneurial lawyers of the 1820s and 1830s created the legal foundation for an economy that gave priority to ambitious individuals interested in maximizing their own wealth.

Not everyone applauded these developments. Andrew Jackson, himself a skillful lawyer-turned-politician, spoke for a large and mistrustful segment of the population when he warned about the abuses of power "which the moneyed interest derives from a paper currency which they are able to control, from the multitude of corporations with exclusive privileges which they have succeeded in obtaining in the different states, and which are employed altogether for their benefit." Jacksonians believed that ending government-granted privileges was the way to maximize individual liberty and economic opportunity.

Booms and Busts

One aspect of the economy that the lawyer-politicians could not control was the threat of financial collapse. The boom years from 1815 to 1818 exhibited a volatility that resulted in the first sharp, large-scale economic downturn in U.S. history, a depression that Americans called a "panic"; the pattern was repeated in the 1830s. Rapidly rising consumer demand stimulated rising prices for goods, and speculative investment opportunities with high payoffs abounded—in bank stocks, western land sales, urban real estate, and commodities markets. Steep inflation made some people wealthy but created hardships for workers on fixed incomes.

When the bubble first burst in 1819, the overnight rich suddenly became the overnight poor. Some suspected that a precipitating cause of the panic of 1819 was the second Bank of the United States. For too long, the bank had neglected to exercise control over state banks, many of which had suspended specie payments—the exchange of gold or silver for banknotes—in their eagerness to make loans and expand the economic bubble. Then, in mid-1818, the Bank of the United States started to call in its loans and insisted that state banks do likewise. The contraction of the money supply created tremors throughout the economy, a foretaste of the catastrophe to come.

What made the crunch worse was a parallel financial crisis in Europe in the spring of 1819. Overseas prices of cotton, tobacco, and wheat plummeted by more than 50 percent. Now when the Bank

of the United States and state banks tried to call in their outstanding loans, debtors involved in the commodities trade could not pay. The number of business and personal bankruptcies skyrocketed. The intricate web of credit and debt relationships meant that almost everyone with even a toe in the new commercial economy was affected by the panic of 1819. Thousands of Americans lost their savings and property and unemployment estimates suggest that a half million people lost their jobs.

Recovery from the panic of 1819 took several years. Unemployment rates fell, but bitterness lingered, ready to be mobilized by politicians in the decades to come. The dangers of a system dependent on extensive credit were now clear: In one memorable, folksy formulation that circulated around 1820, a farmer was said to compare credit to "a man pissing in his breeches on a cold day to keep his arse warm—very comfortable at first but I dare say . . . you know how it feels afterwards."

By the mid-1820s, the booming economy was back on track, driven by increases in productivity and consumer demand for goods, an accelerating international trade, and a restless and calculating people moving goods, human labor, and investment capital in expanding circles of commerce. But an undercurrent of anxiety about rapid economic change continued to shape the political views of many Americans.

The Spread of Democracy

Just as the market revolution held out the promise, if not the reality, of economic opportunity for anyone who worked hard, the political transformation of the 1830s held out the promise of political opportunity for hundreds of thousands of new voters. Between 1828 and 1836, the years of Andrew Jackson's presidency, the second American party system took shape, although not until 1836 would the parties have distinct names and consistent programs that transcended the particular personalities running for office. Over those years, more men could and did vote, responding to new methods of arousing voter interest. In 1828, Jackson's charismatic personality defined his party. By 1836, both parties had institutionalized one of his most successful themes: that politicians had to appear to have the common touch in an era when popularity with voters drove the electoral process.

Popular Politics and Partisan Identity

The election of 1828 was the first presidential contest in which popular votes determined the outcome; in twenty-two out of twenty-four states, voters—and not state legislatures—now designated electors committed to a particular candidate. More than a million voters participated, three times the number in 1824 and nearly half the electorate, reflecting the high stakes voters perceived in the Adams-Jackson rematch. Throughout the 1830s, the number of voters rose to all-time highs. This increase resulted partly from relaxed voting restrictions; by the mid-1830s, all but three states allowed universal white male suffrage, without property qualifications. But the higher turnout also indicated increased political interest.

The 1828 election inaugurated new campaign styles as well. State-level candidates routinely gave speeches to woo the voters, appearing at rallies, picnics, and banquets. Adams and Jackson still declined such activities as too undignified; but Henry Clay of Kentucky, campaigning for Adams, earned the nickname the "Barbecue Orator." Campaign rhetoric, under the necessity to create popular appeal, became more informal and even blunt. The Jackson camp established many Hickory Clubs, trading on Jackson's popular nickname, "Old Hickory," from a common Tennessee tree suggesting resilience and toughness. (Jackson was the first presidential candidate to have an affectionate and widely used nickname.)

Partisan newspapers defined issues and publicized political personalities as never before. Party leaders judiciously dispensed subsidies and other favors to secure the loyalties of papers, even in remote towns and villages. In New York State, where party development was most advanced, a pro-Jackson group called the Bucktails controlled fifty weekly publications. Stories from the leading Jacksonian paper in Washington, D.C., would be reprinted two days later in a Boston or Cincinnati paper, as fast as the mail stage could carry them. Presidential campaigns were now coordinated in a national arena.

Parties declined to adopt official names in 1828, still honoring the fiction of Republican Party unity. Instead, they called themselves the Jackson party or the Adams party. By the 1832 election, labels began to appear; Adams's political heir, Henry Clay, rep-

resented the National Republicans, while Jackson's supporters called themselves Democratic Republicans. Both parties were still claiming the mantle of the Jefferson-to-Monroe heritage by keeping "Republican" in the name, but the National Republicans favored federal action to promote commercial development, while the Democratic Republicans promised to be responsive to the will of the majority. By 1834, a few state-level National Republicans shortened their name to the Whig Party, a term that was in common use by 1836, the same year that Jackson's party became simply the Democrats. Thus, Whig and Democrat crystallized as names only at the end of an eight-year evolution.

The Election of 1828 and the Character Issue

The campaign of 1828 was modern in more ways than just the drawn-out electioneering and the importance of popular votes. It was also the first national election in which scandal and character questions reigned supreme.

John Quincy Adams was vilified by his opponents as an elitist, bookish academic, perhaps even a monarchist. Critics pointed to Adams's White House billiard table and ivory chess set as symbols of his aristocratic degeneracy along with the "corrupt bargain" of 1824, the alleged election deal between Adams and Henry Clay. The Adams men returned fire with fire. They played on Jackson's fatherless childhood to portray him as the bastard son of a prostitute. Worse, the cloudy circumstances around his marriage to Rachel Donelson Robards in 1791 gave rise to the story that Jackson was a seducer and an adulterer, having married a woman whose divorce from her first husband was not entirely legal. Pro-Adams newspapers howled that Jackson was sinful and impulsive, while Adams was portrayed as pious, learned, and virtuous.

Editors in favor of Adams played up Jackson's notorious violent temper, evidenced by the many duels, brawls, and canings they could recount. Jackson men used the same stories to project the old man as a tough frontier hero who knew how to command obedience. As for learning, Jackson's rough frontier education gave him a "natural sense," wrote a Boston editor, which "can never be acquired by reading books—it can only be acquired, in perfection, by reading men."

These stories were not smoke screens to obscure the "real" issues in the election. They became real issues themselves because voters used them to comprehend the kind of public officer each man would make. Character issues conveyed in shorthand larger questions about morality, honor, and discipline; Jackson and Adams presented two radically different styles of masculinity.

Throughout the campaign, Jackson was vague on issues; he was famous for his support of a "judicious tariff," a position that could be endorsed by proponents of both higher and lower taxes on imports. His supporters were thus a diverse group who could be sure only that Jackson favored western expansion and more limited federal powers than Adams. As the incumbent, Adams stood by his record, mainly his promise to promote commerce through federal action, which brought him strength in New England and parts of New York.

Jackson won a sweeping victory, with 56 percent of the popular vote and 178 electoral votes, compared with Adams's 83 (Map 11.2). The victor took most of the South and West and carried Pennsylvania and New York as well. Jackson's vice president was John C. Calhoun, who had just served as vice president under Adams but had broken with Adams's policies.

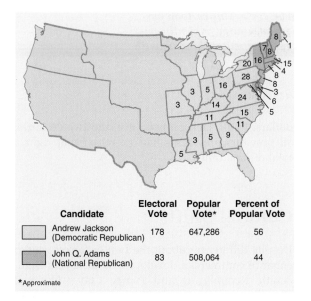

Candidate	Electoral Vote	Popular Vote*	Percent of Popular Vote
Andrew Jackson (Democratic Republican)	178	647,286	56
John Q. Adams (National Republican)	83	508,064	44

*Approximate

MAP 11.2
The Election of 1828

After 1828, national politicians no longer deplored the existence of political parties. They were coming to see that parties mobilized and delivered voters, sharpened candidates' differences, and created party loyalty that surpassed loyalty to individual candidates and elections. Adams and Jackson clearly symbolized and defined for voters the competing ideas of the emerging parties: a moralistic, top-down party ready to make major decisions to promote economic growth competing against a contentious, energetic party ready to embrace liberty-loving individualism.

Jackson's Democratic Agenda

Before the inauguration in March 1829, Rachel Jackson died. The president, certain that the ugly campaign had hastened her death, went into deep mourning. His depression was worsened by constant pain from the 1806 bullet still lodged in his chest and by mercury poisoning from the medicines he took. Sixty-two years old, he carried only 140 pounds on his six-foot-one frame. His adversaries doubted he would make it to a second term. His supporters, however, went wild at the inauguration. Thousands cheered his ten-minute inaugural address, the shortest in history. An open reception at the White House turned into a near-riot as well-wishers jammed the premises, used windows as doors, stood on furniture for a better view of the great man, and broke thousands of dollars' worth of china and glasses.

During his presidency, Jackson continued to offer unprecedented hospitality to the public. Twenty spittoons newly installed in the East Room of the White House accommodated the spit of the throngs that arrived daily to see the president. Some were visitors and others were jobseekers. The courteous Jackson, committed to his image as the president of the "common man," held audience with unannounced visitors throughout his two terms.

Jackson's cabinet appointments marked a departure. Whereas past presidents had tried to lessen party conflict by including men of different factions in their cabinets, Jackson would have only Jackson loyalists, a political tactic followed by most later presidents. The most important position, secretary of state, he offered to Martin Van Buren, one of the shrewdest politicians of the day and newly elected governor of New York.

PRESIDENT JACKSON'S KITCHEN CABINET
Jackson's official cabinet, consisting of party loyalists who were heads of executive departments, did not inspire the president's trust and confidence. Instead, Jackson turned to a set of close friends, quickly dubbed the Kitchen Cabinet by the press, for advice, for patronage decisions, and even for the drafting of state papers. Several were newspapermen; one was an old Tennessee friend, William B. Lewis, who moved into the White House with Jackson. Martin Van Buren was also in this inner circle. This cartoon purports to show a meeting of the Kitchen Cabinet: raucous, argumentative, violently employing the tools of women's work. How does its pointed message reflect the new partisan politics of the time?
Granger Collection.

Jackson's agenda quickly emerged once he was in office. He favored a Jeffersonian limited federal government, fearing that intervention in the economy inevitably favored some groups at the expense of others. He therefore opposed federal support of transportation and grants of monopolies and charters that privileged wealthy investors. Like Jefferson, he anticipated rapid settlement of the country's interior, where land sales would spread economic democracy to settlers. Establishing a federal Indian policy thus had high priority. Unlike Jefferson, however, Jackson exercised full presidential powers over Congress. In 1830, he vetoed a highway project in Kentucky—Henry Clay's home state—that Congress voted to support with federal

dollars. In all, Jackson used the veto twelve times; all previous presidents had exercised that right a total of nine times.

Cultural Shifts

Despite differences about the best or fairest way to enhance commercial development, Jackson's Democratic Republicans and Henry Clay's National Republicans shared enthusiasm for the outcome—a growing, booming economy. For increasing numbers of families, especially in the highly commercialized Northeast, the standard of living rose, consumption patterns changed, and the nature and location of work altered.

All of these changes had a direct impact on the roles and duties of men and women and on the training of youth for the economy of the future. New ideas about gender relations in a commercial economy surfaced in printed material and in public behavior. In Jacksonian America, a widely shared public culture came into being, originating within the new commercial classes and spreading rapidly through rising levels of literacy and an explosion of print.

The Family and Separate Spheres

The centerpiece of new ideas about gender relations held that husbands found their status and authority in the new world of work, leaving wives to tend the hearth and home. Sermons, advice books, periodicals, and novels reinforced the idea that men and women inhabited separate spheres with separate duties. "To woman it belongs . . . to elevate the intellectual character of her household [and] to kindle the fires of mental activity in childhood," wrote Mrs. A. J. Graves in a popular book titled *Advice to American Women*. For men, in contrast, "the absorbing passion for gain, and the pressing demands of business, engross their whole attention." In particular, the home, now the exclusive domain of women, was sentimentalized as the source of intimacy, love, and safety, a refuge from the cruel and competitive world of market relations.

Some new aspects of society gave substance to this formulation of separate spheres. Men's work, especially in the manufacturing, urban Northeast, was undergoing profound change after 1815. Increasingly, men's jobs brought cash to the household. Farmers and tradesmen sold products in a market, and bankers, bookkeepers, shoemakers, and canal diggers got pay envelopes. Furthermore, many men performed jobs outside of the home, at an office or store. For men who were not farmers, work indeed seemed newly disconnected from the home.

A woman's domestic role was more complicated than the cultural prescriptions indicated. Although the vast majority of married white women did not hold paying jobs, the home continued to be a site of time-consuming labor. But the advice books treated household tasks as loving familial duties; housework as work was thereby rendered invisible in an economy that evaluated work by how much

cash it generated. In reality, wives directly contributed to family income in many ways. Some took in boarders, while others engaged in outwork, earning pay for shoebinding, hatmaking, or needlework done at home. Wives in the poorer classes of society, including most free black wives, did not have the luxury of husbands earning adequate wages; for them, work as servants or laundresses helped augment family income.

The Education and Training of Youth

The market economy with its new expectations for men and women required fresh methods of training youth of both sexes. The generation that came of age in the 1820s and 1830s had opportunities for education and work unparalleled in previous eras, at least for children in the middling classes and above. Northern states adopted public schooling between 1790 and the 1820s, and within another decade southern states followed suit. The curriculum produced pupils who were able, by age twelve or fourteen, to read, write, and participate in marketplace calculations. Remarkably, girls usually received the same basic education as boys. Literacy rates for white females climbed dramatically, rivaling the rates for white males for the first time.

The fact that taxpayers paid for children's education created an incentive to seek an inexpensive teaching force. By the 1830s, northeastern school districts were replacing male teachers with young females. Like mill workers, teachers were in their late teens and regarded the work as temporary. In the 1840s, several states opened teacher training schools ("normal" schools) for women students. With the exception of Oberlin College in Ohio, no other colleges admitted women until after the Civil War, but a handful of private "female seminaries" established a rigorous curriculum that rivaled that of the best men's colleges. Two of the most prominent were the Troy Seminary in New York, founded by Emma Willard in 1821, and Mount Holyoke in Massachusetts, founded by Mary Lyon in 1837.

Male youths leaving public school faced two paths. A small percentage continued at private boys' academies (numbering in the several hundreds nationwide), and a far smaller number entered the country's two dozen colleges. More typically, boys left school at fourteen to apprentice to a specific trade or to seek business careers in entry-level clerkships, abundant in the growing urban centers.

WOMEN GRADUATES OF OBERLIN COLLEGE, CLASS OF 1855
Oberlin College was founded in Ohio by evangelical and abolitionist activists in the 1830s; it admitted white and black men and women, although in the early years the black students were all male and the women students were all white. Admission was not exactly equal: The women entered a separate Ladies' Department. By 1855, as this daguerreotype shows, black women had integrated the Ladies' Department. The two older women with bonnets were the principal and a member of the board. The students wear the latest fashion: dark taffeta dresses with sloping shoulders and tight bodice, topped by detachable white lace collars. Hair fashions were similarly uniform for women of all ages throughout the 1850s: a central part, hair dressed with oil and lustrously coiled over the ears. Compare these women with the mill woman pictured on page 241. What differences do you see?
Oberlin College Archives, Oberlin, Ohio.

Young girls also headed for mill towns or for the cities in unprecedented numbers, seeking work in the expanding service sector as seamstresses and domestic servants.

Changes in patterns of youth employment and training meant that large numbers of youngsters in the 1830s and later escaped the watchful eyes of their families. Moralists fretted about the dangers of unsupervised youth, and, following the lead of the Lowell mill owners, some established apprentices' libraries and uplifting lecture series to keep young people honorably occupied. Advice books published by the hundreds instructed youth in the virtues of hard work and delayed gratification.

Public Life, the Press, and Popular Amusements

Many new forms of inexpensive reading matter and public entertainment competed with the moralistic messages for youth. Innovations in printing technology as well as rising literacy rates created a brisk market in the 1830s for publications appealing to popular tastes: adventure and mystery pamphlets, romance novels, and penny press newspapers. In cities, theaters were nightly magnets for audiences in the thousands.

In the 1790s, fewer than ninety newspapers, each printing a few thousand copies per issue, provided news of current events. By 1830, there were eight hundred papers, sixty-five of them urban dailies, and in the 1830s the most successful of these, the new penny press papers, gained circulations of ten to twenty thousand copies daily. Such huge print runs were made possible by the development of steam-driven rotary presses with automatic paper feed devices replacing the old-style hand-presses. Six-cent papers covered politics, banking, and shipping news; the one-cent papers featured breezy political coverage, irreverent editorializing on current events, and crime reporting.

New York had three penny papers by 1835, and Philadelphia, Boston, and Baltimore each had one or two. Their influence extended throughout the nation, facilitated by a regular system of newspaper exchange via the postal system. Town and village papers reprinted the snappy political editorials and sensationalized crime stories, putting very undeferential ideas into the heads of readers new to politics.

Newspapers were not the only new medium for spreading a shared American culture. Starting in the 1820s, traveling lecturers crisscrossed the country, bringing entertainment and instruction to small-town audiences. Speakers gave dramatic readings of plays or poetry or lectured on history, current events, popular science, or controversial topics like advanced female education or anatomy and physiology. Theater also blossomed in the 1830s, providing urban Americans with their most common form of shared entertainment, featuring Shakespearean plays, melodramas, and the newly popular minstrelsy, a blackface musical comedy first performed in 1831 by white performers with blackened faces.

The popularity of theaters exemplified a general cultural turn toward the celebration of brilliant public speech. In this golden age of oration, actors, lawyers, politicians, and ministers could hold crowds spellbound for hours with their flawless elocution and elegant turns of phrase. Criminal trials, for example, were very short by modern standards, but the lawyers' closing arguments might consume many hours, with crowds of spectators hanging on every word. Senator Daniel Webster of Massachusetts was the acknowledged genius of political oration. At a Webster speech commemorating the Pilgrims' arrival, one man in a crowd of fifteen hundred recalled that "three or four times I thought my temples would burst with the gush of blood." Ministers with gifted tongues could in the space of an evening transform crowds of skeptics into

LURID COVER OF A CRIME PAMPHLET, NEW YORK
Cheap and easy printing in the early nineteenth century gave rise to new genres of popular reading matter, including a large pamphlet literature detailing horrific murder stories that invited readers to contemplate the nature of evil. This woodcut cover from 1836 promises to reveal the "interesting particulars" of the murder of Ellen Jewett, a New York City prostitute axed to death in her brothel bed. The pamphlet claims to constitute "an impressive warning" to youth about the tragedies of "dens of infamy." But the crude picture of the female corpse, with bare legs and breasts fully exposed, suggests that alternative, less moralistic readings of the same material were certainly possible for the purchasers.
William L. Clements Library.

Adopting the methods of evangelical ministers, temperance lecturers traveled the country expounding the damage of drink; by 1833, some six thousand local affiliates of the American Temperance Society boasted more than a million members. Middle-class drinking began a steep decline.

In 1836, the temperance leaders regrouped into a new society, the American Temperance Union, which demanded total abstinence of its adherents. The intensified war against alcohol moved beyond individual moral suasion into the realm of politics, as reformers sought to deny taverns liquor licenses. By 1845, temperance advocates had put an impressive dent in alcohol consumption, which had diminished to one-quarter of the per capita consumption of 1830. In 1851, Maine became the first state to ban entirely the manufacture and sale of all alcoholic beverages.

More controversial than temperance was a social movement called "moral reform," which first aimed at public morals in general but quickly narrowed to a campaign to eradicate sexual sin, especially prostitution. In 1833, a group of Finneyite women started the New York Female Moral Reform Society. Its members insisted that uncontrolled male sexual expression posed a serious threat to society in general and to women in particular. The society's nationally distributed newspaper, *The Advocate of Moral Reform*, was the first major woman-edited, woman-written, and woman-typeset paper in the country. In it they condemned men who visited brothels or who seduced innocent victims. Within five years, more than four thousand auxiliary groups of women members had sprung up, mostly in New England, New York, Pennsylvania, and Ohio.

In its analysis of the causes of licentiousness and its conviction that women had a duty to speak out about unspeakable things, the female Moral Reformers pushed the limits of what even the men in the evangelical movement could tolerate. Yet they did not regard themselves as radicals. They were simply pursuing the logic of a gender system that defined home protection and morality as women's special sphere and a religious conviction that called for the eradication of sin.

Organizing against Slavery

More radical still was the movement in the 1830s to abolish the sin of slavery. The only previous antislavery organization, the American Colonization Society, had been founded in 1817 by some Maryland and Virginia planters to promote gradual individual emancipation of slaves followed by colonization in Africa. By the early 1820s, several thousand ex-slaves had been transported to Liberia on the West African coast. But not surprisingly, newly freed men and women were often not eager to emigrate; their African roots were three or more generations in the past. Colonization was too moderate (and expensive) to have much impact on American slavery.

In 1831, an antislavery agitation developed in Boston, centered on William Lloyd Garrison, editor of the *Liberator*, a weekly newspaper. Garrison advocated immediate abolition: "On this subject, I do not wish to think, or speak, or write, with moderation. No! No! Tell a man whose house is on fire to give a moderate alarm; tell him to moderately rescue his wife from the hands of the ravisher; tell the mother to gradually extricate her babe from the fire into which it has fallen;—but urge me not to use moderation in a cause like the present."

Garrison's visibility built on several years of growing local antislavery sentiment. In 1829, a black printer named David Walker published *An Appeal to the Colored Citizens of the World*, which condemned racism, invoked the egalitarian language of the Declaration of Independence, and hinted at racial violence if whites did not change their prejudiced ways. And in 1831, a young black woman, Maria Stewart, delivered public lectures for black audiences in Boston on slavery and racial prejudice. While her arguments against slavery were welcomed, her voice—that of a woman—created problems. Few American-born women had yet engaged in public speaking beyond theatrical performances; Stewart was breaking a social taboo. She retired from the platform in 1833, but Garrison published her lectures, giving them wider circulation.

In 1832, Garrison supporters started the New England Anti-Slavery Society; Philadelphia and New York started similar groups in 1833. Soon there were a dozen antislavery newspapers, along with scores of antislavery lecturers spreading the word and inspiring the formation of new societies, which grew to number thirteen hundred by 1837. Confined to the North, their membership totaled a quarter of a million men and women.

However, many northerners were not prepared to embrace the abolitionist call for emancipation, immediate or gradual. They might oppose slavery as a blot on the country's ideals or as a rival to the free-labor system of the North, but at the same time most white northerners remained antiblack and

ABOLITIONIST PURSES
Female antislavery societies raised many thousands of dollars to support the
abolitionist cause by selling handcrafted items at giant antislavery fairs. Toys, infant
clothes, quilts, caps and collars, purses, needlebooks, wax flowers, inlaid boxes: The list
was endless. Items were often emblazoned with abolitionist mottoes, such as "Let My
People Go," "Liberty," and "Loose the Bonds of Wickedness." These pink silk draw-
string bags were decorated with pictures of the hapless slave woman, an object of com-
passion. Dollars raised at these fairs supported the travels of abolitionist speakers as
well as the publication and distribution of many antislavery books and articles.
The Daughters of the American Revolution Museum, Washington, D.C. Gift of Mrs. Erwin L. Broecker.

therefore antiabolition. From 1834 to 1838, there were more than a hundred eruptions of serious mob violence against abolitionists or free blacks. On one occasion, antislavery headquarters in Philadelphia and a black church and orphanage were burned to the ground; in another incident, Illinois abolitionist editor Elijah Lovejoy was killed by a rioting crowd attempting to destroy his printing press.

Women played a prominent role in abolition, just as they did in moral reform and evangelical religion. They formed women's auxiliaries and engaged in fundraising to support lecturers in the field. They circulated antislavery petitions, presented to the U.S. Congress with tens of thousands of signatures. Garrison particularly welcomed women's activity. When a southern plantation daughter named Angelina Grimké wrote him about her personal repugnance for slavery, Garrison published the letter in the *Liberator* and brought her overnight fame. Grimké and her older sister, Sarah,

now living in Philadelphia, quickly became lecturers for the antislavery movement and started a speaking tour to women's groups in Massachusetts in 1837. Grimké's powerful eyewitness speeches attracted men as well, causing the Congregational church leadership of Massachusetts to issue a warning to all its ministers not to let the Grimké sisters use their pulpits.

In the late 1830s, the cause of abolition divided the nation as no other issue did. Even among the abolitionists, significant divisions emerged. The Grimké sisters, radicalized by the public reaction to their speaking tour, began to write and speak about women's rights. They were opposed by moderate abolitionists who were unwilling to mix a new and controversial issue about women with their first cause, the rights of blacks. A few radical men, like Garrison, embraced women's rights fully, working to get women leadership positions in the national antislavery group.

The many men and women active in reform movements in the 1830s found their initial inspiration in evangelical Protestantism's dual message: Salvation was open to all and society needed to be perfected. Their activist mentality squared well with the interventionist tendencies of the party forming in opposition to Andrew Jackson's Democrats. On the whole, reformers gravitated to the Whig Party.

Jackson Defines the Democratic Party

In his eight years in office, Andrew Jackson worked to implement his vision of a politics of opportunity for all white men. He also greatly enhanced the power of the presidency. He favored rapid western land settlement, which led to conflict with Indian tribes. He had a dramatic confrontation with John C. Calhoun and South Carolina when that state tried to nullify the tariff of 1828. Disapproving of all government-granted privilege, Jackson challenged what he called the "monster" Bank of the United States and took it down to defeat. Jackson's legacy to his successor, Martin Van Buren, was a Democratic Party strong enough to withstand the passing of the powerful old man.

Indian Policy and the Trail of Tears

Improved transportation after 1815 greatly accelerated the westward flow of white settlers, and states containing Indian tribes rapidly joined the Union. But fundamental questions remained unresolved: What was the legal status of the quarter of a million Indians now resident in the United States? Were they subject to state and federal law?

From the 1790s to the 1820s, the federal government negotiated treaties with tribes on the assumption that the tribes were foreign nations. The Indians, though within state borders, asserted their sovereignty and communal rights to their land. Treaty making, however, proved a precarious practice. American negotiators found it hard to strike terms that whole tribes would accept, and all too often a few Indians with no legitimacy to speak for their tribes signed treaties ceding vast acreage.

Privately, Andrew Jackson thought it was "absurd" to call the Indians foreigners. In his view, they were subjects of the United States, entitled perhaps to keep small areas of their improved land but not their large hunting grounds. Jackson also did not think it feasible to promote assimilation of the Indians. From 1790 to the 1820s, various missionary associations had tried to "civilize" native peoples by converting them to Christianity, and presidents from Jefferson to Monroe had promoted assimilation as a peaceable alternative to warfare. In 1819, Congress authorized $10,000 a year for interdenominational missions to instruct Indians in religion, reading and writing, and agricultural practices. Missionaries also tried to get Indians to adopt white gender customs, but Indian women were reluctant to embrace practices that accorded them less power than their tribal system did. The general failure of assimilation moved Jackson to a more drastic policy.

In his first message to Congress in 1829, Jackson declared that Indians within U.S. borders could not remain independent and in sovereign control of tribal lands. Congress agreed and passed the Removal Act of 1830, appropriating $500,000 to relocate tribes west of the Mississippi River (Map 11.3).

For northern tribes, their numbers greatly diminished by years of war, gradual removal was already well under way. But not all the Indians went quietly. In 1832 in western Illinois, Black Hawk, a leader of the Sac and Fox Indians, resisted. Volunteer militias attacked and chased the Indians into southern Wisconsin, where, after several skirmishes and a deadly battle, Black Hawk was captured and more than nine hundred of his people massacred.

Southern tribes proved even more resistant to removal. The powerful Creek, Chickasaw, Choctaw, and Cherokee tribes, whose lands encompassed parts of North Carolina, Tennessee, and northern Georgia, Alabama, and Mississippi, at first refused to relocate. But their land attracted cotton-hungry white settlers, and a rumor of gold on Cherokee land in Georgia in 1829 only intensified the pressure.

Ironically, the seventeen thousand members of the Cherokee tribe had "assimilated" most successfully, spurred by dedicated missionaries living with them. More than two hundred Cherokees had intermarried with whites and had adopted white styles of housing, dress, and cotton agriculture, including the ownership of more than a thousand African American slaves. They had developed a

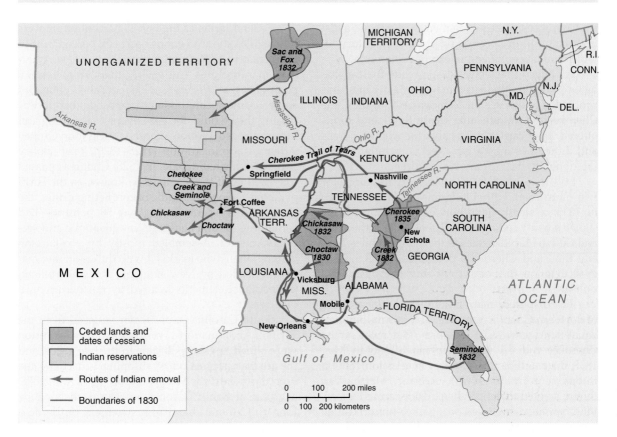

MAP 11.3

Indian Removal and the Trail of Tears

The federal government under President Andrew Jackson pursued a vigorous policy of Indian removal in the 1830s. Tribes were forcibly moved west to land known as the Indian Territory (in present-day Oklahoma). As many as a quarter of the Cherokee Indians died in 1838 on their route, known as the Trail of Tears.

READING THE MAP: From which states were most of the Native Americans removed? Through what states did the Trail of Tears go?

CONNECTIONS: Before Jackson's presidency, how did the federal government view Native Americans, and what policy initiatives were undertaken by the government and private groups? How did Jackson change the government's Native American policies?

www.bedfordstmartins.com/roarkcompact SEE THE ONLINE STUDY GUIDE for more help in analyzing this map.

written alphabet and published a newspaper as well as Christian prayerbooks in their language, and by 1827 had a constitution directly modeled on that of the United States.

In 1831, after Georgia announced it would subject the Indians to state law, the Cherokee tribe responded by suing Georgia before the U.S. Supreme

Court. Chief Justice John Marshall set aside the suit on technicalities but encouraged the Cherokees to seek further legal redress. When Georgia jailed two missionaries under an 1830 law forbidding missionary aid to Indians without state permission, the Cherokees brought suit again. In the 1832 case, *Worcester v. Georgia*, the Supreme Court found for the Cherokees, recognizing their existence as "a distinct community, occupying its own territory, in which the laws of Georgia can have no force."

An angry President Jackson made it clear that he would ignore the Supreme Court's decision and proceeded to enforce the Removal Act. "If they [the Cherokees] now refuse to accept the liberal terms offered, they can only be liable for whatever evils and difficulties may arise. I feel conscious of having done my duty to my red children."

Still, the Cherokee tribe remained in Georgia for two more years without significant violence. Then in 1835, a small, unauthorized part of the tribe signed a treaty ceding all the tribal lands to the state, and Georgia rapidly sold off the land to whites. Several thousand Cherokees petitioned the U.S. Congress to ignore the bogus treaty, but their pleas went unheard.

The disputed treaty relinquished a large piece of northern Georgia in exchange for $5 million and equal acreage west of Arkansas. But most of the Cherokee Indians refused to move, and in May 1838, the deadline for voluntary evacuation, federal troops sent by Jackson's successor, Martin Van Buren, arrived to deport them. Under armed guard, the Cherokees embarked on a twelve-hundred-mile journey that came to be called the Trail of Tears. Nearly a quarter of the Cherokees died en route, from hardship and starvation. They joined the thousands of Creek, Choctaw, and Chickasaw Indians also forcibly relocated to what is now Oklahoma.

In his farewell address to the nation in 1837, Jackson justified Indian removal with high-minded language about the benefit of the policy to the forlorn natives: "This unhappy race . . . are now placed in a situation where we may well hope that they will share in the blessings of civilization and be saved from the degradation and destruction to which they were rapidly hastening while they remained in the states."

The Tariff of Abominations and Nullification

Jackson's Indian policy happened to harmonize with the principle of states' rights: The president supported Georgia's right to ignore the Supreme Court decision in *Worcester v. Georgia*. But in another pressing question of states' rights, Jackson contested South Carolina's claim to ignore federal tariff policy.

Federal tariffs as high as 33 percent on imports like textiles and iron goods had been passed in 1816 and again in 1824, in an effort to favor new American manufactures and shelter them from foreign competition as well as to raise federal revenue. But some southern congressmen opposed steep tariffs, fearing they would decrease overseas shipping and hurt the South's cotton export. During John Quincy Adams's administration (1825–1829), tariff policy generated heated debate. In 1828, Congress passed a revised tariff that came to be known as the Tariff of Abominations. A bundle of conflicting duties, the set of tariffs—some as high as 50 percent—had something for and against every economic and sectional interest. Assembled mostly by pro-Jackson congressmen, who loaded it with duties on raw materials needed by New England, it also contained protectionist elements favored by northern manufacturers.

South Carolina in particular suffered from the Tariff of Abominations. Worldwide prices for cotton were already in sharp decline in the late 1820s, and the further depression of shipping caused by the high tariffs hurt the South's export market. In 1828, a group of South Carolina politicians headed by John C. Calhoun drew up a statement outlining a doctrine called "nullification." The Union, they argued, was a confederation of states that had yielded some but not all power to the federal government. When Congress overstepped its powers, states had the right to nullify Congress's acts; as precedents they pointed to the Virginia and Kentucky Resolutions of 1798, which had attempted to invalidate the Alien and Sedition Acts (see chapter 9). Congress had erred in using tariff policy as an instrument to benefit specific industries, the South Carolinians claimed; tariffs should be used only to raise revenue.

On assuming the presidency in 1829, Jackson ignored the South Carolina statement of nullification and shut out Calhoun, his new vice president, from influence or power. Tariff revisions in early 1832 brought little relief to the South. Sensing futility, Calhoun resigned from the vice presidency in 1832 and accepted election by the South Carolina legislature to a seat in the U.S. Senate, where he could better protect his state's antitariff stance. Strained to their limit, the South Carolina leaders took the radical step of declaring the federal tariffs to be null and void in their state as of February 1, 1833.

Finally, the constitutional crisis was out in the open. Opting for a dramatic confrontation, Jackson sent armed ships to Charleston's harbor and threatened to invade the state. He pushed through Congress a bill, called the Force Bill, defining the Carolina stance as treason and authorizing military action to collect federal tariffs.

At the same time, Congress moved quickly to pass a revised tariff more acceptable to the South. The conciliating Senator Henry Clay rallied support for a moderate bill that gradually reduced tariffs down to the 1816 level. Both the new tariff and the Force Bill were passed by Congress on March 1, 1833. South Carolina responded by withdrawing its nullification of the old tariff—and then nullifying the Force Bill. It was a symbolic gesture, since Jackson's show of muscle was no longer necessary. Both sides were satisfied with the immediate outcome. Federal power had prevailed over a dangerous assertion of states' rights; and South Carolina got the lower tariff it wanted.

Yet the question of federal power versus states' rights was far from settled. The implied threat behind nullification was secession, a position articulated in 1832 by some South Carolinians whose concerns went beyond tariff policy. The growing voice of antislavery activism in the North threatened the South's economic system. If and when a northern-dominated federal government decided to end slavery, the South Carolinians thought, the South must have the right to remove itself from the Union.

The Bank War and the Panic of 1837

President Jackson also did battle over the Bank of the United States. After riding out the panic of 1819, the bank finally prospered. It handled the federal government's deposits, extended credit and loans, and issued banknotes—by 1830 the most stable currency in the country. With twenty-nine branches, it benefited the whole nation. Jackson, however, did not find the bank's functions sufficiently valuable to offset his criticism of the concept of a national bank. In his first and second messages to Congress, in 1829 and 1830, Jackson claimed that the bank concentrated undue economic power in the hands of a few.

National Republican Senators Daniel Webster and Henry Clay decided to force the issue. They convinced the bank to apply for charter renewal in 1832, well before the fall election, even though the existing charter ran until 1836. They fully expected that Congress's renewal would force Jackson to follow through on his rhetoric with a veto. The unpopular veto would then cause Jackson to lose the election, while the bank would survive on an override vote from a new Congress swept into power in the anti-Jackson tide.

At first the plan seemed to work. The bank applied for recharter, Congress voted to renew, and Jackson, angry over being manipulated, issued his veto. But it was a brilliantly written veto, full of fierce language about privileges of the moneyed elite who oppress the democratic masses in order to enrich themselves. Jackson had translated the bank controversy into a language of class antagonism and egalitarian ideals that strongly resonated with many Americans. Old Hickory won the election easily over his National Republican opponent, Henry Clay, gaining 55 percent of the popular vote and a lopsided electoral college vote of 219 to 49. The Jackson party still controlled Congress, so no override was possible. The bank would cease to exist after 1836.

But Jackson wanted to destroy the bank sooner. Calling the bank a "monster," he had the federal deposits removed from its vaults and redeposited into "pet banks," Democratic-leaning institutions throughout the country; because of the high tariffs and high-volume sales of public lands, this government nest egg was quite sizable. In retaliation, the bank raised interest rates and called in loans; this action caused a minor recession in 1833 and actually enhanced Jackson's claim that the bank was too powerful for the good of the country.

Unleashed and unregulated, the economy went into high gear. Perhaps only a small part of the problem arose from irresponsible banking practices; just at this moment, an excess of silver from Mexican mines had made its way into American banks, giving bankers license to print ever more banknotes. Inflation soared from 1834 to 1837; prices of basic goods rose more than 50 percent. Many hundreds of new private banks were quickly chartered by the states, each bank issuing its own banknotes and setting interest rates as high as the market would bear. Entrepreneurs borrowed and invested money, much of it funneled into privately financed railroads and canals.

The market in western land sales heated up. In 1834, about 4.5 million acres of the public domain

FISTFIGHT BETWEEN OLD HICKORY AND BULLY NICK *This 1834 cartoon represents President Andrew Jackson squaring off to fight Nicholas Biddle, the director of the Bank of the United States. Pugilism as a semiprofessional sport gained great popularity in the 1830s; the joke here is that the aged Jackson and the aristocratic Biddle would strip to such revealing tight pants and engage in open combat. To Biddle's left are his seconds, Daniel Webster and Henry Clay; behind the president is his vice president, Martin Van Buren. Whiskey and port lubricate the action.* The Library Company of Philadelphia.

had been sold, the highest annual volume since the peak year 1819; by 1836, the total reached an astonishing 20 million acres. Some of this was southern land in Mississippi and Louisiana, which slave owners rushed to bring under cultivation, but much more was in the North, where land offices were deluged with buyers. The Jackson administration worried that the purchasers were overwhelmingly eastern capitalists, land speculators instead of self-reliant yeoman farmers who intended to settle on the land.

In one respect, the economy attained an admirable goal: The national debt disappeared, and, for the first and only time in American history, from 1835 to 1837, the government had a monetary surplus. But much of it consisted of questionable bank currencies—"bloated, diseased" currencies, in Jackson's vivid terminology.

Jackson decided to restrain the economy. In 1836, the Treasury Department issued the Specie Circular, an order that public land could be purchased only with hard money, federally coined gold and silver. In response, bankers started to reduce their loans, fearing a general contraction of the economy. Compounding the difficulty, the Bank of England also now insisted on hard-money payments for American loans, which had grown large in the years

since 1831 because of a trade imbalance. Failures in various crop markets, a downturn in cotton prices on the international market, and the silver glut, all unrelated to Jackson's fiscal policies, fed the growing economic crisis.

The familiar events of the panic of 1819 unfolded again, with terrifying rapidity. In April 1837, a wave of bank and business failures ensued, and the credit market tumbled like a house of cards. The Specie Circular was only one precipitating cause, but the Whig Party held it and Jackson responsible for the depression. For more than five years after the panic of 1837, the United States suffered from economic hard times.

Van Buren's One-Term Presidency

The election of 1836, which preceded the panic by six months, demonstrated the transformation of the Democrats from coalition to party. The personality of Jackson had stamped the elections of 1824, 1828, and 1832, but now the party apparatus was sufficiently developed to support itself. Local and state committees existed throughout the country. Democratic candidates ran in every state election, succeeding even in old Federalist states like Maine and New Hampshire. More than four hundred newspapers declared themselves Democratic. In 1836, the Democrats repeated an innovation begun in 1832, holding a national convention that nominated Vice President Martin Van Buren of New York for president. Van Buren's running mate was Richard M. Johnson, a slave owner from Kentucky whose principal claim to fame was the unverifiable boast that he had killed Shawnee chief Tecumseh in 1813.

Sophisticated party organization was Martin Van Buren's specialty. Nicknamed the "Little Magician" for his consummate political skills, the Dutch New Yorker had built his career by pioneering many of the loyalty-enhancing techniques the Democrats used in the 1830s. After serving as senator and then governor, he became Jackson's secretary of state in 1828. Four years later he replaced Calhoun as Jackson's running mate. His eight years in the volatile Jackson administration required the full measure of his political deftness, as he sought repeatedly to save Jackson both from his enemies and from his own obstinacy.

Van Buren was a backroom politician, not a popular public figure, and the Whigs hoped that he might be defeatable. In many states, Whigs had captured high office in 1834, shedding the awkward National Republican label and developing statewide organizations to rival those of the Democrats. However, no figure commanded nationwide support. The result was that three candidates opposed Van Buren in 1836, each with a solid regional base. Massachusetts Senator Daniel Webster could deliver New England; Tennessee Senator Hugh Lawson White attracted proslavery, pro-Jackson, but anti–Van Buren voters in the South; and the aging General William Henry Harrison of Indiana, memorable for his Indian war heroics in 1811, pulled in the western, anti-Indian vote. Not one of the three candidates could have won the presidency, but together they came close to denying Van Buren a majority vote. Their combined strength pulled many Whigs into office at the state level. In the end, Van Buren had 170 electoral votes, while the other three received a total of 113.

Van Buren took office in March 1837, and a month later the panic hit. The new president called a special session of Congress to consider creating an independent treasury system to fulfill some of the functions of the defunct Bank of the United States. Such a system, funded by government deposits, would deal only in hard money, forcing commercial banks to restrict their issuance of paper currency. Equally important, the new system would not make

loans and would thus avoid the danger of speculative meddling in the economy. In short, an independent treasury system could exert a powerful moderating influence on inflation and the credit market without itself being directly involved in the market. But Van Buren encountered strong resistance in Congress, even from Democrats. The treasury system finally won approval in 1840; by then, however, Van Buren's chances of a second term in office were virtually nil. The four years had proved to be tumultuous for the economy, with federal bank policy at a stalemate.

In 1840, the Whigs settled on William Henry Harrison, sixty-seven, to oppose Van Buren. The campaign drew on voter involvement as no other presidential campaign ever had. The Whigs borrowed tricks from the Democrats: Harrison was touted as a common man born in a log cabin, although a Virginia plantation was the real site. His Indian-fighting days, now thirty years behind him, were played up to give him a Jacksonian aura. Whigs staged festive rallies all over the country, drumming up mass appeal with candlelight parades and song shows. Women participated in Whig campaign rallies as never before. Some 78 percent of eligible voters cast ballots—the highest percentage ever in American history. Harrison took 53 percent of the popular vote and won a resounding 234 electoral college votes to Van Buren's 60. A Democratic editor lamented, "We have taught them how to conquer us!"

Conclusion: The Second American Party System

From 1828 to 1840, Andrew Jackson created and put his stamp on the newly emergent Democratic Party. Jackson's fame as an aggressive general, Indian fighter, champion of the common man, opponent of aristocracy, and defender of slavery and white privilege allowed him to pull together an unlikely but ultimately workable coalition of rural western farmers, urban laborers, pro-state bank commercial men, and wealthy southern slave owners. These groups embraced personal liberty, free competition, and egalitarian opportunity for all white men, compelling values embodied in the larger-than-life Old Hickory. Jacksonian Democrats accepted drinking and tolerated Sabbath violations, preferring not to legislate morality. They avoided debating the wisdom of slavery at all costs.

In contrast, the Whigs coalesced in the 1830s as the party of activist moralism and state-sponsored entrepreneurship. Wealthy merchants from Boston to Savannah who appreciated a national bank and protective tariffs tended to be Whigs, as did the evangelical middle classes. Personal liberty must be tempered by self-discipline and backed by government controls over moral issues, Whigs asserted, favoring laws that prohibited liquor sales or stagecoach travel on Sundays. Abolitionists tended to vote for Whigs, even though most Whig politicians shied away from antislavery ideas.

National politics in the 1830s were more heated and divisive than at any other time since the 1790s. The new party system of Democrats and Whigs cut far deeper into the electorate than had the previous system of Federalists and Republicans. Innovations in transportation and communication disseminated political information from the city to the backwoods, politicizing voters who now understood what they might gain or lose under the competing economic policies of the two parties. Politics acquired immediacy and excitement, causing four out of five white men to cast a ballot in 1840.

High rates of voter participation would continue into the 1840s and 1850s, because politics remained the arena where different choices about economic development and social change were contested. Unprecedented urban growth, westward expansion, and early industrialism marked those decades, sustaining the Jacksonian-Whig split in the electorate. But other new challenges not easily dealt with by those two parties—critiques of slavery, concerns for free labor, and an emerging protest against women's second-class citizenship—complicated the political scene of the 1840s, leading to third-party movements that splintered from the two parties of the 1830s. One of these third parties, called the Republican Party, would achieve dominance in 1860 with the election of an Illinois lawyer, Abraham Lincoln, to the presidency.

FOR FURTHER READING ABOUT THE TOPICS IN THIS CHAPTER, see the Online Bibliography at www.bedfordstmartins.com/roarkcompact.

FOR ADDITIONAL FIRST-HAND ACCOUNTS OF THIS PERIOD, see pages 164–180 in Michael Johnson, ed., *Reading the American Past*, Second Edition, Volume I.

TO ASSESS YOUR MASTERY OF THE MATERIAL IN THIS CHAPTER, see the Online Study Guide at www.bedfordstmartins.com/roarkcompact.

CHRONOLOGY

1807 Robert Fulton develops first commercially successful steamboat, *Clermont.*

1816 Second Bank of the United States chartered for twenty years.

Import tariff imposed on foreign textiles.

1817 American Colonization Society founded to promote gradual emancipation and removal of African Americans to Liberia.

1818 National Road links Baltimore and Wheeling, West Virginia.

1819 Economic collapse and panic nationwide.

1821 Boston business entrepreneurs start to build mills with power looms at Lowell, Massachusetts.

1824 Congress passes expanded tariff bill.

1825 Erie Canal spans 350 miles in New York State.

1826 Schuylkill Canal—108 miles long— opens in Pennsylvania.

1828 Tariff of Abominations passed.

Andrew Jackson elected president.

1829 David Walker's *An Appeal to the Colored Citizens of the World* published in Boston.

Baltimore and Ohio Railroad lays thirteen miles of track.

1830 Indian Removal Act appropriates money to relocate Indian tribes west of Mississippi River.

1831 William Lloyd Garrison begins publishing abolitionist newspaper *Liberator.*

Charles G. Finney stages evangelical revival in Rochester, New York.

Supreme Court allows Georgia to continue to subject Indians to state laws.

1832 Supreme Court in *Worcester v. Georgia* recognizes Cherokees as distinct community outside legal jurisdiction of Georgia.

Jackson vetoes Bank of the United States charter.

New England Anti-Slavery Society founded.

Andrew Jackson reelected president.

1833 Nullification crisis: South Carolina declares federal tariffs void in the state.

New York and Philadelphia Anti-Slavery Societies founded.

1834, Female mill workers strike in
1836 Lowell, Massachusetts.

1836 Jackson issues Specie Circular.

Martin Van Buren elected president.

1837 Economic panic.

1838 Trail of Tears—Cherokees forced to relocate west.

William Henry Harrison elected president.

SHAKO HAT

American soldiers fighting in the Mexican War were a colorful lot. Their dress uniform was a dark blue wool tailcoat worn with sky-blue wool trousers and topped with the shako, a full-dress cap made of leather, crowned with black feathers, and adorned with a decorative plate showing the eagle spreading its wings—the symbol of manifest destiny. Even everyday uniforms often included lace on collars and cuffs, silk sashes and scarves, and fringed epaulettes.

One veteran criticized the army for "dressing up men within an inch of their lives, until they looked more like a flock of eastern flamingos . . . than the descendants of the race of men who fought and bled to establish civil liberty and republican simplicity in our country." General Winfield Scott, "Old Fuss and Feathers," expected his troops to follow "regulations of dress, hair, whiskers, and so forth." Other commanders, most notably General Zachary Taylor, were notoriously lax. One junior officer serving under Taylor observed: "We wear all kinds of uniforms here, each one to his taste, some shirtsleeves, some white, some purple, some fancy jackets and all colors of cottonelle pants, some straw and some Quaker hats, and that is just the way, too, that our fellows went into battle." However they dressed, American soldiers in Mexico employed some of the world's most modern and innovative weapons.

Chicago Historical Society.

THE FREE NORTH AND WEST

12

1840–1860

EARLY IN NOVEMBER 1842, Abraham Lincoln and his new wife, Mary, moved into their first home in Springfield, Illinois, a rented room measuring eight by fourteen feet on the second floor of the Globe Tavern, the nicest place Abraham had ever lived. Mary Todd Lincoln had grown up in Lexington, Kentucky, attended by slaves in the elegant home of her father, a prosperous merchant, banker, and politician. The small, noisy room above the Globe Tavern was the worst place she had ever lived. Fewer than twenty years later, in March 1861, the Lincolns moved into what would prove to be their last home, the presidential mansion in Washington, D.C. Abraham Lincoln climbed from the Globe Tavern to the White House by relentless work, unslaked ambition, and immense talent, traits he had honed since boyhood.

Born in a Kentucky log cabin in 1809, Lincoln grew up on small, struggling farms. His father, Thomas, never learned to read and, Abraham explained, "never did more in the way of writing than to bunglingly sign his own name." Lincoln's mother, Nancy, could neither read nor write. In December 1816, Thomas Lincoln moved his young family out of Kentucky, crossing the Ohio River to the Indiana wilderness. They lived for two frozen months in a crude lean-to only partially enclosed by limbs and bushes while Thomas, a skilled carpenter, built a new cabin. There Abraham learned the arts of farming practiced by families throughout the nation. Although only eight years old, Abraham "had an axe put into his hands at once" and used it "almost constantly" for the next fifteen years, he recalled. When he could be spared from work, the boy attended school, less than a year in all. "There was absolutely nothing to excite ambition for education," Lincoln recollected. In contrast, Mary Todd, his future wife, received ten years of schooling in Lexington's best academies for young women.

By 1830, Thomas Lincoln decided to start over. The Lincolns moved two hundred miles west to central Illinois and built another log cabin. The next spring Thomas Lincoln moved again, and this time Abraham set out on his own, a "friendless, uneducated, penniless boy," as he described himself.

By dogged striving, Lincoln gained an education and the respect of his Illinois neighbors, although a steady income eluded him for years. He also received help from his father-in-law. Shortly after Lincoln married, Mary's father gave the young couple eighty acres of land and promised a yearly allowance of about $1,100 for six years, helping them to move out of their room above the Globe Tavern. Lincoln eventually built a thriving law practice in Springfield and served in the Illinois legislature and in Congress. His political activity and hard-driving ambition ultimately catapulted him into the White House.

ABRAHAM LINCOLN'S HAT
Abraham Lincoln wore this stovepipe hat, made of beaver pelt, during his years as president of the United States. Stovepipe hats were worn by established, respectable, middle-class men in the 1850s. Workingmen and farmers would have felt out of place wearing such a hat, except perhaps on special occasions like weddings or funerals. Growing up in Kentucky, Indiana, and Illinois, Lincoln may have seen stovepipe hats on the leading men of his community, but he probably never owned one until he became an aspiring Illinois lawyer and politician. Wearing such a hat was a mark that one had achieved a certain success in life, in Lincoln's case the enormous social distance he had traveled from his backwoods origins to the White House. But even as president he continued a backwoods practice he had begun as a young postmaster in New Salem, Illinois, using his hat as a place to store letters and papers. Lincoln's law partner William Herndon termed Lincoln's hat "an extraordinary receptacle [that] served as his desk and memorandum book."
Smithsonian Institution.

Like Lincoln, millions of Americans believed they could make something of themselves, whatever their origins, so long as they were willing to work. Individuals who refused to work—who were lazy, improvident, or foolish—had only themselves to blame if they failed. The promise of rewards from hard work spurred efforts that shaped the contours of America, pushing the boundaries of the nation south to the Rio Grande and west to the Pacific Ocean. That expansion—

economic, political, and geographic—also raised anew the question of slavery that Lincoln ultimately confronted as president.

Economic and Industrial Evolution

During the 1840s and 1850s, Lincoln and other Americans lived amidst profound economic transformation that had been under way since the start of the nineteenth century. By 1860, the nation's population numbered over 31 million and the total output of the American economy had multiplied twelvefold since 1800. Four fundamental changes in American society fueled this phenomenal economic growth.

First, Abraham Lincoln and millions of other Americans left farms behind, boosting the urban population, although farmers still made up 80 percent of the nation's population by 1860. A second major change was that a growing number of Americans worked in factories, by 1860 almost 20 percent of the labor force. This trend contributed to the nation's economic growth because, in general, factory workers were twice as productive (in output per unit of labor input) as agricultural workers. A third fundamental change—from water to steam as a source of energy—permitted factories to be more productive. During the 1830s, extensive mining began in Pennsylvania coal fields and massive quantities of coal became available for industrial fuel. Coal provided heat to power steam engines in factories, railroads, and ships.

This cascade of interrelated developments—steam, coal, factories, cities, railroads—had begun to transform the character of the American economy by the 1850s. Historians have often referred to this transformation as an industrial revolution. However, the profound changes in the American economy in these years did not cause a revolutionary discontinuity in the economy or society. The United States remained overwhelmingly agricultural. Old methods of production continued alongside the new. Before 1860, the American economy underwent a process that might best be termed "industrial evolution."

That evolution was made possible by a fourth fundamental development that propelled American economic growth. Agricultural productivity (defined as crop output per unit of labor input) nearly doubled during Lincoln's lifetime. This dramatic increase contributed more than any other single factor to the economic growth of the era. While cities, factories, and steam engines blossomed throughout the nation—especially in the North and West—the roots of American economic growth lay in agriculture.

Agriculture and Land Policy

The sheer physical labor required to convert unimproved land to cultivated fields limited agricultural productivity. Energy that might have gone to growing crops went instead to clearing land. But as farmers pushed westward, they encountered thinner forests and eventually the Midwest's comparatively treeless prairie, where they could spend less time with an ax and more time at the plow or hoe, significantly boosting agricultural productivity. Rich prairie soils also gave somewhat higher crop yields than eastern farms, and farmers migrated to the Midwest by the tens of thousands between 1830 and 1860.

Labor-saving improvements in farm implements also hiked agricultural productivity. The cast-iron plow in use since the 1820s proved too weak for the thick turf and dense soil of the midwestern prairie. In 1837, John Deere patented a strong, smooth steel plow that sliced through prairie soil so cleanly that farmers called it the "singing plow." Deere's company became the leading plow manufacturer in the Midwest, turning out more than ten thousand plows a year by the late 1850s. By 1860, the energy for plowing still came from two- and four-legged animals, but better plows permitted that energy to break more ground and plant more crops.

Improvements in wheat harvesting also multiplied farmers' productivity. In 1850, most farmers harvested wheat by hand, cutting two or three acres a day with back-breaking labor. Tinkerers throughout the nation tried to fashion a mechanical reaper that would make the wheat harvest easier and quicker. Cyrus McCormick and others experimented with designs until the late 1840s, when mechanical reapers began to appear in American wheat fields. A McCormick reaper that cost between $100 and $150 allowed a farmer to harvest up to twelve acres a day. By 1860, about eighty thousand reapers

had been sold. Although reapers represented the cutting edge of agricultural technology, they still had to be powered by a horse or an ox. Most farmers continued to cut their grain by hand. Reapers and improved plows, however, allowed more land to be brought into cultivation. Without access to fresh, uncultivated land, farmers could not have doubled the corn and wheat harvests between 1840 and 1860, as they did.

In the end, the agricultural productivity that fueled the nation's economy was an outgrowth of federal land policy. Up to 1860, the United States continued to be land rich and labor poor. During the nineteenth century, the nation became a great deal richer in land, acquiring more than a billion acres with the Louisiana Purchase and the annexation of Florida, Oregon, and vast territories following the Mexican War (discussed later in this chapter). The federal government made the land available for purchase to attract settlers and to generate revenues. Although federal land cost only $1.25 an acre, millions of Americans could not afford to pay $50 for a forty-acre farm. They squatted on unclaimed federal land and carved out a farm they neither rented nor owned. Many poor farmers never accumulated enough money to purchase the land on which they squatted, and eventually they moved elsewhere, often to squat again on unclaimed federal land.

In addition to aiding small farmers, government land policy enriched wily speculators who found ways to claim large tracts of the most desirable plots and sell them to settlers at a generous markup. Nonetheless, by making land available to millions of ordinary people, the federal government achieved the goal of attracting settlers to the new territories in the West, which in due course joined the Union as new states. Above all, federal land policy created the basic precondition for the increase in agricultural productivity that underlay the nation's impressive economic growth.

Manufacturing and Mechanization

Changes in manufacturing arose in the context of the nation's land-rich, labor-poor economy. England and other European countries had land-poor, labor-rich economies; there, meager opportunities in agriculture kept factory laborers plentiful and wages low. In the United States, geographical expansion and government land policies buoyed agriculture, keeping millions of people on the farm and thereby limiting the supply of workers for manufacturing and elevating wages. Because of this shortage of workers, manufacturers searched constantly for ways to save labor.

Mechanization marched forward as quickly as manufacturers could turn innovative ideas into workable combinations of gears, levers, screws, and pulleys. Outside the textile industry (see chapter 11), homegrown machines set the pace. The practice of manufacturing and then assembling interchangeable parts spread from gun making to other industries and became known as the "American system." Mechanization became so integral to American manufacturing that some machinists specialized in what was called the machine tool industry, namely making machines that made parts for other machines.

Manufacturing and agriculture meshed into a dynamic national economy. New England led the nation in manufacturing, shipping products like clocks, guns, and axes west and south, while commodities like wheat, pork, whiskey, tobacco, and cotton flowed north and east. Manufacturers specialized in producing for the gigantic domestic market rather than for export. U.S. manufacturers supported tariffs to minimize British competition, but their best protection from British competitors was to strive harder to please their American customers, the vast majority of whom were farmers.

Throughout American manufacturing, hand labor continued to be an essential component of production, despite the advances in mechanization. Even in heavily mechanized industries, factories remained fairly small, few having more than twenty or thirty employees. But the industrial evolution under way before 1860 would quicken later in the nineteenth century; railroads were a harbinger of that future.

Railroads: Breaking the Bonds of Nature

To a degree unequaled by any other industry, railroads incorporated the most advanced developments of the age. No wonder a Swedish visitor in 1849 noticed that American schoolboys constantly doodled sketches of locomotives, always smoking, always in motion. Railroads captured Americans' imaginations in part because they seemed to break the bonds of nature. When canals and rivers froze in winter or became impassable during summer droughts, trains steamed ahead. When becalmed sailing ships went nowhere, locomotives kept on chugging, averaging over twenty miles an hour during the 1850s. Above all, railroads offered cities not blessed with canals or navigable rivers a way to compete for the trade of the countryside.

By 1850, trains steamed along nine thousand miles of track, almost two-thirds of it in New England and the Middle Atlantic states. By 1860, several railroads had crossed the Mississippi River to link frontier farmers to the nation's thirty thousand miles of track, approximately as much as in all the rest of the world combined (Map 12.1). This massive expansion of railroads helped the United States catapult into position as the world's second leading industrial power, behind Great Britain.

In addition to speeding transportation, railroads propelled growth of the iron and coal industries vital to railroad construction and operation. Railroads also stimulated the fledgling telegraph industry. In 1844, Samuel F. B. Morse persuasively demonstrated the potential of his telegraph by transmitting a series of dots and dashes that instantly conveyed an electronic message along forty miles of wire between Washington and Baltimore. By 1861, more than fifty thousand miles of wire stretched across the continent to the Pacific, often alongside railroad tracks. Telegraphy made railroads safer and more efficient, swiftly signaling whether tracks were clear.

Almost all railroads were built and owned by private corporations rather than by governments. Undergirding these private investments was massive government aid, especially federal land grants. Up to 1850, the federal government had granted a total of seven million acres of federal land to various turnpike, highway, and canal projects. In that year, Illinois Senator Stephen A. Douglas obtained congressional approval for a precedent-setting grant to railroads of six square miles of federal land for each mile of track constructed. Railroad companies quickly lined up congressional support for other lucrative land deals. By 1860, Congress had granted railroads more than twenty million acres of federal lands, establishing a generous policy that would last for decades.

The railroad boom of the 1850s was a signal of the growing industrial might of the American econ-

RAILROAD TRAVEL

In addition to carrying people and goods more quickly and reliably than ever before, railroads also brought many Americans face to face for the first time with machinery that was much larger and more powerful than any human being. This painting of a train leaving Rochester, New York, in 1852 contrasts the size and power of human beings and machines. The huge, lovingly portrayed, steam-belching locomotive is barely held back by some unseen brake against which the massive engine strains, ready to pull the long train through the columns of the station, out of the past and into the future. The people, in contrast, appear indistinct, passive, and dependent. Except for the two women and child in the foreground, the people face backward, and all of them avoid looking directly at the locomotive. The painting evokes the way the almost incomprehensible power of the railroads dwarfed human effort.

From the photographic collection of the Rochester Historical Society.

omy. But railroads, like other industries, succeeded because they served farms as well as cities. And older forms of transportation remained significant. By 1857, for example, trains carried about one-third of the mail; most of the rest still went by stagecoach or horseback. In 1860, most Americans were still far more familiar with horses than with iron horses.

The economy of the 1840s and 1850s linked muscles, animals, and farms to machines, steam, railroads, and cities. Abraham Lincoln split rails as a young man and defended railroad corporations as a successful attorney. His legendary upward

MAP 12.1

Railroads in 1860

Railroads were a crucial component of the revolutions in transportation and communications that transformed nineteenth-century America. The railroad system reflected the differences that had developed in the economies of the North and South.

mobility illustrated the direction of economic change and the opportunities that change offered to enterprising individuals.

Free Labor: Promise and Reality

The impressive economic performance did not reward all Americans equally. With few exceptions, women were excluded from the opportunities open to men. Tens of thousands of women worked as seamstresses, laundresses, domestic servants, factory hands, and teachers, but with little opportunity to aspire to more lucrative jobs. In the North and West, slavery was slowly eliminated in the half century after the American Revolution, but free African Americans there found themselves relegated, on the whole, to dead-end jobs as laborers and servants. This discrimination against women and free blacks did not trouble most white men. With certain notable exceptions, they considered it proper and just.

The Free-Labor Ideal: Freedom plus Labor

During the 1840s and 1850s, leaders throughout the North and West emphasized a set of ideas that seemed to explain why the changes under way in their society benefited some more than others. They referred again and again to the advantages of what they termed "free labor." (The word *free* referred to laborers who were not slaves; it did not mean laborers who worked for nothing.) By the 1850s, free-labor ideas described a social and economic ideal that accounted for both the successes and the shortcomings of the economy and society taking shape in the North and West.

Free-labor spokesmen celebrated hard work, self-reliance, and independence. They proclaimed that the door to success was open not just to those who inherited wealth or status but also to self-made men like Abraham Lincoln. Lincoln himself declared, "Free labor—the just and generous, and prosperous system, which opens the way for all—gives hope to all, and energy, and progress, and improvement of condition to all." The free-labor system permitted farmers and artisans to enjoy the products of their own labor and also benefited wage workers. Ultimately, the free-labor system made it possible for hired laborers to become independent property owners, proponents argued. "The prudent, penniless beginner in the world," Lincoln asserted, "labors for wages awhile, saves a surplus with which to buy tools or land, for himself; then labors on his own account another while, and at length hires another new beginner to help him." Wage labor was the first rung on the ladder toward self-employment and, eventually, to hiring others.

The free-labor ideal affirmed an egalitarian vision of human potential. Lincoln and other spokesmen stressed the importance of universal education to permit "heads and hands [to] cooperate as friends." Throughout the North and West, communities supported public schools to make the rudiments of learning available to young children. By 1860, many cities and towns boasted that up to 80 percent of children age seven to thirteen attended school, at least for a few days each year. In rural areas, where the labor of children was more difficult to spare, schools typically enrolled no more than half the school-age children. Lessons included more than arithmetic, penmanship, and a smattering of other subjects. Textbooks and teachers—most of whom were young women—drummed into students the virtues of the free-labor system: self-reliance, discipline, and, above all, hard work. "Remember that all the ignorance, degradation, and misery in the world is the result of indolence and vice," one textbook intoned. Free-labor ideology, whether in school or out, emphasized labor as much as freedom.

Economic Inequality

The free-labor ideal made sense to many Americans, especially in the North and West, because it seemed to describe their own experience. Lincoln frequently referred to his humble beginnings as a hired laborer and silently invited his listeners to consider how far he had come. In 1860, his wealth of $17,000 easily placed him in the top 5 percent of the population. Most Americans, however, measured success in far more modest terms. The average wealth of adult white men in the North in 1860 barely topped $2,000. Only about a quarter of American men possessed that much. Nearly 60 percent owned no land. It is difficult to estimate the wealth of adult white women since property possessed by married women was normally considered to belong to their husbands, but certainly women had less wealth than men. Free African Americans had still less; 90 percent were propertyless.

Free-labor spokesmen considered these economic inequalities a natural outgrowth of freedom, the inevitable result of some individuals being more able, more willing to work, and luckier. These inequalities suggest, however, the gap between the promise and the performance of the free-labor ideal in this era. Economic growth permitted many men to move from landless squatters to landowning farmers and from hired laborers to independent, self-employed producers. But many more Americans remained behind, landless and working for wages. Even those who realized their aspirations had a precarious hold on their independence; bad debts, crop failure, sickness, or death could quickly eliminate a family's gains.

Seeking out new opportunities in pursuit of free-labor ideals created restless social and geographic mobility. Commonly up to two-thirds of the residents of a rural area moved every decade, and the population turnover in cities was even greater. Such constant coming and going weakened community ties to neighbors and friends and threw individuals even more upon their own resources for help in times of trouble.

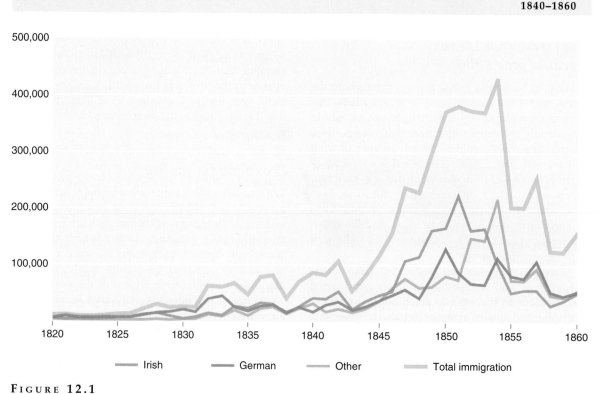

FIGURE 12.1
Antebellum Immigration, 1820–1860
After increasing gradually for several decades, immigration shot up in the mid-1840s.
Between 1848 and 1860, nearly 3.5 million immigrants entered the United States.

Immigrants and the Free-Labor Ladder

The risks and uncertainties of free labor did not deter millions of immigrants from entering the United States during the 1840s and 1850s. Almost four and a half million immigrants arrived between 1840 and 1860, six times more than had come during the previous two decades (Figure 12.1). The half million immigrants who came in 1854 accounted for nearly 2 percent of the entire population, a higher proportion than in any other single year of the nation's history. By 1860, foreign-born residents made up about one-eighth of the American population, a fraction that held steady well into the twentieth century.

Nearly three out of four of the immigrants who arrived between 1840 and 1860 came from either Germany or Ireland. The vast majority of the 1.4 million Germans who entered the United States during these years were skilled tradesmen and their families. They left Germany to escape deteriorating economic conditions and to seize opportunities offered by the expanding economy, where skilled artisans had little difficulty finding work. German butchers, bakers, beer makers, carpenters, shopkeepers, machinists, and others tended to congregate in cities, particularly in the Midwest. Roughly a quarter of German immigrants were farmers, most of whom scattered throughout the Midwest, although some settled in Texas. On the whole, German Americans settled into that middle stratum of sturdy independent producers celebrated by free-labor spokesmen; relatively few Germans occupied the bottom rung of the free-labor ladder as wage laborers or domestic servants.

Irish immigrants, in contrast, entered at the bottom of the free-labor ladder and had difficulty climbing up. Nearly 1.7 million Irish immigrants arrived between 1840 and 1860, nearly all of them desperately poor and often weakened by hunger and disease. Potato blight struck Ireland in 1845 and returned repeatedly in subsequent years, spreading a catastrophic famine throughout the island. Many of the lucky ones, half-starved, crowded into the holds of ships and set out for America, where they congregated in northeastern cities. As one immigrant group declared, "All we want is to get out of Ireland; we must be better anywhere than here."

Roughly three out of four Irish immigrants worked as laborers or domestic servants. Irish men dug canals, loaded ships, built railroad tracks, and took what other work they could find. Irish women hired out to cook, wash and iron, mind children, and clean house. Almost all Irish immigrants were Catholic, a fact that set them apart from the overwhelmingly Protestant native-born residents. Many natives regarded the Irish as hard-drinking, obstreperous, half-civilized folk. Such views lay behind the discrimination that often excluded Irish immigrants from better jobs. Job announcements commonly stated, "No Irish need apply." Despite such prejudices, native residents hired Irish immigrants because they accepted low pay and worked hard.

In America's labor-poor economy, Irish laborers could earn in one day wages that would require several weeks' work in Ireland, if work could be found there. In America, one immigrant explained in 1853, there was "plenty of work and plenty of wages plenty to eat and no land lords thats enough what more does a man want." But some immigrants wanted more, especially respect and decent working conditions. One immigrant complained that he was "a slave for the Americans as the generality of the Irish . . . are."

Such testimony illustrates that the free-labor system, whether for immigrants or native-born laborers, often did not live up to the optimistic vision outlined by Abraham Lincoln and others. Many wage laborers could not realistically aspire to become independent, self-sufficient property holders, despite the claims of free-labor proponents.

Reforming Self and Society

The emphasis on self-discipline and individual effort at the core of the free-labor ideal pervaded America in the 1840s and 1850s. Many Americans believed that insufficient self-control caused the most important social problems of the era. Evangelical Protestants struggled to control individuals' propensity to sin, and temperance advocates exhorted drinkers to control their urge for alcohol. In the midst of the worldly disruptions of geographic expansion and economic change, evangelicals brought more Americans than ever before into churches. Historians estimate that church members accounted for about one-third of the American population by midcentury. Most Americans remained outside churches, as did Abraham Lincoln. But the influence of evangelical religion reached far beyond those who belonged to churches. The evangelical temperament—a conviction of righteousness coupled with energy, self-discipline, and faith that the world could be improved—animated most reformers.

A few activists pointed out that certain fundamental injustices lay beyond the reach of self-control. Transcendentalists and utopians believed that perfection could be attained only by rejecting the competitive values of the larger society. Women's rights activists and abolitionists sought to reverse the subordination of women and to eliminate the enslavement of blacks by changing society. They confronted the daunting challenge of repudiating widespread assumptions about male supremacy and white supremacy and somehow subverting the entrenched institutions that reinforced those assumptions: the family and slavery.

The Pursuit of Perfection: Transcendentalists and Utopians

A group of New England writers that came to be known as transcendentalists believed that individuals should not conform to the materialistic world or to some abstract notion of religion. Instead, people should look within themselves for truth and guidance. The leading transcendentalist, Ralph Waldo Emerson—an essayist, poet, and lecturer—proclaimed that the power of the solitary individual was nearly limitless. Henry David Thoreau, Margaret Fuller, and other transcendentalists agreed with Emerson that "if the single man plant himself indomitably on his instincts, and there abide, the huge world will come round to him." In many ways, transcendentalism represented less an alternative to the values of mainstream society than an exaggerated form of the rampant individualism of the age.

Unlike transcendentalists, a few reformers tried to change the world by organizing utopian communities. Although these communities never involved more than a few thousand people, the activities of their members demonstrated both their dissatisfactions with the larger society and their efforts to realize their visions of perfection. Some communities functioned essentially as retreats for those who did not want to sever their ties with the larger society. Brook Farm, organized in 1841 in West Roxbury, Massachusetts, provided a short-lived haven for literary and artistic New Englanders who agreed to balance bookish pursuits with manual labor.

Other communities set out to become models of perfection that they hoped would point the way toward a better life for everyone. During the 1840s, more than two dozen communities—principally in New York, New Jersey, Pennsylvania, and Ohio—organized around the ideas of Charles Fourier, a French critic of contemporary society. Members of these Fourierist communities (or *phalanxes*, as they were called) believed that individualism and competition were evils that denied the basic truth that "men . . . are brothers and not competitors." Fourierist phalanxes tried to replace competition with harmonious cooperation based on communal ownership of property. The Fourierist communities failed to achieve their ambitious goals. Few survived more than two or three years.

The Oneida community went beyond the Fourierist notion of communalism. John Humphrey Noyes, the charismatic leader of Oneida, believed that individuals who had achieved salvation were literally without sin. The larger society's commitment to private property, however, made even saints greedy and selfish. Noyes believed that the root of private property lay in marriage, in men's conviction that their wives were their exclusive property. With a substantial inheritance, Noyes organized the Oneida community in New York in 1848 to practice what he called "complex marriage." Sexual intercourse was permitted between any man and woman in the community who had been saved. Noyes also required all members to relinquish their economic property to the community, which developed a lucrative business manufacturing animal traps. Oneida's sexual and economic communalism attracted several hundred members, but most of their neighbors considered Oneidans adulterers, blasphemers, and worse. Yet the practices that set Oneida apart from its mainstream neighbors also

MARY CRAGIN, ONEIDA WOMAN
Mary Cragin, one of the founding members of the Oneida community, had a passionate sexual relationship with John Humphrey Noyes even before the community was organized. Within the bounds of complex marriage as practiced by the Oneidans, Cragin's magnetic sexuality made her a favorite partner of many men. In her journal, Cragin confessed that "every evil passion was very strong in me from my childhood, sexual desire, love of dress and admiration, deceit, anger, pride." Oneida, however, transformed evil passion to holy piety. Cragin wrote, "In view of [God's] goodness to me and of his desire that I should let him fill me with himself, I yield and offer myself, to be penetrated by his spirit, and desire that love and gratitude may inspire my heart so that I shall sympathize with his pleasure in the thing, before my personal pleasure begins, knowing that it will increase my capability for happiness." Oneida's sexual practices were considered outrageous and sinful by almost all other Americans. Even Oneidans did not agree with all of Noyes's ideas about sex. "There is no reason why [sex] should not be done in public as much as music and dancing," he declared. It would display the art of sex, he explained, and watching "would give pleasure to a great many of the older people who now have nothing to do with the matter." Nonetheless, public sex never caught on among Oneidans.
Oneida Community Mansion House/James Demarest.

strengthened the community, and it survived long after the Civil War.

Women's Rights Activists

Women participated in the many reform activities that grew out of evangelical churches. Women church members outnumbered men two to one, and they worked to put their religious ideas into practice by joining peace, temperance, antislavery, and other societies. Involvement in reform organizations gave a few women activists practical experience in such political arts as speaking in public, running a meeting, drafting resolutions, and circulating petitions. Along with such experience came confidence. Abolitionist Lydia Maria Child pointed out in 1841 that "those who urged women to become missionaries and form tract societies . . . have changed the household utensil to a living energetic being and they have no spell to turn it into a broom again."

In 1848, about one hundred reformers led by Elizabeth Cady Stanton and Lucretia Mott, gathered at Seneca Falls, New York, for the first women's rights convention in the United States. The Seneca Falls Declaration of Sentiments proclaimed that "the history of mankind is a history of repeated injuries and usurpations on the part of man toward woman, having in direct object the establishment of an absolute tyranny over her." In the style of the Declaration of Independence, the Seneca Falls Declaration listed the ways women had been discriminated against. Through the tyranny of male supremacy, men "endeavored in every way that [they] could to destroy her confidence in her own powers, to lessen her self-respect, and to make her willing to lead a dependent and abject life." The Declaration demanded that women "have immediate admission to all the rights and privileges which belong to them as citizens of the United States," particularly the "inalienable right to the elective franchise."

Nearly two dozen other women's rights conventions assembled before 1860 repeatedly calling for suffrage. But they had difficulty receiving a respectful hearing, much less obtaining legislative action. No state came close to permitting women to vote. Nonetheless, the Seneca Falls Declaration served as a path-breaking manifesto of dissent against male supremacy and of support for woman suffrage, which would become the focus of the women's rights movement during the next seventy years.

Abolitionists and the American Ideal

During the 1840s and 1850s, abolitionists continued to struggle to draw the nation's attention to the plight of slaves and the need for emancipation. Former slaves like Frederick Douglass, Henry Bibb, and Sojourner Truth lectured to reform audiences throughout the North about the cruelties of slavery. Abolitionists published newspapers, held conventions, and petitioned Congress. But they never attracted a mass following among white Americans. Many white Northerners became convinced that slavery was wrong, but they still believed that blacks were inferior. Many other white Northerners shared the common view of white Southerners that slavery was necessary and even desirable. The geographic expansion of the nation during the 1840s offered abolitionists an opportunity to link their unpopular ideal to a goal that many white Northerners found much more attractive—limiting the geographic expansion of slavery, an issue that moved to the center of national politics during the 1850s (see chapter 14).

Black leaders rose to prominence in the abolitionist movement during the 1840s and 1850s. African Americans had actively opposed slavery for decades, but a new generation of leaders came to the forefront in these years. Men like Douglass, Henry Highland Garnet, William Wells Brown, and Martin R. Delany became impatient with white abolitionists' appeals to the conscience of the white majority. Garnet proclaimed in 1843 that slaves should rise in insurrection against their masters, an idea that alienated almost all white people. To express their own uncompromising ideas, black abolitionists founded their own newspapers and held their own antislavery conventions, although they still cooperated with sympathetic whites.

The commitment of black abolitionists to battling slavery grew out of their own experiences with white supremacy. The 250,000 free African Americans in the North and West constituted less than 2 percent of the total population. They confronted the humiliations of racial discrimination in virtually every arena of daily life: at work, at school, at church, in shops, in the streets, on trains, in hotels. Only four states (Maine, Massachusetts, New Hampshire, and Vermont) permitted black men to vote; New York imposed a special property-holding requirement on black—but not white—voters, effectively excluding most black men

ABOLITIONIST MEETING
This rare daguerreotype was made by Ezra Greenleaf Weld in August 1850 at an abolitionist meeting in Cazenovia, New York. Frederick Douglass, who had escaped from slavery in Maryland twelve years earlier, is seated on the platform next to the woman at the table. One of the nation's most brilliant and eloquent abolitionists, Douglass also supported equal rights for women. The man immediately behind Douglass gesturing with his outstretched arm is Gerrit Smith, a wealthy New Yorker and militant abolitionist whose funds supported many reform activities. Note the two black women in similar clothing on either side of Smith and the white woman next to Douglass. Most white Americans considered such voluntary racial proximity scandalous and promiscuous. What messages did abolitionists attempt to convey by attending such protest meetings?
Collection of the J. Paul Getty Museum, Malibu, Calif.

from the franchise. The pervasive racial discrimination both handicapped and energized black abolitionists. African American leaders organized campaigns against segregation, particularly in transportation and education. Their most notable success came in 1855 when Massachusetts integrated public schools. Elsewhere white supremacy continued unabated.

Outside the public spotlight, free African Americans in the North and West contributed to the antislavery cause by quietly aiding fugitive slaves. Harriet Tubman escaped from slavery in Maryland in 1849 and repeatedly risked her free-

dom and her life to return to the South to escort slaves to freedom. When the opportunity arose, free blacks in the North provided fugitive slaves with food, a safe place to rest, and a helping hand. This "underground railroad" ran mainly through black neighborhoods, black churches, and black homes, an outgrowth of the antislavery sentiment and opposition to white supremacy that unified virtually all African Americans in the North. While a few fortunate southern slaves rode the underground railroad to freedom in the North, millions of other Americans uprooted their families and headed west.

The Westward Movement

The 1840s ushered in an era of rapid westward movement. Until then, the overwhelming majority of Americans lived east of the Mississippi River. To the west, Native Americans inhabited the plains, prairies, and deserts to the rugged coasts of the Pacific. The British claimed Oregon Country, and the Mexican flag flew over the vast expanse of the Southwest. But by 1850, the boundaries of the United States stretched to the Pacific, and the nation had more than doubled its size. By 1860, the great migration had carried four million Americans west of the Mississippi River.

Thomas Jefferson, John Quincy Adams, and other government officials had helped clear the way for the march across the continent by aggressively acquiring territory in the east. The nation's revolution in transportation and communication, its swelling population, and its booming economy propelled the westward surge. But the emigrants themselves conquered the continent. Shock troops of the American empire, frontier settlers craving land took the soil and then lobbied their government to follow them with the flag. The human cost of westward expansion was high. Two centuries of Indian wars east of the Mississippi ended during the 1830s, but the old, fierce struggle between native inhabitant and invader continued for another half century in the West.

Manifest Destiny

Most Americans believed that the superiority of their institutions and white culture bestowed on them a God-given right to spread their civilization across the continent. They imagined the West as a howling wilderness, empty and undeveloped. If they recognized Indians and Mexicans at all, they dismissed them as primitive drags on progress who would have to be redeemed, shoved aside, or exterminated. The sense of uniqueness and mission was as old as the Puritans, but by the 1840s the conviction of superiority had been bolstered by the young nation's amazing success. The West needed the civilizing power of the hammer and plow, the ballot box and pulpit, that had transformed the East, most Americans believed.

In the summer of 1845, New York journalist John L. O'Sullivan coined the term *manifest destiny* as the latest justification for white settlers to take the land they coveted. O'Sullivan was an armchair expansionist, but he took second place to no one in his passion for conquest of the West. He called on Americans to resist any foreign power—British, French, or Mexican—that attempted to thwart "the fulfillment of our manifest destiny to overspread the continent allotted by Providence for the free development of our yearly multiplying millions [and] for the development of the great experiment of liberty and federative self-government entrusted to us." Almost overnight, the magic phrase "manifest destiny" swept the nation and provided an ideological shield for conquering the West.

As important as national pride and racial arrogance were to manifest destiny, economic gain made up its core. Land hunger drew hundreds of thousands of average Americans westward. Some politicians, moreover, had become convinced that national prosperity depended on capturing the rich trade of the Far East. To trade with Asia, the United States needed the Pacific ports that stretched from San Francisco to Puget Sound. No one was more eager to extend American trade in the Pacific than Missouri Senator Thomas Hart Benton. "The sun of civilization must shine across the sea: socially and commercially," he declared. The United States and Asia must "talk together, and trade together. Commerce is a great civilizer." In the 1840s, American economic expansion came wrapped in the rhetoric of uplift and civilization.

Oregon and the Overland Trail

Oregon Country, that vast region bounded on the west by the Pacific, on the east by the Rockies, on the south by the forty-second parallel, and on the north by Russian Alaska, caused the pulse of American expansionists to race (Map 12.2). But Americans were not alone in hungrily eyeing the Pacific Northwest. The British traced their interest—and their rights—to the voyage of Sir Francis Drake, who, they argued, discovered the Oregon coast in 1579. Americans matched the British assertion with historic claims of their own. Unable to agree on ownership, the United States and Great Britain decided in 1818 on a "joint occupation" that would leave Oregon "free and open" to settlement by both countries. A handful of American fur traders and "mountain men" roamed the region in the 1820s, but in the 1830s and 1840s expansionists made Oregon Country an early target of manifest destiny.

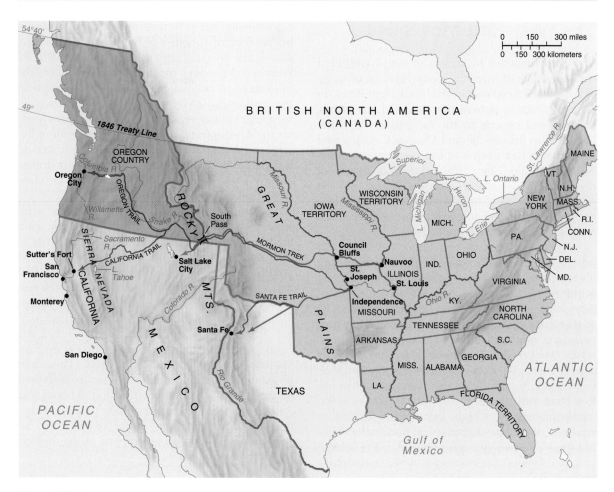

MAP 12.2
Trails to the West
In the 1830s, wagon trains began snaking their way to the Southwest and the Pacific coast. Deep ruts, some of which can still be seen today, soon marked the most popular routes.

By the late 1830s, settlers began to trickle along the Oregon Trail, following a path blazed by the mountain men (see Map 12.2). The first wagon trains hit the trail in 1841, and by 1843 about 1,000 emigrants a year set out from Independence, Missouri. By 1869, when the first transcontinental railroad was completed, something like 350,000 migrants had traveled west to the Pacific in wagon trains.

Emigrants encountered Plains Indians, whose cultures differed markedly from those of the Eastern Woodlands tribes. The quarter of a million Native Americans who populated the area between the Rocky Mountains and the Mississippi River defy easy generalization. Some were farmers who lived peaceful, sedentary lives, but a majority of Plains Indians—the Sioux, Cheyenne, Shoshoni, and Arapaho of the Central Plains and the Kiowa, Wichita, Apache, and Comanche in the Southwest—were horse-mounted, nomadic, nonagricultural peoples whose warriors symbolized the "savage Indian" in the minds of whites.

Horses, which had been brought to the continent by Spaniards in the sixteenth century, permitted the Plains tribes to become highly mobile hunters of buffalo. In time they came to depend on buffalo for most of their food, clothing, shelter, and fuel. As they followed the huge herds over the plains, these peoples bumped into one another. Competition and warfare became a crucial component of their way of life. Young men were introduced to the art of war early, learning to ride ponies at breakneck speed while firing off arrows and, later, rifles with astounding accuracy. "A Comanche on his feet is out of his element," observed George Catlin, an artist of the West, "but the moment he lays his hands upon his horse, I doubt very much whether any people in the world can surpass [him]."

Plains Indians struck fear in the hearts of whites on the wagon trains. But Native Americans had far more to fear from whites. Indians killed fewer than four hundred emigrants on the trail between 1840 and 1860, while whites proved to be deadly to the Indians. Even though they were usually just passing through on their way to the Pacific slope, whites brought alcohol and disease, especially epidemics of smallpox, measles, cholera, and scarlet fever. Moreover, whites killed the buffalo, slaughtering hundreds of thousands for sport. Buffalo still numbered some twelve million in 1860, but the herds were shrinking rapidly, intensifying conflict among the Plains Indians.

As the number of wagon trains increased, emigrants insisted that the federal government provide them more protection. The government responded by constructing a chain of forts along the trail. More important, the United States adopted a new Indian policy of "concentration." To clear the way, the government rescinded the "permanent" buffer it had granted the Indians west of the ninety-fifth meridian, which was only two or three hundred miles west of the Mississippi River. Then, in 1851, it called the Plains tribes to a conference at Fort Laramie, Wyoming. Some ten thousand Dakota, Sioux, Arapaho, Cheyenne, Crow, and other Indians showed up, hopeful that something could be done

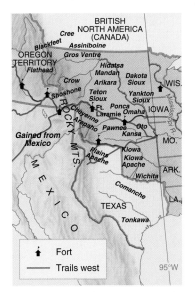

Plains Indians and Trails West in the 1840s and 1850s

to protect them from the ravages of the wagon trains. Instead, government negotiators persuaded the chiefs to sign agreements restricting their people to specific areas that whites promised they would never violate. This policy of isolation became the seedbed for the subsequent policy of reservations. But whites would not keep out of Indian territory, and Indians would not easily give up their traditional way of life. Competition meant warfare for decades to come.

Still, Indians threatened emigrants less than life on the trail did. The men, women, and children who headed west each spring could count on four to six months of grueling travel. With nearly two thousand miles to go and traveling no more than fifteen miles a day, the pioneers endured parching heat, drought, treacherous rivers, disease, physical and emotional exhaustion, and, if the snows closed the mountain passes before they got through, freezing and starvation. Women sometimes faced the dangers of trailside childbirth. It was said that one could walk from Missouri to the Pacific stepping only on the graves of those who had failed to make it.

Everyone experienced hardships on the trail, but no one felt the burden quite as much as the women who made the trip. Since husbands usually decided to pull up stakes and go west, many wives went involuntarily. One miserable woman, trying to keep her children dry in a rainstorm and to calm them as they listened to Indian shouts, wondered "what had possessed my husband, anyway, that he should have thought of bringing us away out through this God forsaken country." Men viewed the privation as a necessary step to land of their own and an independent life; women tended to judge it by the homes, kin, and friends they had left behind to take up what one called "this wild goose chase."

When men reached Oregon, they usually liked what they found. Oregon is "one of the greatest countries in the world," Richard R. Howard declared. From "the Cascade mountains to the Pacific, the whole country can be cultivated." When women reached Oregon, they found a wilderness. "I had all I could do to keep from asking George to turn around and bring me back home," one woman wrote to her mother in Missouri. Neighbors were few and far between, and the isolation weighed heavily. Moreover, things were in a "primitive state." One young wife set up housekeeping with her new husband with only one stew kettle and

WI-JUN-JON, AN ASSINIBOIN CHIEF
*Pennsylvania-born artist George Catlin, the painter of this 1845 dual portrait, was
present in the Assiniboin village when Wi-Jun-Jon returned from Washington, D.C.,
wearing the military uniform that President Andrew Jackson had presented to him. His
uniform and ceaseless boasting bred so much dislike and distrust that a young warrior
from a nearby tribe murdered him. Catlin was convinced that the western Indian
cultures he had begun observing in the 1830s would soon disappear, and he sought to
document Indian life through hundreds of paintings and prints.*
Library of Congress.

www.bedfordstmartins.com/roarkcompact SEE THE ONLINE STUDY GUIDE for more help in
analyzing these images.

three knives. Necessity blurred the traditional division between men's and women's work. "I am maid of all traids," one busy woman remarked in 1853. Work seemed unending. "I am a very old woman," remarked twenty-nine-year-old Sarah Everett. "My face is thin sunken and wrinkled, my hands bony withered and hard." As one wife observed, "A woman that can not endure almost as much as a horse has no business here."

Despite the ordeal of the trail and the difficulties of starting from scratch, emigrants kept coming. By 1845, Oregon counted five thousand Amer-

PIONEER FAMILY ON THE TRAIL WEST
In 1860, W. G. Chamberlain photographed these unidentified travelers momentarily at rest by the Upper Arkansas River in Colorado. We do not know their fates, but we can hope that they fared better than the Sager family, Henry, Naomi, and their six daughters, who set out from St. Joseph, Missouri, in 1844. "Father," one of his daughters remembered, "was one of those restless men who are not content to remain in one place long at a time. [He] had been talking of going to Texas. But mother, hearing much said about the healthfulness of Oregon, preferred to go there." Still far from Oregon, Henry Sager died of fever, and twenty-six days later, Naomi died, leaving seven children, the last delivered on the trail. The Sager children, under the care of other families in the wagon train, pressed on. After traveling 2,000 miles in seven months, the migrants arrived in Oregon, where a couple named the Whitmans, whose daughter had drowned, adopted all of the Sager children.
Denver Public Library, Western History Division # F3226.

ican settlers. And from the beginning, they clamored for the protection of the U.S. government.

The Mormon Migration

Not every wagon train heading west was bound for the Pacific slope. One remarkable group of religious emigrants chose to settle in the heart of the arid West. Halting near the Great Salt Lake in what was

then Mexican territory, the Mormons deliberately chose the remote site as a refuge. After years of persecution in the East, they sought religious freedom and communal security in the West.

In 1830, Joseph Smith Jr., who was only twenty-four, published *The Book of Mormon* and founded the Church of Jesus Christ of Latter-Day Saints (the Mormons). A decade earlier, the upstate New York farm boy had begun to have visions and revelations that were followed, he said, by a visit from an angel who led him to golden tablets buried near his home. With the aid of magic stones, he translated the mysterious language on the tablets. What was revealed was *The Book of Mormon*. It told the story of an ancient Christian civilization in the New World and predicted the appearance of an American prophet who would reestablish Jesus Christ's undefiled kingdom in America. Converts, attracted to the promise of a pure faith in the midst of antebellum America's social turmoil and rampant materialism, flocked to the new church.

"Gentile" neighbors branded Mormons heretics and resented what they considered their religious self-righteousness and their sympathy toward abolitionists and Indians. Persecution drove Smith and his followers from New York to Ohio, then to Missouri, and finally in 1839 to Nauvoo, Illinois, where they built a prosperous community of fifteen thousand. But dissenters within the church accused Smith of advocating plural marriage (polygamy) and published an exposé of the practice. Non-Mormons caught wind of the controversy and eventually arrested Smith and his brother. On June 27, 1844, a mob stormed the jail and shot both men dead.

The embattled church turned to an extraordinary new leader, Brigham Young, who immediately began to plan the exodus of his people from Illinois. In 1846, traveling in 3,700 wagons, twelve thousand Mormons made their way to eastern Iowa and eventually to their new home beside the Great Salt Lake. Young described it as a barren waste, "the paradise of the lizard, the cricket and the rattlesnake." Within ten years, however, the Mormons developed an efficient irrigation system and made the desert bloom. They accomplished the feat through cooperative labor, not the individualistic and competitive enterprise common among most emigrants. Under the stern leadership of Young and other church leaders, the Mormons built a thriving community.

In 1850, only three years after its founding, Deseret, as the Mormons called their kingdom, became annexed to the United States as Utah Territory. But what focused the nation's attention on the Latter-Day Saints was the announcement by Brigham Young in 1852 that many Mormons practiced polygamy. Although only one Mormon man in five had more than one wife (Young had twenty-three), Young's public statement caused an outcry that forced the government to establish its authority in Utah. In 1857, twenty-five hundred U.S. troops in-vaded Salt Lake City in what was known as the Mormon War. The bloodless occupation illustrates that most Americans viewed the Mormons as a threat to American morality, law, and institutions. The invasion did not dislodge the Mormon Church from its central place in Utah, however, and for years to come most Americans perceived the Mormon settlement as a strange, and suitably isolated, place.

The Mexican Borderlands

In the Mexican Southwest, westward-moving Anglo-American pioneers confronted northern-moving Spanish-speaking frontiersmen. On this frontier as elsewhere, cultures, interests, and aspirations collided. Since 1821, when Mexico won its independence from Spain, the Mexican flag had flown over the vast expanse that stretched from the Gulf of Mexico to the Pacific and from Oregon Country to Guatemala. Mexico's borders remained ill defined, and its northern provinces were sparsely populated. Moreover, severe problems plagued the young nation: civil wars, economic crises, quarrels between the Roman Catholic Church and the state, and devastating raids by the Comanche, Apache, and Kiowa. Mexico found it increasingly difficult to defend its borderlands, especially when faced with a northern neighbor that was convinced of its superiority and bent on territorial acquisition.

The American assault began quietly. In the 1820s, when Anglo-American trappers, traders, and settlers began drifting into Mexico's far northern provinces, they discovered that their newly independent neighbor was eager for American business. Santa Fe, a remote outpost in the province of New Mexico, became a magnet for American enterprise. American traders gathered each spring at Independence, Missouri, for the long trek southwest along the Santa Fe Trail (see Map 12.2). They crammed their wagons with inexpensive American manufactured goods and returned with Mexican silver, furs, and mules.

The Mexican province of Texas attracted a flood of Americans who had settlement, not long-distance trade, on their minds (Map 12.3). The Mexican government, which wanted to populate and develop its northern territory, granted the American Stephen F. Austin a huge tract of land, and in the 1820s he established a thriving settlement along the Brazos River. Land was cheap—only ten cents an acre—and thousands of farmers poured over the

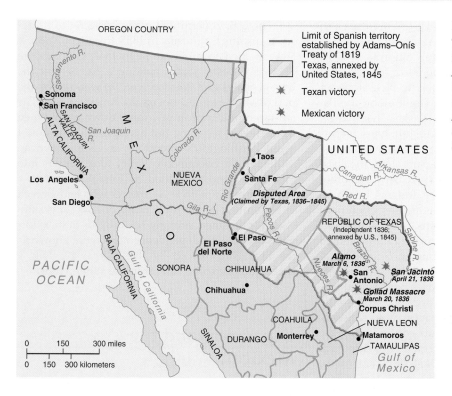

M A P 12.3

Texas and Mexico in the 1830s

As Americans spilled into lightly populated and loosely governed northern Mexico, Texas and then other Mexican provinces became contested territory.

border. Most of the migrants were Southerners, who brought cotton and slaves with them. By 1835, the number of American settlers—free and slave—in Texas had reached thirty thousand, while the Tejano (Spanish-speaking) population was less than eight thousand. Most Anglo-American settlers were not Roman Catholic, did not speak Spanish, and cared little about assimilating into a culture that was so different from their own. In 1829, the Mexican government sought to arrest further immigration with an emancipation proclamation, which it hoped would make Texas less attractive. The settlers sidestepped the decree by calling their slaves servants, but settlers had other grievances, most significantly the puny voice they had in local government. General Antonio López de Santa Anna all but extinguished that voice when he seized political power and concentrated authority in Mexico City.

Faced with what they considered tyranny, the Texan settlers rebelled and declared the independent Republic of Texas. Santa Anna took the field and in February 1836 arrived at the outskirts of San Antonio with nearly 6,000 troops. The rebels, who included the Tennessee frontiersman Davy Crockett and the Louisiana adventurer Jim Bowie, as well

as a number of Tejanos, took refuge in the old Franciscan mission, the Alamo. Wave after wave of Mexicans crashed against the walls until the attackers finally broke through and killed all 187 defenders. A few weeks later in the small town of Goliad, Mexican forces surrounded and captured a garrison of 365 Texans. Following orders from Santa Anna, Mexican firing squads executed the men as pirates. But in April 1836 at San Jacinto, Santa Anna suffered a crushing defeat at the hands of forces under General Sam Houston. Texans had succeeded in establishing their Lone Star Republic, and the following year the United States recognized the independence of Texas from Mexico.

Texas War for Independence, 1836

The distant Mexican province of California also caught the eye of a few Anglo-Americans. Spain had first extended its influence into California in 1769, when it sent a naval expedition north from Mexico to San Francisco Bay in an effort to block Russian fur traders who were moving south along the Pacific Coast from their base in Alaska. The Spanish built garrisoned towns (*presidios*), but, more important, they constructed a string of twenty-one missions, spaced a day's journey apart, along the coast from San Diego to Sonoma. Junípero Serra and other Franciscan friars converted the Indians to Christianity and drew them into the life and often hard agricultural labor of the missions. In 1824, in an effort to increase Mexican migration to thinly settled California, the Mexican government granted *ranchos*—huge estates devoted to cattle raising—to new settlers. *Rancheros* ruled over near-feudal empires worked by Indians whose condition sometimes approached that of slaves. Not satisfied, *rancheros* coveted the vast lands controlled by the Franciscan missions. In 1834, they persuaded the government to confiscate the missions and make their lands available to new settlement, a development that accelerated the decline of California Indians. Devastated by disease, the Indians, who numbered approximately 300,000 when the Spanish arrived in 1769, declined to half that number by 1846.

Despite the efforts of the Mexican government, California in 1840 counted a population of only 7,000 Mexican settlers. Non-Mexican settlers numbered only 380, but among them were Americans who championed manifest destiny. Thomas O. Larkin, a prosperous merchant, John Marsh, a successful *ranchero* in the San Joaquin Valley, and others became boosters who sought to attract Americans from Oregon Country to California. The first overland party arrived in California in 1841. Thereafter, wagon after wagon followed the California Trail, which forked off from the Oregon Trail near the Snake River and led through the Sierra Nevada at Lake Tahoe (see Map 12.2). As the trickle of Americans became a river, Mexican officials grew alarmed, for as a New York newspaper put it in 1845, "Let the tide of emigration flow toward California and the American population will soon be sufficiently numerous to play the Texas game." Not all Americans in California wanted to play the "Texas game," but many dreamed of living again under the American flag.

The U.S. government made no secret of its desire to acquire California. In 1835, President Andrew Jackson tried to purchase it. In 1842, Commodore Thomas Catesby Jones, hearing a rumor that the United States and Mexico were at war, seized the port of Monterey and ran up the American flag. The red-faced officer promptly ran it down again when he learned of his error. But his actions left no doubt about Washington's intentions. In 1846, American settlers in the Sacramento Valley took matters into their own hands. Prodded by John C. Frémont, a former army captain and explorer who had arrived in December 1845 with a party of sixty buckskin-clad frontiersmen spoiling for a fight, the Californians raised an independence movement known as the Bear Flag Revolt. By then, James K. Polk, a champion of expansion, sat in the White House.

Expansion and the Mexican War

Although emigrants acted as the advanced guard of American empire, there was nothing automatic about the U.S. annexation of territory in the West. Acquiring territory required political action, and in the 1840s the difficult problems of Texas, Oregon, and the Mexican borderlands intruded into national politics. The politics of expansion became entangled with sectionalism and the slavery question and thrust the United States into dangerous diplomatic crises with Great Britain and Mexico.

Aggravation between Mexico and the United States escalated to open antagonism in 1845 when the United States annexed Texas. Absorbing territory still claimed by Mexico ruptured diplomatic relations between the two countries and set the stage for war. But it was President James K. Polk's insistence on having Mexico's other northern provinces that made war certain. The war was not as easy as Polk anticipated, but it ended in American victory and acquisition of a new American West.

The Politics of Expansion

The complicated issues of westward expansion and the nation's boundaries ended up on the desk of John Tyler when he became president in April 1841. The Whig William Henry Harrison had been elected president in 1840, but one month after he took office, he died. Tyler, nominally a Whig but actually a Democrat in his political convictions, spent much of his administration beating back the Whig Henry Clay's efforts to turn his party's American System —protective tariffs, a national bank, and internal improvements—into law.

But the issue that stirred John Tyler's blood, and that of much of the nation, was Texas. Texans had sought admission to the Union almost since their independence from Mexico in 1836, but Tyler, an ardent expansionist, understood that Texas was a dangerous issue. Any suggestion of adding another slave state to the Union brought many Northerners to a boil. Annexing Texas also risked precipitating war because Mexico had never relinquished its claim to its lost province.

Cold-shouldered by the United States, Texans explored Great Britain's interest in recognition. Britain was eager to keep Texas independent. In Britain's eyes, Texas provided a buffer against American expansion and a new market for English manufactured goods. American officials worried that Britain's real object was adding Texas to the British Empire. This volatile mix of threat, fear, and opportunity convinced Tyler to risk negotiations with Texas, and he worked vigorously to annex the republic before his term expired. His efforts pushed Texas and the slavery issue to the center of national politics.

In April 1844, after months of secret negotiations between Texas and the Tyler administration, the new secretary of state, John C. Calhoun, laid an annexation treaty before the Senate. But when Calhoun linked annexation to the defense of slavery, he doomed the treaty. Howls of protest erupted across the North. When the Senate soundly rejected the treaty, it appeared that Tyler had succeeded only in inflaming sectional conflict.

The issue of Texas had not died down by the 1844 elections. Henry Clay looked forward to receiving the Whig nomination and waging his campaign on the old Whig economic principles that Tyler had frustrated. But in an effort to appeal to northern voters, Clay came out against the immediate annexation of Texas. "Annexation and war with Mexico are identical," he declared. When news of Clay's statement reached Andrew Jackson at his plantation in Tennessee, he chuckled, "Clay [is] a dead political Duck." In Jackson's shrewd judgment, no man who opposed annexation could be

elected president. But the Whig Party paid no attention and nominated Clay.

The Democrats chose James K. Polk of Tennessee. Polk was as strong for the annexation of Texas as Clay was against it. To make Texas annexation palatable to Northerners, the Democrats shrewdly yoked Texas to Oregon, thus tapping the desire for expansion in the free states of the North as well in the slave states of the South. The Democratic platform called for the "reannexation of Texas" and the "reoccupation of Oregon." The suggestion that the United States was merely reasserting its existing rights was poor history but good politics. According to the Democratic formula, Texas annexation did not give an advantage to slavery and the South. Linked to Oregon, Texas expanded America to the advantage of the entire nation.

During the campaign, Clay finally recognized the groundswell for expansion, and he waffled on Texas, hinting that he might accept annexation under certain circumstances. His retreat won little support in the South and only succeeded in alienating antislavery opinion in the North. James G. Birney, the candidate of the fledgling Liberty Party, picked up the votes of thousands of disillusioned Clay supporters. In the November election, Polk received 170 electoral votes and Clay 105. New York's 35 electoral votes proved critical to Clay's defeat. A shift of just one-third of Birney's 15,000 votes to Clay would have given him the state and the presidency.

The nation did not have to wait for Polk's inauguration to see results from his victory. One month after the election, President Tyler announced that the Democratic triumph provided a mandate for the annexation of Texas "promptly and immediately." In February 1845, after a fierce debate between antislavery and proslavery forces, Congress approved a joint resolution offering the Republic of Texas admission to the United States. Texas entered as the fifteenth slave state.

Tyler had delivered Texas, but Polk had promised Oregon, too. Westerners particularly demanded that the new president make good on the Democrats' campaign slogan—"Fifty-four Forty or Fight"—that is, all of Oregon, right up to Alaska (54°40' being the southern latitude of Russian Alaska). But Polk was close to war with Mexico and could not afford a simultaneous war with Britain over its claims to Canada. After the initial bluster, therefore, Polk buried the Democrats' campaign promise and renewed an old offer to divide Oregon along the forty-ninth parallel. When Britain accepted the compromise, some cried betrayal, but most Americans celebrated the agreement that gave the nation an enormous territory peacefully. Besides, when the Senate finally approved the treaty in June 1846, the United States and Mexico were already at war.

The Mexican War, 1846–1848

From the day he entered the White House, Polk craved Mexico's remaining northern provinces: California and New Mexico, land that today makes up California, Nevada, and Utah, most of New Mexico and Arizona, and parts of Wyoming and Colorado. Polk hoped to buy the territory, but the Mexicans refused to sell off their country. A furious Polk concluded that it would take military force to realize the United States' manifest destiny.

Polk had already ordered General Zachary Taylor to march his 4,000-man Army of Occupation of Texas from its position on the Nueces River, the southern boundary of Texas according to the Mexicans, to the banks of the Rio Grande 150 miles south, the boundary claimed by Texans. The Mexican general in Matamoros viewed the American advance as aggression and ordered Taylor back to the Nueces. Taylor refused, and on April 25 Mexican cavalry attacked a party of American soldiers, killing or wounding 16 and capturing the rest. Even before news of the battle arrived in Washington, Polk had already obtained his cabinet's approval of a war message.

On May 11, 1846, the president told Congress, "Mexico has passed the boundary of the United States, has invaded our territory, and shed American blood upon American soil." Thus "war exists, and, notwithstanding all our efforts to avoid it, exists by the act of Mexico herself." Two days later, Congress passed a declaration of war and began raising an army. Despite years of saber rattling toward Mexico and Britain, the American army was pitifully small, only 7,400 soldiers. Faced with the nation's first foreign war, up against a Mexican army that numbered more than 30,000, Polk called for volunteers. Men rushed to the colors. Eventually, more than 112,000 white Americans (blacks were banned) joined the army to fight in Mexico.

Despite the outpouring of support, the war divided the nation. Northerners were not nearly as hot-blooded about the war as Southerners. North-

ern Whigs in particular loudly condemned the war as the unwarranted bullying of a weak nation by its greedy expansionist neighbor. On January 12, 1848, a gangly freshman Whig representative from Illinois rose from his back-row seat in the House of Representatives to deliver his first important speech in Congress. Before Abraham Lincoln sat down, he had questioned the president's intelligence, honesty, and sanity. President Polk simply ignored the upstart representative, but antislavery, antiwar Whigs kept up the attack throughout the conflict. In their effort to undercut national support, they labeled it "Mr. Polk's War."

Since most Americans backed the war, it was not really Polk's war, but the president acted as if it were. Although he had no military experience, he directed the war personally. Working eighteen hours a day, Polk established overall strategy and oversaw the details of military campaigns. He planned a short war in which American armies would occupy Mexico's northern provinces and defeat the Mexican army in a decisive battle or two, after which Mexico would sue for peace and the United States would keep the territory its armies occupied.

And, indeed, Polk's strategy seemed to work at first. In May 1846, Zachary Taylor's troops drove south from the Rio Grande and routed the Mexican army, first on the plain of Palo Alto and then in a palm-filled ravine known as Resaca de la Palma (Map 12.4). "Old Rough and Ready," as Taylor was affectionately known among his adoring troops, became an instant war hero. Polk rewarded Taylor for his victories by making him commander of the Mexican campaign.

A second prong of the campaign to occupy Mexico's northern provinces centered on Colonel Stephen Watts Kearny, who led a 1,700-man army from Missouri into New Mexico. Without firing a shot, American forces took Santa Fe in August 1846. Kearny promptly proclaimed New Mexico American territory and with 300 troops headed for California. Three months later, Kearny's army marched into San Diego and into a major Mexican rebellion against American rule. In January 1847, after several clashes, the American forces occupied Los Angeles. California and New Mexico were in American hands.

By then, Taylor had driven deep into the interior of Mexico. In September 1846, after a five-day siege and house-to-house fighting, he took the fortified city of Monterrey. With reinforcements and

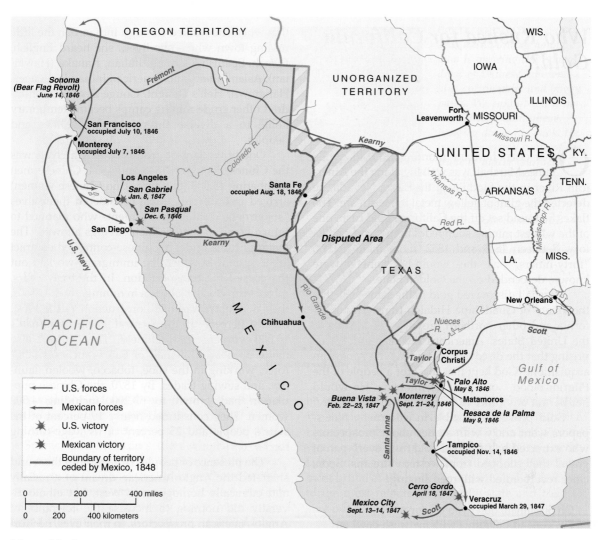

M A P 12.4

The Mexican War, 1846–1848

American and Mexican soldiers skirmished across much of northern Mexico, but the major battles took place between the Rio Grande and Mexico City.

fresh supplies, Taylor pushed his 5,000 troops southwest, where the Mexican hero of the Alamo, General Antonio López de Santa Anna, was concentrating a huge army of 21,000, which he hoped would strike a decisive blow against the invaders from the north.

In February 1847, Taylor's troops met Santa Anna's at Buena Vista. Superior American artillery and accurate musket fire won the day, but the Americans suffered heavy casualties, including Henry Clay Jr., the son of the man who had opposed Texas

annexation for fear it would precipitate war. But the Mexicans suffered even greater losses.

The series of uninterrupted victories in northern Mexico fed the American troops' sense of superiority and very nearly led to a feeling of invincibility. "No American force has ever thought of being defeated by any amount of Mexican troops," one soldier declared. The Americans worried about other hazards, however. "I can assure you that fighting is the least dangerous & arduous part of a soldier's life," one young man said. Of the 13,000

BATTLE OF PALO ALTO

The battle of Palo Alto, fought in May 1846 and captured here by lithographer Carl Nebel, was the first full-scale battle the U.S. Army had fought since the War of 1812. Here we see General Zachary Taylor astride Old Whitey, as he directs the action from the right foreground. On the extreme right Colonel David Twiggs's infantry repulses Anastasio Torrejon's cavalry. On the left smoke from the grass fire conceals 150 additional Mexican cavalrymen. Ferocious American artillery won the day. "The American artillery," one Mexican reported, "much superior to ours, made terrible ravages in the Mexican ranks. . . . The troops, drained by the needless deaths, pleaded to go before the enemy's bayonets and die bravely in close range."

Amon Carter Museum of Western Art, Fort Worth, Texas.

American soldiers who died in Mexico (some 50,000 Mexicans died), only 2,000 fell to Mexican bullets and shells. Disease killed most of the others. Medicine was so primitive and conditions so harsh that army doctors could do little. As a Tennessee man observed, "nearly all who take sick die."

Victory in Mexico

Although Americans won battle after battle, President Polk's strategy misfired. Despite its loss of territory and men, Mexico determinedly refused to trade land for peace. One American soldier captured the Mexican mood: "They cannot submit to be deprived of California after the loss of Texas, and nothing but the conquest of their Capital will force them to such a humiliation." Polk had arrived at the same conclusion. Zachary Taylor had not proven decisive enough for Polk, and the president tapped another general to carry the war to Mexico City. While Taylor occupied the north, General Winfield Scott would land his army on the Gulf coast of Mexico and march 250 miles inland to the capital. Polk's plan entailed enormous risk; it meant that Scott would have to cut himself off from supplies on the coast and lead his men deep into enemy country against a numerically superior foe.

After months of careful planning and the skillful coordination of army and navy, an amphibious landing near Veracruz put 8,600 American troops ashore in five hours without the loss of a single life. After eighty-eight hours of furious shelling, Veracruz surrendered. Scott immediately began preparations for the march west. Transportation alone posed enormous problems. His army required 9,300 wagons and 17,000 pack mules, 500,000 bushels of oats and corn, and 100 pounds of blister ointment before it could begin the mountainous journey. In early April 1847, the army moved out, following the path that had been trodden more than three centuries earlier by Hernán Cortés.

Meanwhile, after the frightful defeat at Buena Vista, Santa Anna had returned to Mexico City. He rallied his ragged troops and marched them east to set a trap for Scott in the mountain pass at Cerro Gordo. But the Americans knifed through Mexican lines, almost capturing Santa Anna, who fled the field on foot. So complete was the victory that Scott gloated to Taylor, "Mexico no longer has an army." But ever resilient, Santa Anna again rallied the Mexican army. Some 30,000 troops took up defensive positions on the outskirts of Mexico City, where

MAP 12.5

Territorial Expansion by 1860

Less than a century after its founding, the United States had spread from the Atlantic seaboard to the Pacific Ocean. War, purchase, and diplomacy had gained a continent.

READING THE MAP: List the countries from which the United States acquired land. Which nation lost the most land because of U.S. expansion?

CONNECTIONS: Who coined the phrase "manifest destiny"? When? What does it mean? What areas targeted for expansion were debated during the presidential campaign of 1844?

www.bedfordstmartins.com/roarkcompact SEE THE ONLINE STUDY GUIDE for more help in analyzing this map.

they hurriedly began melting down church bells to cast new cannon.

In August, Scott began his assault on the Mexican capital. The fighting proved the most brutal of the war. Santa Anna backed his army into the city, fighting each step of the way. At the battle of Churubusco, the Mexicans took 4,000 casualties in a single day and the Americans more than 1,000. At the castle of Chapultepec, American troops scaled the walls and fought the Mexican defenders hand to hand. After Chapultepec, Santa Anna evacuated Mexico City, and on September 14, 1847, General Winfield Scott rode in triumphantly. The ancient capital of the Aztecs had fallen once again to an invading army.

With Mexico City in American hands, Polk sent Nicholas P. Trist, the chief clerk in the State Department, to Mexico to negotiate the peace. On February 2, 1848, Trist and Mexican officials signed the Treaty of Guadalupe Hidalgo. Mexico agreed to give up all claims to Texas above the Rio Grande and to cede the huge provinces of New Mexico and California to the United States. The United States agreed to pay Mexico $15 million and to assume $3.25 million in claims that American citizens had against Mexico. Some Americans clamored for all of Mexico, and others for less, but in March 1848 the Senate ratified the treaty by a vote of thirty-eight to fourteen. The last American soldiers left Mexico a few months later.

Less than three-quarters of a century after its founding, the United States had achieved its self-proclaimed manifest destiny to stretch from the Atlantic to the Pacific (Map 12.5, page 289). With the northern half of Mexico in American hands, California gold, which was discovered almost simultaneously with the transfer of territory, poured into American and not Mexican pockets. (See "Historical Question," page 286.) The war also reinforced the worst stereotypes Mexicans and Americans had of each other. A virulent anti-Yankee sentiment took root in Mexico, while deeply prejudiced views of Mexicans and Mexican culture flourished in the fertile soil of American victory. For Mexico, defeat meant national humiliation, but it also had a positive effect. It generated for the first time a genuine nationalism. In America, victory increased the sense of superiority that was already deeply ingrained.

Conclusion: Free Labor, Free Men

In the 1840s, diplomacy and war handed the United States 1.2 million square miles and more than 1,000 miles of Pacific coastline. To most Americans, vast geographical expansion seemed to be the natural companion of a stunning economic transformation. A cluster of interrelated developments—steam power, railroads, and the growing mechanization of agriculture and manufacturing—resulted in greater productivity, a burst of output from farms and factories, and prosperity for many.

To Northerners, their industrial evolution confirmed the choice they had made to eliminate slavery and to promote free labor as the key to independence, equality, and prosperity. Millions of Northerners, like Abraham Lincoln, could point to personal experience as evidence of the practical truth of the free-labor ideal. But millions of others had different stories to tell. Rather than producing economic equality, the free-labor system saw wealth and poverty continue to rub shoulders. Instead of social independence, more than half of the nation's free-labor workforce toiled for someone else by 1860. Free-labor enthusiasts denied that the problems were built into the system. They argued that most social ills—including poverty and dependency—sprang from individual deficiencies. Consequently, reformers usually focused on the lack of self-control and discipline, on sin and alcohol. They denied that free labor meant exploitation. Slaves suffered, not free workers, they argued. White Southerners, on the other hand, pitied northern free workers, not slaves. By the 1840s, the nation was half slave and half free, and not even victory over Mexico could bridge the deepening differences between North and South.

FOR FURTHER READING ABOUT THE TOPICS IN THIS CHAPTER, see the Online Bibliography at www.bedfordstmartins.com/roarkcompact.

FOR ADDITIONAL FIRST-HAND ACCOUNTS OF THIS PERIOD, see pages 181–195 in Michael Johnson, ed., *Reading the American Past,* Second Edition, Volume I.

TO ASSESS YOUR MASTERY OF THE MATERIAL IN THIS CHAPTER, see the Online Study Guide at www.bedfordstmartins.com/roarkcompact.

CHRONOLOGY

1836   Texas declares independence from Mexico.

1837   John Deere patents his steel plow.

1840s Americans begin harnessing steam power to manufacturing.

Cyrus McCormick and others create practical mechanical reapers.

1841   First wagon trains set out for West on Oregon Trail.

Vice President John Tyler becomes president of the United States when William Henry Harrison dies in office after one month.

1844   Democrat James K. Polk elected president on platform calling for annexation of Texas and Oregon.

Samuel F. B. Morse invents telegraph.

1845   Term *manifest destiny* coined by New York journalist John L. O'Sullivan; used as justification for Anglo-American settlers to take land in West.

United States annexes Texas, which enters Union as slave state.

1846   Bear Flag Revolt, independence movement to secede from Mexico, takes place in California.

May 13. Congress declares war on Mexico.

United States and Great Britain agree to divide Oregon Country at forty-ninth parallel.

1847   Brigham Young leads advance party of Mormons to Great Salt Lake in Utah.

1848   Treaty of Guadalupe Hidalgo ends Mexican War. Mexico gives up all claims to Texas north of Rio Grande and cedes provinces of New Mexico and California to United States.

Oneida community organized in New York.

First women's rights convention in United States takes place at Seneca Falls, New York.

1849   California gold rush begins.

Harriet Tubman escapes from slavery in Maryland.

1850   Mormon community of Deseret annexed to United States as Utah Territory.

1851   Conference in Laramie, Wyoming, between U.S. government and Plains tribes marks beginning of government policy of forcing Indians onto reservations.

Massachusetts integrates public schools as result of campaigns led by African Americans.

CLAY JUG

This ceramic water cooler, made in about 1840, is attributed to Thomas Chandler, a famous potter of Edgefield District, South Carolina. The relatively fine clothes of the African American man and woman portrayed on the vessel suggest that they are house servants. On the wall of the home of Alexander Stephens in Crawfordsville, Georgia, an intriguing letter from Stephens states that two of his favorite slaves are getting married and orders the plantation manager to butcher a hog for their wedding. With its portrait of a couple, a hog, and a jug, it is possible that Stephens commissioned this cooler to commemorate the union.

Potters made vessels for use—they held water and food. Analysis of the form, decoration, and glazes of southern pottery suggests a blend of European, African, and Native American ceramic traditions. Some pottery went beyond the utilitarian and became art. The most renowned slave potter was another Edgefield man by the name of Dave, who skillfully fashioned huge vessels, inscribed poems on their surfaces, and proudly and boldly signed them, "Dave the potter." Although a slave, Dave self-consciously left his mark.

Collection of the High Museum of Art, Atlanta. Purchase in honor of Audrey Shilt, President of the Members Guild of the High Museum of Art, 1996–1997, with funds from the Decorative Arts Endowment & Acquisition Trust 1996.

THE SLAVE SOUTH
1820–1860

13

NAT TURNER WAS BORN A SLAVE IN SOUTHAMPTON COUNTY, VIRGINIA, on October 1, 1800. People in his neighborhood claimed that he had always been different. His parents had noticed special marks on his body, which they said were signs that he was "intended for some great purpose." His master said that he learned to read without being taught. As an adolescent, he adopted a severe lifestyle of Christian devotion and fasting. In his twenties, he received visits from the "Spirit," the same spirit, he believed, that had spoken to the ancient prophets. In time, Nat Turner began to interpret these things to mean that God had appointed him an instrument of divine vengeance for the sin of slaveholding.

In the early morning of August 22, 1831, he set out with six trusted friends—Hark, Henry, Sam, Nelson, Will, and Jack—to punish slave owners and free their suffering slaves. The first blow was that of Nat Turner's ax to the head of his master, Joseph Travis. The rebels killed all of the white men, women, and children they encountered in each household they attacked. By noon, they had visited eleven farms and slaughtered fifty-seven whites and, along the way, added fifty or sixty men to their army. Word spread quickly, however, and soon the militia and hundreds of local whites gathered. By the next day, whites had captured or killed all of the insurgents, except for Nat Turner, who successfully hid out for about ten weeks before being captured in nearby woods. Within a week, he was tried, convicted, and executed. By then, forty-five slaves had stood trial; twenty had been convicted and hanged and another ten had been transported from Virginia. Another hundred or more blacks—rebels and innocent bystanders—had been killed in the whites' frenzied counterattack against the insurrection.

Slave revolts were white Southerners' worst nightmare. Virginia's governor John Floyd asked how Turner with his band of "assassins and murderers" could have assaulted in their sleep the "unsuspecting and defenseless" citizens of "one of the fairest counties in the Commonwealth." Virginians prided themselves on having the "mildest" slavery in the South, but sixty black rebels on a rampage challenged the comforting theory of the contented slave. Nonetheless, whites found explanations that allowed them to feel more at ease. They placed the blame on outside agitators. In 1829, David Walker, a freeborn black man living in Boston, had published his *Appeal . . . to the Colored Citizens of the World*, an invitation to slaves to rise up in bloody rebellion, and copies had fallen into the hands of Virginia slaves. Moreover, on January 1, 1831, William Lloyd Garrison, the Massachusetts abolitionist, had published the first issue of his fiery newspaper, the *Liberator*. But white Virginians also dismissed the rebellion's leader, Nat Turner, as insane. "He is a complete fanatic, or plays his part admirably," wrote Thomas R. Gray, the lawyer who was assigned to defend Turner.

In the months following the insurrection, white Virginians debated the future of slavery in their state. While some expressed substantial doubts, the Virginia legislature reaffirmed the state's determination to beat back threats to white

NAT TURNER
*There are no known contemporary images of Nat Turner. This imagined portrait comes
from William Still's* **The Underground Railroad,** *which was published in 1872. Meeting
secretly at night deep in a forest and thus well out of earshot of whites, an intense
Turner passionately tries to convince four other slaves to join him in rebellion. What do
their faces reveal? What considerations do you suppose entered their calculations about
whether to join Turner? Significantly perhaps, they are holding work tools, not arms.*
Library of Congress.

supremacy. Delegates passed a raft of laws strengthening the institution of slavery and further restricting free blacks. A thirty-year-old professor at the College of William and Mary, Thomas R. Dew, published a vigorous defense of slavery that became the bible of Southerners' proslavery arguments. More than ever, the nation was divided along the "Mason-Dixon line," the surveyors' mark that in colonial times had established the boundary between Maryland and Pennsylvania but half a century later divided the free North and slave South.

Black slavery increasingly dominated the South and shaped it into a distinctive region. In the decades after 1820, Southerners, like Northerners, raced westward, but they spread slavery, cotton, and plantations, whereas Northerners in contrast spread small farms and free labor. Geographic expansion meant that slavery became more vigorous and profitable than ever, embraced more people,

and increased the South's political power. Antebellum Southerners included diverse peoples who at times found themselves at odds with one another—not only slaves and free people, but also women and men; Indians, Africans, and Europeans; and aristocrats and common folk. Nevertheless, beneath this diversity of Southerners there was also forming a distinctively southern society and culture. The South became a slave society, and most white Southerners were proud of it.

The Growing Distinctiveness of the South

From the earliest settlements, inhabitants of southern colonies had shared a great deal with northern colonists. Most whites in both sections were British and Protestant, and they spoke a common language, even if a regional twang or drawl flavored their speech. They shared an exuberant pride in their victorious revolution against British rule. The creation of the new nation under the Constitution in 1789 forged strong political ties that bound all Americans. The beginnings of a national economy fostered economic interdependence and communication across regional boundaries. White Americans everywhere celebrated the achievements of the prosperous young nation, and they looked forward to its seemingly boundless future.

Despite these national similarities, Southerners and Northerners grew increasingly different. The French political observer Alexis de Tocqueville believed he knew why. "I could easily prove," he asserted in 1831, "that almost all the differences which may be noticed between the character of the Americans in the Southern and Northern states have originated in slavery." Slavery made the South different, and it was the differences between the North and the South, not the similarities, that came to shape antebellum American history.

Cotton Kingdom, Slave Empire

In the first half of the nineteenth century, legions of Americans migrated west, but in the South the surge westward was propelled by an insatiable hunger for more and better cotton land. Eager slaveholders seeking virgin acreage for new plantations, struggling farmers looking for patches of good land for small farms, herders and drovers pushing their hogs and cattle toward fresh pastures—anyone who was restless and ambitious felt the pull. Southerners relentlessly pushed westward, until by midcentury the South encompassed nearly a million square miles, much of it planted in cotton.

The South's climate and geography were ideally suited for the cultivation of cotton. Advancing Southerners encountered a variety of terrain, soil, and weather, but the cotton seeds they carried with them were very adaptable. By the 1830s, cotton fields stretched from southern Virginia to central Texas. Production soared, and by 1860 the South produced three-fourths of the world's supply. The South—especially that tier of states from South Carolina west to Texas known as the Lower South—had become the cotton kingdom (Map 13.1).

The cotton kingdom was also a slave empire. The South's cotton boom rested on the backs of slaves, who grew 75 percent of the crop on

plantations, toiling in gangs in broad fields under the direct supervision of whites. As cotton agriculture expanded westward, whites shipped more than 300,000 slaves out of the old seaboard states. Some slaves accompanied masters who were leaving behind worn-out, eroded plantations, but at least two-thirds were victims of a brutal but thriving domestic slave trade. Traders advertised for slaves who were "hearty and well made" and marched black men, women, and children hundreds of miles to the new plantation regions of the Lower South. Cotton, slaves, and plantations moved west together.

The slave population grew enormously. Southern slaves numbered fewer than 700,000 in 1790, about 2 million in 1830, and about 4 million by 1860, an increase of almost 600 percent in seven decades. By 1860, the South contained more slaves than all the other slave societies in the New World combined. The extraordinary growth was not the result of the importation of slaves, which was outlawed in 1808. Instead the slave population grew through natural reproduction. By the nineteenth century, most slaves were black Southerners.

The South in Black and White

By 1860, one in every three Southerners was black (about 4 million blacks and 8 million whites). In the Lower South, the proportion was higher, for whites and blacks lived there in almost equal numbers. In Mississippi and South Carolina, blacks were the majority (Figure 13.1). The contrast with the North was striking: In 1860, only 1 Northerner in 76 was black (about 250,000 blacks to 19 million whites).

The presence of large numbers of African Americans had profound consequences for the South. Southern culture—language, food, music, religion, and even accents—was in part shaped by blacks. But the most direct consequence of the South's biracialism was the response it stimulated in the region's white majority. Southern whites were dedicated to white supremacy. Northern whites were, too, but they lived in a society in which blacks made up barely more than 1 percent of the population. Their commitment to white supremacy lacked the intensity and urgency increasingly felt by white Southerners. White Southerners lived among millions of blacks, whom they simultaneously despised and feared. They despised blacks because they considered them members of an inferior race, further degraded by their status as slaves. They feared blacks because they realized that slaves had every reason

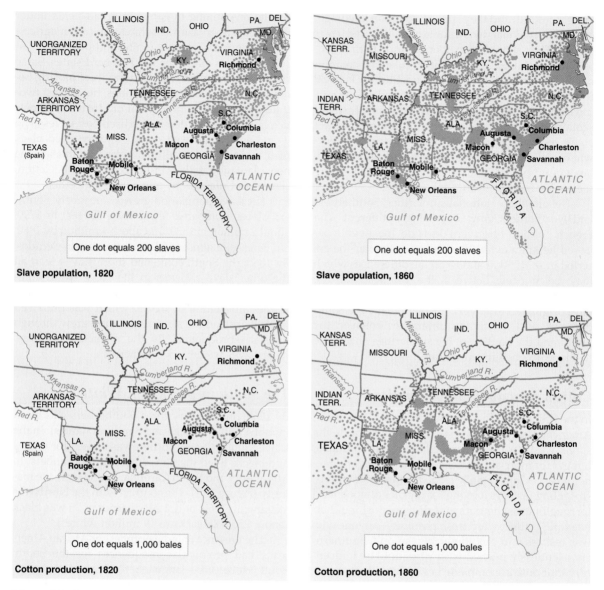

MAP 13.1

Cotton Kingdom, Slave Empire: 1820 and 1860

As the production of cotton soared, the slave population increased dramatically. Slaves continued to toil in tobacco and rice fields along the Atlantic seaboard, but increasingly they worked on cotton plantations in Alabama, Mississippi, and Louisiana.

READING THE MAP: Where was slavery most prevalent in 1820? In 1860? How did the spread of slavery compare with the spread of cotton?

CONNECTIONS: How much of the world's cotton was produced in the American South in 1860? While most slaves worked in agriculture, how else were slaves employed?

www.bedfordstmartins.com/roarkcompact   SEE THE ONLINE STUDY GUIDE for more help in analyzing these maps.

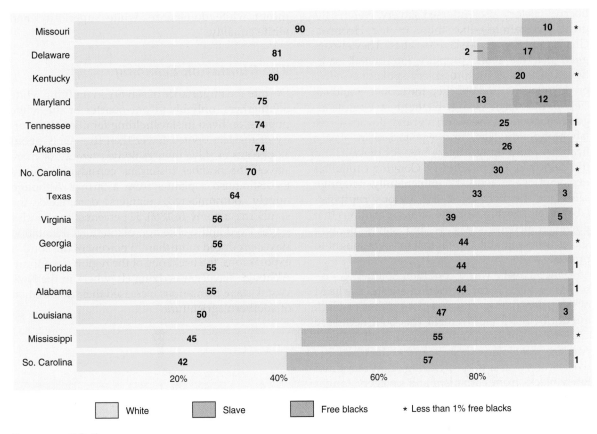

FIGURE 13.1

Black and White Population in the South, 1860
*Blacks represented a much larger fraction of the population in the South than in the
North, but considerable variation existed from state to state. Only one Missourian in
ten, for example, was black, while Mississippi and South Carolina had black majorities.
States in the Upper South were "whiter" than in the Lower South, despite the Upper
South's greater number of free blacks.*

to hate them and to seek to end their oppression, as Nat Turner had, by any means necessary.

Attacks on slavery after 1820—from blacks within and from abolitionists without—jolted southern slaveholders into a distressing awareness that they lived in a dangerous and fragile world. In response, southern leaders initiated fresh efforts to strengthen slavery. State legislatures constructed elaborate slave codes that required the total submission of slaves to their masters and to white society in general. As the Louisiana code stated, a slave "owes his master . . . a respect without bounds, and an absolute obedience." The laws underlined the authority of all whites, not just masters. Any white could "correct" slaves who did not stay "in their place."

Intellectuals joined legislators in the campaign to strengthen slavery. The South's academics, writers, and clergy constructed a proslavery argument that sought to unify the region's whites around slavery and provide ammunition for the emerging war of words with northern abolitionists. Under the intellectuals' tutelage, the white South gradually moved away from defending slavery as a "necessary evil"—the halfhearted argument popular in Jefferson's day—and toward a full-throated, aggressive defense of slavery as a "positive good."

Slavery's champions employed every imaginable defense. The law protected slavery, they observed, for slaves were legal property. And wasn't the security of property the bedrock of American liberty? History also endorsed slavery. Weren't the great civilizations—like those of the Hebrews, Greeks, and Romans—slave societies? They also argued that the Bible, properly interpreted, sanctioned slavery. Some proslavery spokesmen went on the offensive and attacked the economy and society of the North. George Fitzhugh of Virginia argued that behind the North's grand slogans—free labor, individualism, and egalitarianism—lay a heartless philosophy: "Every man for himself, and the devil take the hindmost." Gouging capitalists exploited wage workers unmercifully, Fitzhugh said, and he contrasted the vicious capitalist-laborer relationship with the humane relations that prevailed between masters and slaves because slaves were valuable capital that masters sought to protect.

Since slavery was a condition Southerners reserved exclusively for African Americans, the heart of the defense of slavery rested on claims of black inferiority. Black enslavement was both necessary and proper, antebellum defenders argued, because Africans were inferior beings. Rather than exploitative, slavery was a mass civilizing effort that lifted lowly blacks from barbarism and savagery, taught them disciplined work, and converted them to soul-saving Christianity. According to Virginian Thomas R. Dew, most slaves were grateful. "The slaves of a good master are his warmest, most constant, and most devoted friends," he declared.

Black slavery encouraged whites to unify around race rather than to divide by class. The grubbiest, most tobacco-stained white man could proudly proclaim his superiority to all blacks and his equality with the most refined southern patrician. Because slaves were not recognized as citizens in the South, Georgia attorney Thomas R. R. Cobb observed, every white Southerner "feels that he belongs to an elevated class. It matters not that he is no slaveholder; he is not of the inferior race; he is a freeborn citizen." Consequently, the "poorest meets the richest as an equal; sits at his table with him; salutes him as a neighbor; meets him in every public assembly, and stands on the same social platform." In the South, Cobb boasted, "there is no war of classes."

In reality, slavery did not create perfect harmony among whites or ease every strain along class lines. But by providing every antebellum white Southerner symbolic membership in the ruling class, racial slavery helped whites bridge differences in wealth, education, and culture. Slavery meant white dominance, white superiority, and white equality.

The Plantation Economy

Despite the importance of slavery in unifying white Southerners, only about one-quarter of the white population lived in slaveholding families. A majority of masters owned fewer than five. Only about 12 percent of slave owners owned twenty or more slaves, the number historians consider necessary to distinguish a planter from a farmer. Although hugely outnumbered, planters dominated the southern economy. In 1860, 52 percent of the South's slaves lived and worked on plantations. Plantation slaves produced more than 75 percent of the South's export crops, the backbone of the region's economy. Although slavery was dying elsewhere in the New World, slave plantations increased their domination of southern agriculture.

THE COTTON GIN
By the 1790s, the English had succeeded in mechanizing the manufacture of cotton cloth, but they were unable to get enough raw cotton. The South could grow cotton in unimaginable quantities, but cotton that was stuck to seeds was useless in English textile mills. In 1793, Eli Whitney, a Northerner who was living on a Savannah River plantation, built a simple device for separating the cotton from the seed. Widespread use of the cotton gin broke the bottleneck in the commercial production of cotton and eventually bound millions of African Americans to slavery.
Smithsonian Institution.

MAP 13.2

The Agricultural Economy of the South, 1860
Cotton dominated the South's agricultural economy, but the region grew a diversity of crops and was largely self-sufficient in foodstuffs.

The dominant cash crops of southern agriculture were the four major staples grown on plantations: tobacco, sugar, rice, and cotton (Map 13.2). Tobacco was the original plantation crop in North America, but by the nineteenth century tobacco had shifted westward from the Chesapeake to Tennessee and Kentucky. Large-scale sugar production began in 1795, when Étienne de Boré built a modern sugar mill in what is today New Orleans, and sugar plantations were confined almost entirely to Louisiana. Commercial rice production began in the seventeenth century, and like sugar, rice was confined to a small geographic area, a narrow strip stretching from the Carolinas into Georgia.

If tobacco, sugar, and rice were princes of plantation agriculture, cotton was king. Cotton became commercially significant after the advent of Eli Whitney's cotton gin in 1793, which allowed cotton to be prepared more quickly before being shipped to textile mills. By the early years of the nineteenth century, cotton had displaced tobacco and had begun to dominate the southern economy. It was grown almost everywhere in the South, by

small farmer and planter alike. Nonetheless, plantations produced three-quarters of the South's cotton. While hardscrabble farmer Jessup Snopes grew half a bale, Mississippian Frederick Stanton, who owned more than fifteen thousand prime acres, produced 3,054 bales of cotton worth $122,000 in 1859.

For major slaveholders, then, the Old South's economy was productive and profitable. Further, plantation slavery benefited the national economy. By 1840, cotton alone accounted for more than 60 percent of the nation's exports. Much of the profit from sales of cotton overseas returned to planters, but some went to northern middlemen who bought, sold, insured, warehoused, and shipped cotton to the mills in Great Britain and elsewhere. As they invested their profits in the burgeoning northern economy, industrial development received much-needed capital. Furthermore, planters provided an important market for northern textiles, agricultural tools, and other manufactured goods.

The economies of North and South steadily diverged. While the North developed a mixed economy—agriculture, commerce, and manufacturing—the South remained overwhelmingly agricultural. Since planters were earning healthy profits, they saw little reason to diversify. Year after year, they funneled the profits they earned from land and slaves back into more land and slaves.

With its capital flowing into agriculture, the Old South did not develop as many factories as did the North. By 1860, only 10 percent of the nation's industrial workers were in the South. And the region that produced 100 percent of the nation's cotton manufactured less than 7 percent of its cotton textiles.

Without significant economic diversification, the South developed fewer cities than the North. In 1860, it was the least urban region in the country. While nearly 37 percent of New England's population lived in cities, less than 12 percent of Southerners were urban dwellers. In fact, nine southern states had 5 percent or fewer of their people in cities.

Because the South had so few cities and industrial jobs, it attracted relatively small numbers of European immigrants. Seeking economic opportunity, not competition with slaves, immigrants steered well north of the South's slave-dominated, agricultural economy. In 1860, 13 percent of all Americans were foreign-born. But in nine of the fifteen slave states, only 2 percent or fewer were born abroad.

Not every Southerner celebrated the region's plantation economy. Critics railed against the excessive commitment to cotton and slaves and bemoaned the scarcity of factories. Diversification, reformers promised, would make the South not only economically independent but more prosperous as well. State governments encouraged economic diversification and development by helping to create banking systems that supplied credit for a wide range of projects, industrial as well as agricultural, and by building railroads.

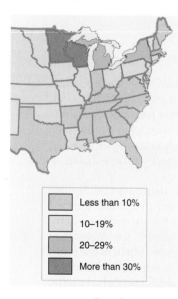

Immigrants as a Percent of State Populations, 1860

Less than 10%

10–19%

20–29%

More than 30%

But encouragement of a diversified economy had clear limits. State governments failed to create some of the essential services modern economies require. By midcentury, for example, no southern legislature had created a statewide public school system. Consequently, the South's illiteracy rate for whites topped 20 percent. Despite the flurry of railroad building, the South's mileage in 1860 was less than half that of the North. While railroads crisscrossed the North carrying manufactured goods as well as agricultural products, most railroads in the South were built primarily to export staple crops to port cities (see Map 12.1).

Northerners claimed that slavery was outmoded and doomed, but few Southerners perceived economic weakness in their region. In fact, the planters' pockets were never fuller than at the end of the antebellum period. Compared with Northerners, Southerners committed less of their capital to investment in industry, transportation, and public education. Planters' decisions to reinvest in staple agriculture ensured the momentum of the plantation economy and the social and political relationships that were rooted in it.

Masters, Mistresses, and the Big House

Nowhere was the contrast between northern and southern life more vivid than in the plantations of the South. Located on a patchwork of cleared fields and dense forests, a plantation typically included a "big house" and slave quarters. Scattered about were numerous outbuildings, each with a special function. Near the big house were the kitchen, storehouse, smokehouse (for curing and preserving meat), and hen coop. More distant were the barns, toolsheds, artisans' workshops, and overseer's house. Depending on the crop, there was a tobacco shed, a rice mill, a sugar refinery, or a cotton gin house.

The plantation was the home of masters, mistresses, and slaves. Slavery shaped the lives of all the plantation's inhabitants, but it affected each differently. A hierarchy of rigid roles and duties governed relationships. Presiding was the master, who ruled his wife, children, and slaves, none of whom had many legal rights and all of whom were designated by the state as dependents under his dominion and protection.

Plantation Masters

While smaller planters supervised the labor of their slaves themselves, larger planters often hired overseers who went to the fields with the slaves, leaving planters free to concentrate on marketing, finance, and general plantation affairs. Planters also found time to escape to town to discuss the weather, to the courthouse and legislature to debate politics, and to the woods to hunt and fish.

Increasingly in the nineteenth century, planters characterized the master-slave relationship in terms of what historians have called "paternalism." The concept of paternalism denied that the form of slavery practiced in the South was brutal and exploitative. Instead, it defined slavery as a set of reciprocal obligations between masters and slaves. In exchange for the slaves' labor and obedience, masters provided basic care and necessary guidance. To northern claims that they were tyrants and exploiters, slaveholders responded that they were stewards and guardians. As owners of blacks, mas-

ters argued, they had the heavy responsibility of caring for a childlike, dependent people. In 1814, Thomas Jefferson captured the essence of the advancing ideal: "We should endeavor, with those whom fortune has thrown on our hands, to feed & clothe them well, protect them from ill usage, require such reasonable labor only as is performed voluntarily by freemen, and be led by no repugnancies to abdicate them, and our duties to them."

Paternalism was part propaganda and part self-delusion. But it was more. Indeed, there was some truth in the assertion that master-slave relationships in the South were unique. Unlike planters elsewhere in the New World, most southern planters lived year-round where their slaves worked, which meant that the relationship between master and slave was face to face, direct, and personal. In addition, after the close of the external slave trade in 1808, masters recognized slaves as assets to be maintained, and they realized that the expansion of the slave labor force could come only from natural reproduction.

One consequence of this paternalism and economic self-interest was a relative improvement in

SOUTHERN MAN WITH CHILDREN AND THEIR MAMMY
Obviously prosperous and projecting the aura of a man accustomed to giving orders and to being obeyed, this patriarch poses around 1848 with his young daughters and their nurse. The absent mother may have been dead, which might in part explain the inclusion of the slave woman in the family circle. But her presence also confirms her importance in the household. Fathers left the raising of children to mothers and nurses. However important, the black woman is clearly a servant, a status indicated by both her race and her attire.
Collection of the J. Paul Getty Museum, Malibu, Calif.

NANCY FORT, HOUSE SERVANT
This rare portrait of a slave woman at the turn of the nineteenth century depicts a strong and dignified person. Some who worked in domestic service took pride in their superior status and identified more with the master than with the slaves. "Honey, I wan't no common eve'day slave," one former servant recalled proudly. "I [helped] de white folks in de big house." But intense interaction with whites did not necessarily breed affection. Most domestic servants remained bound by ties of kinship and friendship, as well as by common oppression, to the slave quarters.
Courtesy of Georgia Department of Archives and History.

SLAVE CARPENTER
Haywood Dixon (1826–c. 1889) was a slave carpenter who worked in Greene County, North Carolina. In this 1854 daguerreotype, he is posed with a symbol of his craft, the carpenter's square. When work was slow on the home plantation, masters could hire out their skilled artisans to neighbors who needed a carpenter, blacksmith, or mason.
Collection of William L. Murphy.

and rest, it made for a long day. For slaves, Lewis Young recalled, "work, work, work, 'twas all they do."

Family, Religion, and Community

At night, when the labor was done, and all day Sundays and usually Saturday afternoons, slaves were left largely to themselves. Bone tired perhaps, they nonetheless used the time and space to develop and enjoy what mattered most: family, religion, and community.

In the quarters, slaves lived lives that their masters were hardly aware of. Temporarily leaving the master-slave relationship at their cabin doors, slaves became husbands and wives, mothers and fathers, sons and daughters, preachers and singers, storytellers and conjurers. Over the generations, they created a community and a culture of their own that buoyed them up during long hours in the fields and brought them joy and hope in the few hours they had to themselves.

One of the most important consequences of the slaves' limited autonomy was the preservation

SLAVE QUARTER, SOUTH CAROLINA
On large plantations, several score of African Americans lived in cabins that were often arranged along what slaves called "the street." The dwellings pictured in this image by Civil War photographer George N. Barnard of a South Carolina plantation were better built than the typical rickety, one-room, dirt-floored slave cabin. Although this photograph is almost certainly posed, it captures the inhabitants of the slave quarter—little children playing in the dirt, girls and women sitting on the steps talking and working at something, and older boys and men driving carts and wagons. During the daylight hours of the work week when most men and women labored in the fields, the quarter was largely empty. But at night and on Sundays, it was a busy place.
Collection of the New-York Historical Society.

and persistence of the family. Perhaps the most serious charge abolitionists leveled against slavery was that it wrecked black family life, a telling indictment in a society that put family at the heart of decent society. Slaveholders sometimes agreed that blacks had no family life, but they placed the blame on the slaves themselves, claiming that blacks chose to lead licentious, promiscuous lives.

Contrary to both abolitionists' and slaveholders' claims, the black family survived slavery. Indeed, family was the chief fact of life in the quarters. Owners sometimes encouraged the creation and maintenance of families, but slave family life grew primarily from slaves' own commitment. While no laws recognized slave marriage, and therefore no master or slave was legally obligated to honor the bond, plantation records show that slave marriages were often long-lasting. Young men and women in the slave quarters fell in love, married, and set up housekeeping in cabins of their own. The primary cause of the ending of slave marriages was death, just as it was in white families. But the second most frequent cause of the end of slave marriages was the sale of the husband or wife, something no white family ever had to fear. Precise figures are unavailable, but one scholar estimates that in the years 1820–1860, sales destroyed 300,000 slave marriages. Years after Moses Grandy was parted from his slave wife, he said, "I have never seen or heard of her from that day to this." And he added, "I loved her as I love my life."

Plantation records also reveal the importance of slave fathers. Not all fathers could live with their children—some men had been sold away and others had married women on neighboring plantations—but fathers were often present. Despite their inability to fulfill the traditional roles of provider and protector, slave fathers gained status by doing what they could to provide for their families: hunting, raising hogs, cultivating a garden, making furniture. Slaves held both their mothers and fathers in high esteem, grateful for the small bits of refuge their parents provided from the rigors of slavery when they were children.

Like families, religion also provided slaves with a refuge and a reason for living. Beginning about the time of the American Revolution, Protestant evangelical sects, particularly the Baptists and Methodists, began trying to convert slaves from their African beliefs. Evangelicals offered an emotional "religion of the heart" to which blacks (and many whites as well) responded enthusiastically. By the mid-nineteenth century, perhaps as many as one-quarter of all slaves claimed church membership, and many of the rest would not have objected to being called Christians.

Planters began promoting Christianity in the quarters because they came to see the slaves' salvation as part of their obligation and to believe that religion made slaves more obedient. Certainly, the Christianity that masters broadcast to slaves emphasized the meeker virtues. White preachers admonished their black congregants to love God and to obey their owners. Many slaves laughed up their sleeves at the message. "That old white preacher just was telling us slaves to be good to our masters," a Virginia ex-slave chuckled. "We ain't cared a bit about that stuff he was telling us 'cause we wanted to sing, pray, and serve God in our own way."

Meeting in their cabins or secretly in the woods, slaves created an African American Christianity that served their needs, not the masters'. Beginning in the 1830s, laws prohibited teaching slaves to read, but some slaves could read enough to struggle with the Bible. With the help of black preachers, they interpreted the Christian message themselves. Rather than obedience, their faith emphasized justice. Nat Turner felt himself to be an avenging angel who would punish whites and end bondage. More often, slaves believed that God kept score, and accounts of this world would be settled in the next. But the slaves' faith also spoke to their experiences in this world. In the Old Testament they discovered Moses, who delivered his people from slavery, and in the New Testament they found Jesus, who offered salvation to all and thereby established the equality of all people. Jesus' message of equality provided a potent antidote to the planters' claim that blacks were an inferior people whom God condemned to slavery and was a crucial buttress to the slaves' self-esteem.

Christianity did not entirely drive out traditional African beliefs. Even slaves who were Christians sometimes continued to believe that conjurers, witches, and spirits possessed the power to protect and defend. Moreover, their Christian music, preaching, and rituals showed the influence of Africa, as did much of the slaves' secular activities, such as wood carving, quilt making, and storytelling.

Resistance and Rebellion

Slaves did not suffer slavery passively. They were, as whites said, "troublesome property." Slaves understood that accommodation to what they could not change was the price of survival, but in a hundred ways they protested their bondage. Theoretically, the master was all-powerful and the slave powerless. But sustained by their culture, religion, and community, slaves engaged in day-to-day resistance against their enslavers.

The spectrum of slave resistance ranged from mild to extreme. Telling a pointed story by the fireside in a slave cabin was probably the mildest form of protest. But when the weak got the better of the strong, as they did in tales of Brer Rabbit and Brer

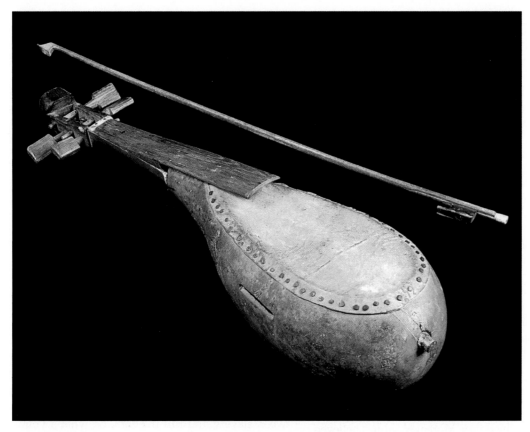

GOURD FIDDLE
*Found in St. Mary's County, Maryland, this slave-made gourd fiddle is an example of
the many musical instruments that African Americans crafted and played throughout
the South. Henry Wright, an ex-slave from Georgia, remembered: "I made a fiddle out
of a large sized gourd—a long wooden handle was used as a neck, and the hair from a
horse's tail was used for the bow. The strings were made of catgut." A hybrid of African
and European elements, this fiddle offers material evidence of the cultural transformation of African slaves. While Africans lost much in their forced journey to the Americas,
Africa remained in their cultural memory. Black men and women drew on the traditions
of their homeland and the South to create something new—an African American culture. Music, a crucial component of that sustaining culture, provided slaves with a
creative outlet and relief from the rigors of slavery.*
Smithsonian Institution/Aldo Tutino/Folio, Inc.

Fox (Brer is a contraction of Brother), listeners could
enjoy the thrill of a vicarious victory over their masters. Protest in the fields was more active than that
around firesides. Slaves were particularly inventive
in resisting their master's demand that they work.
They dragged their feet getting to the fields, put
rocks in their cotton bags before putting them on
the scale to be weighed, feigned illness, and pretended to be so thickheaded that they could not understand the simplest instruction. Slaves broke so

many hoe handles that owners outfitted the hoes
with oversized handles. Slaves so mistreated the
work animals that masters switched from horses to
mules, which could absorb more abuse. While
slaves worked hard in the master's fields, they also
sabotaged his interests.

Running away, a widespread form of protest,
particularly angered masters. By escaping the plantation, runaways denied masters what they wanted
most from their slaves—work. Sometimes runaways

sought the ultimate prize: freedom in the North or in Canada. Over the decades, thousands of slaves, mostly from the Upper South, made it. But from the Lower South, escape to freedom was almost impossible. At most, runaways could hope to escape for a few weeks. They usually stayed close to the plantation, keeping to the deep woods or swamps and slipping back into the quarters at night to get food. "Lying out," as it was known, usually ended when the runaway, worn out and ragged, gave up or was finally chased down by slave-hunting dogs.

While resistance was common, outright rebellion—a violent assault on slavery by large numbers of slaves—was rare. The scarcity of revolts in the antebellum South is not evidence of the slaves' contentedness. Rather, conditions gave rebels virtually no chance of success. By 1860, whites outnumbered blacks two to one and were heavily armed. Moreover, communication between plantations was difficult, and the South provided little protective wilderness into which rebels could retreat and defend themselves. Organized rebellion in the American South, as Nat Turner's experience showed, was virtual suicide.

Given the odds, it is perhaps surprising to find any organized rebellion. But slaves in the antebellum South did rise up. Nat Turner's revolt in 1831 was one of the bloodiest. Moreover, whites believed that that they were surrounded by conspiracies to rebel. In 1822, Denmark Vesey, a free black carpenter in Charleston, was accused of planning to storm the city arsenal, capture its weapons, kill any white who stood in the way, and set fire to the city. The authorities rounded up suspects, and prodded by torture and the threat of death, they implicated others. After three months, whites had banished thirty-seven blacks from the state and executed thirty-five more, including Denmark Vesey.

Although masters often boasted that their slaves were "instinctively contented," steady resistance and occasional rebellion proved otherwise. Slaves did not have the power to end their bondage, but by asserting themselves, they affirmed their humanity and worth. By resisting their masters' will, slaves became actors in the plantation drama, helping to establish limits beyond which planters and overseers hesitated to go.

It would be false to the historical record to minimize what the lack of freedom meant to slaves. Because the essence of slavery was the inability to shape one's own life, slavery blunted and thwarted African Americans' hopes and aspirations. But slav-

ery's destructive power had to contend with the resiliency of the human spirit. Slaves fought back physically, culturally, and spiritually. They not only survived bondage, but they created in the slave quarters a vibrant African American culture and community that would sustain them through more than two centuries of slavery and after.

Black and Free: On the Middle Ground

Not every black Southerner was a slave. In 1860, some 260,000 (approximately 6 percent) of the region's 4.1 million African Americans were free (see Figure 13.1). What is surprising is not that their numbers were small but that they existed at all. "Free black" seemed increasingly a contradiction to most white Southerners. According to the emerging racial thinking, blacks were supposed to be slaves; only whites were supposed to be free. Blacks who were free did not fit neatly into the South's idealized social order. They stood out, and whites made them more and more objects of scrutiny and scorn. Free blacks realized that they stood precariously between slavery and full freedom, on what a young free black artisan in Charleston characterized in 1848 as "a middle ground."

Free Blacks and the White Response

Free blacks were rare in the colonial era, but their numbers swelled after the Revolution, when the natural rights philosophy of the Declaration of Independence and the egalitarian message of evangelical Protestantism joined to challenge slavery. Although probably not more than one slaveholder in a hundred freed his slaves, a brief flurry of emancipation visited the Upper South, where the ideological assault on slavery coincided with a deep depression in the tobacco economy. Other planters permitted favorite slaves to work after hours to accumulate money with which to buy their freedom. By 1810, free blacks numbered more than 100,000 and had become the fastest-growing element of the southern population. Burgeoning numbers of free blacks worried white Southerners, who, because of the cotton boom, wanted desperately to see more slaves, not more free blacks.

In the 1820s and 1830s, state legislatures acted to stem the growth of the free black population and to shrink the liberty of those blacks who had already gained their freedom. Laws denied masters the right to free their slaves. Other laws humiliated and restricted free blacks by subjecting them to special taxes, requiring them to register annually with the state or to choose a white guardian, prohibiting them from interstate travel, denying them the right to have schools and to participate in politics, and requiring them to carry "freedom papers" to prove they were not slaves. Increasingly, whites subjected free blacks to many of the same laws as slaves. They could not testify under oath in a court of law or serve on juries. They were liable to punishment meted out to slaves such as whipping and the treadmill. Like slaves, free blacks were forbidden to strike whites, even to defend themselves. "Free negroes belong to a degraded caste of society," a South Carolina judge summed up in 1848. "They are in no respect on a perfect equality with the white man. . . . They ought, by law, to be compelled to demean themselves as inferiors."

The elaborate system of regulations confined most free African Americans to a constricted life of poverty and dependence. Typically, free blacks were rural, uneducated, unskilled agricultural laborers and domestic servants, scrambling to find work and eke out a living. Opportunities of all kinds—for work, education, community—were slim. Planters looked upon free blacks as degraded parasites, likely to set a bad example for slaves. They believed that free blacks subverted the racial subordination that was the essence of slavery.

Achievement despite Restrictions

Despite increasingly harsh laws and stepped-up persecution, free African Americans made the most of the advantages their status offered. Unlike slaves, free blacks could legally marry. They could protect their families from arbitrary disruption and pass on their heritage of freedom to their children. Freedom also meant that they could choose occupations and own property. For most, these economic rights proved only theoretical, for whites allowed most free blacks few opportunities. Unlike whites, a majority of the antebellum South's free blacks remained propertyless.

Still, some free blacks escaped the poverty and degradation whites thrust upon them. Particularly in urban areas—especially the cities of Charleston,

Mobile, and New Orleans—a small elite of free blacks developed and even flourished. Urban whites enforced many of the restrictive laws only sporadically, allowing free blacks room to maneuver. The elite consisted overwhelmingly of light-skinned African Americans who worked at skilled trades, as tailors, carpenters, mechanics, and the like. Their customers were prominent whites—planters, merchants, and judges—who appreciated their able, respectful service. The free black elite operated schools for their children and traveled in and out of their states, despite the laws. They worshiped with whites (in separate seating) in the finest churches and lived scattered about in white neighborhoods, not in ghettos. And like elite whites, some owned slaves. Blacks could own blacks because, despite all of the restrictions whites placed on free African Americans, whites did not deny them the right to own property, which in the South included human property. Of the 3,200 black slaveholders (barely 1 percent of the free black population), most owned only a few, who were sometimes family members whom they could not legally free. But others owned slaves in large numbers, none of whom were family and all of whom were exploited for labor.

One such free black slave owner, William Ellison of South Carolina, owned a cotton gin manufacturing business that grew so much that by 1835 he was prosperous enough to purchase the home of a former governor of the state. By the time of his death in 1861, he owned sixty-three slaves on his eight-hundred-acre plantation.

Most free blacks neither became slaveholders nor sought to raise a slave rebellion. Rather, they simply tried to preserve their freedom. Increasingly under attack from planters who wanted to eliminate or enslave them and from white artisans who coveted their jobs, they sought to impress whites with their reliability, their economic progress, and their good behavior.

The Plain Folk

Most whites in the South did not own slaves, not even one. In 1860, more than six million of the South's eight million whites lived in slaveless families. Most "plain folk" were small farmers. Perhaps three out of four were yeomen, small farmers who owned their own land. As in the North, farm ownership provided a family with an economic foundation, social respectability, and political standing. Unlike their northern counterparts, however, southern yeomen lived in a region whose economy and society were increasingly dominated by unfree labor.

In an important sense, the South had more than one white yeomanry. The huge southern landscape provided space enough for two yeoman societies, separated roughly along geographical lines. Yeomen throughout the South had a good deal in common, but the life of a small farm family in the plantation belt—the flatlands that spread from South Carolina to East Texas—differed from the life of one in the upcountry—the area of hills and mountains.

Plantation Belt Yeomen

Plantation belt yeomen lived within the orbit of the planter class. Small farms actually outnumbered plantations in the plantation belt, but they were dwarfed in importance. Small farmers grew food crops, particularly corn, but like planters, yeomen devoted a significant portion of their land to growing cotton. With only family labor to draw upon, however, they produced only a couple of four-hundred-pound bales each year, whereas large planters measured their crop in hundreds of bales. The small farmers' cotton tied them to planters. Unable to afford cotton gins or baling presses of their own, they relied on helpful neighborhood slave owners to gin and bale their small crops. With no link to merchants in the port cities, yeomen turned to better-connected planters to ship and sell their cotton.

The Cotton Belt

A dense network of personal relationships laced small farmers and planters together in patterns of reciprocity and mutual obligation. A planter might send his slaves to help a newcomer build a house or a sick farmer get in his crop. He hired out surplus slaves to ambitious yeomen who wanted to expand cotton production. He sometimes chose his overseers from among the sons of local farm families. Plantation mistresses sometimes nursed ailing neighbors. Family ties could span class lines, making rich and poor kin as well as neighbors. Yeomen

shared the planters' commitment to white supremacy and actively defended black subordination. Rural counties required adult white males to ride in slave patrols, which nightly scoured country roads to make certain that no slaves were moving about without permission. On Sundays, plantation dwellers and plain folk came together in church to worship and afterward lingered to gossip and to transact small business.

Plantation belt yeomen may have envied, and at times even resented, wealthy slaveholders, but in general small farmers learned to accommodate. Planters made accommodation easier by going out of their way to provide necessary services, behave as good neighbors, and avoid direct exploitation of slaveless whites in their community. As a consequence, rather than raging at the oppression of the planter regime, the typical plantation belt yeoman sought entry into it. He dreamed of adding acreage to his farm, buying a few slaves of his own, retiring from field work, and perhaps even joining his prosperous neighbors on their shady verandas for a cool drink.

Upcountry Yeomen

By contrast, the hills and mountains of the South resisted the penetration of slavery and plantations. In the western parts of Virginia, North Carolina, and South Carolina, northern Georgia and Alabama, and eastern Tennessee and Kentucky, the higher elevation, colder climate, rugged terrain, and poor transportation made it difficult for commercial agriculture to make headway. For yeomen who lived there, planters and slaves were not everyday acquaintances. Geographically isolated, the upcountry was a yeoman stronghold.

At the core of the distinctive upcountry culture was the independent farm family working its own patch of land; raising a considerable number of hogs, cattle, and sheep; and seeking self-sufficiency and independence. Toward that end, all members of the family worked, their tasks depending on their sex and age. Husbands labored in the fields, and with their sons they cleared, plowed, planted, and cultivated primarily food crops. Although pressed into field labor at harvest time, wives and daughters of upcountry yeomen, like those of plantation belt yeomen, worked in and about the cabin most of the year. One upcountry farmer remembered that his mother "worked in the house cooking, spinning, weaving [and doing] patch-

A BAPTISING ON THE SOUTH BRANCH OF THE POTOMAC NEAR FRANKLIN, VIRGINIA
(DETAIL), 1844
In 1844, noted painter William Thompson Russell Smith undertook a geological expedition to Virginia, and there he encountered this rural baptism. Primarily a landscape painter, Smith in this painting relegates the human figures to minor characters. If one of the participants had sketched the baptism, he or she might have emphasized the human drama, the emotional pitch of what was for evangelical Christians throughout the South a profound religious moment.
The Charleston Renaissance Gallery, Robert M. Hicklin Jr., Inc., Charleston, South Carolina.

work." Women also tended the vegetable garden, kept a cow and some chickens, preserved foods,

Upcountry of the South

cleaned their homes, fed their families, and cared for their children. Male and female tasks were equally crucial to the farm's success, but as in other white southern households, the female domestic sphere was subordinated to the will of the male patriarch.

The typical upcountry yeoman also grew a little cotton or tobacco, but production for home consumption was more important than production for the market. Not much currency changed hands in the upcountry. Credit was common, as was direct barter. A yeoman might trade his small commercial crop to a country store owner for a little salt, lead shot, needles, and nails. Or he might swap extra sweet potatoes with the blacksmith for a plow or with the tanner for leather. Networks of exchange and mutual assistance tied individual homesteads to the larger community. Farm families also joined together in logrolling, house- and barn-raising, and cornhusking. Strong communal ties made the yeoman's goal of maintaining his family's independence realistic.

Yeomen did not have the upcountry entirely to themselves. Even the hills had some plantations and slaves. But they existed in much smaller numbers than in the plantation belt. Most upcountry counties were less than a quarter black, whereas counties in the plantation belt were more than half black. The few upcountry folks who owned slaves usually had only two or three. As a result, slaveholders had much less direct social and economic power, and yeomen had more. But yeoman domination did not mean that the upcountry opposed slavery. As long as they were free to lead their own lives, upcountry plain folk defended slavery and white supremacy just as staunchly as did other white Southerners.

The Culture of Southern Plain Folk

But not all nonslaveholding farmers were yeomen. Perhaps one in four farmers was landless. Landless farm families lived as tenants, renting rather than owning land. Other poor rural Southerners worked as unskilled day laborers, hunters, herders, and fisherman. Some landless whites barely made a go of it, but most were ambitious people scratching to survive and aspiring to climb into the yeomanry. Many succeeded, but in the 1850s upward mobility slowed. Rich planters expanded their operations, often driving the price of land beyond the reach of poor families. Despite these differences, poor rural Southerners shared some common cultural emphases with yeomen farmers.

Whether plain folk lived in the hills or in the flatlands, they did not usually associate "book learning" with the basic needs of life. A northern woman visiting the South in the 1850s observed, "Education is not extended to the masses here as at the North." Private academies charged fees that yeomen could not afford, and public schools were scarce. Although most people managed to pick up a basic knowledge of the "three R's," approximately one southern white man in five was illiterate in 1860, and the rate for white women was even higher. "People here prefer talking to reading," a Virginian remarked. Telling stories, reciting ballads, and singing hymns were important activities in yeoman folk culture.

Plain folk everywhere spent more hours in revival tents than in classrooms. By no means were all rural whites religious, but many were, and the most characteristic feature of their evangelical Christian faith was the revival. The greatest of the early nineteenth-century revivals occurred in 1801 at Cane Ridge, Kentucky, where some twenty thousand people gathered to listen to a host of evangelical preachers who spoke day and night for a week. Ministers sought to convert and save souls by bringing individuals to a personal conviction of sin. Revivalism crossed denominational lines; Baptists and Methodists adopted it wholeheartedly and by mid-century had become the South's largest religious groups. By emphasizing free choice and individual worth, the plain folk's religion was hopeful and affirming. Hymns and spirituals provided guides to right and wrong—praising modesty, condemning drinking and devilish activity like dancing. Above all, hymns spoke of eventual release from worldly sorrows and the assurance of eternal salvation.

The Politics of Slavery

Like every other significant feature of southern society, politics reflected slavery's power. Even after the South's politics became democratic in form for the white male population, political power remained unevenly distributed. The nonslaveholding white majority wielded less political power than their numbers indicated. The slaveholding white minority wielded more. Self-conscious, cohesive, and with a well-developed sense of class interest, slaveholders busied themselves with party politics, campaigns, and officeholding and made demands of state governments. As a result, they received significant benefits. But nonslaveholding whites were concerned mainly with preserving their liberties and keeping their taxes low. Collectively, they asked government for little of an economic nature, and they received little.

Slaveholders sometimes worried about nonslaveholders' loyalty to slavery, but since the eighteenth century, the mass of whites had accepted the planters' argument that the existing social order served all Southerners' interests. Slavery compensated every white man—no matter how poor—with membership in the South's white ruling class. It also provided the means by which nonslaveholders might someday advance into the ranks of the planters. White men in the South fought furiously about many things, but they agreed that they should take land from Indians, promote agriculture, uphold white supremacy, and defend slavery from its enemies.

The Democratization of the Political Arena

The political reforms that swept the nation in the first half of the nineteenth century reached deeply into the South. Southern politics became democratic politics—for white men. Southerners eliminated the wealth and property requirements that had once restricted political participation. Every state extended suffrage to all white males who were at least twenty-one years of age. Most southern states also removed the property requirements for holding state offices. In addition, increasing numbers of local and state officials—justices of the peace, judges, militia officers, and others—were chosen by the voters. To be sure, undemocratic features lingered. Plantation districts still wielded disproportionate power in several state legislatures. Nevertheless, southern politics increasingly took place within a democratic political structure.

White male suffrage ushered in an era of vigorous electoral competition. Eager voters rushed to the polls to exercise their new rights. In South Carolina, for example, in the 1810 election—the last election with voting restrictions in place—only 43 percent of white men cast ballots. In 1824, a remarkable 76 percent of white men voted. High turnouts became a hallmark of southern electoral politics.

As politics became aggressively democratic, it also grew fiercely partisan. From the 1830s to the 1850s, Whigs and Democrats battled for the electorate's favor. Whigs and Democrats both presented themselves as the plain white folk's best friend. All candidates declared their fervent commitment to republican equality and pledged to defend the people's liberty. Each party sought to portray the other as a collection of rich, snobbish, selfish men who had antidemocratic designs up their silk sleeves. Each, in turn, claimed for itself the mantle of humble "servant of the people."

The Whig and Democratic Parties sought to serve the people differently, however. Southern Whigs tended, as Whigs did elsewhere in the nation, to favor government intervention in the economy, and Democrats tended to oppose it. Whigs generally backed state support of banks, railroads, and corporations, arguing that government aid would stimulate the economy, enlarge opportunity, and thus increase the general welfare. Democrats emphasized the threat to individual liberty that government intervention posed, claiming that granting favors to special economic interests would result in concentrated power, which would in turn jeopardize the common man's opportunity and equality. Beginning with the panic of 1837, the parties clashed repeatedly on concrete economic and financial issues.

Planter Power

Whether Whig or Democrat, southern officeholders were likely to be slave owners. The power slaveholders exerted over slaves did not translate directly into political authority over whites, however. In the nineteenth century, political power could be won only at the ballot box, and almost everywhere nonslaveholders were in the majority. Yet year after year, proud and noisily egalitarian common men elected wealthy slaveholders (Table 13.1).

TABLE 13.1

SLAVEHOLDERS AND PLANTERS IN LEGISLATURES, 1860

Legislature	Percent of Slaveholders	Percent of Planters*
Virginia	67.3	24.2
Maryland	53.4	19.3
North Carolina	85.8	36.6
Kentucky	60.6	8.4
Tennessee	66.0	14.0
Missouri	41.2	5.3
Arkansas	42.0	13.0
South Carolina	81.7	55.4
Georgia	71.6	29.0
Florida	55.4	20.0
Alabama	76.3	40.8
Mississippi	73.4	49.5
Louisiana	63.8	23.5
Texas	54.1	18.1

*Planters: Owned 20 or more slaves.

Source: Adapted from Ralph A. Wooster, *The People in Power: Courthouse and Statehouse in the Lower South, 1850–1860* (1969), 41; *Politicians, Planters, and Plain Folks: Courthouse and Statehouse in the Upper South* (1975), 40.

Courtesy of the University of Tennessee Press.

Over time, slaveholders increased their power in state legislatures. By 1860, the percentage of slave owners in state legislatures ranged from 41 percent in Missouri to nearly 86 percent in North Carolina. Legislators not only tended to own slaves—they often owned large numbers. The percentage of planters (individuals with twenty or more slaves) in southern legislatures in 1860 ranged from 5.3 percent in Missouri to 55.4 percent in South Carolina. In North Carolina, where only 3 percent of the state's white families belonged to the planter class, 36.6 percent of the legislature were planters. The democratization of politics in the nineteenth century meant that more ordinary citizens participated in elections, but yeomen and artisans remained rare sights in the halls of southern legislatures.

Upper-class dominance of southern politics reflected, in part, the strength of the rural folk culture, which valued tradition and stability. Since the colonial era, yeomen had looked to the upper class for political leadership. As democracy rose in the nineteenth century, notions of hierarchy and habits of deference declined, but planter status remained important in the South and the surest ticket to political advancement.

But tradition was not enough to ensure planter rule. Slaveholders had to persuade the white majority that what was good for slaveholders was also good for them. Slaveless white men proved to be receptive to the planters' argument. The South had, on the whole, done well by them. Most had farms of their own. They participated as equals in a democratic political system. They enjoyed an elevated social status, above all blacks and in theory equal to all other whites. As patriarchs, they commanded their households. As long as slavery existed, they could dream of joining the planter class, of rising above the drudgery of field labor. Slaveless white men found much to celebrate in the slave South.

Most slaveholders took pains to win the plain folk's trust and to nurture their respect. In the plantation districts especially, where slaveholders and nonslaveholders lived side by side, planters learned that flexing their economic muscle was a poor way to win the political allegiance of common men. Instead, they developed a lighter touch, fully attentive to their own interests but aware of the personal feelings of poorer whites. One South Carolinian told his wealthy neighbor that he had a bright political future because he never thought himself "too good to sit down & talk to a poor man."

Smart candidates found ways to convince wary yeomen of their democratic convictions and egalitarian sentiments, whether they were genuine or not. When young John A. Quitman ran for a seat in the Mississippi legislature, he amazed a boisterous crowd of small farmers at one campaign stop by not only entering but winning contests in jumping, boxing, wrestling, and sprinting. For his finale he outshot the area's champion marksman. Then, demonstrating his deft political touch, he gave his prize, a fat ox, to the defeated rifleman. The electorate showed its approval by sending Quitman to the state capital.

The massive representation of slaveholders ensured that southern legislatures would make every effort to preserve slavery. Georgia politics show how well the planters protected themselves in the political struggle. In 1850, about half of the state's revenues came from taxes on slave property, the characteristic form of planter wealth. However, the tax rate on slaves was trifling, only about one-fifth

the rate on land. Moreover, planters benefited far more than other social groups from public spending: Financing railroads—which carried cotton to market—was the largest state expenditure. The legislature also established low tax rates on land, the characteristic form of yeoman wealth, which meant that the typical yeoman's annual tax bill was small. Still, relative to their wealth, large slaveholders paid less than did other whites. Relative to their numbers, they got more in return. A sympathetic slaveholding legislature protected planters' interests and gave the impression of protecting the small farmers' interests as well.

The South's elite protected slavery in other ways. In the 1830s, whites decided that slavery was too important to debate. "So interwoven is [slavery] with our interest, our manners, our climate and our very being," one man declared in 1833, "that no change can ever possibly be effected without a civil commotion from which the heart of a patriot must turn with horror." A "cotton curtain" descended along the Mason-Dixon line that ended free speech on the slavery question. Slavery's critics were dismissed from college faculties, driven from pulpits, and hounded from political life. Sometimes they fell victim to vigilantes and mob violence. One could defend slavery; one could even delicately suggest mild reforms. But no Southerner could safely call slavery evil or advocate its destruction.

In the antebellum South, therefore, the rise of the common man occurred alongside the continuing, even growing, power of the planter class. Rather than pitting slaveholders against nonslaveholders, elections remained an effective means of binding the region's whites together. Elections affirmed the sovereignty of white men, whether planter or plain folk, and the subordination of African Americans. Those twin themes played well among white women as well. Although unable to vote, white women supported equality for whites and slavery for blacks.

Conclusion: A Slave Society

Antebellum Americans came to see the South as fundamentally different from the rest of the nation. Rural and biracial, the South reflected the power of plantation slavery. Regional differences increased over time, not merely because the South became more and more dominated by slavery, but also because developments in the North rapidly propelled it in a very different direction.

In 1860, one-third of the South's population was enslaved. Bondage saddled blacks with enormous physical and spiritual burdens: hard labor, poor treatment, broken families, and, most important, the denial of freedom itself. Although degraded and exploited, they were not defeated. Out of African memories and New World realities, blacks created a life-affirming African American culture that sustained and strengthened them. Their families, religion, and community provided antidotes to white racist ideas and even to white power. Defined as property, they refused to be reduced to things. Perceived as inferior beings, they rejected the notion that they were natural slaves. Slaves engaged in a war of wills with masters who sought their labor while they sought to live dignified, autonomous lives.

Much more than racial slavery contributed to the South's distinctiveness and to the loyalty and regional identification of its whites. White Southerners felt strong attachments to local communities, to extended families, to personal, face-to-face relationships, to rural life, to evangelical Protestantism, and to codes of honor and chivalry, among other things. But slavery was crucial to the South's economy, society, and culture, as well as to its developing sectional consciousness. After the 1830s, the South was not merely a society with slaves; it was a slave society. Little disturbed the white consensus south of the Mason-Dixon line that racial slavery was necessary and just. By making all blacks a pariah class, all whites gained a measure of equality and harmony.

Racism did not erase stress along class lines. Nor did the other features of southern life that helped confine class tensions: the wide availability of land, rapid economic mobility, the democratic nature of political life, patriarchal power among white men, the shrewd behavior of slaveholders toward poorer whites, kinship ties between rich and poor, and rural traditions. Anxious slaveholders continued to worry that yeomen would defect from the proslavery consensus. But during the 1850s a far more ominous division emerged—that between the "slave states" and the "free states."

FOR FURTHER READING ABOUT THE TOPICS IN THIS CHAPTER, see the Online Bibliography at **www.bedfordstmartins.com/roarkcompact.**

FOR ADDITIONAL FIRST-HAND ACCOUNTS OF THIS PERIOD, see pages 196–211 in Michael Johnson, ed., *Reading the American Past,* Second Edition, Volume I.

TO ASSESS YOUR MASTERY OF THE MATERIAL IN THIS CHAPTER, see the Online Study Guide at **www.bedfordstmartins.com/roarkcompact.**

CHRONOLOGY

1808	External slave trade outlawed.
1810s–1850s	Suffrage gradually extended throughout South to white males over twenty-one years of age.
1820s–1830s	Southern legislatures enact slave codes to strengthen slavery.
	Southern legislatures enact laws to restrict growth of free black population and to limit freedom of free blacks.
	Southern intellectuals begin to fashion systematic defense of slavery.

1820–1860	Cotton production soars from about 300,000 bales to nearly 5 million bales.
1822	Denmark Vesey executed for conspiring to lead a slave rebellion in South Carolina.
1831	Nat Turner's slave rebellion occurs in Virginia.
1860	The slave population of the South surpasses 4 million, an increase of 600 percent in seven decades.

JOHN BROWN'S PIKES
Scorning what he called "milk-and-water" abolitionists who only talked about slavery, John Brown favored "action!" In 1859 when he brought his abolitionist war to Virginia, he carried with him 950 pikes, handsome but deadly spears made by a Connecticut blacksmith, which he expected to put into the hands of rebelling slaves. Bloody pikes, he thought, would end slavery in America. But after Brown's failure at Harpers Ferry, townspeople sold many of the weapons as souvenirs.
Chicago Historical Society.

THE HOUSE DIVIDED
1846–1861

14

OTHER THAN TWENTY CHILDREN, John Brown did not have much to show for his life in 1859. Grizzled, gnarled, and fifty-nine years old, he had for decades lived like a nomad, hauling his large family back and forth across six states as he tried desperately to better himself. He turned his hand to farming, raising sheep, running a tannery, and selling wool, but failure followed failure. The world had given John Brown some hard licks, but it had not budged his conviction that slavery was wrong and ought to be destroyed. He had learned to hate slavery at his father's knee, and in the wake of the fighting that erupted over the issue in Kansas in the 1850s, his beliefs turned violent. On May 24, 1856, he led an eight-man antislavery posse in the midnight slaughter of five allegedly proslavery men at Pottawatomie, Kansas. He told Mahala Doyle, whose husband and two oldest sons he killed, that if a man stood between him and what he thought right, he would take that man's life as calmly as he would eat breakfast.

Kansans knew that John Brown and his men were the Pottawatomie killers, but Brown admitted nothing, slipped away from the territory, and reemerged in the East. More than ever, he was a man on fire for abolition. He spent thirty months begging money from New England abolitionists to support his vague plan for military operations against slavery. He captivated the genteel Easterners, particularly the Boston elite. They shared his antislavery convictions and were awed by his iron-willed determination and courage. They listened when the hypnotic-eyed Brown told them that God had touched him for a great purpose. Eventually, Brown received enough in gifts to gather a small band of antislavery warriors.

On the night of October 16, 1859, John Brown took his war against slavery into the South. With only twenty-one men, including five African Americans, he invaded Harpers Ferry, Virginia. Brown's band quickly seized the town's armory and rifle works, but the invaders were immediately surrounded, first by local militia and then by Colonel Robert E. Lee, who commanded the U.S. troops in the area. When Brown refused to surrender, federal soldiers charged with bayonets. Seventeen men, two of whom were slaves, lost their lives. Although a few of Brown's raiders escaped, federal forces killed ten (including two of his sons) and captured seven, among them Brown.

"When I strike, the bees will begin to swarm," Brown told Frederick Douglass a few months before the raid. As slaves rushed to Harpers Ferry, Brown planned to arm them with the pikes he carried with him and with weapons stolen from the armory. They would then fight a war of liberation. In reality, however, Brown had neglected to inform the slaves that he had arrived in Harpers Ferry, and the few who knew wanted nothing to do with the enterprise. "It was not a slave insurrection," Abraham Lincoln observed. "It was an attempt by white men to get up a revolt among slaves, in which the slaves refused to participate. In fact, it was so absurd that the slaves, with all their ignorance, saw plainly enough it could not succeed."

JOHN BROWN
Was John Brown crazy? The debate about Brown's mental state began with his contemporaries and has raged ever since. Those who argue that he was a madman have asked: Would a sane man have butchered innocent victims at Pottawatomie Creek and set out for Harpers Ferry to overthrow slavery with fewer than two dozen men? But others see a resolute and selfless hero, not a psychotic. Moreover, they ask: If John Brown was a lunatic, what does that make the proper New England abolitionists who supported him?
Boston Athenaeum.

Although Brown's raid ended in utter defeat, it provided white Southerners with proof of their growing suspicion that Northerners actively sought to incite slaves in bloody rebellion. For more than a decade, Northerners and Southerners had hurled accusations at one another, and by 1859, emotions were raw. Sectional tension was as old as the United States, but hostility escalated to unprecedented heights with the outbreak of war with Mexico in May 1846. Only three months after the war began, national expansion and the slavery issue intersected when Representative David Wilmot introduced a bill to prohibit slavery from any territory that might be acquired as a result of the war. After that, the problem of slavery in the territories bitterly divided the nation.

For a decade and a half, the slavery issue poisoned national political debate and contaminated issues that were only distantly related. Slavery proved powerful enough to transform party politics into sectional politics. Rather than Whigs and Democrats confronting one another across party lines, Northerners and Southerners eyed one another hostilely across the Mason-Dixon line. Sectional politics encouraged the South's separatist impulses. A fitful tendency before the Mexican War, southern separatism gained strength with each confrontation. As the nation lurched from crisis to crisis, southern disaffection and alienation mounted and support for compromise and conciliation eroded. The era ended as it began—with a crisis of the Union. As Abraham Lincoln predicted in 1858, "A house divided against itself cannot stand."

Fruits of War

Congress had faced the question of slavery in the national territories before the Mexican War, but history provided contradictory precedents. In 1787, Congress passed the Northwest Ordinance, which banned slavery in territory north of the Ohio River. In 1803, when the United States acquired the Louisiana Territory, where slavery was already legal, Congress allowed slavery to remain. As part of the Missouri Compromise of 1820, Congress voted to prohibit slavery in part of the territory and allow it in the rest.

In 1846, when it appeared that the war with Mexico would mean new U.S. territories, politicians put on the table a variety of different plans, but when the war ended in 1848, Congress had made no headway in solving the great issue of slavery in the territories. Nor did the presidential election that year produce an answer. Instead, the territorial issue battered the Whig and Democratic Parties and raised the political temperature of the nation to the boiling point. In 1850, after four years of strife, Congress patched together a settlement, one that most Americans hoped would be permanent.

The Wilmot Proviso and the Expansion of Slavery

In the years leading up to the Civil War, Americans did not focus on slavery where it existed but on the possibility that it might expand into areas where it did not exist. Except for a few abolitionists who strove to uproot slavery wherever they found it, most Americans agreed that the Constitution had left the issue of slavery to the individual states to decide. Northern states had done away with slavery, while southern states had retained it. But what about slavery in the nation's territories? The Constitution stated that "Congress shall have power to . . . make all needful rules and regulations respecting the territory . . . belonging to the United States." The debate between the North and South about slavery, then, turned toward Congress and the definition of its authority over western lands.

The spark for the national debate was provided in August 1846 by a young Democratic representative from Pennsylvania, David Wilmot, who proposed that Congress bar slavery from all lands acquired in the war with Mexico. Wilmot explained that the Mexicans had already abolished slavery in all of their territory. "God forbid," he declared, "that we should be the means of planting this institution upon it."

Regardless of party affiliation, Northerners lined up behind Wilmot's effort to stop the spread of slavery. Abolitionists, of course, supported "free soil," that is, territory from which slavery was prohibited. Many Whigs also stepped forward on the basis of principle. Whigs often denounced slavery as a sin and emphasized Congress's authority to ban it from the territories. But not all Northerners who opposed slavery's extension did so out of sympathy for slaves. Support also came from Northerners who were not so much antislavery as they were anti-South. New slave territories would eventually mean new slave states, and they opposed any act that would magnify the power of Southerners. From experience, they knew that proslavery Southerners in Congress backed economic policies radically different from those of Northerners, especially in banking, internal improvements, and the tariff.

Further support came from Northerners who were hostile to African Americans and wanted to reserve new lands for whites. Wilmot himself had blatantly encouraged racist support when he declared, "I would preserve for free white labor a fair country, a rich inheritance, where the sons of toil, of my own race and own color, can live without the disgrace which association with negro slavery brings upon free labor." It is no wonder that some called the Wilmot Proviso the White Man's Proviso.

While the specter of new slave territory alarmed most Northerners, the thought that slavery might be excluded outraged almost all white Southerners. Yeoman and planter alike regarded the West as a ladder for economic and social opportunity. In addition, they agreed that the exclusion of slavery was a slap in the face. An Alabaman observed that at least half of the American soldiers in Mexico were Southerners. "When the war-worn soldier returns home," he asked, "is he to be told that he cannot carry his property to the country won by his blood?"

Southern leaders also approached the territorial issue with an eye on political clout. They understood the need for political parity with the North to protect the South's interests, especially slavery. The need never seemed more urgent than in the 1840s, when the North's population and wealth were booming. James Henry Hammond of South Carolina predicted that ten new states would be carved from the acquired Mexican land. If free soil won, the North would "ride over us rough shod" in Congress, he claimed.

In the nation's capital, the two sides squared off. Because Northerners had a majority in the House, they easily passed the Wilmot Proviso over the united opposition of Southerners. In the Senate, John C. Calhoun of South Carolina denied that Congress had constitutional authority to exclude slavery from the nation's territories. He argued that the territories were the "joint and common property" of all the states, that Congress could not justly deprive any state of equal rights in the territories, and that Congress therefore could not bar citizens of one state from migrating with their property (including slaves) to the territories. Because slave states in the Senate outnumbered free states fifteen to fourteen, southern senators successfully stopped the proviso.

Senator Lewis Cass of Michigan offered a compromise between these extremes. He proposed the doctrine of "popular sovereignty": letting the people who actually settled the territories decide for themselves slavery's fate. This solution, Cass argued, sat squarely in the American tradition of democracy and local self-government. It had the added attraction of removing the incendiary issue of the expansion of slavery from the nation's capital and lodging it in distant, sleepy territorial legislatures, where it would excite fewer passions.

But the plan's most attractive feature was its ambiguity about the precise moment when settlers could determine slavery's fate. Northern advocates believed that the decision on slavery could be made as soon as the first territorial legislature assembled. With free-soil majorities likely, they would shut the door to slavery almost before the first slave arrived.

Southern supporters declared that popular sovereignty guaranteed that slavery would be unrestricted throughout the entire settlement period. Only at the very end, when settlers in the territory drew up a constitution and applied for statehood, could they decide the issue of slavery or freedom. By then, slavery would have sunk deep roots. As long as the matter of timing remained vague, popular sovereignty provided some Northerners and some Southerners with common ground.

When Congress ended its session in 1848, no plan had won a majority in both houses. Northerners who demanded no new slave territory anywhere, ever, and Southerners who demanded free entry for their slave property into all territories, or else, staked out their extreme positions. Unresolved in Congress, the territorial question naturally became an issue in the presidential election of 1848.

The Election of 1848

When President Polk—worn out, ailing, and unable to unite the Democratic Party—chose not to seek reelection, the Democratic convention nominated Lewis Cass of Michigan, the man most closely as-

GENERAL TAYLOR CIGAR CASE
This papier-mâché cigar case portrays General Zachary Taylor, Whig presidential candidate in 1848, in a colorful scene from the Mexican War. Shown as a dashing, elegant officer, Taylor was in fact a short, thickset, and roughly dressed Indian fighter who had spent his career commanding small frontier garrisons. The inscription reminds voters that Taylor was a victor in the first four battles fought in the war and directs attention away from the fact that in politics he was a rank amateur.
Collection of Janice L. and David J. Frent.

sociated with popular sovereignty, but in an effort to keep peace between the proslavery and antislavery factions within the party adopted a platform that avoided a firm position on slavery in the territories. The Whigs followed a different strategy in their effort to patch the fissure within their party over slavery. They nominated the Mexican War hero, General Zachary Taylor. The Whigs bet that selection of a military hero combined with total silence on the central issue facing the country would carry the day and thus declined to adopt a party platform. Taylor, who owned more than one hundred slaves on plantations in Mississippi and Louisiana, was hailed by Georgia politician Robert Toombs as a "Southern man, a slaveholder, a cotton planter."

Antislavery Whigs balked and looked for an alternative. The time seemed ripe for a major political realignment. Senator Charles Sumner called for "one grand Northern party of Freedom," and in the summer of 1848 antislavery Democrats and antislavery Whigs founded the Free-Soil Party. Nearly fifteen thousand noisy Free-Soilers gathered in Buffalo, New York, where they welded the factions together by nominating a Democrat, Martin Van Buren, for president and a Whig, Charles Francis Adams, for vice president. The platform boldly proclaimed, "Free soil, free speech, free labor, and free men."

The November election dashed the hopes of the Free-Soilers. Although they succeeded in making slavery the campaign's central issue, they did not carry a single state. The major parties went through contortions to present their candidates favorably in both the North and the South, and their evasions succeeded. Taylor won the all-important electoral vote, 163 to 127, carrying eight of the fifteen slave states and seven of the fifteen free states (Map 14.1). (Wisconsin had entered the Union earlier in 1848 as the fifteenth free state.) Northern voters proved they were not yet ready for Sumner's "one grand Northern party of Freedom," but the struggle over slavery in the territories had shaken the major parties badly.

Debate and Compromise

Zachary Taylor entered the White House in March 1849 and almost immediately shocked the nation. The southern slaveholder championed a free-soil solution to the problem of western land. He sent agents west to persuade settlers in California and when he took the floor on January 29, 1850, "I hold in my hand a series of resolutions which I desire to submit to the consideration of this body. Taken together, in combination, they propose an amicable arrangement of all questions in controversy between the free and slave states, growing out of the subject of slavery." His comprehensive plan sought to balance the interests of the slave and free states. Admit California as a free state, he proposed, but organize the rest of the Southwest without restrictions on slavery. Require Texas to abandon its claim to parts of New Mexico, but compensate it by assuming its preannexation debt. Abolish the slave trade in Washington, D.C., but confirm slavery itself in the nation's capital. Reassert Congress's lack

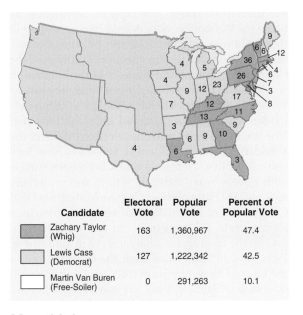

Candidate	Electoral Vote	Popular Vote	Percent of Popular Vote
Zachary Taylor (Whig)	163	1,360,967	47.4
Lewis Cass (Democrat)	127	1,222,342	42.5
Martin Van Buren (Free-Soiler)	0	291,263	10.1

MAP 14.1
The Election of 1848

New Mexico to frame constitutions and apply for admission to the Union as states. Predominately antislavery, the settlers began writing free-state constitutions. "For the first time," Mississippian Jefferson Davis lamented, "we are about permanently to destroy the balance of power between the sections."

When Congress convened in December 1849, anxious citizens packed the galleries, eager for the "Great Debate." They witnessed what proved to be one of the longest, most contentious, and most significant sessions in the history of Congress in which the territorial issue dominated. President Taylor urged Congress to admit California as a free state immediately and to admit New Mexico, which lagged behind, as soon as it applied. Southerners exploded. In their eyes, Taylor had betrayed his region. Southerners who would "consent to be thus degraded and enslaved," a North Carolinian declared, "ought to be whipped through their fields by their own negroes." Calhoun almost lost heart. "As things now stand," he said in February, the South "cannot with safety remain in the Union."

Into this rancorous scene stepped Henry Clay, recently returned to the Senate by his home state of Kentucky. His reputation preceded him: the "Great Pacificator," master of accommodation, architect of Union-saving compromises in the Missouri and nullification crises. "Mr. President," Clay declared

JOHN C. CALHOUN
Hollow-cheeked and dark-eyed in this 1850 daguerreotype by Mathew Brady, Calhoun had only months to live. Still, his passion and indomitable will come through. British writer Harriet Martineau once described the champion of southern rights as "the cast-iron man who looks as if he had never been born and could never be extinguished."
National Portrait Gallery, Smithsonian Institution/Art Resource, N.Y.

of authority to interfere with the interstate slave trade. And enact a more effective fugitive slave law.

Antislavery advocates and "fire-eaters" (as radical southern secessionists were called) both savaged Clay's plan. Senator Salmon Chase of Ohio ridiculed it as "sentiment for the North, substance for the South." Senator Henry S. Foote of Mississippi denounced it as more offensive to the South than the speeches of abolitionists William Lloyd Garrison, Wendell Phillips, and Frederick Douglass combined. The most ominous response came from the mighty Calhoun, who concluded northern agitation on the slavery question had "snapped" many of the "cords which bind these states together in one common Union . . . and has greatly weakened all the others." The fragile political unity of North and South depended on continued equal representation in the Senate, which Clay's plan for a free California destroyed. Without equality, Calhoun declared, Southerners were defenseless and could not remain in the Union.

After Clay and Calhoun had spoken, it was time for the third member of the "great triumvirate," Daniel Webster of Massachusetts. Like Clay, Webster sought to build a constituency for compromise. Admitting that the South had complaints that required attention, he argued forcefully that secession from the Union would mean civil war. He appealed for an end to reckless proposals and, to

the dismay of many Northerners, mentioned by name the Wilmot Proviso. A legal ban on slavery in the territories was unnecessary, he said, because rough climate and terrain effectively prohibited the expansion of cotton and slaves into the Southwest.

Free-soil forces recoiled from what they saw as Webster's desertion. Theodore Parker, a Boston clergyman and abolitionist, could only conclude that "the Southern men" must have offered Webster the presidency. Senator William H. Seward of New York responded that Webster's and Clay's compromise with slavery was "radically wrong and essentially vicious." He flatly rejected Calhoun's argument that Congress lacked constitutional authority to exclude slavery from the territories. In any case, Seward said, in the most sensational moment in his address, there was a "higher law than the Constitution"— the law of God—to ensure freedom in all the public domain. Claiming that God was a Free-Soiler did nothing to cool the superheated atmosphere of Washington.

In May, a Senate committee (with the tireless Clay at its head) reported a bill that joined Clay's resolutions into a single comprehensive package, known as the Omnibus Bill because it was a vehicle on which "every sort of passenger" could ride. Clay bet that a majority of Congress wanted compromise and that while the omnibus contained items individuals disliked, each would vote for the

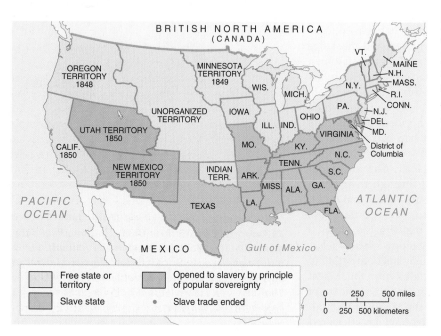

M A P 14.2

The Compromise of 1850
The patched-together sectional agreement was both clumsy and unstable. Few Americans—in either the North or the South— supported all five parts of the Compromise.

package to gain an overall settlement of sectional issues. But the omnibus strategy backfired. Free-Soilers, Conscience Whigs, and proslavery Southerners would support separate parts of Clay's bill, but they would not endorse the whole. After making seventy speeches to defend his plan, Clay saw it go down to defeat.

Fortunately for those who favored a settlement, Senator Stephen A. Douglas, a rising Democratic star from Illinois, stepped into Clay's shoes. Rejecting the omnibus strategy, he broke the bill into its various parts and skillfully ushered each through Congress. The agreement Douglas won in September 1850 was very much the one Clay had proposed in January. California entered the Union as a free state. New Mexico and Utah became territories in which the question of slavery would be decided by popular sovereignty. Texas accepted its present-day boundary with New Mexico and received $10 million from the federal government. Congress ended the slave trade in the District of Columbia yet enacted a more stringent fugitive slave law. In September, Millard Fillmore, who had become president upon the death of Zachary Taylor in July, signed each bill, collectively known as the Compromise of 1850, into law (Map 14.2).

Actually, the Compromise of 1850 was not a true compromise at all. Douglas's parliamentary skill, not a spirit of conciliation, led to legislative success. Only by nimbly allying a small group of true compromisers with larger blocs of Northerners and Southerners who voted along sectional lines did Douglas gain a majority for each separate measure. Nor was the Compromise the "final settlement," as President Fillmore announced.

The Sectional Balance Undone

The so-called final settlement of the Compromise of 1850 began to come apart almost immediately. The thread that unraveled the Compromise was not slavery in the Southwest, the crux of the disagreement, but runaway slaves in New England, a part of the settlement that had previously received relatively little attention. Rather than restore calm, the Compromise brought the horrors of slavery into the North.

Millions of Northerners who never saw a runaway slave nevertheless confronted slavery in the early 1850s. Harriet Beecher Stowe's *Uncle Tom's Cabin*, a novel that vividly depicted the brutality and heartlessness of the South's "peculiar institution," aroused passions so deep that many found goodwill toward white Southerners nearly impossible. But no popular uprising forced Congress to reopen the slavery controversy: Politicians did it themselves. Four years after Congress delicately stitched the sectional compromise together, it ripped the threads out. It once again posed the question of slavery in the territories, the deadliest of all sectional issues.

The Fugitive Slave Act

The Fugitive Slave Act proved the most explosive of the Compromise measures. The issue of runaways was as old as the Constitution, which contained a provision for the return of any "person held to service or labor in one state" who escaped to another. In 1793, a federal law gave muscle to the provision by authorizing slave owners to enter other states to recapture their slave property. Proclaiming the 1793 law a license to kidnap free blacks, northern states in the 1830s began passing "personal liberty laws" that provided fugitives with some protection. Some northern communities also formed vigilance committees to help runaways and to obstruct white Southerners who came north to reclaim them. Each year, a few hundred slaves escaped into free states and found friendly northern "conductors" who put them aboard the "underground railroad," which was not a railroad at all but a series of secret "stations" (hideouts) on the way to Canada.

Furious about northern interference, Southerners in 1850 insisted on the stricter fugitive slave law that was passed as part of the Compromise. To seize an alleged slave, a slaveholder or his agent simply had to appear before a commissioner and swear that the runaway was his. The commissioner earned ten dollars for every black returned to slavery but only five dollars for those set free. Most galling to Northerners, the law stipulated that all citizens were expected to assist officials in apprehending runaways. Theodore Parker, the clergyman and abolitionist, denounced the law as "a hateful statute of kidnappers" and headed a Boston vigilance committee that openly violated it. In February 1851, an angry crowd in Boston overpowered federal marshals and snatched a runaway named Shadrach from a courtroom, put him on the underground railroad, and whisked him off to Montreal, Canada.

To white Southerners, it seemed that fanatics of the "higher law" creed had whipped Northerners into a frenzy of massive resistance. Actually, the overwhelming majority of fugitives claimed before federal commissioners were reenslaved and shipped south peacefully. Spectacular rescues such as the one that saved Shadrach were rare. But brutal enforcement of the unpopular law had a radicalizing effect in the North, particularly in New England. And to Southerners it seemed that Northerners had betrayed the Compromise. As a Tennessee man warned in November 1850, "If the fugitive slave bill is not enforced in the north, the

moderate men of the South . . . will be overwhelmed by the 'fire-eaters.'"

Uncle Tom's Cabin

The spectacle of shackled African Americans being herded south seared the conscience of every Northerner who witnessed such a scene. But even more Northerners were turned against slavery by a fictional account, a novel. Harriet Beecher Stowe, a Northerner who had never seen a plantation, made the South's slaves into flesh-and-blood human beings almost more real than life.

A member of a famous clan of preachers, teachers, and reformers, Stowe despised the slave catch-

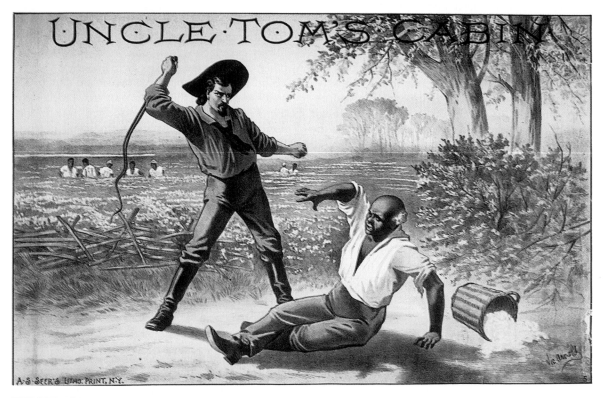

THEATER POSTER
During the 1850s, at least ten individuals, including Harriet Beecher Stowe herself, dramatized the novel **Uncle Tom's Cabin.** *These plays, known as "Tom Shows," drew crowds in America and Britain. Stowe's moral indictment of slavery translated well to the stage. Scenes of Eliza crossing the ice with bloodhounds in pursuit, the cruelty of Legree, and Little Eva borne to heaven on puffy clouds gripped the imagination of audiences and fueled the growing antislavery crusade.*
Smithsonian Institution.

www.bedfordstmartins.com/roarkcompact SEE THE ONLINE STUDY GUIDE for more help in analyzing this image.

ers and wrote to expose the sin of slavery. Published in 1852, her book *Uncle Tom's Cabin* became a blockbuster hit and sold 300,000 copies in its first year. Her characters leaped from the page. Here was the gentle slave Uncle Tom, a Christian saint who forgave those who beat him to death; the courageous slave Eliza, who fled with her child across the frozen Ohio River; and the fiendish overseer Simon Legree, whose Louisiana plantation was a nightmare of torture and death. Herself the mother of seven children, Stowe aimed her most powerful blows at slavery's destructive impact on the family. Her character Eliza succeeds in keeping her son from being sold away, but other mothers are not so fortunate. When told that her infant has been sold, Lucy drowns herself. Driven half mad by the sale of a son and daughter, Cassy decides "never again [to] let a child live to grow up!" She gives her third child an opiate and watches as "he slept to death."

Responses to *Uncle Tom's Cabin* depended on geography. In the North, common people and literary giants alike shed tears and sang its praises. The poet John Greenleaf Whittier sent "ten thousand thanks for thy immortal book," and poet Henry Wadsworth Longfellow judged it "one of the greatest triumphs recorded in literary history." What Northerners accepted as truth, Southerners denounced as slander. Virginian George F. Holmes proclaimed Stowe a member of the "Woman's Rights" and "Higher Law" schools and dismissed the novel as a work of "intense fanaticism." Unfortunately, he said, this "maze of misinterpretation" had filled those who knew nothing about slavery "with hatred for that institution and those who uphold it." Although it is impossible to measure precisely the impact of a novel on public opinion, *Uncle*

Tom's Cabin clearly helped to crystallize northern sentiment against slavery and to confirm white Southerners' suspicion that they no longer had any sympathy in the free states.

Other writers—ex-slaves who knew life in slave cabins firsthand—also produced stinging indictments of slavery. Solomon Northup's compelling *Twelve Years a Slave* (1853) sold 27,000 copies in two years, and the powerful *Narrative of the Life of Frederick Douglass, as Told by Himself* (1845) eventually sold more than 30,000 copies. But no work touched the North's conscience like the novel by the woman who had never set foot on a plantation. A decade after its publication, when Stowe visited Abraham Lincoln at the White House, he reportedly said, "So you are the little woman who wrote the book that made this great war."

The Kansas-Nebraska Act

As national elections approached in 1852, Democrats and Whigs sought to close the sectional rifts that had opened within their parties. For their presidential nominee, the Democrats turned to Franklin Pierce of New Hampshire. Pierce's most valuable asset was his well-known sympathy with southern views on public issues. His leanings caused northern critics to include him among the "doughfaces," northern men malleable enough to champion southern causes. The Whigs were less successful in compromising differences. Adopting the formula that had proved successful in 1848, they chose another Mexican War hero, General Winfield Scott of Virginia. But the Whigs were hopeless divided and suffered a humiliating defeat. The Democrat Pierce carried twenty-seven states to Scott's four, 254 electoral votes to 42 (Table 14.1). In the afterglow of the

TABLE 14.1
THE ELECTION OF 1852

Candidate	Electoral Vote	Popular Vote	Percent of Popular Vote
Franklin Pierce (Democrat)	254	1,601,000	50.9
Winfield Scott (Whig)	42	1,385,000	44.1
John P. Hale (Free-Soil)	0	156,000	5.0

Compromise of 1850, the Free-Soil Party lost almost half of the voters who had turned to it in the tumultuous atmosphere of 1848.

Eager to leave the sectional controversy behind, the new president turned swiftly to foreign expansion. Manifest Destiny remained robust. Pierce's major objective was Cuba, which was owned by Spain and in which slavery flourished, but Pierce's clumsy diplomatic efforts galvanized antislavery Northerners, who blocked Cuba's acquisition. Pierce's fortunes improved in Mexico. In 1853, he sent diplomat James Gadsden, a former army officer and railroad company president, to negotiate a $15 million purchase of some 30,000 square miles of territory south of the Gila River in present-day Arizona and New Mexico. The Gadsden Purchase stemmed from the dream of a transcontinental railroad to California and Pierce's desire to build it through Mexican territory. The booming population of the Pacific coast made it obvious that the vast, loose-jointed republic needed a railroad to bind it together. Talk of a railroad ignited rivalries in cities from New Orleans to Chicago as they maneuvered to become the eastern terminus. Thus, the railroad became a sectional contest, which by the 1850s inevitably involved slavery.

No one played the railroad game more enthusiastically than Senator Stephen A. Douglas, who was an energetic spokesman for western economic development. He badly wanted the transcontinental railroad for Chicago and his home state, Illinois. His chairmanship of the Senate Committee on Territories provided him with an opportunity. Any railroad that ran west from Chicago would pass through a region that Congress in 1830 had designated a "permanent" Indian reserve. Douglas proposed giving this vast area between the Missouri River and the Rocky Mountains an Indian name, Nebraska, and then nullifying Indian titles and throwing the Indians out. Once the region achieved territorial status, whites could survey and sell the land, establish civil government, and build a railroad.

Gadsden Purchase of 1853

Nebraska lay within the Louisiana Purchase north of 36°30′, which, according to the Missouri Compromise of 1820, closed it to slavery. Since Douglas could not count on New England to back western economic development, he needed southern votes to pass his Nebraska legislation. But Southerners had no incentive to create another free territory or to help a northern city win the Pacific railroad. Southerners, however, would help to organize Nebraska—for a price: nothing less than the repeal of the Missouri Compromise. Southerners insisted that Congress organize Nebraska according to popular sovereignty, and that meant giving slavery a chance in the Nebraska Territory and reopening the dangerous issue of slavery expansion that Douglas himself had so ably helped to resolve only four years earlier.

In January 1854, Douglas introduced his bill to organize the Nebraska Territory, leaving to the settlers themselves the decision about slavery. At southern insistence, and even though he knew it would "raise a hell of a storm," Douglas added an explicit repeal of the Missouri Compromise. Indeed, the Nebraska bill raised a storm of controversy. Free-Soilers branded Douglas's plan "a gross violation of a sacred pledge" and an "atrocious plot" to transform free land into a "dreary region of despotism, inhabited by masters and slaves."

Douglas skillfully shepherded the explosive bill through Congress in May 1854. Nine-tenths of all southern members (Whigs and Democrats) and half of the northern Democrats cast votes in favor. Like Douglas, most northern Democrats believed that popular sovereignty would make Nebraska free territory. Ominously, however, half of the northern Democrats broke with their party and opposed the bill. In its final form, the Kansas-Nebraska Act divided the huge territory in two: Nebraska west of the free state of Iowa and Kansas west of the slave state of Missouri (Map 14.3).

The Realignment of the Party System

The Kansas-Nebraska Act marked a fateful escalation of the sectional conflict. Douglas's controversial measure had several consequences, none more crucial than the realignment of the nation's political parties. Since the rise of the Whigs in the early 1830s, Whigs and Democrats had or-

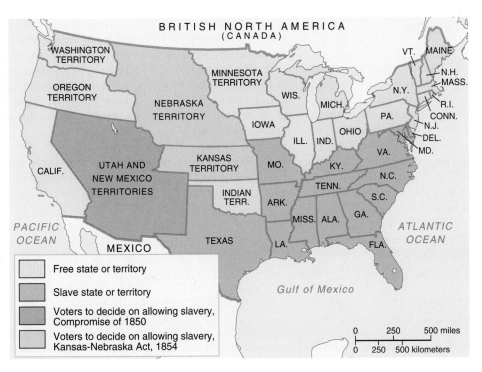

MAP 14.3

The Kansas-Nebraska Act, 1854
*Americans hardly thought twice about dispossessing the Indians of lands guaranteed
them by treaty, but many worried about the outcome of repealing the Missouri
Compromise and opening up lands to slavery.*

READING THE MAP: How many slave states and how many free states does the map show?
Estimate the percentage of territory likely to be settled by slaveholders.
CONNECTIONS: Who would be more likely to support changes in government legislation
to discontinue the Missouri Compromise, slaveholders or free-soil advocates? Why?

www.bedfordstmartins.com/roarkcompact   SEE THE ONLINE STUDY GUIDE for more help in analyzing this map.

ganized and channeled political conflict in the
nation. This party system dampened sectionalism
and strengthened the Union. To achieve national
political power, Whigs and Democrats had to retain strength in both the North and the South.
Strong northern and southern wings required that
each party compromise and find positions acceptable to both wings.

The Kansas-Nebraska controversy shattered
this conservative political system. In place of two
national parties with bisectional strength, the mid-

1850s witnessed the development of one party
heavily dominated by one section and another party
entirely limited to the other section. Rather than
"national" parties, the country had what one critic
disdainfully called "geographic" parties. Parties
now had the advantage of sharpening ideological
and policy differences between the sections and no
longer muffling moral issues, like slavery. But the
new party system also thwarted political compromise and instead promoted political polarization
and further jeopardized the Union.

The Old Parties: Whigs and Democrats

Distress signals could be heard from the Whig camp as early as the Mexican War, when members clashed over the future of slavery in annexed Mexican lands. But the disintegration of the party dated from 1849–1850, when southern Whigs watched in stunned amazement as Whig president Zachary Taylor sponsored a plan for a free California. And above the Mason-Dixon line, the strains of the slav-

ery issue split northern Whigs. Anti-slavery Whigs gained a majority by 1852. The party could please the southern wing or the northern wing but not both. The Whigs' miserable showing in the election of 1852 made clear that they were no longer a strong national party. By 1856, after more than two decades of contesting the Democrats, they were hardly a party at all (Map 14.4).

The decline and eventual collapse of the Whig Party left the Democrats as the country's only national party. Although the Democrats were not im-

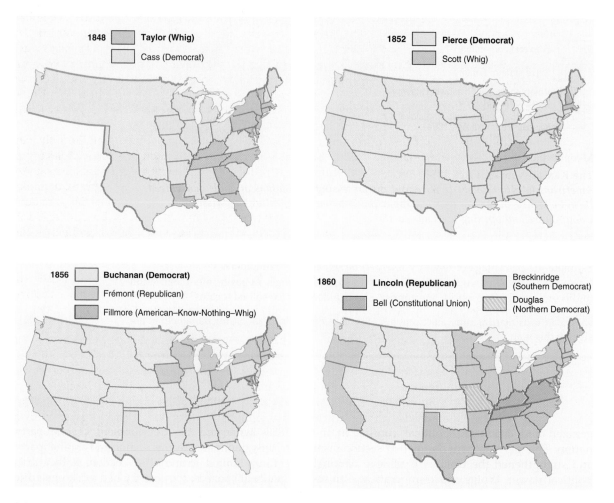

MAP 14.4

Political Realignment, 1848–1860

In 1848, slavery and sectionalism began hammering the country's party system. The Whig Party was an early casualty. By 1860, national parties—those that contended for votes in both the North and the South—had been replaced by regional parties.

mune to the disruptive pressures of the territorial question, they discovered in popular sovereignty a doctrine that many Democrats could support. But popular sovereignty very nearly undid the party as well. When Stephen Douglas applied the doctrine to that part of the Louisiana Purchase where slavery had been barred, he divided northern Democrats and destroyed the dominance of the Democratic Party in the free states. After 1854, the Democrats became a southern-dominated party.

Nevertheless, Democrats remained the dominant party throughout the 1850s. Gains in the South more than balanced losses in the North. During the decade, Democrats elected two presidents and won majorities in Congress in almost every election. But national power required that the party maintain a northern and a southern wing, which in turn required that they avoid the issue of the expansion of slavery.

The breakup of the Whigs and the disaffection of significant numbers of northern Democrats set many Americans politically adrift. As they searched for new political harbors, Americans found that the death of the old party system created a multitude of fresh political alternatives. The question was which party would attract the drifters.

The New Parties: Know-Nothings and Republicans

Dozens of new political organizations vied for voters' attention, but two emerged as true contenders. One grew out of the slavery controversy, a spontaneous coalition of indignant antislavery Northerners. The other arose from an entirely different split in American society, that between Roman Catholic immigrants and native Protestants.

The tidal wave of immigrants that broke over America in the decade from 1845 to 1855 produced a nasty backlash among Protestant Americans, who believed they were about to drown in a sea of Roman Catholics from Ireland and Germany (see Figure 12.1). When the immigrants entered American politics, they largely became Democrats because they perceived that party as more tolerant of newcomers than were the Whigs. But in the 1850s they met sharp political opposition when nativists (individuals who were anti-immigrant) began to organize, first into secret fraternal societies and then

into a political party. Recruits swore never to vote for either foreign-born or Roman Catholic candidates and not to reveal any information about the organization. When questioned, they said: "I know nothing." Officially, they were named the American Party, but most Americans called them Know-Nothings.

The Know-Nothings exploded onto the political stage in 1854 and 1855 with a series of dazzling successes. They captured state legislatures in the Northeast, West, and South and claimed dozens of seats in Congress. Their greatest triumph came in Massachusetts, a favorite destination for the Irish. Know-Nothings elected the Massachusetts governor, all of the state senators, all but two of the state representatives, and all of the congressmen. The American Party attracted both Democrats and Whigs, but with their party crumbling, more Whigs responded to the attraction. In 1855, an observer might reasonably have concluded that the Know-Nothings had emerged as the successor to the Whigs.

But Know-Nothings were not the only new party making noise. Among the new antislavery organizations provoked by the Kansas-Nebraska Act, one called itself Republican. Republicans attempted to unite under their banner all the dissidents and political orphans—Whigs, Free-Soilers, anti-Nebraska Democrats, even Know-Nothings—who opposed the extension of slavery into any territory of the United States.

The Republican creed tapped basic beliefs and values of the northern public. Slave labor and free labor, Republicans argued, had spawned two incompatible civilizations. In the South, they said, slavery degraded the dignity of white labor by associating work with blacks and servility. They argued slavery repressed every Southerner, except planter aristocrats. Those insatiable slave lords, whom antislavery Northerners called the Slave Power, now conspired to expand slavery, subvert liberty, and undermine the Constitution through the Democratic Party.

Only by restricting slavery to the South, Republicans believed, could free labor flourish elsewhere. The system of free labor respected the dignity of work and provided anyone willing to toil an opportunity for a decent living and for advancement. These powerful images attracted a wide range of Northerners to the Republican cause.

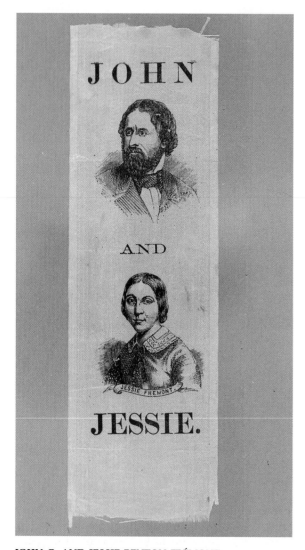

JOHN C. AND JESSIE BENTON FRÉMONT
The election of 1856 marked the first time a candidate's wife appeared on campaign items. Smart and ambitious, Jessie Benton Frémont made the breakthrough. Seen here on a silk ribbon with her husband, John C. Frémont, Republican Party presidential nominee, Jessie helped plan Frémont's campaign, coauthored his election biography, and drew northern women into political activity as never before. "What a shame that women can't vote!" declared abolitionist Lydia Maria Child. "We'd carry 'our Jessie' into the White House on our shoulders, wouldn't we." Critics of Jessie's violation of women's traditional sphere ridiculed both Frémonts. A man who met the couple in San Francisco pronounced her "the better man of the two." Jessie Frémont was, as Abraham Lincoln observed ambivalently, "quite a female politician."
Collection of Janice L. and David J. Frent.

The Election of 1856

By the mid-1850s, the Know-Nothings had emerged as the principal champion of nativism and the Republicans as the primary advocate of antislavery. But the election of 1856 revealed that the Republicans had emerged as the Democrats' main challenger, and slavery in the territories became the election's only issue. The Know-Nothings came apart when party leaders insisted on a platform that endorsed the Kansas-Nebraska Act, causing most Northerners to walk out. The Know-Nothings who remained nominated ex-president Millard Fillmore.

The Republicans, in contrast, adopted a platform that focused almost exclusively on "making every territory free." When they labeled slavery a "relic of barbarism," Republicans signaled that they had written off the South. For president, they nominated the dashing soldier and California adventurer John C. Frémont. Though a celebrated explorer, Frémont lacked political credentials. Political know-how resided in his wife, Jessie, who, as a daughter of Senator Thomas Hart Benton of Missouri, knew the political map as well as her husband knew western trails. Although careful to maintain a proper public image, the vivacious thirty-two-year-old mother and antislavery zealot helped draw ordinary women into electoral politics. (See "Documenting the American Promise," page 336.)

The Democrats, successful in 1852 in bridging sectional differences by nominating a northern man with southern principles, chose another "doughface," James Buchanan of Pennsylvania. The Democrats took refuge in the ambiguity of popular sovereignty and portrayed Republicans as extremists whose support for the Wilmot Proviso risked pushing the South out of the Union.

The Democratic strategy helped carry the day for Buchanan, but Frémont did astonishingly well. Buchanan won 174 electoral votes against Frémont's 114 and Fillmore's 8. Frémont carried all but five of the states north of the Mason-Dixon line. The election made clear that the Whigs had disintegrated, that the Know-Nothings would not ride nativism to national power, and that the Democrats were badly strained (see Map 14.4). But the big news was what the press called the "glorious defeat" of the Republicans. Despite being a brand-new party and purely sectional, Republicans challenged other parties for national power. Sectionalism had fashioned

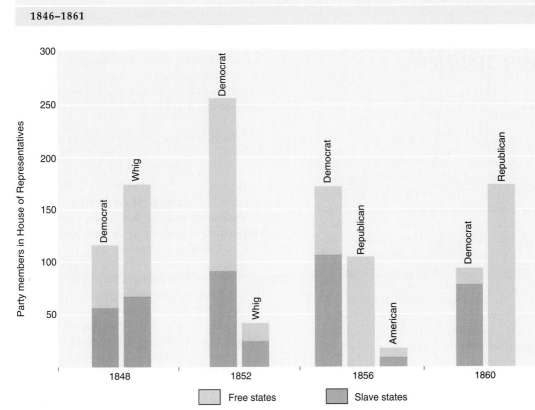

FIGURE 14.1
Changing Political Landscape, 1848–1860
The polarization of American politics between the free states and slave states occurred in little more than a decade.

a new party system, one that spelled danger for the Republic (Figure 14.1).

Freedom under Siege

The "glorious defeat" of the Republicans meant that the second party in the new two-party system was entirely sectional. It felt no compelling need to compromise, to conciliate, to keep a southern wing happy. Indeed, the Republican Party organized around the premise that the slaveholding South provided a profound threat to "free soil, free labor, and free men."

Events in distant Kansas Territory provided the young Republican organization with an enormous boost. Kansas reeled with violence between proslavery and antislavery settlers, which Republicans argued was southern in origin. They claimed that the Kansas frontier offered a window onto southern

values and intentions. Republicans also pointed to the brutal beating by a Southerner of a respected northern senator on the floor of Congress. Even the Supreme Court, in the Republicans' view, reflected the South's drive toward tyranny and minority rule. Then, in 1858, the issues dividing North and South received an extraordinary airing in a senatorial contest in Illinois, when the nation's foremost Democrat debated a resourceful Republican.

"Bleeding Kansas"

Three days after the House of Representatives approved the Kansas-Nebraska Act, Senator William H. Seward of New York boldly challenged the South. "Come on then, Gentlemen of the Slave States," he cried, "since there is no escaping your challenge, I accept it in behalf of the cause of freedom. We will engage in competition for the virgin soil of Kansas, and God give the victory to the side which is stronger in numbers as it is in right."

Women's Politics

*A*lthough women could not vote before the Civil War, many women nevertheless participated in public political activity. Uncle Tom's Cabin, Harriet Beecher Stowe's searing indictment of slavery, galvanized support for the Republican Party's campaign against the extension of slavery. The novel's moral power stemmed from its author's vivid description of how slavery assaulted cherished American institutions and values— Christian duty, female domesticity, and the family. Throughout her life, Jessie Benton Frémont sought to fulfill her domestic roles as wife and mother, even though she found them constraining. She also sought unabashedly to influence politics. She, like many other women, wrote to men of influence on behalf of her husband. "Do not suppose Sir, that I lightly interfere in a matter properly belonging to men," she began a letter to President James Polk in 1842, "but in the absence of Mr. Frémont I attend to his affairs at his request." During the 1850s, she became one of her husband's principal political analysts and advisers.

DOCUMENT 1. Jessie Benton Frémont's Letter to Elizabeth Blair Lee, 1856

On October 20, 1856, Jessie Frémont offered a clear-eyed interpretation of the significance of the Republican Party's paper-thin but devastating loss in the October 14 Pennsylvania state election.

I heartily regret the defeat we have met and do not look for things to change for the better. The Democrats will follow up their advantage with the courage of success & our forces are unorganized and just now surprised and inactive. I wish the cause had triumphed. I do wish Mr. Frémont had been the one to administer the bitter dose of subjection to the South for he has the coolness & nerve to do it just as it needs to be done—without passion & without sympathy—as coldly as a surgeon over a hospital patient would he have cut off their

right hand Kansas from the old unhealthy southern body. . . . Tell your Father he must come to us for example & comfort in November for I don't think we will wear any but black feathers this year.

SOURCE: Pamela Herr and Mary Lee Spence, eds., *The Letters of Jessie Benton Frémont* (Urbana and Chicago: University of Illinois Press, 1993), 140.

DOCUMENT 2. Harriot K. Hunt's Letter "to . . . [the] Treasurer, and the Assessors, and other Authorities of the city of Boston, and the Citizens generally," 1852

Some activist women challenged the domesticity that Stowe and Frémont honored, however, arguing that women's equality depended on their liberation from tradition. These women not only attended women's rights conventions but also signed petitions asking legislators to change laws that discriminated against women and worked to put the ideas of equal rights into practice in their personal lives. Harriot K. Hunt protested having to pay taxes when she was prohibited from voting. A physician who had practiced medicine in Boston since 1835, Hunt had been refused admission to Harvard Medical School and finally received her medical degree in 1853 from the Female Medical College of Philadelphia.

Harriot K. Hunt, physician, a native and permanent resident of the city of Boston, and for many years a taxpayer therein, in making payment of her city taxes for the coming year, begs leave to protest against the injustice and inequality of levying taxes upon women, and at the same time refusing them any voice or vote in the imposition and expenditure of the same. The only classes of male persons required to pay taxes, and not at the same time allowed the privilege of voting, are aliens and minors. The objection in the case of aliens is their supposed want of interest in our institutions and knowledge of them. The objection in the case of minors, is the want of sufficient understanding. These objections can not apply to women, natives of the city, all of whose property interests are here, and who have accumulated, by their own sagacity and industry, the very property on which they are taxed. But this is not all; the alien, by going through the forms of naturalization, the minor on coming of age, obtain the right of voting; and so long as they continue to pay a mere poll-tax of a dollar and a half, they may continue to exercise it, though so ignorant as not to be able to sign their names, or read the very votes they put into the ballot-boxes. Even drunkards, felons, idiots, and lunatics, if men, may still enjoy that right of voting to which no woman, however large the amount of taxes she pays, however respectable her character, or useful her life, can ever attain. Wherein, your remonstrant would inquire, is the justice, equality, or wisdom of this?

SOURCE: Elizabeth Cady Stanton, Susan B. Anthony, and Matilda Joslyn Gage, eds., *History of Woman Suffrage*, vol. 1 (New York: Fowler & Wells, 1881), 259.

DOCUMENT 3. Lucy Stone–Henry B. Blackwell Marriage Agreement, 1855

Marriage typically made women legally inferior to their husbands, but women's rights activists refashioned marriage vows to honor equality rather than subordination. When women's rights leader Lucy Stone married Henry B. Blackwell in 1855, both signed the following statement.

While acknowledging our mutual affection by publicly assuming the relationship of husband and wife, yet in justice to ourselves and a great principle, we deem it a duty to declare that this act on our part implies no sanction of, nor promise of voluntary obedience to such of the present laws of marriage, as refuse to recognize the wife as an independent, rational being, while they confer upon the husband an injurious and unnatural superiority, investing him with legal powers which no honorable man would exercise, and which no man should possess. We protest especially against the laws which give to the husband:

1. The custody of the wife's person.
2. The exclusive control and guardianship of their children.
3. The sole ownership of her personal [property], and use of her real estate. . . .

4. The absolute right to the product of her industry.
5. Also against laws which give to the widower so much larger and more permanent an interest in the property of his deceased wife, than they give to the widow in that of the deceased husband.
6. Finally, against the whole system by which "the legal existence of the wife is suspended during marriage," so that in most States, she neither has a legal part in the choice of her residence, nor can she make a will, nor sue or be sued in her own name, nor inherit property.

We believe that personal independence and equal human rights can never be forfeited, except for crime; that marriage should be an equal and permanent partnership, and so recognized by law; that until it is so recognized, married partners should provide against the radical injustice of present laws, by every means in their power. . . .

Thus reverencing law, we enter our protest against rules and customs which are unworthy of the name, since they violate justice, the essence of law.

(signed) Henry B. Blackwell
Lucy Stone

SOURCE: Elizabeth Cady Stanton, Susan B. Anthony, and Matilda Joslyn Gage, eds., *History of Woman Suffrage*, vol. 1 (New York: Fowler & Wells, 1881), 260–61.

QUESTIONS FOR ANALYSIS AND DEBATE

1. Jessie Frémont did not interpret the Republican defeat in Pennsylvania in 1856 as a "glorious defeat." Can you suggest possible reasons why she did not?
2. On what grounds, according to Harriot Hunt, should women be accorded the vote? Do you agree with her argument? Why or why not?
3. What legal disabilities for women was the marriage contract of Henry Blackstone and Lucy Stone designed to overcome?

Because of Stephen Douglas, popular sovereignty would determine whether Kansas became slave or free. Free-state and slave-state settlers each sought majorities at the ballot box, claimed God's blessing, and kept their rifles ready.

In the North, emigrant aid societies sprang up to promote settlement from the free states. The most famous, the New England Emigrant Aid Company, sponsored some 1,240 settlers in 1854 and 1855. In the South, tiny rural communities from Virginia to Texas raised money to support proslavery settlers. Missourians, already bordered on the east by the free state of Illinois and on the north by the free state of Iowa, especially thought it important to secure Kansas for slavery.

In theory, popular sovereignty meant an orderly tallying of ballots. In Kansas, however, elections became violent circuses. Thousands of hell-for-leather frontiersmen from Missouri, egged on by Missouri senator David Rice Atchison, invaded Kansas. "There are eleven hundred coming over from Platte County to vote," Atchison reported, "and if that ain't enough we can send five thousand—enough to kill every God-damned abolitionist in the Territory." Not surprisingly, proslavery candidates swept the early elections. When the first territorial legislature met, it enacted some of the most severe proslavery laws in the nation. Antislavery men, for example, were barred from holding office or serving on juries. Ever-pliant President Pierce endorsed the work of the fraudulently elected proslavery legislature. Free-state Kansans did not. They elected their own legislature, which promptly banned both slaves and free blacks from the territory. Organized into two rival governments and armed to the teeth, Kansans verged on civil war.

Fighting broke out on the morning of May 21, 1856, when a mob of several hundred proslavery men entered the town of Lawrence, the center of free-state settlement. Only one man died—a proslavery raider who was killed when a burning wall collapsed—but the "Sack of Lawrence," as free-soil forces called it, inflamed northern opinion. News of Lawrence provoked John Brown, a free-soil settler, to "fight fire with fire." Announcing that "it was better that a score of bad men should die than that one man who came here to make Kansas a Free State should be driven out," he led the posse that massacred five allegedly proslavery settlers along the Pottawatomie Creek. After that, guerrilla war engulfed the territory.

By providing graphic evidence of a dangerously aggressive Slave Power, "Bleeding Kansas" gave the fledgling Republican Party fresh ammunition. The Republicans received additional encouragement from an event that occurred in the national capital. On May 19 and 20, 1856, Senator Charles Sumner of Massachusetts delivered a scathing speech entitled "The Crime against Kansas." He damned the administration, the South, and proslavery Kansans. He also indulged in a scalding personal attack on the elderly South Carolina senator Andrew P. Butler, whom Sumner described as a "Don Quixote" who had taken as his mistress "the harlot, slavery."

"Bleeding Kansas," 1850s

Preston Brooks, a young South Carolina member of the House and a kinsman of Butler, felt compelled to defend the honor of both his aged relative and his state. On May 22, armed with a walking cane, Brooks entered the Senate, where he found Sumner working at his desk. He began beating Sumner over the head with his cane, and within a minute, Sumner lay bleeding and unconscious on the Senate floor. Brooks resigned his seat in the House, only to be promptly reelected. In the North, the southern hero became an archvillain. Like Bleeding Kansas, "Bleeding Sumner" provided the Republican Party with a potent symbol of the South's twisted and violent "civilization."

The Dred Scott Decision

Only the Supreme Court speaks definitively about the meaning of the Constitution, and in 1857, in the *Dred Scott* case, the Court announced its judgment of the issue of slavery in the territories. The Court proved that it enjoyed no special immunity from the sectional and partisan passions that convulsed the land.

In 1833, John Emerson, an army doctor, bought the slave Dred Scott and took him as his personal servant to Fort Armstrong, Illinois. Two years later,

Scott accompanied Emerson when he was transferred to Fort Snelling in Wisconsin Territory. Emerson eventually returned Scott to St. Louis, where in 1846, Scott sued to prove that he, his wife Harriet, and their two daughters, Eliza and Lizzie, were legally entitled to their freedom. Scott's claim was based on his travels and residences in a free state, Illinois, and free territory, Wisconsin.

Eleven years after the Scotts first sued for freedom, the U.S. Supreme Court ruled in the case. The Court saw the case as an opportunity to settle once and for all the vexing question of slavery in the territories. Chief Justice Roger B. Taney hated Republicans and detested racial equality, and the Court's decision reflected those prejudices. First, the Court ruled that Dred Scott could not legally claim violation of his constitutional rights because he was not a citizen of the United States. At the time of the Constitution, Taney said, blacks "had for more than a century before been regarded as beings of an inferior order . . . so far inferior, that they had no rights which the white man was bound to respect." Second, the laws of Dred Scott's home state, Missouri, determined his status, and thus his travels in free areas did not make him free. Third, Congress's power to make "all needful rules and regulations" for the territories did not include the right to prohibit slavery. The Court then explicitly declared the Missouri Compromise unconstitutional, even though it had already been voided by the Kansas-Nebraska Act.

Republicans exploded in outrage. By declaring unconstitutional the Republican program of federal exclusion of slavery in the territories, the Court had cut the ground from beneath the party. Moreover, as the *New York Tribune* lamented, the decision cleared the way for "all our Territories . . . to be ripened into Slave States." Particularly frightening to African Americans in the North was the Court's declaration that blacks were not citizens and had "no rights which the white man was bound to respect."

The Republican rebuttal to Taney's decision relied heavily on the brilliant dissenting opinion of Justice Benjamin R. Curtis. Scott *was* a citizen of the United States, Curtis argued. At the time of the writing of the Constitution, free black men could vote in five states and participated in the ratification process. Scott *was* free: Because slavery was prohibited in Wisconsin, the "involuntary servitude of a slave, coming into the Territory with his master, should cease to exist." And the Missouri Compro-

mise *was* constitutional. The Founders meant exactly what they said: Congress had the power to make "all needful rules and regulations" for the territories, including barring slavery.

But by a seven-to-two majority, the Court had validated the most extreme statement of the South's territorial rights. John C. Calhoun's claim that Congress had no authority to exclude slavery now became the law of the land. While southern Democrats cheered, northern Democrats feared that the *Dred Scott* decision annihilated not just the Wilmot Proviso but popular sovereignty as well. If Congress did not have the authority to exclude slavery, how could a territorial government assume that right? The Kansas-Nebraska Act had opened the territory to popular sovereignty, and now, contrary to Douglas's promise, it appeared that free-soilers could not keep slavery out. No one could exclude slavery until the moment of statehood. By draining the last drop of ambiguity out of popular sovereignty, the *Dred Scott* decision jeopardized the ability of the Democratic Party to hold its northern and southern wings together.

Ironically, the *Dred Scott* decision strengthened the young Republican Party by giving credence to its claim that a hostile Slave Power conspired against northern liberties. Only the capture of the Supreme Court by the "slavocracy," Republicans argued, could explain the *Dred Scott* decision. As for Dred Scott, although the Court rejected his suit, he did in the end gain his freedom. In May 1857, Taylor Blow, the son of his first owner, purchased and freed Scott and his family. On September 17, 1858, Dred Scott died in obscurity.

Prairie Republican: Abraham Lincoln

The reigniting of sectional flames provided Republican politicians, including Abraham Lincoln of Illinois, with fresh challenges and fresh opportunities. Lincoln had long since put behind him his hardscrabble log-cabin beginnings in Kentucky and Indiana. At the time of the *Dred Scott* decision, he lived in a fine two-story house in Springfield, brought in enough business from the Illinois Central Railroad to be known as the "railroad lawyer," and by virtue of his marriage into a well-to-do family and successful law practice associated with men and women of reputation and standing.

The law provided Lincoln's living, but politics was his life. "His ambition was a little engine that

THE DRED SCOTT FAMILY

The **Dred Scott** *case in 1857 not only produced a fierce political storm, but also fueled enormous curiosity about the family suing for freedom. The correspondent for the popular* **Frank Leslie's Illustrated** *met Dred Scott in St. Louis and reported: "We found him on examination to be a pure-blooded African, perhaps fifty years of age, with a shrewd, intelligent, good-natured face, of rather light frame, being not more than five feet six inches high." But as this illustration makes clear, Northerners wanted to see all of the Scotts: Harriet, who was a slave when Dred Scott married her in Wisconsin Territory in about 1836; daughter Eliza, who was born in 1838 on board a ship traveling in free territory north of Missouri; and daughter Lizzie, born after the Scotts returned to St. Louis.*
Library of Congress.

knew no rest," observed his law partner William Herndon. At age twenty-six, he served his first term in the Illinois state legislature. Between 1847 and 1849, he enjoyed his only term in the House of Representatives, where he fired away at "Mr. Polk's War" and cast dozens of votes for free soil but otherwise served inconspicuously. When he returned to Springfield, he kept his eye fixed on public office.

But, like Whigs everywhere in the mid-1850s, Lincoln had no political home. His credo—opposition to "the extension of slavery"—made the Democrats an impossible choice. The Republicans made free soil their principal tenet, and in 1856 Lincoln joined the party. Convinced that slavery was a "monstrous injustice," a "great moral wrong," and an "unqualified evil to the negro, the white man, and the State," Lincoln condemned Douglas's Kansas-Nebraska Act of 1854 for giving slavery a new life. He accepted that the Constitution sanctioned slavery in those states where it existed, but he believed that the Founders planned to contain its spread. Penned in, Lincoln believed, plantation slavery would exhaust southern soil and in time Southerners would have no choice but to end slavery themselves. In Lincoln's eyes, by providing fresh land in the territories, Douglas put slavery "on the high road to extension and perpetuity."

Just as Lincoln staked out the middle ground on antislavery, he held what were, for his times, moderate racial views. Like a majority of Republicans, Lincoln defended black humanity without challenging white supremacy. He denounced slavery as immoral and believed that it should end, but he also viewed black equality as impractical and unachievable. "Negroes have natural rights . . . as other men have," he said, "although they cannot enjoy them here." Insurmountable white prejudice made it impossible to extend full citizenship and equality to blacks in America, he said. Freeing blacks and allowing them to remain in this country would lead to race war. In Lincoln's mind, social stability and black progress required that slavery end and that blacks leave the country.

Lincoln envisioned the western territories as "places for poor people to go to, and better their conditions." The "free labor system," he said, "opens the way for all—gives hope to all, and energy, and progress, and improvement of condition to all." In Lincoln's view, slavery's expansion threatened this freedom to succeed. He became persuaded that slaveholders formed an aggressive and dangerous conspiracy to nationalize slavery. The Kansas-Nebraska Act repealed the restriction on slavery's advance in the territories. The *Dred Scott* decision denied Congress the right to impose fresh restrictions. The next step, Lincoln warned, would be "another Supreme Court decision, declaring that the Constitution of the United States does not permit a State to exclude slavery from its limits." Unless its citizens woke up, he warned, the Supreme Court would make "Illinois a slave State."

In Lincoln's view, the nation could not "endure, permanently half slave and half free." Either opponents of slavery would arrest its spread and place it on the "course of ultimate extinction" or its advocates would push it forward until it became legal in "all the States, old as well as new—North as well as South." Lincoln's convictions that slavery was wrong, that Congress must stop its spread, and that it must be put on the road to extinction formed the core of the Republican ideology. By 1858, he had so impressed his fellow Republicans in Illinois that they put him forward to challenge the nation's premier Democrat, who was seeking reelection to the Senate.

The Lincoln-Douglas Debates

When Stephen Douglas learned that the Republican Abraham Lincoln would be his opponent for the Senate, he confided in a fellow Democrat: "He is the strong man of the party—full of wit, facts, dates—and the best stump speaker, with his droll ways and dry jokes, in the West. He is as honest as he is shrewd, and if I beat him my victory will be hardly won."

Not only did Douglas have to contend with a formidable foe, but he also carried the weight of a burden not of his own making. The previous year, the nation's economy experienced a sharp downturn. Prices plummeted, thousands of businesses failed, and unemployment rose. Although Illinois suffered less than the Northeast, Douglas had to go before the voters in 1858 as a member of the Democratic Party, whose policies stood accused of causing the "panic" of 1857.

Douglas's response to another crisis in 1857, however, helped shore up his standing with his constituents. Proslavery forces in Kansas met in the town of Lecompton, drafted a proslavery constitution, and applied for statehood. Everyone knew that free-soilers outnumbered proslavery settlers by at least two to one, but President Buchanan instructed Congress to admit Kansas as the sixteenth slave state. Republicans denounced

ABRAHAM LINCOLN
Lincoln actively sought the Republican presidential nomination in 1860. When in New York City to give a political address, he had his photograph taken by Mathew Brady. "While I was there I was taken to one of the places where they get up such things," Lincoln explained, sounding more innocent than he was, "and I suppose they got my shadow, and can multiply copies indefinitely." Multiply they did. Copies of the dignified photograph of Lincoln soon replaced the less flattering drawings. Later, Lincoln credited his victory to his New York speech and to Mathew Brady.
The Lincoln Museum, Fort Wayne, Indiana. Photo: #0-17; drawing: #2024.

"among the gravest of crimes" and confirmed the security of slavery in the South.

Republicans cast about for a moderate candidate to go with their evenhanded platform. The foremost Republican, William H. Seward, had made enemies with his radical "higher law" doctrine and "irrepressible conflict" speech. Since bursting onto the national scene in 1858, Lincoln had demonstrated his clear purpose, good judgment, and solid Republican credentials. That, and his residence in Illinois, a crucial state, made him attractive to the party. Masterful maneuvering by Lincoln's managers converted his status as the second choice of

many delegates into a majority on the third ballot. Defeated by Douglas in a state contest less than two years earlier, Lincoln now stood ready to take him on for the presidency.

The election of 1860 was like none other in American politics. It took place in the midst of the nation's severest crisis. Moreover, four major candidates crowded the presidential field. Rather than a four-cornered contest, however, the election broke into two contests, each with two candidates. In the North, Lincoln faced Douglas, and in the South, Breckinridge confronted Bell. Southerners did not even permit Lincoln's name to appear on the ballot

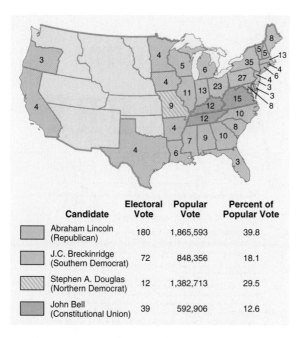

Candidate	Electoral Vote	Popular Vote	Percent of Popular Vote
Abraham Lincoln (Republican)	180	1,865,593	39.8
J.C. Breckinridge (Southern Democrat)	72	848,356	18.1
Stephen A. Douglas (Northern Democrat)	12	1,382,713	29.5
John Bell (Constitutional Union)	39	592,906	12.6

MAP 14.5
The Election of 1860

in ten of the fifteen slave states, so outrageous did they consider the Republican Party.

An unprecedented number of voters cast ballots on November 6, 1860. Approximately 82 percent of eligible northern men and nearly 70 percent of eligible southern men went to the polls. Lincoln swept all of the eighteen free states except New Jersey, which split its votes between him and Douglas. While Lincoln received only 39 percent of the popular vote, he won easily in the electoral balloting, gaining 180 votes, 28 more than he needed for victory. Lincoln did not win because his opposition was splintered. Even if the votes of his three opponents were combined, Lincoln would still have won. Ominously, however, Breckinridge, running on a southern-rights platform, won the entire Lower South plus Delaware, Maryland, and North Carolina. Two fully sectionalized parties swept their regions, but the northern one won the presidency (Map 14.5).

Secession Winter

Although Breckinridge had carried the South, a vote for "southern rights" was not necessarily a vote for secession. In fact, Breckinridge steadfastly denied that he was a secession candidate. Besides, slightly

more than half of the Southerners who voted cast ballots for Douglas and Bell, two stout defenders of the Union. During the winter of 1860–61, Southerners debated what to do.

Southern Unionists tried to calm the fears that Lincoln's election triggered. Let the dust settle, they pleaded. Extremists in both sections, they argued, had created the crisis. Alexander Stephens of Georgia eloquently defended the Union. He asked what Lincoln had done to justify something as extreme as secession. Had he not promised to respect slavery where it existed? In Stephens's judgment, the fire-eater cure would be worse than the Republican disease. Secession might lead to war, which would loosen the hinges of southern society, possibly even open the door to slave insurrection or a revolt by nonslaveholding whites. "Revolutions are much easier started than controlled," Stephens warned. "I consider slavery much more secure in the Union than out of it."

Secessionists emphasized the urgency of the moment and the dangers of delay. No Southerner should mistake Republican intentions, they argued. "Mr. Lincoln and his party assert that this doctrine of equality applies to the negro," Howell Cobb of Georgia asserted, "and necessarily there can exist no such thing as property in our equals." Lincoln's election without a single electoral vote from the South meant that Southerners were unable to defend themselves within the Union, they argued. Why wait, Cobb asked, for abolitionist emissaries to arrive? Secession would not result in war; the Union was a voluntary compact, and Lincoln would not coerce patriotism. If Northerners did resist with force, secessionists argued, the conflict would be brief, for one southern woodsman could whip five of Lincoln's greasy mechanics.

For all their differences, southern whites were generally united in their determination to defend slavery, to take slave property into the territories, and to squeeze from the North an admission that they were good and decent people. They disagreed about whether the mere presence of a Republican in the White House made it necessary to exercise what they considered a legitimate right to secede.

The debate about what to do was briefest in South Carolina. It seceded from the Union on December 20, 1860. By February 1861, the six other Deep South states marched in South Carolina's footsteps. Only South Carolinians voted overwhelmingly in favor of secession, however; elsewhere, the vote was close. In general, the nonslaveholding inhabitants of the pine barrens and mountain counties displayed the greatest attachment to the Union. Slaveholders spearheaded secession. On February 4, representatives from South Carolina, Georgia, Florida, Alabama, Mississippi, Louisiana, and Texas met in Montgomery, Alabama, where three days later they celebrated the birth of the Confederate States of America. Jefferson Davis became president and Alexander Stephens, who had spoken so eloquently about the dangers of revolution, became vice president.

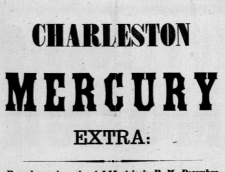

Secession of the Lower South, Dec. 1860–Feb. 1861

Lincoln's election had split the Union. Now secession split the South. Seven slave states seceded during the winter, but eight did not. Citizens of the Upper South debated just as furiously whether the South could defend itself better inside or outside the Union, but they came down opposite the Lower South, at least for the moment. The fact was that the Upper South had a smaller stake in slavery. Just over half as many white families in the Upper South held slaves (21 percent) as did those in the Lower South (37 percent). Slaves represented twice as large a percentage of the population in the Lower South (48 percent) as in the Upper South (23 percent). Consequently, whites in the Upper South had fewer fears that Republican ascendancy meant economic catastrophe, racial war, and social chaos. Lincoln would need to do more than just be elected to provoke them into secession.

The nation had to wait until March 4, 1861, to see what Lincoln would do. (Presidents-elect waited four months to take office until 1933, when the Twentieth Amendment to the Constitution shifted the inauguration forward to January 20.) In his inaugural address, Lincoln began with reassurances to the South. He had "no lawful right" to interfere with slavery where it existed, he said again, adding for emphasis that he had "no inclination to do so." There would be "no invasion—no using of force against or among the people anywhere." In filling federal posts, he would not "force obnoxious strangers" on the South. Conciliatory toward Southerners, Lincoln proved inflexible about the Union.

CHARLESTON MERCURY

EXTRA:

Passed unanimously at 1.15 o'clock, P. M., December 20th, 1860.

AN ORDINANCE

To dissolve the Union between the State of South Carolina and other States united with her under the compact entitled "The Constitution of the United States of America."

We, the People of the State of South Carolina, in Convention assembled, do declare and ordain, and it is hereby declared and ordained,

That the Ordinance adopted by us in Convention, on the twenty-third day of May, in the year of our Lord one thousand seven hundred and eighty-eight, whereby the Constitution of the United States of America was ratified, and also, all Acts and parts of Acts of the General Assembly of this State, ratifying amendments of the said Constitution, are hereby repealed; and that the union now subsisting between South Carolina and other States, under the name of "The United States of America," is hereby dissolved.

THE UNION IS DISSOLVED!

"THE UNION IS DISSOLVED!"
On December 20, 1860, the Charleston Mercury put out this special edition of the paper to celebrate South Carolina's secession from the Union. Six weeks earlier, upon hearing the news that Lincoln had won the presidency, it had predicted as much. "The tea has been thrown overboard," the Mercury announced. "The revolution of 1860 has been initiated."
Chicago Historical Society.

The Union, he declared, is "perpetual." Secession was "anarchy" and "legally void." The Constitution required him to execute the law "in all the States." He would hold federal property, collect federal duties, and deliver the mails.

The decision for civil war or peace rested in the South's hands, Lincoln warned. "You can have no conflict, without being yourselves the aggressors. You have no oath registered in Heaven to destroy the government, while I shall have the most solemn one to 'preserve, protect, and defend' it." What Southerners in Charleston held in their hands at that very moment were the cords for firing the cannons that they aimed at the federal garrison at Fort Sumter.

Conclusion: The Failure of Compromise

As their economies, societies, and cultures diverged in the early nineteenth century, Northerners and Southerners increasingly expressed different concepts of the American promise. Their differences crystallized in 1846 when David Wilmot proposed banning slavery in any territory won in the Mexican War. "As if by magic," a Boston newspaper observed, "it brought to a head the great question that is about to divide the American people." During the extended crisis of the Union that stretched from 1846 to 1861, the nation's attention fixed on the expansion of slavery. From the beginning, though, both Northerners and Southerners recognized that the controversy had less to do with the expansion of slavery than with the future of slavery in America.

For more than seventy years, imaginative statesmen had found compromises that accepted slavery and preserved the Union. Few Americans easily gave up the national experiment in republican democracy. But accommodation had limits. In 1859, John Brown had pushed white Southerners to the edge. Lincoln's election in 1860 convinced whites in the Deep South that slavery and the society they had built on it were at risk in the Union, and they seceded. In his inaugural, Lincoln pleaded, "We are not enemies but friends. We must not be enemies." By then, however, the Deep South had ceased to sing what he called "the chorus of the Union." It remained to be seen whether disunion would mean war.

FOR FURTHER READING ABOUT THE TOPICS IN THIS CHAPTER, see the Online Bibliography at

www.bedfordstmartins.com/roarkcompact.

FOR ADDITIONAL FIRST-HAND ACCOUNTS OF THIS PERIOD, see pages 212–223 in Michael Johnson, ed., *Reading the American Past*, Second Edition, Volume I.

TO ASSESS YOUR MASTERY OF THE MATERIAL IN THIS CHAPTER, see the Online Study Guide at

www.bedfordstmartins.com/roarkcompact.

CHRONOLOGY

1846 Wilmot Proviso proposes barring slavery from all lands acquired in Mexican War.

1847 John C. Calhoun challenges Wilmot Proviso on constitutional grounds, stating that Congress has no power to exclude slavery from territories.

Senator Lewis Cass offers compromise of "popular sovereignty," allowing people of territories to determine fate of slavery.

1848 Opponents of expansion of slavery found Free-Soil Party.

Whig candidate General Zachary Taylor elected president of United States, defeating Democrat Lewis Cass and Free-Soil candidate Martin Van Buren.

1850s Vigilance committees in North challenge and sometimes thwart Fugitive Slave Act.

1850 **July 9.** President Zachary Taylor dies; succeeded by Vice President Millard Fillmore.

Senator Henry Clay proposes Omnibus Bill to avert territorial crisis over slavery; bill ultimately defeated.

Senator Stephen Douglas's compromise bills (Compromise of 1850) pass Congress, signed into law by President Fillmore.

1852 Harriet Beecher Stowe's *Uncle Tom's Cabin* published in book form.

Democrat Franklin Pierce elected president of the United States, defeating Whig Winfield Scott.

1853 Gadsden Purchase adds 30,000 square miles of territory in present-day Arizona and New Mexico.

1854 American Party (Know-Nothings) emerges, advocating nativist positions.

Kansas-Nebraska Act opens the Kansas and Nebraska Territories to popular sovereignty.

Republican Party emerges on platform opposing extension of slavery in territories.

1856 Armed conflict between proslavery and antislavery forces erupts in Kansas.

Preston Brooks of South Carolina brutally assaults Charles Sumner of Massachusetts on Senate floor.

Democrat James Buchanan elected president of United States, defeating Republican John C. Frémont.

1857 *Dred Scott* decision declares that African Americans have no constitutional rights, that Congress cannot exclude slavery in the territories, and that the Missouri Compromise is unconstitutional.

Nation experiences economic downturn, panic of 1857.

1858 In Illinois senatorial campaign, Abraham Lincoln and Stephen A. Douglas debate slavery; Douglas defeats Lincoln for Senate seat.

1859 **October 16.** John Brown's attempt to foment slave uprising in Harpers Ferry, Virginia, further alienates South and moves nation toward war.

1860 Republican Abraham Lincoln elected president in four-way race that divides electorate along sectional lines.

December 20. South Carolina secedes from Union.

1861 Representatives of seven southern states, meeting in Montgomery, Alabama, form Confederate States of America.

DAGUERREOTYPE OF UNION DRUMMER BOY

The Civil War is often called a "brother's war." Families sometimes split and offered up soldiers for both the Union and the Confederate armies. But the war was also a children's war, as this daguerreotype of the twelve-year-old Johnny Clem, a Union drummer boy, reminds us. Clem ran away from his Ohio home when he was ten, joined the Twenty-second Michigan Regiment, and fought with it in all its major battles from Shiloh to Atlanta. He became a hero in the North when, during the retreat of Union soldiers at Chickamauga, he shot and wounded a Confederate officer with a sawed-off musket cut down to his small size. When he retired from the U.S. Army in 1915, Major General John L. Clem was the last federal soldier who had fought in the Civil War. Clem's face shows no trace of the horrors he had seen, but even children who stayed at home often experienced the heartbreak of youth destroyed and innocence lost.

Library of Congress.

THE CRUCIBLE OF WAR
1861–1865

15

I N 1838, A TWENTY-YEAR-OLD MARYLAND SLAVE by the name of Frederick Bailey fled north to freedom. The young runaway took a new name, Frederick Douglass, and might understandably have settled into obscurity, content just to avoid the slave catchers and to live quietly as a free man. Instead, he chose to wage war against slavery. In 1841, an agent for the Massachusetts Anti-Slavery Society observed that "the public have itching ears to hear a colored man speak, and particularly a slave." No fugitive slave stripped away the myth of the contented slave more eloquently than Frederick Douglass. In 1845, he published his immensely popular autobiography. In 1847, he began the *North Star,* an antislavery newspaper that reached thousands. Douglass's powerful denunciations of slavery and moving pleas for emancipation made him the most famous African American in the English-speaking world.

But after two decades of speaking and writing, Douglass feared that the country was no closer to ending slavery. In some ways the situation had grown worse. When Douglass fled slavery in 1838, two million Americans were in bondage. By 1860, the number of slaves had doubled to four million. Every step forward—the birth of the Republican Party, for instance—was followed by a giant step back, such as the *Dred Scott* decision. "How long! How long! O Lord God of Sabbath!" he cried at the end of the 1850s, "shall the crushed and bleeding bondsman wait?"

During the secession winter of 1860–61, Douglass found himself torn between hope and despair. Abraham Lincoln's election in November had revived his optimism. "The slaveholders know that the day of their power is over," Douglass exulted. But he realized that the Republican Party's free-soil principles fell short of abolition. Republicans opposed slavery's right to expand into the national territories, not slavery's right to exist in the South. Indeed, Douglass feared that the Republicans would become "the best protectors of slavery where it now is."

When news came from Charleston in April 1861 that Southerners had fired on the American flag, Douglass celebrated the outbreak of fighting. He realized that in going to war Lincoln was striking out against "treason and rebellion," but much earlier than most, he also understood that a war to save the Union would inevitably affect slavery. The South had initiated a "war for slavery," Douglass said, and it followed that a war to crush southern independence must become a war against slavery. Even though "the Government is not yet on the side of the oppressed, events mightier than the Government are bringing about that result," Douglass declared. "Friends of freedom!" he cried, "be up and doing;—now is your time." Few Northerners, certainly not Abraham Lincoln, agreed that the outbreak of fighting marked the beginning of the end of slavery. For eighteen months, Union soldiers fought solely to uphold the Constitution and preserve the nation. But in 1863, as Douglass foresaw, the northern war effort took on a dual purpose: to save the Union and to free the slaves.

FREDERICK DOUGLASS, 1852
*Samuel J. Miller made this daguerreotype of
Frederick Douglass in Akron, Ohio, a hotbed of
abolitionism. Douglass self-consciously employed
an aggressive posture and fiery expression to fashion
his identity as a free man dead set on eradicating
slavery. Fellow abolitionists understood that the
"very look and bearing of Douglass are an irresistible
logic against the oppression of his race."*
Art Institute of Chicago.

Even if the Civil War had not touched slavery, the conflict still would have transformed America. As the world's first modern war, it mobilized entire populations, harnessed the productive capacities of entire economies, and enlisted millions of troops, with single battles fielding 200,000 soldiers and producing casualties in the tens of thousands. The carnage lasted four years and cost the nation an estimated 633,000 lives, nearly as many as in all of its other wars before and after combined. The war helped mold the modern American nation-state. The federal government emerged with new power and responsibility over national life. War

furthered the emergence of a modern industrializing nation. But because the war to preserve the Union also became a war to destroy slavery, the northern victory had truly revolutionary meaning. Defeat and emancipation destroyed the slave society of the Old South and gave birth to a different society.

Years later, remembering the Civil War years, Douglass said, "It is something to couple one's name with great occasions." It was something—for millions of Americans. Whether they battled or defended the Confederacy, whether they labored behind the lines to produce goods for northern or southern soldiers, whether they kept the home fires burning for Yankees or rebels, all Americans experienced the crucible of war. But the war affected no group more than the four million African Americans who saw its beginning in 1861 as slaves and emerged in 1865 as free people.

"And the War Came"

New to high office, Abraham Lincoln faced the worst crisis in the history of the nation: the threat of disunion. Lincoln revealed his strategy on March 4, 1861, in his inaugural address, which he carefully crafted to combine firmness and conciliation. First, he sought to stop the contagion of secession. Eight of the fifteen slave states had said no to disunion, but they remained suspicious and skittish. Lincoln wanted to avoid any act that would push the Upper South (North Carolina, Virginia, Maryland, Delaware, Kentucky, Tennessee, Missouri, and Arkansas) into leaving. Second, he sought to buy time so that emotions could cool in the Deep South. By reassuring South Carolina, Georgia, Florida, Alabama, Mississippi, Louisiana, and Texas that slavery would not be abolished, he would provide Unionists there the opportunity to reassert themselves and to overturn the secession decision. Always, Lincoln expressed his uncompromising will to oppose secession and to uphold the Union.

His counterpart, Jefferson Davis, fully intended to establish the Confederate States of America as an independent republic. Neither man sought war. Both wanted to achieve their objectives peacefully. But as Lincoln later observed, "Both parties deprecated war, but one of them would make war rather than let the nation survive, and the other would accept war rather than let it perish. And the war came."

Attack on Fort Sumter

Although within newly seceded territory, Fort Sumter was occupied by Major Robert Anderson and some eighty U.S. soldiers. Sitting at the entrance to Charleston harbor, the fort became a hateful symbol of the nation Southerners had abandoned, and they wanted federal troops out. But Sumter was also a symbol to Northerners, a beacon affirming federal sovereignty in the seceded states.

The situation at Fort Sumter presented the new president with hard choices. Ordering the fort's evacuation would play well in the Upper South, whose edgy slave states threatened to bolt to the Confederacy if Lincoln resorted to military force. But yielding the fort would make it appear that Lincoln accepted the Confederacy's existence. Lincoln decided to hold Fort Sumter. But to do so, he had to provision it, for Anderson was running dangerously short of food. In the first week in April, Lincoln authorized a peaceful expedition to bring supplies, but not military reinforcements, to the fort. The president understood that he risked war, but his plan honored his inaugural promises to defend federal property and to avoid using military force unless first attacked. Masterfully, Lincoln had shifted the fateful decision of war or peace to Jefferson Davis.

On April 9, 1861, Jefferson Davis and his cabinet met to consider the situation in Charleston harbor. The territorial integrity of the Confederacy demanded the end of the federal presence, Davis argued. But his secretary of state, Robert Toombs of Georgia, pleaded against military action. "Mr. President," he declared, "at this time it is suicide, murder, and will lose us every friend at the North. You will wantonly strike a hornet's nest which extends from mountain to ocean, and legions now quiet will swarm out and sting us to death." Davis rejected Toombs's prophecy and sent word to the commander of Confederate troops in Charleston to take the fort before the relief expedition arrived. Thirty-three hours of bombardment on April 12 and 13 reduced the fort to rubble, but, miraculously, not a single Union soldier died. On April 14, with the fort ablaze, Major Anderson offered his surrender. The Confederates had Fort Sumter, but they also had war.

The response of the free states was thunderous. On April 15, Lincoln called for seventy-five thousand militia to serve for ninety days to put down the rebellion, and several times that number rushed to defend the flag. Democrats responded as fervently as Republicans. Stephen A. Douglas, the recently defeated Democratic candidate for president, pledged his support. "There are only two sides to the question," he told a massive crowd in Chicago. "Every man must be for the United States or against it. There can be no neutrals in this war, only patriots—or traitors." No one faced more acutely the dilemma of loyalty than the men and women of the Upper South.

The Upper South Chooses Sides

Many who had only months earlier rejected secession now embraced the Confederacy. To oppose southern independence was one thing; to fight fellow Southerners was another. Thousands felt betrayed, believing that Lincoln had promised to achieve a peaceful reunion by waiting patiently for Unionists to reassert themselves in the seceding states. One man furiously denounced the conflict as a "politician's war," conceding that "this is no time now to discuss the causes, but it is the duty of all who regard Southern institutions of value to side with the South, make common cause with the Confederate States and sink or swim with them."

One by one the states of the Upper South jumped off the fence. Within weeks, Virginia, Arkansas, North Carolina, and Tennessee had joined the Confederacy (Map 15.1). But in the border states of Delaware, Maryland, Kentucky, and Missouri, Unionism triumphed. Only in Delaware, though, where slaves accounted for less than 2 percent of the population, was the victory easy. In Maryland, Unionism needed a helping hand. Rather than allow the state to secede and make Washington, D.C., a federal island in a Confederate sea, Lincoln suspended the writ of habeas corpus, essentially setting aside normal constitutional guarantees such as trial before a jury of peers, and marched troops into Baltimore. Maryland's legislature, frightened by the federal invasion and aware of the strength of Union sentiment in the western counties, rejected secession.

The struggle turned violent in the West. In Missouri, Unionists won a narrow victory, but southern-sympathizing guerrilla bands roamed the

would stand idle. Without southern planters purchasing northern manufactured goods, northern factories would drown in their own surpluses. Without the foreign exchange earned by the overseas sales of cotton, the financial structure of the entire Yankee nation would collapse. One Virginian spoke for most Confederates when he declared that in the South's ability to "withhold the benefits of our trade, we hold a power over the North more powerful than a powerful army in the field."

King Cotton would also make Europe a powerful ally of the Confederacy, Southerners reasoned. After all, they said, England's economy (and to a lesser degree, France's) depended on cotton. Of the 900 million pounds of cotton England imported annually, more than 700 million came from the South. If the supply were interrupted, sheer economic need would make England (and perhaps France) a Confederate ally. And because the British navy ruled the seas, the North would find Britain a formidable foe.

Southerners' confidence may seem naive today, but even tough-minded European military observers picked the South to win. Offsetting the North's power was the South's expanse. The North, Europeans predicted, could not conquer the vast territory (750,000 square miles) from the Potomac to the Rio Grande, with its rugged terrain and bad roads. It would require raising a massive invading army, supplying it with huge quantities of provisions and arms, and protecting supply lines that would stretch farther than any in modern history.

Indeed, the South enjoyed major advantages, and the Confederacy devised a military strategy to exploit them. Jefferson Davis called it an "offensive-defensive" strategy. It recognized that a Union victory required the North to defeat and subjugate the South. A Confederate victory required only that the South stay at home, blunt invasions, avoid battles that risked annihilating its army, and outlast the northern will to fight. When an opportunity presented itself, the South would strike the invaders. Like the American colonists, the South could win independence by not losing the war.

If the North did nothing, the South would by default establish itself as a sovereign nation. The Lincoln administration therefore adopted an offensive strategy. On April 19, four days after the president issued the proclamation calling for a militia to put down the rebellion, he issued another proclamation declaring a naval blockade of the Confederacy. He sought to deny the Confederacy the use of its most valuable commodity—cotton. Without the sale of cotton abroad, the South would have far fewer dollars to pay for war goods. Even before the North could mount an effective blockade, however, Jefferson Davis decided voluntarily to cease exporting cotton. He wanted to create a cotton "famine" that would enfeeble the northern economy and precipitate European intervention.

Southerners were not the only ones with illusions. Lincoln's call for 75,000 men for ninety days illustrates his failure to predict the magnitude and duration of the war. He was not alone. Most Americans thought of war in terms of their most recent experience, the Mexican War in the 1840s. In Mexico, fighting had taken place between relatively small armies, had cost relatively few lives, and had inflicted only light damage on the countryside. Americans on the eve of the Civil War could not know that four ghastly years of bloodletting lay ahead.

Lincoln and Davis Mobilize

Mobilization required effective political leadership, and at first glance it appeared that the South had the decided advantage. An aristocrat from a Mississippi planter family, Jefferson Davis brought to the Confederate presidency a distinguished political career, including experience in the U.S. Senate. He was also a West Point graduate, a combat veteran of the Mexican War, and a former secretary of war. Dignified and erect, with "a jaw sawed in steel," Davis appeared to be everything a nation could want in a wartime leader.

In contrast, Lincoln, an Illinois lawyer-politician, occupied the White House. He brought with him one lackluster term in the House of Representatives, almost no administrative experience, and his sole brush with anything military was as a captain in the militia in the Black Hawk War, a brief struggle in Illinois in 1832 in which whites expelled the last Indians from the state. The lanky, disheveled Westerner looked anything but military or presidential in his bearing, and even his friends feared that he was in over his head.

Davis, however, proved to be less than he appeared. Possessing little capacity for broad military strategy and yet vain about what he regarded as his own superior judgment, he intervened constantly in military affairs. He was an even less able political leader. Quarrelsome and proud, he had an acid tongue that made enemies the Confederacy could ill afford. The Confederacy's intimidating problems might have defeated an even more talented leader, however. For example, state sovereignty, which was enshrined in the Confederate constitution, made Davis's task of organizing a new nation and fighting a war difficult in the extreme.

In Lincoln, however, the North got far more than met the eye. He proved himself a master politician and a superb leader. He never allowed personal feelings to get in the way of his objectives. When forming his cabinet, for example, Lincoln shrewdly appointed representatives of every Republican faction, men who were often his chief rivals and critics. He made Salmon P. Chase secretary of the treasury, knowing that Chase had presidential ambitions. As secretary of state, he chose his chief opponent for the Republican nomination in 1860, William H. Seward, who mistakenly expected to twist Lincoln around his little finger and formulate policy himself. Despite his civilian background, Lincoln displayed an innate understanding of military strategy. In time, no one was more crucial in mapping the Union war plan. Further, Lincoln was an enormously eloquent man who reached out to the North's people, galvanizing them in defense of the nation he called "the last best hope of earth."

Guided by Lincoln and Davis, the North and South began gathering their armies. Southerners had the task of building almost everything from scratch, and Northerners had to mobilize their superior numbers and industrial resources for war. In 1861, the puny federal army numbered only 16,000 men. The navy was in better shape. Forty-two ships were in service, and a large merchant marine would in time provide more ships and sailors. Most of the officers and men were Northerners and loyal to the Union. The Confederate navy was never a match for the Union fleet, and thus the South pinned its hopes on its armies. Military companies sprang up everywhere.

From the beginning, the South exhibited more enthusiasm than ability to provide its soldiers with supplies and transportation. The Confederacy made prodigious efforts to build new factories to produce tents, blankets, shoes, and uniforms, but many soldiers slept in the open air without proper clothes and sometimes without shoes. Even when factories managed to produce what soldiers needed, southern railroads—constructed to connect plantations with ports—often could not deliver the goods. And with each year of the war, more railroads were captured, destroyed, or left in disrepair. Food production proved less of a problem, but food sometimes

rotted before it reached the soldiers. The one bright spot was the Confederacy's Ordnance Bureau, headed by Josiah Gorgas, a near miracle worker when it came to manufacturing gunpower, cannons, and rifles. In April 1864, Gorgas observed: "Where three years ago we were not making a gun, a pistol nor a sabre, no shot nor shell . . .—a pound of powder—we now make all these in quantities to meet the demands of our large armies."

Recruiting and supplying huge armies required enormous public spending. Before the war, the federal government's tiny income had come primarily from tariff duties and the sale of public lands. Massive wartime expenditures made new revenues imperative. At first, both the North and the South resorted to selling war bonds, which essentially were loans from patriotic citizens. In time, both sides began printing paper money. Inflation soared, but the South suffered more because it financed a greater part of its wartime costs through the printing press. Prices in the North rose by about 80 percent during the war, while in the South inflation topped 9,000 percent. Eventually, the Union and the Confederacy turned to taxes, but whereas the North raised one-fifth of its wartime revenue from taxes, the South raised only one-twentieth.

Within months of the bombardment of Fort Sumter, both sides had found men to fight and people to supply and support them. But the underlying strength of the northern economy gave the Union the decided advantage. With their military and industrial muscles beginning to ripple, Northerners became itchy for action. Northerners wanted an invasion that would once and for all smash the rebellion. Horace Greeley's *New York Tribune* began the chant: "Forward to Richmond! Forward to Richmond!"

The Battlefields, 1861–1862

During the first year and a half of the war, armies fought major campaigns in two theaters: in Virginia-Maryland in the East and in Tennessee-Kentucky in the West. With the rival capitals of Richmond and Washington, D.C., only ninety miles apart and each threatened more than once with capture, the eastern campaign was more dramatic and commanded public attention. But the battles in the West proved more decisive. And as Yankee and rebel armies pounded each other on land, their navies fought it out on the seas and their diplomats sought advantage in the corridors of power in Europe. All the while, casualty lists reached appalling lengths.

Stalemate in the Eastern Theater

As commander in chief, Lincoln appointed Mexican War veteran Irvin McDowell to be commanding general of the army assembling outside Washington. McDowell had no thought of taking his raw recruits into battle during the summer of 1861, but Lincoln ordered McDowell to prepare his 30,000 greenhorn troops for an attack on the Confederate army gathered at Manassas, a railroad junction in Virginia about thirty miles southwest of Washington.

On July 21, the Union army forded Bull Run, a branch of the Potomac River, and engaged the southern forces effectively (Map 15.2). But fast-moving southern reinforcements blunted the Union attack and then counterattacked. What began as an orderly retreat turned into a panicky stampede.

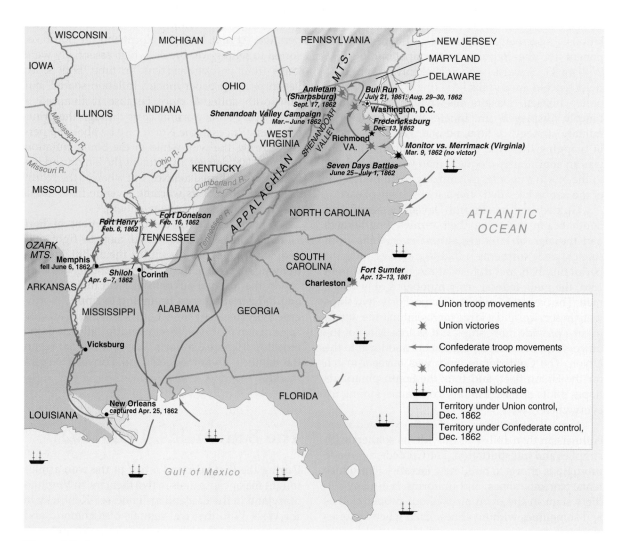

MAP 15.2

The Civil War, 1861–1862

While eyes focused on the eastern theater, especially the tiny geography between the two capitals of Washington and Richmond, strategic victories were being won by Union troops in the West.

Demoralized soldiers ran over shocked civilians as they raced back to Washington.

By Civil War standards, casualties at Bull Run (or Manassas, as Southerners called the battle) were light; the significance of the battle lay in the lessons Northerners and Southerners drew from it. For Southerners, it confirmed the superiority of rebel fighting men and the inevitability of Confederate nationhood. Manassas was "one of the decisive battles of the world," a Georgian proclaimed. It "has secured our independence." While victory elevated southern pride, defeat sobered Northerners. It was a major setback, admitted the *New York Tribune,* but "Let us go to work, then, with a will." Manassas taught Lincoln that victory would be neither quick nor easy. Within four days of the disaster, the president signed bills authorizing the enlistment of 1 million men for three years.

Lincoln also found a new general, replacing McDowell with the arrogant young George B. McClellan. Born in Philadelphia of well-to-do parents, educated in the best schools before graduating from West Point second in his class, the thirty-four-year-old McClellan believed that he was a great soldier and that Lincoln was a dunce, the "original Gorilla." A superb administrator and organizer, McClellan was brought to Washington as commander of the newly named Army of the Potomac. In the months following his appointment, McClellan energetically whipped his dispirited army into shape, yet was reluctant to send them into battle. McClellan, for all his energy, lacked decisiveness. Lincoln wanted a general who would advance, take risks, and fight, but McClellan went into winter quarters without budging from the Potomac. "If General McClellan does not want to use the army I would like to borrow it," Lincoln declared in frustration.

Finally, in the spring of 1862, McClellan launched his long-awaited offensive. He transported his highly polished army, now 130,000 strong, down the Chesapeake Bay to the mouth of the James River and began moving up the peninsula toward Richmond. McClellan took two and a half months to advance sixty-five miles. When he was within six miles of the Confederate capital, Confederate general Joseph Johnston hit him like a hammer. In the assault, Johnston was wounded and was replaced by Robert E. Lee of Virginia, a reluctant Confederate who would become the South's most celebrated general. Lee named his command the Army of Northern Virginia.

The contrast between Lee and McClellan could hardly have been greater. McClellan overflowed with conceit and braggadocio, while Lee was courteous and reserved. But on the battlefield, where McClellan grew timid and irresolute, Lee became audaciously, even recklessly, aggressive. And Lee had at his side in the peninsula campaign military men of real talent: General Thomas J. Jackson, nicknamed Stonewall for holding the line at Manassas, and James E. B. (Jeb) Stuart, the dashing twenty-nine-year-old cavalry commander who rode circles around Yankee troops. Lee's assault initiated the Seven Days Battle and began McClellan's backward march down the peninsula. By the time McClellan reached

Peninsula Campaign, 1862

the water and the safety of the Union navy, 30,000 men from both sides had died or been wounded. Although Southerners suffered twice the casualties of Northerners, Lee had saved Richmond and achieved a strategic success. Lincoln wired McClellan to abandon the peninsula campaign and replaced him with General John Pope.

In August, just north of Richmond, Pope had his own rendezvous with Lee. At the Second Battle of Bull Run, Lee's smaller army battered Pope's forces and sent them scurrying back to Washington. Lincoln ordered Pope to Minnesota to pacify Indians and again put McClellan in command. Lincoln had not changed his mind about McClellan's capacity as a warrior. Instead, he reluctantly concluded, "If he can't fight himself, he excels in making others ready to fight."

Sensing that he had his enemy on the ropes, Lee sought to land the knockout punch. He pushed the Army of Northern Virginia across the Potomac and invaded Maryland. A victory on northern soil would dislodge Maryland from the Union, Lee reasoned, and might even cause Lincoln to sue for

THE BATTLE OF SAVAGE'S STATION, ROBERT KNOX SNEDEN, 1862
In 1862, thirty-year-old Robert Sneden joined the 40th New York Volunteers and soon found himself in Virginia, part of George McClellan's peninsula campaign. A gifted artist in water colors, as well as an eloquent writer, Sneden captures here an early Confederate assault in what became known as the Seven Days Battle. "The immense open space in front of Savage's [house] was densely thronged with wagon trains, artillery, caissons, ammunition trains, and moving troops," Sneden observed. The "storm of lead was continuous and deadly on the approaching lines of the Rebels. They bravely rushed up, however, to within twenty feet of our artillery, when bushels of grape and canister from the cannon laid them low in rows." Over the next three years, Sneden produced hundreds of vivid drawings and eventually thousands of pages of remembrance, providing one of the most complete accounts of a Union soldier's Civil War experience.
Virginia Historical Society.

peace. On September 17, 1862, McClellan's forces finally engaged Lee's army at Antietam Creek (see Map. 15.2). Earlier, a Union soldier had found a copy of Lee's orders to his army wrapped around some cigars dropped by a careless Confederate officer. McClellan had a clear picture of Lee's position, but his characteristic slowness meant that he missed a great opportunity to destroy the opposing army. Still, he did it severe damage. With "solid shot . . . cracking skulls like egg-shells," according to one observer, the armies went after each other. By nightfall the battlefield lay littered with 6,000 men dead or dying and 17,000 more wounded, making the Battle of Antietam the bloodiest day of the

war. Badly damaged and deeply disappointed, Lee turned back to Virginia. When McClellan, who had 33,000 fresh troops in reserve (more men than Lee had in his entire army), failed to renew the attack, Lincoln removed him from command of the Army of the Potomac and appointed General Ambrose Burnside.

Lee remained alert for an opportunity to punish his enemy, and in December, Burnside provided the Virginian a fresh chance. At Fredericksburg, Virginia, Burnside's 122,000 Union troops faced 78,500 Confederates dug in behind a stone wall on the heights above the Rappahannock River. Half a mile of open ground lay between the armies. A Confederate artillery officer predicted that "a chicken could not live on that field when we open on it." Yet Burnside ordered a frontal assault. Wave after wave of bluecoats crashed against impregnable defenses. When the guns finally ceased, the federals counted nearly 13,000 casualties while the Confederates suffered fewer than 5,000. It was one of the Union's worst defeats. At the end of 1862, the North seemed no nearer to ending the rebellion than it had been when the war began. Rather than checkmate, military struggle in the East had reached stalemate.

Union Victories in the Western Theater

While most eyes focused on the East, the decisive early encounters of the war took place between the Appalachian Mountains and the Ozarks. The West's rivers—the Mississippi, the Tennessee, and the Cumberland—became the keys to the military situation. Southerners looked northward along the rivers and spied Missouri and Kentucky, states they claimed but did not control. Looking southward, Northerners knew that by taking the Mississippi they would split Arkansas, Louisiana, and Texas from the Confederacy. And the Cumberland and Tennessee waterways penetrated Tennessee, one of the Confederacy's main producers of food, mules, and iron—all vital resources.

General Ulysses S. Grant became the key northern figure on the western battlefields. Although Grant had graduated from West Point, when war broke out he was a thirty-nine-year-old dry-goods clerk in Galena, Illinois. Gentle at home, he became pugnacious on the battlefield. "The art of war is simple," he said. "Find out where your enemy is, get at him as soon as you can and strike him as hard as you can, and keep moving on." Grant's philosophy of war as annihilation took a huge toll in human life, but it played to the North's strength: superior manpower. In time, the North fashioned victory from it. In his old uniform and slouch hat, with his tired, sad, nondescript face, Grant did not look much like a general. But Lincoln, who did not look much like a president, knew his worth.

In February 1862, operating in tandem with navy gunboats, Grant captured Fort Henry on the Tennessee River and Fort Donelson on the Cumberland (see Map 15.2). Defeat forced the Confederates to withdraw from all of Kentucky and most of Tennessee. Grant pushed after the retreating rebels until, on April 6, General Albert Sidney Johnston's army surprised him at Shiloh Church in Tennessee. Although his troops were badly mauled the first day, Grant remained cool and brought up reinforcements throughout the night. The next morning, the Union army counterattacked, driving the Confederates before it. The battle was terribly costly; there were 20,000 casualties, including the death of Johnston. Manassas had disabused Lincoln of the illusion of a short war; and, after Shiloh, Grant "gave up all idea of saving the Union except by complete conquest."

Although no one knew it at the time, Shiloh inflicted a mortal wound to the Confederacy's bid to control the Western theater. In short order, the Yankees captured the strategic town of Corinth, Mississippi, the river city of Memphis, and the South's largest city, New Orleans. By the end of 1862, most—but not all—of the Mississippi valley lay in Union hands.

War and Diplomacy in the Atlantic Theater

With a blockade fleet of only about three dozen ships at the beginning of the war and more than thirty-five hundred miles of southern coastline to patrol, the U.S. navy faced an impossible task. At first, rebel ships slipped in and out of port nearly at will. Taking on cargoes in the Caribbean, the sleek, fast blockade runners brought in vital supplies—guns and medicine—and also small quantities of luxury goods such as tea and liquor. But with the U.S. navy commissioning a new blockader almost weekly, the fleet eventually reached 150 ships on duty, and the Union navy dramatically improved its score.

Unable to build a conventional navy equal to the expanding federal fleet, the Confederates experimented with a radical new maritime design: the ironclad warship. At Norfolk, Virginia, they layered the wooden hull of the frigate *Merrimack* with two-inch-thick armor plate. Rechristened *Virginia*, it steamed out in March 1862 to engage the federal blockade. Within a few hours, it sank two large federal ships, killing at least 240 sailors. But when the *Virginia* returned the following morning to finish its work, it found the *Monitor*, a federal ironclad that had arrived from Brooklyn during the night. The *Monitor*, a ship of even more radical design than the *Virginia*, was topped by a revolving turret containing two eleven-inch guns. Although the two ships hurled shells at each other for two hours, neither could penetrate the other's armor and the duel ended in a draw (see Map 15.2).

The Confederacy never found a way to break the blockade. Each month the northern navy tightened its noose until by 1865 the Union fleet intercepted about half of the southern ships that attempted to break through. By 1863, the South had abandoned its embargo policy and desperately wanted to ship cotton to pay for imports it needed to fight the war. But the growing effectiveness of the federal blockade, a southern naval officer observed, "shut the Confederacy out from the world, deprived it of supplies, weakened its military and naval strength."

What they could not achieve on saltwater, Confederates sought through foreign policy. According to the theory of King Cotton, cotton-starved European nations had no choice but to break the blockade and recognize the Confederacy. Although European nations granted the Confederacy "belligerent" status, which enabled it to buy goods and build ships in European ports, none recognized Confederate nationhood, a bolder act that probably would have drawn them into war with the United States.

King Cotton diplomacy failed for several reasons. A bumper cotton crop in 1860 meant that the warehouses of British textile manufacturers bulged with surplus cotton throughout 1861. In 1862, when Europe began to feel the pinch of the cotton famine, manufacturers found new sources of cotton in Egypt and India. In addition, a brisk trade developed between the Union and Britain—British war materiel for American grain and flour—which helped offset the decline in textiles and encouraged Britain to remain neutral.

Europe's temptation to intervene disappeared for good in 1862. Union military successes on the rivers of the West made Britain and France think twice about linking their fates to the Confederacy. And in the fall of 1862, Lincoln announced a new policy that made an alliance with the Confederacy an alliance with slavery. The president finally acknowledged that it was impossible to fight for union without fighting against slavery.

Union *and* Freedom

For a year and a half, Lincoln insisted that emancipation was not a goal; the war he said was strictly to save the Union. But the war for union did become a war for African American freedom. Each

month the conflict dragged on, it became clearer that the Confederate war machine depended heavily on slavery. Rebel armies used slaves to build fortifications, haul materiel, tend horses, and perform camp chores. On the home front, slaves labored in ironworks and shipyards, and they grew the food that fed both soldiers and civilians. Slavery undergirded the Confederacy as certainly as it had the Old South. In the field among military commanders, in the halls of Congress, and in the White House, the truth gradually came into focus: To defeat the Confederacy, the North would have to destroy slavery. "I am a slow walker," Lincoln said, "but I never walk back."

From Slaves to Contraband

Personally, Lincoln detested human bondage, but as president he felt compelled to act prudently in the interests of the Union. He doubted his right under the Constitution to tamper with the "domestic institutions" of any state, even those in rebellion. An astute politician, Lincoln worked within the limits of public opinion, and in 1861 he believed those limits were tight. The issue of black freedom was particularly explosive in the loyal border states, where slaveholders threatened to jump into the arms of the Confederacy at even the hint of emancipation. Black freedom also attracted attention in the free states. The Democratic Party gave notice that emancipation would kill the bipartisan alliance and make the war strictly a Republican affair. Democrats were as ardent for union as Republicans, but they marched under the banner "The Constitution As It Is, the Union As It Was."

Moreover, many white Northerners were not about to risk their lives to satisfy abolitionist "fanaticism." "We Won't Fight to Free the Nigger," one popular banner read. They feared that emancipation would propel "two or three million semi-savages" northward, where they would crowd into white neighborhoods, compete for white jobs, and mix with white "sons and daughters." A surge of anti-emancipation, antiblack sentiment, then, threatened to dislodge the loyal slave states from the Union, alienate the Democratic Party, deplete the armies, and perhaps even spark race warfare.

Yet proponents of emancipation pressed Lincoln as relentlessly as the anti-emancipation forces. Abolitionists argued that by seceding, Southerners had forfeited their right to the protection of the Constitution. Lincoln could now—as the price

CONTRABANDS
*These refugees from slavery crossed the Rappahannock River in Virginia in August 1862
to seek the sanctuary of a federal army. Most slaves fled with little more than the
clothes on their backs, but not all escaped slavery empty-handed. The oxen, wagon, and
goods seen here could have been procured by a number of means—purchased during
slavery, "borrowed" from the former master, or gathered during flight. Refugees who
possessed draft animals and a wagon had much more economic opportunity than those
who had only their labor to sell.*
Library of Congress.

of treason—legally confiscate their property in slaves. When Lincoln refused, abolitionists scalded him. Frederick Douglass labeled Lincoln "the miserable tool of traitors and rebels."

The Republican-dominated Congress refused to leave slavery policy entirely in Lincoln's hands. In August 1861, Congress approved the Confiscation Act, which allowed the seizure of any slave who was employed directly by the Confederate military. The House and the Senate also fulfilled the free-soil dream of prohibiting slavery in the territories and abolished slavery in Washington, D.C. Democrats and border-state representatives voted against even these mild measures, but little by little, Congress displayed a stiffening of attitude as it cast about for a just and practical slavery policy.

But slaves, not politicians, became the most insistent force for emancipation. By escaping their masters by the tens of thousands and running away to Union lines, they forced slavery on the North's wartime agenda. Union officials could not ignore the flood of fugitives, and runaways precipitated a series of momentous decisions on the part of the military, Congress, and the president. Were the runaways now free, or were they still slaves who, according to the fugitive slave law, had to be returned to their masters? At first, most Yankee military commanders believed that administration policy required them to send the fugitives back. But Union armies needed laborers, and some officers accepted the runaways and put them to work. At Fort Monroe, Virginia, General Benjamin F. Butler not only refused to turn them over to their owners but also provided them with a new status. He called them "contraband of war," meaning "confiscated property." Congress established national policy in

March 1862 when it forbade the practice of returning fugitive slaves to their masters. Slaves were still not legally free, but there was a tilt toward emancipation.

Gradually, Lincoln's policy of noninterference with slavery crumbled. To calm Northerners' racial fears, which he considered the chief obstacle to Union acceptance of emancipation, Lincoln offered colonization, the deportation of African Americans from the United States to Haiti, Panama, or elsewhere. In the summer of 1862, he defended colonization to a delegation of black visitors to the White House. He told them that deep-seated racial prejudice made it impossible for blacks to achieve equality in this country. An African American from Philadelphia spoke for the group when he told the president, "This is our country as much as it is yours, and we will not leave it." Congress voted a small amount of money to underwrite colonization, but after one miserable experiment on a small island in the Caribbean, practical limitations and black opposition sank further efforts.

At the same time that Lincoln was developing his own initiatives, he snuffed out actions he believed jeopardized northern unity. He was particularly alert to Union commanders who tried to dictate slavery policy from the field. In August 1861, when John C. Frémont, commander of federal troops in Missouri, impetuously freed the slaves belonging to Missouri rebels, Lincoln forced the general to revoke his edict and then removed him from command. The following May, when General David Hunter issued a proclamation freeing the slaves in the southeast, Lincoln countermanded his order. Events moved so rapidly, however, that Lincoln found it impossible to control federal policy on slavery.

From Contraband to Free People

On August 22, 1862, Lincoln replied to an angry abolitionist who demanded that he go after slavery. "My paramount objective in this struggle is to save the Union," Lincoln said deliberately, "and is not either to save or destroy slavery. If I could save the Union without freeing any slave I would do it, and if I could save it by freeing all the slaves I would do it; and if I could save it by freeing some and leaving others alone I would also do that." At first glance, it seemed a restatement of his old position: that union was the North's sole objective. But what

marked it as a radical departure was Lincoln's refusal to say that slavery was safe. Instead, he said that he would emancipate every slave if it would preserve the Union.

By the summer of 1862, events were tumbling rapidly toward emancipation. On July 17, Congress adopted a second Confiscation Act. The first had confiscated slaves employed by the Confederate military; the second declared all slaves of rebel masters "forever free of their servitude." In theory, this breathtaking measure freed most of the slaves in the Confederacy, for slaveholders formed the backbone of the rebellion. Congress had traveled far since the war began. Lincoln had too. On July 21, the president informed his cabinet that he was ready "to take some definitive steps in respect to military action and slavery." The next day, he read a draft of a preliminary emancipation proclamation that promised to free all slaves in the seceding states on January 1, 1863.

Lincoln described emancipation as an "act of justice," but it was the lengthening casualty lists that finally brought him around. Emancipation, he declared, was "a military necessity, absolutely essential to the preservation of the Union." Only freeing the slaves would "strike at the heart of the rebellion." His cabinet favored Lincoln's plan but advised him to wait for a military victory before announcing it so that critics would not call it an act of desperation. Although Antietam was actually a draw, Lincoln called it a victory, and on September 22, five days after the battle, he served notice that if the rebel states did not lay down their arms and return to the Union by January 1, 1863, their slaves "shall be then, thenceforward, and forever free."

The limitations of the proclamation—it exempted the loyal border states and the Union-occupied areas of the Confederacy—caused some to ridicule the act. The *London Times* observed cynically, "Where he has no power Mr. Lincoln will set the negroes free, where he retains power he will consider them as slaves." But Lincoln had no power to free slaves in loyal states, and invading Union armies would liberate slaves in the Confederacy as they advanced.

By presenting emancipation as a "military necessity," Lincoln hoped he had disarmed his conservative critics. Emancipation would shorten the war and thus save lives. Instead, Democrats exploded with rage. They charged that the "shrieking and howling abolitionist faction" had captured the

White House and made it "a nigger war." The fall 1862 elections were only weeks away, and Democrats sought to make political hay out of Lincoln's action. They gained thirty-four congressional seats. When House Democrats proposed a resolution branding emancipation "a high crime against the Constitution," the Republicans, who maintained narrow majorities in both houses, beat it back. As promised, on New Year's Day, Lincoln issued the final Emancipation Proclamation. In addition to freeing the slaves in the states that were in rebellion, the edict also committed the federal government to the fullest use of African Americans to defeat the Confederate enemy.

War of Black Liberation

Even before Lincoln proclaimed freedom a Union war aim, African Americans in the North had volunteered to fight. But the War Department, doubtful of their abilities and fearful of white reaction to serving side by side with them, refused to make black men soldiers. Instead, the army employed black men as manual laborers; black women sometimes found employment as laundresses and cooks. The navy, however, from the outset accepted blacks as sailors. They usually served in noncombatant roles, but within months a few blacks served on gun crews.

BAND OF THE 107TH U.S. COLORED INFANTRY, ARLINGTON, VIRGINIA, 1865
Photographed carrying their music and over-the-shoulder instruments, the members of this military band represent only a tiny fraction of the African Americans who served in the federal military during the Civil War. The Lincoln administration was slow to accept black soldiers, in part because of lingering doubts about their ability to fight. Colonel Thomas W. Higginson, a white Massachusetts clergyman and abolitionist, commanded the First South Carolina Infantry, which was made up of former slaves. After his regiment's first skirmish with Confederate soldiers, Higginson celebrated his men's courage: "No officer in this regiment now doubts that the key to the successful prosecution of this war lies in the unlimited employment of black troops. . . . Instead of leaving their homes and families to fight they are fighting for their homes and families." After the spring of 1863 the federal government did all it could to maximize the number of black soldiers. Throughout the war, however, policy required that blacks serve under white commissioned officers, such as the man on the left of this photograph.
Library of Congress.

As the Union experienced manpower shortages, Northerners gradually and reluctantly turned to African Americans to fill blue uniforms. With the Militia Act of July 1862, Congress authorized enrolling blacks in "any military or naval service for which they may be found competent." Lingering resistance to black military service largely disappeared in 1863. After the Emancipation Proclamation, whites—like it or not—were fighting and dying for black freedom, and few were likely to insist that blacks remain out of harm's way behind the lines. Indeed, rather than resist black military participation, whites insisted that blacks share the danger, especially after March 1863, when Congress resorted to the draft to fill the Union army.

Black soldiers discovered that the military was far from color blind. The Union army established segregated black regiments, paid black soldiers $10 per month rather than the $13 it paid to whites, refused blacks the opportunity to become commissioned officers, punished blacks as if they were slaves, and assigned blacks to labor battalions rather than to combat units. But nothing deterred black recruits. When the war ended, 179,000 African American men had served in the Union forces, approximately 10 percent of the army total. An astounding 71 percent of black men ages eighteen to forty-five in the free states wore Union blue, a participation rate that was substantially higher than that of white men. More than 130,000 black soldiers came from the slave states, perhaps 100,000 of them ex-slaves.

In time, whites allowed blacks to put down their shovels and to shoulder rifles. At the battles of Port Hudson and Milliken's Bend on the Mississippi River and at Fort Wagner in Charleston harbor, black courage under fire finally dispelled notions that African Americans could not fight. More than 38,000 black soldiers died in the Civil War, a mortality rate that was higher than that of white troops. Blacks played a crucial role in the triumph of the Union and the destruction of slavery.

The South at War

During the secession winter of 1860–61, a Louisiana planter had declared confidently that the creation of the Confederate States of America would "guarantee order, security, tranquility, as well as liberty." Instead, by seceding Southerners brought on themselves a firestorm of unimaginable fury. Monstrous losses on the battlefields nearly bled the Confederacy to death. But white Southerners at the home front were also under attack.

The most surprising thrust came from their own government. Richmond's efforts to centralize power to fight the war effectively convinced many men and women that the Confederacy had betrayed them. Wartime economic changes hurt everyone, but some suffered more than others; by 1863, planters and yeomen who had stood together began to drift apart. Most disturbing of all, slaves became open participants in the destruction of slavery and the Confederacy.

Revolution from Above

When Jefferson Davis arrived in Richmond in 1861, he faced the gargantuan task of building an army and navy from scratch, supplying them from factories that were scarce and anemic, and paying for it all from a treasury that did not exist. As one Confederate general observed, Southerners were engaged in a total war "in which the whole population and the whole production . . . are to be put on a war footing, where every institution is to be made auxiliary to war." Building the army proved easiest. Hundreds of officers defected from the federal army, and hundreds of thousands of eager young rebels volunteered to join them. Very quickly, the Confederacy developed formidable striking power.

The Confederacy's economy and finances proved tougher. Because of the Union blockade, the government had no choice but to build an industrial sector itself. Government-owned clothing and shoe factories, mines, arsenals, and powder works "sprung up almost like magic," according to one Mississippian. In addition, the government harnessed private companies, such as the huge Tredegar Iron Works in Richmond, to the war effort. The financial task proved most difficult because Southerners had invested their capital in land and slaves, which were not easily tapped for the war. Richmond came up with a mix of bonds, taxes, and paper money to finance the war effort.

Despite its bold measures, however, the Davis administration failed to transform the slave-labor, staple-producing agricultural economy into a modern industrial one. The Confederacy manufactured much more than most people imagined possible, but it never produced all that the South needed. Each month, the gap between the North's and the South's production widened. Moreover, the flood of paper money coming from Richmond caused debilitating inflation. By 1863, Charlestonians paid ten times more for food than they had at the start of the war. By Christmas 1864, a Confederate soldier's monthly pay no longer bought a pair of socks.

Richmond's war-making effort meant that government intruded in unprecedented ways into the private lives of Confederate citizens. In April 1862, the Confederate Congress passed the first conscription (draft) law in American history. All able-bodied white males between the ages of eighteen and thirty-five (later seventeen and fifty) were liable to serve in the rebel army for three years. The Confederate government adopted a policy of impressment, which allowed officials to confiscate food, horses, wagons, or whatever they wanted from private citizens and to pay for them at below-market rates. After March 1863, the Confederacy also legally impressed slaves, employing them as government military laborers. In addition, Richmond took control of the South's railroads and shipping. The war necessitated much of the government's unprecedented behavior, but citizens found it arbitrary and inequitable. In time, Southerners named Jefferson Davis as the politician they hated most, after Lincoln.

Hardship Below

Richmond's centralizing efforts ran head-on into the South's traditional values of states' rights and unfettered individualism. The states lashed out at what Georgia governor Joseph E. Brown denounced as the "dangerous usurpation by Congress of the reserved right of the States." A tug-of-war between Richmond and the states ensued for control of money, supplies, and soldiers, with damaging consequences for the war effort. Individual citizens also remembered that Davis had promised to defend southern "liberty" against Republican "despotism."

Hardships were widespread, but they fell most heavily on the poor. Inflation, for example, threatened the poor with starvation. Salt—necessary for preserving meat—shot up from $2 to $60 a bag during the first year of the war. Flour that cost three or four cents a pound in 1861 cost thirty-five cents in 1863. The draft depopulated yeomen farms of men, leaving the women and children to grow what they ate. When farm wives succeeded in bringing in a harvest, government agents took 10 percent of it as a "tax-in-kind" on agriculture. Like inflation, shortages also afflicted the entire population, but the rich

MARIA ISABELLA ("BELLE") BOYD, SPY
Most white southern women, in addition to keeping their families fed and safe, served the Confederate cause by sewing uniforms, knitting socks, rolling bandages, and nursing the sick and wounded. But Belle Boyd became a spy. Only seventeen when the war broke out, she became in the words of a northern journalist "insanely devoted to the rebel cause." Her first act for the Confederacy came on July 3, 1861, when she shot a drunken federal soldier who barged into her Virginia home and insulted her mother. Her relations with occupying northern troops improved, and soon this compelling young woman was eavesdropping on officers' conversations and slipping messages to Confederate armies. Boyd's information handed Stonewall Jackson an easy victory at Front Royal, Virginia, in May 1862. "I thank you," the general wrote Boyd, ". . . for the immense service that you have rendered your country today." Imprisoned several times for spying, Boyd took up a theatrical career when the war ended.
Courtesy Warren Rifles Confederate Museum, Front Royal, Va. Photo by Larry Sherer.

When the Republican-dominated Congress enacted the draft law in March 1863, Democrats had another grievance. Grim news from the battlefields had dried up the stream of volunteers, and the North, like the South a year earlier, turned to military conscription to fill the ranks. The law required that all men between the ages of twenty and forty-five enroll and make themselves available for a lottery, which would decide who went to war. What poor men found particularly galling were provisions that allowed a draftee to hire a substitute or simply to pay a $300 fee and get out of his military obligation. As in the South, common folk could be heard chanting, "A rich man's war and a poor man's fight."

Linking the draft and emancipation, Democrats argued that Republicans employed an unconstitutional means (the draft) to achieve an unconstitutional end (emancipation). In the summer of 1863, antidraft, antiblack mobs went on rampages in northern cities. New York experienced an explosion of unprecedented proportions. Solidly Democratic Irish workingmen, crowded into stinking, disease-ridden tenements, gouged by inflation, enraged by the inequities of the draft, and dead set against fighting to free blacks, erupted in four days of rioting. By the time police and soldiers restored order, at least 105 people, most of them black, lay dead, and the Colored Orphan Asylum was a smoking ruin.

The riots stunned black Northerners, but the racist mobs failed to achieve their purpose: the subordination of African Americans. Free black leaders had lobbied aggressively for emancipation, and after Lincoln's proclamation they fanned out over the North agitating for equality. They won some small wartime successes. Illinois and Iowa overturned laws that excluded blacks from entering the states. Illinois and Ohio began permitting blacks to testify in court. But defeat was more common. Indiana, for example, continued to forbid blacks to vote, testify, and attend public schools, and additional blacks were not allowed to enter the state.

Grinding Out Victory, 1863–1865

In the early months of 1863, the Union's prospects looked bleak, while the Confederate cause stood at high tide. But in July 1863, the tide began to recede. The military man who was most responsible for seeing that it never rose again was Ulysses S. Grant.

Lifted from obscurity by brilliant successes in the West in 1862 and 1863, Grant became "the great man of the day," one man observed in July 1864, "perhaps of the age." Elevated to supreme command, Grant knit together a powerful war machine that integrated a sophisticated command structure, modern technology, and complex logistics and supply systems. But the arithmetic of this plain man remained unchanged: killing more of the enemy than he kills of you equaled "the complete overthrow of the rebellion."

The North ground out the victory, battle by bloody battle. The balance tipped in the Union's favor in 1863, but if the Confederacy was beaten, Southerners clearly did not know it. The fighting reached new levels of ferocity in the last two years of the war. As national elections approached in the fall of 1864, a discouraged Lincoln expected a war-weary North to make him a one-term president. Instead, northern voters declared their willingness to continue the war in the defense of the ideals of union and freedom.

Vicksburg and Gettysburg

Perched on the bluffs above the eastern bank of the Mississippi River, Vicksburg, Mississippi, bristled with cannon and dared Yankee ships to try to pass. This Confederate stronghold stood between Union forces and complete control of the river. Impenetrable terrain made it impossible to take the city from the north, and to get his army south of Vicksburg, Grant marched it down the swampy western bank of the Mississippi. Union forces crossed the Mississippi River, marched north more than one hundred miles, and attacked the city. When the Confederates beat back the assault, Grant began siege operations to starve out the enemy. Civilian inhabitants took to living in caves to escape incessant Union cannon bombardment, and to survive they soon began eating mules and rats.

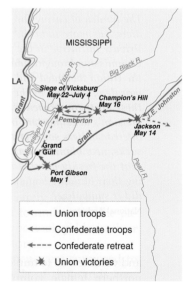

Vicksburg Campaign, 1863

Eventually, the siege succeeded. On July 4, 1863, nearly 30,000 rebels marched out of Vicksburg, stacked their arms, and surrendered unconditionally. A Yankee captain wrote home to his wife: "The backbone of the Rebellion is this day broken. The Confederacy is divided. . . . Vicksburg is ours. The Mississippi River is opened, and Gen. Grant is to be our next President."

On the same Fourth of July that a grateful nation received the news of Vicksburg, word arrived that Union forces had crushed General Lee at Gettysburg, Pennsylvania (Map 15.3). Lee's triumph two months earlier at Chancellorsville, Virginia, over Joseph "Fighting Joe" Hooker had revived his confidence, even though the battle cost him his favorite commander, the incomparable Stonewall Jackson, accidentally shot in the dark by his own troops. Lee wanted to relieve Virginia of the burden of the fighting, and he felt bold enough to think that he could deliver a morale-crunching defeat to the Yankees on their home turf.

In June, Lee's 75,000-man Army of Northern Virginia invaded Pennsylvania. On June 28, the Army of the Potomac, under its new commander, General George G. Meade, moved quickly to intercept it. Advanced units of both armies met at the small town of Gettysburg, where Union forces occupied the high ground. Three days of furious fighting, involving 165,000 soldiers, could not dislodge them from the ridges and hills. But Lee ached for a decisive victory, and on July 3 he ordered a major assault against the Union center on Cemetery Ridge. The open, rolling fields provided the dug-in Yankees with three-quarters of a mile of clear vision, and they raked the mile-wide line of Confederates with cannon and rifle fire. Time and again, the rebels closed ranks and raced on, until finally their momentum failed.

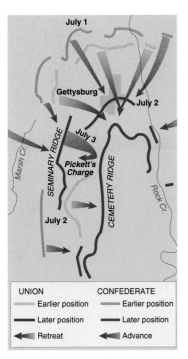

Battle of Gettysburg, July 1–3, 1863

Gettysburg cost Lee more than one-third of his army—28,000 casualties. "It's all my fault," he said. In a drenching rain on the night of July 4, 1863, he marched his battered army back to Virginia.

The twin disasters at Vicksburg and Gettysburg proved to be the turning point of the war. The Confederacy could not replace the nearly 60,000 soldiers who were captured, wounded, or killed. Lee never launched another major offensive north of the Mason-Dixon line. But it is hindsight that permits us to see the pair of battles as decisive. At the time, the Confederacy still controlled the heartland of the South, and Lee, back on the defensive in Virginia, still had a vicious sting. War-weariness threatened to erode the North's will to win before Union armies destroyed the Confederacy's ability to go on.

Grant Takes Command

In September 1863, Union general William Rosecrans placed his army in a dangerous situation in Chattanooga, Tennessee, where he had retreated after taking a whipping at the battle of Chickamauga (see Map 15.3). Rebels surrounded the disorganized bluecoats and threatened to starve them into submission. Ulysses S. Grant, whom Lincoln had made commander of all Union forces between the Mississippi River and the Appalachians, arrived in Chattanooga in October. Within weeks, he opened an effective supply line, broke the siege, and then (largely because troops disobeyed orders and charged wildly up Missionary Ridge) routed the Confederate army. The victory at Chattanooga had immense strategic value. It opened the door to Georgia. It also confirmed Lincoln's estimation of Grant. In March 1864, the president asked the commander to come east to become the general in chief of all Union armies.

In Washington, Grant implemented his grand strategy of a war of annihilation. He ordered a series of simultaneous assaults from Virginia to Louisiana. Two actions proved more significant than the others. In one, General William Tecumseh Sherman, whom Grant appointed his successor to command the western armies, plunged southeast toward Atlanta. In the other, Grant, who took control of the Army of the Potomac, went head-to-head with Lee for almost four straight weeks in Virginia.

Grant and Lee met in early May 1864 at the Wilderness, a dense tangle of scrub oaks and small

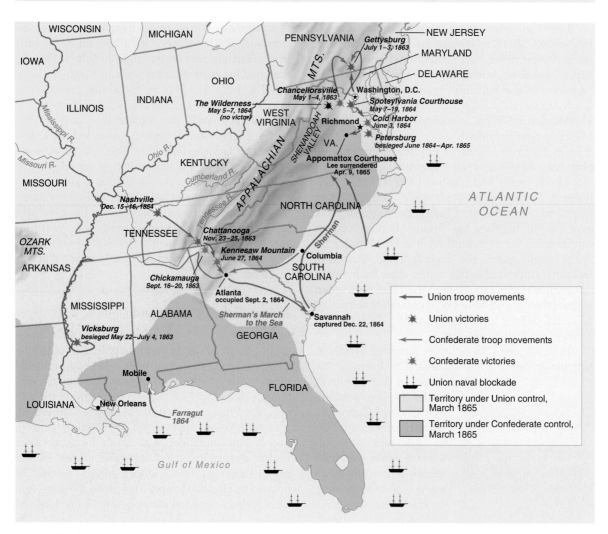

MAP 15.3
The Civil War, 1863–1865
Ulysses S. Grant's victory at Vicksburg divided the Confederacy at the Mississippi River. William Tecumseh Sherman's march from Chattanooga to Savannah divided it again. In northern Virginia, Robert E. Lee fought fiercely, but Grant's larger, better-supplied armies prevailed.

READING THE MAP: Describe the difference between Union and Confederate naval strength. Were the battles shown fought primarily in Union-controlled or Confederate-controlled territory?

CONNECTIONS: Did former slaves serve in the Civil War? If so, on which side(s)? Describe their efforts.

www.bedfordstmartins.com/roarkcompact SEE THE ONLINE STUDY GUIDE for more help in analyzing this map.

pines that proved to be Lee's ally, for it helped off-set the Yankees' numerical superiority. Often unable to see more than ten paces, the armies pounded away at each other until approximately 18,000 Yankees and 11,000 rebels had fallen. But the savagery of the Wilderness did not compare with that at Spot-sylvania Court House a few days later. Frenzied men fought hand to hand for eighteen hours in the rain. One veteran remembered men "piled upon each other in some places four layers deep, ex-hibiting every ghastly phase of mutilation." Spot-sylvania cost Grant another 18,000 casualties and Lee 10,000. But the Yankee bulldog would not let go. Grant kept moving and tangled with Lee again at Cold Harbor, where he lost 13,000 additional troops to Lee's 5,000. (See "Historical Question," page 378.)

Twice as many Union soldiers as rebel soldiers died in the four weeks of fighting in Virginia in the spring of 1864. Yet Grant did not consider himself defeated. Since Lee had only half the number of troops, he lost proportionally as many men as Grant. Ever the mathematician of war, Grant knew that the South could not replace the losses. More-over, the campaign had carried Grant to the out-skirts of Petersburg, just south of the Confederate capital. Since most of the major railroad lines sup-plying Richmond ran through Petersburg, Lee had little choice but to defend the city. Grant abandoned the costly tactic of the frontal assault and began a siege that immobilized both armies and dragged on for nine months.

There was no pause in Sherman's invasion of Georgia. Grant had instructed Sherman to "get into the interior of the enemy's country as far as you can, inflicting all the damage you can against their War resources." In early May Sherman moved 100,000 men south against the 65,000 rebels in the rugged mountains of northern Georgia. Skillful maneuver-ing, constant skirmishing, and one pitched battle (Kennesaw Mountain) brought Sherman to Atlanta, which fell on September 1.

Sherman was only warming up. Intending to "make Georgia howl," he marched out of Atlanta on November 15 with 62,000 battle-hardened vet-erans, heading for Savannah, 285 miles away. Fed-eral troops cut a swath from twenty-five to sixty miles wide. One veteran remembered, "[We] de-stroyed all we could not eat, stole their niggers, burned their cotton & gins, spilled their sorghum, burned & twisted their R. Roads and raised Hell generally." Sherman's "March to the Sea" aimed at

GRANT AT COLD HARBOR
Seated next to his chief of staff, John A. Rawlins, at his Cold Harbor, Virginia, headquarters, Ulysses S. Grant plots his next move against Robert E. Lee. On June 3, 1864, Grant ordered frontal assaults against entrenched Confederate forces, resulting in enormous Union losses. "I am disgusted with the generalship displayed," young Brigadier General Emory Upton exclaimed. "Our men have, in many cases, been fool-ishly and wantonly slaughtered." Years later, Grant said that he regretted the assault at Cold Harbor, but in 1864 he kept pushing toward Richmond.
Chicago Historical Society.

Why Did So Many Soldiers Die?

FROM 1861 TO 1865, Americans killed Americans on a scale that had never before been seen. Not until the First World War, a half century later, would the world match (and surpass) the killing fields at Shiloh, Antietam, and Gettysburg (Figure 15.2). Why were the Civil War totals so huge? Why did 260,000 rebel soldiers and 373,000 Union soldiers die?

The balance between the ability to kill and the ability to save lives had tipped disastrously toward death. The sheer size of the armies—some battles involved more than 200,000 soldiers—ensured that battlefields would turn red with blood. Moreover, armies fought with antiquated strategy. In the generals' eyes, the ideal soldier remained the veteran of Napoleonic warfare, a man trained to advance with his comrades in a compact, close-order formation. Theory also emphasized frontal assaults. In classrooms at West Point and on the high plains of Mexico in the 1840s, men who would one day be officers in rival armies learned that infantry advancing shoulder to shoulder, supported by artillery, carried the day.

But by the 1860s, modern technology had made such strategy appallingly deadly. Weapons with ri-

WOUNDED MEN AT SAVAGE'S STATION
Misery did not end when the cannon ceased firing. This heap of mangled humanity strewn on the ground was but a fraction of the cost of General George McClellan's campaign on the Virginia peninsula in 1862.
Library of Congress.

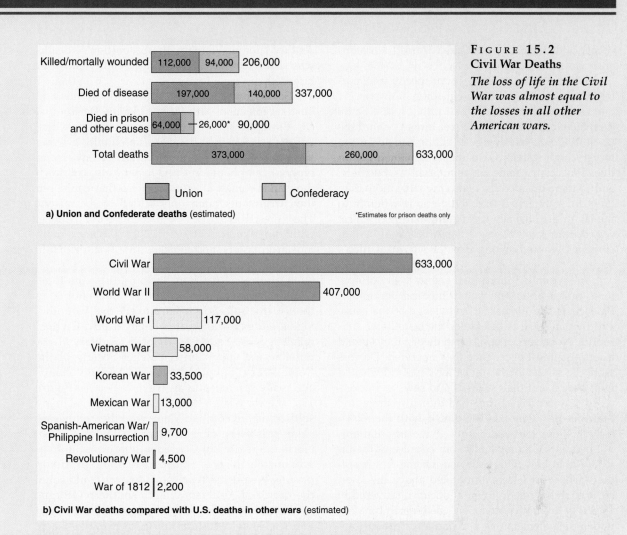

FIGURE 15.2
Civil War Deaths
The loss of life in the Civil War was almost equal to the losses in all other American wars.

Killed/mortally wounded 112,000 94,000 206,000

Died of disease 197,000 140,000 337,000

Died in prison and other causes 64,000 26,000* 90,000

Total deaths 373,000 260,000 633,000

■ Union ☐ Confederacy

a) Union and Confederate deaths (estimated)

*Estimates for prison deaths only

Civil War 633,000

World War II 407,000

World War I 117,000

Vietnam War 58,000

Korean War 33,500

Mexican War 13,000

Spanish-American War/ Philippine Insurrection 9,700

Revolutionary War 4,500

War of 1812 2,200

b) Civil War deaths compared with U.S. deaths in other wars (estimated)

fled barrels (that is, with spiral grooves cut into the bore) were replacing old smoothbore muskets. Whereas muskets had an effective range of only about eighty yards, rifles propelled spinning bullets four times as far. The rifle's greater range and accuracy, along with cannons firing canisters filled with flesh-ripping, bone-breaking steel shot, made sitting ducks of charging infantry units and gave enormous advantage to entrenched defensive forces. As a result, battles took thousands of lives in a single day. On July 2, 1862, the morning after the battle at Malvern Hill in eastern Virginia, a Union officer surveyed the scene: "Over five thousand dead and wounded men were on the ground . . . enough were alive and moving to give to the field a singular crawling effect."

Soldiers who littered the battlefields often lay for hours, sometimes days, without water or care of any kind. When the war began, no one anticipated casualty lists with thousands of names. Union and Confederate medical departments could not cope with skirmishes, much less large-scale battles. They had no ambulance corps to lift the wounded from the scene. They had no field hospitals to deliver them to. At first, the Quartermaster Department, which was responsible for constructing Union hospitals, answered demands that it do something by saying: "Men need guns, not beds." It took the shock of massive casualties to compel reform. Although a lack of resources meant that the South lagged behind the North, both North and South gradually organized effective ambulance *(Continued)* corps, built hospitals, and hired trained surgeons and nurses.

Soldiers did not always count speedy transportation to a field hospital as a blessing, however. As one Union soldier said, "I had rather risk a battle than the Hospitals." Real danger lurked behind the lines. While the technology of killing had advanced to very high standards, medicine remained primitive. Physicians gained a reputation as butchers, and soldiers dreaded the operating table more than they did entrenched riflemen. Serious wounds to the leg or arm usually meant amputation, the best way doctors knew to save lives. After major battles, surgeons worked among piles of wounded men's limbs.

The wounded man's real enemy was not doctors' callousness, but rather medical ignorance. Physicians had almost no knowledge of the cause and transmission of disease or the benefits of antiseptics. Not aware of basic germ theory, they spread infection almost every time they operated. Doctors wore the same bloody smock for days and washed their hands and their scalpels and saws in buckets of dirty water. When they had difficulty threading their needles, they wet the thread with their own saliva. Soldiers often did not survive amputations, not because of the operation but because of the infection that inevitably followed. Of the Union soldiers whose legs were amputated above the knee, more than half died. A Union doctor discovered in 1864 that bromine (previously used in combination with other elements as a sedative) arrested gangrene, but the best most amputees could hope for was maggots, which ate dead flesh on the stump and thus inhibited the spread of infection. During the Civil War, nearly one of every five wounded rebel soldiers died, and one in every six Yankees. A

century later, in Vietnam, the proportion of deaths was one wounded American soldier in four hundred.

Soldiers who avoided battlefield wounds and hospital infections still faced sickness. Deadly diseases swept through crowded army camps, where latrines were often in dangerous proximity to water supplies. The principal killers were dysentery and typhoid, but pneumonia and malaria also cut down thousands of men. Doctors did what they could, but their treatments often only added to the misery. They prescribed doses of turpentine for patients with typhoid, fought respiratory problems with mustard plasters, and attacked intestinal disorders with blisters and sulfuric acid.

Dorothea Dix, Clara Barton, Juliet Ann Opie Hopkins, and thousands of other female nurses in the North and South improved the wounded men's odds and alleviated their misery. Civilian relief agencies, such as the U.S. Sanitary Commission and the Women's Relief Society of the Confederacy, promoted hygiene in army camps and made some headway. Nevertheless, as Figure 15.2 shows, disease killed nearly twice as many soldiers as did combat. Many who died of disease were prisoners of war. Approximately 30,000 Northerners died in Confederate prisons, and approximately 26,000 Southerners died in Union prisons. No northern prison, however, could equal the horror of Andersonville in southern Georgia. In August 1864, about 33,000 emaciated men lived in unspeakable conditions in a twenty-six-acre barren stockade with no shelter except what the prisoners were able to construct. More than 13,000 perished.

In the end, 633,000 northern and southern soldiers died, a staggering death toll.

destroying the will of the southern people. A few weeks earlier, General Philip H. Sheridan had tried as much in the Shenandoah Valley, complying with Grant's order to turn the valley into "a barren waste . . . so that crows flying over it for the balance of this season will have to carry their provender [food] with them." When Sherman's troops entered an undefended Savannah in the third week of December,

the general telegraphed Lincoln that he had "a Christmas gift" for him.

The Election of 1864

In the fall, white men in the Union states turned to the election of a president. Never before had a nation held general elections in the midst of war. "We can not have free government without elections," Lincoln explained, "and if the rebellion could force us to forgo or postpone a national election, it might fairly claim to have already conquered and ruined us."

Lincoln's determination to hold elections is especially noteworthy because the Democratic Party smelled victory. The Union war effort had stalled during the summer, and frustration had settled over the North. Rankled by inflation, the draft, the attack on civil liberties, and the commitment to blacks, Northerners appeared ready for a change. Lincoln himself concluded in the gloomy summer of 1864, "It seems exceedingly probable that this administration will not be re-elected."

Democrats were badly divided, however. "Peace" Democrats insisted on an armistice, while "war" Democrats supported the conflict but opposed Republican means of fighting it. They tried to paper over the chasm by nominating a war candidate, General George McClellan, but adopting a peace platform that demanded that "immediate efforts be made for a cessation of hostilities."

Lincoln was no shoo-in for renomination, much less reelection. Conservatives believed he had acted precipitously in emancipating the slaves, and radicals criticized him for moving too slowly to free them and for failing to champion black equality. But frightened by the strength of the peace Democrats, the Republican Party stuck with Lincoln. In an effort to reach out to the largest number of voters, however, the Republicans made two changes. First, they chose the new name the Union Party, making it easier for prowar Democrats to embrace Lincoln. Second, they chose a new vice presidential candidate, Andrew Johnson of Tennessee.

The capture of Atlanta in September turned the political tide in favor of the Republicans. Lincoln received 55 percent of the popular vote, but his electoral margin was a whopping 212 to McClellan's 21. The Republicans also stormed back in the congressional elections, gaining large margins over the Democrats in the Senate and the House. The Union Party bristled with factions, but they united for a resounding victory. The victory gave Lincoln a mandate to continue the war until slavery and the Confederacy were dead.

The Confederacy Collapses

Jefferson Davis found little to celebrate as the new year of 1865 dawned in Richmond. Military disaster littered the Confederate landscape. With the

destruction of John B. Hood's army at Nashville in November, the interior of the Confederacy lay in Yankee hands (see Map 15.3). Sherman's troops, resting momentarily in Savannah, eyed South Carolina hungrily. Lee's army remained, but Grant had it pinned down in Petersburg just a few miles from Richmond. Southerners took out their frustration and bitterness on their president. Kinder than most, Alexander Stephens, vice president of the Confederacy, likened Davis to "my poor old blind and deaf dog."

In the final months of the war, more and more Confederates turned their backs on the rebellion. News from the battlefields made it difficult not to conclude that the Yankees had beaten them. Soldiers' wives begged their husbands to return home to keep their families from starving, and the stream of deserters became a flood. In most cases, they lost the will to continue not so much because they lost faith in southern independence but because they had been battered into submission. Despite all the divisions and conflicts within the Confederacy and the loss of heart in the final months, white Southerners had shown remarkable endurance for their cause. Half of the 900,000 Confederate soldiers had been killed or wounded, and ragged, hungry women and children had sacrificed for four years. Confederates had shown remarkable staying power through the bloodiest war then known to history.

The end came with a rush. On February 1, 1865, Sherman's troops stormed out of Savannah into South Carolina, the "cradle of the Confederacy." But before Sherman could push through North Carolina and arrive at the rear of Lee's army at Petersburg, Lee abandoned the city. Davis fled Richmond, and the capital city fell a few days later. Grant pursued Lee for one hundred miles, until Lee surrendered on April 9, 1865, in a farmhouse near the town of Appomattox Court House, Virginia. The beaten man arrived in an immaculate full-dress uniform, complete with sash and sword; the victor came in his usual mud-splattered private's outfit. Grant offered a generous peace. He allowed Lee's men to return home and to take their horses to help "put in a crop to carry themselves and their families through the next winter." With Lee gone, the remaining ragtag Confederate armies lost hope and gave up. After four years, the war was over.

The day after Lee's surrender, a brass band led a happy crowd of three thousand to the White House, where they pleaded with Lincoln for a speech. He begged off and asked the band to strike up "Dixie." He knew that the rebels had claimed

RUINS OF RICHMOND
A Union soldier and a small boy in a Union cap contemplate the silence and devastation of Richmond, Virginia, the Confederacy's capital. On their way out of the city on the evening of April 2, 1865, Confederate demolition squads set fire to tobacco warehouses and ammunition dumps. Huge explosions tore holes in the city, and windswept fires destroyed much of what was left standing. As one Confederate observed, "The old war-scarred city seemed to prefer annihilation to conquest."
Library of Congress.

the tune as their own, he said, but it was one of his favorites, and now he was taking it back. The crowd roared its approval, and the band played "Dixie," following it with "Yankee Doodle." No one was more relieved than Lincoln that the war was over, but his celebration was restrained. He told his cabinet that his postwar burdens would weigh almost as heavily as those of wartime. But Lincoln had other things on his mind when he attended Ford's Theatre on the evening of Good Friday, April 14, 1865. While he and his wife, Mary, enjoyed *Our American Cousin,* a British comedy, John Wilkes Booth, an actor with southern sympathies, slipped into the president's box and mortally wounded Lincoln with a single shot to his head. The man who had led the nation through the war would not lead it in its postwar search for a just peace.

Conclusion: The Second American Revolution

The Civil War had a profound effect on the nation and its people. It devastated the South. Three-fourths of southern white men of military age served in the army, and at least half of them were captured, wounded, or killed or died of disease. The war destroyed two-fifths of the South's livestock, wrecked half of the farm machinery, and blackened dozens of cities and towns. The immediate impact of the war on the North was more paradoxical. Putting down the slaveholders' rebellion cost the North a heavy price: 373,000 lives. But rather than devastating the land, war set the countryside and cities humming with business activity.

A transformed nation emerged from the crucible of war. Antebellum America was decentralized politically and loosely integrated economically. To bend the resources of the country to a Union victory, Congress enacted legislation that reshaped the nation's political and economic character. It adopted policies that established the sovereignty of the federal government and the dominance of industrial capitalism. Moreover, the common sacrifice of northern people to save the nation created an even fiercer national loyalty. The shift in power from South to North and the creation of a national government, a national economy, and a national spirit led one historian to call the American Civil War the "Second American Revolution."

Most revolutionary of all, the war ended slavery. As Frederick Douglass had predicted, the South's war to preserve slavery killed it. Because that ancient labor and racial system was entangled in almost every aspect of southern life, slavery's uprooting would mean fundamental change. But the full meaning of abolition remained unclear in 1865. The task of determining the new economic, political, and social status of four million ex-slaves would be the principal task of the era known as Reconstruction.

For further reading about the topics in this chapter, see the Online Bibliography at

www.bedfordstmartins.com/roarkcompact.

For additional first-hand accounts of this period, see pages 224–241 in Michael Johnson, ed., *Reading the American Past,* Second Edition, Volume I.

To assess your mastery of the material in this chapter, see the Online Study Guide at

www.bedfordstmartins.com/roarkcompact.

CHRONOLOGY

1861   **April.** Union nurse Dorothea Dix named superintendent of female nurses.

April 12–13. Confederate forces attack Fort Sumter, South Carolina, the opening engagement of the Civil War.

April–May. Four Upper South states secede and join Confederacy.

July. Union forces routed at Manassas, Virginia, in first major clash of war.

August. Congress approves first Confiscation Act, which allows seizure of any slave employed by Confederate military.

1862   **February.** Legal Tender Act creates first national currency, called "greenbacks."

Union forces in West under General Ulysses S. Grant capture Fort Henry and Fort Donelson and drive Confederates from Kentucky and most of Tennessee.

April. Battle of Shiloh in Tennessee results in huge casualties and ends Confederate bid to control Mississippi Valley.

Confederate Congress passes first draft law in American history.

May. Homestead Act offers western land to those who would live and labor on it.

May–July. General George McClellan's Union forces defeated during peninsula campaign in Virginia.

July. Congress approves second Confiscation Act, freeing all slaves of rebel masters.

Congress passes Militia Act, authorizing enrollment of blacks in Union military.

September 17. Battle of Antietam stops Lee's advance into Maryland, but Confederate forces escape back to Virginia.

September 22. Lincoln announces preliminary emancipation proclamation.

1863   **January 1.** Emancipation Proclamation becomes law, freeing slaves in areas still in rebellion.

February. National Banking Act creates system of national banks.

March. Congress authorizes draft.

July. Vicksburg falls to Union forces under Grant, effectively cutting Confederacy in two along Mississippi River.

Battle of Gettysburg results in Confederate defeat and Lee's last offensive in North.

1864   **March.** Grant appointed general in chief of all Union forces.

May–June. Grant's forces engage Confederates in Virginia in bloodiest fighting of war, from Wilderness campaign to beginnings of siege of Petersburg.

September. Atlanta falls to Union forces under General William Tecumseh Sherman.

November. Lincoln reelected president.

December. Sherman occupies Savannah after scorched-earth campaign in Georgia.

1865   **April 9.** Lee surrenders to Grant at Appomattox Court House, Virginia, triggering the end of resistance.

April 14. Lincoln shot by John Wilkes Booth at Ford's Theatre in Washington. He dies on April 15, succeeded by Vice President Andrew Johnson.

ba be bi bo bu	ra re ri ro ru	
da de di do du	sa se si so su	
fa fe fi fo fu	ta te ti to tu	
ka ke ki ko ku	va ve vi vo vu	

Top.   Hen and chickens.   Drum.

la le li lo lu	ya ye yi yo yu	
na ne ni no nu	*ca ce ci co cu	
pa pe pi po pu	ga ge gi go gu	

Bugle.

ab eb i
ab ed id
af ef if
ag eg i

Zebra.   Hobby-horse.

Fire Engine.   Snake.

Turkey.   Hoopoe

Squirrel.

AMERICAN
ONE CENT
PRIMER.

NEW YORK:
KIGGINS & KELLOGG, PUBLISHERS,
Nos. 123 & 125 WILLIAM STREET,
Between John & Fulton.

ONE-CENT PRIMER

"The people are hungry and thirsty after knowledge," a former slave from South Carolina observed after the Civil War. Future African American leader Booker T. Washington remembered "a whole race trying to go to school. Few were too young, and none too old, to make the attempt to learn." Inexpensive elementary textbooks (this humble eight-page primer cost a penny) offered poor ex-slaves the basic elements of literacy—the letters of the alphabet and the sounds they make. For people who had been forbidden to learn to read and write as slaves, literacy symbolized freedom. It also meant that deeply religious people could experience the joy of reading the Bible. Literacy provided a crucial tool for negotiating the hostile world of the post-war South. Reading and writing permitted African Americans to understand labor agreements, sign contracts, and participate knowledgeably in politics.

The William Gladstone Collection.

RECONSTRUCTION
1863–1877

Y ORK DISAPPEARED ON YESTERDAY MORNING," David Golightly Harris noted in his journal on June 6, 1865. "I suppose that he has gone to the yankey. I wish they would give him a good whipping & hasten him back." York, a black field hand, had once belonged to Harris, a white slaveholder in Spartanburg District, South Carolina. When York disappeared, however, the war had been over for two months, and York was a free man. In Harris's mind, however, simply declaring York free did not make him so. In July, Harris noted that another field hand, Old Will, had left "to try to enjoy the freedom the Yankey's have promised the negroes." Two weeks later, black freedom still seemed in doubt. "There is much talk about freeing the negroes. Some are said already to have freed them," Harris declared. But Harris had not freed anyone. He did not inform his former slaves of their freedom until federal military authorities required him to. *"Freed the Negroes,"* he declared on August 16, four months after Appomattox.

Like many ex-slaveholders, Harris had trouble coming to grips with emancipation. "Family well, Horses well, Cattle well, Hogs well & everything else are well so far as I know, if it was not for the free negroes," Harris wrote on September 17. "On their account everything is turned upside down. So much so that we do not know what to do with our land, nor who to hire if we want it worked. . . . We are in the midst of troublesome times & do not know what will turn up." Harris had owned ten slaves, and now he faced what seemed to him an insoluble problem. He needed black labor to cultivate his farm, but like most whites he did not believe that blacks would work much when free. Some kind of compulsion would be needed. But slavery was gone, leaving the South upside down. Some white men in Harris's neighborhood sought to set it straight again. "In this district several negroes have been badly whipped & several have been hung by some unknown persons," he noted in November. "This has a tendency to keep them in their proper bounds & make them more humble." But the violence did not keep ex-slaves from acting like free people. On Christmas Day 1865, Harris recorded, "The negroes leave today to hunt themselves a new home while we will be left to wait upon ourselves."

Across the South, ex-masters predicted that emancipation would mean economic collapse and social anarchy. Carl Schurz, a Union general who undertook a fact-finding mission to the ex-Confederate states in the summer of 1865, encountered this dire prediction often enough to conclude that the Civil War was a "revolution but half accomplished." Northern victory had freed the slaves, but it had not changed former slaveholders' minds about the need for slavery. Left to themselves, Schurz believed, whites would "introduce some new system of forced labor, not perhaps exactly slavery in its old form but something similar to it." To defend their freedom, blacks would need federal protection, land of their own, and voting rights, Schurz concluded. Until whites "cut loose from the past, it will be a

BLACK WOMAN IN COTTON FIELDS, THOMASVILLE, GEORGIA
Few images of everyday black women during the era of Reconstruction survive. This photograph was taken in 1895, but it nevertheless goes to the heart of the labor struggle after the Civil War. As slaves, black women worked in the fields, and white landlords wanted them to continue working there after emancipation. Freedom allowed some women to escape field labor, but not this Georgian, who no doubt worked to survive. Despite her plight, the photograph reveals a strong person with a clear sense of who she is. Although worn to protect her head and body from the fierce heat, her intricately wrapped headdress dramatically expresses her individuality. However, what do her feet reveal about her life?
Vanishing Georgia Collection, Georgia Department of Archives and History, Atlanta, Georgia.

dangerous experiment to put Southern society upon its own legs." The end of the war did not mean the beginning of peace. Instead, the nation entered one of its most chaotic and conflicted eras—Reconstruction, an era that would define the status of the defeated South within the Union and the meaning of freedom for ex-slaves.

The status of the South and the nature of black freedom were determined by the political debate in the nation's capital and in the state legislatures and county seats of the South and through the active participation of blacks themselves. In the midst of the flux and chaos, a small band of crusading women sought to achieve gender equality. The years of reconstruction were characterized by struggle in which white Southerners eventually prevailed. Though they largely defined the "New South," it was a very different South from the one to which whites like David Golightly Harris wished to return.

Wartime Reconstruction

Reconstruction did not wait for the end of war. As the odds of a northern victory increased, thinking about reunification quickened. Immediately, a question arose: Who had authority to devise a plan for reconstructing the Union? Lincoln believed firmly that reconstruction was a matter of executive responsibility. Congress just as firmly asserted its jurisdiction. Fueling the argument about who had authority to set the terms of reconstruction were significant differences about the terms themselves. Lincoln's primary aim was the restoration of national unity, which he sought through a program of speedy, forgiving political reconciliation. Congress feared that the president's program amounted to restoring the old southern ruling class to power. It wanted greater assurances of white loyalty and greater guarantees of black rights.

In their eagerness to formulate a plan for political reunification, neither Lincoln nor Congress gave much attention to the South's land and labor problems. But the war rapidly eroded slavery and traditional plantation agriculture, and Yankee military commanders in the Union-occupied areas of the Confederacy had no choice but to oversee the emergence of a new labor system.

"To Bind Up the Nation's Wounds"

On March 4, 1865, President Abraham Lincoln delivered his second inaugural address. He surveyed the history of the long, deadly war and then looked ahead to peace. "With malice toward none; with charity for all; with firmness in the right, as God gives us to see the right," Lincoln said, "let us strive on to finish the work we are in; to bind up the nation's wounds . . . to do all which may achieve and cherish a just, and a lasting peace." Lincoln had contemplated reunion for nearly two years. Deep compassion for the enemy guided his thinking about peace. But kindness is not the key to understanding Lincoln's program. His reconstruction plan aimed primarily at shortening the war and ending slavery.

In his Proclamation of Amnesty and Reconstruction, issued in December 1863, Lincoln offered a full pardon to rebels willing to renounce secession and to accept the abolition of slavery. (Pardons were valuable because they restored all property, except slaves, and full political rights.) His offer excluded several groups of Confederates, such as high-ranking civilian and military officers. When only 10 percent of men who had been qualified voters in 1860 had taken an oath of allegiance, they could organize a new state government. Lincoln's plan did not require ex-rebels to extend social or political rights to ex-slaves, nor did it anticipate a program of long-term federal assistance to freedmen. Clearly, the president sought to restore the broken Union, not to reform it.

Lincoln's easy terms enraged abolitionists like Bostonian Wendell Phillips, who charged that the president "makes the negro's freedom a mere sham." He "is willing that the negro should be free but seeks nothing else for him," Phillips declared. Phillips and other northern radicals called instead for a thorough overhaul of southern society. Their ideas proved to be too drastic for most Republicans during the war years, but Congress agreed that Lincoln's plan was inadequate. In July 1864, Congress put forward a plan of its own.

Congressman Henry Winter Davis of Maryland and Senator Benjamin Wade of Ohio jointly sponsored a bill that threw out Lincoln's "10 percent plan" and demanded that at least half of the voters in a conquered rebel state take the oath of allegiance before reconstruction could begin. Moreover, the Wade-Davis bill banned ex-Confederates from participating in the drafting of new state constitutions. Finally, the bill guaranteed the equality of freedmen before the law. Congress's reconstruction would be neither as quick nor as forgiving as Lincoln's. Still, the Wade-Davis bill angered radicals because it did not include a provision for black suffrage. When Lincoln exercised his right not to sign the bill and let it die instead, Wade and Davis published a manifesto charging the president with usurpation of power. They warned Lincoln to confine himself to "his executive duties—to obey and execute, not make the laws—to suppress by arms armed rebellion, and leave political organization to Congress."

Undeterred, Lincoln continued to nurture the formation of loyal state governments under his own plan. Four states—Louisiana, Arkansas, Tennessee, and Virginia—fulfilled the president's requirements, but Congress refused to seat representatives from the "Lincoln states." In his last public address in April 1865, Lincoln defended his plan but for the first time expressed publicly his endorsement of suffrage for southern blacks, at least "the very intelligent, and . . . those who serve our cause as soldiers." The announcement demonstrated that Lincoln's thinking about reconstruction was still evolving. Four days later, he was dead.

Land and Labor

Of all the problems raised by emancipation, none proved more critical than the transition from slave to free labor. As federal armies proceeded to invade and occupy the Confederacy during the war, hundreds of thousands of slaves became free workers. Moreover, northern occupation meant that Union armies controlled vast territories where legal title to land had become unclear. The wartime Confiscation Acts punished "traitors" by taking away their property. What to do with federally occupied land and how to organize labor on it engaged former slaves, former slaveholders, Union military commanders, and federal government officials long before the war ended.

Occupying federal troops announced a new labor code. The code required planters to sign contracts with ex-slaves and to pay wages. It also obligated employers to provide food, housing, and medical care. It outlawed whipping, but it reserved to the army the right to discipline blacks who refused to work. The code required black laborers to enter into contracts, work diligently, and remain subordinate and obedient. Military leaders clearly had no intention of promoting a social or economic revolution. Instead, they sought to restore plantation agriculture with wage labor. The effort resulted in a hybrid system of "compulsory free labor" that satisfied no one. Depending on one's point of view, it either provided too little or too much of a break with the past.

Planters complained because the new system fell short of slavery. Blacks could not be "transformed by proclamation," a Louisiana sugar planter warned. Yet under the new system, blacks "are expected to perform their new obligations without coercion, & without the fear of punishment which is essential to stimulate the idle and correct the vicious." Without the right to whip, he argued, the new labor system did not have a chance.

African Americans found the new regime too reminiscent of slavery to be called "free labor." Of its many shortcomings, none disappointed ex-slaves more than the failure to provide them land of their own. "What's the use of being free if you don't own land enough to be buried in?" one man asked. Freedmen believed they had a moral right to land because they and their ancestors had worked it without compensation for more than two centuries. Moreover, several wartime developments led them to believe that the federal government planned to strengthen black freedom with landownership.

In January 1865, General William T. Sherman set aside part of the coast south of Charleston for black settlement. He devised the plan to relieve himself of the burden of thousands of impoverished blacks who trailed desperately after his army. By June 1865, some forty thousand freedmen sat on 400,000 acres of "Sherman land." In addition, in March 1865, Congress established the Bureau of Refugees, Freedmen, and Abandoned Lands. The Freedmen's Bureau, as it was called, distributed food and clothing to destitute Southerners and eased the transition of blacks from slaves to free persons. Congress also authorized the agency to divide abandoned and confiscated land into 40-acre plots, to rent them to freedmen, and eventually to sell them "with such title as the United States can convey." By June 1865, the bureau had situated nearly ten thousand black families on a half million acres that had been abandoned by fleeing planters. Hundreds of thousands of other ex-slaves eagerly anticipated farms of their own.

Despite the flurry of activity, wartime reconstruction had settled nothing. Two years of controversy had failed to produce agreement about whether the president or Congress had the authority to devise and direct policy or what proper policy should be. Clearly, the nation faced dilemmas almost as trying as those of the war.

The African American Quest for Autonomy

Ex-slaves never had any doubt about what they wanted freedom to mean. They had only to contemplate what they had been denied as slaves. (See "Documenting the American Promise," page 392.) Slaves had to remain on their plantations; freedom allowed blacks to go wherever they pleased. Thus, in the first heady weeks after emancipation, freedmen often abandoned their plantations just to see what was on the other side of the hill. Slaves had to be at work in the fields by dawn; freedom permitted blacks to taste the forbidden pleasure of sleeping through a sunrise. Freedmen also tested the etiquette of racial subordination. "Lizzie's maid passed me today when I was coming from church without speaking to me," huffed one plantation mistress.

To whites, it looked like pure anarchy. Without the discipline of slavery, they said, blacks had reverted to their natural condition: lazy, irresponsible, and wild. Actually, these former slaves were experimenting with freedom, but they could not long afford to roam the countryside, neglect work, and casually provoke whites. Soon, most were back on plantations, at work in the fields and kitchens.

But other items on ex-slaves' agenda of freedom endured. Freedmen did not easily give up their quest for economic independence. In addition, slavery had deliberately kept blacks illiterate, and freedmen emerged from slavery eager to read and write. Moreover, bondage had denied slaves secure family lives, and the restoration of their families became a persistent black aspiration. As a consequence, thousands of black men and women took to the roads in 1865 to look for relations who had been sold away. Couples who emerged from slavery with their marriages intact often rushed to northern military chaplains to legalize their unions.

Another hunger that freedom permitted African Americans to satisfy was independent worship. Under slavery, blacks had often prayed with whites in biracial churches. Intent on religious independence, blacks greeted freedom with a mass exodus from white churches. Some joined the newly established southern branches of all-black northern churches, such as the African Methodist Episcopal Church. Others formed black versions of the major southern denominations, Baptists and Methodists. Slaves had comprehended their tribulations through the lens of their deeply felt Christian faith, and freedmen continued to interpret the events of the Civil War and reconstruction as people of faith.

Presidential Reconstruction

Abraham Lincoln died on April 15, 1865, just hours after John Wilkes Booth had shot him at a Washington, D.C., theater. Chief Justice Salmon P. Chase immediately administered the oath of office to Vice President Andrew Johnson of Tennessee. Congress had adjourned in March, which meant that legislators were away from Washington when Lincoln was killed. They would not reconvene until December. Throughout the summer and fall, therefore, the "accidental president" made critical decisions about the future of the South. Like Lincoln, Johnson believed that responsibility for restoring the Union lay with the president. With dizzying speed, he drew up and executed a plan of reconstruction.

Congress returned to the capital in December to find that, as far as the president and former Confederates were concerned, reconstruction was over. To most Republicans, Johnson's modest demands of ex-rebels made a mockery of the sacrifice of Union soldiers. In an 1863 speech dedicating the cemetery at Gettysburg, Lincoln had spoken of the "great task remaining before us . . . that we here highly resolve that these dead shall not have died in vain— that this nation, under God, shall have a new birth of freedom." Instead, Johnson had acted as midwife to the rebirth of the Old South. He had achieved political reunification at the cost of black liberty. To let his program stand, Republican legislators said, would mean that the North's dead had indeed died in vain.

Johnson's Program of Reconciliation

Born in 1808 in Raleigh, North Carolina, Andrew Johnson was the son of poor, illiterate parents. Unable to afford to send her son to school, Johnson's widowed mother apprenticed him to a tailor. Self-educated and ambitious, he later worked as a tailor in Tennessee, accumulated a fortune in land, acquired five slaves, and built a career in politics championing the South's common white people and assailing its "illegitimate, swaggering, bastard, scrub aristocracy." The only senator from a Confederate state to remain loyal to the Union, Johnson held slaveholders responsible for secession. Less than two weeks before he became president, he made it clear what he would do to the rascals if he ever had the chance: "I would arrest them—I would try them—I would convict them and I would hang them."

In reality, however, Johnson was no friend of northern radicals. A southern Democrat all his life, Johnson occupied the White House only because the Republican Party in 1864 had needed to broaden its appeal to loyal, Union-supporting Democrats. Johnson favored traditional Democratic causes, vigorously defending states' rights (but not secession) and opposing Republican efforts to expand the power of the federal government.

Moreover, Johnson had been a steadfast defender of slavery. He had owned slaves until 1862, when Tennessee rebels, angry at his Unionism, confiscated them. He only grudgingly accepted emancipation. When he did, it was more because of his hatred for slaveholders than sympathy for slaves. "Damn the negroes," he said. "I am fighting those traitorous aristocrats, their masters." At a time when the nation faced its moment of truth regarding black Americans, the new president harbored unshakable racist convictions. Africans, Johnson said, were "inferior to the white man in point of intellect—better calculated in physical structure to undergo drudgery and hardship."

Johnson presented his plan of reconstruction as a continuation of Lincoln's plan, and in some ways it was. Like Lincoln, he stressed reconciliation between the Union and the defeated Confederacy and rapid restoration of civil government in the South. He offered to pardon most ex-rebels. Johnson recognized the state governments created by Lincoln and set out his own requirements for restoring the rebel states to the Union. All that the citizens of a state had to do was to renounce the right of secession, deny that the debts of the Confederacy were legal and binding, and ratify the Thirteenth Amendment abolishing slavery, which became part of the Constitution in December 1865. Johnson's plan ignored Lincoln's acceptance near the end of his life of some form of limited black voting.

The Meaning of Freedom

*O*n *New Year's Day 1863, President Abraham Lincoln issued the Emancipation Proclamation. It states that "all persons held as slaves" within the states still in rebellion "are, and henceforward shall be, free." Although it did not in and of itself free any slaves, it transformed the character of the war. Despite often intolerable conditions, black people focused on the possibilities of freedom.*

DOCUMENT 1. Letter from John Q. A. Dennis to Edwin M. Stanton, July 26, 1864

John Q. A. Dennis, formerly a slave in Maryland, wrote to Secretary of War Edwin M. Stanton to ask his help in reuniting his family.

Boston

Dear Sir I am Glad that I have the Honour to Write you afew line I have been in troble for about four yars my Dear wife was taken from me Nov 19th 1859 and left me with three Children and I being a Slave At the time Could Not do Anny thing for the poor little Children for my master it was took me Carry me some forty mile from them So I Could Not do for them and the man that they live with half feed them and half Cloth them & beat them like dogs & when I was admitted to go to see them it use to brake my heart & Now I say again I am Glad to have the honour to write to you to see if you Can Do Anny thing for me or for my poor little Children I was keap in Slavy untell last Novr 1863. then the Good lord sent the Cornel borne [federal Colonel William Birney?] Down their in Marland in worsester Co So as I have been recently freed I have but letle to live on but I am Striveing Dear Sir but what I went too know of you Sir is it possible for me to go & take my Children from those men that keep them in Savery if it is possible will you pleas give me a permit from your hand then I think they would let them go. . . .

Hon sir will you please excuse my Miserable writeing & answer me as soon as you can I want get the little Children out of Slavery, I being Criple would like to know of you also if I Cant be permited to rase a Shool Down there & on what turm I Could be admited to Do so No more At present Dear Hon Sir

SOURCE: Excerpt from "Letter from John Q. A. Dennis to Edwin M. Stanton, July 26, 1864." In *Freedom: A Documentary History of Emancipation 1861–1867*, Series 1, Volume 1, The Destruction of Slavery, p. 386, by Ira Berlin, Joseph

P. Reidy, and Leslie S. Rowland, eds. Copyright © 1985. Reprinted with the permission of Cambridge University Press.

DOCUMENT 2. Report from Reverend A. B. Randall, February 28, 1865

Freedom also prompted ex-slaves to seek legal marriages, which under slavery had been impossible. Writing from Little Rock, Arkansas, A. B. Randall, the white chaplain of a black regiment, in a report of February 1865 to the adjutant general of the Union army, affirmed the importance of marriage to freed slaves and emphasized their conviction that emancipation was just the first step toward full freedom.

Weddings, just now, are very popular, and abundant among the Colored People. They have just learned, of the Special Order No. 15. of Gen Thomas [Adjutant General Lorenzo Thomas] by which, they may not only be lawfully married, but have their Marriage Certificates, Recorded; in a book furnished by the Government. This is most desirable. . . . Those who were captured . . . at Ivy's Ford, on the 17th of January, by Col Brooks, had their Marriage Certificates, taken from them; and destroyed; and then were roundly cursed, for having such papers in their posession. I have married, during the month, at this Post; Twenty five couples; mostly, those, who have families; & have been living together for years. I try to dissuade single men, who are soldiers, from marrying, till their time of enlistment is out: as that course seems to me, to be most judicious.

The Colord People here, generally consider, this war not only; their exodus, from bondage; but the road, to Responsibility; Competency; and an honorable Citizenship—God grant that their hopes and expectations may be fully realized.

SOURCE: Excerpt from "Report from Reverend A. B. Randall, February 28, 1865." In *Freedom: A Documentary History of Emancipation 1861–1867*, Series 2, Volume 1, The Black Military Experience, p. 712, by Ira Berlin, Joseph P. Reidy, and Leslie S. Rowland, eds. Copyright © 1982. Reprinted with the permission of Cambridge University Press.

DOCUMENT 3. Petition "to the Union Convention of Tennessee Assembled in the Capitol at Nashville," January 9, 1865

Early efforts at political reconstruction prompted petitions from former slaves demanding civil and political rights. In January 1865, black Tennesseans petitioned a convention of white Unionists debating the reorganization of state government.

We the undersigned petitioners, American citizens of African descent, natives and residents of Tennessee, and devoted friends of the great National cause, do most respectfully ask a patient hearing of your honorable body in regard to matters deeply affecting the future condition of our unfortunate and long suffering race.

First of all, however, we would say that words are too weak to tell how profoundly grateful we are to the Federal Government for the good work of freedom which it is gradually carrying forward; and for the Emancipation Proclamation which has set free all the slaves in some of the rebellious States, as well as many of the slaves in Tennessee. . . .

We claim freedom, as our natural right, and ask that in harmony and co-operation with the nation at large, you should cut up by the roots the system of slavery, which is not only a wrong to us, but the source of all the evil which at present afflicts the State. For slavery, corrupt itself, corrupted nearly all, also, around it, so that it has influenced nearly all the slave States to rebel against the Federal Government, in order to set up a government of pirates under which slavery might be perpetrated.

In the contest between the nation and slavery, our unfortunate people have sided, by instinct, with the former. We have little fortune to devote to the national cause, for a hard fate has hitherto forced us to live in poverty, but we do devote to its success, our hopes, our toils, our whole heart, our sacred honor, and our lives. We will work, pray, live, and, if need be, die for the Union, as cheerfully as ever a white patriot died for his country. The color of our skin does not lessen in the least degree, our love either for God or for the land of our birth. . . .

We know the burdens of citizenship, and are ready to bear them. We know the duties of the good citizen, and are ready to perform them cheerfully, and would ask to be put in a position in which we can discharge them more effectually. . . .

This is a democracy—a government of the people. It should aim to make every man, without regard to the color of his skin, the amount of his wealth, or the character of his religious faith, feel personally interested in its welfare. Every man who lives under the Government should feel that it is his property, his treasure, the bulwark and defence of

himself and his family, his pearl of great price, which he must preserve, protect, and defend faithfully at all times, on all occasions, in every possible manner.

This is not a Democratic Government if a numerous, law-abiding, industrious, and useful class of citizens, born and bred on the soil, are to be treated as aliens and enemies, as an inferior degraded class, who must have no voice in the Government which they support, protect and defend, with all their heart, soul, mind, and body, both in peace and war. . . .

The possibility that the negro suffrage proposition may shock popular prejudice at first sight, is not a conclusive argument against its wisdom and policy. No proposition ever met with more furious or general opposition than the one to enlist colored soldiers in the United States army. The opponents of the measure exclaimed on all hands that the negro was a coward; that he would not fight; that one white man, with a whip in his hand could put to flight a regiment of them; that the experiment would end in the utter rout and ruin of the Federal army. Yet the colored man has fought so well, on almost every occasion, that the rebel government is prevented, only by its fears and distrust of being able to force him to fight for slavery as well as he fights against it, from putting half a million of negroes into its ranks.

The Government has asked the colored man to fight for its preservation and gladly has he done it. It can afford to trust him with a vote as safely as it trusted him with a bayonet.

Source: Excerpt from "Petition to the Union Convention of Tennessee Assembled in the Capitol at Nashville, January 9, 1865." In *Freedom: A Documentary History of Emancipation 1861–1867*, Series 2, Volume 1, The Black Military Experience, p. 811-16, by Ira Berlin, Joseph P. Reidy, and Leslie S. Rowland, eds. Copyright © 1982. Reprinted with the permission of Cambridge University Press.

QUESTIONS FOR ANALYSIS AND DEBATE

1. How does John Q. A. Dennis interpret his responsibility as a father?
2. Why do you think ex-slaves wanted their marriages legalized?
3. Why, according to the Union Convention of Tennessee, did blacks deserve voting rights?

Johnson's eagerness to normalize relations with southern states and his lack of sympathy for blacks also led him to instruct military and government officials to return to pardoned ex-Confederates all confiscated and abandoned land, even if it was in the hands of freedmen. Reformers were shocked. They had expected the president's vendetta against planters to mean the permanent confiscation of the South's plantations and the distribution of the land to loyal freedmen. Instead, his instructions canceled the promising beginnings made by General Sherman and the Freedmen's Bureau to settle blacks on land of their own. As one freedman observed, "Things was hurt by Mr. Lincoln getting killed."

Southern Resistance and Black Codes

In the summer of 1865, delegates across the South gathered to draw up the new state constitutions required by Johnson's plan of reconstruction. While they had been defeated, clearly whites had not been subdued. Rather than take their medicine, delegates choked on even the president's mild requirements. Refusing to declare their secession ordinances null and void, the South Carolina and Georgia conventions merely "repudiated" their ordinances, preserving in principle their right to secede. In addition, South Carolina and Mississippi refused to repudiate their Confederate war debts. Finally, Mississippi rejected the Thirteenth Amendment outright, and Alabama rejected it in part. Despite these defiant acts, Johnson did not demand that Southerners comply with his lenient terms. By failing to draw a hard line, he rekindled southern resistance. White Southerners began to think that by standing up for themselves they—not victorious Northerners—would shape the transition from slavery to freedom. In the fall of 1865, newly elected southern legislators attempted to do just that.

State governments across the South adopted a series of laws known as the black codes. While emancipation had brought freedmen important rights that they had lacked as slaves—to own property, to make contracts, to marry legally, and to sue and be sued in court—the black codes made a travesty of freedom. They sought to keep blacks subordinate to whites by subjecting blacks to every sort of discrimination. Several states made it illegal for blacks to own a gun. Mississippi made insulting gestures and language by blacks a criminal offense. Blacks were barred from jury duty. Not a single southern state granted any black—no matter how educated, wealthy, or refined—the right to vote.

At the core of the black codes, however, lay the matter of labor. Faced with the death of slavery and the disintegration of plantations, legislators sought to hustle freedmen back into traditional tasks. South Carolina attempted to limit blacks to either farmwork or domestic service by requiring them to pay annual taxes of $10 to $100 to work in any other occupation. Mississippi declared that blacks who did not possess written evidence of employment could be declared vagrants and be subject to fines or involuntary plantation labor. Most states allowed judges to bind black children—orphans and others whose parents they deemed unable to support them—to white employers. Under these so-called apprenticeship laws, courts bound out thousands of black children to planter "guardians."

Johnson refused to intervene decisively. A staunch defender of states' rights, he believed that the citizens of every state, even those citizens who had attempted to destroy the Union, should be free to write their own constitutions and laws. Moreover, since Johnson was as eager as other white Southerners to restore white supremacy and black subordination, the black codes did not offend him.

But Johnson also followed the path he believed offered him the greatest political return. A conservative Tennessee Democrat at the head of a northern Republican Party, he began to look southward for political allies. By pardoning planters and Confederate officials, by acquiescing in the South's black codes, and by accepting the new southern governments even when they failed to satisfy his minimal demands, he won useful friends.

If Northerners had any doubts about the mood of the South, they evaporated in the elections of 1865. To represent them in Congress, white Southerners chose former Confederates, not loyal Unionists. Of the eighty senators and representatives they sent to Washington, fifteen had served in the Confederate army, ten of them as generals. Another sixteen had served in civil and judicial posts in the Confederacy. Nine others had served in the Confederate Congress. One—Alexander Stephens—had been vice president of the Confederacy. In December, this remarkable group arrived on the steps of the nation's Capitol building to be seated in Congress. As one Georgian later remarked: "It looked as though Richmond had moved to Washington."

Expansion of Black Rights and Federal Authority

Southerners had blundered monumentally. They had assumed that what Andrew Johnson was willing to accept, the northern public and Congress would accept as well. But southern intransigence compelled even moderate Republicans to conclude that ex-rebels were a "generation of vipers," still dangerous and untrustworthy.

The black codes in particular soured moderate Republicans on the South. The codes became a symbol of southern intentions not to accept the verdict

THE LOST CAUSE

While politicians in Washington, D.C., debated the future of the South, white Southerners were coming to grips with their emotions and history. They began to refer to their failure to secede from the Union as the "Lost Cause." They enshrined the memory of certain former Confederates, especially Robert E. Lee, whose nobility and courage represented the white South's image of itself. This quilt from about 1870, with Lee stitched in the center, illustrates how common whites incorporated the symbols of the Lost Cause into their daily lives. The maker of the quilt, a woman whose name is unknown, also included miniature Confederate flags and memorial ribbons.

Valentine Museum, Cook Collection.

of the battlefields, but instead to "restore all of slavery but its name." Northerners were hardly saints when it came to racial justice, but black freedom had become a hallowed war aim. "We tell the white men of Mississippi," the *Chicago Tribune* roared, "that the men of the North will convert the State of Mississippi into a frog pond before they will allow such laws to disgrace one foot of the soil in which the bones of our soldiers sleep and over which the flag of freedom waves."

Moderates represented the mainstream of the Republican Party and wanted only assurance that slavery and treason were dead. They did not champion black equality or the confiscation of plantations or black voting, as did the Radicals, a minority faction within the Republican Party. In December 1865, however, when Congress convened in Washington, it became clear that southern obstinacy had succeeded in forging unity (at least temporarily) among Republican factions. Exercising Congress's right to determine the qualifications of its members, Republicans refused to seat the southern representatives. Rather than accept Johnson's claim that the "work of restoration" was done, Congress challenged his executive power. Congressional Republicans enjoyed a three-to-one majority over the Democrats, and if they could agree on a program of reconstruction, they could easily pass legislation and even override presidential vetoes.

The moderates took the initiative. Senator Lyman Trumbull of Illinois declared that the president's policy of trusting southern whites proved that the ex-slave would "be tyrannized over, abused, and virtually reenslaved without some legislation by the nation for his protection." Early in 1866, the moderates produced two bills that strengthened the federal shield. The first, the Freedmen's Bureau bill, prolonged the life of the agency established by the previous Congress. Since the end of the war, it had distributed food, supervised labor contracts, and sponsored schools for freedmen. Arguing that the Constitution never contemplated a "system for the support of indigent persons," President Andrew Johnson vetoed the Freedmen's Bureau bill. Congress failed by a narrow margin to override the president's veto.

Johnson's shocking veto galvanized nearly unanimous Republican support for the moderates' second measure, the Civil Rights Act. Designed to nullify the black codes, it affirmed the rights of blacks to enjoy "full and equal benefit of all laws and proceedings for the security of person and property as is enjoyed by white citizens." The act boldly required the end of legal discrimination in state laws and represented an extraordinary expansion of black rights and federal authority. The president argued that the civil rights bill amounted to an "unconstitutional invasion of states' rights" and vetoed it. In essence, he denied that the federal government possessed authority to protect the civil rights of blacks.

The president did not have the final word. In April 1866, an incensed Republican Party again pushed a civil rights bill through Congress and overrode another presidential veto. In July, it sustained another Freedmen's Bureau Act. For the first time in American history, Congress had overridden presidential vetoes of major legislation. As a worried South Carolinian observed, Johnson had succeeded in uniting the Republicans and probably touched off "a fight this fall such as has never been seen."

Congressional Reconstruction

By the summer of 1866, President Andrew Johnson and Congress had dropped their gloves and stood toe to toe in a bare-knuckled contest unprecedented in American history. Moderate Republicans made a major effort to resolve the dilemma of reconstruction by amending the Constitution, but the obstinacy of Johnson and white Southerners pushed Republican moderates ever closer to the Radicals and to acceptance of additional federal intervention in the South. In time, white men in Congress debated whether to give the ballot to black men. Outside of Congress, blacks raised their voices on behalf of color-blind voting rights, while women argued to make voting sex-blind as well.

The Fourteenth Amendment and Escalating Violence

In April 1866, Republican moderates introduced the Fourteenth Amendment to the Constitution, Congress passed it in June, and two years later it gained the necessary ratification of three-fourths of the states. The most important provisions of this complex amendment made all native-born or naturalized persons American citizens and prohibited states from abridging the "privileges and immunities" of citizens, depriving them of "life, liberty, or property without due process of law," and denying them "equal protection of the laws." By making blacks national citizens, the amendment nullified the *Dred Scott* decision of 1857 and provided a national guarantee of equality before the law. In essence, it protected the rights of citizens against violation by their own state governments.

The Fourteenth Amendment also dealt with voting rights. Rather than explicitly granting the vote to blacks, as Radicals wanted, the amendment gave Congress the right to reduce the congressional representation of states that withheld suffrage from some of its adult male population. In other words, white Southerners could either allow their former slaves to vote or see their representation in Washington slashed.

Tennessee approved the Fourteenth Amendment in July, and Congress promptly welcomed its representatives and senators back. Had Johnson counseled other southern states to ratify this relatively mild amendment and warned them that they faced the fury of an outraged Republican Party if they refused, they might have listened. Instead, Johnson advised Southerners to reject the Fourteenth Amendment and to rely on him to trounce the Republicans in the fall congressional elections.

Johnson had decided to make the Fourteenth Amendment the overriding issue of the 1866 congressional elections and to gather its white opponents into a new conservative party, the National Union Party. In August, his supporters met in Philadelphia. Democrats came, but Republicans did not—Johnson failed to forge a new conservative party behind him.

The president's strategy had already suffered a setback two weeks earlier when whites in several southern cities went on rampages against blacks. It was less an outbreak of violence than an escalation of the violence that had never ceased. In New Orleans, a mob assaulted delegates to a black suffrage convention, and thirty-four blacks died. In Memphis, white mobs hurtled through the black sections of town and killed at least forty-six people. The slaughter shocked Northerners and renewed skepticism about Johnson's claim that southern whites could be trusted. "Who doubts that the Freedmen's Bureau ought to be abolished forthwith," a New Yorker observed sarcastically, "and the blacks remitted to the paternal care of their old masters, who 'understand the nigger, you know, a great deal better than the Yankees can.'"

MEMPHIS RIOTS, MAY 1866
On May 1, 1866, two carriages, one driven by a white man and the other by a black man, collided on a busy Memphis street. This minor incident spiraled into three days of bloody racial violence in which dozens of blacks and two whites died. Racial friction was common in postwar Memphis, and white newspapers routinely heaped abuse on black citizens. "Would to God they were back in Africa, or some other seaport town," the Memphis **Argus** *shouted two days before the riot erupted, "anywhere but here." South Memphis, pictured in this lithograph from* **Harper's Weekly,** *was a shantytown where the families of black soldiers stationed at nearby Fort Pickering lived. The army commander refused to send troops to protect soldiers' families and property, and white mobs ran wild.*
Library of Congress.

The 1866 election resulted in an overwhelming Republican victory in which the party retained its three-to-one congressional majority. Johnson had bet that Northerners would not support federal protection of black rights. But the Fourteenth Amendment was not radical enough to drive Republican voters into Johnson's camp, and the war was still fresh in northern minds. As one Republican explained, southern whites "with all their intelligence were traitors, the blacks with all their ignorance were loyal."

Radical Reconstruction and Military Rule

The elections of 1866 should have taught southern whites the folly of relying on Andrew Johnson as a guide through the thicket of reconstruction. But

when Johnson continued to urge Southerners toward rejection of the Fourteenth Amendment, every southern state except Tennessee voted it down. In the void created by the South's rejection of the moderates' program, the Radicals seized the initiative.

Each act of defiance by southern whites had boosted the standing of the Radicals within the Republican Party. At the core was a small group of men who had cut their political teeth on the antebellum campaign against slavery, who had goaded Lincoln toward making the war a crusade for freedom, and who had carried into the postwar period the conviction that only federal power could protect the rights of the freedmen. Except for freedmen themselves, no one did more to make freedom the "mighty moral question of the age." Men like Senator Charles Sumner, that pompous but sincere

Massachusetts crusader, and Thaddeus Stevens, the caustic representative from Pennsylvania, did not speak with a single voice, but they united in calling for civil and political equality. They insisted on extending to ex-slaves the same opportunities that northern working people enjoyed under the free-labor system. The southern states were "like clay in the hands of the potter," Stevens declared in January 1867, and he called on Congress to begin reconstruction all over again.

In March 1867, moderates joined the Radicals to overturn the Johnson state governments and initiate military rule of the South. The Military Reconstruction Act (and three subsequent acts) divided the ten unreconstructed Confederate states into five military districts. Congress placed a Union general in charge of each district and instructed him to "suppress insurrection, disorder, and violence" and to begin political reform. After the military had completed voter registration, which would include black men and exclude all those barred by the Fourteenth Amendment from holding public office, voters would elect delegates to conventions that would draw up new state constitutions. Each constitution would guarantee black suffrage. When the voters of each state had approved the constitution and its legislature had ratified the Fourteenth Amendment, the state could submit its work to Congress. If Congress approved, the state's senators and representatives could be seated and political reunification would be accomplished.

Reconstruction Military Districts, 1867

Radicals proclaimed the provision for black suffrage "a prodigious triumph." The doggedness of the Radicals and of African Americans, along with the pigheadedness of Johnson and the white South, had swept the Republican Party far beyond the limited suffrage provisions of the Fourteenth Amendment. Republicans finally agreed with Sumner that only the voting power of ex-slaves could bring about a permanent revolution in the South. Indeed, suffrage provided blacks with a powerful instrument of change and self-protection. When combined with the disfranchisement of thousands of ex-rebels, it promised to cripple any neo-Confederate resurgence and guarantee Republican governments in the South.

Despite its bold suffrage provision, the Military Reconstruction Act of 1867 disappointed those who advocated the confiscation and redistribution of southern plantations. Thaddeus Stevens believed that at bottom reconstruction was an economic problem. He agreed wholeheartedly with the ex-slave who said, "Give us our own land and we take care of ourselves, but without land, the old masters can hire us or starve us, as they please." But most Republicans believed they had already provided blacks with the critical tools: equal legal rights and the ballot. If blacks were to get forty acres, they would have to gain it themselves.

Declaring that he would rather sever his right arm than sign such a formula for "anarchy and chaos," Andrew Johnson vetoed the Military Reconstruction Act. Congress overrode his veto the very same day, dramatizing the shift in power from the executive to the legislative branch of government. With the passage of the Reconstruction Acts of 1867, congressional reconstruction was virtually completed. Congress had left white folks owning most of the South's land, but in a radical departure it had given black men the ballot. More than any other provision, black suffrage justifies the term "radical reconstruction." In 1867, the nation began an unprecedented experiment in interracial democracy—at least in the South, for Congress's plan did not touch the North. Soon the former Confederate states would become the primary theater for political struggle. But before the spotlight swung away from Washington, the president and Congress had one more scene to play.

Impeaching a President

Despite his defeats, Andrew Johnson had no intention of yielding control of reconstruction. In a dozen ways he sabotaged Congress's will and encouraged white belligerence and resistance. He issued a flood of pardons to undermine efforts at political and economic change. He waged war against the Freedmen's Bureau by removing officers who sympathized too fully with ex-slaves. And he replaced Union generals eager to enforce Congress's Reconstruction Acts with conservative men who were eager to defeat them. Johnson claimed that he was merely defending the "violated Constitution." At bottom, however, the president subverted congressional reconstruction to protect southern whites from what he considered the horrors of "Negro domination."

When Congress learned that overriding Johnson's vetoes did not ensure victory, it attempted to tie the president's hands. Congress required that all orders to field commanders pass through the General of the Army, Ulysses S. Grant, who Congress believed was sympathetic to southern freedmen, Unionists, and Republicans. It also enacted the Tenure of Office Act in 1867, which required the approval of the Senate for the removal of any government official who had been appointed with Senate consent. Congress intended that the Tenure of Office Act would protect Secretary of War Edwin M. Stanton, the last remaining friend of radical reconstruction in the cabinet. Some Republicans, however, believed that nothing less than removing Johnson from office could save reconstruction, and they initiated a crusade to impeach the president.

As long as Johnson refrained from breaking a law, however, impeachment languished. The Republicans got their chance in August 1867 when Johnson suspended Secretary of War Stanton from office. As required by the Tenure of Office Act, he requested the Senate to consent to dismissal. When the Senate balked, the president removed Stanton anyway. "Is the President crazy, or only drunk?" asked a dumbfounded Republican moderate. "I'm afraid his doings will make us all favor impeachment."

News of Johnson's open defiance of the law did indeed convince every Republican in the House to vote for a resolution impeaching the president. Chief Justice Salmon Chase presided over the Senate trial, which lasted from March until May 1868. Chase refused to allow Johnson's opponents to raise the broad issues of misuse of power and forced them to argue their case exclusively on the narrow legal grounds of Johnson's removal of Stanton. Johnson's lawyers argued that he had not committed a criminal offense, that the Tenure of Office Act was unconstitutional, and that in any case it did not apply to Stanton, who had been appointed by Lincoln. When the critical vote came, seven moderate Republicans broke with their party and joined the Democrats in voting not guilty. With thirty-five in favor and nineteen opposed, the impeachment forces fell one vote short of the two-thirds needed to convict.

Johnson survived, but he did not come through the ordeal unscathed. After his trial he called a truce, and for the remaining ten months of his term reconstruction proceeded unhindered by presidential interference.

The Fifteenth Amendment and Women's Demands

In February 1869, Republicans passed the Fifteenth Amendment to the Constitution. The amendment prohibited states from depriving any citizen of the right to vote because of "race, color, or previous condition of servitude." The Reconstruction Acts of 1867 had already required black suffrage in the South, but the Fifteenth Amendment extended black voting to the entire nation. Partisan advantage played an important role in the amendment's passage. Gains by northern Democrats in the 1868 elections worried Republicans, and black voters now represented the balance of power in several northern states. By giving ballots to northern blacks, Republicans could lessen their political vulnerability. As one Republican congressman observed, "Party expediency and exact justice coincide for once."

Some Republicans, however, found the final wording of the Fifteenth Amendment "lame and halting." Rather than absolutely guaranteeing the right to vote, the amendment merely prohibited exclusion on grounds of race. The distinction would prove to be significant. In time, inventive white Southerners would devise tests of literacy and property and other apparently nonracial measures that would effectively disfranchise blacks and yet not violate the Fifteenth Amendment. But an amendment that guaranteed the right to vote courted defeat in the North. Rising antiforeign sentiment—against the Chinese in California and against European immigrants in the Northeast—caused states to resist giving up control of suffrage requirements. In March 1870, after three-fourths of the states had ratified it, the Fifteenth Amendment became part of the Constitution. Republicans generally breathed a sigh of relief, confident that black suffrage had been "the last great point that remained to be settled of the issues of the war."

But the Republican Party's reappraisal of suffrage had ignored completely the small band of politicized and energized women who had emerged from the war demanding "the ballot for the two disenfranchised classes, negroes and women." Founding the Equal Rights Association in 1866, Susan B. Anthony and Elizabeth Cady

SUSAN B. ANTHONY
Like many outspoken suffragists, Anthony, depicted here in 1852, had begun her public career working on behalf of temperance and abolition. But she grew tired of laboring under the direction of male clergymen—"white orthodox little saints," she called them—who controlled the reform movements and who routinely dismissed the opinions of women. Anthony's continued passion for other causes—improving working conditions for labor, for example—led some conservatives to oppose women's political rights because they equated the suffragist cause with radicalism in general. Women could not easily overcome such views, and the long struggle for the vote eventually drew millions of women into public life.
Susan B. Anthony House, Inc.

Stanton lobbied for "a government by the people, and the whole people; for the people and the whole people." They felt betrayed when their old antislavery allies, who now occupied positions of national power, proved to be fickle and refused to work for their goals. "It was the Negro's hour," Frederick Douglass later explained. The Republican Party had to avoid anything that might jeopardize black gains, Charles Sumner declared. He suggested that woman suffrage could be "the great question of the future."

It was not the first time women's expectations had been dashed. The Fourteenth Amendment had provided for punishment of any state that excluded voters on the basis of race but not on the basis of sex. It had also introduced the word *male* into the Constitution when it referred to a citizen's right to vote. Stanton had predicted that "if that word 'male' be inserted, it will take us a century at least to get it out." The Fifteenth Amendment proved to be no less disappointing. Although women fought hard to include the word *sex*, the amendment denied states the right to forbid suffrage only on the basis of race. Stanton and Anthony condemned the Republicans' "negro first" strategy and concluded that woman "must not put her trust in man."

Although the Fifteenth Amendment left women with more work to do, northern Republicans declared victory and scratched the "Negro question" from the agenda of national politics. As the crusader for equality Wendell Phillips argued, the black man held "sufficient shield in his own hands. . . . Whatever he suffers will be largely now, and in future, his own fault." Reformers like Phillips had no idea of the violent struggles that lay ahead.

The Struggle in the South

While Northerners believed they had discharged their responsibilities with the Reconstruction Acts and the amendments to the Constitution, Southerners knew that the battle had just begun. Black suffrage and large-scale rebel disfranchisement that came with congressional reconstruction had destroyed traditional southern politics and established the foundation for the rise of the Republican Party in the South. Gathering together outsiders and outcasts, the southern Republicans won elections, wrote new state constitutions, and formed new state governments.

Challenging the established class for political control was dangerous business. Equally dangerous were the confrontations that took place on farms and plantations across the South. In the countryside, blacks sought to give practical, everyday meaning to their newly won legal and political equality. But ex-masters like David Golightly Harris and other whites had their own ideas about the social and economic arrangements that should replace slavery. Freedom remained contested territory, and Southerners fought pitched battles with one another to determine the contours of their postemancipation world.

Freedmen, Yankees, and Yeomen

African Americans made up the majority of southern Republicans. Freedmen realized that without the ballot they were almost powerless, and they threw themselves into the suffrage campaign. Southern black men gained voting rights in 1867, and within months virtually every eligible black man had registered to vote. Black women, like white women, remained disfranchised, but black women mobilized along with black men. They attended political rallies and parades and in the 1868 presidential election bravely wore buttons supporting the Republican candidate, General Ulysses S. Grant. Southern blacks did not have identical political priorities, but almost all voted Republican, and they united in their desire for education and equal treatment before the laws.

Northern whites who decided to make the South their home after the war were a second element of the South's Republican Party. Conservative white Southerners called any northern migrant a "carpetbagger," a man so poor that he could pack all his earthly belongings in a single carpet-sided suitcase and swoop southward like a buzzard to "fatten on our misfortunes." But most Northerners who moved south were restless, relatively well-educated young men, often former Union officers and Freedmen's Bureau agents who looked upon the South as they did the West—as a promising place to make a living. They expected that a South without slavery would prosper, and they wanted to be part of it. Northerners in the southern Republican Party consistently supported programs that encouraged vigorous economic development along the lines of the northern free-labor model.

Southern whites made up the third element of the Republican Party in the South. Approximately one out of four white Southerners voted Republican. The other three cursed those who did. They condemned southern-born white Republicans as traitors to their region and their race and called them "scalawags," a term for runty horses and lowdown, good-for-nothing rascals. Yeoman farmers accounted for the vast majority of white Republicans in the South. Some were Unionists who

emerged from the war with bitter memories of Confederate persecution. Some small farmers also welcomed the Republican Party because it promised to end favoritism toward the interests of plantation owners. Yeomen usually supported initiatives for public schools and for expanding economic opportunity in the South.

The Republican Party in the South, then, was made up of freedmen, Yankees, and yeomen—an improbable coalition. The mix of races, regions, and classes inevitably meant friction as each group maneuvered to define the party. But reconstruction represents an extraordinary moment in American politics: Through the Republican Party, blacks and whites joined together to pursue political change. Formally, of course, only men participated in politics—casting ballots and holding offices—but women also played parts in the political struggle. Women joined in parades and rallies, attended stump speeches, and even campaigned.

Reconstruction politics was not for cowards. Any political act took courage. Most whites in the South condemned the entire political process as illegitimate and felt justified in doing whatever it took to stamp out Republicanism. Violence against blacks—the "white terror"—took brutal institutional form in 1866 with the formation of the Ku Klux Klan, a social club of Confederate veterans that quickly developed into a paramilitary organization armed against Republicans. The Klan went on a rampage of whipping, hanging, shooting, burning, and throat-cutting to defeat reconstruction and restore white supremacy. Rapid demobilization of the Union army after the war left only twenty thousand troops to patrol the entire South, a vast territory. Without effective military protection, southern Republicans had to take care of themselves.

Republican Rule

The Reconstruction Acts required southern states to draw up new constitutions before they could be readmitted to Congress. Beginning in the fall of 1867, states held elections for delegates to constitutional conventions. About 40 percent of the white electorate stayed home, either because they had been disfranchised or because they were boycotting politics. Republicans won three-fourths of the seats. About 15 percent of the Republican delegates were Northerners who had moved south, 25 percent were African Americans, and 60 percent were white

down his secretary of war and secretary of the navy as well as his private secretary. Grant's dogged loyalty to liars and cheats only compounded the damage. While never personally implicated in any scandal, Grant was aggravatingly naive and his administration filled with rot.

Anti-Grant Republicans grew increasingly disgusted, and in 1872 they bolted and launched the Liberal Party. The Liberals condemned the Grant regime of crude graft, tasteless materialism, and blatant anti-intellectualism. To clean up the mess, they proposed ending the spoils system, by which victorious parties rewarded loyal workers with public office, and replacing it with a nonpartisan civil service commission that would oversee competitive examinations for appointment to office. Moreover, they demanded that the government remove federal troops from the South and restore "home rule" (white control). Democrats especially liked the southern policy of the Liberals, and the Democratic Party endorsed the Liberal presidential candidate, Horace Greeley, the longtime editor of the *New York Tribune*. However, the nation still felt enormous affection for the man who had saved the Union, and in 1872 reelected Grant with 56 percent of the popular vote.

Northerners increasingly wanted to shift their attention from reconstruction to other issues, especially after the nation slipped into a devastating economic depression in 1873. More than eighteen thousand businesses collapsed, and more than a million workers lost their jobs. But the old issues of reconstruction would not go away. When southern Republicans pleaded for federal protection from Klan violence—the Klan had murdered hundreds of black and white Republicans during the 1868 election—Congress enacted three laws in 1870 and 1871 that were intended to break the back of white terrorism. The severest of the three, the Ku Klux Klan Act, made interference with voting rights a felony and authorized the use of the army to enforce it. Intrepid federal marshals arrested thousands of suspected Klansmen. While the government came close to destroying the Klan, it did not end terrorism against blacks. Congress also passed the Civil Rights Act of 1875, which boldly outlawed racial discrimination in transportation, public accommodations, and juries. But federal authorities did little to enforce the law, and segregated facilities remained the rule throughout the South.

In reality, the retreat from reconstruction had begun in 1868 with Grant's election. Grant genuinely wanted to see blacks' civil and political rights protected, but he felt uneasy about an open-ended commitment that seemed to ignore constitutional limitations on federal power. In May 1872, Congress restored the right of officeholding to all but three hundred ex-rebels. By the early 1870s, reform had lost its principal spokesmen to death or defeat at the polls. Many Republicans concluded that the quest for black equality was mistaken or hopelessly naive. In the minds of many, traditional white leaders offered the best hope for honesty, order, and prosperity in the South.

Underlying the North's abandonment of reconstruction was unyielding racial prejudice. During the war, Northerners had learned to accept black freedom, but deep-seated prejudice prevented many from equating freedom with equality. Even the actions they took on behalf of blacks often served partisan political advantage. Northerners generally supported Indiana Senator Thomas A. Hendricks's declaration that "this is a white man's Government, made by the white man for the white man."

The U.S. Supreme Court also did its part to undermine reconstruction. In the 1870s, a series of Court decisions significantly weakened the federal government's ability to protect black Southerners under the Fourteenth and Fifteenth Amendments. In the *Slaughterhouse* cases (1873), the Court distinguished between national and state citizenship and ruled that the Fourteenth Amendment protected only those rights that stemmed from the federal government, like voting in federal elections and interstate travel. Since the Court decided that most rights derived from the states, it sharply curtailed the federal government's authority to protect black citizens. Even more devastating, the *United States v. Cruikshank* ruling (1876) said that the reconstruction amendments gave Congress power to legislate only against discrimination by states, not by individuals. The "suppression of ordinary crime," such as assault, remained a state responsibility. The Supreme Court did not declare reconstruction unconstitutional, but it gradually undermined its legal foundation.

The mood of the North found political expression in the election of 1874, when for the first time in eighteen years the Democrats gained control of the House of Representatives. Reconstruction had come apart. Congress gradually abandoned it. President Grant grew increasingly unwilling to enforce it. The Supreme Court busily denied the constitutionality of significant parts of it. And the people sent unmistakable messages that they were tired of it. Rather than defend reconstruction from its southern enemies, Northerners steadily backed away from the challenge. After the early 1870s, southern blacks faced the forces of reaction largely on their own.

White Supremacy Triumphs

Republican governments in the South attracted more bitterness and hatred than any other political regimes in American history. In the eyes of the majority of whites, each day of Republican rule produced fresh insults: Black militiamen patrolled town streets, black laborers negotiated contracts with former masters, black maids stood up to former mistresses, black voters cast ballots, and black legislators enacted laws. The northern retreat from reconstruction permitted southern Democrats to harness this white rage to politics. Taking the name "Redeemers," they promised to replace "bayonet rule" (some federal troops continued to be stationed in the South) with "home rule." They branded Republican governments a carnival of extravagance, waste, and fraud and promised that honest, thrifty Democrats would supplant the irresponsible tax-and-spend Republicans. Above all, Redeemers swore to save southern civilization from a descent into African "barbarism" and "negro rule." As one man put it, "We must render this either a white man's government, or convert the land into a Negro man's cemetery."

By the early 1870s, Democrats understood that race was their most potent weapon. They adopted a two-pronged racial strategy to overthrow Republican governments. First, they sought to polarize the parties around color, and, second, they relentlessly intimidated black voters. They went about gathering all the South's white voters into the Democratic Party, leaving the Republicans to depend on blacks. The "straight-out" appeal to whites promised great advantage because whites made up a majority of the population in every southern state except Mississippi, South Carolina, and Louisiana.

Democrats employed several devices to dislodge whites from the Republican Party. First and foremost, they fanned the flames of racial prejudice. In South Carolina, a Democrat crowed that his party appealed to the "proud Caucasian race, whose sovereignty on earth God has proclaimed." Ostracism also proved effective. Local newspapers published the names of whites who kept company with blacks. So complete was the ostracism that one of its victims said, "No white man can live in the South in the future and act with any other than the Democratic party unless he is willing and prepared to live a life of social isolation."

In addition, Democrats exploited the small white farmer's severe economic plight by blaming it on Republican financial policy. Government spending soared during reconstruction, and small farmers saw their tax burden skyrocket. When cotton prices fell by nearly 50 percent in the 1870s, yeomen farmers without enough cash to pay their taxes lost their land. In 1871, Mississippi reported that one-seventh of the state's land—3.3 million acres—had been forfeited for nonpayment of taxes. The small farmer's economic distress had a racial dimension. Because few freedmen succeeded in acquiring land, they rarely paid taxes. From the perspective of the small white farmer, Republican rule meant not only that he was paying more taxes but that he was paying them to aid blacks. Democrats asked whether it was not time for hard-pressed yeomen to join the white man's party.

Democrats also turned to terrorism. "Night riders" targeted scalawags as well as blacks for murder and assassination. By the early 1870s, then, only a fraction of southern whites any longer professed allegiance to the party of Lincoln. Racial polarization became a reality as rich and poor whites united against southern Republicanism.

The second prong of Democratic strategy—intimidation of black voters—proved equally devastating. Antiblack political violence escalated to unprecedented levels. In 1873 in Louisiana, a clash between black militiamen and gun-toting whites killed two white men and an estimated seventy black men. Although the federal government indicted more than one hundred white men, local juries failed to convict a single one of them.

Even before adopting the all-out white supremacist tactics of the 1870s, Democrats had already captured Virginia, Tennessee, and North Carolina. The new campaign brought fresh gains. The Redeemers retook Georgia in 1871, Texas in 1873, and Arkansas and Alabama in 1874. In 1876, Mississippi fell. The story in Mississippi was one of open, unrelenting, and often savage intimidation of black voters and their few remaining white allies. As the state election approached in 1876, Governor Adelbert Ames appealed to Washington for federal troops to control the violence, only to hear from the attorney general that the "whole public are tired of these annual autumnal outbreaks in the South." Abandoned, Mississippi Republicans succumbed to the Democratic onslaught in the fall elections. By 1876, only three Republican state governments—in Florida, Louisiana, and South Carolina—survived (Map 16.2).

An Election and a Compromise

The centennial year of 1876 witnessed one of the most tumultuous elections in American history. Its chaos and confusion provided a fitting conclusion

to the experiment known as Reconstruction. The election took place in November, but not until March 2 of the following year, at 4 A.M., did the nation know who would be inaugurated president on March 4. For four months the country suffered through a constitutional and political crisis. Sixteen years after Lincoln's election, Americans feared that a presidential contest would again precipitate civil war.

The Democrats had nominated New York's reform governor, Samuel J. Tilden, who immediately targeted the corruption of the Grant administration and the despotism of Republican reconstruction. The Republicans put forward a reformer of their

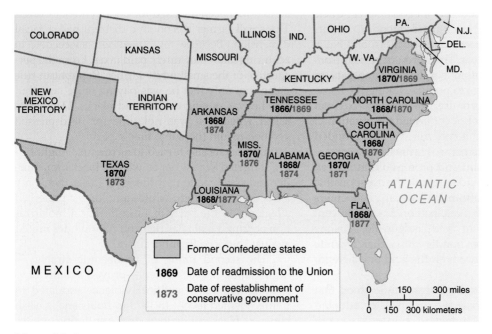

MAP 16.2
The Reconstruction of the South
Myth has it that Republican rule of the former Confederacy was not only harsh but long. In most states, however, conservative southern whites stormed back into power in only a matter of a few months or a very few years. By the election of 1876, Republican governments could be found in only three states. And they soon fell.

READING THE MAP: List in chronological order the readmission of former states to the Union. Which states reestablished conservative governments most quickly?
CONNECTIONS: What did the former Confederate states need to do in order to be readmitted to the Union? How did reestablished conservative governments react to reconstruction?

www.bedfordstmartins.com/roarkcompact SEE THE ONLINE STUDY GUIDE for more help in analyzing this map.

own, Rutherford B. Hayes, governor of Ohio. Privately, Hayes considered "bayonet rule" a mistake, but he concluded that waving the "bloody shirt," that is, reminding the voters that the Democrats were the "party of rebellion," remained the Republicans' best political strategy.

On election day, Tilden tallied 4,284,000 votes to Hayes's 4,036,000. Yet in the all-important electoral college, Tilden fell one vote short of the majority required for victory. However, the electoral votes of three states remained in doubt and thus were uncounted. Both Democrats and Republicans claimed the nineteen votes of South Carolina, Louisiana, and Florida, the only remaining Republican governments in the South. To win, Tilden needed only one of the contested votes. Hayes had to have all of them.

Congress had to decide who had actually won the elections in the three southern states and thus who would be president. The Constitution provided little guidance. Moreover, Democrats controlled the House, and Republicans the Senate. To break the deadlock, Congress created a special electoral commission to arbitrate the disputed returns. A cumbersome compromise, the commission was made up of five representatives (two Republicans, three Democrats), five senators (two Democrats, three Republicans), and five justices of the Supreme Court (two Republicans, two Democrats, and one justice who was considered an independent). But before the commission could meet, the Illinois legislature elected the independent justice to the Senate, and his place on the commission was filled with a Republican. The commissioners all voted the straight party line, giving every state to the Republican Hayes and putting him over the top in electoral votes (Map 16.3).

Some outraged Democrats vowed to resist Hayes's victory. But the impasse was broken when negotiations behind the scenes between Hayes's lieutenants and some moderate southern Democrats resulted in an informal understanding, known as the Compromise of 1877. In exchange for a Democratic promise not to block Hayes's inauguration and to deal fairly with the freedmen, Hayes vowed not to use the army to uphold the remaining Republican regimes. The South would also gain substantial federal subsidies for internal improvements. Two days later, the nation celebrated Hayes's peaceful inauguration.

Stubborn Tilden supporters bemoaned the "stolen election" and damned "His Fraudulency,"

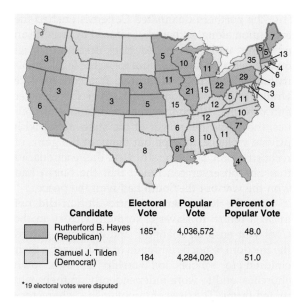

Candidate	Electoral Vote	Popular Vote	Percent of Popular Vote
Rutherford B. Hayes (Republican)	185*	4,036,572	48.0
Samuel J. Tilden (Democrat)	184	4,284,020	51.0

*19 electoral votes were disputed

MAP 16.3
The Election of 1876

Rutherford B. Hayes. Old-guard Radicals such as William Lloyd Garrison denounced Hayes's bargain as a "policy of compromise, of credulity, of weakness, of subserviency, of surrender." But the nation as a whole celebrated, for the Republic had weathered a grave crisis. The last three Republican state governments fell quickly once Hayes abandoned them and withdrew the army. Reconstruction had ended.

Conclusion: "A Revolution but Half-Accomplished"

In 1865, when General Carl Schurz visited the South, he discovered "a revolution but half accomplished." Defeat had not prepared the South for an easy transition from slavery to free labor, from white racial despotism to equal justice, and from white political monopoly to biracial democracy. Ex-masters like David Golightly Harris had trouble seeing former slaves like York and Old Will as free people. The old elite wanted to get "things back as near to slavery as possible," while ex-slaves and whites who had lacked power in the slave regime were eager to exploit the revolutionary implications of defeat and emancipation.

The northern-dominated Congress pushed the revolution along. Although it refused to provide an economic underpinning to black freedom, it required defeated Confederates to accept legal equality and share political power. But conservative whites fought ferociously to recover their power and privilege. When they regained control of politics, they used the power of the state, along with private violence, to wipe out many of the gains of reconstruction. So successful were the reactionaries that one observer concluded that the North had won the war but the South had won the peace.

But the Redeemer counterrevolution did not mean a return to slavery. Northern victory in the Civil War ensured abolition, and ex-slaves gained the freedom to not be whipped or sold, to send their children to school, to worship in their own churches, and to work independently on their own rented farms. The lives of impoverished sharecroppers overflowed with hardships, but even sharecropping provided more autonomy and economic welfare than bondage had. It was limited freedom, to be sure, but it was not slavery.

The Civil War and emancipation set in motion the most profound upheaval in the nation's history, and nothing whites did entirely erased its revolutionary impact. War destroyed the richest and largest slave society in the New World, and abolition overturned the social and economic order that had dominated the region for nearly two centuries. The world of masters and slaves succumbed to that of landlords and sharecroppers. In addition, for the first time sovereignty rested uncontested in the federal government. Moreover, the South returned to the Union, but as a junior partner. The victorious North now possessed the power to establish the nation's direction, and the new Republican leaders in the North set its compass toward the expansion of industrial capitalism.

Still, in one significant respect, the Civil War remained only a "half accomplished" revolution. As such, reconstruction represents a tragedy of enormous proportions. The nation did not fulfill the promises that it seemed to hold out to black Americans at war's end. The failure had enduring consequences. Almost a century after reconstruction, the nation would embark on what one observer called a "second reconstruction," another effort to fulfill nineteenth-century promises. The solid achievements of the Thirteenth, Fourteenth, and Fifteenth Amendments to the Constitution would provide a legal foundation for the renewed commitment. It is worth remembering, though, that it was only the failure of the first reconstruction that made a modern civil rights movement necessary.

For further reading about the topics in this chapter, see the Online Bibliography at

www.bedfordstmartins.com/roarkcompact.

For additional first-hand accounts of this period, see pages 242–256 in Michael Johnson, ed., *Reading the American Past,* Second Edition, Volume I, or pages 1–16 in Volume II.

To assess your mastery of the material in this chapter, see the Online Study Guide at

www.bedfordstmartins.com/roarkcompact.

CHRONOLOGY

1863 **December.** Lincoln issues Proclamation of Amnesty and Reconstruction.

1864 **July.** Congress offers more stringent plan for reconstruction, Wade-Davis bill.

1865 **January.** General William T. Sherman sets aside land in South Carolina for black settlement.

March. Congress establishes Freedmen's Bureau.

March 4. Lincoln sworn in for second term as president of United States.

April 14. Lincoln shot, dies on April 15, succeeded by Vice President Andrew Johnson.

Fall. Southern legislatures enact discriminatory black codes.

December. Thirteenth Amendment abolishing slavery becomes part of U.S. Constitution.

1866 **April.** Congress approves Fourteenth Amendment making native-born blacks American citizens and guaranteeing all American citizens "equal protection of the laws." Amendment becomes part of Constitution in 1868.

April. Congress passes Civil Rights Act over President Johnson's veto.

May. Susan B. Anthony and Elizabeth Cady Stanton found Equal Rights Association to lobby for vote for women.

July. Congress extends Freedmen's Bureau over President Johnson's veto.

Summer. Ku Klux Klan founded in Tennessee.

November. Republicans triumph over Johnson's Democrats in congressional elections.

1867 **March.** Overriding Johnson's veto, Congress passes Military Reconstruction Act imposing military rule on South and requiring states to guarantee vote to black men.

1868 **March–May.** Senate impeachment trial of President Johnson results in acquittal.

November. Ulysses S. Grant elected president of the United States.

1869 **February.** Congress approves Fifteenth Amendment prohibiting racial discrimination in voting rights. Amendment becomes part of Constitution in 1870.

1871 **April.** Congress enacts Ku Klux Klan Act in effort to end white terrorism in South.

1872 **November.** President Grant reelected.

1873 Economic depression sets in for remainder of decade.

1874 **November.** Elections return Democratic majority to House of Representatives.

1875 **February.** Civil Rights Act of 1875 outlaws racial discrimination, but federal authorities do little to enforce law.

1877 **March.** Special congressional committee awards disputed electoral votes to Republican Rutherford B. Hayes, making him president of United States; Hayes agrees to pull military out of South.

Appendix I. Documents

For additional documents see the Online Appendix at
www.bedfordstmartins.com/roarkcompact.

THE DECLARATION OF INDEPENDENCE

In Congress, July 4, 1776,

THE UNANIMOUS DECLARATION OF THE
THIRTEEN UNITED STATES OF AMERICA

When in the course of human events, it becomes necessary for one people to dissolve the political bands which have connected them with another, and to assume, among the powers of the earth, the separate and equal station to which the laws of nature and of nature's God entitle them, a decent respect to the opinions of mankind requires that they should declare the causes which impel them to the separation.

We hold these truths to be self-evident, that all men are created equal; that they are endowed by their Creator with certain unalienable rights; that among these, are life, liberty, and the pursuit of happiness. That, to secure these rights, governments are instituted among men, deriving their just powers from the consent of the governed; that, whenever any form of government becomes destructive of these ends, it is the right of the people to alter or to abolish it, and to institute a new government, laying its foundation on such principles, and organizing its powers in such form, as to them shall seem most likely to effect their safety and happiness. Prudence, indeed, will dictate that governments long established, should not be changed for light and transient causes; and, accordingly, all experience hath shown, that mankind are more disposed to suffer, while evils are sufferable, than to right themselves by abolishing the forms to which they are accustomed. But, when a long train of abuses and usurpations, pursuing invariably the same object, evinces a design to reduce them under absolute despotism, it is their right, it is their duty, to throw off such government and to provide new guards for their future security. Such has been the patient sufferance of these colonies, and such is now the necessity which constrains them to alter their former systems of government. The history of the present King of Great Britain is a history of repeated injuries and usurpations, all having, in direct object, the establishment of an absolute tyranny over these States. To prove this, let facts be submitted to a candid world:

He has refused his assent to laws the most wholesome and necessary for the public good.

He has forbidden his governors to pass laws of immediate and pressing importance, unless suspended in their operation till his assent should be obtained; and, when so suspended, he has utterly neglected to attend to them.

He has refused to pass other laws for the accommodation of large districts of people, unless those people would relinquish the right of representation in the legislature; a right inestimable to them, and formidable to tyrants only.

He has called together legislative bodies at places unusual, uncomfortable, and distant from the depository of their public records, for the sole purpose of fatiguing them into compliance with his measures.

He has dissolved representative houses repeatedly for opposing, with manly firmness, his invasions on the rights of the people.

He has refused, for a long time after such dissolutions, to cause others to be elected; whereby the legislative powers, incapable of annihilation, have returned to the people at large for their exercise; the state remaining in the mean-time exposed to all the danger of invasion from without, and convulsions within.

He has endeavoured to prevent the population of these States; for that purpose, obstructing the laws for naturalization of foreigners, refusing to pass others to encourage their migration hither, and raising the conditions of new appropriations of lands.

He has obstructed the administration of justice, by refusing his assent to laws for establishing judiciary powers.

He has made judges dependent on his will alone, for the tenure of their offices, and the amount and payment of their salaries.

He has erected a multitude of new offices, and sent hither swarms of officers to harass our people, and eat out their substance.

He has kept among us, in times of peace, standing armies, without the consent of our legislature.

He has affected to render the military independent of, and superior to, the civil power.

He has combined, with others, to subject us to a jurisdiction foreign to our Constitution, and unacknowledged by our laws; giving his assent to their acts of pretended legislation:

For quartering large bodies of armed troops among us:

For protecting them by a mock trial, from punishment, for any murders which they should commit on the inhabitants of these States:

For cutting off our trade with all parts of the world:

For imposing taxes on us without our consent:

For depriving us, in many cases, of the benefit of trial by jury:

For transporting us beyond seas to be tried for pretended offences:

For abolishing the free system of English laws in a neighboring province, establishing therein an arbitrary government, and enlarging its boundaries, so as to render it at once an example and fit instrument for introducing the same absolute rule into these colonies:

For taking away our charters, abolishing our most valuable laws, and altering, fundamentally, the powers of our governments:

For suspending our own legislatures, and declaring themselves invested with power to legislate for us in all cases whatsoever.

He has abdicated government here, by declaring us out of his protection, and waging war against us.

He has plundered our seas, ravaged our coasts, burnt our towns, and destroyed the lives of our people.

He is, at this time, transporting large armies of foreign mercenaries to complete the works of death, desolation, and tyranny, already begun, with circumstances of cruelty and perfidy scarcely paralleled in the most barbarous ages, and totally unworthy the head of a civilized nation.

He has constrained our fellow citizens, taken captive on the high seas, to bear arms against their country, to become the executioners of their friends, and brethren, or to fall themselves by their hands.

He has excited domestic insurrections amongst us, and has endeavored to bring on the inhabitants of our frontiers, the merciless Indian savages, whose known rule of warfare is an undistinguished destruction of all ages, sexes, and conditions.

In every stage of these oppressions, we have petitioned for redress; in the most humble terms; our repeated petitions have been answered only by repeated injury. A prince, whose character is thus marked by every act which may define a tyrant, is unfit to be the ruler of a free people.

Nor have we been wanting in attention to our British brethren. We have warned them, from time to time, of attempts made by their legislature to extend an unwarrantable jurisdiction over us. We have reminded them of the circumstances of our emigration and settlement here. We have appealed to their native justice and magnanimity, and we have conjured them, by the ties of our common kindred, to disavow these usurpations, which would inevitably interrupt our connections and correspondence. They, too, have been deaf to the voice of justice and consanguinity. We must, therefore, acquiesce in the necessity which denounces our separation, and hold them as we hold the rest of mankind, enemies in war, in peace, friends.

We, therefore, the representatives of the United States of America, in general Congress assembled, appealing to the Supreme Judge of the world for the rectitude of our intentions, do, in the name, and by authority of the good people of these colonies, solemnly publish and declare, that these united colonies are, and of right ought to be, free and independent states: that they are absolved from all allegiance to the British Crown, and that all political connection between them and the state of Great Britain is, and ought to be, totally dissolved; and that, as free and independent states, they have full power to levy war, conclude peace, contract alliances, establish commerce, and to do all other acts and things which independent states may of right do. And, for the support of this declaration, with a firm reliance on the protection of Divine Providence, we mutually pledge to each other our lives, our fortunes, and our sacred honor.

The foregoing Declaration was, by order of Congress, engrossed, and signed by the following members:

JOHN HANCOCK

New Hampshire
Josiah Bartlett
William Whipple
Matthew Thornton

Massachusetts Bay
Samuel Adams
John Adams
Robert Treat Paine
Elbridge Gerry

Rhode Island
Stephen Hopkins
William Ellery

Connecticut
Roger Sherman
Samuel Huntington
William Williams
Oliver Wolcott

New York
William Floyd
Phillip Livingston
Francis Lewis
Lewis Morris

New Jersey
Richard Stockton
John Witherspoon
Francis Hopkinson
John Hart
Abraham Clark

Pennsylvania
Robert Morris
Benjamin Rush
Benjamin Franklin
John Morton
George Clymer
James Smith
George Taylor
James Wilson
George Ross

Delaware	North Carolina	Virginia	Georgia
Caesar Rodney	William Hooper	George Wythe	Button Gwinnett
George Read	Joseph Hewes	Richard Henry Lee	Lyman Hall
Thomas M'Kean	John Penn	Thomas Jefferson	George Walton
		Benjamin Harrison	
Maryland	**South Carolina**	Thomas Nelson, Jr.	
Samuel Chase	Edward Rutledge	Francis Lightfoot Lee	
William Paca	Thomas Heyward, Jr.	Carter Braxton	
Thomas Stone	Thomas Lynch, Jr.		
Charles Carroll,	Arthur Middleton		
of Carrollton			

Resolved, That copies of the Declaration be sent to the several assemblies, conventions, and committees, or councils of safety, and to the several commanding officers of the continental troops; that it be proclaimed in each of the United States, at the head of the army.

THE CONSTITUTION OF THE UNITED STATES*

Agreed to by Philadelphia Convention, September 17, 1787. Implemented March 4, 1789.

Preamble

We the people of the United States, in order to form a more perfect union, establish justice, insure domestic tranquility, provide for the common defense, promote the general welfare, and secure the blessings of liberty to ourselves and our posterity, do ordain and establish this Constitution for the United States of America.

Article I

Section 1 All legislative powers herein granted shall be vested in a Congress of the United States, which shall consist of a Senate and a House of Representatives.

Section 2 The House of Representatives shall be composed of members chosen every second year by the people of the several States, and the electors in each State shall have the qualifications requisite for electors of the most numerous branch of the State Legislature.

No person shall be a Representative who shall not have attained to the age of twenty-five years, and been

seven years a citizen of the United States, and who shall not, when elected, be an inhabitant of that State in which he shall be chosen.

Representatives and direct taxes shall be apportioned among the several States which may be included within this Union, according to their respective numbers, *which shall be determined by adding to the whole number of free persons, including those bound to service for a term of years and excluding Indians not taxed, three-fifths of all other persons.* The actual enumeration shall be made within three years after the first meeting of the Congress of the United States, and within every subsequent term of ten years, in such manner as they shall by law direct. The number of Representatives shall not exceed one for every thirty thousand, but each State shall have at least one Representative; *and until such enumeration shall be made, the State of New Hampshire shall be entitled to choose three, Massachusetts eight, Rhode Island and Providence Plantations one, Connecticut five, New York six, New Jersey four, Pennsylvania eight, Delaware one, Maryland six, Virginia ten, North Carolina five, South Carolina five, and Georgia three.*

When vacancies happen in the representation from any State, the Executive authority thereof shall issue writs of election to fill such vacancies.

The House of Representatives shall choose their Speaker and other officers; and shall have the sole power of impeachment.

*Passages no longer in effect are in italic type.

Section 3 The Senate of the United States shall be composed of two Senators from each State, *chosen by the legislature thereof,* for six years; and each Senator shall have one vote.

Immediately after they shall be assembled in consequence of the first election, they shall be divided as equally as may be into three classes. The seats of the Senators of the first class shall be vacated at the expiration of the second year, of the second class at the expiration of the fourth year, and of the third class at the expiration of the sixth year, so that one-third may be chosen every second year; *and if vacancies happen by resignation or otherwise, during the recess of the legislature of any State, the Executive thereof may make temporary appointments until the next meeting of the legislature, which shall then fill such vacancies.*

No person shall be a Senator who shall not have attained to the age of thirty years, and been nine years a citizen of the United States, and who shall not, when elected, be an inhabitant of that State for which he shall be chosen.

The Vice-President of the United States shall be President of the Senate, but shall have no vote, unless they be equally divided.

The Senate shall choose their other officers, and also a President *pro tempore,* in the absence of the Vice-President, or when he shall exercise the office of President of the United States.

The Senate shall have the sole power to try all impeachments. When sitting for that purpose, they shall be on oath or affirmation. When the President of the United States is tried, the Chief Justice shall preside: and no person shall be convicted without the concurrence of two-thirds of the members present.

Judgment in cases of impeachment shall not extend further than to removal from the office, and disqualification to hold and enjoy any office of honor, trust or profit under the United States: but the party convicted shall nevertheless be liable and subject to indictment, trial, judgment and punishment, according to law.

Section 4 The times, places and manner of holding elections for Senators and Representatives shall be prescribed in each State by the legislature thereof; but the Congress may at any time by law make or alter such regulations, except as to the places of choosing Senators.

The Congress shall assemble at least once in every year, and such meeting *shall be on the first Monday in December, unless they shall by law appoint a different day.*

Section 5 Each house shall be the judge of the elections, returns and qualifications of its own members, and a majority of each shall constitute a quorum to do business; but a smaller number may adjourn from day to day, and may be authorized to compel the atten-

dance of absent members, in such manner, and under such penalties, as each house may provide.

Each house may determine the rules of its proceedings, punish its members for disorderly behavior, and with the concurrence of two-thirds, expel a member.

Each house shall keep a journal of its proceedings, and from time to time publish the same, excepting such parts as may in their judgment require secrecy; and the yeas and nays of the members of either house on any question shall, at the desire of one-fifth of those present, be entered on the journal.

Neither house, during the session of Congress, shall, without the consent of the other, adjourn for more than three days, nor to any other place than that in which the two houses shall be sitting.

Section 6 The Senators and Representatives shall receive a compensation for their services, to be ascertained by law and paid out of the treasury of the United States. They shall in all cases except treason, felony and breach of the peace, be privileged from arrest during their attendance at the session of their respective houses, and in going to and returning from the same; and for any speech or debate in either house, they shall not be questioned in any other place.

No Senator or Representative shall, during the time for which he was elected, be appointed to any civil office under the authority of the United States, which shall have been created, or the emoluments whereof shall have been increased, during such time; and no person holding any office under the United States shall be a member of either house during his continuance in office.

Section 7 All bills for raising revenue shall originate in the House of Representatives; but the Senate may propose or concur with amendments as on other bills.

Every bill which shall have passed the House of Representatives and the Senate, shall, before it become a law, be presented to the President of the United States; if he approve he shall sign it, but if not he shall return it with objections to that house in which it shall have originated, who shall enter the objections at large on their journal, and proceed to reconsider it. If after such reconsideration two-thirds of that house shall agree to pass the bill, it shall be sent, together with the objections, to the other house, by which it shall likewise be reconsidered, and, if approved by two-thirds of that house, it shall become a law. But in all such cases the votes of both houses shall be determined by yeas and nays, and the names of the persons voting for and against the bill shall be entered on the journal of each house respectively. If any bill shall not be returned by the President within ten days (Sundays excepted) after it shall have been presented to him, the same shall be a law, in like manner as if he had signed it, unless the Congress by their adjournment prevent its return, in which case it shall not be a law.

Every order, resolution, or vote to which the concurrence of the Senate and House of Representatives may be necessary (except on a question of adjournment) shall be presented to the President of the United States; and before the same shall take effect, shall be approved by him, or being disapproved by him, shall be repassed by two-thirds of the Senate and House of Representatives, according to the rules and limitations prescribed in the case of a bill.

Section 8 The Congress shall have power

To lay and collect taxes, duties, imposts, and excises, to pay the debts and provide for the common defense and general welfare of the United States; but all duties, imposts and excises shall be uniform throughout the United States;

To borrow money on the credit of the United States;

To regulate commerce with foreign nations, and among the several States, and with the Indian tribes;

To establish an uniform rule of naturalization, and uniform laws on the subject of bankruptcies throughout the United States;

To coin money, regulate the value thereof, and of foreign coin, and fix the standard of weights and measures;

To provide for the punishment of counterfeiting the securities and current coin of the United States;

To establish post offices and post roads;

To promote the progress of science and useful arts by securing for limited times to authors and inventors the exclusive right to their respective writings and discoveries;

To constitute tribunals inferior to the Supreme Court;

To define and punish piracies and felonies committed on the high seas and offences against the law of nations;

To declare war, grant letters of marque and reprisal, and make rules concerning captures on land and water;

To raise and support armies, but no appropriation of money to that use shall be for a longer term than two years;

To provide and maintain a navy;

To make rules for the government and regulation of the land and naval forces;

To provide for calling forth the militia to execute the laws of the Union, suppress insurrections and repel invasions;

To provide for organizing, arming, and disciplining the militia, and for governing such part of them as may be employed in the service of the United States, reserving to the States respectively the appointment of the officers, and the authority of training the militia according to the discipline prescribed by Congress;

To exercise exclusive legislation in all cases whatsoever, over such district (not exceeding ten miles square) as may, by cession of particular States, and the acceptance of Congress, become the seat of the government of the United States, and to exercise like authority over all places purchased by the consent of the legislature of the State, in which the same shall be, for erection of forts, magazines, arsenals, dock-yards, and other needful buildings;—and

To make all laws which shall be necessary and proper for carrying into execution the foregoing powers, and all other powers vested by this Constitution in the government of the United States, or in any department or officer thereof.

Section 9 *The migration or importation of such persons as any of the States now existing shall think proper to admit shall not be prohibited by the Congress prior to the year one thousand eight hundred and eight; but a tax or duty may be imposed on such importation, not exceeding ten dollars for each person.*

The privilege of the writ of habeas corpus shall not be suspended, unless when in cases of rebellion or invasion the public safety may require it.

No bill of attainder or ex post facto law shall be passed.

No capitation, or other direct, tax shall be laid, unless in proportion to the census or enumeration herein before directed to be taken.

No tax or duty shall be laid on articles exported from any State.

No preference shall be given by any regulation of commerce or revenue to the ports of one State over those of another; nor shall vessels bound to, or from, one State be obliged to enter, clear, or pay duties in another.

No money shall be drawn from the treasury, but in consequence of appropriations made by law; and a regular statement and account of the receipts and expenditures of all public money shall be published from time to time.

No title of nobility shall be granted by the United States: and no person holding any office of profit or trust under them, shall, without the consent of the Congress, accept of any present, emolument, office, or title, of any kind whatever, from any king, prince, or foreign state.

Section 10 No State shall enter into any treaty, alliance, or confederation; grant letters of marque and reprisal; coin money; emit bills of credit; make anything but gold and silver coin a tender in payment of debts; pass any bill of attainder, ex post facto law, or law impairing the obligation of contracts, or grant any title of nobility.

No State shall, without the consent of Congress, lay any imposts or duties on imports or exports, except what may be absolutely necessary for executing its inspection laws: and the net produce of all duties and imposts, laid by any State on imports or exports, shall be for the use of the treasury of the United States; and all such laws shall be subject to the revision and control of the Congress.

No State shall, without the consent of Congress, lay any duty of tonnage, keep troops, or ships of war in time of peace, enter into any agreement or compact with another State, or with a foreign power, or engage in war, unless actually invaded, or in such imminent danger as will not admit of delay.

Article II

Section 1 The executive power shall be vested in a President of the United States of America. He shall hold his office during the term of four years, and, together with the Vice-President, chosen for the same term, be elected as follows:

Each State shall appoint, in such manner as the legislature thereof may direct, a number of electors, equal to the whole number of Senators and Representatives to which the State may be entitled in the Congress; but no Senator or Representative, or person holding an office of trust or profit under the United States, shall be appointed an elector.

The electors shall meet in their respective States, and vote by ballot for two persons, of whom one at least shall not be an inhabitant of the same State with themselves. And they shall make a list of all the persons voted for, and of the number of votes for each; which list they shall sign and certify, and transmit sealed to the seat of government of the United States, directed to the President of the Senate. The President of the Senate shall, in the presence of the Senate and House of Representatives, open all the certificates, and the votes shall then be counted. The person having the greatest number of votes shall be the President, if such number be a majority of the whole number of electors appointed; and if there be more than one who have such majority, and have an equal number of votes, then the House of Representatives shall immediately choose by ballot one of them for President; and if no person have a majority, then from the five highest on the list said house shall in like manner choose the President. But in choosing the President the votes shall be taken by States, the representation from each State having one vote; a quorum for this purpose shall consist of a member or members from two-thirds of the States, and a majority of all the States shall be necessary to a choice. In every case,

after the choice of the President, the person having the greatest number of votes of the electors shall be the Vice-President. But if there should remain two or more who have equal votes, the Senate shall choose from them by ballot the Vice-President.

The Congress may determine the time of choosing the electors, and the day on which they shall give their votes; which day shall be the same throughout the United States.

No person except a natural-born citizen, *or a citizen of the United States at the time of the adoption of this Constitution,* shall be eligible to the office of President; neither shall any person be eligible to that office who shall not have attained to the age of thirty-five years, and been fourteen years a resident within the United States.

In cases of the removal of the President from office or of his death, resignation, or inability to discharge the powers and duties of the said office, the same shall devolve on the Vice-President, and the Congress may by law provide for the case of removal, death, resignation, or inability, both of the President and Vice-President, declaring what officer shall then act as President, and such officer shall act accordingly, until the disability be removed, or a President shall be elected.

The President shall, at stated times, receive for his services a compensation, which shall neither be increased nor diminished during the period for which he shall have been elected, and he shall not receive within that period any other emolument from the United States, or any of them.

Before he enter on the execution of his office, he shall take the following oath or affirmation:—"I do solemnly swear (or affirm) that I will faithfully execute the office of the President of the United States, and will to the best of my ability preserve, protect and defend the Constitution of the United States."

Section 2 The President shall be commander in chief of the army and navy of the United States, and of the militia of the several States, when called into the actual service of the United States; he may require the opinion, in writing, of the principal officer in each of the executive departments, upon any subject relating to the duties of their respective offices, and he shall have power to grant reprieves and pardons for offenses against the United States, except in cases of impeachment.

He shall have power, by and with the advice and consent of the Senate, to make treaties, provided two-thirds of the Senators present concur; and he shall nominate, and by and with the advice and consent of the Senate, shall appoint ambassadors, other public ministers and consuls, judges of the Supreme Court, and all other officers of the United States, whose appointments are not herein otherwise provided for, and which shall be established by law: but Congress may by law vest the appointment of such inferior officers, as they think proper, in the President alone, in the courts of law, or in the heads of departments.

The President shall have power to fill up all vacancies that may happen during the recess of the Senate, by granting commissions which shall expire at the end of their next session.

Section 3   He shall from time to time give to the Congress information of the state of the Union, and recommend to their consideration such measures as he shall judge necessary and expedient; he may, on extraordinary occasions, convene both houses, or either of them, and in case of disagreement between them, with respect to the time of adjournment, he may adjourn them to such time as he shall think proper; he shall receive ambassadors and other public ministers; he shall take care that the laws be faithfully executed, and shall commission all the officers of the United States.

Section 4   The President, Vice-President and all civil officers of the United States shall be removed from office on impeachment for, and on conviction of, treason, bribery, or other high crimes and misdemeanors.

Article III

Section 1   The judicial power of the United States shall be vested in one Supreme Court, and in such inferior courts as the Congress may from time to time ordain and establish. The judges, both of the Supreme and inferior courts, shall hold their offices during good behavior, and shall, at stated times, receive for their services a compensation which shall not be diminished during their continuance in office.

Section 2   The judicial power shall extend to all cases, in law and equity, arising under this Constitution, the laws of the United States, and treaties made, or which shall be made, under their authority;—to all cases affecting ambassadors, other public ministers and consuls;—to all cases of admiralty and maritime jurisdiction;—to controversies to which the United States shall be a party;—to controversies between two or more States;—*between a State and citizens of another State;*—between citizens of different States;—between citizens of the same State claiming lands under grants of different States, and between a State, or the citizens thereof, and foreign states, citizens or subjects.

In all cases affecting ambassadors, other public ministers and consuls, and those in which a State shall be party, the Supreme Court shall have original jurisdiction. In all the other cases before mentioned, the Supreme Court shall have appellate jurisdiction, both as to law and fact, with such exceptions, and under such regulations, as the Congress shall make.

The trial of all crimes, except in cases of impeachment, shall be by jury; and such trial shall be held in the State where said crimes shall have been committed; but when not committed within any State, the trial shall be at such place or places as the Congress may by Law have directed.

Section 3   Treason against the United States shall consist only in levying war against them, or in adhering to their enemies, giving them aid and comfort. No person shall be convicted of treason unless on the testimony of two witnesses to the same overt act, or on confession in open court.

The Congress shall have power to declare the punishment of treason, but no attainder of treason shall work corruption of blood, or forfeiture except during the life of the person attainted.

Article IV

Section 1   Full faith and credit shall be given in each State to the public acts, records, and judicial proceedings of every other State. And the Congress may by general laws prescribe the manner in which such acts, records, and proceedings shall be proved, and the effect thereof.

Section 2   The citizens of each State shall be entitled to all privileges and immunities of citizens in the several States.

A person charged in any State with treason, felony, or other crime, who shall flee from justice, and be found in another State, shall on demand of the executive authority of the State from which he fled, be delivered up, to be removed to the State having jurisdiction of the crime.

No Person held to service or labor in one State, under the laws thereof, escaping into another, shall, in consequence of any law or regulation therein, be discharged from such service or labor, but shall be delivered up on claim of the party to whom such service or labor may be due.

Section 3   New States may be admitted by the Congress into this Union; but no new State shall be formed or erected within the jurisdiction of any other State; nor any State be formed by the junction of two or more States, or parts of States, without the consent of the legislatures of the States concerned as well as of the Congress.

trying to protect, others argue that the Ninth Amendment should be read as providing a constitutional "presumption of liberty" that allows people to act in any way that does not violate the rights of others.

Amendment X

The powers not delegated to the United States by the Constitution, nor prohibited by it to the States, are reserved to the States respectively, or to the people.

◆◆◆

The Antifederalists were especially eager to see a "reserved powers clause" explicitly guaranteeing the states control over their internal affairs. Not surprisingly, the Tenth Amendment has been a frequent battleground in the struggle over states' rights and federal supremacy. Prior to the Civil War, the Democratic Republican Party and Jacksonian Democrats invoked the Tenth Amendment to prohibit the federal government from making decisions about whether people in individual states could own slaves. The Tenth Amendment was virtually suspended during Reconstruction following the Civil War. In 1883, however, the Supreme Court declared the Civil Rights Act of 1875 unconstitutional on the grounds that it violated the Tenth Amendment. Business interests also called on the amendment to block efforts at federal regulation.

The Court was inconsistent over the next several decades as it attempted to resolve the tension between the restrictions of the Tenth Amendment and the powers the Constitution granted to Congress to regulate interstate commerce and levy taxes. The Court upheld the Pure Food and Drug Act (1906), the Meat Inspection Acts (1906 and 1907), and the White Slave Traffic Act (1910), all of which affected the states, but struck down an act prohibiting interstate shipment of goods produced through child labor. Between 1934 and 1935, a number of New Deal programs created by Franklin D. Roosevelt were declared unconstitutional on the grounds that they violated the Tenth Amendment. (See Chapter 24.) As Roosevelt appointees changed the composition of the Court, the Tenth Amendment was declared to have no substantive meaning. Generally, the amendment is held to protect the rights of states to regulate internal matters such as local government, education, commerce, labor, and business, as well as matters involving families such as marriage, divorce, and inheritance within the state.

Unratified Amendment

Reapportionment Amendment (proposed by Congress September 25, 1789, along with the Bill of Rights)

After the first enumeration required by the first article of the Constitution, there shall be one Representative for every thirty thousand, until the number shall amount to one hundred, after which the proportion shall be so regulated by Congress, that there shall be not less than one hundred Representatives, nor less than one Representative for every forty thousand persons, until the number of Representatives shall amount to two hundred; after which the proportion shall be so regulated by Congress, that there shall not be less than two hundred Representatives, nor more than one Representative for every fifty thousand persons.

◆◆◆

If the Reapportionment Amendment had passed and remained in effect, the House of Representatives today would have more than 5,000 members rather than 435.

Amendment XI
[Adopted 1798]

The judicial power of the United States shall not be construed to extend to any suit in law or equity, commenced or prosecuted against one of the United States by citizens of another State, or by citizens or subjects of any foreign state.

◆◆◆

In 1793, the Supreme Court ruled in favor of Alexander Chisholm, executor of the estate of a deceased South Carolina merchant. Chisholm was suing the state of Georgia because the merchant had never been paid for provisions he had supplied during the Revolution. Many regarded this Court decision as an error that violated the intent of the Constitution.

Antifederalists had long feared a federal court system with the power to overrule a state court. When the Constitution was being drafted, Federalists had assured worried Antifederalists that section 2 of Article 3, which allows federal courts to hear cases "between a State and citizens of another State," did not mean that the federal courts were authorized to hear suits against a state by citizens of another state or a foreign country. Antifederalists and many other Americans feared a powerful federal court system because they worried that it would become like the British courts of this period, which were accountable only to the monarch. Furthermore, Chisholm v. Georgia prompted a series of suits against state governments by creditors and suppliers who had made loans during the war.

In addition, state legislators and Congress feared that the shaky economies of the new states, as well as the country as a whole, would be destroyed, especially if Loyalists who had fled to other countries sought reimbursement for land and property that had been seized. The day after the Supreme Court announced its decision, a resolution proposing the Eleventh Amendment, which overturned the decision in Chisholm v. Georgia, was introduced in the U.S. Senate.

Amendment XII
[Adopted 1804]

The electors shall meet in their respective States, and vote by ballot for President and Vice-President, one of whom, at least, shall not be an inhabitant of the same State with themselves; they shall name in their ballots the person voted for as President, and in distinct ballots the person voted for as Vice-President, and they shall make distinct lists of all persons voted for as President, and of all persons voted for as Vice-President, and of the number of votes for each, which lists they shall sign and certify, and transmit sealed to the seat of government of the United States, directed to the President of the Senate;—the President of the Senate shall, in the presence of the Senate and House of Representatives, open all the certificates and the votes shall then be counted;—the person having the greatest number of votes for President shall be the President, if such number be a majority of the whole number of electors appointed; and if no person have such majority, then from the persons having the highest numbers not exceeding three on the list of those voted for as President, the House of Representatives shall choose immediately, by ballot, the President. But in choosing the President, the votes shall be taken by States, the representation from each State having one vote; a quorum for this purpose shall consist of a member or members from two-thirds of the States, and a majority of all the States shall be necessary to a choice. And if the House of Representatives shall not choose a President whenever the right of choice shall devolve upon them, before *the fourth day of March* next following, then the Vice-President shall act as President, as in the case of the death or other constitutional disability of the President.

The person having the greatest number of votes as Vice-President shall be the Vice-President, if such number be a majority of the whole number of electors appointed; and if no person have a majority, then from the two highest numbers on the list the Senate shall choose the Vice-President; a quorum for the purpose shall consist of two-thirds of the whole number of Senators, and a majority of the whole number shall be necessary to a choice. But no person constitutionally ineligible to the office of President shall be eligible to that of Vice-President of the United States.

◆◆◆

The framers of the Constitution disliked political parties and assumed that none would ever form. Under the original system, electors chosen by the states would each vote for two candidates. The candidate who won the most votes would become president, while the person who won the second-highest number of votes would become vice president. Rivalries between Federalists and Antifederalists led to the formation of political parties, however, even before

George Washington had left office. Though Washington was elected unanimously in 1789 and 1792, the elections of 1796 and 1800 were procedural disasters because of party maneuvering (see Chapters 9 and 10). In 1796, Federalist John Adams was chosen as president, and his great rival, the Antifederalist Thomas Jefferson (whose party was called the Republican Party), became his vice president. In 1800, all the electors cast their two votes as one of two party blocs. Jefferson and his fellow Republican nominee, Aaron Burr, were tied with seventy-three votes each. The contest went to the House of Representatives, which finally elected Jefferson after thirty-six ballots. The Twelfth Amendment prevents these problems by requiring electors to vote separately for the president and vice president.

Unratified Amendment
Titles of Nobility Amendment
(proposed by Congress May 1, 1810)

If any citizen of the United States shall accept, claim, receive or retain any title of nobility or honor or shall, without the consent of Congress, accept and retain any present, pension, office or emolument of any kind whatever, from any emperor, king, prince or foreign power, such person shall cease to be a citizen of the United States, and shall be incapable of holding any office of trust or profit under them, or either of them.

◆◆◆

This amendment would have extended Article 1, section 9, clause 8 of the Constitution, which prevents the awarding of titles by the United States and the acceptance of such awards from foreign powers without congressional consent. Historians speculate that general nervousness about the power of the Emperor Napoleon, who was at that time extending France's empire throughout Europe, may have prompted the proposal. Though it fell one vote short of ratification, Congress and the American people thought the proposal had been ratified and it was included in many nineteenth-century editions of the Constitution.

The Civil War and Reconstruction Amendments (Thirteenth, Fourteenth, and Fifteenth Amendments)

In the four months between the election of Abraham Lincoln and his inauguration, more than two hundred proposed constitutional amendments were presented to Congress as part of a desperate attempt to hold the rapidly dissolving Union together. Most of these were efforts to appease the southern states by protecting the right to own slaves or by disfranchising African Americans through constitutional amendment. None were able to win the votes required from Congress to send them to the states. The relatively innocuous Corwin Amendment seemed to be the only hope for preserving the Union by amending the Constitution.

The northern victors in the Civil War tried to restructure the Constitution just as the war had restructured the nation. Yet they were often divided in their goals. Some wanted to end slavery; others hoped for social and economic equality regardless of race; others hoped that extending the power of the ballot box to former slaves would help create a new political order. The debates over the Thirteenth, Fourteenth, and Fifteenth Amendments were bitter. Few of those who fought for these changes were satisfied with the amendments themselves; fewer still were satisfied with their interpretation. Although the amendments put an end to the legal status of slavery, it took nearly a hundred years after the amendments' passage before most of the descendants of former slaves could begin to experience the economic, social, and political equality the amendments had been intended to provide.

Unratified Amendment
Corwin Amendment (proposed by Congress March 2, 1861)

No amendment shall be made to the Constitution which will authorize or give to Congress the power to abolish or interfere, within any State, with the domestic institutions thereof, including that of persons held to labor or service by the laws of said State.

◆◆◆

Following the election of Abraham Lincoln, Congress scrambled to try to prevent the secession of the slaveholding states. House member Thomas Corwin of Ohio proposed the "unamendable" amendment in the hope that by protecting slavery where it existed, Congress would keep the southern states in the Union. Lincoln indicated his support for the proposed amendment in his first inaugural address. Only Ohio and Maryland ratified the Corwin Amendment before it was forgotten.

Amendment XIII
[Adopted 1865]

Section 1   Neither slavery nor involuntary servitude, except as a punishment for crime whereof the party shall have been duly convicted, shall exist within the United States, or any place subject to their jurisdiction.

Section 2   Congress shall have power to enforce this article by appropriate legislation.

◆◆◆

Although President Lincoln had abolished slavery in the Confederacy with the Emancipation Proclamation of 1863, abolitionists wanted to rid the entire country of slavery. The Thirteenth Amendment did this in a clear and straightforward manner. In February 1865, when the proposal was approved by the House, the gallery of the House was newly opened to black Americans who had a chance at last to see their government at work. Passage of the proposal was greeted by wild cheers from the gallery as well as tears on the House floor, where congressional representatives openly embraced one another.

The problem of ratification remained, however. The Union position was that the Confederate states were part of the country of thirty-six states. Therefore, twenty-seven states were needed to ratify the amendment. When Kentucky and Delaware rejected it, backers realized that without approval from at least four former Confederate states, the amendment would fail. Lincoln's successor, President Andrew Johnson, made ratification of the Thirteenth Amendment a condition for southern states to rejoin the Union. Under those terms, all the former Confederate states except Mississippi accepted the Thirteenth Amendment, and by the end of 1865 the amendment had become part of the Constitution and slavery had been prohibited in the United States.

Amendment XIV
[Adopted 1868]

Section 1   All persons born or naturalized in the United States, and subject to the jurisdiction thereof, are citizens of the United States and of the State wherein they reside. No State shall make or enforce any law which shall abridge the privileges or immunities of citizens of the United States; nor shall any State deprive any person of life, liberty, or property, without due process of law; nor deny to any person within its jurisdiction the equal protection of the laws.

Section 2   Representatives shall be appointed among the several States according to their respective numbers, counting the whole number of persons in each State, excluding Indians not taxed. But when the right to vote at any election for the choice of Electors for President and Vice-President of the United States, Representatives in Congress, the executive and judicial officers of a State, or the members of the legislature thereof, is denied to any of the male inhabitants of such State, being twenty-one years of age and citizens of the United States, or in any way abridged, except for participation in rebellion, or other crime, the basis of representation therein shall be reduced in the proportion which the number of such male citizens shall bear to the whole number of male citizens twenty-one years of age in such State.

Section 3 No person shall be a Senator or Representative in Congress, or Elector of President and Vice-President, or hold any office, civil or military, under the United States, or under any State, who, having previously taken an oath, as a member of Congress, or as an officer of the United States, or as a member of any State legislature, or as an executive or judicial officer of any State, to support the Constitution of the United States, shall have engaged in insurrection or rebellion against the same, or given aid or comfort to the enemies thereof. Congress may, by a vote of two-thirds of each house, remove such disability.

Section 4 The validity of the public debt of the United States, authorized by law, including debts incurred for payment of pensions and bounties for services in suppressing insurrection or rebellion, shall not be questioned. But neither the United States nor any State shall assume or pay any debt or obligation incurred in aid of insurrection or rebellion against the United States, or any claim for the loss or emancipation of any slave; but all such debts, obligations, and claims shall be held illegal and void.

Section 5 The Congress shall have power to enforce, by appropriate legislation, the provisions of this article.

◆ ◆ ◆

Without Lincoln's leadership in the reconstruction of the nation following the Civil War, it soon became clear that the Thirteenth Amendment needed additional constitutional support. Less than a year after Lincoln's assassination, Andrew Johnson was ready to bring the former Confederate states back into the Union with few changes in their governments or politics. Anxious Republicans drafted the Fourteenth Amendment to prevent that from happening. The most important provisions of this complex amendment made all native-born or naturalized persons American citizens and prohibited states from abridging the "privileges or immunities" of citizens; depriving them of "life, liberty, or property, without due process of law"; and denying them "equal protection of the laws." In essence, it made all ex-slaves citizens and protected the rights of all citizens against violation by their own state governments.

As occurred in the case of the Thirteenth Amendment, former Confederate states were forced to ratify the amendment as a condition of representation in the House and the Senate. The intentions of the Fourteenth Amendment, and how those intentions should be enforced, have been the most debated point of constitutional history. The terms due process *and* equal protection *have been especially troublesome. Was the amendment designed to outlaw racial segregation? Or was the goal simply to prevent the leaders of the rebellious South from gaining political power?*

The framers of the Fourteenth Amendment hoped Article 2 would produce black voters who would increase the power of the Republican Party. The federal government, however, never used its power to punish states for denying blacks their right to vote. Although the Fourteenth Amendment had an immediate impact in giving black Americans citizenship, it did nothing to protect blacks from the vengeance of whites once Reconstruction ended. In the late nineteenth and early twentieth centuries, section 1 of the Fourteenth Amendment was often used to protect business interests and strike down laws protecting workers on the grounds that the rights of "persons," that is, corporations, were protected by "due process." More recently, the Fourteenth Amendment has been used to justify school desegregation and affirmative action programs, as well as to dismantle such programs.

Amendment XV
[Adopted 1870]

Section 1 The right of citizens of the United States to vote shall not be denied or abridged by the United States or by any State on account of race, color, or previous condition of servitude.

Section 2 The Congress shall have power to enforce this article by appropriate legislation.

◆ ◆ ◆

The Fifteenth Amendment was the last major piece of Reconstruction legislation. While earlier Reconstruction acts had already required black suffrage in the South, the Fifteenth Amendment extended black voting rights to the entire nation. Some Republicans felt morally obligated to do away with the double standard between North and South since many northern states had stubbornly refused to enfranchise blacks. Others believed that the freedman's ballot required the extra protection of a constitutional amendment to shield it from white counterattack. But partisan advantage also played an important role in the amendment's passage, since Republicans hoped that by giving the ballot to northern blacks, they could lessen their political vulnerability.

Many women's rights advocates had fought for the amendment. They had felt betrayed by the inclusion of the word male *in section 2 of the Fourteenth Amendment and were further angered when the proposed Fifteenth Amendment failed to prohibit denial of the right to vote on the grounds of sex as well as "race, color, or previous condition of servitude." In this amendment, for the first time, the federal government claimed the power to regulate the franchise, or vote. It was also the first time the Constitution placed limits on the power of the states to regulate access to the franchise. Although ratified in 1870, however, the amendment was not enforced until the twentieth century.*

The Progressive Amendments (Sixteenth–Nineteenth Amendments)

No amendments were added to the Constitution between the Civil War and the Progressive Era. America was changing, however, in fundamental ways. The rapid industrialization of the United States after the Civil War led to many social and economic problems. Hundreds of amendments were proposed, but none received enough support in Congress to be sent to the states. Some scholars believe that regional differences and rivalries were so strong during this period that it was almost impossible to gain a consensus on a constitutional amendment. During the Progressive Era, however, the Constitution was amended four times in seven years.

Amendment XVI
[Adopted 1913]

The Congress shall have power to lay and collect taxes on incomes, from whatever source derived, without apportionment among the several States, and without regard to any census or enumeration.

◆◆◆

Until passage of the Sixteenth Amendment, most of the money used to run the federal government came from customs duties and taxes on specific items, such as liquor. During the Civil War, the federal government taxed incomes as an emergency measure. Pressure to enact an income tax came from those who were concerned about the growing gap between rich and poor in the United States. The Populist Party began campaigning for a graduated income tax in 1892, and support continued to grow. By 1909, thirty-three proposed income tax amendments had been presented in Congress, but lobbying by corporate and other special interests had defeated them all. In June 1909, the growing pressure for an income tax, which had been endorsed by Presidents Roosevelt and Taft, finally pushed an amendment through the Senate. The required thirty-six states had ratified the amendment by February 1913.

Amendment XVII
[Adopted 1913]

Section 1 The Senate of the United States shall be composed of two Senators from each State, elected by the people thereof, for six years; and each Senator shall have one vote. The electors in each State shall have the qualifications requisite for electors of [voters for] the most numerous branch of the State legislatures.

Section 2 When vacancies happen in the representation of any State in the Senate, the executive authority of such State shall issue writs of election to fill such vacancies: Provided, that the Legislature of any State may empower the executive thereof to make temporary appointments until the people fill the vacancies by election as the Legislature may direct.

Section 3 This amendment shall not be so construed as to affect the election or term of any Senator chosen before it becomes valid as part of the Constitution.

◆◆◆

The framers of the Constitution saw the members of the House as the representatives of the people and the members of the Senate as the representatives of the states. Originally senators were to be chosen by the state legislators. According to reform advocates, however, the growth of private industry and transportation conglomerates during the Gilded Age had created a network of corruption in which wealth and power were exchanged for influence and votes in the Senate. Senator Nelson Aldrich, who represented Rhode Island in the late nineteenth and early twentieth centuries, for example, was known as "the senator from Standard Oil" because of his open support of special business interests.

Efforts to amend the Constitution to allow direct election of senators had begun in 1826, but since any proposal had to be approved by the Senate, reform seemed impossible. Progressives tried to gain influence in the Senate by instituting party caucuses and primary elections, which gave citizens the chance to express their choice of a senator who could then be officially elected by the state legislature. By 1910, fourteen of the country's thirty senators received popular votes through a state primary before the state legislature made its selection. Despairing of getting a proposal through the Senate, supporters of a direct-election amendment had begun in 1893 to seek a convention of representatives from two-thirds of the states to propose an amendment that could then be ratified. By 1905, thirty-one of forty-five states had endorsed such an amendment. Finally, in 1911, despite extraordinary opposition, a proposed amendment passed the Senate; by 1913, it had been ratified.

Amendment XVIII
[Adopted 1919; Repealed 1933 by Amendment XXI]

Section 1 After one year from the ratification of this article the manufacture, sale, or transportation of intoxicating liquors within, the importation thereof into, or the exportation thereof from the United States and all territory subject to the jurisdiction thereof, for beverage purposes, is hereby prohibited.

Section 2 The Congress and the several States shall have concurrent power to enforce this article by appropriate legislation.

Section 3 This article shall be inoperative unless it shall have been ratified as an amendment to the Constitution by the legislatures of the several States, as provided by the Constitution, within seven years from the date of the submission thereof to the States by the Congress.

◆◆◆

The Prohibition Party, formed in 1869, began calling for a constitutional amendment to outlaw alcoholic beverages in 1872. A prohibition amendment was first proposed in the Senate in 1876 and was revived eighteen times before 1913. Between 1913 and 1919, another thirty-nine attempts were made to prohibit liquor in the United States through a constitutional amendment. Prohibition became a key element of the Progressive agenda as reformers linked alcohol and drunkenness to numerous social problems, including the corruption of immigrant voters. While opponents of such an amendment argued that it was undemocratic, supporters claimed that their efforts had widespread public support. The admission of twelve "dry" western states to the Union in the early twentieth century and the spirit of sacrifice during World War I laid the groundwork for passage and ratification of the Eighteenth Amendment in 1919. Opponents added a time limit to the amendment in the hope that they could thus block ratification, but this effort failed. (See also Amendment XXI.)

Amendment XIX
[Adopted 1920]

Section 1 The right of citizens of the United States to vote shall not be denied or abridged by the United States or by any State on account of sex.

Section 2 Congress shall have the power to enforce this article by appropriate legislation.

◆◆◆

Advocates of women's rights tried and failed to link woman suffrage to the Fourteenth and Fifteenth Amendments. Nonetheless, the effort for woman suffrage continued. Between 1878 and 1912, at least one and sometimes as many as four proposed amendments were introduced in Congress each year to grant women the right to vote. While over time women won very limited voting rights in some states, at both the state and federal levels opposition to an amendment for woman suffrage remained very strong. President Woodrow Wilson and other officials felt that the federal government should not interfere with the power of the states in this matter. Others worried that granting suffrage to women would encourage ethnic minorities to exercise their own right to vote. And many were concerned that giving women the vote would result in their abandoning traditional gender roles. In 1919, fol-lowing a protracted and often bitter campaign of protest in which women went on hunger strikes and chained themselves to fences, an amendment was introduced with the backing of President Wilson. It narrowly passed the Senate (after efforts to limit the suffrage to white women failed) and was adopted in 1920 after Tennessee became the thirty-sixth state to ratify it.

Unratified Amendment
Child Labor Amendment
(proposed by Congress June 2, 1924)

Section 1 The Congress shall have power to limit, regulate, and prohibit the labor of persons under eighteen years of age.

Section 2 The power of the several States is unimpaired by this article except that the operation of State laws shall be suspended to the extent necessary to give effect to legislation enacted by Congress.

◆◆◆

Throughout the late nineteenth and early twentieth centuries, alarm over the condition of child workers grew. Opponents of child labor argued that children worked in dangerous and unhealthy conditions, that they took jobs from adult workers, that they depressed wages in certain industries, and that states that allowed child labor had an economic advantage over those that did not. Defenders of child labor claimed that children provided needed income in many families, that working at a young age developed character, and that the effort to prohibit the practice constituted an invasion of family privacy.

In 1916, Congress passed a law that made it illegal to sell goods made by children through interstate commerce. The Supreme Court, however, ruled that the law violated the limits on the power of Congress to regulate interstate commerce. Congress then tried to penalize industries that used child labor by taxing such goods. This measure was also thrown out by the courts. In response, reformers set out to amend the Constitution. The proposed amendment was ratified by twenty-eight states, but by 1925, thirteen states had rejected it. Passage of the Fair Labor Standards Act in 1938, which was upheld by the Supreme Court in 1941, made the amendment irrelevant.

Amendment XX
[Adopted 1933]

Section 1 The terms of the President and Vice-President shall end at noon on the 20th day of January, and the terms of Senators and Representatives at noon on the 3rd day of January, of the years in which such terms would have ended if this article had not been ratified; and the terms of their successors shall then begin.

Section 2   The Congress shall assemble at least once in every year, and such meeting shall begin at noon on the 3rd day of January, unless they shall by law appoint a different day.

Section 3   If, at the time fixed for the beginning of the term of the President, the President-elect shall have died, the Vice-President-elect shall become President. If a President shall not have been chosen before the time fixed for the beginning of his term, or if the President-elect shall have failed to qualify, then the Vice-President-elect shall act as President until a President shall have qualified; and the Congress may by law provide for the case wherein neither a President-elect nor a Vice-President-elect shall have qualified, declaring who shall then act as President, or the manner in which one who is to act shall be selected, and such person shall act accordingly until a President or Vice-President shall have qualified.

Section 4   The Congress may by law provide for the case of the death of any of the persons from whom the House of Representatives may choose a President whenever the right of choice shall have devolved upon them, and for the case of the death of any of the persons from whom the Senate may choose a Vice-President whenever the right of choice shall have devolved upon them.

Section 5   Sections 1 and 2 shall take effect on the 15th day of October following the ratification of this article.

Section 6   This article shall be inoperative unless it shall have been ratified as an amendment to the Constitution by the Legislatures of three-fourths of the several States within seven years from the date of its submission.

◆◆◆

Until 1933, presidents took office on March 4. Since elections are held in early November and electoral votes are counted in mid-December, this meant that more than three months passed between the time a new president was elected and when he took office. Moving the inauguration to January shortened the transition period and allowed Congress to begin its term closer to the time of the president's inauguration. Although this seems like a minor change, an amendment was required because the Constitution specifies terms of office. This amendment also deals with questions of succession in the event that a president- or vice president-elect dies before assuming office. Section 3 also clarifies a method for resolving a deadlock in the electoral college.

Amendment XXI
[Adopted 1933]

Section 1   The eighteenth article of amendment to the Constitution of the United States is hereby repealed.

Section 2   The transportation or importation into any State, Territory, or Possession of the United States for delivery or use therein of intoxicating liquors, in violation of the laws thereof, is hereby prohibited.

Section 3   This article shall be inoperative unless it shall have been ratified as an amendment to the Constitution by conventions in the several States, as provided in the Constitution, within seven years from the date of the submission thereof to the States by the Congress.

◆◆◆

Widespread violation of the Volstead Act, the law enacted to enforce prohibition, made the United States a nation of lawbreakers. Prohibition caused more problems than it solved by encouraging crime, bribery, and corruption. Further, a coalition of liquor and beer manufacturers, personal liberty advocates, and constitutional scholars joined forces to challenge the amendment. By 1929, thirty proposed repeal amendments had been introduced in Congress, and the Democratic Party made repeal part of its platform in the 1932 presidential campaign. The Twenty-First Amendment was proposed in February 1933 and ratified less than a year later. The failure of the effort to enforce prohibition through a constitutional amendment has often been cited by opponents to subsequent efforts to shape public virtue and private morality.

Amendment XXII
[Adopted 1951]

Section 1   No person shall be elected to the office of the President more than twice, and no person who has held the office of President, or acted as President, for more than two years of a term to which some other person was elected President shall be elected to the office of President more than once. But this article shall not apply to any person holding the office of President when this Article was proposed by the Congress, and shall not prevent any person who may be holding the office of President, or acting as President, during the term within which this Article becomes operative from holding the office of President or acting as President during the remainder of such term.

Section 2   This article shall be inoperative unless it shall have been ratified as an amendment to the Constitution by the legislatures of three-fourths of the several States within seven years from the date of its submission to the States by the Congress.

◆◆◆

George Washington's refusal to seek a third term of office set a precedent that stood until 1912, when former President Theodore Roosevelt sought, without success, another term as an independent candidate. Democrat Franklin Roosevelt was the only president to seek and win a fourth term, though he did so amid great controversy. Roosevelt died in April 1945, a few months after the beginning of his fourth term. In 1946, Republicans won control of the House and the Senate, and early in 1947 a proposal for an amendment to limit future presidents to two four-year terms was offered to the states for ratification. Democratic critics of the Twenty-Second Amendment charged that it was a partisan posthumous jab at Roosevelt.

Since the Twenty-Second Amendment was adopted, however, the only presidents who might have been able to seek a third term, had it not existed, were Republicans Dwight Eisenhower and Ronald Reagan, and Democrat Bill Clinton. Since 1826, Congress has entertained 160 proposed amendments to limit the president to one six-year term. Such amendments have been backed by fifteen presidents, including Gerald Ford and Jimmy Carter.

Amendment XXIII
[Adopted 1961]

Section 1   The District constituting the seat of Government of the United States shall appoint in such manner as the Congress may direct: A number of electors of President and Vice-President equal to the whole number of Senators and Representatives in Congress to which the District would be entitled if it were a State, but in no event more than the least populous State; they shall be in addition to those appointed by the States, but they shall be considered for the purposes of the election of President and Vice-President, to be electors appointed by a State; and they shall meet in the District and perform such duties as provided by the twelfth article of amendment.

Section 2   The Congress shall have the power to enforce this article by appropriate legislation.

◆◆◆

When Washington, D.C., was established as a federal district, no one expected that a significant number of people would make it their permanent and primary residence. A proposal to allow citizens of the district to vote in presidential elections was approved by Congress in June 1960 and was ratified on March 29, 1961.

Amendment XXIV
[Adopted 1964]

Section 1   The right of citizens of the United States to vote in any primary or other election for President or Vice-President, for electors for President or Vice-President, or for Senator or Representative in Congress, shall not be denied or abridged by the United States or any State by reason of failure to pay any poll tax or other tax.

Section 2   The Congress shall have the power to enforce this article by appropriate legislation.

◆◆◆

In the colonial and Revolutionary eras, financial independence was seen as necessary to political independence, and the poll tax was used as a requirement for voting. By the twentieth century, however, the poll tax was used mostly to bar poor people, especially southern blacks, from voting. While conservatives complained that the amendment interfered with states' rights, liberals thought that the amendment did not go far enough because it barred the poll tax only in national elections and not in state or local elections. The amendment was ratified in 1964, however, and two years later, the Supreme Court ruled that poll taxes in state and local elections also violated the equal protection clause of the Fourteenth Amendment.

Amendment XXV
[Adopted 1967]

Section 1   In case of the removal of the President from office or of his death or resignation, the Vice-President shall become President.

Section 2   Whenever there is a vacancy in the office of the Vice-President, the President shall nominate a Vice-President who shall take office upon confirmation by a majority vote of both Houses of Congress.

Section 3   Whenever the President transmits to the President pro tempore of the Senate and the Speaker of the House of Representatives his written declaration that he is unable to discharge the powers and duties of his office, and until he transmits to them a written declaration to the contrary, such powers and duties shall be discharged by the Vice-President as Acting President.

Section 4   Whenever the Vice-President and a majority of either the principal officers of the executive departments or of such other body as Congress may by law provide, transmit to the President pro tempore of the Senate and the Speaker of the House of Representatives their written declaration that the President is unable to discharge the powers and duties of his office, the Vice-President shall immediately assume the powers and duties of the office as Acting President.

Thereafter, when the President transmits to the President pro tempore of the Senate and the Speaker of the House of Representatives his written declaration that no inability exists, he shall resume the powers and duties of his office unless the Vice-President and a majority of either the principal officers of the executive department[s] or of such other body as Congress may by law provide, transmit within four days to the President pro tempore of the Senate and the Speaker of the House of Representatives their written declaration that the President is unable to discharge the powers and duties of his office. Thereupon Congress shall decide the issue, assembling within forty-eight hours for that purpose if not in session. If the Congress, within twenty-one days after receipt of the latter written declaration, or, if Congress is not in session, within twenty-one days after Congress is required to assemble, determines by two-thirds vote of both Houses that the President is unable to discharge the powers and duties of his office, the Vice-President shall continue to discharge the same as Acting President; otherwise, the President shall resume the powers and duties of his office.

◆◆◆

The framers of the Constitution established the office of vice president because someone was needed to preside over the Senate. The first president to die in office was William Henry Harrison, in 1841. Vice President John Tyler had himself sworn in as president, setting a precedent that was followed when seven later presidents died in office. The assassination of President James A. Garfield in 1881 posed a new problem, however. After he was shot, the president was incapacitated for two months before he died; he was unable to lead the country, while his vice president, Chester A. Arthur, was unable to assume leadership. Efforts to resolve questions of succession in the event of a presidential disability thus began with the death of Garfield.

In 1963, the assassination of President John F. Kennedy galvanized Congress to action. Vice President Lyndon Johnson was a chain smoker with a history of heart trouble. According to the 1947 Presidential Succession Act, the two men who stood in line to succeed him were the seventy-two-year-old Speaker of the House and the eighty-six-year-old president of the Senate. There were serious concerns that any of these men might become incapacitated while serving as chief executive. The first time the Twenty-Fifth Amendment was used, however, was not in the case of presidential death or illness, but during the Watergate crisis. When Vice President Spiro T. Agnew was forced to resign following allegations of bribery and tax violations,

President Richard M. Nixon appointed House Minority Leader Gerald R. Ford vice president. Ford became president following Nixon's resignation eight months later and named Nelson A. Rockefeller as his vice president. Thus, for more than two years, the two highest offices in the country were held by people who had not been elected to them.

Amendment XXVI
[Adopted 1971]

Section 1 The right of citizens of the United States, who are eighteen years of age or older, to vote shall not be denied or abridged by the United States or by any State on account of age.

Section 2 The Congress shall have power to enforce this article by appropriate legislation.

◆◆◆

Efforts to lower the voting age from twenty-one to eighteen began during World War II. Recognizing that those who were old enough to fight a war should have some say in the government policies that involved them in the war, Presidents Eisenhower, Johnson, and Nixon endorsed the idea. In 1970, the combined pressure of the antiwar movement and the demographic pressure of the baby boom generation led to a Voting Rights Act lowering the voting age in federal, state, and local elections.

In Oregon v. Mitchell (1970), the state of Oregon challenged the right of Congress to determine the age at which people could vote in state or local elections. The Supreme Court agreed with Oregon. Since the Voting Rights Act was ruled unconstitutional, the Constitution had to be amended to allow passage of a law that would lower the voting age. The amendment was ratified in a little more than three months, making it the most rapidly ratified amendment in U.S. history.

Unratified Amendment
Equal Rights Amendment (proposed by Congress March 22, 1972; seven-year deadline for ratification extended June 30, 1982)

Section 1 Equality of rights under the law shall not be denied or abridged by the United States or by any State on account of sex.

Section 2 The Congress shall have the power to enforce, by appropriate legislation, the provisions of this article.

Section 3 This amendment shall take effect two years after the date of ratification.

◆◆◆

In 1923, soon after women had won the right to vote, Alice Paul, a leading activist in the woman suffrage movement, proposed an amendment requiring equal treatment of men and women. Opponents of the proposal argued that such an amendment would invalidate laws that protected women and would make women subject to the military draft. After the 1964 Civil Rights Act was adopted, protective workplace legislation was removed anyway.

The renewal of the women's movement, as a by-product of the civil rights and antiwar movements, led to a revival of the Equal Rights Amendment (ERA) in Congress. Disagreements over language held up congressional passage of the proposed amendment, but on March 22, 1972, the Senate approved the ERA by a vote of eighty-four to eight, and it was sent to the states. Six states ratified the amendment within two days, and by the middle of 1973 the amendment seemed well on its way to adoption, with thirty of the needed thirty-eight states having ratified it. In the mid-1970s, however, a powerful "Stop ERA" campaign developed. The campaign portrayed the ERA as a threat to "family values" and traditional relationships between men and women. Although thirty-five states ultimately ratified the ERA, five of those state legislatures voted to rescind ratification, and the amendment was never adopted.

Unratified Amendment

D.C. Statehood Amendment (proposed by Congress August 22, 1978)

Section 1   For purposes of representation in the Congress, election of the President and Vice President, and article V of this Constitution, the District constituting the seat of government of the United States shall be treated as though it were a State.

Section 2   The exercise of the rights and powers conferred under this article shall be by the people of the District constituting the seat of government, and as shall be provided by Congress.

Section 3   The twenty-third article of amendment to the Constitution of the United States is hereby repealed.

Section 4   This article shall be inoperative, unless it shall have been ratified as an amendment to the Constitution by the legislatures of three-fourths of the several states within seven years from the date of its submission.

◆◆◆

The 1961 ratification of the Twenty-Third Amendment, giving residents of the District of Columbia the right to vote for a president and vice president, inspired an effort to give residents of the district full voting rights. In 1966, President Lyndon Johnson appointed a mayor and city council; in 1971, D.C. residents were allowed to name a nonvoting delegate to the House; and in 1981, residents were allowed to elect the mayor and city council. Congress retained the right to overrule laws that might affect commuters, the height of federal buildings, and selection of judges and prosecutors. The district's nonvoting delegate to Congress, Walter Fauntroy, lobbied fiercely for a congressional amendment granting statehood to the district. In 1978, a proposed amendment was approved and sent to the states. A number of states quickly ratified the amendment, but, like the ERA, the D.C. Statehood Amendment ran into trouble. Opponents argued that section 2 created a separate category of "nominal" statehood. They argued that the federal district should be eliminated and that the territory should be reabsorbed into the state of Maryland. Although these theoretical arguments were strong, some scholars believe that racist attitudes toward the predominantly black population of the city was also a factor leading to the defeat of the amendment.

Amendment XXVII
[Adopted 1992]

No law, varying the compensation for the services of the Senators and Representatives, shall take effect, until an election of Representatives shall have intervened.

◆◆◆

While the Twenty-Sixth Amendment was the most rapidly ratified amendment in U.S. history, the Twenty-Seventh Amendment had the longest journey to ratification. First proposed by James Madison in 1789 as part of the package that included the Bill of Rights, this amendment had been ratified by only six states by 1791. In 1873, however, it was ratified by Ohio to protest a massive retroactive salary increase by the federal government. Unlike later proposed amendments, this one came with no time limit on ratification. In the early 1980s, Gregory D. Watson, a University of Texas economics major, discovered the "lost" amendment and began a single-handed campaign to get state legislators to introduce it for ratification. In 1983, it was accepted by Maine. In 1984, it passed the Colorado legislature. Ratifications trickled in slowly until May 1992, when Michigan and New Jersey became the thirty-eighth and thirty-ninth states, respectively, to ratify. This amendment prevents members of Congress from raising their own salaries without giving voters a chance to vote them out of office before they can benefit from the raises.

Appendix II. FACTS AND FIGURES: GOVERNMENT, ECONOMY, AND DEMOGRAPHICS

For additional facts and figures see the Online Appendix at
www.bedfordstmartins.com/roarkcompact.

PRESIDENTIAL ELECTIONS

Year	Candidates	Parties	Popular Vote	Percentage of Popular Vote	Electoral Vote	Percentage of Voter Participation
1789	**GEORGE WASHINGTON (Va.)***				69	
	John Adams				34	
	Others				35	
1792	**GEORGE WASHINGTON (Va.)**				132	
	John Adams				77	
	George Clinton				50	
	Others				5	
1796	**JOHN ADAMS (Mass.)**	Federalist			71	
	Thomas Jefferson	Democratic-Republican			68	
	Thomas Pinckney	Federalist			59	
	Aaron Burr	Dem.-Rep.			30	
	Others				48	
1800	**THOMAS JEFFERSON (Va.)**	Dem.-Rep.			73	
	Aaron Burr	Dem.-Rep.			73	
	John Adams	Federalist			65	
	C. C. Pinckney	Federalist			64	
	John Jay	Federalist			1	
1804	**THOMAS JEFFERSON (Va.)**	Dem.-Rep.			162	
	C. C. Pinckney	Federalist			14	
1808	**JAMES MADISON (Va.)**	Dem.-Rep.			122	
	C. C. Pinckney	Federalist			47	
	George Clinton	Dem.-Rep.			6	
1812	**JAMES MADISON (Va.)**	Dem.-Rep.			128	
	De Witt Clinton	Federalist			89	
1816	**JAMES MONROE (Va.)**	Dem.-Rep.			183	
	Rufus King	Federalist			34	
1820	**JAMES MONROE (Va.)**	Dem.-Rep.			231	
	John Quincy Adams	Dem.-Rep.			1	

*State of residence when elected president.

Year	Candidates	Parties	Popular Vote	Percentage of Popular Vote	Electoral Vote	Percentage of Voter Participation
1824	**JOHN Q. ADAMS (Mass.)**	Dem.-Rep.	108,740	30.5	84	26.9
	Andrew Jackson	Dem.-Rep.	153,544	43.1	99	
	William H. Crawford	Dem.-Rep.	46,618	13.1	41	
	Henry Clay	Dem.-Rep.	47,136	13.2	37	
1828	**ANDREW JACKSON (Tenn.)**	Democratic	647,286	56.0	178	57.6
	John Quincy Adams	National Republican	508,064	44.0	83	
1832	**ANDREW JACKSON (Tenn.)**	Democratic	687,502	55.0	219	55.4
	Henry Clay	National Republican	530,189	42.4	49	
	John Floyd	Independent			11	
	William Wirt	Anti-Mason	33,108	2.6	7	
1836	**MARTIN VAN BUREN (N.Y.)**	Democratic	765,483	50.9	170	57.8
	W. H. Harrison	Whig			73	
	Hugh L. White	Whig	739,795	49.1	26	
	Daniel Webster	Whig			14	
	W. P. Magnum	Independent			11	
1840	**WILLIAM H. HARRISON (Ohio)**	Whig	1,274,624	53.1	234	80.2
	Martin Van Buren	Democratic	1,127,781	46.9	60	
	J. G. Birney	Liberty	7,069		—	
1844	**JAMES K. POLK (Tenn.)**	Democratic	1,338,464	49.6	170	78.9
	Henry Clay	Whig	1,300,097	48.1	105	
	J. G. Birney	Liberty	62,300	2.3	—	
1848	**ZACHARY TAYLOR (La.)**	Whig	1,360,967	47.4	163	72.7
	Lewis Cass	Democratic	1,222,342	42.5	127	
	Martin Van Buren	Free-Soil	291,263	10.1	—	
1852	**FRANKLIN PIERCE (N.H.)**	Democratic	1,601,117	50.9	254	69.6
	Winfield Scott	Whig	1,385,453	44.1	42	
	John P. Hale	Free-Soil	155,825	5.0	—	
1856	**JAMES BUCHANAN (Pa.)**	Democratic	1,832,995	45.3	174	78.9
	John C. Frémont	Republican	1,339,932	33.1	114	
	Millard Fillmore	American	871,731	21.6	8	
1860	**ABRAHAM LINCOLN (Ill.)**	Republican	1,865,593	39.8	180	81.2
	Stephen A. Douglas	Democratic	1,382,713	29.5	12	
	John C. Breckinridge	Democratic	848,356	18.1	72	
	John Bell	Union	592,906	12.6	39	
1864	**ABRAHAM LINCOLN (Ill.)**	Republican	2,206,938	55.0	212	73.8
	George B. McClellan	Democratic	1,803,787	45.0	21	
1868	**ULYSSES S. GRANT (Ill.)**	Republican	3,012,833	52.7	214	78.1
	Horatio Seymour	Democratic	2,703,249	47.3	80	
1872	**ULYSSES S. GRANT (Ill.)**	Republican	3,597,132	55.6	286	71.3
	Horace Greeley	Democratic; Liberal Republican	2,834,125	43.9	66	
1876	**RUTHERFORD B. HAYES (Ohio)**	Republican	4,036,572	48.0	185	81.8
	Samuel J. Tilden	Democratic	4,284,020	51.0	184	
1880	**JAMES A. GARFIELD (Ohio)**	Republican	4,454,416	48.5	214	79.4
	Winfield S. Hancock	Democratic	4,444,952	48.1	155	

Year	Candidates	Parties	Popular Vote	Percentage of Popular Vote	Electoral Vote	Percentage of Voter Participation
1884	**GROVER CLEVELAND (N.Y.)**	Democratic	4,879,507	48.5	219	77.5
	James G. Blaine	Republican	4,850,293	48.2	182	
1888	**BENJAMIN HARRISON (Ind.)**	Republican	5,439,853	47.9	233	79.3
	Grover Cleveland	Democratic	5,540,309	48.6	168	
1892	**GROVER CLEVELAND (N.Y.)**	Democratic	5,555,426	46.1	277	74.7
	Benjamin Harrison	Republican	5,182,690	43.0	145	
	James B. Weaver	People's	1,029,846	8.5	22	
1896	**WILLIAM McKINLEY (Ohio)**	Republican	7,104,779	51.1	271	79.3
	William J. Bryan	Democratic-People's	6,502,925	47.7	176	
1900	**WILLIAM McKINLEY (Ohio)**	Republican	7,207,923	51.7	292	73.2
	William J. Bryan	Dem.-Populist	6,358,133	45.5	155	
1904	**THEODORE ROOSEVELT (N.Y.)**	Republican	7,623,486	57.9	336	65.2
	Alton B. Parker	Democratic	5,077,911	37.6	140	
	Eugene V. Debs	Socialist	402,283	3.0	—	
1908	**WILLIAM H. TAFT (Ohio)**	Republican	7,678,908	51.6	321	65.4
	William J. Bryan	Democratic	6,409,104	43.1	162	
	Eugene V. Debs	Socialist	420,793	2.8	—	
1912	**WOODROW WILSON (N.J.)**	Democratic	6,293,454	41.9	435	58.8
	Theodore Roosevelt	Progressive	4,119,538	27.4	88	
	William H. Taft	Republican	3,484,980	23.2	8	
	Eugene V. Debs	Socialist	900,672	6.1	—	
1916	**WOODROW WILSON (N.J.)**	Democratic	9,129,606	49.4	277	61.6
	Charles E. Hughes	Republican	8,538,221	46.2	254	
	A. L. Benson	Socialist	585,113	3.2	—	
1920	**WARREN G. HARDING (Ohio)**	Republican	16,143,407	60.5	404	49.2
	James M. Cox	Democratic	9,130,328	34.2	127	
	Eugene V. Debs	Socialist	919,799	3.4	—	
1924	**CALVIN COOLIDGE (Mass.)**	Republican	15,725,016	54.0	382	48.9
	John W. Davis	Democratic	8,386,503	28.8	136	
	Robert M. LaFollette	Progressive	4,822,856	16.6	13	
1928	**HERBERT HOOVER (Calif.)**	Republican	21,391,381	58.2	444	56.9
	Alfred E. Smith	Democratic	15,016,443	40.9	87	
	Norman Thomas	Socialist	267,835	0.7	—	
1932	**FRANKLIN D. ROOSEVELT (N.Y.)**	Democratic	22,809,638	57.4	472	56.9
	Herbert Hoover	Republican	15,758,901	39.7	59	
	Norman Thomas	Socialist	881,951	2.2	—	
1936	**FRANKLIN D. ROOSEVELT (N.Y.)**	Democratic	27,751,597	60.8	523	61.0
	Alfred M. Landon	Republican	16,679,583	36.5	8	
	William Lemke	Union	882,479	1.9	—	
1940	**FRANKLIN D. ROOSEVELT (N.Y.)**	Democratic	27,244,160	54.8	449	62.5
	Wendell Willkie	Republican	22,305,198	44.8	82	
1944	**FRANKLIN D. ROOSEVELT (N.Y.)**	Democratic	25,602,504	53.5	432	55.9
	Thomas E. Dewey	Republican	22,006,285	46.0	99	
1948	**HARRY S. TRUMAN (Mo.)**	Democratic	24,105,695	49.5	303	53.0
	Thomas E. Dewey	Republican	21,969,170	45.1	189	
	J. Strom Thurmond	State-Rights Democratic	1,169,021	2.4	38	
	Henry A. Wallace	Progressive	1,156,103	2.4	—	

Year	Candidates	Parties	Popular Vote	Percentage of Popular Vote	Electoral Vote	Percentage of Voter Participation
1952	**DWIGHT D. EISENHOWER (N.Y.)**	Republican	33,936,252	55.1	442	63.3
	Adlai Stevenson	Democratic	27,314,992	44.4	89	
1956	**DWIGHT D. EISENHOWER (N.Y.)**	Republican	35,575,420	57.6	457	60.6
	Adlai Stevenson	Democratic	26,033,066	42.1	73	
	Other	—	—		1	
1960	**JOHN F. KENNEDY (Mass.)**	Democratic	34,227,096	49.9	303	62.8
	Richard M. Nixon	Republican	34,108,546	49.6	219	
	Other	—	—		15	
1964	**LYNDON B. JOHNSON (Texas)**	Democratic	43,126,506	61.1	486	61.7
	Barry M. Goldwater	Republican	27,176,799	38.5	52	
1968	**RICHARD M. NIXON (N.Y.)**	Republican	31,770,237	43.4	301	60.9
	Hubert H. Humphrey	Democratic	31,270,533	42.7	191	
	George Wallace	American Indep.	9,906,141	13.5	46	
1972	**RICHARD M. NIXON (N.Y.)**	Republican	47,169,911	60.7	520	55.2
	George S. McGovern	Democratic	29,170,383	37.5	17	
	Other	—	—		1	
1976	**JIMMY CARTER (Ga.)**	Democratic	40,828,587	50.0	297	53.5
	Gerald R. Ford	Republican	39,147,613	47.9	241	
	Other	—	1,575,459	2.1	—	
1980	**RONALD REAGAN (Calif.)**	Republican	43,901,812	50.7	489	54.0
	Jimmy Carter	Democratic	35,483,820	41.0	49	
	John B. Anderson	Independent	5,719,722	6.6	—	
	Ed Clark	Libertarian	921,188	1.1	—	
1984	**RONALD REAGAN (Calif.)**	Republican	54,455,075	59.0	525	53.1
	Walter Mondale	Democratic	37,577,185	41.0	13	
1988	**GEORGE BUSH (Texas)**	Republican	47,946,422	54.0	426	50.2
	Michael S. Dukakis	Democratic	41,016,429	46.0	112	
1992	**WILLIAM J. CLINTON (Ark.)**	Democratic	44,908,254	42.3	370	55.9
	George Bush	Republican	39,102,282	37.4	168	
	H. Ross Perot	Independent	19,721,433	18.9	—	
1996	**WILLIAM J. CLINTON (Ark.)**	Democratic	47,401,185	49.2	379	49.0
	Robert Dole	Republican	39,197,469	40.7	159	
	H. Ross Perot	Independent	8,085,294	8.4	—	
2000	**GEORGE W. BUSH (Texas)**	Republican	50,456,062	47.8	271	51.2
	Al Gore	Democratic	50,996,862	48.4	267	
	Ralph Nader	Green Party	2,858,843	2.7	—	
	Patrick J. Buchanan	—	438,760	.4	—	

PRESIDENTS, VICE PRESIDENTS, AND SECRETARIES OF STATE

The Washington Administration (1789–1797)

Vice President	John Adams	1789–1797
Secretary of State	Thomas Jefferson	1789–1793
	Edmund Randolph	1794–1795
	Timothy Pickering	1795–1797

The John Adams Administration (1797–1801)

Vice President	Thomas Jefferson	1797–1801
Secretary of State	Timothy Pickering	1797–1800
	John Marshall	1800–1801

The Jefferson Administration (1801–1809)

Vice President	Aaron Burr	1801–1805
	George Clinton	1805–1809
Secretary of State	James Madison	1801–1809

The Madison Administration (1809–1817)

Vice President	George Clinton	1809–1813
	Elbridge Gerry	1813–1817
Secretary of State	Robert Smith	1809–1811
	James Monroe	1811–1817

The Monroe Administration (1817–1825)

Vice President	Daniel Tompkins	1817–1825
Secretary of State	John Quincy Adams	1817–1825

The John Quincy Adams Administration (1825–1829)

Vice President	John C. Calhoun	1825–1829
Secretary of State	Henry Clay	1825–1829

The Jackson Administration (1829–1837)

Vice President	John C. Calhoun	1829–1833
	Martin Van Buren	1833–1837
Secretary of State	Martin Van Buren	1829–1831
	Edward Livingston	1831–1833
	Louis McLane	1833–1834
	John Forsyth	1834–1837

The Van Buren Administration (1837–1841)

Vice President	Richard M. Johnson	1837–1841
Secretary of State	John Forsyth	1837–1841

The William Harrison Administration (1841)

Vice President	John Tyler	1841
Secretary of State	Daniel Webster	1841

The Tyler Administration (1841–1845)

Vice President	None	
Secretary of State	Daniel Webster	1841–1843
	Hugh S. Legaré	1843
	Abel P. Upshur	1843–1844
	John C. Calhoun	1844–1845

The Polk Administration (1845–1849)

Vice President	George M. Dallas	1845–1849
Secretary of State	James Buchanan	1845–1849

The Taylor Administration (1849–1850)

Vice President	Millard Fillmore	1849–1850
Secretary of State	John M. Clayton	1849–1850

The Fillmore Administration (1850–1853)

Vice President	None	
Secretary of State	Daniel Webster	1850–1852
	Edward Everett	1852–1853

The Pierce Administration (1853–1857)

Vice President	William R. King	1853–1857
Secretary of State	William L. Marcy	1853–1857

The Buchanan Administration (1857–1861)

Vice President	John C. Breckinridge	1857–1861
Secretary of State	Lewis Cass	1857–1860
	Jeremiah S. Black	1860–1861

The Lincoln Administration (1861–1865)

Vice President	Hannibal Hamlin	1861–1865
	Andrew Johnson	1865
Secretary of State	William H. Seward	1861–1865

The Andrew Johnson Administration (1865–1869)

Vice President	None	
Secretary of State	William H. Seward	1865–1869

PRESIDENTS, VICE PRESIDENTS, AND SECRETARIES OF STATE

The Grant Administration (1869–1877)

Vice President	Schuyler Colfax	1869–1873
	Henry Wilson	1873–1877
Secretary of State	Elihu B. Washburne	1869
	Hamilton Fish	1869–1877

The Hayes Administration (1877–1881)

| Vice President | William A. Wheeler | 1877–1881 |
| Secretary of State | William M. Evarts | 1877–1881 |

The Garfield Administration (1881)

| Vice President | Chester A. Arthur | 1881 |
| Secretary of State | James G. Blaine | 1881 |

The Arthur Administration (1881–1885)

| Vice President | None | |
| Secretary of State | F. T. Frelinghuysen | 1881–1885 |

The Cleveland Administration (1885–1889)

| Vice President | Thomas A. Hendricks | 1885–1889 |
| Secretary of State | Thomas F. Bayard | 1885–1889 |

The Benjamin Harrison Administration (1889–1893)

Vice President	Levi P. Morton	1889–1893
Secretary of State	James G. Blaine	1889–1892
	John W. Foster	1892–1893

The Cleveland Administration (1893–1897)

Vice President	Adlai E. Stevenson	1893–1897
Secretary of State	Walter Q. Gresham	1893–1895
	Richard Olney	1895–1897

The McKinley Administration (1897–1901)

Vice President	Garret A. Hobart	1897–1901
	Theodore Roosevelt	1901
Secretary of State	John Sherman	1897–1898
	William R. Day	1898
	John Hay	1898–1901

The Theodore Roosevelt Administration (1901–1909)

Vice President	Charles Fairbanks	1905–1909
Secretary of State	John Hay	1901–1905
	Elihu Root	1905–1909
	Robert Bacon	1909

The Taft Administration (1909–1913)

| Vice President | James S. Sherman | 1909–1913 |
| Secretary of State | Philander C. Knox | 1909–1913 |

The Wilson Administration (1913–1921)

Vice President	Thomas R. Marshall	1913–1921
Secretary of State	William J. Bryan	1913–1915
	Robert Lansing	1915–1920
	Bainbridge Colby	1920–1921

The Harding Administration (1921–1923)

| Vice President | Calvin Coolidge | 1921–1923 |
| Secretary of State | Charles E. Hughes | 1921–1923 |

The Coolidge Administration (1923–1929)

Vice President	Charles G. Dawes	1925–1929
Secretary of State	Charles E. Hughes	1923–1925
	Frank B. Kellogg	1925–1929

The Hoover Administration (1929–1933)

| Vice President | Charles Curtis | 1929–1933 |
| Secretary of State | Henry L. Stimson | 1929–1933 |

The Franklin D. Roosevelt Administration (1933–1945)

Vice President	John Nance Garner	1933–1941
	Henry A. Wallace	1941–1945
	Harry S. Truman	1945
Secretary of State	Cordell Hull	1933–1944
	Edward R. Stettinius Jr.	1944–1945

The Truman Administration (1945–1953)

Vice President	Alben W. Barkley	1949–1953
Secretary of State	Edward R. Stettinius Jr.	1945
	James F. Byrnes	1945–1947
	George C. Marshall	1947–1949
	Dean G. Acheson	1949–1953

The Eisenhower Administration (1953–1961)

Vice President	Richard M. Nixon	1953–1961
Secretary of State	John Foster Dulles	1953–1959
	Christian A. Herter	1959–1961

The Kennedy Administration (1961–1963)

| Vice President | Lyndon B. Johnson | 1961–1963 |
| Secretary of State | Dean Rusk | 1961–1963 |

The Lyndon Johnson Administration (1963–1969)

| Vice President | Hubert H. Humphrey | 1965–1969 |
| Secretary of State | Dean Rusk | 1963–1969 |

The Nixon Administration (1969–1974)

Vice President	Spiro T. Agnew	1969–1973
	Gerald R. Ford	1973–1974
Secretary of State	William P. Rogers	1969–1973
	Henry A. Kissinger	1973–1974

The Ford Administration (1974–1977)

| Vice President | Nelson A. Rockefeller | 1974–1977 |
| Secretary of State | Henry A. Kissinger | 1974–1977 |

The Carter Administration (1977–1981)

Vice President	Walter F. Mondale	1977–1981
Secretary of State	Cyrus R. Vance	1977–1980
	Edmund Muskie	1980–1981

The Reagan Administration (1981–1989)

Vice President	George H. W. Bush	1981–1989
Secretary of State	Alexander M. Haig	1981–1982
	George P. Shultz	1982–1989

The George H. W. Bush Administration (1989–1993)

Vice President	J. Danforth Quayle	1989–1993
Secretary of State	James A. Baker III	1989–1992
	Lawrence S. Eagleburger	1992–1993

The Clinton Administration (1993–2001)

Vice President	Albert Gore	1993–2001
Secretary of State	Warren M. Christopher	1993–1997
	Madeleine K. Albright	1997–2001

The George W. Bush Administration (2001–)

| Vice President | Dick Cheney | 2001– |
| Secretary of State | Colin Powell | 2001– |

SUPREME COURT JUSTICES

Name	Service	Appointed by	Name	Service	Appointed by
John Jay*	1789–1795	Washington	Henry B. Livingston	1806–1823	Jefferson
James Wilson	1789–1798	Washington	Thomas Todd	1807–1826	Jefferson
John Blair	1789–1796	Washington	Gabriel Duval	1811–1836	Madison
John Rutledge	1790–1791	Washington	Joseph Story	1811–1845	Madison
William Cushing	1790–1810	Washington	Smith Thompson	1823–1843	Monroe
James Iredell	1790–1799	Washington	Robert Trimble	1826–1828	J. Q. Adams
Thomas Johnson	1791–1793	Washington	John McLean	1829–1861	Jackson
William Paterson	1793–1806	Washington	Henry Baldwin	1830–1844	Jackson
John Rutledge†	1795	Washington	James M. Wayne	1835–1867	Jackson
Samuel Chase	1796–1811	Washington	**Roger B. Taney**	1836–1864	Jackson
Oliver Ellsworth	1796–1799	Washington	Philip P. Barbour	1836–1841	Jackson
Bushrod Washington	1798–1829	J. Adams	John Catron	1837–1865	Van Buren
Alfred Moore	1799–1804	J. Adams	John McKinley	1837–1852	Van Buren
John Marshall	1801–1835	J. Adams	Peter V. Daniel	1841–1860	Van Buren
William Johnson	1804–1834	Jefferson	Samuel Nelson	1845–1872	Tyler
			Levi Woodbury	1845–1851	Polk
			Robert C. Grier	1846–1870	Polk
			Benjamin R. Curtis	1851–1857	Fillmore
			John A. Campbell	1853–1861	Pierce

*Chief Justices appear in bold type.
†Acting Chief Justice; Senate refused to confirm appointment.

Name	Service	Appointed by	Name	Service	Appointed by
Nathan Clifford	1858–1881	Buchanan	Owen J. Roberts	1930–1945	Hoover
Noah H. Swayne	1862–1881	Lincoln	Benjamin N. Cardozo	1932–1938	Hoover
Samuel F. Miller	1862–1890	Lincoln	Hugo L. Black	1937–1971	F. Roosevelt
David Davis	1862–1877	Lincoln	Stanley F. Reed	1938–1957	F. Roosevelt
Stephen J. Field	1863–1897	Lincoln	Felix Frankfurter	1939–1962	F. Roosevelt
Salmon P. Chase	1864–1873	Lincoln	William O. Douglas	1939–1975	F. Roosevelt
William Strong	1870–1880	Grant	Frank Murphy	1940–1949	F. Roosevelt
Joseph P. Bradley	1870–1892	Grant	**Harlan F. Stone**	1941–1946	F. Roosevelt
Ward Hunt	1873–1882	Grant	James F. Byrnes	1941–1942	F. Roosevelt
Morrison R. Waite	1874–1888	Grant	Robert H. Jackson	1941–1954	F. Roosevelt
John M. Harlan	1877–1911	Hayes	Wiley B. Rutledge	1943–1949	F. Roosevelt
William B. Woods	1880–1887	Hayes	Harold H. Burton	1945–1958	Truman
Stanley Matthews	1881–1889	Garfield	**Frederick M. Vinson**	1946–1953	Truman
Horace Gray	1882–1902	Arthur	Tom C. Clark	1949–1967	Truman
Samuel Blatchford	1882–1893	Arthur	Sherman Minton	1949–1956	Truman
Lucious Q. C. Lamar	1888–1893	Cleveland	**Earl Warren**	1953–1969	Eisenhower
Melville W. Fuller	1888–1910	Cleveland	John Marshall Harlan	1955–1971	Eisenhower
David J. Brewer	1889–1910	B. Harrison	William J. Brennan Jr.	1956–1990	Eisenhower
Henry B. Brown	1890–1906	B. Harrison	Charles E. Whittaker	1957–1962	Eisenhower
George Shiras	1892–1903	B. Harrison	Potter Stewart	1958–1981	Eisenhower
Howell E. Jackson	1893–1895	B. Harrison	Byron R. White	1962–1993	Kennedy
Edward D. White	1894–1910	Cleveland	Arthur J. Goldberg	1962–1965	Kennedy
Rufus W. Peckham	1896–1909	Cleveland	Abe Fortas	1965–1969	L. Johnson
Joseph McKenna	1898–1925	McKinley	Thurgood Marshall	1967–1991	L. Johnson
Oliver W. Holmes	1902–1932	T. Roosevelt	**Warren E. Burger**	1969–1986	Nixon
William R. Day	1903–1922	T. Roosevelt	Harry A. Blackmun	1970–1994	Nixon
William H. Moody	1906–1910	T. Roosevelt	Lewis F. Powell Jr.	1972–1988	Nixon
Horace H. Lurton	1910–1914	Taft	William H. Rehnquist	1972–1986	Nixon
Charles E. Hughes	1910–1916	Taft	John Paul Stevens	1975–	Ford
Willis Van Devanter	1910–1937	Taft	Sandra Day O'Connor	1981–	Reagan
Joseph R. Lamar	1911–1916	Taft	**William H. Rehnquist**	1986–	Reagan
Edward D. White	1910–1921	Taft	Antonin Scalia	1986–	Reagan
Mahlon Pitney	1912–1922	Taft	Anthony M. Kennedy	1988–	Reagan
James C. McReynolds	1914–1941	Wilson	David H. Souter	1990–	Bush
Louis D. Brandeis	1916–1939	Wilson	Clarence Thomas	1991–	Bush
John H. Clarke	1916–1922	Wilson	Ruth Bader Ginsburg	1993–	Clinton
William H. Taft	1921–1930	Harding	Stephen Breyer	1994–	Clinton
George Sutherland	1922–1938	Harding			
Pierce Butler	1923–1939	Harding			
Edward T. Sanford	1923–1930	Harding			
Harlan F. Stone	1925–1941	Coolidge			
Charles E. Hughes	1930–1941	Hoover			

Federal Spending and the Economy, 1790–1998

Year	Gross National Product (in billions)	Foreign Trade (in millions) Exports	Imports	Federal Budget (in billions)	Federal Surplus/Deficit (in billions)	Federal Debt (in billions)
1790	NA	20	23	0.004	0.00015	0.076
1800	NA	71	91	0.011	0.0006	0.083
1810	NA	67	85	0.008	0.0012	0.053
1820	NA	70	74	0.018	−0.0004	0.091
1830	NA	74	71	0.015	0.100	0.049
1840	NA	132	107	0.024	−0.005	0.004
1850	NA	152	178	0.040	0.004	0.064
1860	NA	400	362	0.063	−0.01	0.065
1870	7.4	451	462	0.310	0.10	2.4
1880	11.2	853	761	0.268	0.07	2.1
1890	13.1	910	823	0.318	0.09	1.2
1900	18.7	1,499	930	0.521	0.05	1.2
1910	35.3	1,919	1,646	0.694	−0.02	1.1
1920	91.5	8,664	5,784	6.357	0.3	24.3
1930	90.4	4,013	3,500	3.320	0.7	16.3
1940	99.7	4,030	7,433	9.6	−2.7	43.0
1950	284.8	10,816	9,125	43.1	−2.2	257.4
1960	503.7	19,600	15,046	92.2	0.3	286.3
1970	977.1	42,700	40,189	195.6	−2.8	371.0
1980	2,631.7	220,600	244,871	590.9	−73.8	907.7
1990	5,764.9	393,600	495,300	1,253.2	−221.2	3,266.1
1998	8,490.5	682,100	911,900	1,652.5	69.2	5,555.5

Source: Historical Statistics of the U.S., Colonial Times to 1970 (1975), Statistical Abstract of the U.S., 1996 (1996), and Statistical Abstract of the U.S., 1999 (1999).

Population Growth, 1630–2000

Year	Population	Percent Increase	Year	Population	Percent Increase
1630	4,600	—	1820	9,638,453	33.1
1640	26,600	473.3	1830	12,866,020	33.5
1650	50,400	89.1	1840	17,069,453	32.7
1660	75,100	49.0	1850	23,191,876	35.9
1670	111,900	49.1	1860	31,443,321	35.6
1680	151,500	35.4	1870	39,818,449	26.6
1690	210,400	38.9	1880	50,155,783	26.0
1700	250,900	19.3	1890	62,947,714	25.5
1710	331,700	32.2	1900	75,994,575	20.7
1720	466,200	40.5	1910	91,972,266	21.0
1730	629,400	35.0	1920	105,710,620	14.9
1740	905,600	43.9	1930	122,775,046	16.1
1750	1,170,800	30.0	1940	131,669,275	7.2
1760	1,593,600	36.1	1950	150,697,361	14.5
1770	2,148,100	34.8	1960	179,323,175	19.0
1780	2,780,400	29.4	1970	203,302,031	13.4
1790	3,929,214	41.3	1980	226,542,199	11.4
1800	5,308,483	35.1	1990	248,718,301	9.8
1810	7,239,881	36.4	2000	281,421,906	11.0

Source: Historical Statistics of the U.S. (1960), Historical Statistics of the U.S., Colonial Times to 1970 (1975), Statistical Abstract of the U.S., 1996 (1996), and United States Census, 2000 (2000).

Birthrate, 1820–2000

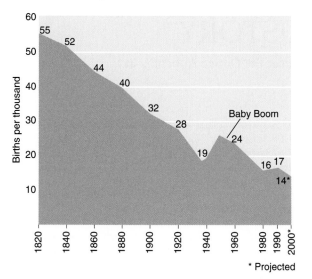

Source: Data from *Historical Statistics of the U.S., Colonial Times to 1970* (1975) and *Statistical Abstract of the U.S., 1996* (1996).

Life Expectancy, 1900–2000

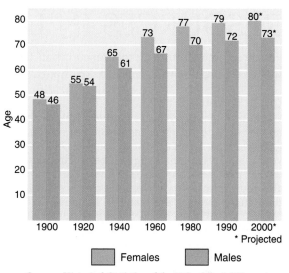

Source: *Historical Statistics of the U.S., Colonial Times to 1970* (1975) and *Statistical Abstract of the U.S., 1996* (1996).

Major Trends in Immigration, 1820–1998

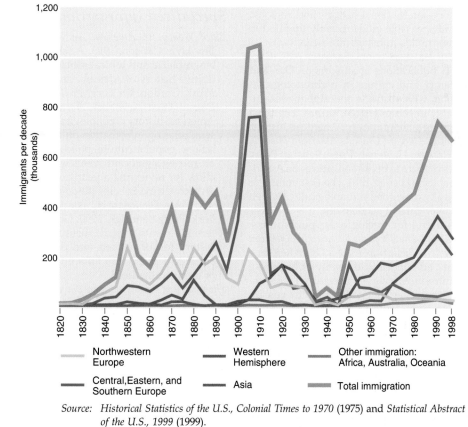

Source: *Historical Statistics of the U.S., Colonial Times to 1970* (1975) and *Statistical Abstract of the U.S., 1999* (1999).

Appendix III. RESEARCH RESOURCES IN U.S. HISTORY

For direct links to the internet resources in this appendix see the Online Appendix at www.bedfordstmartins.com/roarkcompact.

WHILE DOING RESEARCH IN HISTORY, you will use the library to track down primary and secondary sources and to answer questions that arise as you learn more about your topic. This appendix suggests helpful indexes, references, periodicals, and sources of primary documents. It also offers an overview of electronic resources available through the Internet. The materials listed here are not carried at all libraries, but they will give you an idea of the range of sources available. Remember, too, that librarians are an extremely helpful resource. They can direct you to useful materials throughout your research process.

Bibliographies and Indexes

American Historical Association Guide to Historical Literature. 3rd ed. New York: Oxford University Press, 1995. Offers 27,000 citations to important historical literature, arranged in forty-eight sections covering theory, international history, and regional history. An indispensable guide recently updated to include current trends in historical research.

American History and Life. Santa Barbara: ABC-Clio, 1964–. Covers publications of all sorts on U.S. and Canadian history and culture in a chronological/ regional format, with abstracts and alphabetical indexes. Available in computerized format. The most complete ongoing bibliography for American history.

Freidel, Frank Burt. *Harvard Guide to American History.* Cambridge: Harvard University Press, Belknap Press, 1974. Provides citations to books and articles on American history published before 1970. The first volume is arranged topically, the second chronologically. Though it does not cover current scholarship, it is a classic and remains useful for tracing older publications.

Prucha, Francis Paul. *Handbook for Research in American History: A Guide to Bibliographies and Other Reference Works.* 2nd rev. ed. Lincoln: University of Nebraska Press, 1994. Introduces a variety of research tools, including electronic ones. A good source to consult when planning an in-depth research project.

General Overviews

Dictionary of American Biography. New York: Scribner's, 1928–1937, with supplements. Gives substantial biographies of prominent Americans in history.

Dictionary of American History. New York: Scribner's, 1976. An encyclopedia of terms, places, and concepts in U.S. history; other more specialized sets include the *Encyclopedia of North American Colonies* and the *Encyclopedia of the Confederacy.*

Dictionary of Concepts in History. New York: Greenwood, 1986. Contains essays defining concepts in historiography and describing how the concepts were formed; excellent bibliographies.

Encyclopedia of American Social History. New York: Scribner's, 1993. Surveys topics such as religion, class, gender, race, popular culture, regionalism, and everyday life from pre-Columbian to modern times.

Encyclopedia of the United States in the Twentieth Century. New York: Scribner's, 1996. An ambitious overview of American cultural, social, and intellectual history in broad articles arranged topically. Each article is followed by a thorough and very useful bibliography for further research.

Specialized Information

Black Women in America: An Historical Encyclopedia. Brooklyn: Carlson, 1993. A scholarly compilation of biographical and topical articles that constitute a definitive history of African American women.

Carruth, Gordon. *The Encyclopedia of American Facts and Dates.* 10th ed. New York: HarperCollins, 1997. Covers American history chronologically from 986 to the present, offering information on treaties, battles, explorations, popular culture, philosophy, literature, and so on, mixing significant events with telling trivia. Tables allow for reviewing a year from a variety of angles. A thorough index helps pinpoint specific facts in time.

Cook, Chris. *Dictionary of Historical Terms.* 2nd ed. New York: Peter Bendrick, 1990. Covers a wide variety of terms—events, places, institutions, and topics—in history for all periods and places in a remarkably small package. A good place for quick identification of terms in the field.

Dictionary of Afro-American Slavery. New York: Greenwood, 1985. Surveys important people, events, and topics, with useful bibliographies; similar works include *Dictionary of the Vietnam War, Historical Dictionary of the New Deal,* and *Historical Dictionary of the Progressive Era.*

Knappman-Frost, Elizabeth. *The ABC-Clio Companion to Women's Progress in America.* Santa Barbara: ABC-Clio, 1994. Covers American women who were notable for their time as well as topics and organizations that have been significant in women's quest for equality. Each article is brief; there are a chronology and a bibliography at the back of the book.

United States Bureau of the Census. *Historical Statistics of the United States, Colonial Times to 1970.* Washington, D.C.: Government Printing Office, 1975. Offers vital statistics, economic figures, and social data for the United States. An index at the back helps locate tables by subject. For statistics since 1970, consult the annual *Statistical Abstract of the United States.*

Primary Resources

There are many routes to finding contemporary material for historical research. You may search your library catalog using the name of a prominent historical figure as an author; you may also find anthologies covering particular themes or periods in history. Consider also the following special materials for your research.

THE PRESS

American Periodical Series, 1741–1900. Ann Arbor: University Microfilms, 1946–1979. Microfilm collection of periodicals from the colonial period to the turn of the century. An index identifies periodicals that focused on particular topics.

Herstory Microfilm Collection. Berkeley: Women's History Research Center, 1973. A microfilm collection of alternative feminist periodicals published between 1960 and 1980. Offers an interesting documentary history of the women's movement.

New York Times. New York: New York Times, 1851–. Many libraries have this newspaper on microfilm going back to its beginning in 1851. An index is available to locate specific dates and pages of news stories; it also provides detailed chronologies of events as they were reported in the news.

Readers' Guide to Periodical Literature. New York: Wilson, 1900–. This index to popular magazines started in 1900; an earlier index, *Poole's Index to Periodical Literature,* covers 1802–1906, though it does not provide such thorough indexing.

DIARIES, PAMPHLETS, BOOKS

The American Culture Series. Ann Arbor: University Microfilms, 1941–1974. A microfilm set, with a useful index, featuring books and pamphlets published between 1493 and 1875.

American Women's Diaries. New Canaan: Readex, 1984–. A collection of reproductions of women's diaries. There are different series for different regions of the country.

The March of America Facsimile Series. Ann Arbor: University Microfilms, 1966. A collection of more than ninety facsimiles of travel accounts to the New World published in English or English translation from the fifteenth through the nineteenth century.

Women in America from Colonial Times to the Twentieth Century. New York: Arno, 1974. A collection of reprints of dozens of books written by women describing women's lives and experiences in their own words.

GOVERNMENT DOCUMENTS

Congressional Record. Washington, D.C.: Government Printing Office, 1874–. Covers daily debates and proceedings of Congress. Earlier series were called *Debates and Proceedings in the Congress of the United States* and *The Congressional Globe.*

Foreign Relations of the United States. Washington, D.C.: Department of State, 1861–. A collection of documents from 1861, including diplomatic papers, correspondence, and memoranda, that provides a documentary record of U.S. foreign policy.

Public Papers of the Presidents. Washington, D.C.: Office of the Federal Register, 1957–. Includes major documents issued by the executive branch from the Hoover administration to the present.

Serial Set. Washington, D.C.: Government Printing Office, 1789–1969. A huge collection of congressional documents, available in many libraries on microfiche, with a useful index.

LOCAL HISTORY COLLECTIONS

State and county historical societies often house a wealth of historical documents; consider their resources when planning your research—you may find yourself working with material that no one else has analyzed before.

Internet Resources

The Internet has been a useful place for scholars to communicate and publish information in recent years. Electronic discussion lists, electronic journals, and primary texts are among the resources available for historians. The following sources are good places to find historical information. You can also search the World Wide Web using any of a number of search engines. However, bear in mind that there is no board of editors screening Internet sites for accuracy or usefulness, and the search engines generally rely on free-text searches rather than subject headings. Be critical of all of your sources, particularly those found on the Internet. Note that when this book went to press, the sites listed below were active and maintained.

American Memory: Historical Collections for the National Digital Library Program. <http://rs6.loc.gov/amhome.html> An Internet site that features digitized primary source materials from the Library of Congress, among them African American pamphlets, Civil War photographs, documents from the Continental Congress and the Constitutional Convention of 1774–1790, materials on woman suffrage, and oral histories.

Supreme Court Collection. <http://supct.law.cornell.edu/supct> This database can be used to search for information on various Supreme Court cases. Although the site primarily covers cases that occurred after 1990, there is information on some earlier historic cases. The justices' opinions, as originally written, are also included.

Directory of Scholarly and Professional E-Conferences. <http://kovacs.com/directory> A good place to find out what electronic conversations are going on in a scholarly discipline. Includes a good search facility and instructions on how to connect to e-mail discussion lists, newsgroups, and interactive chat sites with academic content. Once identified, these conferences are good places to raise questions, find out what controversies are currently stirring the profession, and even find out about grants and jobs.

Douglass Archives of American Public Address. <http://douglassarchives.org> An electronic archive of American speeches and documents by a variety of people from Jane Addams to Jonathan Edwards to Theodore Roosevelt.

Historical Text Archive. <http://historicaltextarchive.com> A Web interface for the oldest and largest Internet site for historical documents. Includes sections on Native American, African American, and U.S. history, in which can be found texts of the Declaration of Independence, the U.S. Constitution, the Constitution of Iroquois Nations, World War II surrender documents, photograph collections, and a great deal more. These can be used online or saved as files.

History Links from Yahoo! <http://dir.yahoo.com/Arts/Humanities/History> A categorically arranged and frequently updated site list for all types of history. Some of the sources are more useful than others, but this can be a helpful gateway to some good information.

Index of Civil War Information on the Internet. <http://www.cwc.lsu.edu/cwc/civlink.htm> Compiled by the United States Civil War Center, this index lists everything from diaries to historic battlefields to reenactments.

Index of Native American Resources on the Internet. <http://www.hanksville.org/NAresources> A vast index of Native American resources organized by category. Within the history category, links are organized under subcategories: oral history, written history, geographical areas, timelines, and photographs and photographic archives. A central place to come in the search for information on Native American history.

WWW-VL History Index. <http://www.ukans.edu/history/VL> A vast list of more than 1,700 links to sites of interest to historians, arranged alphabetically by general topic. Some links are to sources for general reference information, but most are on historical topics. A good place to start an exploration of Internet resources.

Internet Resources for Students of Afro-American History and Culture. <http://www.libraries.rutgers.edu/rul/rr_gateway/research_guides/history/afrores.shtml> A good place to begin research on topics in African American history. The site is indexed and linked to a wide variety of sources, including primary documents, text collections, and archival sources on African American history. Individual documents such as slave narratives and petitions, the Fugitive Slave Acts, and speeches by W. E. B. Du Bois, Booker T. Washington, and Martin Luther King Jr. are categorized by century.

The Martin Luther King Jr. Papers Project. <http://www.stanford.edu/group/King> Organized by Stanford University, this site gives information about Martin Luther King Jr. and offers some of his writings.

NativeWeb. <http://www.nativeweb.org> One of the best-organized and most-accessible sites available on Native American issues, *NativeWeb* combines an events calendar and message board with history, statistics, a list of news sources, archives, new and updated related sites each week, and documents. The text is indexed and can be searched by subject, nation, and geographic region.

Perry-Castañeda Library Map Collection. <http://www.lib.utexas.edu/maps/index.html> The University of Texas at Austin library has put over seven hundred United States maps on the Web for viewing by students and professors alike.

Smithsonian Institution. <http://www.si.edu> Organized by subject, such as military history or Hispanic/Latino American resources, this site offers selected links to sites hosted by Smithsonian Institution museums and organizations. Content includes graphics of museum pieces and relevant textual information, book suggestions, maps, and links.

United States History Index. <http://www.ukans.edu/history/VL/USA> Maintained by a history professor and arranged by subject, such as women's history, labor history, and agricultural history, this index provides links to a variety of other sites. Although the list is extensive, it does not include a synopsis of each site, which makes finding specific information a time-consuming process.

United States Holocaust Memorial Museum. <http://www.ushmm.org> This site contains information about the Holocaust Museum in Washington, D.C., in particular and the Holocaust in general, and it lists links to related sites.

Women's History Resources. <http://www.mcps.k12.md.us/curriculum/socialstd/Women_Bookmarks.html> An extensive listing of women's history sources available on the Internet. The site indexes resources on subjects as diverse as woman suffrage, women in the workplace, and celebrated women writers. Some of the links are to equally vast indexes, providing an overwhelming wealth of information.

INDEX

READING THE AMERICAN PAST

Selected Historical Documents

Second Edition

Michael P. Johnson
Johns Hopkins University

READING THE AMERICAN PAST

SELECTED HISTORICAL DOCUMENTS

VOLUME I: TO 1877

Vol. I (to 1877)
2002/paper
268 pages

This highly regarded two-volume primary-source collection provides a broad range of voices and perspectives from our nation's past, while emphasizing important social, political, and economic themes of most U.S. history survey courses. Edited by one of the authors of *The American Promise* and designed to complement the textbook, the second edition of *Reading the American Past* offers a rich selection of over 125 documents and revised and expanded editorial apparatus to aid students' understanding of the sources.

Selections that offer a generous cross section of the diverse experiences that constitute the American past. Classic documents such as James Madison's Federalist Number 10, the Gettysburg Address, and Ronald Reagan's "Evil Empire" speech are juxtaposed with lesser known but no less significant sources such as advertisements for runaway slaves, immigrant memoirs, and working people's letters to New Dealers.

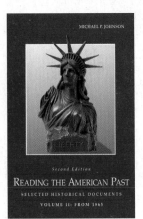

READING THE AMERICAN PAST

SELECTED HISTORICAL DOCUMENTS

VOLUME II: FROM 1865

Vol. II (from 1865)
2002/paper
290 pages

A wide array of primary sources. Diaries, letters, and inventories; speeches and manifestos; court and congressional testimonies; White House tape recordings; essays, poems, and satires; confessions, interviews, and magazine articles: all these sources and more vividly illustrate for students the diversity of materials with which historians work.

User-friendly editorial apparatus. An Introduction for Students appearing at the beginning of each volume explains the significance of documents to the study of history and outlines basic questions that students should consider to understand and interpret primary sources. Brief chapter introductions and headnotes to each document aid students in exploring the sources and making their own discoveries. Three to six Questions for Reading and Discussion following each document help students think critically about the source. Four to five broader Comparative Questions conclude each chapter, inviting students to compare and contrast the documents and to examine the larger historical themes they reveal.

"I have looked at nearly every document reader on the market and have never before seen one that matches the quality of *Reading the American Past*. The selections are not only well chosen and just plain interesting, but they are followed by great questions. . . . I especially admire the mix of major historical figures and ordinary Americans."

— Mary Ann Barber, *University of Pittsburgh at Titusville*